KU-113-824

SI

WITHDRAWN
FROM STOCK
QMUL LIBRARY

QMW LIBRARY

23 0925513 7

01 4687
5. 7. 50.

A DICTIONARY OF MEDIEVAL
ROMANCE AND ROMANCE WRITERS

UNIFORM WITH THIS VOLUME

DICTIONARIES
TO FAMOUS AUTHORS

IN which the various Characters and Scenes are alphabetically arranged and described. Synopses of the Author's various works are also included.

DICKENS. A. J. PHILIP.

THOMAS HARDY. With 2 Maps of Wessex. F. SAXELBY.

KIPLING. W. A. YOUNG.

SCOTT. (Waverley Novels). M. F. A. HUSBAND.

THACKERAY. I. G. MUDGE and E. N. SEARS.

OSCAR WILDE. STUART MASON.

ZOLA. (Rougon-Macquart Novels). With Map. J. G. PATTERSON.

"Not much honour is generally gained by doing such work as is represented in these dictionaries. When, however, it is done with the thoroughness and completeness shown by the compilers in this case, the work ought to be warmly acknowledged. It is a labour which will save much labour to others."—*The Scotsman.*

A DICTIONARY

OF

MEDIEVAL ROMANCE AND ROMANCE WRITERS

BY

LEWIS SPENCE

AUTHOR OF "A DICTIONARY OF NON-CLASSICAL MYTHOLOGY," "THE MYTHS
OF MEXICO AND PERU," "THE CIVILISATION OF ANCIENT
MEXICO," ETC., ETC.

WESTFIELD COLLEGE
LIBRARY
UNIVERSITY OF LONDON

LONDON
GEORGE ROUTLEDGE & SONS, LIMITED
NEW YORK: E. P. DUTTON & CO.

First printed in August, 1913.

PREFACE

THE term "romance" is so wide in its modern acceptance, and so loose in its application, that it will be well at the outset to attempt to formulate a definition of the word, which will also serve to define the scope of this work. Briefly, a romance may be described as a tale written at any period between the eleventh and fourteenth centuries, which deals with the age of chivalry. The narrower meaning of the word can only be applied to such tales of chivalry and love as were written in the "Roman" (that is, in Old French).

Jean Bodel, a French romancer who flourished in the twelfth century, sings—

> "Ne sont que trois matières a nul home entendant,
> De France, de Bretagne, et de Rome la grant."

Thus the tales of Charlemagne, Arthur, and Rome (that is, of ancient history), alluded to in the verse, were held by Jean as the only themes which a contemporary poet might worthily sing of.

But no such bounds can be set to the great Empire of Romance by its modern students. Since Bodel's day its frontiers have been extended into regions that he did not know of. But it is necessary to exercise care in fixing its limits in order that territory which does not rightly belong to it is not included; in other words, that only those bodies of literature which have been evolved from it, have affinities with it, or are of the same *genre* or class, should be included.

Thus, the Celtic prototypes of the Arthurian romance deserve inclusion, as do those Italian and Spanish tales which were adapted in the Peninsulas from the romances of Arthur and Charlemagne. The British Isles also produced a wealth of Arthurian romance of their own, and examples of this have been included.

As regards the great Teutonic cycles of story, it has been thought well to include these. They are of the same *genre*, and, at least, as much romantic in spirit, as the subjects of the *Matière de Bretagne*, or, at any rate, that part of it which emanated from France. Many of the Icelandic saga-stories have also been included for a similar reason. A dividing line has been drawn where the tale is either purely historical or mythological in its purport. Such examples must be relegated to their proper sphere—that of pure myth : they have no place in a dictionary of romance. But wherever the elements or traces of myth have been observed in a romance, such a circumstance has not militated against its inclusion, and an effort has been made in each case to elucidate the mythological references and obscurities where these occur.

Such being the scope of the work, the reader will look in vain through its pages for reference to such works as are included in the term "romance" in its more modern sense. Thus the "romances" of the school of Mlle. de Scudéry and the extravagant fictions of the later "romantic revival" are not

represented.   These are only romances inasmuch as they partook of the
" prodigious " element of romance proper, and have nothing else in common
with it.   Moreover, such a lapse of time separates them from the older romances
that they must be regarded as altogether a separate form of literature.

Several of the articles will be remarked as more extended in scope than
others.   This applies to that on Guyot, whom I regard as important as being
the probable originator of the Grail legend.   The *Morte d'Arthur* I have also
summarized at length, as being the greatest English example of the Arthurian
legend, and a treasure-house of Arthurian lore.

It is not claimed that every example which comes under the heads above
outlined is dealt with.   But, while I shall welcome all corrections and sugges-
tions for a possible new edition, it will be found, I hope, that by far the larger
number have been included, and that no outstanding romance has been
altogether neglected.   Many romances still remain in MS. in the seclusion of
small Continental libraries, and to include some of these has been found im-
practicable.   But it is hoped that the work will provide a trustworthy book
of reference on a subject which is yearly attracting greater attention, and that
it will prove of assistance not only to the general reader, but also to the
student of comparative literature and folklore.

L. S.

6, SYLVAN PLACE,
   EDINBURGH.

A DICTIONARY OF MEDIEVAL ROMANCE AND ROMANCE WRITERS

A

ACCOLON OF GAUL. A knight loved by Morgan le Fay (*q.v.*), who gave him the scabbard of Arthur's sword Excalibur, which prevented its owner from bleeding, however sorely he might be wounded. By reason of his possession of this scabbard, he nearly succeeded in slaying Arthur. He died of the wounds he received in combat with the king.

ACHEFLOUR. The mother of Percyvelle and sister of Arthur. Alluded to in the Thornton MS. of the Grail legend. (*Vide* "Bliocadrans.")

ADDANC OF THE LAKE. Evidently a water-spirit or monster. Alluded to in the Mabinogi tale of *Peredur*. It slays the inhabitants of the palace of the King of the Tortures daily. Peredur receives a magic stone from a certain damsel, by which he is enabled to see the Addanc whilst remaining invisible to it, and succeeds in slaying the monster.

ADLAND, KING. Mentioned in the romance of *King Estmere* as the father of the lady who wedded King Estmere (*q.v.*). He was beset by two kings who desired his daughter. The solution of his dilemma was the death of one of the lovers at the hands of the other.

ADLER. A companion of King Estmere (*q.v.*), in the romance of that name. He receives the credit in the romance of successfully winning for King Estmere the daughter of King Adland.

AED THE FAIR. Chief sage of Ireland. Author of the *Voyage of Maeldun* (*q.v.*).

AEDA. In Irish romance, dwarf of King Fergus mac Leda (*q.v.*). The lover and slayer of Vivionn. He is mentioned in the tale of the Fair Giantess, to be found in the *Colloquy of the Ancients* (*q.v.*).

AEI. In Irish romance, the death plain of the bull of Ailill (*q.v.*) and Maev (*q.v.*).

AGARAN. Alluded to in the *Queste del Saint Graal* as the nephew of a hermit encountered by Lancelot.

AGLOVALE, SIR. Knight of King Arthur, nephew to the Queen of Orkney, and brother of Perceval. He meets his death at the hands of Lancelot in carrying out the punishment of Guinever. (*Vide* "Morte d'Arthur.")

AGOLANT. A romance of the Charlemagne cycle (*q.v.*) contained in an MS. in the British Museum (King's Library, 15 E. VI.) together with other of the Carlovingian tales. It depicts the fusing of the Carlovingian sub-cycle proper, and of the allied feudal sub-cycles, and is in heroic pentameters, generally, though rather irregular, running into rhyme. The subject is a war of the Franks against the Saracens under their king Agolant; Charlemagne, in order to give them battle, having to cross Aspremont, by which is meant either the Alps or the Pyrenees. The romance has left a deep impression upon Italian literature, and was one of the most popular stories of the Middle Ages. It exhibits a more modern character when compared with such poems as *The Song of Roland* or *Garin*, and many marvels are recounted concerning Aspremont and its inhabitants. The early adventures of Naymes (*q.v.*), and the love of a paynim queen for him, as well as the first exploits of Roland, are dealt with; but the poem is full of imitations and elaborations of the *Song of Roland*. In the great battle which is described in the course of the romance the Franks bestow a crushing defeat on the Saracens, whilst Hiaumont, Agolant's son, is, like Roland by Oliver, vainly pressed by a friend to sound his horn to obtain succour from his father. Thus the story of Roncevaux is simply reversed. At this battle Roland is dubbed knight by Charles, who girds his famous sword, Durandal, by his side. From many accompanying circumstances the date of the poem may be fixed about the middle of the twelfth century. (Cf. Bekker, introduction to the Provençal poem of *Fierabras*, Berlin, Reinier, 1829.)

AGRAMANT. (See "Orlando Innamorato" and "Orlando Furioso.") King of Africa, invaded France to revenge his father Troyano, slain by the Christians. He besieged Paris, was defeated with great slaughter, then retired to Arli. He was latterly slain by Orlando.

AGRAVAINE, SIR. Son of the Queen of Orkney, brother to Mordred, Gawaine, Gareth, and Gaheris. He plotted against Lancelot and Guinevere, and was subsequently slain by the former. (*Vide* "Morte d'Arthur.")

AGRETES. King of Camelot. He is alluded to in the *Grand Saint Graal* as being angered at Josephes for Christianizing his folk, and, pretending to become a Christian himself, grievously persecuted the converts among his people on the departure of Josephes. For so doing he was punished with madness and death.

AGUIGRENONS, MARSHAL. In Grail romance, King Clamadex's general, whom Sir Perceval fights with and overcomes in defence of a beauteous maiden, Blanchefleur. He is sent to King Arthur's court, where he is soon followed by King Clamadex (*q.v.*).

AIDEEN. Wife of Oscar, a champion of the Fianna (*q.v.*). She died of grief after he was slain at the battle of Gowra, and was buried by Oscar's father, Oisin, on Ben Edar in Howth, where a dolmen was raised over her.

AIFA (Eefa). An amazonian chieftainess, in early Irish romance. Skatha, a warrior-woman of the Land of Shadows (perhaps the Isle of Skye), made war upon her, in which campaign Cuchulain (*q.v.*) took a prominent part. He met Aifa in single combat, and succeeded in vanquishing her by the stratagem of arousing her fears for her horses and chariot during the encounter. Whilst she turned to view the imagined catastrophe which had overtaken them, she was seized by Cuchulain, who fled with her to the army of Skatha, with whom she cemented a truce. She had a son by Cuchulain, whom in after-years he slew unwittingly.

AILILL (1). "Edge of Battle," Father of Maeldun (*q.v.*). Encamping with his king, during a foray into foreign territory, near a convent of nuns, he had the opportunity of offering his love to one of them as she came out to strike the midnight bell. In due time she gave birth to a posthumous son, whom she named Maeldun. Ailill was burnt, with the church of Doocloone, by reavers from Leix.

AILILL (2). Brother of Eochy, High King of Ireland, alluded to in the Cycle of Ulster. He fell sick by reason of his great love for Etain, daughter of Etar, and wife of his brother. Eochy went on a journey, and left Etain to care for the sick Ailill, who avowed his passion for her. She made a tryst with him in a house near Tara. But on the night before it, Ailill was cast into a deep sleep, and failed to arrive at the appointed time. His apparition, however, visited the queen, and spoke of his illness, departing wearily. In his sleep his madness for Etain had vanished, and she on her part became aware that she was once a goddess, and that the apparition who visited her was none other than Midar the Proud, her god-spouse of the divine tribe of Danaan, with whom she afterwards disappeared. (*Vide* "Etain.")

AILILL (3). In Irish romance, son of Laery (*q.v.*); treacherously slain by his uncle Covac (*q.v.*).

AILILL (4). King of Connacht, husband of Maev (*q.v.*). He assisted Angus Og (*q.v.*) to besiege Ethal

Anubal (*q.v.*), with whose daughter the latter had fallen in love, and as the husband of Maev he took a foremost part in the Cattle Raid of Quelgny (*q.v.*). Finally he was slain by Conall (*q.v.*).

AILILL OLUM. King of Munster. He cruelly stole the love of the Goddess Ainé (*q.v.*), and in consequence met his death by means of her magic arts.

AIMERI DE NARBONNES. (*Vide* "Garin De Montglane.")

AINÉ. An Irish love-goddess. In Irish romance, the patroness of Munster, daughter of the Danaan Owel. She was loved by many a mortal, among whom are to be noted Ailill Olum (*q.v.*), King of Munster, and a Fitzgerald. By her the latter became the father of the semi-divine wizard Earl Gerald, the fourth Earl of Desmond, from whom many aristocratic families of Munster trace their descent. Her name is to be found in Knockainey ("Hill of Ainé"). Like the other Danaan deities, she was a goddess of the earth, and she figures prominently in Munster folk-lore. On one occasion, at the bidding of Earl Gerald, she planted her hill with pease in a single night. On Midsummer Eve her peasantry would walk round Knockainey, carrying lighted torches of hay and straw. Then they would depart to their own fields, waving the torches over their crops and cattle, that good luck might attend them the next year. D. Fitzgerald, in his *Popular Tales of Ireland*, in the *Revue Celtique*, vol. iv., tells us that on St. John's Eve this annual ceremony was omitted, as a neighbour had died. That night, however, the torches blazed in greater numbers, and at the head of the procession walked the goddess herself. Again, it is related that on a similar occasion some girls remained longer upon the hill to watch the torches and to join in the games. To these Ainé suddenly appeared to thank them for the honour, and to request them to return home ; as she required the hill to herself and her fairy company. These invisible beings several of the maidens perceived through a ring held up by the goddess.

AINLE. Brother of Naisi (*q.v.*), mentioned in the Ulster cycle.

AJOUB. (*Vide* "Florice and Blanchfleur.") Principal Imam of the great mosque. Urged by Mohady, his religious brother, he persecuted Blanchfleur, and was killed in a duel by Florice, who defended her.

ALAINS LE GROS. The youngest son of Brons (*q.v.*), chosen by Josephes (*q.v.*) as the Keeper of the Grail. He was instructed by Josephes to take the net from the Grail table and cast it into a certain lake. Alains caught one great fish, which his hungry company considered was insufficient to feed them all. But Alains having prayed and shared it in three, all are sufficed. He was called in consequence "The Rich Fisher," and all the Grail-Keepers after him bore this name, "but they were more blessed than he, being crowned kings, whereas he never wore a crown." The incident is described in the *Grand Saint Graal*.

ALAIS. In the Charlemagne cycle, wife of Raoul of Cambray (*q.v.*).

ALBERICH or **ANDWARI.** (*Vide* "Nibelungenlied.") A dwarf who guards a treasure, possessor of a magic ring, symbolic of wealth and of the reproductivity of nature. In the stories of the Volsungs (*q.v.*), he transformed himself into a pike, and brought from the river gold for Loki (*q.v.*) and Ram. The Nibelung story shows him to be the owner of a cap of darkness, the power of which he gave to Siegfried (*q.v.*), whose treasure he guarded until after his death.

ALBRACCA. The capital city of Galafron, King of Cathay. It was besieged by Agrican, King of Tartary, who had been an unsuccessful suitor for the hand of Angelica, Galafron's daughter. Angelica obtained the assistance of many knights, both pagan and the peers of Charlemagne, among them Sacripant, King of Circassia, but to no avail, for Agrican succeeded in taking the city. Angelica, however, escaped. (*Vide* "Orlando Furioso.")

ALDA. Sister of Oliver (*q.v.*), and the betrothed of Roland (*q.v.*). She first espied him from the walls of Viana, invested at the time by Charlemagne, and, although an enemy, greeted him courteously and kindly. On hearing of his death at Roncevaux, she died suddenly of grief.

ALEINE. The niece of Gauvain or Gawaine. She is alluded to in the *Didot Perceval* as inciting Perceval to take part in an Easter tournament at the court of King Arthur, from which he had hitherto refrained. She sent him a suit of red armour ; he entered the lists unknown, overthrew all his opponents, and won a vacant place at the Round Table.

ALEXANDER THE GREAT. (*Vide* "Roman d'Alexandre.")

ALEXANDER and **DINDIMUS.** The letters of Alexander the Great to Dindimus, King of the Brahmans, and his replies, constitute an alliterative romance translated from the Latin about 1340–50. The unique MS. is housed in the Bodleian Library, at Oxford. The general contents of the work, which is fragmentary, relate how that after Alexander had slain Perseus, King of India, he came to the country of the Oxydracca, the people of which are called Gymnosophists. Their king informs him that he has nothing to gain by subduing them. Alexander offers them peace, and promises to grant them a boon, upon which they ask him to give them everlasting life. He replies that such is not within his power to grant. Next he sees wonderful trees which only grow during sunlight, and disappear into the darkness. These trees are guarded by birds that spit deadly fire. His journey resumed, he arrives on the banks of the Ganges, a river impassable except in July and August. He sends messengers across the river in a boat with a letter to the king of that country. This king is called Dindimus. The rest of the poem concerns five letters which pass between him and Alexander. In the first letter, Alexander asks Dindimus to inform him of the habits of his subjects. The second letter, which is Dindimus's reply, outlines the customs of that people. Dindimus states that his subjects live simple lives; they never plough, fish nor hunt, live frugally, and die at a fixed age. They avoid lusts, eat fruits, drink milk or water, speak truthfully, never covet, nor make war. "Your gods," says he, "likewise are evil,—each one presides over some member; your idols lead you into sins, for which you shall endure endless torture." The third letter contains Alexander's reply. He asks, "Why blame us? Your account of yourself is a miserable one, to be neither envied nor imitated. Ye are beasts, but we are men. We work hard and earn pleasure. You dishonour your Creator, and your deeds are but foolish." Dindimus replies, "We are but pilgrims on earth. Your boastful deeds only make you proud. The gold which you prize cannot satisfy thirst; and we are wiser in treading it underfoot. You know not how you err, and it is a kindness to tell you. The men who do not fear death deserve to be struck down by lightning." Alexander concludes the correspondence by replying thus : " Ye are so set on an island that no strangers can come to you. God has decreed for you misery in this life, and pain in the hereafter." After the letters had ended, Alexander erects a pillar of marble to mark the farthest spot which he had succeeded in reaching. He and his men then begin their homeward journey. The two leading ideas, which are both theological, display the contrast between the active life and the contemplative life—the European and the Asiatic. Though the poem deals with India and attempts an account of the life of the Brahmans, there is little Oriental thought in its composition. A point of interest is the name of Dindimus given to the supposed King of the Brahmans. It should more properly be Dandamis, and is not really a proper name, but a title.

ALEXANDRE DE BERNAY. Sometimes called Alexandre of Paris, a French poet of the twelfth century. Little or nothing is known about his life, and he is remembered simply by his *Roman d'Alexandre*, an epic treating of the exploits of Alexander the Great. This poem is based largely on an earlier one on the same subject, the work of Lambert - li - Gros, occasionally styled Lambert-le-Court ; but Alexandre de Bernay employed a wholly different manner from this writer, and is generally considered much his superior. He eliminated his predecessor's crudeness, and eschewed his multiplicity of assurances ; while he created for his use what is known nowadays as Alexandrine verse, and indeed the term traces its origin to Alexander's invention. Apart from its literary worth, the *Roman d'Alexandre* has considerable antiquarian interest ; for the matter which the author borrowed from Lambert was in turn gleaned in great measure from obscure Byzantine romancers of the seventh and eighth centuries ; while moreover, Alexandre is a discursive poet, and accordingly his pages illuminate the manners and customs of his own time— the age of chivalry and the Crusades. Many early manuscript copies of the poem are extant, the Bibliothèque Nationale alone possessing no fewer than twenty, and this goes far to prove that the work enjoyed exceptional popularity throughout the Middle Ages. As regards recent criticisms thereof, the best is one edited by M. N. Michelant for the Literary Society of Stuttgart, 1846. Besides the foregoing, Alexandre de Bernay is credited with a poem entitled *Athis et Prophylias*, but the ascription is not well supported, resting as it does merely on a line in the first verse : " Oez del savoir Alexandre."

Literature : Cf. Michelant's preface to his edition of the *Roman d'Alexandre*, and more particularly *Alexandre de Bernay et les Vers Alexandrines*, contained in the *Bulletin de la Société de l'Eure*, 1833.

ALFASEM. King of Terre Foraine, and alluded to in the *Grand Saint Graal* as being converted and baptized by Alain (*q.v.*). He is wounded through both thighs by an angel for sleeping where the Grail rests, and later dies.

ALFRED OF BEVERLEY. An English author who flourished about the beginning of the twelfth century. He made an abridgment of Geoffrey of Monmouth's *Historia Regum Britanniæ*. He tells us that, hearing people talk of British kings of whom he knew nothing, he became ashamed of his ignorance, and with difficulty borrowed a copy of Geoffrey's new history. Delighted with it, he desired to possess a copy himself. But lacking the time to copy it or money for materials for a full transcript, he made an abridgment of it in the days of an imposed silence among the clergy— probably at a period of contest between the two rival archbishops who took opposite sides in the civil war in Stephen's reign (1141–1154). Having curtailed Geoffrey's book, he determined to continue his work down to Norman times, and thus he produced a chronicle which ends, like Turgot's, the last from which he took material, with the year 1129.

(Cf. *Aluredi Beverlacensis Annales, sive Historia de Gestis Regum Britanniæ*, Libris x., ed. by Thomas Hearne, Oxford, 1716.)

ALGARVA, SULTAN OF (*vide* "Florice and Blanchfleur"), who was instrumental in despatching his physician Averroes to the aid of Florice, who lay sick.

ALGOLUFRE. (*Vide* "Sir Ferumbras.") A fierce giant who guarded the bridge of Mantribe for Laban. He was killed by Richard of Normandy.

ALI. (*Vide* "Grettir Saga.") The unruly house-carl of Thorbiorn Oxmain (*q.v.*). Ill-treated and expelled by his master, he took service with Atli (*q.v.*), to whom he proved very useful.

ALICE. Daughter of Louis le Debonair and Queen Blancheflower, in Carlovingian romance, and niece of William of Orange (*q.v.*). She was instrumental in bringing about a reconciliation between her mother and uncle on the occasion of a serious quarrel between them. (*Vide* "Blancheflower," and "Arleschans, Battle of.")

ALICE. (*Vide* "Garin the Lorrainer.") Daughter of Duke Milo of Gascony. King Pepin asked her father if he desired that his daughter should marry one of the counts at his court, and gave her to Garin. The marriage was a very happy one, and she only survived her husband a few days.

ALICE LA BEALE PILGRIM. Daughter of Duke Ansirus (*q.v.*). She married Alisander (*q.v.*), and became the mother of Bellongerius (*q.v.*). (*Vide* "Morte d'Arthur.")

ALISANDER, SIR. Son of Bondwin (*q.v.*). His mother Anglides (*q.v.*), after her husband's death, presents him to Arthur. He then resolves to avenge himself on King Mark of Cornwall for his father's death (*q.v.*). He marries Alice la Beale Pilgrim (*q.v.*). According to Arthurian romance, he is subsequently slain by his father's murderer. (*Vide* "Morte d'Arthur.")

ALISCANS, BATTLE OF. (*Vide* "Arleschans, Battle of.")

ALONZO OF AGUILAR, DEATH OF. This romance tells how Fernando, King of Arragon, desires to rid the mountains of the Moors, who refuse to accept his religion. He chooses Alonzo of Aguilar to be his champion. With a thousand horse Alonzo reaches Nevada, but before they can reach the ravine, they are detected by the Moors, who hurl rocks down upon them. Alonzo with a handful more escapes into a field, but is killed from afar by bolt and javelin. The Moors then come down from their hiding-place, and take Alonzo's body and lay it upon the village green for all to view.

ALORY. In Carlovingian romance, a Lombard standard-bearer of the Frankish army, who, in fighting against the Saracens in Italy, took fright and fled. He was stopped by Ogier the Dane (*q.v.*), who reclaimed the day for the Franks.

ALPHAR. King of Aquitaine, father of Walthar of Aquitaine (*q.v.*). (*Vide* "Dietrich of Bern.")

ALPHART'S TOD. A Bavarian poem of the latter part of the thirteenth century, connected with the Saga-cycle of Dietrich of Bern (*q.v.*). The poem recounts how Heine acts as herald from Ermenrich to Dietrich, bearing a declaration of war. Alphart is sent by Dietrich to keep watch for the enemy. One of Ermenrich's heroes approaches with eighty followers, of of whom Alphart slays all but eight. Witege, a renegade from Dietrich's army, attacks Alphart and lies at his mercy, when Heine rushes from behind a tree and suggests that the contest should be discontinued. Alphart refuses, with the result that both attack him, and he is slain. (Cf. *Deutsches Heldenbuch*, 1866–78 ; Ludlow, *Popular Epics of the Middle Ages*, 1865.)

ALSWID. (*Vide* " Volsungs.") Son of Heimar and Bekkhild (*q.v.*). He advised Sigurd (*q.v.*) against Brynhild (*q.v.*).

AMADIS DE GAUL. The origin of this romance is a matter of some controversy. By most authorities the Portuguese Vasco Lobeira is held to be the author, but at all events the Amadis romances are genuinely Spanish in their colouring, and tinged by a glow of Oriental fancy. The story tells how Garinter, King of Brittany, has two daughters, one of whom marries Languines, King of Scotland, and the other Elisena, is beloved by Perion, King of Gaul. To this latter pair is attributed the birth of Amadis, whose mother, anxious to conceal his birth, launches him in an ark into a stream, which carries him to the Scottish coast, where he is picked up by the knight Gandales. The foundling he named " Child of the Sea," and a parchment roll, which he finds around the babe's neck, declared him to be the son of a king. There are also tokens which in due time will disclose his identity. The King and Queen of Scotland become interested in the child, and, unconscious of their relationship, order him to be reared at their court along with the knight's son, Grandalin. Meanwhile King Perion had openly married Elisena. They had another son Galaor, who had been stolen away from them by a giant named Gandalar, under whose instructions he became a mirror of chivalry. Perion had another son, Florestan. Some

time after the three sons perform many exploits together, unaware of their connection. Perion comes on a visit to the court of his Scottish brother-in-law, who had also a guest, Lisuarte, King of Great Britain, with his daughter Oriana. To her young Amadis acts as page. She succeeds in getting Perion to knight him, and he repays the honour by his prowess against Abies, King of Ireland. The young knight then learns, as the tokens of his cradle prove, that he is the son of Perion, and accordingly he dubs as knight his long-lost brother Galaor. The interest of the story now centres around the fair Oriana, toward whom he remains faithful. But she, deceived as to his constancy, writes him such cruel letters, that at the height of his renown he renounces friends, arms, and fame, and goes off under the name of Beltenebros, the " Fair Forlorn," to live in seclusion upon an island known as the Poor Rock, inhabited only by a hermit. The difficulty between the lovers is eventually overcome ; Lisuarte, quarrelling with the hero, would have married his daughter to a brother of the emperor, had not Amadis intervened by defeating him. He carries off Oriana to the Firm Island, where both achieve the " Arch of Lovers " and the " Forbidden Chamber," an enterprise to be achieved by only the bravest of knights and the fairest of ladies. (Cf. Nuñez de Liao, *Origem da Lingoa Portugueza ; Cancionero de Romances*, Antwerp, 1555 ; Bouterwek, *History of Spanish Literature*. There is an English translation of *Amadis* by Southey.)

AMANGONS. King of Logres. Alluded to in the *Conte du Graal*.

In the wells and springs of Logres
dwelt damsels who fed the way-
farers with meat, pasties, and
bread. But Amangons wronged
one, and carried off her golden
cup, so that never more came
damsels out of the springs to
comfort the wanderer. The men
of King Amangons followed his
evil example, so that the land grew
waste.

AMANT, SIR. A knight of the Court
of Arthur. He was slain by Mark,
King of Cornwall (*q.v.*). (*Vide*
"Morte d'Arthur.")

AMERGIN (1). A Milesian bard, son
of Miled, mentioned in the myths
of the Irish invasion. When he
first landed in Ireland with the
Milesian hosts he sang a strange
pantheistic lay, probably expres-
sive of the esoteric and bardic
philosophy of the Celts. He
uttered the first judgment which
was given in Ireland, to the effect
that the invading Milesians must
not take the native Danaans by
surprise, but should withdraw the
length of nine waves from the
shore, and then return. As they
did so, the Danaans raised a mist
and tempest by their sorceries,
whereupon the vessels of the
Milesians were scattered. Amergin, however, dispelled these by
means of an incantation, and the
Milesians were about to land, when
once more the tempest arose, and
sank many of their ships. A
number of the Milesians succeeded
in landing in the Boyne, and proceeded on their path of conquest.

AMERGIN (2). Father of Conall of
the Victories (*q.v.*).

AMFORTAS. The Fisher King. (*Vide*
"Grail, Holy.") By Chrétien he
is represented on Perceval's first
meeting with him as angling from
a boat steered by his companion ;

he directs Perceval to his castle.
Perceval is afterwards informed
that, being wounded and consequently unable to mount on horseback, fishing is his only solace,
whence the name applied to him.
He is also known as the Keeper
of the Holy Grail, but how it
came into his possession is not
definitely known, though conjecture would point to his being
the descendant of Joseph. From
Manessier we learn that Joseph,
"having converted the land, died
therein ; " that " the Fisher King
is of his seed, and that if God wills
the Grail will never have its
dwelling elsewhere than with him."
He is also known as " The Maimed
King " (*q.v.*), having been brought
to this pass by indulging in illicit
loves. In all the old French works
of the cycle the soubriquet " rich "
is applied to the Fisher. He is a
character in Wagner's well-known
Opera " Parsifal." (*Vide* "Fisher
King.")

AMINADAP. One of the Grail-
Keepers and Kings alluded to as
such in the *Grand Saint Grail* (*q.v.*).

AMYS AND AMYLION. An English
romance of great length, believed
to be of French origin. The tale
opens with the marriage of two
knights of Lombardy, who had
been from infancy fast friends.
It happened that both their wives
were on the same day delivered
of sons, one of whom is christened Amys, the other Amylion.
These children become playmates,
while as they grow older, they
develop a striking similarity to
each other. The Duke of Lombardy holds a festival, which
is attended by the two knights,
who bring with them their sons.
The duke instantly becomes
attached to them, requests their
fathers to leave them in his care,

assuring them of his increasing attention toward them. To this request the fathers agree, and, leaving their sons with the duke, they repair to their respective castles. Shortly afterwards the two fathers die. Living in the court, and receiving the same instruction, the two friends become deeply attached to each other. Their education having been completed, the duke knights them, and subsequently appoints Sir Amys to the office of butler, and Sir Amylion to that of steward of the household. This latter appointment, however, awakens the envy of the chief steward, a man of most malicious character. Soon after, Sir Amylion succeeds to his father's estates. This parting naturally causes much sorrow ; and, making two gold cups, Amys presents one to his friend, while the other he himself retains. The steward, none the less malicious, quarrels with Amys. The duke's daughter, who by this has taken up residence at the court, falls madly in love with Sir Amys, and as the attachment is mutual the steward, who learns of it, hastens to inform his master. The duke, enraged at what has become a scandal, immediately summons Sir Amys, who untruthfully declares his innocence. Hardly satisfied by this denial, the duke fixes a day on which the steward and Amys must fight. The duchess and Belisante stand as pledges for Amys, who, fearing defeat, hastens to seek the aid of his friend. Sir Amylion gladly agrees to fight for the cause of Amys, and, exchanging their armour, Amylion proceeds to the scene of battle, while Amys remains with his friend's wife. The disguise which they both adopt completely deceives both Amylion's wife and

the duke and his steward. Amylion arrives, slays the wicked steward, thus winning the duke's favour, who offers him Belisante and the succession to the kingdom. Sir Amylion returns to his castle, and informs Amys of his success. Amys then hastens to the duke's court, where he is married to Belisante. This event is followed shortly afterwards by his succession to the duke's kingdom. Sir Amylion's wife meanwhile learns from her husband the story of the affair. Her annoyance at her husband's deception causes her to reject him. He becomes afflicted with leprosy as the result of a dream which he previously had, warning him not to fight in the cause of his friend. His repulsive appearance, combined with hatred for the deception practised upon him prompts his wife to banish him from the castle. All his attendants but one desert him. This faithful page, Childe Oneys, and Sir Amylion quit the castle. For three years the afflicted knight and his page tramp the country. Destitute almost beyond recognition, the hapless pair one day arrive at a city, and hearing of a generous duke who resides there, they proceed in the direction of the castle. The page makes his appearance along with the rest, before the sergeant, who, surprised at his powerful build, asks to see his companion. This done, the youthful Oneys is offered a position in the castle ; but, refusing to quit his master, he leaves the sergeant in a state of surprise. The sergeant immediately reports the incident to his master, Amys, who fills the gold cup with wine, commanding him to carry it to the afflicted man. Immediately Amylion sees the cup, he produces his own, which he had faithfully preserved, and compares the two, to find them similar. The sergeant immediately relates the incident to Sir Amys, who, thinking the sick man had stolen the cup from his friend Sir Amylion, rushes upon the afflicted knight, and would have slain him had not the page disclosed his master's name. At this Sir Amys leads him into the castle, where he is welcomed by Belisante. The same night the two friends dream of an angel appearing before them, and commanding that the two children of Sir Amys must be sacrificed and Sir Amylion anointed with their blood, in which manner his leprosy is to be cured. The following morning the knights relate their dreams, and finding them the same, decide that the two children must be sacrificed. Sir Amys succeeds in decoying his wife from the house, while he kills his children, with whose blood he anoints Sir Amylion. Belisante returns, and is informed of her husband's deed, but learning the reason of the sacrifice, she is consoled. Amylion is now restored to youth and vigour. They return to the fatal room, and to their astonishment find the two children awaking from a refreshing sleep, little the worse. Amylion bids farewell to his hospitable comrade, and, accompanied by Childe Oneys, he arrives in his own land, to find his wife on the point of taking another husband. He immediately prevents the union, banishes her from his lands, and places the faithful Oneys in charge over them. He returns to his friend, and the two give up the remainder of their lives to the cause of charity. (Cf. Ellis, *Specimens of Early English Metrical Romances*.)

ANDREA. An Italian chronicler and ecclesiastic of the ninth century. The work by which he is remembered deals with the history of Italy from its shadowy dawn till the advent of the Lombards on the death of the Emperor Louis II., and is of the nature of pseudo-history. The reader will find it in the first volume of *Antiquitates Italiæ*, edited by Muratori, and also in the third volume of *Monumentæ Ecumeniæ*, edited by Pertz. Nothing is known about Andrea's life save that for some time he was Canon of Bergame.

ANDVARIS. (*Vide* "Volsungs.") A dwarf in league with Loki (*q.v.*).

ANGANTYR, YARL. (*Vide* "Frithjof Saga.") The chief to whom Helgi (*q.v.*) sent Frithjof to wrest from him the tribute due to the sons of Bele. But the yarl had been the friend of both Thorsten, Frithjof's father, and of King Bele to whom he had given presents, not tribute. He welcomed the son of his friend.

ANGELICA. (*Vide* "Orlando Innamorato" and "Orlando Furioso.") Daughter to Galaphron, King of Cathay. She first loved Orlando, then discarded him for Rinaldo. She ultimately sailed for India with Medoro, whom she married.

ANGHARAD LAW EURA WC. Alluded to in the tale of *Peredur the Son of Evrawc* (*q.v.*) in the Welsh *Mabinogion*. The name signifies "Angharad with the Golden Hand," probably bestowed upon her to typify her liberality. Peredur pledges his faith that he will not speak a word to any Christian again until she come to love him. After performing various adventures he meets her again, and she declares her love for him, so that his self-inflicted penance comes to an end.

ANGLIDES, DAME. Wife of Bondwin (*q.v.*) and mother to Alisander (*q.v.*). She flees from the wrath of King Mark, who slays her husband in her presence. (*Vide* " Morte d'Arthur.")

ANGUISH. In Arthurian romance, King of Scotland. He was one of those who advised Arthur to withstand the Romans and refuse to pay their tribute, and assisted him in his war with them with twenty thousand men.

ANGURVADEL. (*Vide* " Frithjof Saga.") The wonderful golden-hilted sword inherited by Frithjof (*q.v.*). It was made by the dwarfs, blazed like the Northern Lights, and upon its blade were unintelligible runes that dulled and paled in time of peace and reddened fierce and fiery when the battle raged.

ANGUS OG (Angus the Young). In Irish romance and myth, the son of Dagda, supreme Danaan god, and father of Maga (*q.v.*). He was the Irish God of Love. His palace was reported to be at New Grange, on the Boyne. It was said that his kisses took the form of four beautiful birds that hovered continually about his head, and by their singing inspired with love both youths and maidens. His own passion was for a maiden whom he had beheld in a dream, and who, the Dagda and Boanna failing in their search for her, was at last found by Bov the Red (*q.v.*), King of the Munster Danaans, at the Lake of the Dragon's Mouth. Unable to carry her off from her hundred and fifty companions as she walked the lake-shores, Angus sought the aid of Ailill (*q.v.*) and Maev (*q.v.*), the King and Queen of Connacht. These, however, had no authority over Ethal Anubal

(*q.v.*), sovereign of the Danaans of Connacht, and parent of the maiden, whose name was Caer. Her father refusing to give her up, he was besieged and taken prisoner by Ailill and the Dagda. But in vain, for his daughter had more power than he, as she took the form of a swan on the first of November every alternate year. Angus Og, calling to her on the first day of her transformation, was changed into a swan, and plunged into the lake. Then together they flew to the Boyne palace, lulling all who heard their singing into a charmed sleep which lasted three days and nights.

ANLUAN. In Irish romance, son of Maga, brother of Ket. He accompanied Maev (*q.v.*), the Queen of Connacht, on a foray into Ulster, the famous Cattle Raid of Quelgny (*q.v.*). But after the Ulster peace he was slain by Conall (*q.v.*), and his head produced to Ket on the occasion of those warriors' rivalry in boasting.

ANSIRUS, DUKE. " The Pilgrim," so called for his love of holy travel. He was the father of Alice, who married Alisander (*q.v.*). (*Vide* " Morte d'Arthur.")

ANSEIS. (*Vide* "Garin the Lorrainer.") King of Cologne. He went with a huge army to aid Hervi in defending Metz from the Saracens. Hervi was killed and Anseis took possession of Metz, as he had driven off the invaders. He afterwards lost it, and Garin, son of Hervi, won it back.

ANSWERER. Fragarach, the Irish Sea-god Lir's (*q.v.*) magical sword, which could pierce any armour. It was brought by Lugh (*q.v.*) from the " Land of the Living," *i.e.* the " Celtic Otherworld."

AOIFE. The second wife of Lir, a god of the Danaans, mentioned in the Irish invasion myth, and cognate with the British Celtic deity Llyr. Lir's first wife had borne him four children, and so jealous was Aoife of them that she took them to the court of King Bov the Red, and on the journey requested her retainers to slay them. They refused, and not possessing the courage to undertake the deed herself, she cast a spell upon them, by which they became swans. (*Vide* "Lir, Children of.") King Bov, horrified at her act, changed her into a demon of the air, and with discordant cries she quitted the palace, and was seen no more.

AONBARR. The magical horse of Manaanan, son of the Irish Sea-god Lir (*q.v.*), which could gallop on land or sea.

ARAWN, Lord of Annwn (alluded to in the *Mabinogion* tale of *Pwyll, Prince of Dyfed* (*q.v.*)). He was the King of Annwn, or the Celtic Otherworld in its later mythological aspect of a country adjoining the dominions of Pwyll, a Welsh princeling, and not as a land across the misty ocean. It is doubtful if he can be identified with Arawn ap Cynvarch, whom the Welsh triads celebrate as one of the three knights of counsel, or with that Arawn mab Dewinoin whose grave is alluded to in the verses of Beddau.

ARBRIORES. A Knight alluded to in Gautier's portion of the *Conte du Graal* (*q.v.*) as being overcome by Percival and sent to King Arthur.

ARDAN. Brother of Naisi (*q.v.*), an Ultonian warrior.

ARDANATA. Daughter of the King of Satyn (*q.v.*), who, according to the romance of *Eglamour of Artoys*

(*q.v.*), offered herself in marriage to Eglamour, but was refused. She waited fifteen years in the hope of winning her desire ; but in the end was married to Degrabell (*q.v.*).

ARGASTES. Son of King Helain, and master of the black knights mentioned in the *Queste del Saint Graal*, as observed by Lancelot tourneying with a band of white knights in a meadow by a castle. They captured. but afterwards released him.

ARIDES OF CAVALON. Alluded to in Manessier's portion of the *Conte du Graal*, as oppressing a damsel of Blanchefleur's (*q.v.*). He was overcome by Perceval, who sent him to Arthur's court, bidding him announce his arrival at Whitsuntide.

ARIES, the Cowherd, in Arthurian romance, foster-father of Sir Tor. (Cf. Malory's *Morte d'Arthur*, Book III. chap. iii.)

ARIOSTO, The author of the celebrated romantic poem *Orlando Furioso* (*q.v.*), was born at Reggio in Modena, in 1474. His father was an officer in the forces of the Duke of Ferrara, whose son, Cardinal d'Este, chancing to see a number of the poetical effusions of the young Ariosto, gave him a position in his household, and sent him on various missions. In 1516, at the age of forty-two, Ariosto completed his great work, *Orlando Furioso*, in which he drew with a vivid and vivacious pen the adventures of various knights belonging to the court of Charlemagne, and of their pagan foes. This wonderful and entertaining work cost him no less than ten years of arduous labour, and was first published at Ferrara, in 1516, in forty and afterwards in forty-six cantos. Shortly afterwards Ariosto joined the household of the Duke of Ferrara, brother of his late master, and in 1522 was appointed to the governorship of Garfagnana, in the Apennines, a brigand-ridden district. During the three years he resided there he succeeded in reducing the province to a semblance of order, his rank and reputation assisting him considerably in this task. On his return to Ferrara he resumed life as an author and produced several theatrical pieces under his own direction. He died in 1533. His talent for description was of a high order, and his invention assisted him greatly in the weaving of original plots. In character-study and sketches he is not so successful, but this is compensated for by the sweetness and elegance of his versification. The harmony of his poetry is incomparable, and every description is felt to be a picture. He never attempted the epic style of poetry, and even wrote at times like an *improvisatore*. But this is practically concealed by the polish of his verse, and his irregularities partake of the art which conceals art. At times he rises to a poignant pathos which will bear comparison with that of the most gifted lyrists. His plays are only mediocre, and are entitled *La Cassaria*, *I Suppositi*, and *La Calandra*. He also wrote sonnets, madrigals, and canzoni. (*Vide* " Orlando Furioso.")

ARLESCHANS or ALISCANS, BATTLE OF. A romance of the William of Orange sub-cycle of the Charlemagne Saga. It is a sequel to *Le Covenant de Vivien* (*q.v.*), but was probably written by a different hand. The Saracens are being driven towards the sea by Vivien, when the French espy a new enemy—the men of Gorant, " horned in front and rear." The Saracens turn, and take many of

William of Orange's men, and Vivien falls wounded under a tree. William, endeavouring to escape, finds Vivien dying. He gives him some consecrated bread, and when he passes, carries the lad's body off on his horse. The death-scene of Vivien is most exquisitely touching, and one of the most tender and beautiful in romance. Attacked, William is forced to put down the body, but, returning, he watches by it the whole night. Disguised in the body-armour of a dead Saracen, he returns to Orange, where his wife Guibor fails to recognize him at first. She counsels him to seek succour from King Louis, and dresses with her women in armour, to make the Saracens believe that Orange is well garrisoned. William swears that he will not change his clothes until he kisses his lady again. He reaches the French Court, where he is jeered at because of his rough attire. He learns that his sister Blanchflower, the queen, is about to be crowned. Louis accords him an interview, and in sheer terror of him grants his request to be supplied with an army. With this force and with Reuouart, the gigantic brother of his wife Guibor, he returns, and inflicts a crushing defeat upon the Saracens. The rest of the romance is taken up with the recital of the deeds of Reuouart, who, stolen from his parents in early youth, was until this time a scullion in the king's kitchen. He marries Alice, the King's daughter, and his subsequent adventures are detailed in *The Battle of Loquifer* (*q.v.*).

The romance of *Arleschans* undoubtedly rests upon historical tradition. M. E. Gautier holds that it represents the welding together of the defeat of William of Aquitaine by the Saracens at

Villedaigne in 793, and the defeat of the Saracens by William I. of Provence in 976.

Literature: *Aliscans, Recueil des Anciens Poëtes de la France*, vol. x. 1875; critical ed. by E. Weinbeck, 1903. An early MS. of *Arleschans* was discovered in England in 1904. It was printed under the title *La Cancun de Willame* (see M. Paul Meyer's articles in *Romania*, vols. xxxii. xxxiv.). Wolfram von Eschenbach translated *Arleschans* under the title of *Willehalm* (see the complete edition of his works by Lochmann, 5th edition).

ARTHUR, KING. Son of Uther Pendragon (*q.v.*), King of England, and Igraine (*q.v.*), wife of Gorlois, a Lord of Cornwall, who subsequently married Uther. Given by Merlin after his birth to Sir Ector, he was reared by him, and on Uther's demise established his right to the Kingship by drawing an enchanted sword from a block of stone. The circumstances of his life will be found detailed at length in the article on the *Morte d'Arthur*. It is probable that Arthur was a sixth-century British leader or chieftain who bore the not very common name of a British deity. The deeds of the god probably became confounded with those of the hero, and the *Historia Regum Brittaniæ* (*q.v.*) for ever fixed the type of the romance and rendered the figure of Arthur human, whereas in earlier Celtic times it undoubtedly loomed through a mythological mist. Indeed its mythologic origin is patent to the student in the circumstances which surround the story. Arthur's career begins in darkness and mystery. He possesses a magic weapon (Excalibur). He begets a son (Mordred)

upon his sister unwitting of the relationship. In a word, his myth parallels the circumstances of a hundred others. All the details which occur in the career of a great mythological hero are represented in his story. He is probably a British leader on whose memory were grafted tales relating to an ancient British solar deity, his Round Table possibly represents the sun itself, and his knights the host which accompanies the luminary.

(See "Morte d'Arthur," "Excalibur," and the titles of the various Arthurian romances; "Historia Britonum," "Historia Regum Brittaniæ," and especially "Arthurian Romance," as to his historicity. For Literature on the subject, see that at end of the above articles.)

ARTHURIAN ROMANCE, RISE AND EVOLUTION OF. The historicity of Arthur, his existence as a veritable personage, is a much-debated point. There are several theories as to the manner in which his myth grew into prominence. One is that he was the *Comes Brittaniæ* or Protector of the Romano-Britons on the withdrawal of the Roman forces from the island. Another would derive him from a Celtic deity, Arturus or Artus, and would make the alleged historical matter concerning him part of a mythological process. It is probable that the truth lies between these extremes; that the figure of the Arthur of romance was derived from that of the sixth-century British commander who bore the name of the god, and around whom, as a hero of considerable fame in his day, the attributes of the deity clustered and clung. The first historical notice we have of Arthur is in the *Historia*

Britonum, ascribed to Nennius (*c.* 800). In its pages Arthur is alluded to as " Emperor " of Britain, and his battles with the Saxon invaders are described. The exact region over which he held sway is variously debated, Wales, the South of Scotland and even Brittany being claimed by different authorities, and natural objects bearing his name being encountered over the length and breadth of Britain. The lack of direct allusion to Arthur in Bede and *The Anglo-Saxon Chronicle* is scarcely an argument in favour of his non-existence, as some authorities appear to think. The real Arthur may have been a leader of importance, as his deeds are frequently alluded to in Welsh legendary and semi-mythical literature, and it is not surprising that he is unnoticed in the very scanty Saxon literature of the three or four centuries which followed his death. But it is almost certain that the circumstance that he was of one name with a native deity assisted to raise him to a pedestal of heroship in the popular imagination. It is not until the twelfth century that we have any definite evidence that his story had awakened interest in the minds of men. Whatever the amount of enthusiasm that accrued to it between the fifth and twelfth centuries, there is no mistaking the note of passionate admiration struck by its chroniclers and perusers of the latter era. The circumstances of Arthur's life were on all men's lips, and were matter of general discussion. His story appealed to the martial and romantic spirit of the time, and probably had a vogue in Britain greater and more extended than that of any literary subject-matter either before or since. The tale was probably in an inchoate condition, hawked about the country by jongleurs and minstrels when it was seized upon by Geoffrey of Monmouth, who for ever placed upon it that veritable stamp of chivalric romance which was to be so often imitated but seldom surpassed, and which fixed it for all time as a world-story of the first magnitude. Geoffrey maintained that he had received the matter of his *Historia Regum Brittaniæ* from a Breton or Welsh source. This is generally doubted, without much show of reason. Some such source must undoubtedly have existed behind his pseudo-history, as he certainly did not invent its basis, however much he may have elaborated it. A host of continuators, imitators, and authors of tales which threw light upon the lesser known portions of Arthurian story pursued the subject. And the Arthuriad became practically the only theme of song and fiction in England and France, and in great measure in Italy and Germany for at least a century and a half.

That the original matter of Arthurian romance emanated from Wales or Brittany is certain. It arose from Celtic myth, and is closely interwoven with the deathless tales of the Cymric deities. But it is more probable that the impulses which went to the making of English Arthurian romance came rather from Brittany than from Wales. Geoffrey of Monmouth states that he merely translated from " a certain most ancient book in the British Language," which " Walter Archdeacon of Oxford, brought hither from Brittany," and it is merely ludicrous to discount the existence of such a volume of lore or some traditional equivalent on the ground that it is not now extant, and to allude to this source of the *Historia Regum Brittaniæ* as " one of the great ruses of English Literary History."

Regarding the evolution of Arthurian Romance from a chronological standpoint and dating a review of such from the probable period of the historical Arthur's death (which occurred in the first third of the sixth century), we are justified in concluding that heroic poems commemorating the struggle between Briton and Saxon were in existence by the beginning of the seventh century. The development of the legend may be observed in Nennius' *History of the Britons*, which dates from the eighth or ninth century. By 1050 or thereabouts the settlement of Normandy had in all probability made the Arthurian stories known to the Normans by reason of their close contact with Brittany, and these they carried with them to their colonies in Italy and Sicily. The last quarter of the eleventh century witnessed considerable literary activity in Wales, when a renaissance of national literature was marked chiefly by the popularity of the work of the sixth-century bards, of which several of the *Mabinogi* tales are good examples. Geoffrey's works reflected the outburst in England, and he was followed by Wace, who translated his history into French, Marie de France (who wrote *c.* 1150–1165), Béroul (*c.* 1150), and Thomas (*c.* 1170), the last two of whom wrote on the subject of Tristan (*q.v.*). Then Chretien de Troyes (*q.v.*) followed with *Erec, Cliges* and *Le Chevalier de Charette*, and finally the *Conte du Graal* (1182), and the prose romances such as the *Lancelot*. In this subject he had been preceded by Guyot (*q.v.*). We observe in the titles of the works alluded to that two new subjects have by this time been added to the Arthurian story, the sub-cycle of *Tristan* (*q.v.*) and the Grail story (*q.v.*). Later Arthurian romantic effort includes the spread of the purely French romances of the cycle into Wales, giving rise to new Welsh versions, and the vogue of Malory's compilation. It would scarcely be untrue to say that the evolution of the Arthurian romances had ceased, with the echoes of the deathless works of Tennyson, Swinburne and many other nineteenth-century poets still ringing in the ears of the present generation.

(*Vide* also articles on Arthurian Romance, for example " Grail," " Tristram," the articles on the several romances themselves, and " Chrétien de Troies," " Geoffrey of Monmouth," " Walter Map," " Lancelot," " Gawain," etc., etc.)

Literature : Nennius, *Historia Britonum ;* Geoffrey of Monmouth, *Historia Regum Brittaniæ ;* Professor A. Brown, *The Round Table before Wace,* " Harvard Studies and Notes," vol. viii. ; Dr. Lewis Mott, *The Round Table,* Mod. Lang. Assoc. of America, xx. 2 ; Skene, *Four Ancient Books of Wales,* Edinburgh, 1868 ; Fletcher, *Arthurian Matter in the Chronicles,* " Harvard Studies and Notes," 1906 ; Alfred Nutt, *Celtic and Mediæval Romance ;* Sir John Rhys, *The Arthurian Legend,* 1891 ; Jessie P. Weston, *King Arthur and his Knights* (" Popular Studies in Mythology and Folklore "). For a good resumé of the subject see W. Lewis Jones's *King Arthur in History and Legend* (" Cambridge Manuals of Science and Literature ").

ARUNDEL. A kingdom ruled over by King Jovelin. Tristram (*q.v.*)

during his wanderings in that land assisted Jovelin to rid it of robbers and once more made the throne secure. (*Vide* "Morte d'Arthur.")

ASAL. King of the Golden Pillars, in Irish Celtic Myth. He possessed seven swine which might be killed and eaten every night, yet which were found alive every morning. (*Vide* "Turenn, Sons of.")

ASCAPARD. (*Vide* "Bevis of Hampton.") A giant whose life was spared by Bevis at the request of Josyan (*q.v.*). He became their page and served them faithfully till Bevis gave up his estates, when Ascapard went back to his pagan master. Saber killed him when he rescued Josyan.

ASDIS. (*Vide* "Grettir Saga.") Mother of Grettir; wife of Asmund.

ASENATH. A French Mediæval romance which relates how Asenath, the daughter of Poti-pherah, Chief Priest of Egypt, was scornful of men, and immured herself in a high tower to be without their reach. Joseph, being sent by Pharaoh to gather corn throughout Egypt in face of famine, sent for Poti-pherah, who desired to give him Asenath to wife. But Asenath was sore vexed, and declared that only the son of a King should wed her. But she espied Joseph from her tower and repented of her words. Joseph inquired what woman had looked from the tower, and was told by Poti-pherah that it was his daughter. Joseph, hating woman as much as Asenath disliked men, announced that he would be "as a brother to her." But he refused to kiss her because of her idolatry to the gods of Egypt. At this she sought her chamber, and renounced the gods. When Joseph departed Asenath

grieved mightily, but an angel appeared to her, and announced that her name was written in the Book of Life, and that she should become Joseph's wife. She supplied the angel with bread, but when he requested honey she could not supply it, so he brought it miraculously from Paradise. The angel further blessed her seven handmaidens, and, Joseph arriving, Asenath was given him to wife.

ASKELDART. (*Vide* "Guy of Warwick.") A Saracen knight.

ASMUND. (*Vide* "Grettir Saga.") Father of Grettir; husband of Asdis.

ASPERAUNT. (*Vide* "Sir Otuel.") A favourite adviser of King Garsie, who consulted him when he found himself in danger from the French army as to how he could punish Otuel and defeat the French. Asperaunt thought no headway could be made so long as Roland and Olivier were alive and Otuel still held his famous sword, Corrouge.

ASTOLPHO. (*Vide* "Orlando Innamorato" and "Orlando Furioso.") Son of Otho, King of England. He was transformed into a myrtle by Alcina. He regained his former shape through Melissa, then travelled to Logistilla. He took Caligorant the giant prisoner in his own net. He cured Orlando of his madness.

ATHELSTAN. A pseudo-history in metre, of the reign of that king. As the son of Edward the Elder, Alfred's successor, he ascended the throne of England in the year 925. He was the first monarch who exercised actual kingly power over all the divisions of the Heptarchy. According to tradition, he was not without opponents to the crown of England ; these aspirants he is said to have cleared out of his way by successively bribing his cup-bearer, a personage of importance, to remove them. Ælfred, who coveted the throne, accused Athelstan of murdering his brother, Prince Ethelwald ; but the mob to whom he appealed assaulted him, dragged his mutilated body through the lanes, and cried, " Up with Athelstan ! " His greatest enemy was Sigrig the Dane, who married Eadritha, the king's sister. By this union Sigrig, who was king over Northumbria, promised to renounce the worship of Odin and form an alliance of peace with his brother-in-law. Such a treaty he never fulfilled. The spirit of his god reclaimed his soul, and he perished through fear. The fires of Odin consumed him, and when his warriors entered his chamber the final flames of the fatal fire passed away. With Sigrig dead, Athelstan united Northumbria to England. Anlaf, son of Sigrig, opposed Athelstan. He visited York, while his brother Gunthforth journeyed to the court of the Scottish king Constance. As a result of their visits, the Scots and Welsh, who were, (according to this romantic history), but tributary nations to Athelstan, joined Anlaf and his Irish hosts. The king, who had, meanwhile, strengthened himself by forming various alliances with foreign princes, prepared for battle. The rival armies met at Brunnanburh (938 A.D.), where Anlaf and his allies were routed. The son of Sigrig fled from the field, leaving no less than five kings dead. The kingdom prospered under Athelstan's rule ; and, after laying the foundations of England's maritime greatness, he retired to Glou-

cester, where he died in 941. At the express wish of the dying monarch, Edmund, his brother, assumed the kingship of the rising nation.

ATLI (1). (*Vide* "Volsungs, Lay of the.") A monarch who married Gudrun (*q.v.*). His thirst for gold led him to war against the sons of Giuki, whom he took prisoners. He slew Helge and cast Gunnar into a pit of vipers. He was slain in revenge by Gudrun and Niblung.

ATLI (2). (See "Frithjof Saga.") The fiercest of Yarl Angantyr's vikings. Desiring to prove the reputed qualities of Frithjof's magic sword, Angurvadel, he engaged that hero in combat. Frithjof's blade cut his sword in twain, but his opponent thought him too brave to die, and became his friend.

ATLI (3). (See "Grettir Saga.") Eldest son of Asmund and brother of Grettir. Mild and peace-loving, he was treacherously slain by Thorbiorn Oxmain (*q.v.*), who thus avenged the death of his brother Thorbiorn the Tardy (*q.v.*) at the hands of Grettir.

ATTILA or **ETZEL**. King of the Huns, and ally of Dietrich of Bern (*q.v.*).

AUBRY. (*Vide* "Garin the Lorrainer.") Son of Duke of Burgundy, nephew of the Lorrainers. He was one of the party who went to help King Thierry of Savoy. He was besieged in Dijon by Bernard, but Bego relieved him. When Bego was wounded and unable to fight, he sent out Aubry in his place. He hated Bernard, but was overthrown by him in the attack on Naisil. He and Garin went to the assistance of Huo in a fierce fight with the Bordelais. He fought bravely on the side of the Lorrainers in time of battle, and gave good advice to them on several occasions.

AUCASSIN AND NICOLETE. A French *cantefable* or romance partly in prose, partly in verse, dating from the thirteenth century, and one of the most beautiful examples of Mediæval literature. It has evoked the enthusiasm of some of the best English writers of the last half century, notably Swinburne, Pater, and Lang, and it is admitted by literary critics of eminence to possess elements of originality and intrinsic loveliness which make it at once one of the most intense and delicately fragrant love stories of the Middle Ages. In every page we catch the far-off, dreamy beauty which characterizes the literary craftsmanship of the period, and, if the audacity, extravagance, and even puerility of certain passages force us to smile, we are in turning the next page rapt by the wonderfully human descriptions of passion and the intricate workmanship in words which we encounter. By some critics an Eastern origin has been ascribed to *Aucassin and Nicolete*. The name, Aucassin, it is insisted, is merely the Moorish Al Cassim, and the "Saracen" birth of Nicolete is adduced as a further proof of the Oriental genesis of the tale. It relates how Aucassin, a noble youth, falls in love with Nicolete, a Saracen captive maid. Count Garin of Beaucaire, enraged at his son's choice, promises him the noblest lady in the land if he will break off the attachment. This Aucassin refuses to do ; whereupon Count Garin commands Nicolete's guardian to send her away, ere evil befall her. So she is imprisoned in an upper chamber of her guardian's palace. While Aucassin seeks the solitude of his chamber and laments the loss of Nicolete, Count Bougars of Valence, who had a family feud against Garin, attempts to storm the castle. Garin seeks his son, upbraids him for his craven indifference to their danger, and begs him to take his place in the fight, for his presence will instil courage into the people. Aucassin at first refuses, but for the sake of a promised interview with his beloved, he dons his armour and sallies forth. But Aucassin, obsessed with the thought of Nicolete, allows himself to be taken prisoner. Awaking from his day-dream as the soldiers are preparing to hang him, he draws his sword, and makes a wild dash for freedom. Winning clear of the melée, he rides swiftly on, and encounters Count Bougars of Valence. Taking him prisoner, he delivers him to his father, and demands the fulfilment of their bargain—his interview with Nicolete. Count Garin, thinking the danger over, refuses, whereupon Aucassin extracts a promise from his prisoner, that as long as he lived he would harry and make war on the Count of Beaucaire. Leading his prisoner safely out of the castle precincts, he sets him free. Aucassin is thrown into prison again, and one is left to wonder how he could not make his own escape while freeing the Count of Bougars. Meanwhile Nicolete escapes from her tower, and hides in the woods, where she makes herself a bower of leaves and branches. The cry is raised that she is lost, or that Count Garin has killed her. Aucassin is set free in honour of a great feast given by the Count, to induce his son to become enamoured of some other fair lady. But he slips away, and rides in search of Nicolete. Coming upon the bower in the woods, he dismounts, and in doing so, stumbles, and dislocates his shoulder. Crawling in, he decides to spend the night, and lies bewailing the loss of his Nicolete. The girl overhearing him, enters, and they embrace each other. Discovering his hurt, she deftly sets the bone, and bandages his arm. Aucassin then mounts his horse, and placing Nicolete in front, they set off in the direction of the sea. Boarding a ship with some merchants, they are driven by a mighty storm to a far country. They dwell for some time at the mad court of Torelore, the environment of which mirrors all that is grotesque in the period of the tale. The castle of Torelore is seized by the Saracens, who bear the lovers off to captivity. Aucassin and Nicolete are placed in different ships. A storm arises, and the vessels are scattered. Aucassin is driven ashore near the Castle of Beaucaire, where he learns that his father and mother are dead and that he is the heir. Nicolete is carried to Carthage, where she is proved to be the daughter of the king of that city. On the eve of her marriage with a rich Paynim monarch, she stains her face, and disguises herself as a minstrel. Taking her viol, she manages to get a passage in a ship bound for Provence. Arrived there, she wanders about the country playing her viol, till she comes to the castle of Beaucaire, where she discovers herself to Aucassin, and the romance ends with their marriage.

The tale has been frequently edited, the best editions being that of the late Mr. Andrew Lang (1887), and Mr. Bourdillon (1887). A facsimile of the original and only MS. was also edited by Mr. Bourdillon, in 1896.

AUCHINLECK MS. A manuscript

containing the only copy of the famous romance, *Sir Tristrem*, doubtfully attributed to Thomas the Rymour (*q.v.*). It was discovered in the Advocates' Library at Edinburgh, by Ritson, the celebrated critic of antique poetry, and forms part of a vellum manuscript volume presented to the library in 1744 by Alexander Boswell of Auchinleck, father of James Boswell, Johnson's biographer. It contains upwards of forty poems and fragments, which are treated by Sir W. Scott in his appendix to *Sir Tristrem*. The volume has been considerably mutilated by the excision of the illuminated initials, and the latter part of the romance of *Sir Tristrem* is lost. This work is connected with the name of Thomas Rymour because of the circumstance that Robert Manning, an English monk, a native of Malton, in Yorkshire, who translated into English verse the *Chronicle of England* by Peter Langtoft, and who dwelt at the Priory of Brunne from which he took the territorial nomenclature of Robert de Brunne, refers to Thomas as the author of the *Tristrem*, as follows :—

" I see in song in sedgeyng tale
Of Erceldoun and of Kendale
Non tham says as thai tham wroght,
And in ther sayng it semes noght
That may thou here in Sir Tristrem ;
Ouer gestes it has the 'steem,
Ouer all that is or was,
If men it said as made Thomas ;
Bot I here it no man so say,
That of som copple som is away."

There is considerable diversity of opinion as to the exact meaning of these lines. But it may be regarded as establishing the fact that Brunne was familiar with a poem of *Sir Tristrem* that was held in universal esteem in his day, and that its author's name was Thomas. He also states that he heard no man say it as Thomas made it, which implies that he must either have heard Thomas recite it or have seen the original MS. It will be observed that he couples the names of Erceldoun and Kendale. Warton thinks that these are the names of romances, and says he can find no traces of the latter in ancient British poetry. Nor can Ritson find any trace of Kendale, but Sir Frederick Madden, who regards the authorship of Thomas Rymour as fictitious, states that a passage in the unedited portion of De Brunne shows that Kendale's Christian name was also Thomas, and that he wrote a romance about Flayn, the brother of the giant Skardyng the lord of Scarborough Castle. He does not give the passage, which is unfortunate, and he does not enumerate his reasons for the belief that the *Tristrem* was not the work of a native of Scotland. Scott had deemed that the *Tristrem* of Thomas the Rymour was famous and popular on the continent. But he forgot or was unaware that there was such a poet as Thomas of Brittany. The first two lines of the poem read :

"I was at
With Thomas spak Y thare."

Scott thought the missing word in the first line is " Ercildoun," and it suits both the metre and the rhyme, as the third line ends in the word "roune." Further, the first line, used as a " catch-line " at the bottom of the preceding page, is conclusive on the point, as it includes the word " Ercildoune." For a summary of the *Tristrem* romance, *vide* one of the entries under " Tristrem."

AVERROES. (*Vide* " Florice and Blanchfleur.") Physician to the Sultan of Algarva, who was commanded by his imperial master to hasten to the sick-bed of Florice. By his skill his patient was cured of his malady.

AVILION. (*Vide* "Morte d'Arthur.") A mystic land to where the soul of King Arthur (*q.v.*), is wafted by maidens after his death, at the hands of Mordred (*q.v.*). Here he is healed, and here he rests for evermore. It is probably a Mediæval form of the Celtic Otherworld across the sea.

AVOWING OF ARTHUR. This early English romance relates an incident which occurred near Carlisle. King Arthur is hunting with Sir Gawain, Sir Kay and Sir Baldwin, and all four undertake separate vows. Arthur is to capture single-handed a ferocious bear ; Sir Kay to fight all who oppose him. The king is successful, but Sir Kay falls before a knight who is carrying off a beautiful maiden. The victor, however, is afterwards overcome in a fight with Gawain, and then ensues a significant contrast in the matter of behaviour. Sir Kay sustains his earlier reputation by cruelly taunting the beaten knight ; while Sir Gawain, on the other hand, mindful of the claims of chivalry, is studiously kind and considerate towards his fallen foe.

AWNTYRS OF ARTHURE AT THE TERN WATHELYN, THE. An Arthurian poem, probably of the fourteenth century, but possibly of the fifteenth, written in stanzas of thirteen lines each, rhymed in a very intricate manner, and full of the alliteration common to the metrical romances of the period. It is difficult to say whether it should be claimed by Scotland or the North of England,

and the dialect forms no accurate solution to this question, for throughout the Middle Ages there was little difference between the speech of the southern Scots and that of their neighbours across the border. The poem is usually considered Scottish, however, but the authorship is a debated point; and the only light thereon consists in the fact that, in its style throughout, the *Awntyrs* bears an exceedingly close resemblance to another Arthurian poem, *Gologras and Gawane*, attributed sometimes to Huchown of the Awle Ryle and sometimes to one Clerk of Tranent. Andrew of Wynton ascribes it to the former, saying in his *Orygynale Cronykil of Scotland* that Huchown

" Made the gret Gest of Arthure
  And the Awntyrs of Gawane ; "

but William Dunbar, on the other hand, in his *Lament for the Makaris*, speaks of

" Clerk of Tranent eik he has tane
  That made the anteris of Sir Gawane."

Now Wynton lived fully a century before Dunbar, and thus his testimony is the more valuable of the two. Accordingly, then, *Gologras and Gawane* may reasonably be accepted as Huchown's work, and from this it may be deduced that he too wrote the *Awntyrs*.

The scene of the poem is laid in the wilds of Cumberland, Arthur having established his Court at Carlisle; and the opening stanzas tell how the king, along with his queen Guinevere—or Geyenour as the poet calls her— go to hunt in the forest of Inglewood accompanied by their favourite knight, Sir Gawane. He and the queen, while at a distance from the rest of the party, are overtaken by darkness, and much to their surprise the ghost of the queen's mother appears to them. Speaking of the torments to which it had been subjected, the apparition implores that prayers be offered up for its soul; and the queen and Sir Gawane promise to do this, and thereafter they return to Carlisle. Here, in the course of the evening, a knight called Sir Galaron comes upon the scene, and, claiming from the king certain lands which the latter had wrested from him, he offers to prove his rights by fighting any one of Arthur's henchmen in the lists. Sir Gawane is appointed to confront him on the following day, and in the fight which ensues both men are wounded, Sir Galaron getting back his territory in consequence, and at the same time being appointed a knight of the Round Table as a mark of the king's admiration for his prowess. Nor is the staunch Sir Gawane forgotten, his royal master granting him an estate in Wales; while the queen, remembering the injunctions of the ghost, orders millions of masses to be sung on its behalf.

The *Awntyrs* possesses considerable literary merit, the supernatural element therein being well handled, and the tourney described vividly. There are several Mediæval manuscript copies of the poem, and of these the most important are one in the Bodleian Library, and one in the Cathedral Library, Lincoln.

Literature : In *Scottish Poems reprinted from Scarce Editions*, edited by John Pinkerton (1792), the *Awntyrs* is given from the Bodleian manuscript under the title of *Sir Gawane and Sir Galloran of Galloway ;* while the

Lincoln version, which differs slightly from the other, is contained in *Select Remains of the Ancient Popular and Romance Poetry of* *Scotland*, edited by David Laing (1822). (*Vide* also articles " Clerk of Tranent," " Gologras and Gawane," and " Huchown.")

B

BAGDEMAGUS, SIR. Son of King Pellinore, and a knight of the court of Arthur. (*Vide* " Morte d'Arthur.")

BAGOMMEDES. A knight alluded to in Gautier's portion of the *Conte du Graal* as being discovered by Perceval hanging by his feet from a tree, and released by him. He had been thus secured by Kay, and upon his return to Arthur's court challenged Kay, and was only hindered by Arthur from slaying him.

BALAN. (*Vide* " Morte d'Arthur.")

BALDOLF OF AQUILENT. (*Vide* " Sir Otuel.") One of Garsie's generals ; fought against the Christians.

BALDWIN, SIR. (*Vide* " Sir Otuel.") One of Charlemagne's knights who attended to the dying needs of Roland at Roncesvalles.

BALDWIN THE FLEMING. (*Vide* " Garin the Lorrainer.") Count of Flanders. He was persuaded by Droo of Amiens to ask his sister to marry Fromont, not knowing he had been defeated by Garin and had lost Soissons and other lands. On learning the truth he set out with a large army to attack Cambrai, the property of Huo, nephew of Garin. When the king summoned Fromont to answer for his misdeeds, he also threatened Baldwin with the loss of Flanders. The royalists were successful. Afterwards

at the affray at the king's marriage Baldwin was taken prisoner. He fought at the great fight between Fromondin and Rigaut, and was killed by Bego.

BALIGAND. (*Vide* " Sir Otuel.") A Saracen king who bribed Ganelon, ambassador of Charlemagne, to lead the French troops into the Forest of Roncesvalles. Slain at Saragossa by Turpin.

BALIN. An Arthurian knight, whose adventures are given at length in Book II. of the *Morte d'Arthur* (*q.v.*).

BALOR. A mighty King of the Fomorians, mentioned in the Irish invasion myths. He was generally alluded to as " Balor of the Evil Eye," because if he cast his glance in anger upon any one, that person was instantly destroyed. When the Danaans (*q.v.*) refused to continue their tribute to the Fomorians (*q.v.*), Balor gave instructions to his captains to anchor their vessels to the island of Ireland, and to tow it into the gloomy Fomorian Sea, of which he was the lord. In the battle which ensued with the Danaans, Balor, who was now aged, had his drooping eyelid raised by means of ropes and pulleys, and cast his baleful glance on Nuada, and other Danaan chiefs, who were smitten down by it. But Lugh, the sun-god (*q.v.*), his grandson, stole near him as the eyelid drooped momentarily and hurled at him a great stone, which sunk through eye and brain and slew him.

BAN, KING. In Arthurian legend, an ally, with King Bors, of Arthur. They assisted him against the league of the eleven kings, and are always mentioned as in close *entente* with him. Ban was King of Benwick, Bors of Gaul.

BANBA. In Irish romance, wife of McCuill, a Danaan king.

BANK, ELAINE DE. Daughter of Sir Bernard of Astolat. She falls madly in love with Sir Lancelot (*q.v.*), but failing to win his heart she perishes. (*Vide* "Morte d'Arthur.")

BARBOUR, JOHN. A Scottish poet of the fourteenth century, remembered chiefly by *The Bruce*, an epic poem of some fourteen thousand octosyllabic lines, rhymed in pairs, which recounts the deeds of the hero of Bannockburn, King Robert the Bruce. The exact date of Barbour's birth is uncertain, but it is commonly supposed to have been about 1316. Entering the Church, he became Archdeacon of Aberdeen in 1357, and subsequently enjoyed considerable favour from the King, Robert II, becoming Clerk of Audit of the Royal Household, and also one of the Auditors of the Exchequer. Again, in 1377, Barbour received from his sovereign a present of £10, a considerable sum in those days—while in the following year he was granted a pension of £1 *per annum ;* and it would seem that this was given him in recognition of his achievements in literature, for, in the *Exchequer Rolls of Scotland*, the annuity is accounted for as being bestowed on the poet " qui compilavit librum de gestis illus-

trissimi principis quondam domini regis Roberti Bruys . . ." Barbour died in 1395, but it appears that, ere this, he wrote various poems besides the epic on which his fame rests. An historian who lived just after him, Andrew Wynton, speaks in his *Orygynale Cronykil of Scotland* of a lengthy poem by Barbour, its subject the genealogy of the House of Stuart. No trace of this work exists nowadays, yet Wynton's statement is quite credible withal, as in 1388, Barbour received a further annual grant of £10 ; and this points to his having completed some important piece of writing at the time, while simultaneously it supports the idea that the missing poem was concerned with the reigning dynasty. Another poem ascribed to Barbour is *The Buik of the most noble and vailyeand Conqueror, Alexander the Great*, first published in 1580, and reprinted by the Bannatyne Club in 1831 ; and the ascription in this case is based on the similarity between the poem in question and *The Bruce*, while mainly for a like reason Barbour is credited with sundry further works notably *Legends of the Saints* and the *Legend of Troy*, the former a translation of *Legenda Aurea*, and the latter a rendering of Guido de Colonna's *Historia Destructionis Troiœ*.

Whether actually Barbour's or not, these minor writings need not be discussed here. As regards *The Bruce*, it need hardly be said that the original document is not extant but in the Advocates' Library, Edinburgh, there are two manuscript copies, both of the fifteenth century. So far as can be ascertained, the earliest printed edition of the poem is one dated Edinburgh, 1616 ; but the poet, Patrick Gordon, writing prior to this time, refers to Barbour's *Bruce* as the 'old printed book," and indeed it is reasonable to suppose that Chepman and Myllar printed an edition thereof. Be that as it may, Barbour's epic was issued by the famous Foulis press of Glasgow in 1648, while at least two other editions were published during the remaining half of the seventeenth century. In Scotland the poem enjoyed very considerable popularity till its phraseology became outmoded, and in the main this popularity was merited. Barbour is often crude, and appears to have been easily contented with whatever he wrote ; but, if the rank and file of his lines were but mediocre, flashes of genuine poetry break out ever and again, and these flashes are the more delightful by reason of a seeming absolute spontaneity as if they had grown up like a flower. Take, for instance, this passage on the subject of liberty :

" A ! freedome is a nobill thing !
Freedome mayss man to haiff liking !
Freedome all solace to man giffis
He levys at ess that frely levys !
A noble hart may haiff nane ess
Na ellys nocht that may him bless,
Giff freedome fail : for fre liking
Is yharnit our all othir thing
Na, he, that ay has levyt fre,
May nocht know weill the propyrte
The angyr, na the wrechyt dome
That is cuplyt to foule thryldome."

And like Scotland's other epic poet, Blind Harry, Barbour is never languid, but on the contrary invariably vigorous, while his descriptions of martial actions are singularly vivid. This is true in particular of his long account of the Battle of Bannockburn, especially the lines describing the preliminary duel between Bruce and de Bohun, and again the closing passage which details the rout of the English :

" Than mycht men heir ensenzeis cry
And Scottismen cry hardely,
' On thame ! On thame ! On thame !
  thai faill !
With that so hard thai can assaill,
And slew all that thai mycht our-ta,
And the Scottis archeris
Schot amang thame so sturdely,
Ingrevand them so gretumly. . . .
For thai that with thame fechtand
  weit
Set hardyment, and strynth, and
  will,
With hart and courage als thar- till,
And all thait mayn and all that
  mycht,
To put thame foully to the flycht."

Like several of the early Scottish historians, Barbour confounds King Robert the Bruce with his grandfather, Robert de Bruce, known as "the Competitor"; and numerous other deviations from fact are contained in his work, yet despite this it is one of the most valuable authorities on the Scottish War of Independence. It has been pointed out that Chaucer and Barbour are distinctly similar in places, but it is unlikely that the English poet ever read his great predecessor in Scotland, or even heard of him. As to the writings which influenced Barbour himself in this relation it is possible to speak more definitely, for in many passages the Scottish singer discloses an almost transparent debt to the French *Roman d'Alexandre*. And this is interesting and important, showing as it does that, so early as the fourteenth century, Scotland was imbibing that French teaching destined in later years to leave an indelible mark on all her arts, notably her painting, engraving and architecture.

Literature : The best modern editions of *The Bruce* are one edited by Jamieson, Edinburgh, 1830, and another issued by the Scottish Text Society in 1894, annotated by Professor Skeat. (Cf.

also article in the *Scottish Anti-quary* and the *Athenæum* for 1896, and a German work by Dr. Albert Hermann, *Untersuchungen über das Scöttishe Alexanderbuch*, 1893.)

BARROK. (*Vide* " Sir Ferumbras.") A giantess, wife of Estragott (*q.v.*). She used a scythe to mow down the Christians, when she was defending the walls of Aigremor. She was killed by Charlemagne.

BARUCH. Lord of the Red Branch, mentioned in the Ulster cycle of the Irish romances as inviting Fergus (*q.v.*) to a feast as he was conveying Deirdre and the sons of Usna to Emain Macha. Fergus consented, but on his return from the feast to Emain Macha, he found the sons of Usna slain, and Deirdre dead by her own act. (*Vide* " Deirdre.")

BASCNA CLAN. In Ossianic litera-ture, one of the two divisions of the Fianna (*q.v.*). Its first leader was Cumhal, Finn's father, its last Oscar, Finn's grandson. These clans were continually at war with each other for the supre-macy, but in the Battle of Gowra (*q.v.*), they were almost exter-minated. (*Vide* " Sgeimh Solais.")

BATTLE OF LOQUIFER, THE. A romance of the William of Orange sub-cycle of the Charlemagne saga. (*Vide* " William of Orange.") Gaston Paris did not suppose it to be earlier than the end of the twelfth century. It details the military prowess of Renouart (*q.v.*), the gigantic brother-in-law of Wil-liam of Orange, and is singular in having the sea for its chief scene of action. Renouart, with his barons, is on the sands before Porpaillart, when he espies a Saracen fleet in the roads. The Paynim persuade him to enter one

of their vessels, on the pretext of showing him some merchandise. They set sail, and Isembert, a monster who had been a fish, but who had been metamorphosed into a more hideous shape by the fairies, tells Renouart that he is to be flayed alive by the Saracens. Renouart slays the monster, and, armed only with a great bar of wood, forces the Saracens to let him go and to return themselves to Baratron, their capital. A new Saracen army is placed under the leadership of one Loquifer, a fairy-giant, so called because he is armed with a log. He and Renouart agree to meet in single combat, on which the issue of the war will depend. They meet in an island near Porpaillart. Loquifer has in the hollow of his club a fairy balm which imme-diately heals his wounds, and this circumstance assists him greatly in the combat, which goes against Renouart. God sends angels seve-ral times to assist Renouart, and at length he succeeds in depriving Loquifer of his club, so that the giant's strength departs. Renou-art slays him, and the devil carries off his soul. But the Saracens attack William of Orange, and Guibor, his wife, falls into the hands of Tybalt, her first husband. The Saracens are soon at the gates of Orange. Here a single combat takes place between William and Desramé, the father of Renou-art. William prevails, and Des-ramé's head is cut off. William hangs it to a pillar in his hall, and whilst there it ceases not to blow, to rain, to thunder and to lighten, till at last he has it taken down and cast into the sea. Renouart, grieving over the slain, goes to the sea-shore, where he is met by three fairies, one of whom holds in her hands a purple veil in which are seen trees, flowery meads, robes, mantles, rivers, fountains; a second shows a carbuncle which changes days and hours, the third a staff which contains the most delicate meats and drinks. They bear Renouart to Avalon, where he finds King Arthur, Gauvain and Roland (*q.v.*). Arthur, desirous of judging the hero's prowess, summons a monster, Chapalu, with the head of a cat and the body of a horse, who is doomed to remain so until he can suck the blood from Renouart's heel. He does so, and regains his human form. Renouart falls deeply in love with Morgue (Morgana), and from their union springs Corbon, a fiend who "did nought save evil." Renouart, desirous of seeing his son Maillefer, who is a prisoner with the Saracens, betakes him to Odierne, and Morgue, jealous of the child, bids Chapalu sink the ship. Renouart is wrecked, but succoured by the mermaids, and awakes to the memory of his woes on the shore opposite Porpaillart. In this romance we can perceive how the Mediæval poets were affected by the mythology of Greece, and perhaps by Celtic folklore elements, with which we find intermingled the fairy mythology of their own time.

BAUCENT. The good horse of William of Orange, in Carlovingian romance. On being addressed by his master in the midst of fight, he rallied to his encouraging words. The faithful steed was slain at the Battle of Arleschans or Aliscans (*q.v.*).

BAUDWIN, SIR. Of Brittany. He dwelt in England under the guise of a hermit. He was known among the Arthurian knights as a good surgeon. (*Vide* "Morte d'Arthur.")

BAVE. In the Ultonian legend, "The Cattle Raid of Quelgny" (*q.v.*), daughter of the wizard Calatin (*q.v.*). Wishing to lead Niam (*q.v.*) away from Cuchulain (*q.v.*), she took the form of one of her handmaids, and beckoned her forth to wander helplessly in the woods.

BEÄLCHU. A champion of Connaught, mentioned in the Ulster cycle of Irish romance. He discovered Conall (*q.v.*), bleeding to death after his fight with Ket. Conall requested Beälchu to slay him, but he refused, and took him home and healed his wounds. His three sons, noting Conall's might, resolved to slay the hero before he recovered. But Conall so contrived that they killed their father instead, after which he slew all three, and took their heads to Ulster.

BEALM, KING OF. A character in *The History of Roswall and Lillian* (*q.v.*). A friend of the King of Naples, he promises to receive the latter's son Roswall, but is deceived by Roswall's steward, who escorts the prince on the journey. This person, posing as Roswall, succeeds in receiving from the king the hand of his daughter Lillian. The king does not suspect the steward, and enforces Lillian against her will to accept him as her husband. Meanwhile he had engaged Dissawar (Roswall's *alias*) as servant to his daughter. In response to the discoveries of three lords soon after the marriage, the king orders the pretended prince to be put to death, and places the wronged "Dissawar" in his rightful position; further consenting to the marriage of his daughter and Roswall.

BEATRICE. (*Vide* "Garin the Lorrainer.") Daughter of Duke Milo of Gascony, and wife of Bego. She lived at Belin very happily with her husband, and remonstrated with him when he left on his last journey to visit Garin. She never re-married, although advised to do so, and died, like her sister, a few days after Garin's death.

BEAUMAINS, SIR. Brother to Sir Gawaine, and a knight of Arthur. He went on a quest to relieve Dame Liones (*q.v.*), who was captive to the Knight of the Red Laundes (*q.v.*). (*Vide* "Morte d'Arthur.")

BEBO. Wife of Iubdan (*q.v.*), a King of the Wee Folk, mentioned in an Irish Ultonian romance.

BEDEVERE, SIR. A knight of King Arthur. He was present at the battle between Arthur and Mordred (*q.v.*), and after Arthur's death he caused a history to be written of the event. (*Vide* "Morte d'Arthur.")

BEDUERS. A knight alluded to in the Grail romance of *Didot Perceval*, as taking upon himself the Grail quest at the same time as Perceval. He is perhaps identical with Bedivere.

BEGO. (*Vide* "Garin the Lorrainer.") Son of Hervi, Duke of Metz. Reared at the court of France by Count Hardre, he was a favourite of King Pepin (*q.v.*), and was a chivalrous knight, always ready to fight for any of his kinsmen who needed help. He displayed great courage on many occasions, both in single combat and at the head of his forces. He married Beatrice (*q.v.*), daughter of Duke Milo (*q.v.*), and lived happily with her, but, weary to

see his brother again, he set out to hunt a boar in order that he might take the head to Garin, and this resulted in his death.

BEKKHILD. (*Vide* "Volsungs.") Sister to Brynhild, wife of Heimar (*q.v.*) and mother of Alsund (*q.v.*).

BELE, KING. (*Vide* "Frithjof Saga.") Father of Ingebjorg, Helgi, and Halfdan.

BELISANTE. (*Vide* "Amys and Amylion.") Daughter of the Duke of Lombardy (*q.v.*) and wife of Amys. She was concerned in the treason which the steward brought against Amys, and was the mother of the two children whom her husband sacrificed for the sake of Amylion.

BELISENT. (*Vide* "Sir Otuel.") Daughter of Charlemagne. Married to Sir Otuel.

BELLIANCE, SIR, LE ORGULUS. Brother to Sir Frol, who was slain by Lancelot during the fight for Guinever at the stake. (*Vide* "Morte d'Arthur.")

BELLONGERIUS, SIR, LE BREUSE. Son of Sir Alisander (*q.v.*). He is mentioned in Arthurian romance as having avenged both his father's and grandfather's death by killing King Mark. (*Vide* "Morte d'Arthur.")

BEN BULBEN, THE BOAR OF. In Irish romance, the transformed step-brother and destroyer of Dermot (*q.v.*). The legend runs : Donn (*q.v.*), Dermot's father, gave his son to be brought up by Angus Og (*q.v.*). His mother proved unfaithful to her husband and bore a child to Roc, the steward of Angus. One day his child, in fear of some hounds that were fighting on the floor of the hall, ran between the knees of Donn. His stepfather then squeezed him to death and flung the body to the dogs. On discovering with Finn's aid the cause of his son's death, Roc, by virtue of a druidic rod, transformed the body into a huge living boar without ears or tail, and bade it bring Dermot to his death. The beast then rushed from the hall, and roamed about the forests of Ben Bulben till the fatal day when it slew Dermot.

BEOWULF. An Anglo-Saxon epic poem of great antiquarian and philological interest. The events which are described in it are referred to the middle of the fifth century, and the lay itself was perhaps brought to England by Teutonic settlers from their original home in Germany. The MS. in the Cottonian Library is the only one known to exist, and that was unfortunately seriously injured by fire in 1731. It is in two portions which exhibit obvious signs of having been written at different periods and by different hands, and is certainly a copy of an older manuscript, executed about the beginning of the eighth century. That the poem is of the antiquity ascribed to it appears probable from the admixture of Christianity and paganism which its text contains, and it would seem from this circumstance that it must have originated at a period when the elder Teutonic faith was in process of elimination. There can be little doubt that Beowulf is one of the great army of Sons of the Light, Sun-heroes, or Men of the Sun, whose business it was to wage eternal war against the powers of darkness until they themselves fell before the shaft that flies in gloom, or were slain by the night-dragon. He comes to land in the traditional sun-boat as a child. We find that the

Saxons called their harvest month Beo or Bewod, and we know that gods of light are invariably connected with fertility and the raising of crops. Grendel, as the peruser of the myth in the appended synopsis will observe, is the gloomy demon in one of his most dread forms. He is akin to the night-dragon, the Sphinx, the Dragon of Wantley, and the throttling snake Ahi. Slain, his dam comes to avenge him. She is merely his prototype, as is the later dragon encountered typifying the night-forces first conquered by the sun, and then victorious over him. Like all mythical monsters this pair are the guardians of a great treasure, and when, like Herakles, Beowulf lies dying of the dragon's venom, he beholds in the lustre of the gained hoard the splendour of the gates of the setting sun. Beowulf was a mighty warrior and saved his country from defeat by the Swedes. At a feast of victory a wandering minstrel sang of how he had come from the court of Hrodgar of Jutland, King of the Skioldungs, whose realm was being devastated by the monster Grendel, descendant of the daughters of Cain and evil demons (*q.v.*), and he called upon Beowulf to slay the giant. Promising his aid, Beowulf, after a trial of strength with Breka (*q.v.*) set out with fifteen noble Goths for the castle of King Hrodgar, who received them with joy. Beowulf was so confident of victory that he laid aside his armour, deciding to fight Grendel with his hands. At midnight Grendel entered the hall where Beowulf lay among his warriors, and after a fierce struggle Beowulf defeated him, the monster escaping only by leaving his arm, wrenched out at the socket, in the hero's grip. Highly was Beowulf honoured next day, and great rejoicings took place, but that night there came out of the sea another monster—Grendel's mother, who came to avenge her son. She slew many of the Skioldungs, and Beowulf, learning at morning of the havoc she had wrought, vowed to seek out and slay her. He dived to the bottom of the sea, encountering many dangers, and in the hall of the mer-woman's palace, where Grendel lay dead, Beowulf slew her, after a fierce fight. Laden with gifts and acclaimed as a mighty hero, Beowulf returned to his own country. There he passed many years in peace, till the Frisians raided Gothland, and King Hygelak was slain in a punitive expedition to Friesland. Hygelak's son Hardred (*q.v.*) was but a child, and while his mother Hygd mourned for her husband the barons quarrelled among themselves till the queen roused herself from her grief, and calling a meeting of the notables advised that Beowulf be elected king, as Hardred was too young to rule. The assembly cheered, but Beowulf refused to deprive Hardred of his rights, saying that rather would he act as regent till the young king could govern for himself. This Beowulf did faithfully, but soon after attaining sovereign power Hardred (*q.v.*) was slain, and the Gothic Allthing unanimously elected Beowulf King, which office he now accepted. He defeated those who raided the country, the last being the Swedes (*vide* " Eadgils,"), after which he reigned in peace, and with wisdom, for about forty years. Then the land was laid waste by a dragon, roused to wrath and grief by the loss of a gold pot stolen by a fugitive slave from the treasure that the monster guarded. The

flame of its breath devastated the land, and Beowulf, despite the remonstrances of his friends, resolved to attack it. He had a three-fold shield made, and set out with Wichstan (*q.v.*) and ten other warriors. A dreadful struggle took place between Beowulf and the dragon, till at last the smoke and fire from the monster's mouth cleared momentarily, and his companions saw Beowulf in the dragon's jaws. They all sought refuge save Wichstan, who went to his master's aid, so that finally Beowulf was able to slay the dragon, though he was poisoned by its fangs and knew himself doomed. He bade Wichstan bring the treasure out of the dragon's cave as the king's last gift to his people, and presently he died. He was buried on a height named Hronesnas. He was so beloved by his people that they refused to take the treasure his death had won for them, placing it in his grave.

It is obvious that this poem did not originate in Scandinavia or the North, but probably in Sleswig, the names of the various characters being purely Saxon. It perhaps relates to veritable occurrences in the history of our Teutonic forefathers ere they yet left their original land of Angeln.

BERGTHORA. (*Vide* " Burnt Njal.") Wife of Njal. Her bitter enmity with Hallgerda, Gunnar's wife, brought about her own and her husband's fiery death.

BERNARD, SIR. Of Astolat, Father to Elaine de Banke (*q.v.*), Tirre and Lavaine. He is especially known for his hospitality to the Knights of the Round Table. (*Vide* " Morte d'Arthur.")

BERNARD OF NAISIL. (*Vide* " Garin the Lorrainer.") A crafty unscrupulous man. He began life as a monk, and being nearly killed at the battle at Verdun was hidden in the same monastery. He had a struggle with Garin for the golden cup at the king's marriage, and another fight with Garin when Galopin's message came to him. He had a great hatred of the Lorrainers, and fought against them on every possible occasion.

BERNI, FRANCESCO. A satiric poet of Florence, near which city he was born about the year 1490. He remodelled the *Orlando Innamorato* of Boiardo (*q.v.*) in a free and lively style, and so characteristic was the light and elegant mockery of his verse, that his countrymen attached to it the appellation of *bernesque*. Berni was of noble but not opulent family, and received a post in the Apostolic Datary, employment in which was uncongenial to him. He made many enemies by his biting satires, and though he made much pretence to a love of liberty, did nothing to enfranchise himself from the condition of dependence in which he remained for the whole of his life. He was incorrigibly lazy, and his chief pleasure was dozing in bed. As he refused to poison the Cardinal Ippolito at the request of that Churchman's cousin the Duke Alessandro de' Medici, he was himself poisoned a few days afterwards, probably in order to ensure that he would not betray the illustrious instigator of the crime. Under his hand everything was transformed into ridicule. Like Ariosto, Berni treated chivalry with a degree of mockery, and if he has not travestied the tale of Boiardo, he has indulged in inextinguishable laughter at the absurdities he has himself created. He also wrote many satirical sonnets and other verses in *terza rima*, among which are eulogies upon Aristotle and on the Plague.

BERNIER. (*Vide* "Raoul of Cambrai.") The Squire of Raoul of Cambrai. He was a natural son of Ybert, a lord of Vermandois. Raoul sacks the convent of Bernier's mother, Marsent, and incurs his implacable enmity, being finally slain by him. This brings about a feud, which is later patched up, at which Charlemagne is highly displeased, insults Bernier, and is overthrown. He is affianced to the daughter of Red Guerry, one of his principal enemies, and is then reconciled to him. Charles, the emperor, takes Bernier's wife prisoner, and gives her to another, but Bernier regains her. Guerry, repenting of his friendship with Bernier, treacherously slays him.

BEVIS OF HAMPTON. An English romance of the thirteenth century. Some romances represent Bevis as a son of Ogier the Dane (*q.v.*). Like Arthur or Tristrem he is born to greatness, he is a match for any number of men who may assail him, is the victim of treacherous letters ordering him to be slain, is imprisoned in a dragon-haunted dungeon, but escapes once more into the light —passing from obscurity to light and gloom to light again. Incidents in his myth are common to those of Odysseus and the Hindoo legend of Logedas Raja. Like Odysseus he returns in traveller's attire to the home of his lady-love, and is known by his horse like Ogier. The writer of Bevis was obviously destitute of imagination, but the nature of the material which he sought to mould into a story is none the less evident, for the adventures of the hero are obviously superimposed upon the ancient matter of the sun-myth. The romance tells how Guy, Earl of Southampton, spent his youth in defending his territory, which was exposed to foreign invasion, and late in life married a daughter of the King of Scotland. She had a lover, Sir Murdour, and hated her husband. She sent for her lover and with him made a pact to get her husband into the forest, on the pretext of procuring some game for her, where Sir Murdour met him and brutally killed him. She had one son, Bevis, whom she disliked also, and to get rid of him after first trying to get his uncle Saber to kill him, she had him sold as a slave and sent " into Heathenesse." He arrived at the court of Ermyn, a Saracen King, who, taking a fancy to the clever boy, completed his education, knighted him and made him his chamberlain. He proposed to Bevis to marry his daughter Josyan, but this offer Bevis declined. Bradmond, King of Damascus, sent Ermyn a proposal for Josyan's hand, threatening if she did not marry him, that he would ravage her father's country. Incensed at this threat, Ermyn prepared to fight, and Josyan armed Bevis, gave him a very swift horse called Arundel and a famous sword called Morglay. Bevis returned victorious, and was greatly honoured, and Josyan paid him every attention, indeed, made violent love to him. But it was only when she promised to renounce paganism that he avowed his passion for her. Two knights whom Bevis had befriended and who saw Josyan and Bevis together and heard their conversation went to Ermyn and told him all. They suggested to the king to send Bevis with a letter to Bradmond, in which the king charged him to take Bevis prisoner. In good faith Bevis set out, not even providing himself with sufficient food, but on the way he was entertained by a palmer who turned out to be the son of Saber. Saber had gone to the Isle of Wight, hating the rule of his dead master's successors, and had defended the island against them. He had sent his son disguised as a palmer to try to find Bevis and bring him back to help them. Bevis did not reveal himself to Terry, but said he knew Bevis, and would relate this news to him and that Saber would get help as soon as possible. Bevis then went on to Damascus, and the magnificence of Bradmond's palace impressed him. But the sight of the people preparing a sacrifice for an idol enraged him so much that he seized it and cast it to the ground, thereby rousing the indignation of the populace, who tried to seize him. He made such good use of an ordinary sword, however, that he forced his way to the king and showed him the letter. Bradmond, after complaining to Bevis of his sacrilege, ordered his men to put him in a dungeon inhabited by two dragons which devoured those cast to them, and he pretended that Ermyn had arranged this punishment. Bevis slew the monsters, but for seven years he was kept in the dungeon on most wretched fare. Josyan had meanwhile married Inor, King of Mounbraunt, being told that Sir Bevis had gone to England and had married. Bevis escaped, and having armed himself and taken a good horse, he rode out to the forest. After many adventures a knight he met told him of Josyan's marriage to Inor, so he went to find her. Disguised as a palmer he arrived at her tower and heard her praying, and his own name was not forgotten. She gave dole to poor pilgrims daily, so Sir Bevis went next morning and was fed by her and spoke of his travels, and when she asked him if he knew anything of a Sir Bevis, he said he was a friend that had been sent in search of a horse called Arundel. The queen then took him to the stable, and whenever she saw him mount the horse she recognized him. The pair, reunited, wished to set out together at once, but were advised by Boniface, Josyan's confidential chamberlain, to wait till the king came back from hunting and pretend that Bevis had come from Syria, and that his brother had been defeated by King Syrak, and had no means of sending for help. This ruse succeeded, and the king set out with all his men to Syria to rescue his brother. Sir Bevis then donned the best armour he could find, mounted Arundel, and with Boniface they made their escape to a cave. While Sir Bevis was out hunting one day Josyan was attacked in the cave by two lions. They killed and devoured Boniface, but instead of hurting Josyan, they lay down with their heads in her lap. When Sir Bevis returned and found what had happened, he rejoiced in the knowledge of Josyan's chastity, and, killing the lions, they left the cave and continued their journey. They soon met a great giant called Ascapard, whom Bevis overcame. At Josyan's request, he made him their page. Seeing a ship bound for Germany they went on board, but some Saracens objected to their presence. Ascapard drove them out, and carrying Bevis and Josyan on board, set sail, and

they soon arrived at Cologne. The Bishop of Cologne was Bevis's uncle, and was much interested in hearing his adventures. Josyan was christened as also the pagan giant. Sir Bevis's next adventure was with a dragon which he killed, taking its head back to Cologne. The grateful Bishop of Cologne gave Bevis a hundred knights to accompany him to England to avenge his father, and leaving Josyan in care of Ascapard, Bevis set out. He landed near Southampton, and sent a messenger to Sir Murdour to the effect that a knight of Brittany had arrived with one hundred men who were willing to offer him service if he desired. If not, they would assist his rival. Bevis had taken the name of Sir Jarrad, and under his assumed name heard a very garbled version of his own history. He offered to go to the Isle of Wight in the interests of Sir Murdour against Saber. He had no sooner joined Saber, than he sent word to Sir Murdour of his real name and purpose. Meanwhile Josyan was being persecuted by the attentions of a German earl, Sir Mile. To save herself she promised to marry him, and on the night of their wedding strangled him with her girdle. For this, she was condemned to be burned. Prior to this she had sent a message to Sir Bevis to come to her help. He arrived in time, and he and Ascapard rescued her at the stake, subsequently returning together to the Isle of Wight. A great battle then took place between Sir Bevis and Sir Murdour. Sir Murdour was slain by Bevis, with the assistance of Ascapard, and this decided the struggle. The countess threw herself down from a tower and was killed. The Bishop of Cologne came to marry

Josyan and Bevis, and Bevis got back his own territories, and was then made earl-marshal by the king. The king's son begged Sir Bevis to give him Arundel, but Sir Bevis declined, and Edgar tried to steal the horse, but it kicked him so severely that he died. The king ordered Sir Bevis to be hanged for this. But the barons objected, and in expiation Sir Bevis proposed to leave England and hand over his estates to Saber. He left the country immediately with his wife and nephew, Terry. Ascapard, turning traitor, thought that he would fare better now with his old master, so he hastened to King Inor at Mounbraunt and got from him a company of Saracens to help him to take back Josyan to the king. Josyan became the mother of twin sons when she was alone in the forest, and at this juncture she was carried off by Ascapard. When Bevis and Terry came back they found the two babes, and guessed what had happened. They left the children, one who was to be called Guy, to the care of a forester, the other to be called Mile, to a fisherman, and both were christened. Bevis and Terry went on to find Ascapard and Josyan. On their way they entered a tournament and gained the prize—the wealthy daughter of a Duke. As Bevis was already married they arranged she should remain with him till he found his wife and then marry Terry. Sir Saber meanwhile had a dream. Ernebrough, his wife, interpreted dreams, and she concluded from it that some misfortune had overtaken Sir Bevis. Saber set out with twelve knights encased in armour under pilgrim's dress, and he soon overtook Ascapard, and, killing him, rescued Josyan. She

made an ointment which disguised her, and she remained with Saber for seven years till accidentally they came to the town where Sir Bevis was, where they were happily united and her children joined them. King Inor met Sir Bevis in single combat, but by the help of his famous sword, Morglay, Sir Bevis slew him. Bevis put on Inor's armour and entered the garrison at Mounbraunt and conquered that country and converted it to Christianity. After this Saber's wife arrived to tell them that Edgar of England had deprived their son Robert of his estates and given them to a favourite, Sir Bryant of Cornwall. Sir Bevis set out with a great army, and having inflicted much damage upon Edgar, that monarch to obtain peace, offered his only daughter to Mile, son of Bevis, and through this marriage Mile became King of England. Josyan, Bevis and Sir Guy went back to Ermonry first, where Sir Guy reigned as King, and Bevis resumed his sway at Mounbraunt.

BIBUNG. (*Vide* "Dietrich of Bern.") He styled himself the unconquerable protector of Queen Virginal (*q.v.*).

BIORN (1). (*Vide* "Grettir Saga.") The chief of Thorkel's men and enemy of Grettir. Having fled from the bear that ravaged the land he was mocked and jeered at by Grettir, and, therefore, in revenge he cast his enemy's cloak into the bear's den. Both men had promised to keep the peace while they dwelt with Thorkel, but upon landing in Norway they met, and Biorn was slain.

BIORN (2). A daring fellow who harboured Grettir, and urged him to give the dandy Gisli (*q.v.*) a lesson.

BIROG. In Irish romance, a Druidess who by her magic brought Kian (*q.v.*) and Ethlinn (*q.v.*) together.

BISCLAVARET. (*Vide* " Were-Wolf, Lay of the.")

BISHOP OF COLOGNE. (*Vide* "Bevis of Hampton.") Uncle of Sir Bevis. In gratitude to Bevis for delivering the people of Cologne from a dragon, he supplied him with a hundred knights when he went to England. Afterwards he, himself, went there to perform the marriage ceremony between Bevis and Josyan.

BITEROLF AND DIETRICH. (*Vide* " Dietrich of Bern.")

BITEROLF AND DIETLIEB. A poem of great length and tediousness, believed by Gervinus to belong to the end of the twelfth century. The legend, in brief, is as follows :

Biterolf, a gallant knight of the capital of Toledo, hearing wonderful stories about King Etzel's (Attila's) court, secretly leaves his wife, Dietlint, and his son, Dietlieb, to go in search of it. In his absence, the son grows up, and, in like manner, sets out in search of his father. In crossing Burgundy, he is attacked by King Gunthar, but is victorious. On reaching Etzel's court, a fight occurs between father and son, their relationship being unknown. A mutual recognition takes place, and they proceed homewards, along with an army sent by Etzel to avenge the outrage perpetrated by the Burgundians on young Dietlieb. Gunthar meets them with a host of valiant guests, invited under pretext of a tournament. They fight together, and the mock battle turns into a real one, which remains indecisive. A general reconciliation follows,
after which, Biterolf and Dietlieb continue their way homeward.

The poem contains over 13,000 lines, and is undoubtedly connected with the *Nibelungenlied* cycle. It is written in doggerel verse, and is perhaps by the same author as *Klage*. Its chief value is that it presents to us all the leading characters of the *Nibelungenlied* with others of the cycle, such as Walther, often in connection with details which seem to belong to a lost portion of the original cycle.

BITEROLF, YARL. Father of Dietlieb (Ilmenrick). (*Vide* " Dietrich of Bern.")

BJORN. (*Vide* "Frithjof Saga.") The sworn companion of Frithjof after the death of the latter's father, Thorsten.

BLACK SAINGLEND. Cuchulain's (*q.v.*) last horse. When the Ulster hero was fatally struck by Lewry (*q.v.*), it broke away from the chariot.

BLAI. In Irish Ossianic romance, the Danaan mother of Oisin (*q.v.*).

BLAISE. Alluded to in the *Didot Perceval* as the " Master " of Merlin, resident in " Ortoberland." He alone could tell Merlin the use of the Grail. He " writed down these things, and by his writings we know them." The whole passage is one of much obscurity. In the romance of *Merlin* (Auchinleck MS.) he is alluded to as a holy hermit who tried to keep Merlin's mother and aunts from wrong-doing, and when Merlin, the offspring of Satan, was born as the fruit of their sin, baptised him ere his infernal parent could intervene.

BLAMORE, SIR DE GANIS. Brother to Bleoberis (*q.v.*). He was one of the knights taken by Lancelot to Benwick, which they ruled over for a time. (*Vide* "Morte d'Arthur.")

BLANCHFLEUR or WHITE FLOWER. In Arthurian legend the beauteous damsel whom Sir Perceval defends against Climadex's (*q.v.*) marshal, Aguigrenons (*q.v.*). She favours Sir Perceval with her amorous embraces the night before the onslaught, but withholds them the next day in order to urge him to greater prowess in the contest.

BLANCHFLEUR. (*Vide* "Florice and Blanchfleur.") Daughter of Topase the daughter of the Duke of Ferrara. She was friendly with Florice, son of Felix, King of Murcia, from infancy, and gave him a mystic ring. Florice was banished for his love of the Christian maiden, and she was sentenced to death, but was shipped to Alexandria instead, there to be sold as a slave. But Florice discovered her there, partly by means of the ring she had given him, and they were happily united. There are several versions of the tale, which is told by Boccaccio in his *Filocopo*.

BLANCHE-FLEUR. (*Vide* "Guy of Warwick.") Daughter of Reignier, Emperor of Germany. A tournament was held in her honour, in which Sir Guy took the prize.

BLANCHEFLOWER. In Carlovingian romance, sister of William of Orange, and Queen to Louis Le Debonair. On his return from the Battle of Arleschans or Aliscans (*q.v.*) to plead for succour against the Saracens, she mocks William for his sorry array, but he puts her to shame, tearing the crown from her head, seizing her by the hair, and abusing her foully. He is even about to behead her, when their mother Hermengard takes her away. A reconciliation is, however, brought about between them through the mediation of the holy Alice, the queen's daughter.

BLANCHFLOWER. (*Vide* "Garin of Lorraine.") Daughter of King Thierry of Savoy (*q.v.*). She was betrothed to Garin at the age of fifteen years, which event was followed by the death of her father. She arrived in Paris, when the Lorrainers and Bordelais met to settle their dispute, and was much admired by Pepin (*q.v.*), who through the advice of the Archbishop of Rheims (*q.v.*), married her. Her first love was present at the wedding. She afterwards assisted the brothers, Bego and Garin, who plotted against the king. She once went on an errand of peace to Garin.

BLANID. Wife of Curoi, King of Munster, mentioned in the Ulster cycle of Irish romance. She conceived a violent passion for Cuchulain (*q.v.*) and requested him to abduct her from her husband's dwelling. Knowing that Cuchulain was in hiding hard by, she sent him word to wait until a certain stream should grow white. She poured the milk of three cows into the brook, and on this signal Cuchulain attacked the abode of Curoi, slew him, and carried off Blanid. Fercartna, the Sennachie or bard of Curoi, followed them, and waiting until the party had gained the edge of the cliff of Beara, seized Blanid, and leaped with her into the depths below.

BLEHERIS. A poet "born and bred in Wales," alluded to by Gautier de Denain, one of the continuators of Chrétien de Troyes, as his authority for the stories of Gawain, and believed to be identical with the Bledhericus mentioned by Giraldus Cambrensis, as *famosus ille fabulator*, and the Bréris quoted by Thomas of Brittany as an authority for the story of Tristan.

BLEOBERIS DE GANIS, SIR. Brother to Blamore, and cousin to Sir Lancelot. He is for a while, according to Arthurian Romance, Duke of Poictiers in Benwick, the duchy of which is given him by Lancelot (*q.v.*). (*Vide* "Morte d'Arthur.")

BLIANT, SIR. A noble knight and defender of Lancelot (*q.v.*), whom he harbours during his insane period.

BLIHOS BLIHERIS. A person alluded to in the *Conte du Graal*, as being conquered by Gauvain or Gawain, and as recounting to Arthur's Court the tale of the wandering damsels sprung from those ravished by King Amangons (*q.v.*). "So long would they wander till God gave them to find the Court, whence joy and splendour would come to the land." They were regained by Arthur's knights.

BLIND HARRY. A Mediæval Scottish poet. His name is sometimes spelt Hary, while occasionally he is styled Henry the Minstrel. He lived in the fifteenth century, but he is included here because the work by which he is remembered, a long poem, entitled *Schir William Wallace*, which recounts the deeds of that hero, is based largely on traditions handed down orally since Wallace's own time, that is to say, the end of the thirteenth century.

One of the earliest trustworthy Scottish historians, John Major in his *Historia Majoris Britanniæ*, tells that "There was one Henry, blind from his birth, who in the

time of my childhood fabricated a whole book about William Wallace, and herein he wrote down in our native rhymes—and this was a kind of composition in which he had much skill—all that passed current amongst the people in his day. I, however, can give but a partial evidence to such writings as these. This Henry used to recite his tales in the houses of the nobles, and thereby he procured food and clothing." Major was born in 1469, so Harry's birth must have been considerably anterior to that, but hardly anything is known definitely about his life. On the 1st April, 1490, as the *Accounts of the Lord High Treasurer of Scotland* show, he was granted a small pension by James IV., then resident at Stirling. The amount was only eighteen shillings per annum, but, though this figure appears diminutive, if not actually ridiculous, it must be borne in mind that the purchasing value of such a sum was much greater in the middle-ages than now. The last payment of Harry's pension recorded in the treasurer's books is in 1492, and as James was invariably generous towards poets, and usually paid a pension very regularly up till the time of the annuitant's death, the year in question was probably that in which Blind Harry died. Moreover, he is mentioned by Dunbar in his *Lament for the Makaris*, composed in 1507, so he must have been dead by that time.

Major's statement that Harry was blind from his birth has often been questioned, and with good reason ; for the poem of *Wallace* is not the output of an illiterate man, but rather the work of one who had received a fairly good education, as good at least as that of the average ecclesiastic of the period. Indeed, Harry's verse frequently suggests obligations to Chaucer, and proclaims the author to have been acquainted with the Arthurian legends, and the tales of ancient Greece ; while although, to repeat, the poem is based chiefly on tradition, Harry also utilised several Latin authorities. He acknowledges this repeatedly, laying particular stress on his debt to

> " the Latin buk,
> Quhilk Maister Blair in his time
> undertuk " ;

And the person cited thus has always been assumed to have been one Arnold Blair, a chaplain to Wallace, who wrote a biography of the latter.

Harry's epic is written in ten-syllable lines of heroic verse, and as regards its historical value, this has been much impugned, but perhaps unduly so, for the poem corroborates nearly all that is known about Wallace from other sources. At the same time, the minstrel was distinctly a hero-worshipper and not a mere chronicler, and he crowds the life of Scotland's liberator with endless valiant deeds of which other writers have nothing to say. For instance, he relates that Wallace defeated Edward I. at Biggar long before the memorable Battle of Stirling Bridge in 1297, and of this event there is no trace in history. True it is that, in 1303, the Scots won a victory over the English at Roslin, and perhaps Harry's statement is a confusion with this event, the supposition being the more reasonable inasmuch as the poet's chronology is usually inaccurate ; but then, there is no proof that Wallace took part in the fight at Roslin, the Scottish forces having been commanded on that occasion by John Comyn and Simon Fraser. Again, the poet represents his hero as receiving a visit from the Queen of England at a time when no such person existed ; while not content with this, he even depicts this mythological queen as enamoured of Sir William. Numerous other examples might be given of Harry's perversion of fact, and, in short, it is clear that he allowed his own family to flower at large round the life of his hero ; while it is natural, besides, that the name and fame of Wallace should have gathered about them many extravagant legends during the two centuries between Sir William's own time and Harry's.

Blind Harry is hardly in the forefront of the Mediæval Scottish poets. He is by no means the equal of his predecessor, James I., nor yet of his mighty successor, William Dunbar, and even his best passages can hardly be ranked beside the finest in John Barbour's *Bruce*. Nevertheless, the general level of excellence in *Wallace* is fully equal to that in the last-named poem ; and, whatever Harry's limitations, his verse is always manly and decisive. Vigour seems to have attended him perennially, and it is impossible to conceive him hesitating, or searching for the right word, the right phrase. On the contrary, spontaneity characterises his work throughout ; while it abounds in very vivid descriptions—descriptions so vivid, indeed, that their existence supports the contention that the poet was not blind all his life.

In the Advocates' Library, Edinburgh, there is a complete manuscript copy of *Schir William Wallace*, dated 1488, the scribe who wrote this being one John Ramsay. As the whole poem was copied so early as this—at least four years before the poet's death —it may be assumed that it was very popular during his lifetime ; and the mere fact that Harry was universally known by his Christian name, while his surname has not come down to posterity, likewise points to his having been an idol of the people in his own day. Nor did his reputation die with him, and it should be noted that Burns, in one of his letters, speaks of *Wallace* with great enthusiasm, saying it was one of the first books he read in boyhood with real delight, and adding that it left an indelible mark on his memory. A fine tribute was this to the old poet, while further homage has been offered him in the shape of many editions of his works. Carlyle's friend, David Laing, in his preface to *Gologras and Gawain* mentions having seen an edition of *Wallace* printed by the first Scottish press, that conducted by Chepman and Myllar, during the reign of James IV. Such an edition, however, is not known to exist nowadays, and perhaps Laing was in error. Be that as it may, Harry's poem was certainly printed again and again during the sixteenth and seventeenth centuries, while notable editions of recent years are one edited by John Jamieson in 1820, and another published by the Scottish Text Society in 1885–86.

Literature : Despite the scanty materials therefor, Blind Harry's life has been repeatedly written, notably by David Irvine in *Lives of the Scottish Poets*, Edinburgh, 1810. The merits of *Wallace* are discussed by T. F. Henderson in *Scottish Vernacular Literature*, and by J. H. Millar in *A Literary History of Scotland ;* while the question of Chaucer's influence on Harry was debated by Professor Walter W. Skeat in *The Modern Language Quarterly* of November, 1897.

BLIOCADRANS. Mentioned in the *Conte du Graal* as the father of Perceval. He of the twelve knights of the land of Wales alone survived, so eager were they for tournaments and combats. He goes forth to a tourney held by the King of Wales against the folk of the Waste Fountain, in which he is slain. His wife, who has borne a son, Perceval, pretends a pilgrimage to St. Brandan in Scotland, but removes to the Waste Forest, far from all men. Here she brings up Perceval, warning him against men in armour, who, she tells him, are "Devils." (*Vide* "Perceval.")

BOANNA. (The river Boyne), in Irish romance, Mother of Angus Og (*q.v.*).

BOCTUS AND SIDRAC. (*Vide* "Sidrac.")

BODEL, JEAN. A French poet of the thirteenth century, remembered mainly by his drama of *St. Nicholas* and an epic poem, *Les Saisnes* or *Song of the Saxons* (*q.v.*). Arras was his native town, and there he lived for a number of years, gaining his livelihood—as was the fashion among poets of the Middle Ages—by acting as a herald. He appears to have early acquired considerable fame, and to have been a jovial and reckless character ; yet it would seem that a strain of piety ran through his nature, for it is recorded that, about the year 1269, he commenced making preparations to follow a body of crusaders to the Holy Land. It is possible, of course, that it was not religious ardour which prompted him to this step, and that he was simply called upon to accompany the troops in his official capacity ; but be that as it may, his project was suddenly cut short by a terrible misfortune, unmistakable signs of leprosy now showing themselves on his hands and face. In accordance with the law of the time he had to cut himself off from all his relations and friends, but his townsfellows, moved by pity, procured him admittance to a lazar-house at Meulan. He was thus rescued from that life of wandering which was the sorry fate of so many lepers, yet the incarceration to which he was doomed henceforth was scarcely less terrible, and how deeply he suffered is shown by his poem, *Les Congés*, in which he bids a touching farewell to his old associates at Arras, alike the rich who had patronized him, and the gay fellows with whom he had fraternized in the taverns. Bodel is supposed to have spent the rest of his days entirely at Meulan, and it was probably in that uncongenial atmosphere that he penned the majority of his extant poems, these including a series of Pastorals besides the things cited above. Save for *Les Congés*, however, the writer's work is by no means tinged with the melancholy which would naturally imbrue the productions of a dweller in a lazar-house ; and, indeed, *St. Nicholas*, which is based on a story in *The Apocrypha*, contains several rollicking tavern scenes, each of them drawn with unflinching realism, and being obviously based on the personal experience and observation of the author. The piece is especially interesting, moreover, as being one of the first miracle plays in French literature ; while as regards *Les Saisnes*, this has considerable historical as well as literary value. It treats of one of Charlemagne's campaigns, and the writer is thought to have gleaned his information largely from early poems current in his day but now lost. Bodel's description of the threefold territory of romance is frequently quoted :—

"Ne sont que troîs matières à nul
   homme entendant,
  De France, et de Bretagne, et de
   Rome la grant."

BOIARDO, MATTEO MARIE. Count of Scandiano, a famous Italian poet, was born at Scandiano in Lombardy 1430–94, and educated at the Court of the Duke Borso d'Este, and was subsequently made Governor of Reggio (1478), then of Modena (1481), and once more of Reggio, shortly before his death, which occurred on 21st December, 1494. The greatest of his poems is the *Orlando Innamorato*, based on the Charlemagne cycle. With a freshness and splendour of fancy, he portrays the loves of Orlando and the fair Angelica in a manner which gives the work perpetual popularity among lovers of fantastic poetry. Between 1545 and the date of the *editio princeps* (1495), the poem appears to have been much relished, for it had passed through no fewer than sixteen editions. From then, and not until 1836, when Panizzi published an excellent edition, it was unpublished. It has been translated into most of the languages of Western Europe.

BOLFIANA. (*Vide* "Dietrich of Bern.") She was presented in marriage by King Ermenrich to Wittich (*q.v.*).

BONDWIN, SIR. Brother to King Mark (*q.v.*) and father of Alisander (*q.v.*). He was treacherously slain by Mark, who dispersed his dependents. (*Vide* "Morte d'Arthur.")

BONIFACE. (*Vide* "Bevis of Hampton.") Confidential chamberlain to Josyan at Mounbraunt. He assisted her and Bevis to escape from Inor, and was devoured by two lions when he was hiding Josyan.

BOOK OF LEINSTER. An Irish manuscript of the twelfth century containing among other romances *The Cattle Raid of Quelgny* (*q.v.*).

BOOK OF THE DUN COW. An Irish manuscript of about the year 1100 A.D. In it the Legend of Tuan mac Carell (*q.v.*), the story of the reappearance of Cuchulain (*q.v.*), and The Voyage of Maeldun (*q.v.*) are given.

BORGHILD. First wife of Sigmund (*q.v.*) and mother of Helgi (*q.v.*) and Hammund (*q.v.*). She poisoned Sinfjötli (*q.v.*), in consequence of which her husband destroyed her. (*Vide* "The Lay of the Volsungs.")

BORS, KING. (*Vide* "Ban.")

BORS, BOHORS or **BOORT.** A famous knight in the Arthurian cycle—associated with Sir Galahad and Lancelot in their quest of the Holy Grail. During this sojourn he is exhorted by a hermit to abandon the quest unless he can free himself from sin. He confesses and receives absolution from the holy man, and until the quest be finished he abjures all nourishment save bread and water. He achieves several notable feats, such as that of overcoming Priadam the Black, who is the champion of the oppressor of a castle, which once belonged to a lady whom Bors reinstates in her ownership. He refuses her hospitality nevertheless. On the morrow, he goes to the rescue of "a very fair maiden," whom he saves from her would-be ravisher. He relieves his brother,

among other things, and a picturesque incident during his quest is that related in which a young damsel offers him her love, and on his refusal threatens with twelve other damsels to throw herself from a tower. Bors, although full of the milk of human kindness, thinks they had better lose their souls than he his. They fall from the tower, Bors crosses himself, and the whole vanishes, being a deceit of the devil. His brother's corpse, shown him, is also proved to be a figment of the imagination. Then a hermit and a knight, Calogrenant, would fain stop him, and Bors is compelled to draw in self-defence, but a voice tells him to flee, and a fiery brand comes from heaven between them. Bors follows the command of the voice directing him towards the sea, where Perceval awaits him. After the accomplishment of the quest and the deaths of Galahad and Perceval, Bors sets sail for Britain, and comes to Camelot where all are glad to welcome him ; he tells the adventures of the Holy Grail, which, according to the story, were written down and kept in the Abbey of Salisbury.

BOV THE RED. King of the Danaans or Immortals of Munster, and brother of the Irish deity, Dagda. He figures in the mythical Irish "Book of Invasions," and was deeply skilled in magic and enchantments. He it was who found the dream-maiden of Angus Og (*q.v.*), who had fallen sick of love for his visionary mistress. He had in his service a goldsmith named Len, who gave their name to the Lakes of Killarney, once known as Locha Lein.

BRADAMANTE. (*Vide* "Orlando Innamorato" and "Orlando Furioso.") Daughter to Amon, and sister to Rinaldo (*q.v.*). She formed an attachment for Rogero. She slew Pinabello for decoying her into Merlin's cave. Three kings, and Marphisa, were unhorsed by her. She married Rogero.

BRADMOND KING OF DAMASCUS. (*Vide* "Bevis of Hampton.") Quarrelled with Ermyn because he could not get Josyan as wife, but was defeated. He kept Bevis a prisoner for seven years in Damascus.

BRANDILES, SIR. A frequent visitor to the Court of Arthur. (*Vide* "Morte d'Arthur.")

BRANWEN, DAUGHTER OF LLYR. A Welsh romance included in Lady Charlotte Guest's *Mabinogion* (*q.v.*) and originally found in the fourteenth century manuscript known as *The Red Book of Hergest*. It is connected with the story of *Pwyll* (*q.v.*) by the third in the series, that of *Manawyddan* (*q.v.*). It tells how Bran the Blessed, son of Llyr, with his brother Manawyddan and his half-brothers Nissyen the peacemaker, and Evnissyen the mischief-maker, are seated one day on a rock by the sea at Harlech. They observe thirteen ships draw near the coast, one of which lands Matholwch, King of Ireland, who has come to crave the hand of Branwen, Bran's sister. Evnissyen, angered at his consent to Branwen's marriage not having been asked, mutilates the horses of Matholwch, and the Irish king, deeply offended at the outrage, departs in his ships, but returns on being assured that Bran knew nothing of the affair, and that he is willing to make ample amends. Bran, noticing that Matholwch's mood is still heavy, gives him a magic cauldron which has the property of resuscitating any dead warrior thrown into it in a short space. He informs Matholwch that it was brought from Ireland by Llasas Llaesgyfnewid and his wife Kymideu Kymeinvoll when they escaped from the white-hot iron house in that country. Matholwch is conversant with the rest of the story; how one day he was sitting by a lake when a giant made his appearance followed by a still greater woman, and bearing a cauldron on his back; how the woman was soon to give birth to a fully-armed warrior; how these people became a pest in Ireland, and how they with their offspring were imprisoned in an iron house which was made white-hot; and how the man and his wife alone escaped, and came to Britain, where, Bran assures him, they have multiplied, and bred a race of mighty warriors. In this tale we are for the first time introduced to the family of Llyr, who, with that of Don and Pwyll, make up the four branches of the *Mabinogi*. The tale of the cauldron has undoubtedly been interpolated by the story-teller as one which might quite possibly be told by an Irish visitor, and may be equated with an incident in the *Mesce Ulad*, a tale of the Ulster heroic cycle. It has no real connection with the story of Branwen. Matholwch takes Branwen to Ireland, and all prospers for a twelvemonth, when the matter of the outrage on the horses is revived, and Branwen is ignominiously buffeted into the kitchen-quarters, where she is thrashed every morning by the butcher. This goes on for three years, and as all communication is cut off between Ireland and Britain Branwen cannot convey her sad condition to her brother. At last she contrives to rear a starling, which carries a letter to

Bran. He sets out for Ireland, his men by ship, he himself wading through the ocean with his musicians on his back. Matholwch and his men retreat across the Shannon which the Britons cross, using Bran's body as a bridge. The Irish surrender, but Bran will not come to terms until they promise to build for him a house large enough to hold him, a thing not before accomplished. They resolve to make the house a trap, and men are concealed around it in bags. Evnissyen, however, discovers this, and kills them all singly. Peace is on the point of being concluded in the great hall, when suddenly Evnissyen casts Branwen's child on the blazing fire. A dreadful slaughter ensues, and the Irish make use of the cauldron of regeneration, until Evnissyen, concealing himself among the Irish slain, is thrown in and bursts it, breaking his own heart in the effort. Seven of the Britons escape, along with Bran, who is wounded by a poisoned lance. He requests the seven to cut off his head and to bury it in the White Hill (the site of the Tower), in London, with the face towards France. He tells them on the way back of the various hardships that they will endure before they arrive at London; how they will feast for seven years at Harlech, while the birds of Rhiannon will sing to them, and that at Gwales in Pembroke they will rest eighty years, until one of them opens a door looking upon Cornwall. On landing in Britain, Branwen, thinking of the misery she has unwittingly caused, dies of a broken heart. Bran's head is eventually buried in London. Ireland, we are told, was re-peopled by the offspring of five pregnant women, all that were left of the inhabitants on Bran's departure. This tale, it has been pointed out, bears analogies to the Gudrun and Nibelung cycles, and it is probable that the Brythonic inhabitants of Wales received it, or the outlines of it, from the Danish folk in Ireland, or those Danes who settled in the peninsula of Gower in Wales. But, probably only the form is Teutonic, not the matter. (*Vide The Mabinogion*, edited by Alfred Nutt.)

BRASTIAS. (*Vide* " Ulfius.")

BREA. The death-field of Finn (*q.v.*), the Ossianic hero.

BREGON. In Irish romance, Great-grandfather of Miled, father of Ith (*q.v.*). His name is mentioned in the Milesian invasion of Ireland.

BREKA. A Gothland warrior mentioned in the legend of Beowulf (*q.v.*). Before Beowulf set out for Jutland to fight Grendel, Breka proposed that he and the hero should fight the monsters of the sea, to prove which of them was the better man, King Hygelak (*q.v.*) to give a gold chain to the victor. Breka returned to shore first, receiving the gold chain, but when Beowulf came he brought with him the dead body of a nixie whom he had slain in the sea, thus proving himself the greater warrior. Hygelak gave him his own sword, Nagling.

BRENNOR, SIR. An evil knight and an oppressor of the Knights of the " Round Table." He was slain by Sir Tristram (*q.v.*). (*Vide* " Morte d'Arthur.")

BRES (1). In Irish romance, the Danaan (*q.v.*) representative sent to parley with the natives on the occasion of the entrance into Ireland of the People of Dana. He was slain in the Battle of

Moytura, which settled the question of the superiority of the People of Light.

BRES (2). Son of a Danaan woman Eri, by an unknown father. He was elected King of the Danaans in place of the mutilated Nuada of the Silver Hand (*q.v.*). He failed, however, to uphold his people's superiority. In addition, he laid heavy taxes upon them, and refused hospitality to chiefs, nobles, and harpers. This refusal in the end cost him his kingship, for the poet Corpry (*q.v.*), being despicably housed in the royal Court, spread abroad a satire upon his host, and Nuada came into his own again. Bres then sought his mother, from whom he learned that his father was Glatha, a Fomorian king. Her lover had left with her a ring, and had bidden her give it to the man whose finger it fitted. This was Bres, and together they sailed for Glatha's home. He recognized the ring, gave his son an army for the re-conquest of Ireland, and sent him to seek further aid from the greatest of the Fomorian kings, Balor. Then ensued the second Battle of Moytura, between the Fomorians and the Danaans, in which the latter were decisively victorious.

BRES (3). Son of Balor. In the Tale of the Quest of the Sons of Turenn (*q.v.*), Lugh (*q.v.*) is said to have advanced from the west, his face shining like the Sun. Bres wondered why that day dawned on the west, till he was told that "yonder light came not from the sun, but from the face of Lugh."

BRIAN (1), **SIR.** An evil knight who through his wickedness is deprived of his authority over the Castle Pendragon, which Sir Lancelot afterwards presented to Sir La Côte Male-tailé. (*Vide* "Morte d'Arthur.")

BRIAN (2). In Irish romance, the chief of the three sons of Turenn (*q.v.*).

BRICCRIU. (Surnamed "of the Poisoned Tongue.") A chief of Ulster, alluded to in the myth of Cuchulain in the Ultonian cycle of Irish romance. On one occasion he invited the heralds of the Red Branch (*q.v.*) to a feast, and instigated them to strife upon the vexed question as to who was the most renowned warrior in Ireland. The assembly selected Conall, Laery, and Cuchulain, and a demon named "The Terrible" was summoned to decide the order of precedence. He gave it as his opinion that the most courageous man of the trio would best deserve the title of champion, and proposed that he who would cut off his (the demon's) head to-day and submit to having his own head cut off on the morrow would prove himself the bravest. Cuchulain decapitated the demon, who at once seized his head and disappeared. On the morrow he appeared in his usual shape to claim the right of beheading Cuchulain, who placed his head on the block, but the demon bade him arise, and acknowledged him champion of Erin.

BRIOS. Alluded to in the *Conte du Graal*, as persuading Percival to join in the tourney held by Arthur at the Castle Orguellous, as he must have the prize of Knighthood before coming to the Castle of the Fisher King. Percival visits his castle and carries off the prize unknown.

BRISIN. An enchantress, who plays an important part in the Annunciation of Galahad, and the allurement of Lancelot (*q.v.*). (*Vide* "Morte d'Arthur.")

BRITAN. According to Irish story the chief of one of the three surviving Nemedian families (*vide* " Nemed ") after the Fomorian (*q.v.*) victory. Tradition has it that he settled in Britain, and hence the name given to that country.

BRITOMARTE. (*Vide* " Sir Ferumbras.*") Refused to help Floripas to release Roland and Oliver from the dungeon at Laban's palace, and was killed by her in consequence.

BROCELIANDE. A magic forest in Brittany connected with Arthurian romance. There it was that Merlin was enchanted by Nimue or Viviana (*q.v.*), Lady of the Lake, and imprisoned underneath a great stone. Wace (*q.v.*) actually travelled to the spot to " verify " its legends. The name " Broceliande " is often employed as typical of the *mise en scene* of romance, and as symbolic of the dim unreality of legendary scenery.

BROIFFORT. Ogier's horse, which he had won in the Saracen wars, and which was renowned for its swiftness. (*Vide* " Ogier the Dane.")

BRONS, BRON, or **HEBRON.** In Grail romance brother-in-law of Joseph, whose sister Enygeus he married. They have twelve sons, about whom they are greatly concerned and demand of Joseph what is to be done with them. Joseph prays before the Holy Grail: eleven of them will marry and one remain single—this one is Alain (*q.v.*), to whom descended the custody of the Holy Grail.

BROWN BULL. (*Vide* " Cattle Raid of Quelgny.")

BRUILLANT. Mentioned in the *Grand Saint Graal* as an enemy of Lambor (*q.v.*). Fighting with Lambor, he is pursued to the seashore where he finds and enters Solomon's ship, where he discovers the Grail sword. With this he slays Lambor. But this use of the holy weapon was accompanied with great woes, for no wheat grew within Britain, nor fruit trees bare, nor was fish found in the waters. Bruillant fell dead as a punishment for using the sword.

BRUNAMONT. King of Maiolgre (Majorca). A pagan monarch who arrived with 10,000 men to assist the Saracens against the army of Charlemagne in Italy. Corsuble, a Saracen Emir, offered him his daughter Glorianda who was betrothed to Karaheut, King of India (*q.v.*), but the latter monarch succeeded in gaining her. (*Vide* " Ogier of Denmark.")

BRUNHILD. (*Vide* " Nibelungenlied " and " Volsunga Saga.") A valkyr or warrior-maiden, who was imprisoned by Odin the Scandinavian deity, in a castle on Isenstein surrounded by flames. In the *Volsunga Saga* she is awakened by Sigurd, who pledges troth with her, only to forget her by reason of a magic draught. He again penetrates the flames in the shape of Gunnar, for whom he succeeds in winning Brunhild. She quarrels with Gudrun, the wife of Sigurd, and is instrumental in having him slain. In the *Nibelungenlied* she is won for Gunther by the wiles of Siegfried, who beats her in sports, she having agreed to marry the man who can conquer her at her favourite games. She quarrels with Siegfried's wife, Kriemhild, and compasses his death. The myth of her imprisonment is probably originally a nature-myth. She is the sun-maiden who sleeps the charmed sleep caused by the prick of the thorn of winter.

BRUNSTEIN, KING. A character in the romance of *Samson* (*q.v.*), who succeeded to the throne of Salern after the death of his brother, Rodgeier. He also is slain by Samson.

BRUT D'ANGLETERRE or **LI RO-MANS DE BRUT.** A chronicle of British pseudo-history, written by Richard Wace (*q.v.*) in French, of the early twelfth century, and based upon the famous British History of Geoffrey of Monmouth (*q.v.*) under *Historia Regum Britanniæ.* The British histories are generally supposed to have been called Bruts from Brutus, the great-grandson of Æneas, who is represented in them as the first king of the Britons. But it is more probable that the meaning of the word is " repute " or " rumour," in the sense of the expression " bruit " or news. The subject-matter of the poem practically coincides with that of the *Historia Regum Britanniæ* (*q.v.*).

Literature : Li Romans de Brut, edited by Leroux de Lincy, 2 vols., 1835–38.

BRYANT OF CORNWALL, SIR. (*Vide* " Bevis of Hampton.") A wicked favourite of Edgar, King of England, who was the origin of the cruel strife between Edgar and Sir Bevis.

BRYER, SIR. (*Vide* " Sir Ferumbras.") Duke of Brittany. A French Peer, one of the twelve sent as a delegate to demand Roland's liberation. He was killed in a sally he made from Labans' palace when he was imprisoned there.

BUDDVAN. (*Vide* " Gododin.") Son of Bleidovan the Bold. He was a Cymric warrior and was slain in the battle of Cattreath. " His armour has been thoroughly washed in his gore."

BULL FIGHT OF GANZUL, THE. This tale is one in which the dexterity of the Moorish cavaliers in the bull fight is described. King Almanzor of Granada summons the Moorish Lords to a bull fight in honour of the Baptist's feast. Eight lords go into the ring and are defeated. Then come Ganzul, the Alcaydé of Agalva, and the poem tells how he succeeds in fighting and killing three bulls, one of them, Harpado, being enormously strong and fierce.

BURNT NJAL. An Icelandic romance dating from the eleventh century. Njal was the most esteemed and beloved man in Iceland. He dwelt at Bergthorsknoll, and his ability in law was praised by everybody. His gentle disposition surrounded him with many friends, but chief among those was Gunnar of Lithend, the most famous warrior in Iceland. These two vowed lifelong friendship, a vow which they kept in spite of many difficulties, for Gunnar's wife, Hallgerda and Njal's, Bergthora, were at ceaseless feud with each other, slaying and counter-slaying house-carles and freemen belonging to each. This enmity arose through Hallgerda telling Bergthora, who was then her hostess, that she had thieves' fingers, Bergthora retaliating by referring to Hallgerda's murdered husbands. Gunnar was drawn into much strife on his wife's account. In famine time she stole from the store of the avaricious Otkell, for which theft Gunnar gave her a blow on the face. This insult she never forgot. By dint of Njal's wisdom the angry husband suffered no loss. But Otkell, unsatisfied with the court's decision, sought to slay Gunnar, himself, however, with his fawning friend Skamkell, falling at his enemy's hands. Then the cunning Mord learnt that Njal had warned his friend not to slay twice in the same stock. He, therefore, advised Thorgeir who ' sought Gunnar's death, to incense Otkell's son, an honest and peace-loving youth, against their enemy. Their end was accomplished. Gunnar thrust his bill through the youth's body, and was accordingly banished from Iceland for three years. But his love for his home swelled so greatly within him as he set out for another land, that he was unable to leave Lithend. Mord, Thorgier, and Sigurd the White then plotted his destruction, which they accomplished in his own home. With his bow-string broken, and with a scanty supply of arrows, Gunnar bade his wife twist two locks of her hair into a bow-string. Remembering the blow he had given her, she only laughed, and left him to his death. Gunnar's elder son Hogni then took upon him the management of the farm, while the hated Hallgerda was driven by her mother-in-law, Rannveig, to seek a home elsewhere. She, therefore, went to live with Thrain her son-in-law and took her son Grani with her. Hogni was destined to avenge his father's death, for one day as he laid his hand upon Gunnar's war-bill it sang so loudly that Rannveig knew that this son was the chosen avenger. With the aid of Skarp-hedinn, Njal's son, Hogni slew Thorgeir and three of the other suitors, Mord, however, receiving his life at a great price of money. Grim and Helgi, Njal's sons, went sea-roving about the Orkneys. Here they fell in with Kari, a viking, who generously succoured them in their need. He again lent his aid when they sought his protection from Yarl Hacon of Norway, for, being falsely accused of screening a felon, Hrapp, who was concealed in Thrain's ship, Hacon would have put them to death. But the king made atonement to Njal's sons for all they had suffered unjustly, and they became his friends. Kari went home with them to Iceland, and they wedded their sister Helga to him. Now all Thrain's household, which included Hrapp, all save his son Hanskuld, hated Njal's household. Insulted and reviled by their three enemies, Njal's sons and Kari slew Thrain and Hrapp, granting mercy, however, to Grani. For this slaying Njal paid the blood-money, and having made friends with the generous-minded Hanskuld, took him back to Bergthorsknoll as his foster-son. Elected the priest of White-ness, Hanskuld married Hildegunna, the beautiful but hard-hearted daughter of Flosi. But Mord hated Hanskuld as a rival priest, and when his father was dying he had promised him to revenge upon Skarp-hedinn their great loss of money in the Gunnar murder case. He, therefore, set to work upon the destruction of his enemies. Making friends with both by lying tale-bearing he incensed Njal's sons and Kari against Hanskuld, and with them fell upon him. For this foul murder the sorrowing Njal sought to pay a large fine and thus to keep the peace. But with mutual insults Flosi and Skarp-hedinn refused the money decision. Then Hanskuld's father-in-law gathered together a large company, including Grani, and set fire to Bergthors-Knoll. Njal, Bergthora, Skarp-hedinn, Grim and Helgi's little son were all burnt, while Helgi, seeking to escape, was slain by Flosi. Kari, however, did escape, and with the now satisfied Mord as pleader sought redress for the burning. But the case dwindling into a question of contempt of court on the part of Mord or his opponent, Kari and his men laid about them in the court, where several persons were slain. The Thing then settled the question, and sent into banishment or outlawry Flosi and the burners. Flosi fared home, did penance there, and received absolution from the Pope's own hands. Then he returned to Swinefeld, his home. Driven by storm on his enemy's shore, Kari yet sought Flosi's assistance, and was kindly received and cared for. The two foes then became friends, and some time after Helgi's death Kari married Hildegunna.

C

CAER. Daughter of Ethal Anubal, Prince of the Danaans of Connaught, loved by Angus Og (*q.v.*), and mentioned in the Irish mythical books. She lived, year about, in the form of a maiden and a swan, and upon calling to her, Angus found himself transformed into a swan. He joined her, and all who heard the rapturous music uttered by the swan-lovers were plunged into a deep sleep lasting for three days and nights.

CAERLEON (near Carlisle). A town mentioned in the *Morte d'Arthur* as the chief seat of Arthur's court.

CAIAPHAS. Alluded to in the *Grand St. Graal* as the jailor of Joseph of Arimathea (*q.v.*). He permitted Joseph to starve, but Christ supplied his necessities. Caiaphas was latterly set adrift in a boat. He is, of course, the Caiaphas mentioned in Scripture as the High Priest of the Jews.

CAIRBRY. In Irish romance, son of Cormac mac Art (*q.v.*), and High-King of Ireland. Father of Sgeim Solais (*q.v.*).

CALATIN CLAN. A noisome multiform creature composed of a father and his twenty-seven sons, any one of whose weapons would bring to his death in nine days the man who was but grazed by it. This hideous monster was sent against Cuchulain (*q.v.*), and hurled at him its eight and twenty spears which he, however, caught on his shield. But as he was about to lop off the spears the clan threw him down and ground his face in the gravel. Fiacha, son of Firaba, an Ulster exile, indignant at the unequal combat, then cut off their heads, when Cuchulain hacked the creature to pieces. But again was a monster loosed against the Hound of Cullan. This was the posthumous three sons of three daughters, born at a birth, of the wizard Calatin. These Maev (*q.v.*) had sent through Ireland and Alba and as far as Babylon to learn the magic arts, that she might revenge herself upon the Ulster hero. Then did the children of Calatin fall upon the mind of Cuchulain and conjure up horror, despondency and apparitions of war. And in the form of Niam (*q.v.*), the Sorceress Bave (*q.v.*) bade the warrior arouse himself to rescue Ulster.

E

CALAYNOS THE MOOR. This Spanish tale is believed to be one of the most ancient, and certainly was among the most popular of all the ballads in the *Cancionero*, or Spanish *Book of Romances*. Calaynos, wishing to win the favour of a maid of Spain, offers her gold and riches. These she refuses and asks for the heads of certain peers—Ronald's and Oliver's. The ballad then narrates how Charlemagne is met when at the chase by a Moor, who brings defiance to every lord on behalf of Calaynos. A knight, Sir Baldwin, takes up the challenge, and fights Calaynos, who strikes him down. Then another knight, Sir Ronald (uncle to Sir Baldwin), on seeing his kinsman fall, calls Calaynos to combat. They fight and Calaynos is killed.

CARADOC OF LLANCARVEN. A Welsh author of the twelfth century, alluded to by Geoffrey of Monmouth in the epilogue to his *Historia Regum Britanniæ* (*q.v.*), as "my contemporary." To him Geoffrey leaves the task of writing "the deeds of the kings who succeeded in Wales" from the date at which his history closes to the period in which he flourished. The work hinted at by Geoffrey, if it was ever written, is not now extant, and one which bears the name of Caradoc, and the date, 1156, is generally regarded with suspicion. It is likely, however, that the Latin *Life of Gildas*, found in the twelfth century MS. in the library of Corpus Christi College, Cambridge, is his. It presents several aspects of the Arthurian legend, which are not to be found in Geoffrey's work. In its pages Gildas is alluded to as a contemporary of Arthur. His brother Hueil, King of Scotland, fought a battle with Arthur in the "Isle of Minau" (Man?), and was slain. But Gildas, true to his saintly character, pardoned Arthur the slaying of his brother. The incident is described in the *Mabinogion* story of *Kulhwch and Olwen*. The *Life* also relates the story of the abduction of Guinevere by Melwas, King of the Summer Country (see *Chevalier de la Charrette*), who carried her to Glastonbury, where he was besieged by Arthur. But strife between the kings was avoided by the good offices of Gildas. (*Cf.* Rhys, *Arthurian Legend*.)

CARADY, Count of. (*Vide* "Gudrun Lay," first division of, under heading "Hagen.") He rescued Hagen (*q.v.*) and his three girl companions from the coast where the griffins had carried them. The count had suffered loss at the hands of Hagen's father, King Sigebant, and wished to keep Hagen as a hostage, but the latter fought and conquered the count, and carried him to Ireland, where he became reconciled to Sigebant.

CARAHIES. The brother of Gauvain. His adventures are given at length in Gautier's portion of the *Conte du Graal*, but are of no importance in connection with the Grail legend.

CARCHELOIS, CASTLE OF. According to Grail romance, situated in the March of Scotland. The inmates attack Sir Galahad and his companions, but all are slain by him. On Sir Galahad expressing contrition to a priest, he is told they are all heathens, and that he had done a good deed, as the three knights who had held the castle had ravished their sister and done their father, Count Ernous, to death.

CARDUEL. Famous as the spot where Sir Perceval demanded knighthood of King Arthur, and from where the Red Knight—whom Sir Perceval defeated—carried off King Arthur's cup for the fifth time. (*Vide* "Sir Percyvelle.")

CARTAGE OF NÎMES. (*Vide* "Charroi de Nîmes.")

CASTLE DANGEROUS. (*Vide* "Morte d'Arthur.") The home of the Knight of the Red Laundes (*q.v.*), an oppressor of good knights.

CATHBAD. A druid who was overheard by Cuchulain (*q.v.*) to say that the youth who should take up arms upon that day he spoke would become Erin's champion, but would spend a short life (*cf.* Achilles). He prophesied that Deirdre (*q.v.*) should be the fairest woman in Ireland, that she should wed a king, and that through her ruin should fall upon Ulster. He figures in the Ultonian cycle of Irish myth.

CATHELOYS. Alluded to in the *Grand Saint Graal* as one of the Kings and Keepers of the Grail.

CATTLE RAID OF QUELGNY, THE. A famous Irish poem, in which Cuchulain (*q.v.*), the great Ulster hero, figures. (*Vide* "Maev.")

CELIDOINE. In Grail romance, son of Nasciens and ancestor of Sir Galahad and Lancelot. It is related of him that he knew the "stars in their courses," and was seen in Lancelot's vision surrounded by stellar bodies, and that nine streams issued from his body, representing nine descendants, of whom seven were kings and two knights. In romance "he was the first King of Scotland" (*sic*).

CHANAAN. A companion of Joseph, alluded to in the *Grand Saint Graal*.

A white hart, accompanied by four stags, led Joseph's band across a great water, all except Chanaan, who crossed later in a fisherman's boat. Enraged that the Graal refused him sustenance, Chanaan slew twelve of the band. After death his grave burst out in flames which might not be quenched till the coming of Lancelot.

CHANSONS DE GESTE. The old French epical poems, written in the dialect of the north, or *langue d'oïl*, and having for their subject-matter the adventures and pseudo-history of Charlemagne, and his twelve peers. They are the oldest examples of elaborate verse in any modern language, with the exception of English and Norse, and the last to become known to modern critics. Homogeneous and well-marked in character, they date in time from the eleventh to the thirteenth century, with a few straggling examples in the fourteenth ; but the forms in which we possess most of them are comparatively late and un-original. They "stand in a real, positive, ancestral relation to all modern literature ; there is something of them in all the poetry of Europe."

Designated *matière de France* by the *trouvère* Jean Bodel (*q.v.*), they are intimately connected with the pseudo-history of that country, even as the Arthurian cycle, called *matière de Bretagne* by the same singer, deals in part with the mythi-history of our own island. More racy and more romantic than the romance pure and simple, they were in the aggregate less human, and the softer passions are less insisted upon in their pages. The style is simple, to suit a mixed audience and the necessities of vocal interpretation, and thus dramatic subtlety is seldom achieved. There is a strong family resemblance in the literary machinery employed in all these tales, and this is also the case as regards their psychology. The theory that they owed their origin to the fabulous *Chronicle* of Archbishop Turpin of Rheims, the warrior-priest of Charlemagne, is now discredited, as that monk is known to be later in date than the majority of the *chansons*. Another discarded hypothesis is that which would refer their origin to earlier ballads on the same theme. But not a trace of such ballads has been discovered.

Singularly complete in form, the older poems are written in batches of lines varying from one to several score, each of which derives unity from an assonant vowel-rhyme. These are known as *laisses* or *tirades*. Later, this assonance was discarded in favour of rhyme, the entire *laisse* ending with one rhyme-sound. Still later, the decasyllabic line gave way to the Alexandrine ; but the substitution of rhyme for assonance, and of the twelve-syllabled for the ten-syllabled line were all the mechanical changes admitted by the *chansons* in the space of three hundred years.

In these poems the character of Charlemagne, as has been pointed out in the article which deals with his personality, plays a part which can scarcely be designated heroic ; but he is ever the head and front of Christendom against the Saracens, if at home he is capriciously savage and tyrannical and not a little pusillanimous. His peers are the more romantic figures—Roland, Oliver, Naymes, Ogier, William of Orange ; and concerning one or other of these the numerous *chansons*, which circle round the figure and court of the aged emperor are written. Three principal subjects may be enumerated around which the various *chansons* appear to crystallise : the deeds of Charlemagne himself ; those of Garin, which includes the exhaustive sub-cycle of William of Orange (*q.v.*), and the doings of the hereditary princelings and peers of Charles's period, and those of his enemies, such as Ogier the Dane.

Of these poems, M. Leon Gautier has published a list of no less than one hundred and ten, the average length of which is probably six thousand lines each, *without later additions and interpolations.* Of this enormous body of verse about half the total number dates from the twelfth century, the most esteemed examples being *Aliscans Aspremont, Battaille Loquifer, Charroi de Nîmes, Covenant Vivien, Garin the Lorrainer, Huon de Bordeaux, Ogier, Renouart, Moniage Guillaume, Song of the Saxons,* and the *Voyage of Charlemagne* (all of which see). By far the larger portion of the remainder date not later than the thirteenth century, and of these the most outstanding are : *Enfances Vivien, Fierabras, Garin de Montglane, The Four Sons of Aymon,* and the *Departement des Enfants Aimeri* (*q.v.*). The *Song of Roland* dates from the end of the eleventh century.

Most of this immense body of verse remains unprinted, and no very systematic attempt has been made to embody it into a corpus. A few of the poems are in Provençal, but all attempts to refer the entire cycle in its original condition to that language have signally failed. The great mass of the work is entirely anonymous. Here and there in the MSS. we encounter names which may be those of the authors or copyists or of the *jongleurs* who sang their productions. The *chansons* of Richard the Pilgrim—*Les Chétifs*, *Antioche*, and *Jerusalem*, were refashioned by Graindor of Douai. *Garin the Lorrainer* was the work of Jehan de Flagy, and the *Song of the Saxons* that of Jean Bodel (*q.v.*). Adenès le Roi remodelled parts of *Ogier* and other *chansons*. There are other names—the shadows of shadows—Bertrand of Bar sur Aube, Raimbert of Paris, Pierre de Rieu, Gerard d'Amiens, Brianchon, Nicolas of Padua, Gautier of Douai, Guillaume de Bapaume, Huon de Villeneuve, Herbert de Dammartin—of the owners of which nothing is known except the name.

"They lived their golden day,
They sang—and passed away."

But those of them who wrote assisted in the erection of a palace of song, fantastic and precious, into which the literary Europe of to-day is entering as upon a splendid inheritance.

On the coming of the romance proper, degradation followed, and the *chansons de geste* were forced into the market-place and the scullions' hall. But many of the better examples continued their hold on the upper ranks of society. Reading came into fashion, and the *chansons*, once invariably sung or declaimed, were transferred to written books. Here and there we / discover romance invading the domain of the *chansons*, from which the romance-writers were not disinclined to borrow. But gradually they dropped out of public favour, as did their themes, until such time as the

genius of Boiardo, Pulci and Ariosto was called to clothe their dry bones with sweet flesh, and make resound a new music which was to the magnificent sea-surge of their heroic *laisses* as the horns of Oberon to the clamour of trumpets in the day of battle.

Full bibliographical notes will be found at the end of each article dealing with the numerous *chansons de geste* noticed in this work.

CHAPEL PERILOUS. (*Vide* " Morte d'Arthur.") Mentioned in the quest of the Holy Grail, when Lancelot (*q.v.*) enters the chapel to meet with the body of King Evalach (*q.v.*).

CHARLEMAGNE, Carolus Magnus, or Karl der Grosse, the greatest of Frankish Kings, and the first Teutonic monarch to have conferred upon him the dignity of Roman Emperor. He was the elder son of Pepin the Short, and succeeded, on the death of his father in 768 A.D., to a kingdom which extended from the Low Countries to the borders of Spain. On the death of his brother Karlmann he seized Burgundy, Alsace, and Provence from his nephews, and later plunged into a war against the Saxon tribes dwelling between the Rhine, Weser, and Elbe, which continued for a generation. Lombardy, Switzerland, and Bavaria soon acknowledged the Frankish rule, and thousands of hostile Saxons were forced to submit to Christian baptism. Charles intervened in the affairs of the Spanish Moors by assisting the Abbasside faction against the Ommiad Caliph of Cordova, but was recalled from the peninsula by the great insurrection of Wittikind on the Rhine. It was on the way back from Spain to quell this revolt that the ambuscade of his rear-guard took place at Roncesvaux, by Basques of the Pyrenees, and not by "Saracens," as related in the *Song of Roland* (*q.v.*) and elsewhere. Successful in campaigns against the Slavs of the Elbe and Oder and the Huns, Charles was hard pressed by the apostasy and revolt of the Saxons, and the invasion of Aquitaine by the Saracens in 793. Three years later the celebrated *Karoline Books*, inveighing against heresy and idolatry, were published after the Council of Frankfort, and in 800 Charles was crowned King of the Romans for assisting and countenancing Pope Leo III. On the dawning of the ninth century the inroads of the various pagan races dwelling on his frontiers indicated to the emperor the necessity for remaining strictly on the defensive, and he cemented peace with them. In 811 he crowned Hlodowiz, his only re-maining son, as emperor, and thenceforth gave himself up to good works and devotional exer-cises. He died at Aix-la-Chapelle on Jan. 28, 814, and was buried there. His life, by his secretary, Eginhard, depicts him as simple, desirous for the promotion of learn-ing, affectionate in family affairs, and deeply religious. He was undoubtedly the most powerful monarch of his time in Europe, a wise legislator, and he ruled his extensive empire with justice and liberal-mindedness. He possessed a keen sense of his duty as the defender of Christendom, strongly menaced in his day, and is to be regarded as the relentless foe of the heathendom by which he was surrounded.

A very different picture is drawn of him in the *chansons de geste* (*q.v.*), which purport to chronicle many of the circum-stances of his reign. In these he is depicted as a ferocious and capricious tyrant, gullible and irascible, ever ready to hearken to traitors, and act upon their advice with unrelenting harshness even where his own family are concerned. His heroism is dubious, and in many of the *chansons* he is drawn as pitifully deficient in all manly qualities. In others, how-ever, an impressive picture is afforded, which exhibits him as a venerable, white-bearded poten-tate, surrounded by a glittering court, the defender and champion of the Cross, and the deadly foe of heathenesse. Which of the portraits as outlined by contem-porary history or the *chansons* is the more correct, it would probably be fruitless to inquire. The pro-bability is that both contain a portion of the truth, and that by fusing the two accounts we can procure something like a picture of the real Charlemagne—a man and monarch of his age, with all its rude virtues and its ruder passions.

(*Vide* "Chansons de Geste," and the various romances alluded to in that article.)

CHARLEMAGNE CYCLE. (*Vide* "Chansons de Geste.")

CHARLES THE GRETE, LYFE OF. Is a translation by William Caxton from French histories. It de-scribes how Charles inherited the kingdom of France on the death of his father Pepin. His brother, who also would have shared with him the sovereignty of that vast empire, died, thus leaving Charles supreme master of his inheritance.

His labours for the Church of Rome were unceasing during the whole period of his illustrious reign; and at a very early date after his ascension to the throne he was chosen Emperor of Rome by Pope Leo III. (A.D. 800). According to Turpin, Charles was over eight feet in height, stout and broad-shouldered, and large of limb. He wore a beard a foot long, and his complexion was fair, his eyes bright and sparkling. His waist measured eight feet in circumference. For strength he had no equal. He could lift an armed knight with one hand; he was liberal to all, just and merciful, and careful in his language. Charles had his sons taught religion and science, and his daughters were trained to use the needle, and in the duties of the home. Churches were built at his command and endowed with imperial liberality; he was never idle, but fond of study. The welfare of his subjects was jealously guarded and commissioners were sent to study and report on the state of his kingdom and the laws of other nations. The Saracen nations were his greatest foes, and his whole reign of thirty-three years was marked by repeated excursions into pagan lands for the purpose of crushing their heathen spirit. By these acts of Christian valour he met with the approval of the whole Catholic world.

The siege of Jerusalem by the Saracens causes him to hasten to the aid of the patriarch of that city. With a huge army he enters the Holy Land and puts the Saracens to flight. The thankful patriarch presents the imperial deliverer with the sacred crown of thorns, and also a piece of the Holy Cross, with the holy napkin and other relics. With these sacred treasures he returns to his people, and, by their aid, performs many miracles. Roland, nephew

to Charles, and one of his faithful knights, accuses his uncle of sneering at him. The emperor in his rage strikes his nephew on the cheek with his glove. Roland immediately draws his sword: Charles orders his nephew to be seized: his knights hesitate to execute their royal master's orders, but Ogier, a faithful paladin, interposes and brings about a reconciliation.

Fierabras, a Saracen chief, who continuously harassed the Christians, sends a challenge to the court of Charles. Oliver, a brave knight, accepts it, much to Charles' displeasure. The duel, which is of a very sanguinary nature, lasts for some considerable time. The Saracen chief, nevertheless, displays a noble chivalry equalled by his valorous opponent. Oliver loses his sword. The French knights would have rushed on Fierabras; but Charles holds them back, while the cool Saracen offers to pick up the fallen weapon for his rival. Oliver, however, refuses the chivalrous advance. Their shields are next destroyed, followed by the loss of their helmets. Oliver's horse is slain under him, and the sanguinary battle is continued on foot. Charles threatens to destroy every church in the land, should Oliver lose his life, while the wounded combatants engage in a sportive conversation. Finally the Saracen is brought to the ground. He then discloses a plot laid by his accomplices, and a formal truce is declared between the heroes. No sooner is the treaty sealed than Oliver and numbers of French knights are carried away to a dungeon. Floripas, a beautiful maiden, hears their cries, and offers to rescue them provided they grant her a request: this Oliver pledges to do, and the damsel straightway releases them. Floripas heals Oliver's wounds with a magic draught. Charles about this time sends Roland and six other paladins on an embassy to the treacherous Balan, who, on the other hand, despatches fifteen knights to demand the release of Fierabras. Charles' messengers meet with Balan's: Maradas, the chief of the rival embassy, challenges the French paladins: the result is that all the Saracens are slain but one. Roland, pursues his mission, and on arriving at the court of Balan, presents him with the heads of his ambassadors. Much ill luck befalls Charles and his army during these incidents, and he very prudently orders a retreat. As he does so, he sees Richard approaching in his direction. Richard, who is an ally of the emperor, informs Charles how and where his noble knights are imprisoned. Charles disguises himself as a merchant, and followed by a similarly attired host sets out for Martrible, a town which he reaches, and slays its defender Galafre. He enters the captured city and cuts down the aggressive giant Ampleon. The Saracens then release their prisoners, and Ganelon and Fierabras are highly commended for their valorous assault of the city. The giant's children are baptized.

On hearing of this defeat, Balan, in his rage, smashes the image of the god Mahoun, and hurries off to encounter the valiant emperor. The two warriors meet in combat, and Balan is defeated. He renounces paganism.

Saint James appears to Charles in a dream and bids him go and conquer Galicia. Its Saracen defender, Pampeluna, is captured by a miracle, as is the town of Lucerne by a similar miracle.

Charles destroys the idols of his enemy, but Salancadys, an image which he had overlooked, drops a symbolic key as a sign of Christian conquest and victory over its worshippers. The Saracens are next routed at Argolant; Gascony is invaded, and under disguise Charles marches to Agenne, a town which he captures, but Pampeluna, who had previously promised to observe the order of baptism, refuses to submit to it, and consequently is slain by Charles.

The King of Navarre, who had also defied the Frankish monarch's rule, receives a crushing humiliation. A battle between Roland and Ferragus takes place; the latter is slain: the former soon after dies. Charles laments over the loss of his faithful knight, and orders Ganelon, who is believed to have incited the duel, to be put to death. (*Vide* "Roland and Ferragus.") The emperor, in great sadness of heart, retires to Aeon, where he dies at the age of 72 years, leaving behind him three sons and the same number of daughters.

Charles is buried with great magnificence in a tomb over which is set a figure of himself crowned and seated on his throne.

Caxton, in his *Lyfe of Charles*, divides his biography into three books. The first treats of the emperor's youth. The second portion relates the duel between Oliver and Fierabras. The third part deals with the conquest of Spain by Charles, of the treason of Ganelon, and of the emperor's death.

CHARLOT. (See "Ogier the Dane.")

CHARROI DE NÎMES. (The Cartage of Nîmes.) A romance of the William of Orange sub-cycle of the

Charlemagne saga. (*Vide* "William of Orange.") It is by far the most vigorous and remarkable poem of the series. It tells how William of Orange took Nîmes by "the mounted car," how he conquered the city of Orange, and had Guibor baptized, whom he took from "King Tybalt the Slavon" (who in other romances figures as a "Saracen"), and married as his wife. William reproaches the King (Louis) for his ingratitude, as the monarch has gifted almost all his inheritances away, and has taken no thought of him who has done such deeds for France and the throne. For him there is no gift of honour, his men die of hunger, his hair is white, and he is unprovided for. Louis offers him the lands of orphans and widows, but William scorns to listen to such proposals. The king then offers him a fourth of his kingdom, and William is about to retire in disgust at the weakling's meaningless proposal, when Bertram advises him to ask a fief which none would dispute with him, to wit, Spain (meaning those provinces of Southern France at that time in the hands of the Saracens). The king consents. William collects thirty thousand poor knights without estates. At Puy the host fall in with a villein leading a cart on which is a barrel filled with salt. Garnier, a knight, observes that with a thousand such barrels the French could take Nîmes. William seizes all the carts, barrels, and oxen in the fields on which he can lay hands, and the knights attire themselves in the garb of peasants. Thus disguised, they enter the city as merchants from Canterbury. William is brought before the king of the Saracens, who mocks him, and a certain Herpin pulls his beard.

William reveals himself, and attacks the Paynim. His knights, concealed within the barrels, which he has brought into the town, rush forth from their hiding-places and make great slaughter. William kills Herpin with a blow of his fist. He seizes the king, and casts him from a tower, and the town is taken. Trogus Pompeius tells of a similar strategem, by which King Comanus took Marseilles, and mentions a like device at Treves in 1017. Jonckbloet attributes the taking of Nîmes to William I. of Provence.

CHATELAINE OF VERGI, THE. A French romance, probably of the twelfth century. In high favour with the Duke of Burgundy, in the days of this story, was a noble and brave knight. Secretly he cherished, and was cherished by, his master's niece, the Chatelaine of Vergi. In the shades of night they met and told o'er their tale of love; but the lady made covenant that none should know their sweet secret. Now, the duchess yearned after this knight, and, as he refused her love, falsely accused him to the duke. Exile from his native land and from his sweet friend now awaited the knight, or he must break his covenant with the chatelaine. Urged by the duke's promises of secrecy, he therefore opened his heart to his lord, who witnessed that night the tender meeting of the lovers. But the duchess had noted with what favour her husband treated this despiser of her love, and by her woman's wiles drew the secret from her trusting lord. Death, however, he told her, would immediately ensue, were she to breathe a syllable of the tale. She now sought an opportunity to humiliate her servant. This occasion came at the Feast of Pentecost. The duchess showed the chatelaine that her secret was known, whereupon the unhappy lady sought the tiring chamber, and having bewailed her betrayed love, tightly clasped her arms over her breast and died. Dead her knight found her there, and learning the truth from a maiden who had lain at the foot of the bed unperceived by the heart-broken chatelaine, found death upon his own sword. The maiden sped to the duke and showed him what had happened. Without a word he sought his wife and smote her on the head with the knight's own sword. The dancing and mirth were changed to weeping, while the duke told o'er the sad tale of these lovers. And nevermore he smiled, but took the Cross and became a Knight Templar far from his own land.

CHEVALIER DE LA CHARRETTE, LE. (Knight of the Cart.) A romance written in French by Chrétien de Troyes in the latter part of the twelfth century, but completed by another hand. The matter it contains has been transferred almost literally into the prose *Lancelot*. It is the first piece of literature which deals with the adventures of Sir Lancelot du Lac. It tells how Guinevere is abducted by Meleagaunt, son of the king of a land whence no man returns, and in these *dramatis personæ* we can descry the same figures who appear in the Latin *Life of Gildas*, preserved in a twelfth-century MS. in the Library of Corpus Christi College, Cambridge, in which Guinevere is alluded to as having been abducted by one Melwas. She is rescued in Chrétien's poem by Lancelot, who is compelled for the sake of strategem to ride in a cart used to convey prisoners to execution, hence his nickname of "The Knight of the Cart." In this romance the Queen is represented for the first time as the lady love of Lancelot, and, according to Chrétien's own account, he got the material of his poem from Marie de Champagne, who was probably deeply versed in the love-lore of the Courts of Gallantry of her day. See the edition of Chrétien's works by Dr. W. Förster (vol. iv.). It is obvious that a myth of considerable antiquity underlies this romance, probably evolved from an incident in which the wife of the sun-god or "Son of the Sun" is abducted, and taken to the Land Whence no one Returns (the west, or place of the setting sun), by a son of its monarch, or, perhaps the monarch himself. This land is also alluded to as "the Summer Country," possibly Somerset.

CHILDHOOD OF WILLIAM. (See "Enfance Guillaume.")

CHILDREN OF LIR. (See "Lir.")

CHRÉTIEN DE TROYES. Sometimes styled Chrestien or Crétien, a French poet of the Middle Ages, possibly the originator of the Grail poems. His name indicates that he was a native of Troyes, a small village in Champagne ; and it is commonly supposed that, like the majority of mediæval troubadours, he was a herald by profession. Nevertheless, his career, and even the date of his birth, are wrapped in mystery, but he himself records that he was a protégé of Philip Augustus, Count of Flanders and Vermandois ; and, as that nobleman is known to have perished in the Crusade of 1191, this gives an idea as to the period at which Chrétien lived and wrote.

When Sancho heard of this he said, "My brother has broken the oath he made to my father and disinherited Donna Urraca, my sister." So he consulted Rodrigo, as Ferdinand had advised him. The Cid urged him to meet Alfonso at Sahagen. But Alfonso refused to join forces with him, as he would not go against the will of his father. Sancho afterwards passed through Alfonso's country, taking many lands in Galicia. Then he marched into Portugal, and besieged his brother Garcia at Santarem. There he would have been vanquished had not the Cid gained the victory for him against Garcia, capturing Galicia and Portugal. Sancho next requested Alfonso to yield up Leon to him. Alfonso, however, prepared to defend his kingdom from the usurper. Don Pedro Ansures commanded King Alfonso's army, and the Cid upheld Don Sancho's standard. In this onslaught great was the slaughter on either side, but the courage of the Cid prevailed. Alfonso again attacked his brother at Vulpegera, fighting for the kingdom of Leon. This time the Leonese had the victory, for the Cid was not in the field, and Don Sancho fled. While the Leonese were sleeping at break of day in Vulpegera, the Cid arose early and took them unawares. Alfonso fled to Carrion. Sancho was captured by thirteen knights, but the Cid galloped after them without his lance, and cried, " Give me my lord, and I will yield up yours." But they refused him, until he challenged them, saying, " Hand me but a lance, and I will rescue my lord from all of ye." They complied ; then he attacked them so bravely, slaying eleven and leaving only two alive, that he rescued the king. Thereafter

Sancho went to Burgos, taking with him his brother prisoner. Thereupon Donna Urraca besought the Cid to intercede with Sancho for her brother. Alfonso having fled from Leon to King Alimaymon of Toledo, Sancho captured the citadel. Bent on conquest, Sancho now sent the Cid to Zamora, bidding Donna Urraca yield up the city to him. But she refused to give up what her father had bequeathed her. Persisting, Sancho besieged Zamora, until Vellido Dolfos, under pretence of showing how to win Zamora, slew Don Sancho for breaking the oath which he made unto Ferdinand his father.

When Alfonso arrived at Zamora he pitched his tents at Santiago, and took counsel with his sister Urraca. The Leonese and the Galegos came to Zamora and received him as their king. Then the Castilians arrived, and the men of Navarre. All kissed Alfonso's hand in homage, save Rodrigo the Cid. This incensed the king, who inquired the cause of such disloyalty. Rodrigo arose and said, " Sir, all whom you see here present suspect that you caused your brother Sancho's death. Unless you clear yourself of this I will never kiss your hand nor receive you as my king." Alfonso took the oath in the Church of St. Gadea at Burgos before his sisters Urraca and Elvira, and all his knights. When he had cleared his name of the imputation the Cid replied, " If you gave command that such a thing should be done may you die by the hand of a villain whom you trust." From that day forward Alfonso bore no love toward the Cid. Rodrigo, after despoiling Logrono, Navarre, and Calahorra, besieged the castle of Faro, and took it. Alfonso now commanded the Cid to do battle with Ximen Garcia de Tiogelos, the bravest knight in Navarre. They fought for three castles, and Rodrigo being victorious, Alfonso gained them. The Cid's next combat was in Medina Celi with a Moor called Furos, whom he slew. Alfonso now set Rodrigo to demand tribute from the Kings of Seville and of Cordova. War was then being waged between Almocanis, King of Seville, and Almundafar, King of Granada. Five Castilian counts aided Almundafar, who boldly entered Seville. Rodrigo overcame them, taking them prisoners. In three days he set them free, then returned with great honour to Seville. Almocanis paid him the tribute due to his king, and gave him many gifts, so that the Cid departed enriched for Castile. Thereafter King Alfonso went against the Moors, and Rodrigo being sick abode at home. While the king was going through Andalusia, the Moors assembled, and besieged the castle of Gormaz. When the Cid recovered strength he confronted the Moors at Toledo, bringing back several thousand prisoners. Rodrigo's enemies charged him with broken faith. Alfonso believed these slanderers, so he sent for the Cid to meet him between Burgos and Bivar. The Cid would have kissed Alfonso's hand, but the king withheld it, saying angrily, "Rodrigo, quit my land." The Cid spurred his mule, vaulted into his own property, then replied, "Sir, I am not in your land, but my own." Albeit Alfonso ordered him out of the kingdom without delay. The king even decreed that no man should give Rodrigo a lodging, so he took up his abode on the sands. All were forbidden to supply the Cid with food in Burgos. But Martin Antolinez, a good Burgolese, supplied the Cid and all his company with bread and wine abundantly. "Campeador," said he to the Cid, "I have incurred the king's displeasure, but when you regain the royal favour Alfonso will have me for his friend."

Having left the kingdom of Alfonso, the Cid entered the country of the Moors. He stormed the castle of Castrejon, slaying eleven men who defended the gates, and gaining great booty. He informed Alfonso of the conquest. Rodrigo next attacked Alcocer, saying, "Lay on, knights, by God's mercy the spoil is our own." Three hundred Moors were slain, and the Cid entered the castle in triumph. Alcamin, King of Valencia, sent three hundred horsemen to bring Rodrigo to him alive. Great numbers joined them ; but when three hundred lances charged every man slew his Moor. "Smite them, knights, for the love of charity," cried the Campeador. "I am Rodrigo, the Cid of Bivar." Seeing that the Moors had killed the horse of Alvar Fanez, and that his lance was broken, the Cid went to his aid. He gave him the horse of an alguazil whom he slew, saying, "Mount, Minaya, for you are my right hand." Thus remounted, Alvar Fanez fell upon the Moors so fiercely that they began to give way. Then the Cid, seeing King Fariz, made towards him, smiting down all who were in his way. Two blows failed, but the third went through his cuirass, and wounded him, so that he fled. With that blow were the Moors vanquished. As a gift, Rodrigo sent thirty horses to Alfonso, who pardoned Minaya, but still withheld his favour from the Cid. Now, Don Ramon of

Barcelona vowed to capture the booty of the Cid, and to slay him in the pine-forest of Tebar. But Rodrigo charged his Frenchmen on horseback so valiantly that every man was unseated. King Pedro of Arragon now came out against him, but the Cid took the castle of Monzon in his sight. Next he won Xerica, Onda, and Almenar, besides all the lands of Borriana and Murviedro. After he had plundered all that country he returned to Tamarit, where Zulema of Zaragoza then was. While the Cid was absent besieging the castle of Estrada, which he took by force, Zulema and his brother Abenalfange, King of Denia, together with Count Ramon, stormed Almenar. Rodrigo hastened to the rescue, and after much bloodshed, he was victorious. For this conquest Zulema honoured Rodrigo greatly, giving him power in all his dominions. Now, King Almofalez invited Alfonso to a feast in the castle of Rueda. Suspecting treachery, Alfonso held back, although Don Sancho, Don Nuno, Don Gonzalo, and fifteen other knights, entered. Thereupon the Moors threw down great stones and killed them all. To avenge this villainy Alfonso sent for the Cid. Rodrigo, however, refused to return to Castile until Alfonso had granted just and lawful rights to every subject. Alfonso consented, and the Cid stormed Rueda, capturing Almofalez and his accomplices, whom he sent to Alfonso for justice. Zulema and the Cid next entered Arragon, plundered the country, then returned to Monzon with great booty. Abenalfange's country was next attacked, and the castle of Moriella destroyed. King Pedro of Arragon aided Abenalfange, but the Campeador took Pedro captive, and defeated Abenalfange, who fled. Rodrigo returned to Zaragoza, tarried for a few days, then set out for Castile, with great riches, full of honour, was welcomed by Alfonso, who gave him the castles of Duenas, Orcejon, Hia, Campo, Gana, Berviesca, and Berlanga.

In these days King Tahia reigned in Toledo, but was so cruel that all men desired his death. The Muzarabes therefore exhorted Alfonso to win Toledo from the King of Badajoz, who then maintained it. When attacked he retreated, but Alfonso pursued him, despoiling his country for four years. Alfonso fought Abenalfange, but the Christians were defeated, and Diego, son of the Cid, slain. Thereafter Abenalfange was defeated by Alvar Fanez. Toledo being still unconquered, all Christendom placed itself under the banner of the Cid. After fifteen days' siege Rodrigo entered the city in the year of Christ 1085. Valencia was being besieged by the French under Count Ramon, but at the Cid's request he departed. Again Ramon attacked the Cid, who this time took a thousand prisoners. Next Rodrigo besieged Liria, the people paying him two thousand maravedis. When Ali Abenaxa besieged Aledo, Alfonso besought the Cid's aid. The Moors departed, flying, even before Rodrigo arrived. The Cid's enemies told the king that his delay was intended, so Alfonso took back the Campeador's lands, then sent for his wife and daughters. Alfonso attacked Valencia, demanding tribute formerly paid to the Cid. Feeling dishonoured, Rodrigo marched against the king, sacking Logrono, and Alfaro then returned to Zaragoza. *Now*

Alfonso saw his error in having listened to evil counsellors. So once more he besought the Cid to come to Castile. Rodrigo, however, tarried at Zaragoza, after which he took Valencia. King Yahia escaped in woman's apparel, but was afterwards slain by Abenaif. But this traitor to his lord was cast into prison by Rodrigo. Thus the Cid possessed all the castles and fortresses in Valencia. The Campeador now sent Alvar Fanez and Martin Antolinez to Castile to visit Ximena, Elvira, and Sol, the Cid's wife and daughters, and to present Alfonso with a hundred horses. This magnanimity overcame the king, who made Rodrigo Lord of Valencia, and restored his wife and daughters.

Three months had Ximena been in Valencia when King Yucef of Morocco besieged the city. "My wife and my daughters shall see me fight," said Rodrigo the Cid. Ximena's heart failed her, but her husband reassured her. Alvar Fanez took three hundred horse, went out, and lay in ambush. Four thousand went out with the Campeador to meet fifty thousand. As the Moors were contending with Rodrigo, Minaya sprang from his ambush to succour him, and scattered them, Yucef escaping. Great joy had Ximena and her daughters when Rodrigo came riding in. Holding up a bloody sword, he cried, "This is the way that we conquer the Moors." Besides King Yucef's tent the Cid sent two hundred horses saddled and bridled to Alfonso, who was greatly pleased. But Garcia Ordonez spitefully said, "It seems there is not a man left in the land of the Moors, that the Cid can thus do his pleasure!" Alfonso sternly replied, "Hold thy peace,

for in all things he serves me better than thou." Two brothers, counts of Carrion, had resolved on a marriage with the daughters of the Cid, to obtain possession of his wealth. In a wild, mountainous desert they stripped the garments from the ladies, bound and beat them till pain choked their cries, then departed with the money. A trusty servant delivered them from their wretched situation. The Cid demanded justice, and the king helped him to obtain it. Rodrigo insisted on a combat, so champions were chosen, a duel fought, but the dishonoured counts were spared their lives. The Cid's last exploit was the capture of Saguntum, after which he died at Valencia in the seventy-fourth year of his age, in 1099. He was buried in Castile, at the convent of St. Peter of Gardena, in a tomb which was honoured by emperors and kings. There rests the noble Ximena, and under the trees before the convent lies the faithful horse Babieca.

CLAREL. (*Vide* "Sir Otuel.") A Saracen king, taken prisoner by Charlemagne's knights, but liberated. He afterwards took Ogier prisoner. He fought Otuel in single combat and was slain by him.

CLARICE. (*Vide* "Florice and Blanchfleur.") A slave in the service of the Amiral of Babylon. She was Blanchfleur's companion, and after Florice had entered the castle, contrived to bring the lovers together. She married her master, who proclaimed her queen.

CLARIODUS. A romance written about the year 1550, or perhaps somewhat later. Like many English romances, it is derived from a French original. The story, however, in a great measure concerns England. The hero himself is the son of the Earl of Esture, or of the Asturias; but his lady-love, Meliades, is the daughter and heiress of Philippon, King of England, and the most material incidents and adventures are connected with the court of that monarch. There is a French prose version of this romance, but the two stories differ. Soon after the days of King Arthur, there reigned in England a worthy king named Philippon. He espoused a lady belonging to a very high family of Gascony, and the only issue of the marriage was a daughter named Meliades. The king had a brother, Thomas de Langarde, who was much younger than himself, but of an evil disposition. When Philippon had grown old he solicited the aid of his friend, the Count of Esture, to assist him in the government of his people. The count repairs to England, accompanied by his son Clariodus, and is made the king's lieutenant, while his son likewise meets with the monarch's favour. There are four gentlemen in the count's train, whose names frequently recur in the course of the narrative. Two of them, Amadour de Bruslaut and Palixes, were his sister's sons; the third was of Scotland, and named Richard de Mataint. The fourth was of Wales, Guillaume de Forest.

Clariodus falls madly in love with Meliades. One day a knight, attended by six squires, enters the palace, and delivers a message from the Duc de Jennes; setting forth that, during the said duke's minority, Philippon had, without cause and without reason, seized upon the post of Claire-Fontaine, and declaring that unless he signified his willingness to make restitution he would defy him " with fire and blood." The knight, however, added that he was authorized to leave the decision of their claims to the issue of a single combat, and was prepared to meet with any knight who would appear on the king's behalf.

Clariodus tenders his services, and after being knighted by the king, enters the lists with his adversary. With this incident the romance is continued by a Scottish hand. Clariodus defeats the knight. Beyond this the tale consists of mere repetition, saving that the wedding of Clariodus is described.

CLARISSE or **CLARISSANT**. (Montpellier MS.) Is mentioned in Arthurian legend as being the sister of Gauvain, a dweller in the Magic Castle. Her lover is Guireomelant, whom Sir Percyvelle fights.

CLAUDIUS. Alluded to in the Grail legend of the *Queste del Saint Graal* (*q.v.*), as one of the messengers who carried a message from Bors, Perceval, and Galahad to Arthur's court.

CLEENA. A maiden of the Danaans in Irish myth, who dwelt in the Land of Youth. She fled from there with a mortal, Keevan of the Curling Locks, who, on their arrival in Glandore Bay, went to hunt in the neighbouring woods. Cleena, left behind, heard the lay of a minstrel of her own country, which lulled her to sleep, and a mighty wave catching her up from the seashore bore her back to the land of her youth. The spot is known as the " Wave of Cleena."

CLEGES, SIR. An old English romance of the fourteenth century, probably an adaptation of the

F

Cliges of Marie de France. It tells how Cleges, in the days of King Arthur's father, beggared himself by liberality. But when his fortunes were at a low ebb he and his wife, Claris, would not despair. On Christmas Eve, when all was merry-making, he grieved that he could not as of yore feed " both free and bond," but his spouse cheered him, called him to his frugal meal, and bade him be glad in honour of the day. So they made merry, played with their children, and on the morrow went to the church. On returning home he knelt beneath a cherry tree, and thanked God for all his trials. Arising, he observed that the tree was green, and was covered with cherries. Travelling as a poor man, staff in hand, he and his eldest son carried the fruit to King Uther at Cardiff. The porter would not grant them admittance unless they gave him a third of what they would receive from the king. The usher made a similar bargain, as did a steward. Uther, delighted with the un-seasonable gift, promised the poor man whatever he might ask. Cleges then requested that he might give twelve heavy strokes to his enemies in the palace, and dealt out a fitting punishment to those who had barred his pro-gress. Returning to the hall, he found a harper to whom he had once been kind singing his praises. The king was reminded by his song of his old knight. Cleges then disclosed himself, and re-ceived suitable raiment, and the gift of Cardiff Castle. The last part of the MS. is wanting.

CLEMADEX, KING. In Grail ro-mance, alluded to in connection with the damsel Blanchfleur (*q.v.*), whom Sir Perceval shields. He is overcome by Sir Perceval, and is sent, along with his marshal Aguigrenons (*q.v.*), to Arthur's court.

CODRE. Le, The twin daughter of one of the " two knights " re-ferred to in the *Lay le Fraine* (*q.v.*) and sister to Le Fraine. She soon after her birth lost her sister, who suffered desertion at her mother's hands, She was brought forward as bride to Sir Guroun (*q.v.*), which marriage was after-wards annulled, on her husband discovering his former lover to be her sister. She subsequently married a neighbouring lord.

COLBRAND. (*Vide* " Guy of War-wick.") A Danish giant, slain by Sir Guy in single combat.

COLDRAN. Amiral in the Saracen Army. (*Vide* " Guy of Warwick.")

COLGREVANCE, SIR. A Knight of the Round Table. He was on one occasion severely wounded by Sir Lionel for interfering in a quarrel between him and his brother, Sir Bors (*q.v.*). Latterly, however, he met his death at the hands of Lancelot, in connection with the scandal concerning Queen Guin-ever (*q.v.*). (*Vide* " Morte d'Arthur.")

COLIDES. A knight mentioned in the *Conte du Graal* as warring upon the Dame of the Castle of Maidens, who was delivered from him by Saigremors.

COLLOQUY OF THE ANCIENTS. A collection of Ossianic tales welded into one about the thirteenth and fourteenth centuries. The *Collo-quy* opens by introducing us to the Fian heroes, Keelta and Oisin, who with their eight warriors each met for the last time at the dun of the chieftainess Camha to talk over the glorious past. Oisin then returns to the Fairy Mound of his mother, Blai (*q.v.*), and Keelta eventually falls in with St. Patrick and his monks at Drumderg. The saint and his company listen, enchanted, to some hundred fairy tales, interspersed by lyrics, related by their strange visitor: while St. Patrick on his side baptizes the heathen warriors and gives absolution to many more of their comrades.

COLOGRENANT. A knight mentioned in the *Queste del Saint Graal* as having been slain by Percival. In the *Conte du Graal* he interposes between the quarrelling brothers, Boort and Lyonel, and pays for his interference with his life. He is the same as Sir Colgrevance (*q.v.*) alluded to in the *Morte d'Arthur*.

CONALL OF THE VICTORIES. A Fomorian chief, first alluded to in the Irish myths as a hostage to Conary (*q.v.*). At the Battle of Hostel he cut his way to Teltin, where he found his father, Amergin, at his house. He was covered with a hundred and fifty wounds. Later he is found under the curse of weakness placed by Macha (*q.v.*) on the men of Ulster. He avenged the death of Cuchulain by the slaughter of Lewy (*q.v.*). He made a missle or "brain ball" from lime mingled with the brains of Mesgedra, King of Leinster, whom he had slain. It was placed in King Conor's treasurehouse at Emain Macha, where Ket (*q.v.*) found it, and using it as a sling-stone, nearly slew with it Conor himself at the ford of Athnurchar in Westmeath, but Conor recovered, although the stone remained in his forehead. For further details of Conall's brain-ball, see "Conor."

CONAN MAC LIA. An outlaw of Ireland, who was at enmity with the Fians. It is related in the Ossianic cycle of romance how, cornered by the Fians at Carn Lewy in Munster, he surprised Finn as he rested after the hunt, and clasped him in his arms from behind. Finn asked him what he required to release him, and he replied that he desired to enter his service. The request was granted, and Conan became one of the champions of the Fians.

CONAN MAC MORNA. A champion of the Fianna (*q.v.*). He is described in the Ossianic cycle of Irish romance as being a scoffer and derider of all that was lofty and noble. It is related of him that while hunting he with others of the Fians entered a stately palace which they found empty, and where they sat down to feast. Soon, however, the walls shrank to the size of a fox-earth, and the heroes became aware that they had been lured to their destruction by the enchantment of the fairy folk. Conan, devouring the viands on the table, was oblivious of the danger, and could not stir from his chair. But two of the Fians, seeing his plight, pulled him from the seat, to which his skin stuck. To ease his pain they placed a black sheepskin upon his back, and it grew there, and he wore it till his death-day. He slew Liagan, a piratical invader, at the Battle of the Hill of Slaughter by a stratagem. He told him that a hero had stolen behind him, and whilst he looked round, decapitated him with one blow of his sword.

CONARY MOR. In Irish romance, High King of Ireland, whose figure predominates in a special legend-cycle. The introductory tale to his history is that of the immortals Midir (*q.v.*) and Etain (*q.v.*). Etain's mortal husband, Eochy (*q.v.*), in revenge for the theft of his wife by Midir, destroyed the Fairy Mound of Bri-Leith, and thus brought down the ill fate that attended his great grandson, Conary Mor. Conary left his three foster-brothers after a game with them on the Plains of Liffey, and followed to the sea-shore a flock of marvellously beautiful birds. These took the form of armed men, whose leader, Nemglan, protected him, and informed him that the birds belonged to his father and were his kin. His *geise* or *taboos* were made known to him, and Nemglan told him in what manner to approach Tara. Thus he was proclaimed King of Erin. His reign was good, happy, and prosperous, until the time of his undoing, the Danaan folk eventually luring him to the breaking of his *geise*. While resting with his retinue in Da Derga's hostel, he was attacked by the hosts of Ingcel, the exiled son of the King of Britain and the three reaver foster-brothers. Dying of thirst after the fury of his fighting, and finding the river that flowed through the hostel dried up by the magic of the reavers' wizards, he sent the warrior Mac Cecht, (*q.v.*) to fill his cup. After much searching the water was obtained, but too late, as when Mac Cecht returned he found Conary slain by the reavers. But to the mouth of the bodyless head of the King the cup was raised, and the head thanked Mac Cecht for the deed.

CONN. One of the children of Lir (*q.v.*).

CONNAN. A King of the Fomorians, a mythical folk of Ireland. He was killed in Tory Island by the Nemedian chief, Fergus, in a battle which resulted from the latter's revolt against the Fomorian monarch.

CONNLA. Son of Cuchulain and Aifa. (*Vide* "Cuchulain.") He arrived from the Land of Shadows in a boat of bronze, and, landing in Ulster, was ordered by the king to leave the country. He refused, and overcame the champions who were sent against him, till at length Cuchulain, his father, was himself despatched to deal with the invader. They fought, and in the combat the boy's feet sank deep into the stone of the shore, whence the Strand of Footprints has its name. Cuchulain, on the point of drowning, thrust the Gae Bolg weapon (*q.v.*) into Connla's body, inflicting a mortal wound. Seeing the ring he had given his mistress Aifa on the lad's finger, Cuchulain knew him to be his son, and presented him to the most famous warriors of Ulster before he died. The story is recounted in the *Yellow Book of Lecan*, but several other forms of it exist.

CONNLA'S WELL. (Well of Knowledge.) (*Vide* "Sinend.")

CONOR MAC NESSA. Son of Fachtna and Nessa. It is stated in early Irish myth that he was proclaimed King of Ulster in preference to Fergus. The mighty hero Cuchulain was bred at his court, and received the arms of manhood at his hands. He plays some considerable part in the legend of Deirdre (*q.v.*), and suffered under the debility curse of the Ultonians. (*Vide* "Macha.") Numerous Christian conceptions have crystallized around the legend of his later years. He was wounded at the ford of Athnurchar by a brain-ball missile made from the brains of King Mesgedra. (*Vide* "Conall of the Victories.") The bolt was permitted to remain in his head. Remarking one day to his arch-druid that the sky had become overcast, he was informed by the priest that nature was lamenting the death of the Son of God which was taking place on a hill many thousands of miles away. Infuri-ated that such a being should suffer at the hands of wicked men, Conor drew his sword, and shout-ing, "Thus would I serve His enemies," he fell upon the neigh-bouring trees, and cut and hacked fiercely at them. But the brain-ball in his forehead became loosened with the exertion, and he fell and expired.

CONRAD or KONRAD VON WURTZ-BOURG. A German poet of the second half of the thirteenth century. He is occasionally styled Priest Conrad, but whether he was in holy orders is not definitely recorded, while even the date of his birth is uncertain, and very little is known about his career. Considering his name, it may reasonably be supposed that the greater part of his life was passed in or near Wurtzbourg, but it would seem that he also lived for a while at Strassbourg, while his later years were spent at Basel, and there he died in 1287. In some degree he was a disciple of Gottfried von Strassbourg, and, like him, he strove to introduce greater variety into the rather monotonous metre in vogue among most narrative poets of his era. Conrad was a voluminous writer, and he left behind him two poems of enormous length, *Der Trojaner-krieg* and *Partonopier und Meliur ;* but these can hardly be said to contain his best work, and he is really seen to better advantage in some of his shorter and less ambitious efforts, notably *Die*

Herzmoere and *Engelhard.* A number of his productions have been revived during modern times, and some of his smaller pieces will be found in *Erzählungen und Schwänke des Mittelalters,* edited by Lambel (second edition, 1883) ; while *Der Trojanerkrieg* was issued at Stuttgart in 1858 along with annotations by Roth and Keller, and *Partonopier und Meliur* was published at Vienna in 1870 under the editorship of Bartsch.

CONSTANTINE. Emperor of Rome and father of Viatdur (*q.v.*) who commanded his daughter to heal Eglamour (*q.v.*) after his encounter with the dragon. (*Vide* " Eglamour of Artoys.")

CONSTANTINE. Sir. (*Vide* " Roland and Ferragus.") A Knight of Rome. He was sent by Charle-magne to fight Ferragus, and was slain by him.

CONSTANTIUS. (*Vide* " Roland and Ferragus.") Emperor of Constan-tinople. The Christians appealed to him for help against the per-secution by Ibrahim, and he was directed by an angel to apply to Charlemagne, in order that the Saracens might be defeated. Charle-magne paid a visit to Con-stantinople, and was offered many gifts, although he only accepted a few relics, in the presence of which wonderful miracles took place.

CONTE DEL GRAAL. One of the " Quest " versions of the legend of the Holy Grail (*q.v.*) and an extensive compilation of over 60,000 verses of poetry, written between 1180 and 1240. Verses 1283 to 10,601 were composed by the twelfth-century French poet, Chrétien de Troyes (*q.v.*), who states that he took the story from a book given him by a Count Philip of Flanders, who was Regent of France in 1180–81. The rest of the compilation is by different hands. Chrétien's portion tells how Perceval was reared to the life of a forester by his mother, who had sought the shelter of the woodland. Meeting one day with a band of knights and their retainers, he follows them, despite the entreaties of his mother, to the court of King Arthur, where he becomes an *habitué*, and gains a certain celebrity. Setting forth upon the career of a knight-errant, he meets with Gonemans, who trains him in all manner of knightly exercises. He assists Blanchefleur, an oppressed damsel, the niece of Gonemans, with whom he sojourns for a space. Faring forth once more, he comes upon two fishermen, whom he asks for shelter. He is directed to a neighbouring castle, wherein he beholds an old man stretched upon a couch, who gives him a sword bearing an inscription to the effect that it will not break except in the direst peril, and a lance dripping with blood. At supper a damsel enters bearing "a Grail," the supernatural light from which extinguishes that from the candles. Awakening in the morning, he discovers that the castle is deserted and, mounting his horse, enters the forest, where he encounters a damsel weeping over a dead knight. She explains to Perceval that the fisherman who had directed him to the castle was none other than the old man who had presented him with the sword and lance, and who had at one time been wounded through both legs by a spear, an injury which prevented him from taking any other exercise than fishing, whence he was called the Fisher King. Had Perceval asked the meaning of the mysteries he had beheld, the Fisher King would

have been cured of his malady. It transpires that the damsel is Perceval's cousin. Perceval returns to Arthur's court, when a hideous woman appears, and denounces him for not asking about the mysteries. She tells of adventures perilous at Castle Orgellous and Montesclaire. Gauvain or Gawain goes to Montesclaire to rescue an imprisoned damsel, Giflès to the Castle Orgellous, and Perceval to seek information concerning the Grail. The adventures of Gauvain are fully detailed. Perceval wanders for five years in a state of mind bordering upon godlessness, when at last on a Good Friday he chances to meet with a band of pilgrims. These remonstrate with him for riding armed on that holy day, and he turns aside to confess to a hermit, who proves to be his uncle. From him he learns that only the sinless can ask concerning the Grail, and that he has sinned in abandoning his mother, thus causing her death. The adventures of Gauvain are reverted to, in the midst of which the tale breaks off. The first continuation of the legend is by a poet Gautier, who continues the adventures of Gauvain, who in a certain castle sees lance, sword and Grail, asks concerning them, but falls asleep whilst listening to the reply. On the next day he wakes to find what had been a wilderness blossoming because of the proximity of the Grail. But he is cursed by the peasantry for not having wholly succeeded in his quest. Perceval now returns to the Fisher King, asks the necessary questions, but is told that he must first weld together the Grail sword, now broken. He mends it all except a small rift, and is greatly honoured by the Fisher King. The poem is then continued by Manessier, who recounts how Perceval slew Partinans of the Red Tower, who had killed by guile Goon Desert, brother of the Fisher King, in revenge for the death of Espinogre. On beholding the head of Partinans, the Fisher King is made whole, tells Perceval that he is his uncle, and makes him his heir. Gerbert then takes up the tale, and tells how Perceval, having forsaken Blanchefleure, slays a witch who had murdered her uncle Gornumant, and returns to the damsel, whom he espouses. He is told in a dream that one of his descendants would deliver the Holy Sepulchre. The nature and origin of the Grail are described in these continuations. (*Vide* " Grail," " Parzival," " Peredur," " Sir Percevelle.")

CORBENIC. Castle, mentioned in Arthurian legend as the Castle where the Holy Grail was kept. It was guarded by two lions, and Lancelot was fain to enter, trusting rather to his own strength than that of his Creator. In consequence he is struck dumb by a fiery wind, and remains so without food or drink for the space of fourteen days.

CORMAC (1). Son of Art, King of Ireland. He is supposed to have been imbued with Christian ideals before the coming of St. Patrick to Ireland, and refused to be buried in pagan ground.

CORMAC (2). King of Ulster. He married Etain Oig, daughter of Etain, but as she bore him no children save a girl, he divorced her. (*Vide* " Etain Oig.")

CORMAC (3). Son of Conor Mac Nessa. He revolted against Conor for his treatment of the sons of Usna (*q.v.*), and assisted Maev in her invasion of Ulster.

CORNWALL. Duke of, He warred with Uther Pendragon (*q.v.*) and was defeated and slain by his forces. Uther coveted his wife, Igraine (*q.v.*), and assumed her husband's shape to win her.

CORONEMENT DU ROI LOEYS. (The Crowning of King Louis.) A romance of the William of Orange sub-cycle of the Charlemagne saga. (*Vide* " William of Orange.") Charlemagne before he dies wishes to have his son Louis crowned. Louis is so fearful of the royal duties, however, that he dare not accept the honour. His father in anger threatens to make a monk of him. Hernaut of Orleans counsels three years' delay, but William of Orange, seeing through his treacherous design, kills him with a single blow of his fist. He then takes the crown and places it upon Louis' head. Charlemagne gives his son lengthy and good advice, and tells him to trust in William and Bernard of Breban, his brother. William, however, asks the dying monarch for leave to go to Rome on a pilgrimage. He sets out with forty knights, and finds the Holy City besieged by the Saracens, France itself being also invaded. The issue of the war is staked on the result of a combat between William and King Corsolt, the champion of the Saracens. Corsolt bids a feast be prepared beforehand, as he will soon slay the Frenchman. Corsolt, in the combat which ensues, cuts off William's nose, and cleaves his horse in two. William cannot reach the giant's head, and Corsolt stuns him with a mighty blow. The Saracen attempts to carry him off on the crupper of his horse, but William strikes him such a blow as renders him insensible, and then shears off his head. He next mounts the giant's horse, and returns to the French, who offer battle next day, in which King Galafer, the Saracen, is overcome, but offers to release a certain King Gaifer if he is spared, with thirty thousand of his men. To this William agrees, and William is about to marry the grateful Gaifer's daughter when a messenger arrives announcing Charlemagne's death, and that Louis is menaced by Richard of Normandy. Renouncing his nuptials, William hurries back to France, where he learns that Louis is concealed in the crypt of St. Martin's Church. Arrived at Tours, where Louis is in hiding, he proceeds to St. Martin's Church, where he is advised by Walter, a clerk, to slay all the clergy, as they are traitors. The clerk fetches the young king, William slays Acelin, the son of Richard of Normandy, for refusing homage to the King, and beats the clergy out of the minster. Richard himself clings to the altar. William fells him with a blow of his fist, shaves his head, and strips him. They are, however, outwardly reconciled. Louis is reinstated, and William spends six years in conquering the land for him. Richard, taken prisoner in an ambush, dies in prison. William hastens back to Rome on receiving news of the invasion of that city by Guy of Almain, whom he slays. M. Jonckbloet infers from the circumstances of this romance, that though there was a conspiracy against the crowning of Louis le Debonair, in the poem now under notice there has been welded with it an account of the enthronement of Louis d'Outremer, whose faithful defender was William of Poitiers.

Literature: Jonckbloet, *Guillaume d'Orange, chanson de geste des 11e. et 12e. Siècles*, 1854.

CORPRÉ. In Irish romance, a poet who obtained wretched hospitality at the court of the Irish King Bres (*q.v.*). In return for his treatment he dethroned the unpopular monarch by a scathing satire.

CORSAPIAS. An old knight who set out in search of Nasciens (*q.v.*) as guardian of his wife, Flegentyne. He is mentioned in the *Grand Saint Graal*.

COSTROYE. (*Vide* "Sir Ferumbras.") A Saracen amiral, who when going to the bridge of Mantribe with a convoy of provisions, was overtaken by the ten French peers from Aigremor and killed.

COVAC. Younger son of Ugainy, an Irish king. Envying his brother Laery (*q.v.*) his kingdom, he procured the assistance of a druid in order to gain the throne. Laery suspected treachery, and therefore would never see his brother, unless armed. So by the druid's advice Covac feigned death, and was visited by the king, whom he stabbed to the heart. Having also murdered one of his nephews, he mounted the throne.

COVENANT VIVIEN, LE. A romance of the William of Orange subcycle of the Charlemagne Saga. Vivien, the nephew of William, on receiving knighthood, registers a solemn vow never to flee before the Saracens "more than a lance-length." A great Saracen armada appears near Aliscans or Arleschans (probably Arles Champs or the Fields of Arles, but identified by others with Alis Camps, Elysian Fields, a famous cemetery outside the walls of Arles). Vivien and his comrades attack the invaders, although these are a hundred to one. The Christians are overmatched, and Vivien, who is wounded, permits one of his friends to ride to William of Orange for assistance. The messenger, Gerard of Commarchis, reaches Orange, of which city the romancer draws a beautiful and vivid picture. William is dismayed, but Guibor, his wife, who has nurtured Vivien from childhood, encourages him. Ten thousand men are brought together. Guichard, Vivien's younger brother, desires to follow the host, but is refused permission. But he cuts himself a great staff, fetches a charger out of the stable, and follows William without weapon or armour. Guibor sends after him, and he goes forth once more armed and knighted. He meets fifteen Saracens, kills three, and finally reaches William. Vivien, wounded four times, remains in possession of the field with thirty or forty men. He has his wounds dressed, and meeting his uncle William, strikes him under a misapprehension. They recognize each other. For the continuation of the matter of the romance, *vide* article "Arleschans, Battle of."

COWARD KNIGHT. The, A knight alluded to in the *Conte del Graal* (q.v.) (Manessier's portion) as being afraid to attack the ravishers of two damsels. Perceval attacks them, and the Coward Knight is drawn into the struggle, and quits himself manfully. He subsequently bears himself equally well at a tournament in the company of Perceval, who, because of his courage, gives him the title of "Le Hardis."

CRAFTINY. A harper in early Irish romance, who cut down a willow tree to make a harp. The tree chanced to be that to which King Maon, called Labra the Mariner, had confided the secret that he had horse's ears. The instrument, on being performed upon in the king's hall, sang the words, "Labra the Mariner hath two horse's ears." The secret being out, Labra, who was king, cared nothing more for his deformity which had before galled him much. Craftiny was also instrumental in curing Labra's dumbness.

CREDNE. In Irish romance, the artificer of the Danaans (q.v.). Along with Goban the Smith and Luchta the Carpenter, he kept repairing the weapons of the Danaans during their battle with the Fomorians (q.v.).

CROWNING OF KING LOUIS. (*Vide* "Coronement du Roi Loeys.")

CRUDEL. King of Great Britain. He threw Joseph and his son Josephes, together with many other Christians, into prison for forty days, and forbade food to be given them, but they had the life-sustaining Holy Grail with them. They were ultimately delivered by Mordrains and his brother-in-law Seraphe with their host.

CRUNDCHU. (*Vide* "Macha.")

CRYSTABELL. Daughter of Sir Prinsamour (q.v.), a count of Artois, and for whose sake Sir Eglamour (q.v.) undertook three adventures. She was the mother of Degrabell (q.v.), begotten of Sir Eglamour. Her father subsequently banished her from his court. Her son was stolen from her by a griffin, which carried him into Israel. She eventually arrived in Egypt, where she lived for a while under the guardianship of her uncle, the king of that country. She afterwards married her son, as the result of a tourney given by her uncle; but discovering her husband's real identity, her marriage was revoked. Later, at another tourney for the same purpose, in which Eglamour took part, she discovered him to be her long-lost lover. They and their son return to Artois, where they are married. The latter subsequently married Aradanta. (See the romance of " Sir Eglamour of Artoys.")

CUCHULAIN. The most heroic figure in Irish romance, and the great Ulster warrior who dominates the Ultonian cycle. Son of the solar god Lugh (*q.v.*) and Dectera (*q.v.*), he had also a reputed father, Sualtam (*q.v.*). For his child-life, *vide* " Setanta." Soon after he had received the name of " the Hound of Cullan," he overheard Cathbad, his maternal grandfather, divine that on that day he who should take up arms would become the most famous in deeds in Ireland. Cuchulain then asked King Conor (*q.v.*) that he might take the arms of manhood, a request which was immediately granted him. The men of Ulster now asked him to take a wife, but Emer, daughter of Forgall, alone pleased him. So he set out in his chariot for her father's dun, to learn that she would not marry him until he had slain his hundreds. He therefore sought through black forests and desert paths, through quagmires and seas, the Land of Shadow and the Warrior-goddess Skatha. He passed the Plain of Ill-Luck, crossed unaided the Bridge of Leaps, and presented himself to the warrior-goddess. For a year and a day he dwelt with her, learning all manner of feats, and lastly the use of the Gae Bolg (*q.v.*), a most deadly weapon. With this he was to do much havoc among his enemies. During this time of training he sealed a great

friendship with Ferdia (*q.v.*), which was to have a tragic ending. Skatha, making war with Aifa (*q.v.*), the mightiest of the warrior-women of the world, did not wish Cuchulain to tax his fighting powers, still immature, and therefore gave him a sleeping potion. This should have lasted for twenty-four hours, but the hero awoke after one hour and scattered death upon the host of the enemy. Finally, Aifa inciting Skatha to single combat, Cuchulain accepted the challenge for himself, and by his victory made an end of the war. Aifa then became his friend and lover, and before he departed for the court of Conor he gave her a ring which he bade her fit upon the finger of their son, should they have one, and send him to Ulster. Connla (*q.v.*) was to be the name of the boy, but neither his lineage nor his name was he to reveal. This secrecy brought about the death of this only son at the hands of his father. Cuchulain's first exploit after his pupilage with Skatha was with the sons of Nechtan (*q.v.*), whom he slew and whose heads he fastened to his chariot's rim. Returning in his battle fury with sixteen swans and two stags yoked to his chariot, he was met by naked women of Emania, became ashamed of his battle fury, and after several plunges in vats of cold water he regained his natural mood and aspect. Upon the next day he won Emer, having slain Forgall and many of his men and hundreds of the host of Forgall's sister. For the manner in which he gained the championship of Ireland, *vide* " Briccriu." But the name Cuchulain stands out in the most gigantic lines in the famous Cattle Raid of Quelgny (*q.v.*). Single-handed, and unaffected by the curse of Macha (*q.v.*), he harried and slew by hundreds the host of Maev (*q.v.*). Then he made a compact with the queen that he would cease to harry her host if she sent against him but one champion at a time. Each warrior he would meet at the Ford of Ferda. Even Fergus challenged his old pupil. But Cuchulain pretended to run from him, Fergus having promised to do the same when required. After the capture of the Brown Bull (*q.v.*), the Morrigan, a goddess of war, appeared to Cuchulain as a king's daughter and offered him her love. He refused it, and was beset by her in his fight with Loch (*q.v.*), and through her means was wounded several times by this Connacht champion. She afterwards became his friend. Then worn and despondent with his hard fighting, he beheld his father Lugh, who bade him sleep for three days while he kept the Ford. After the allotted time he arose refreshed, to deal still greater death and destruction on the invaders. For, while he rested, the boys' corps of one hundred and fifty sons of the chieftains of the Ulster princes, had marched against the Maevian army, only to be annihilated. Champion after champion went down before him, and the Clan Calatin (*q.v.*) had been hacked to pieces when Ferdia, the last and mightiest of the warriors of Maev, urged by the fear of satire, went unwillingly against his companion of the Skathan days. After three days of sore wounding on both sides, Cuchulain, by the use of the Gae Bolg, conquered, and Ferdia fell. Then the mighty warrior, overwrought by his efforts and overpowered by grief at the death of his old friend, lay in a death-like swoon for many days. He awoke

to find their debility had passed from the men of Ulster, and, his battle-frenzy coming on him, he completely conquered the host of Connacht and its queen, sparing, however, her life. For with Fergus, who had kept his promise to fly from Cuchulain when required, the men of Leinster and Munster had gone out of the battle. One day, tired with the hunt, Cuchulain lay down to rest, and in his sleep had a vision of two maidens who alternately beat him. For a year and a day afterwards he lay sick until an unknown man bade him seek the face of his vision and learn its meaning. Here he heard of the love that Fand, the Pearl of Beauty, wife of Mananan (*q.v.*) the sea-god, bore him. For the story of this amour, *vide* "Fand." Full of the desire of revenge, Maev set the posthumous three sons of three daughters of the wizard Calatin against Cuchulain. He was then tended in his despondency in a solitary glen by Niam (*q.v.*) and other princesses, until urged by Bave (*q.v.*), in Niam's form, he went forth to battle. At the touch of his lips the wine that Dectera gave him turned to blood; at the ford upon the plain of Emania he beheld a maiden weeping and washing bloody garments and arms, his own; and he partook unwillingly (for he was breaking his *geis* or *taboo*) of the roasted dog offered him by the three crones, Calatin's daughters. His end was at hand; near to Slieve Ford, south of Armagh, he met his foes, and, thrice requested by a satirist to give him his spear, he fell at the third return of it, by the hand of Lewy (*q.v.*). Having drunk at the loch-side and bathed his wounds, upright against a pillar he died, by the sword of the son of Curoi. His vast figure reappears in the twelfth century *Book of the Dun Cow*. Here he is summoned from hell by St. Patrick to relate its horrors to the pagan Laery mac Neill, King of Ireland. Laery accepted Christianity and Cuchulain is granted heaven. We see in Cuchulain a typical solar hero. We are informed at once that he is the son of the sun-god. His youth, like that of Arthur, Tristram, and other similar champions, is passed in obscurity, during his zenith of power his battle-fury is greatest, and at length he weakens, and is slain with comparative ease. He does not, however, exhibit the characteristics of a culture-hero as do some sons of the sun. He does not introduce the arts as does Quetzalcoatl in Mexico, nor does he remedy abuses or undertake gigantic tasks like Hercules. But the essential characteristics of the sun-hero are in his case ever abundantly present. (*Vide* Miss E. Hull's *Cuchullin Saga*, 1898 ; Standish O'Grady, *Silva Gadelica*, 1893 ; L. Winifred Faraday, *The Cattle Raid of Cualnge*, 1904.)

CULLAN. A smith of Quelgny in Ulster, who figures in the Cuchulain myth. He invited King Conor and his followers, and feasted them royally, closing the gates of his house, and letting loose a huge hound for the protection of the mansion. The boy Setanta (*q.v.*), whom the company expected, arrived at the house of Cullan, and, being attacked by the monstrous hound, slew it. Cullan was grieved that his guardian was killed, and, seeing this, Setanta offered to train up one of his whelps to perform the same duty as its sire, and meanwhile to undertake that duty himself, from which circumstance he was afterwards known as Cuchulain, that is " the Hound of Cullan." (*Vide* " Cuchulain.")

CUMHAL. In Irish romance, chief of the clan Bascna, and son of Trenmor, husband of Murna of the White Neck, and father of Finn. He was slain at the Battle of Knock, fighting against the Clan Morna.

CUROI. In the Ultonian cycle of Irish romance, father of Lewy, husband of Blanid, the King of Munster. He was slain by Cuchulain who abducted his wife. (*Vide* " Blanid.")

CYVWLCH THE TALL. (*Vide* " Gododin.") A Cymric warrior slain at the Battle of Cattraeth.

D

DA DERGA. (*Vide* " Conary.")

DAG. Son of King Hogni (*q.v.*) and brother to Sigrun (*q.v.*). (*Vide* the " Lay of the Volsungs.") In revenge for his father's death he slew Helgi (*q.v.*) with the aid of Odin's sword.

DAGONET, SIR. Jester to King Arthur and his knights. (*Vide* " Morte d'Arthur.")

DALAN. In the Irish legend-cycle of Conary Mor (*q.v.*), the druid who revealed to Eochy (*q.v.*) that Etain (*q.v.*) was in the Fairy Mound of Bri-Leith.

DAMAN. In Irish romance, a Firbolg, father of Ferdia (*q.v.*).

DANAANS, THE, *i.e.* the people of the goddess Dana, frequently alluded to in Irish romance, were one of the three Nemedian families who survived the Fomorian victory. They returned at a later period to Ireland. According to Tuan mac Carrell (*q.v.*), they came " out of heaven," and later tradition has it that they sprang from four cities, Falias, Gorias, Finias, and Murias (*q.v.*). In each of these cities at the foot of the throne of a great sage they learned science and craftsmanship, and from each they brought away a magical treasure. From Falias came the Stone of Destiny (Lia Fail) (*q.v.*), from Gorias the invincible sword of Lugh of the Long Arm, from Finias a magical spear, and from Murias the Cauldron of the Dagda. Thus armed, as the *Book of Invasions* tells us, the Danaans were wafted into Ireland in a magic cloud and appeared in Western Connacht. Here they were found by another Nemedian surviving family, the Firbolgs, in the fortified Moyrein camp. Sreng and Bres, ambassadors each, one from the Firbolgs, the other from the Danaans, examined the weapons of either, the light sharp-pointed spears of the latter, the heavy and blunt spears of the former. The new-comer then proposed that Ireland be divided among and protected by the Firbolgs and the Danaans. But Sreng's people would not agree to the proposal, and the first Battle of Moytura ensued. Under Nuada of the Silver Hand (*q.v.*) the Danaans prevailed, and the Firbolg King, mac Cecht, was slain. Then the victors allotted Connacht to the conquered, and took possession of the remaining Irish territory. Nuada being maimed, Bres (*q.v.*) was chosen king, but was satirized out of his throne by the poet Corpré (*q.v.*), and Nuada, now provided with a hand of flesh and blood by the art of Diancecht (*q.v.*), was re-crowned. Bres then sought revenge, and the Danaans groaned under the Fomorian Balor until Lugh (*q.v.*) appeared to deliver them. In the second Battle of Moytura the powers of darkness and brute force, represented by the Fomorians, were crushed by those of science and poetry in the shape of the Danaans. In their turn the Danaans were conquered by the Sons of Miled (*q.v.*) in the Battle of Teltown, and withdrew for good into the realm of faëry. The interpretation of the Danaan myth is the conquest of light and intellect over dulness and stupidity, impersonated by the Firbolgs, and, lastly, over the Fomorians, the powers of " evil " or darkness. The chief Danaan gods and goddesses were the Dagda, Dana or Brigit, his daughter, Angus Og and Midir the Proud, his sons, Bov the Red his brother, Lugh, Fir and his son Mananan, the Morrigan and Ainé. To the bard they were the embodiment of power and beauty, of science and poetry ; to the peasant. gods of earth, upon whom depended his agricultural and pastoral welfare. And this latter conception of them, as it has endured longer than the druidic, so is it most probably the older. Again, in their conflicts with each other and with mortals, they are accessible to death, while it is by magical powers they conquer their mortal foes.

DANEMONT. In Carlovingian romance, son of the Saracen Emir Corsuble. Irritated that his sister Glorianda should be " so light," as to go to behold her lover, Karaheut of India, fight with Ogier the Dane, he interrupted the combat. He was afterwards slain by Ogier. (*Vide* " Ogier the Dane.")

DANKWART. (*Vide* " Nibelungenlied.") Brother of Hagen. He fought against the treacherous Huns, and, single-handed, he mowed his way into King Etzel's court, and informed Hagen and Gunther of their danger.

DARA. Son of Fachtna, in Irish romance, owner of the Brown Bull of Quelgny. (*Vide* " Quelgny.")

DARES AND DICTYS. Dares Phrygius and Dictys Cretensis, two authors, supposed to be contemporary with the siege of Troy, whose apocryhal accounts coloured all Mediæval conceptions of that event. Dictys, a companion of Idomeneus, was supposed to represent the Greek side, whilst Dares, priest of Hephæstus, supported the Trojans. These works exist at present in Latin prose only. But it is highly probable that Dictys was originally a Greek forgery. An introduction to Dictys, which is presumably the older, purports to be a letter from Lucius Septimius to one Quintus Aradius, who states that the book had been written by Dictys in Punic letters, which Cadmus and Agenor had introduced into Greece, and that certain shepherds discovered the manuscript written on linden-bark paper in a tin case in Dictys' tomb at Gnossos, that their superior turned the Punic letters into Greek, which had always been the language of the work, and gave the MS. to Nero. Dares, on the other hand, purports to be introduced by Cornelius Nepos to Sallustius Crispius, and to have been translated by the former from MS. in the handwriting of Dares which he discovered at Athens. Dictys may

have been written by some Greek about the time of Nero, whilst Dares may be as late as the twelfth century. Dictys, the full title of whose book is *Ephemerie Belli Trojani*, is the longer and the better written. But Dares was the more popular of the two in Mediæval times. Dares commences his *De Exidio Trojœ* with the episode of the Golden Fleece. Coming to the matter of Troy, Dares runs quickly through the incidents of the slaughter of Patroclus and the battle at the ships, and tells of the plot of Palamedes against Agamemnon. The Greeks are usually worsted, as behoved the spirit of an author who probably wrote for the delectation of princes who imagined themselves sprung from the loins of those who builded windy Ilium. Agamemnon petitions for a three years' truce, which is granted by Hector. This is speedily leaped over, and the fortunes of war having gone against the Trojans, they in turn sue for a three months' armistice. For twelve days the combatants engage in giant strife, when in turn the Greeks crave a thirty days' cessation of hostilities. Hector's death at the hand of " fierce Achilles " is then described. Palamedes succeeds in supplanting Agamemnon as Polydeuces, and conducts the war with spirit. Achilles, desirous of espousing Polyxena is told that he can gain her by directing his efforts towards the establishment of peace. He abstains from fighting, and another battle takes place at the ships, the hero of which is Troilus. Agamemnon attempts to placate Achilles, but to no purpose. Troilus makes great havoc among the Hellenes in another battle, but is at last slain through Achilles wounding his horse. The death of Achilles by ambush in the temple of Apollo—the vulnerable heel being ignored—is followed by those of Ajax and Paris. The Amazons appear and defeat the Greeks heavily. The war ends with the treacherous admittance of the Greeks into Troy, and the Trojan emigration in twenty-two ships. The work possesses no literary merit, and is actually an attempt to differ from Homer for the political reasons alluded to above. It was from these works that Chaucer derived his ideas of the Tale of Troy, and also through the medium of Guido delle Colonne's *Romance of Troy* (*Storia della Guerra di Troja*). This work was translated by Lydgate, who called it the *Troie Boke*, in 1420, and printed by command of Henry VIII. in 1513. *Dares and Dictys* was also the groundwork of a new compilation in French on the subject of Troy, written by Raoul le Feure, chaplain to the Duke of Burgundy, in 1464, and partly translated into English prose in 1471 by Caxton under the title of the *Recuyel of the Histories of Troy*.

DARK, THE. In Irish romance, a Druid, who sought in vain the love of Saba (*q.v.*), and in revenge turned her into a fawn.

DAYRE. (*Vide* "Florice and Blanchfleur.") A slave in the service of the Amiral of Babylon. He entertained Florice in his quest of Blanchfleur. By his counsel Florice managed to gain admittance to the amiral's castle.

DEATH OF DON PEDRO. A romantic poem of Mediæval Spain, which tells how Don Pedro, the hero of many atrocious and tragical stories, was driven out of Castille by his natural brother, Don Henry of Transtamara, who had spent many years in exile. Owing to the cruelties and insults which Pedro had heaped upon members of French Royalty, including his wife, Queen Blanche, he received no assistance from the French, but Edward the Black Prince took up his cause and marched into Spain with a considerable army, when Henry was defeated at the Battle of Nejara. After the Black Prince left Spain in 1368, Henry, with some of his followers, among whom was the famous Duguesclin, encountered Pedro at the head of a large army, which soon had to give way to the Frenchmen. Pedro escaped with a few men, and took shelter with a knight, who betrayed his hiding-place to Henry. Henry entered his room, and in insulting terms called on him to step forward, which Pedro fearlessly did. The brothers grappled like lions, the Frenchmen looking on, and as they swayed in deadly wrestle, one breathing triumphant fury and the other despair and mortal hatred, Pedro had the vantage of Henry, who fell underneath him. A page of Henry caught Pedro by the waist, thus helping the fallen man, who stabbed his brother to the heart, and "the fiercest soul that ever dwelt in the bosom of a Christian fled." Pedro's head was then cut off and his body meanly buried. The ballad which describes his death is often quoted by Cervantes in *Don Quixote*.

DEBILITY OF THE ULTONIANS. (*Vide* "Macha.") This curse fell upon the Ulster warriors during the Cattle Raid of Quelgny (*q.v.*).

DECTERA. In Irish romance, mother of Cuchulain (*q.v.*) and daughter of Cathbad the Druid. She disappeared from the court of Conor mac Nessa with fifty young female companions. After a lapse of three years a flock of birds settled on the fields of Emain Macha, and laid waste the crops. The King Conor and his courtiers went out to drive them off, but the birds only fled a little way, and at each flight lured the party further on, until they ultimately brought them to the magic mound of Angus on the river Boyne. Night fell, and the king despatched Fergus to find a place for repose. The scouting party came upon a splendid palace, where they were greeted by a youth of noble mien, accompanied by a lovely woman and fifty maidens. Fergus recognized the ladies as Dectera and her missing maidens, and the youth as Lugh the sun-god. King Conor, on hearing this news, summoned Dectera to him, but she sent him her new-born son Cuchulain.

DEGRABELL, SIR. Son of Eglamour (*q.v.*) and Crystabell (*q.v.*), plays an important part in the romance of *Eglamour of Artoys* (*q.v.*). Along with his mother he was banished from the home of the latter's father, Prinsamour (*q.v.*). He was stolen from his mother by a griffin, and subsequently discovered by the King of Israel, who acted as his foster-father. He mistakenly married his own mother, which marriage was, on the same day, revoked. He subsequently discovered his father and married Ardanata.

DEIRDRE. Daughter of Felim. In the chief of the preliminary tales to the Irish romance of the Cattle Raid of Quelgny (*q.v.*), it is related that an Ulster lord, Felim, invited King Conor to a feast. During the merrymaking a messenger brought word of the birth of a daughter to the host. Then Cath-

bad, the King's Druid, foretold : " The infant shall be fairest among the women of Erin, and shall wed a king, but because of her, shall death and ruin come upon the Prince of Ulster." Conor sought to avert this doom by sending the child Deirdre with her nurse Levarcam to a solitary dun in a great wood. Here she was visited by the king, who intended to wed her when she was of marriageable age, nor did she see any other man save Cathbad. One winter's day, however, near the approach of her bridal morn, she beheld on the window upon the white snow the blood of a newly-slain calf and a raven lapping it. Such, she told her nurse, was the man whom she wished to wed : with hair black as the raven's wing, cheek red as the blood of the calf, and skin white as the snow. She had pictured Naisi, a member of the Red Branch, one of Conor's household. Levarcam then, upon the entreaties of Deirdre got her access to Naisi, who at last, conquered by the woman's beauty, and her prayers to be saved from Conor, fled with her to Scotland. Here her lover took service with the King of the Picts, but when the latter beheld the beauty of Deidre, he wished to take her from Naisi, so Naisi and his two brothers who had accompanied him escaped with Deirdre and Levarcam to shelter in Glen Etive. Years had passed, and Conor had been kept in knowledge of Naisi and the maiden. Then, at an invitation brought him by his bosom friend, Fergus mac Roy, to return to Ulster, where all would be well, the fugitive, though Deirdre foresaw evil, left his hiding-place for Ireland. Here they were met by Baruch of the Red Branch, and Fergus was invited to a feast which he unwillingly attended. So, protected by his two sons, the party arrived at Emain Macha, and were received into the House of the Red Branch. Conor did not see them, however, but he sent for Levarcam, and inquired for all. Deirdre, she told him, had lost her beauty. Trendhorn was then sent to spy upon the sons of Usna. Arriving at their lodging, he found bolt and bar fast, and therefore he climbed to an upper window, whence, spell-bound by the beauty of the maiden, he beheld Naisi and Deirdre playing chess, and the others talking, cleaning their arms, or preparing for rest. But Trendhorn was discovered, and Naisi struck out his eye with a chessman. Then Conor sent his guards to fetch the sons of Usna, who had maimed his messenger. Buino, the son of Fergus, however, drove them back at the sword's point, but was bought off by a great gift of lands from the king. His brother Illan then defended the Red Ranch, but was slain by Conor's two sons. So Naisi and his brothers protected themselves, until by the spells of Cathbad they were seized and brought to Conor. The king had promised his druid to do the captives no hurt, but when they were bound he called upon man after man to slay them. None responded, save Owen, son of Duracht and Prince of Ferney, who with one sweep of Naisi's sword, shore off the heads of the three brothers. Then Deirdre dwelt a year with Conor in Emain Macha, but all that time she never smiled. Asked by the king what she hated most, she replied, "Thou thyself, and Owen, son of Duracht." So Conor sent her to Owen for a year; but she, being tormented by the king as

she stood behind Owen in the chariot, flung herself against the rock and died. It is said that the two yew trees above her and Naisi's graves met and intertwined above the church of Armagh.

DEOCA. (The "Woman of the South.") In Irish romance, a Princess of Munster, who asked Lairgnen, to whom she was be-trothed, to give her as a wedding gift the famous children of Lir, who by the enchantments of their step-mother had been changed into four wonderful singing swans. Their guardian hermit refused them to the chief, when the "man of the North" seized them violently by their silver chains. But in the presence of Deoca they assumed their human, not their Danaan, form, and the princess now gazed upon four withered, white-haired, miserable beings. Lairgnen fled from the place, but the hermit administered baptism ere they died, and sorrowed for them until he himself was laid in the grave.

DEPARTURE OF THE SONS OF AYMERY. (*Vide* "Enfances Guill-aume.")

DERMOT OF THE LOVE-SPOT. (Dermot O'Dyna.) The typical lover of Irish legend. He was the son of Donn (*vide* "Ben Bul-ben, The Boar of"), and his foster-father was Angus Og (*q.v.*). A folk-tale relates how he got the love-spot. With his companions Goll, Conan, and Oscar, he entered a hut for a night's shelter after hunting. Here dwelt an old man, a young girl, a wether, and a cat. As the Fianna sat down to eat, the sheep jumped upon the table, and only Goll managed to fling her off, but was with the others finally trodden upon by the animal. Then the man sent the cat to tether it, which it did. The wether was the World, the cat Death. Again, at night the girl lay down in the same room with the huntsmen and repelled each of them as they approached her. She was Youth, but she put the love-spot on Dermot's forehead, and henceforth no woman could behold him without loving him. A follower of Finn (*q.v.*), he was looked upon as the most sprightly and untiring and the boldest of the Fianna. Many a deed he had done for Finn, but his unwilling theft of Grania (*q.v.*) outdid in MacCumhal's estimation all his previous services. The story of that rape runs thus : Grania, the daughter of the High King Cormac mac Art, was betrothed to Finn, but had set her love upon Dermot. She therefore sent a sleeping draught by the hand of her maid to Finn and the rest of the wedding party, save the Fianna chiefs. After seeking courtship from Oisin (*q.v.*), but unfruitfully, as she had guessed, she turned to Dermot. He would not elope with her, but she made it *geis* or unlucky for him to refuse, and they left Tara by a private wicket-gate in her bower. On the way he again sought to escape his fate, but to no purpose. Finn set out in pursuit, and Dermot defended himself by his own strength and ability and by the aid of his foster-father. All over Ireland they were pursued, and peasant tradition calls the dolmens there " Beds of Dermot and Grania." But after sixteen years of outlawry peace was made through Angus Og, and Dermot returned to his patrimony and to prosperity. He had four sons and a daughter. Grania, however, wished to feast at her palace the two best men in Ireland, Cormac and Finn. Dermot had a misgiving, but the party

was invited. Toward the end of the year of feasting, however, he was awakened thrice by the baying of a hound. Next morning with sword and sling he started off to learn the cause of the baying, and on Ben Bulben in Sligo met Finn and some of the Fianna. They were not hunting, but were being hunted by a boar, and thirty of their number had been slain by the beast. Dermot then addressed himself to the contest, when Finn informed him that he was under *geis* not to hunt pig, and related the story of the murder of Dermot's half-brother, and his identity with this boar. Finn's purpose was now clear, and after a hard defence Dermot and his destined slayer fell together. But before he died he prayed Finn to use his magical powers and revive him with water. After much delay and dropping of the water through his fingers as he came from the well, Finn at last brought it, but too late. The Fianna chiefs then covered the body with their cloaks, and returned to Rath Grania, Finn leading Dermot's hound. Grania immediately understood, and swooned on the rampart of the palace. But the People of Dana bore away the corpse on a gilded bier, and into the lifeless body Angus Og sent a soul that Dermot might be able to talk with him each day. The framework of the tales of Naisi and Dermot are identical, but the earlier tale is simpler, more heroic, richer, and more beautiful. Deirdre's love for Naisi is not so much an all-sacrificing passion as a deep devotion : while Grania loves, not so sweetly as masterfully. Both have fascination, but the one maiden is mediæval, whilst the other appears quite *nouveau siècle* of the twentieth century, and not a little "neurotic." Again, the older story has a nobler, though a more painful, ending, while the latter revolts us with the heartless return of Grania to Finn. Dermot is of that class of hero who, like Achilles, is invulnerable save at one point. The myth of Dermot and Grania somewhat recalls the general features of that of Tristan and Ysolt. Dermot is plainly a solar hero. In many world-myths the light and darkness are half brothers, who end in slaying each other. Again, it is noticeable, as in the case of Sigurd, that Dermot receives a "soul," so that Angus Og might be able to talk with him each day—that is, the sun returns daily, and cannot be regarded as "dead." The gilded bier on which the Danaan folk bear Dermot's corpse away is, of course, the sunset.

DESA. In Irish romance, foster-father of Conary Mor (*q.v.*), High King of Ireland.

DEWY-RED. In Irish romance, the horse of Conall of the Victories. At the slaying of Cuchulain (*q.v.*) the steed tore a piece out of Lewy's (*q.v.*) side, and Conall thereupon cut off his head.

DIANCECHT. In Irish story, the Danaan physician who restored to Nuada of the Silver Hand (*q.v.*) his lost limb and thus his throne.

DICTYS. (*Vide* "Dares and Dictys.")

DIDOT PERCEVAL. This romance is so called because the only MS. of it discovered belonged to the well-known collector A. F. Didot. It lays great stress on the malady of the Fisher King (*vide* "Grail"), and has been called "an incongruous jumble of hints from Borron's work." Its intention was undoubtedly to provide a sequel to Borron's poems. The tale commences with the enchanter retailing how he constructed the Table Round, Christ having made the first one, Joseph of Arimathea the second, and Merlin the third. He tells also about the wealthy Fisher King, who is old and infirm, and may not be healed nor made well until a holy knight comes to ask concerning the Grail. The adventures of Sir Perceval, who is the son of Alein le Gros, are then taken up at the point where his father dies. The Holy Grail tells Alein to send his son to King Arthur's Court, where he attains the adventure of the Perilous seat, learns about the Fisher King and the Grail, and vows to seek them. Many knights make the same vow. Perceval then undertakes adventures much the same as those in Gautier's portion of the *Conte del Graal,* especially those at the Chessboard Castle and the Stag-hunt. He comes then to the Fisher King's castle, and sees a lance and a silver plate and goblet in which was the Lord's blood. He would have inquired concerning them, but fears to offend the king, remembering the command laid upon him to be incurious. In the morning all the inhabitants of the castle have gone, and on going forth he is abused. After more adventures, the incident of Good Friday occurs, as in the other Grail romances. Merlin then arrives and tells Perceval to go to his grandfather, which he does, and asks concerning the Grail. The king regains his health, and certain enchantments of Britain come to an end. Perceval is informed about the lance with which Longus pierced Jesus' side, and the Grail. The Holy Ghost tells Brons the secret words which Christ on the cross whispered to Joseph, but these are not included.

Brons is then carried off by angels, and Perceval, who has been instructed in the mystic expressions, remains behind.

DIETHER. (*Vide* "Dietrich of Bern." Son of Dietmar (*q.v.*) and brother to Dietrich.

DIETLINDE. (*Vide* "Nibelungenlied.") Daughter of Rudiger, Margrave of Bechlarn, and Gotelind. She receives with affectionate service Kriemhild (*q.v.*) on her journey to wed Etzel (*q.v.*). Later, with her mother and Rudiger, she helps to lavishly entertain the Burgundians on their way to Etzel's court. Ere they leave she is betrothed to Giselher (*q.v.*), the youngest brother of Kriemhild.

DIETMAR. Uncle to King Samson (*q.v.*), who assisted the latter to secure the throne of Salern.

DIETMAR. Brother to Ermenrich (*q.v.*), husband to Odilia (*q.v.*), and father of Dietrich (*q.v.*). (*Vide* "Dietrich of Bern.")

DIETRICH OF BERN, SAGA-CYCLE OF. A body of semi-traditional matter, the central figure of which is Theodoric, King of the Ostrogoths, who conquered Italy in the fifth century. In the course of ages the facts concerning Theodoric became so altered by traditional processes as to be almost unrecognizable. The oldest version of the saga is that found in a fragmentary collection known as *Hildebrandslied* (c. 700), copied by two monks of Fulda early in the ninth century. It related how Dietrich or Theodoric was expelled from his kingdom by Otonier, in whom we recognize Odoacer, the Vandal monarch who ruled over Italy in the fifth century, and who was in reality dethroned by Theodoric. This early version details how Dietrich, accompanied

by Hildebrand, a faithful retainer, took refuge at the court of Attila, eventually returning with a large force to regain his crown. The chief incident is the meeting of Hildebrand with his son Hadubrant, whom he had left behind to take care of his mother. Hadubrant, having heard rumours of his father's death from mariners, refuses to believe in his identity, and the fragment concludes with an unfinished combat between son and sire. We next find Dietrich referred to in an Old Low German ballad entitled *Ermenrichs Tod*, in which the ancient Gothic King Ermanaric is introduced as Dietrich's mortal foe. Defeated by Dietrich, Ermenrich shut himself up in a certain stronghold with 350 men. Dietrich came up with him with only eleven men at his back. The Gothic monarch, amused at such a puny investment of his fortalice, threw the gates open, when Dietrich and his companions rushed in and succeeded in slaying Ermenrich. In subsequent poems of the Dietrich cycle, we find the hero undertaking all manner of martial deeds, most of which appear to be placed in the period of his sojourn at Attila's court. He slays a formidable ogre who dwelt in its vicinity ; accompanies the Huns in their warlike expeditions ; espouses Herrat, Attila's niece ; leads twelve Hunnish warriors to Worms to do battle with an equal number of Teutonic warriors ; and conquers the Burgundian heroes, Gunter and Hagen. In the *Dietrichs Flucht* of Heinrich der Vogler we read how one Sibecke plots with Ermenrich (in this tale the uncle of Dietrich) against Dietrich's life, but the hero, warned of his danger, escapes. Here for the first time, perhaps, we find Dietrich connected with Bern (*i.e.* Verona in the north of Italy), where it is stated that Ermenrich, disappointed at the failure of his conspiracy, marched upon that city, but was defeated by Dietrich with great loss. Witege, a follower of Dietrich, goes over to Ermenrich, and surrenders to him the fortress of Ravenna. But Dietrich, with a new army of Huns, defeats his uncle, who shuts himself up in Bologna. Dietrich's forces are too few to invest the city, and he returns to the court of Attila. In his *Rabenschlacht* (Battle of Ravenna), Vogler continues his account of Dietrich's adventures. Its central incident is the deaths of the hero's brothers and the two sons of Attila. In the *Nibelungenlied* (*q.v.*) and the *Thidrekssaga* (*q.v.*), based upon it, strangely enough we encounter Dietrich taking part in the incident of the slaughter of the Burgundians, or, rather, standing aside as a mere spectator, whilst his friends slay each other. His follower, Wolfhart, however, involves his comrades in the broil, and all perish save old Hildebrand. Dietrich avenges their fall by delivering the surviving Burgundians to their enemies, who slay them in an effort to discover the treasure of the Nibelungs. In the *Thidrekssaga* (*q.v.*), Siegfried (*q.v.*) is brought into contact with Dietrich, who worsts him by craft. Probably it was inevitable that the two great heroes of romance should be regarded as contemporaries. In the *Biterolf und Dietlieb*, an Austrian poem of the early thirteenth century, Dietrich and twelve of Attila's warriors defeat Siegfried and his picked heroes, and a similar combat is the motive of the *Rosengarten zu Worms*, an Austro-Bavarian poem of the same date. A number of lesser poems have crystallized around the saga, among which the *Alpharts Tod*, *Das Eckenlied*, *Sigenôt*, and *Laurin* (all of which see) may be alluded to. All these were grafted together under the title of *Das Heldenbuch* (*q.v.*) by one Kaspar von der Roen, and published by him in 1472. In many such German myths Dietrich, by reason of his popularity, has replaced the original hero. Such are the tales of his victory over the giants Ecke and Fasolt. It is not necessary to see in the conqueror of these gods or demons of the storm (the remnants of a dying mythology) a mythical being or hero-god, but merely Dietrich as a popular hero who had replaced the original "giant-killer" or true hero-god. Most of the poems of the cycle are silent concerning Dietrich's death, but tradition recounts that he was carried off to Hell by Satan. Later romances describe his disappearance into a desert, there to combat with dangers until the Day of Judgment, or into a hollow mountain, whilst in popular belief he has joined the band of Odin's Wild Huntsmen. In the Dietrich saga-cycle we behold the entire process of the manufacture of a legendary hero from a once living monarch concerning whom there is trustworthy historical data. Theodoric the Ostrogoth by reason of his romantic seizure of Italy and the general circumstances of his life appealed to the men of his own Germanic race as the *beau-ideal* of a hero-king and so widespread did his popularity become that, like that of King Arthur, his figure collected around itself poems, incidents, and lesser epics which in the first instance had no connection with either his historical or legendary personality.

DIETWAR. The Emperor of Rome (Romaburg). A legend belonging to the Amelung cycle of romance. This illustrious emperor, desirous of marriage, sends an embassy to King Ladmer of Westenmer to ask for the hand of his daughter. Ladmer is overjoyed at such an honour, and begs that Dietwar would come to Westenmer and see the princess. To this proposal Dietwar readily consents, and after an adventurous passage, he arrives at his destination, accompanied by one hundred of his bravest warriors. Ladmer, after receiving his guest with all courtesy, told him how delighted he would feel to have Dietwar as a son-in-law, but, the king added, the princess herself must choose who she would have as her husband, nor would he constrain her against her will. A feast is given in Dietwar's honour, and dressing himself in similar apparel to that of his men, he is easily recognized by the princess, whose duty it was to offer the wine to her father's guests. She fills his goblet first. After the guests had retired Ladmer asked his daughter's opinion of her admirer. She thought him very noble, but added that she would not be satisfied until she had learned of his ways, which must be pleasant in her sight. The next day a hunt is arranged, and the princess implores her father that she might be permitted to join in the chase. Knowing her to be very fond of the sport and skilled in the use of the bow he willingly gives his consent. But Dietwar thinks her unmaidenly, and whispers amongst his friends that he would prefer to confine his searchings for a wife to the limits of his own country than wed one so masculine in her sport. But, however, it becomes his duty, along with the rest, to

see that the heedless girl comes to no danger through her rashness. The hunt grows very exciting, and passing through a narrow glen Minnie wounds a fine stag. Drawing another arrow from her quiver she hastens after her dogs, which had pursued the wounded animal. Suddenly the hounds set up a hideous howl, and rush out of the thicket. The hunters realize their danger, and dreading an attack from a dragon, hasten up the hill-side. Minnie, in her foolhardiness, awaits the monster, which appears from between the bushes, hissing dreadfully and trampling everything that obstructs its path. Arrow after arrow the princess shoots at the dragon, but these only rebounded from its scales. At last, Minnie turns to go, when she trips over a branch. Dietwar and his men rush forward, and the dragon advances. Dietwar attacks it with a spear. But its assailants are devoured one after another. The fight becomes desperate. Dietwar's skill is useless against its scales, and the monster tears his breast with its talons. At last, thrusting his spear down its throat he succeeds, after a terrible struggle, in overcoming the dragon. The hero falls in a faint to the ground, the dying dragon above him. He is released and brought back to the castle, where he lies in a critical condition. The poison from the dragon's claws has entered his wounded breast, and his life is despaired of. No leech could save him. But coming to the bedside one morning the princess poured some liquid from a bottle into his wound, which lessened the pain. For several days the dose is repeated, and he grows quite well again. The princess then told him that the magic liquid was given to her by her mother when she died, that it was to be used only on those she loved. They grow strong in love, while King Ladmer inwardly rejoices. The occasion of their wedding is marked by a feast, where in the centre of the table is placed as an ornament one of the dragon's teeth. Dietwar and his wife soon after return to Rome to enjoy their married life amongst his subjects. But the romance tells us they lived for four hundred years, during which time they have forty-four children, of whom one son, Sigeher, alone survives them.

DINADEN, SIR. Knight of the Round Table, brother to Sir Lancelot. He was the composer of " The Lay of King Mar." (*Vide* " Morte d'Arthur.")

DITHORBA. In Irish romance, brother of Red Hugh and Kimbay. He was slain by his niece Macha (*q.v.*), who refused to yield to him the sovereignty of Ireland. Dithorba's five sons were expelled from Ulster, and resolved to regain the kingdom from Macha. But she followed them into the forest where they were in hiding, overpowered them by her mesmeric influence, bound them, and, placing them upon her back, returned to her palace. Under her supervision they built the famous Irish city of Emain Macha.

DIU KLAGE. A continuation of the *Nibelungenlied* (*q.v.*), which as a whole is regarded as being more modern than the " Lied." It is ascribed by some critics to a period so late as the fourteenth century. It is artificial in conception, inartistic in form, and inferior to the poem to which it professes to be an addition. It is obvious, however, as stated by Grimm, that in writing it the author did not have before him the *Nibelungenlied* as we know it, but an earlier version ; and this probably constitutes its greatest value, as by its aid we are enabled to discover several of the discrepancies between the older MS. and that in our possession. The *Klage* is a lament for those who have fallen in the terrific strife in Etzel's palace described in the *Nibelungenlied*. It tells of the search among the dead in the house of slaughter, their obsequies, the journey of Etzel's minstrel Swemmelin to the Rhine to give the tidings to Queen Brunhilt, and the final parting from Etzel of Dietrich and his wife Herrat. Dietrich, desirous of sparing his niece Gotelinde, Rüdiger's wife, directs his friends not to mention the terrible event which has happened, but to say that he and Rüdiger will soon follow. The messengers deliver the false tidings. Gotelinde and her daughter are doubtful, and at length Swemmelin tells the truth. Gotelinde and old Queen Ute die soon after hearing the news. Brunhilt survives, and is prevailed upon by her vassals to have her son crowned. Etzel, after parting with Dietrich, becomes insane. Dietelint, the young margaravine, is taken under Dietrich's protection, who promises to find her a husband. Bishop Pilgrin desires to have the story written out in Latin letters, " that men should deem it true." A writer, Master Konrad (*q.v.*), then commenced to set it down in writing.

DIU KRÔNE. A German Grail poem by Heinrich von dem Türlin. (*Vide* " Grail, Holy.") It reproduces a lost French original. It possesses many parallelisms with those of Wolfram and Chretien, for example, the tournament for the hand of Tiebaut of Tingaguel's daughter, the episode of the two sisters and the combat with Melians de Lis. The father is named Leigamar, the eldest daughter Fursensephin (Fleur sans épine), the youngest Quelbelpluz, where the author has mistaken a French phrase signifying the damsel's beauty for her name. The name of the castle is Karamphi. The wounded knight Lohenis and his lady, Emblie, deprive Gawain of his horse, after which the incident of the Castle of Wonders and the enchanted bed are dealt with. The plucking of a flower from an enchanted garden at the bidding of a damsel named Mancipicelle (the Orgueilleuse of Chretien) and the meeting with Giremelanz follow. Giremelanz challenges Gawain, and Arthur's court comes to the Castle of Wonders to witness the combat. The champions are reconciled, and Giremelanz marries Gawain's sister. Gawain sets forth in search of the Grail, and wins several talismans which will aid him in his quest. He comes to the sister of the magician Gansguoter (Klinschor in Wolfram), who tells him that if he wishes to behold the Grail, he must not be overcome by sleep, that he must not drink excessively, and that as soon as he sees it and its accompanying damsels he must ask concerning it. He meets with many adventures and marvels on his way to the Grail castle, and after a space meets with Lancelot and Calocreant, who inform him that Kay, attempting to enter the Grail castle, has been cast into prison. The three knights then come to the castle. In a splendid hall lies an old man who watches two youths playing chess. The hall fills with knights and dames, and a youth enters who lays a sword before the old man. Gawain is offered drink. He refuses, but his two companions accept, and soon after fall asleep. There enter two maidens bearing lights, followed by two knights bearing a spear, and two other maidens with a great dish of gold and jewels. After them comes the fairest woman ever made by God, and with her a maiden weeping. The spear is laid on the table beside the great dish, in which are three drops of blood. The fair woman bears a box in which is bread, whereof she gives a third part to the old man. Gawain recognizes in her Gansguoter's sister, and asks her what these marvels mean. At once the entire company rise from the table with a great cry of joy, the old man tells Gawain that the dish he has seen is the Grail, and that by his question Gawain has delivered from long waiting and suffering many both dead and living. The old man and his companions are really dead, though they do not seem to be so, but the lady and her maidens are living. They partake of food annually with the old man because of their purity. Gawain receives as the prize of his valour the Grail sword, which will help him in every danger. After him no man shall see the Grail, and he must ask no more concerning it. At daybreak the old man ceases speaking, and vanishes with his whole court, leaving only the lady and her maidens. Gawain releases Kay, and returns to Arthur's court.

DIURAN THE RHYMER. (*Vide* "Maeldune.")

DODINEL. A character in Manessier's portion of the *Conte del*

Graal (*q.v.*), whose lady-love is delivered by Perceval from a felon knight.

DOLOROUS, CASTLE. Connected in Arthurian legend with Sir Perceval (or Percyvelle), and as the spot where two of the Knights of the Round Table lost their wits.

DONN (1). In Irish romance, son of Midir the Proud (*q.v.*). He is mentioned in the *Colloquy of the Ancients* (*q.v.*), as entertaining Finn and Kelta and five other champions at the Brugh of Slievenamon. These were hunting one day at Torach when they roused a beautiful fawn and chased it as far as Slievenamon. Here it vanished underground, and night falling with snow and storm, they sought shelter in the wood. Entering a great illuminated hall of a noble mansion or brugh, they beheld twenty-eight warriors and as many beautiful maidens. After feasting on the best of wine and viands they were informed that their hosts were Donn mac Midir

and his brother, and that the aid of the Fianna was sought against the rest of the Danaan folk, for thrice yearly their chieftains had had to do battle with their fairy foes on the green in front of the brugh. Each of the eight and twenty warriors had once a thousand followers, but all these were now dead, and therefore the warriors had sent one of the maidens in the form of a fawn to seek the aid of the Fianna. After a year of successful fighting, the assailants were compelled to make peace and to give hostages.

DONN (2). "Father of Dermot" (*q.v.*).

DROO. (*Vide* "Garin the Lorrainer.") Count of Amiens, friend of Fromont. He heard from Fromont the story of Garin and Blanchflower, which he treated with contempt, but went to Baldwin the Fleming and persuaded him to allow his sister to marry Fromont, concealing the true story.

DURANDAL. The wondrous sword of Roland (*q.v.*).

E

EADZILS. (Legend of *Beowulf*.) Brother of Eanmund (*q.v.*) son of Ohtere, King of Sweden. After the murder of King Hardred (*q.v.*) and the death of Eanmund, Eadzil fled back to Sweden, and soon after succeeded his father on the Swedish throne. He then led a large army into Gothland to avenge Eanmund's death, but was defeated and slain.

EANMUND. (Legend of *Beowulf*.) Son of Ohtere, King of Sweden, against whom he rebelled. He subsequently fled to the court of King Hardred (*q.v.*). Resenting a reproof from the young king, he

stabbed him in a fit of passion, and was himself slain immediately by Wickstan (*q.v.*).

EBEL. Sir, In Arthurian romance, knight to King Hermance of the Red City (*q.v.*). (*Vide* "Morte d'Arthur.")

EBER DONN. In Irish romance, a leader of the Milesian invaders of Ireland. He exulted so fiercely in the hope of putting the defenders of Ireland to the sword that the Danaans, or original inhabitants, raised a tempest by enchantment which sank his ship and many others of the Milesian host.

EBER FINN. In Irish romance, a leader of the Milesian invaders of Ireland. He was slain by Eremon, first Milesian King of Ireland, in a contest for the crown.

ECKE, THE LAY OF. A poem of the *Heldenbuch* (*q.v.*), which opens with three heroes—Fasolt, Ecke and Ebenrot—sitting together in the town of Cologne, relating deeds of valour. The talk is chiefly about Lord Dietrich of Bern, who all agree to be the bravest man of his time. But Lord Ecke is jealous of the praise bestowed on the Knight of Bern, and inquires if he is not as brave and worthy of esteem as Lord Dietrich. Ecke resolves to go in search of this valiant hero, fight him, and so gain equal renown, or else lose his own life. He goes on to describe his own deeds of valour, and how it would cast more distinction on him to slay one such as Dietrich of Bern than a dozen of weaker strength. Three queens were sitting by, listening to the talk ; the greatest, Queen Seburk, bewails her fate at not having seen this famous lord, and wishes Ecke success in his quest ; at the same time, promising him the wonderful breastplate that had belonged to King Otnit of Lombardy, on condition that, if he find and overcome the Prince of Bern, he will spare him. Ecke promised to bring back Dietrich, or lose his life. An old man warns Ecke of the dangers of his quest, which caution the headstrong youth ignores. He is promised, in reward, the love of any of the three queens he may choose. The best horse in the land is offered him, which he declines, and sets off on foot, fully armed, and wearing the famous breastplate. On entering the town of Bern, the people fly before him, for his armour glows like fire. Hildegrand, seeing him, remarks that a quieter garb would be more suited for an interview with his lord. Ecke makes reply that three renowned queens desire to behold Dietrich, and have sent Ecke as their messenger, who will use force, if need be. Hildegrand answers that his errand is useless ; his lord only fights with those who come on horseback, and advises him to quit Bern. After some more parley, he informs Ecke that Lord Dietrich is from home—journeying through the forest towards Tyrol. Continuing his way, Ecke has an encounter with a centaur, which he kills. Coming upon a wounded man, he asks who has left him in such a plight, and is told it was the Prince of Bern. After hearing some more tales of the knight's courage, which inflame his ardour, he binds up the man's wounds, declares he will avenge him, and proceeds on his way. Ecke at last meets Dietrich in a dark valley, and gives him his message ; he also praises his own armour, and tells Dietrich he has a chance of winning it. The latter replies that, if his sword is so sharp as to hurt giants, it is useless for him to strive against so formidable a foe. Ecke is bitterly disappointed at his unwillingness to fight, and upbraids him with cowardice. Dietrich replies that he will not fight, for he (Ecke) has done him no harm ; but, if he must fight, to wait till it is daylight. Goaded by Ecke's taunts, Dietrich dismounts, and they engage in combat. In the end Ecke is killed. Dietrich, sorely grieved, laments over the death of so brave and rash a hero.

The *Ecke* is a continuation of *Sigenôt* (*vide* "Dietrich of Bern"). The lay was a very popular one, but, in its present shape, we appear to have only a late rehash of the originals.

ECKEHART. A trusty friend of Dietrich of Bern (*q.v.*), and a lover of adventure. As a figure in the Rose Garden (*q.v.*) Battle, he is conspicuous. He fought with Dietrich against King Waldemar (*q.v.*).

ECNE. (Knowledge or Poetry.) In Irish romance, the only son of the three sons of Dana or Brigit, the supreme Danaan goddess.

ECTOR, SIR. In Arthurian romance, the foster-father of Arthur. He received him immediately on his birth on the recommendation of Merlin, and brought him up with his own son Kay, or Kai (*q.v.*), afterwards Arthur's seneschal. It was upon Arthur succeeding in drawing out the magic sword from the anvil placed in the great church of London that he revealed to him that he was not his father. Consult the *Morte d'Arthur*, First Book, chapters iii. and v.

EDDAS, THE. Two Icelandic collections of matter dealing with the divine and heroic mythology of the Scandinavian race. (1) The "Elder" or "poetic" Edda was brought to light by the Icelandic bishop, Brynjulf Sveinsson, about 1643. It was at first attributed to the historian Saemund (*c.* 1050), but is now considered as the work of other hands. The thirty-five poems which it contains are anonymous, and older than the MS. which contains them, which is of the thirteenth century. It is known as the *Codex Regius*, and is preserved in the Royal Library at Copenhagen. Most of the poems it contains date from about the tenth century. It includes prototypes of many of the later Teutonic romantic cycles; for example, early poems relating to the *Volsunga Saga* and the *Nibelungenlied*. The *Edda* throws great light on the mythology of the Scandinavian race, but here we will treat of such of its contents as have a bearing on the later Teutonic romance-cycles, and will omit further reference to the purely mythological matter it contains. Some of the poems contained in the *Edda* are little more than lyrics, presenting as they do perhaps an idyll of a single scene. Others, again, give an abstract of an entire history, as in the case of the *Prophecy of Gripir*, in which the whole history of the Volsungs is summarized. The *Edda* contains poems belonging to the following heroic cycles : Weland the Smith, Sigurd and the Nibelungs, the Ermanric cycle and the Helgi lays, all of which are dealt with under their several headings. The versions of these stories as given in the *Edda* are in many respects divergent from that in which they appear in later times, and each of these cycles is made up of several poems which represent more or less the several portions of the later sagas. For example, the *Lay of Gudrun*, a portion of the prototype of the Volsung story, leaves the details of that saga very much in neglect, and shows up the grief of Gudrun in contradistinction to that of Brunhild in the *Volsunga Saga*. In short, the *Edda* may be said to assist the theory that the first stage of epic is ballad, and that not only do structural changes take place in such compositions in the course of generations, through political and other reasons, but that popular taste demands such alterations. (2) The "Younger" or "prose" *Edda* was compiled by the historian Snorre Sturluson (1178–1241). It also contains many references to the old Scandinavian mythology, but the *Skaldskaparmal* a portion of it, is a treatise on the art of poetry. The work was first discovered in MS. in 1625. It is preserved in three MSS., one a fine copy at Upsala. In it Snorre explained the mythical references available for the poetry of his day, the outlook of which was naturally very different to that of the makers of the elder *Edda*. Practically nothing is touched upon in it which deals with the matter of romance.

EGLAMOUR OF ARTOYS, SIR. A mediæval English romance of French origin. The commencement of the poem refers to the period when the country of Artois was a self-dependent state. During its independence a native count Sir Prinsamour reigned over that country. He made his court a training school in the art of chivalry, and his daughter Christabell became the centre of admiration. She is especially adored by Sir Eglamour of Artoys, who, although a poor knight, aspires very nobly to win her. The princess, in return, encourages Eglamour to approach her father. Eglamour does so, but the princess's father, aware of Eglamour's poverty, and anxious that his daughter's position might rather be elevated than lowered, rejects indirectly her suitor's appeal ; but adds, that he will grant his wish and the lands of Artois, if he fulfils three adventures. The count then directs Eglamour to defy the giant Sir Maroke, by hunting in the latter's preserves, after which he must return with a trophy. The young knight departs on the first adventure.

He enters the forest of the giant, and slays three harts by the aid of a hound which his love bestowed upon him. He then meets the giant. The encounter lasted two days, at the end of which the knight stabbed the giant through the heart. He then cut off his head, and departed with the trophy to the court of the count. Prinsamour now orders him to bring from the distant land of Satyn the head of a prodigious boar, whose tusks were of exceptional length, and which had devoured a large number of knights. He is successful in slaying the monster, and towards the close of the conflict the noise of the boar attracts the attention of Edmond, King of Satyn, who, on learning the cause, hastens to the scene of combat. The king, delighted with the victory, immediately offers to the victor the hand of his daughter Ardanata. This offer the knight politely but firmly refuses ; but the princess, who had instantly fallen in love with the stranger, decides to wait in the hope of gaining him. Hardly had this taken place, when there appears before them a previous claimant to the princess. This lover is the giant Manas, brother to Sir Maroke whom Eglamour had slain, and closely allied in friendship to the dead boar. Immediately he espies his slain friend and learns the story of the tragedy, he assails Eglamour, but is slain by him. Bearing the two grisly heads, and wearing a ring which Ardanata had bestowed upon him, the brave knight enters the capital of Prinsamour. But the count, who still hoped for Eglamour's death, showed but little pleasure at the knight's victories. Crystabell, on the other hand, displays much delight at her lover's conflicts, and welcomes his return with joy. The lovers, anticipating the easy accomplishment of the third feat, now give way to the impulse of their passions. A few weeks of tranquillity soon pass, and once more Eglamour sets off to complete the last adventure, leaving with his mistress the enchanted ring. This time he is directed towards Rome, for the purpose of killing a powerful dragon, which had long ravaged the neighbourhood of that city. This final enterprise is likewise successful. The dragon falls after a stubborn fight, but not before wounding Eglamour with his poisonous claws. Eglamour then deprives the slain monster of his tail, wings, and head. He falls ill as a result of the poison, and Constantine the Roman Emperor keeps him under the care of his daughter, Viatdur, who soon through her remedies restores the victor to health. This project having lasted longer than the previous adventure, raises hopes in the count as to the death of Eglamour. But Crystabell gives birth to a boy. Such an event puts to an end all Prinsamour's high hopes for his daughter ; and vowing vengeance, he banishes her from the land. She and her infant son are placed in a vessel without mariners, sails, oars, or rudder, and abandoned to the winds and waves. The vessel brings her to an uninhabited island, where a griffin carries off her son, who is enveloped in a scarlet mantle and who wears a golden girdle. The hopeless mother, who has remained in the vessel, arrives on the shores of Egypt, where she is discovered and conveyed to the king, who fortunately turns out to be her uncle. Here she remains under his guardianship. Her infant son

meanwhile is carried to Israel, and is discovered by the king of that country, who names the child Degrabell. He receives a good education, and becomes in process of time an accomplished knight. Sir Eglamour returns with the dragon's head to Artois, to learn the whole extent of his misfortune. After depriving the heartless Prinsamour of his lands and driving him to his castle, Eglamour sets out on a visit to the Holy Land, where during fifteen years he distinguishes himself against the unbelievers. At this time the King of Israel, anxious that his adopted son should marry, sets out together with Degrabell, whom he had lately knighted, to visit the King of Egypt, who, as the former knew, possessed a beautiful niece. The latter king willingly consents to the union of his niece to the former's adopted son, and as a consequence the wedding takes place—a union in marriage of mother and son. Hardly were the festivities over, when the bride casts her eyes upon the shield of Degrabell, which bore a griffin holding in its talons an infant wrapped in a scarlet mantle. She immediately bursts into tears, and relating the whole story, is at once released from the unnatural union. The King of Israel, however, still maintains that his niece should marry, and acting accordingly he announces a tournament. The challenge brings together the best knights of which the surrounding countries could boast. There also arrives Sir Eglamour, but only as a spectator. The conditions of the fight make it necessary for the victor to overcome Degrabell ; but the latter proves too powerful for the contestants. This causes no little alarm to the king, who, observing Eglamour, requests him, as a last resort, to enter the lists. This the latter does, but very reluctantly. Degrabell is however overcome by this last rival, and the king, in accordance with his promise, offers his niece to the victor. Crystabell then comes forward, and on observing the new-comer's shield finds thereon the representation of a ship of gold, containing a lady and an infant surrounded by waves. These armorial bearings lead her to dis-cover the victor's identity. Egla-mour is delighted at their reunion, and amid general rejoicings their marriage takes place. They return to Artois, to find that the count having fallen from his tower was dead. Ardanata's constancy is rewarded by her marriage to Degrabell.

EISIRT. In Irish Ossianic romance, a bard to Iubdan, King of Faylinn, the abode of a dwarfish race. He heard of the Fomorian folk in Ulster, and, taunting the king concerning the size of the inhabi-tants of the respective kingdoms, was imprisoned for his insolence. He was freed on the understanding that he would seek out this land of giants, which he accordingly did, and arrived at Ulster, whence he returned with the king's dwarf Æda. The people of Faylinn were terrified at the sight of Æda, and Iubdan was so taunted by Eisirt that he resolved to visit Ulster himself. (*Vide* "Iubdan.")

ELAINE. Daughter of King Pelles and mother of Galahad, son of Lancelot (*q.v.*). She is despised by Queen Guinevere (*q.v.*), because of her love for Lancelot. (*Vide* "Morte d'Arthur.")

ELBEGAST. A dwarf friendly to-ward Dietrich (*q.v.*) during the latter's search for the giant Grim (*q.v.*). (*Vide* "Dietrich of Bern.")

ELEVEN KINGS, THE. Who allied themselves against Arthur, as they suspected his royal birth. They were King Brandegoris of Strang-gore, the Duke of Cambenet, King Clariance of Northumberland, the King of the Hundred Knights, King Lot of Lothian and Orkney (*q.v.*), King Urience of the Land of Gore, King Idres of Cornwall, King Cradelmas, King Agwisance of Ireland, King Nentres, and King Carados. They were defeated by Arthur in a great battle with the assistance of King Ban and King Bors (*q.v.*).

ELIDUC, THE LAY OF. A French romance written by Marie de France (*q.v.*), and according to her, of Breton origin. Eliduc stood high in the favour of his suzerain, the King of Brittany, and upon that monarch's absence from his realm, was his lord's justice and seneschal. But jealous tongues accused Eliduc of meddling with the royal affairs, and he was banished from the court. In vain he prayed the king to name his offence. With ten followers he therefore set out, accompanied for some distance by Guildeluec, his wife. In her hands he had placed his fief, and to each other husband and wife had sworn fidelity. Eliduc then sailed across to the realm of Totenois, and, hearing that the King of Logres, near Exeter, was sorely pressed by an importunate lover of his fair daughter, took service with the old man. Learning of the enemy's entrance and exit through a certain wood-path, he trapped him and freed the kingdom of his assaults. The old king greatly rejoiced in his new knight, and after a year's service appointed him seneschal and constable of his realm. But the young princess had not seen this knight, and therefore sent her chamberlain to ask him to visit her. Eliduc and Guillardun, the maid, loved with an unspoken love. But the princess desiring to learn if her father's seneschal returned her love, sent him a girdle and a ring. These he took from her chamberlain, put the one about his body, the other upon his finger. For a year the lovers exchanged gifts, embraces, and sweet words. Then having put an end to the invader's war, Eliduc fared Brittany-wards to the succour of his king. For this monarch, being sore beset by a strong enemy, diligently sought for tidings of his lost seneschal. Learning of his whereabouts, he prayed him by their former love and his oath of fealty to return to Brittany. Guillardun having set a term to his absence, Eliduc then crossed to his home, where all, and especially his wife, welcomed him with rejoicing. He vanquished the foe, but ever he went sad and thoughtful. Care sat heavy upon Guildeluec's heart, nor could she learn what ailed her lord. As promised, he returned upon the appointed day to the land of his love. Waiting without the city, he sent his chamberlain to tell the lady of his arrival. She attired herself for the journey, and entered with Eliduc into his vessel. But a storm arose. Dismayed and in terror, one of the company advised Eliduc to cast the lady overboard, for on her account had God sent His tempest. The unfortunate Guillardun then learned that her lover was already wed, and straightway fell into a death-like swoon. Then the sorrowing knight, upon reaching land, bore her to a chapel in a wood near his

home, and laid her in his cloak upon the altar. Hither he came daily to mourn her death. But his wife, grown suspicious, sent a varlet to follow her lord. The fellow returned to relate how he had seen the knight enter the chapel and mourn loudly. Guildeluec, thinking it strange that her husband should so grievously lament the death of the hermit whom he had so often visited in previous years, followed her varlet to the wood, entered the chapel with him, and beheld the fair maiden upon the altar. And she too wept for sorrow that such a lovely lady should be laid in the dust, and forthwith understood her lord's lamentation. As she gazed upon the princess's beautiful face a weasel scampered across the body and was immediately slain by her varlet's staff. Then its companion, finding that it could not rise, hastened distractedly to the wood and brought back a vermeil flower. This she put in the dead weasel's mouth, when he rose to his feet. Guildeluec immediately commanded her varlet to seize that flower. She then put it in the maiden's mouth, who after a time awoke, and told the dame her story. And learning that Eliduc was no felon who had deserted her, she was much comforted. The wife, desiring to take the veil, prayed her husband to loose her of her marriage ties, and to install her as abbess in a new-built church near that chapel. Eliduc then wedded Guillardun, and together they lived for many years in peace and happiness. After some time the knight built a church beside his castle, entered into the service of God, and set his wife under Guildeluec's care. Messages were exchanged from monastery and convent, and all three lovers died in peace and salvation.

ELIEZER. Son of King Pelles, alluded to in the *Queste del Saint Graal* (*q.v.*) as master of the white knights whom Lancelot encounters in tourney with a band of black knights who take him prisoner. (*Vide* " Argastes.")

ELLIDE. (*Vide* " Frithjof Saga.") The dragon-like ship of Frithjof. Golden-headed and with open jaws, its under part scaled with blue and gold, its tail twisted and of silver, its sails red-bordered and black, it would skim the calmest seas when its wings were outspread. Aegir, the sea-god, had given this ship to one of Frithjof's ancestors as a reward for having befriended him unknown.

ELSUNG, YARL. (Earl) of Berne (Verona), who refused King Samson's (*q.v.*) demands. He was consequently assailed and slain by Samson, who died through a wound which Elsung inflicted.

EMER. Daughter of Forgall. (*Vide* " Cuchulain.")

ENFANCES GARIN DE MONTGLANE. (*Vide* " Garin de Montglane.")

ENFANCE GUILLAUME. (The Childhood of William.) A romance of the William of Orange sub-cycle of the Charlemagne cycle. (*Vide* " William of Orange.") It tells how Aymery of Narbonne has seven sons, for the four eldest of whom the emperor sends, promising that after a few years' service he will enrich them. William the younger son, refuses, as he wishes to carve out his own fortune. His brothers Guibert, Hernaut, Bevis and Guerin wish to accompany him, but Bernard, the eldest son, desires to serve the emperor, and

sneers at the others for following a younger brother. William declares that he is in reality the head of the family, and that he will vouch for the fortunes of all. He is at last persuaded to go by Aymery, and obeys his father, but declares that when he is a knight he will conquer Spain to endow his brothers. The rest of the poem is occupied with details of the early prowess of William, armed with a great staff, his love-passages with Orable of Orange, and his rescue of Narbonne, besieged by the Arab King Tybalt, Orable's husband.

ENFANCES VIVIEN. (The Childhood of Vivien.) A romance of the William of Orange sub-cycle of the Charlemagne cycle. (*Vide* " William of Orange.") In this romance William's nephew, Vivien, is introduced. He bears a strong resemblance to Roland (*q.v.*). The story of his childhood, as told in this poem, is later than the other branches of his story, which belong to the sub-cycle of *William of Orange*, and does not agree with them in its circumstances. He is exchanged for his father, Garin of Anséune (*q.v.*), of the race of Aymery, who has been taken prisoner by the " Saracens " at Roncevaux. Garin tells his wife by messenger not to give up the boy, who is seven years old. A family council is held, and William of Orange proposes that he should go. In the *Covenant Vivien* (*q.v.*), the sequel to this romance, the further events in the life of the hero are recounted.

ENGUERRAUD. (*Vide* " Garin the Lorrainer.") Knight of Courcy, sent by Fromont to the court, to complain of Aubrey giving his land to Rigaut to fight against the Bordelais.

ENYGEUS, ENYSGEUS, or ANYSGEUS. Alluded to in Robert de Borron's romance of Joseph of Arimathea (*q.v.*), as the sister of Joseph and wife of Brons (*q.v.*). She follows him to far-off lands. It is commanded by a voice from the Holy Ghost that a certain seat at the common table of the Grail company must not be filled up until she have a child by Brons, who shall fill it.

EOCHY (1). Son of Erc, King of the Firbolgs, in Irish romance, and husband of Taltiu (*q.v.*).

EOCHY (2). King of Ireland. The nobility of Ireland urged him to take a wife, and refused to bring their own spouses to the assembly at Tara until he had done so. He wed Etain, daughter of Etar (*q.v.*), but Midir the Proud (*q.v.*) came to him at Tara, and challenged him to a game of chess. He permitted Eochy to consider himself the better player, and, having agreed with him that the stakes should be at the pleasure of the winner, defeated him, and carried off Etain. (*Vide* also " Ailill.")

EPONOGRIS, SIR. Son of the King of Northumberland (*q.v.*). He was constantly in love, but does not loom very large in Arthurian romance. (*Vide* " Morte d'Arthur.")

EQUITAN, THE LAY OF. A romance of Brittany, written by Marie de France (*q.v.*). Equitan was King of Nantes, and, fond of pleasure, he would often put his business into the hands of his seneschal. Now this lord had a very beautiful wife, for whom the king fell sick of love. Equitan, therefore, went ahunting in his woods. After the chase he found an opportunity to unbosom himself to the lady. Discreet as beautiful, she at first refused to listen to him. Eventually, however, the king overcame her scruples, and till death those lovers kept their secret. But their day of reckoning did not fail to come. The lady learning that the king would wed her upon her husband's death, prepared a speedy end for her lord. He and his master were to hunt in her domains, to be bled together for their health, and to bathe at the same time. Her husband's bath, however, she was to fill with boiling water. All this was done. The evil day arrived. The king and the lady, awaiting the seneschal's approach, sat on his bed in a loving embrace. They had set a maiden to watch for his coming, but he, being impatient, thrust by her and came upon the lovers clasped in each others' arms. Thinking only of his dishonour, the king jumped into the bath prepared for the lady's husband ; while he, divining all, thrust his faithless wife head first after her lover.

ERC. King of Ireland, and enemy of Cuchulain (*q.v.*). At the last battle of that hero, Erc seized one of his spears, and wounded his celebrated horse, the Grey of Macha, to the death.

EREC, SIR. One of the five knights —Gauvain, Sagremore, Beduers, Hurgains—with whom Sir Perceval makes a solemn covenant that he will not sleep twice on the same spot until he had discovered the whereabouts of the " rich " fisher, the keeper of the Holy Grail.

EREMON. The first Milesian King of Ireland, said to have been contemporary with King David. He was the elder of two brothers, but after the victory of the Milesians over the Danaans, Eber his brother refused to obey him,

H

and war ensued, in which Eber was slain.

ERI. The mother of King Bres (*q.v.*), in Irish romance, and a woman of the Danaan folk. The father of Bres was unknown when the Danaans chose him for king. But Nuada of the Silver Hand (*q.v.*) being made king in his stead, Bres went to consult his mother Eri as to his course of conduct, who told him that his father was a King of the Fomorians called Elatha, and through the representations of that monarch he received aid from the Fomorians, who oppressed Ireland sorely for many years.

ERIC, YARL. (*Vide* " Gunnlaug Saga.") Co-ruler of Norway with his brother Svein.

ERIN. Wife of the Danaan King Mac Grené (*q.v.*). The poetical name of Ireland is taken from the dative case of her name.

ERLE OF THOULOUSE, THE. An English metrical romance, written in the reign of Henry VI., probably by Thomas Chestre, or rather adapted by him from a French or Breton *lai* of the same name. It tells how Diocletian, the Emperor of Germany, has a rupture with Barnard, Earl of Thoulouse, concerning boundaries of territory. Although dissuaded by his beautiful consort from taking the field, the emperor meets Barnard in battle and is worsted by him. Among other prisoners the earl takes is Sir Tralabas of Turkey, whom he adopts as a companion. They talk of the charms of the empress. The earl waxes curious to see her, and offers Tralabas his freedom if he can succeed in guiding him to the emperor's court, and obtain for him a sight of her without jeopardy or dis-

covery to himself. Arrived at the emperor's court, Tralabas turns traitor, and proposes to the empress that the earl should be assassinated. She rejects the proposal with scorn, pledges Tralabas not to mention the matter to anyone else, and desires to see the earl next day in the chapel at Mass. On leaving the chapel the earl asks an alms of the empress, receives a valuable ring, and returns home. The emperor, called away to war, leaves his wife in the care of three noblemen who, unable to gain her love, resolve to besmirch her good name. She is thrown into prison, and on the emperor's return he credits the scandal trumped up against her. She is sentenced to be burned ; but if a champion can defeat her accusers she is to be set at liberty and her honour cleared. The Earl of Thoulouse privately undertakes her quarrel. He appears at the emperor's court in the guise of a monk, and receives permission to act as her confessor. He publishes the fact of her innocence, but the knights accuse him of being bribed to make the announcement. On this he challenges them to combat, overthrows them, and the empress is declared innocent. The earl then openly avows himself in his true character, and a solemn reconciliation ensues. The emperor appoints him his seneschal, and only lives three years after this event, when the earl is rewarded for his faithful love with the hand of the empress.

ERMENRICH. (*Vide* " Dietrich of Bern.") Brother to Dietmar (*q.v.*), and husband of Swanhild (*q.v.*). His attitude toward the court of Dietrich was for a time friendly ; but his weak nature led him to place too great a trust in his advisors, who subsequently drove him to commit errors which could never be effaced. Listening to the treason of his marshal Sibich (*q.v.*), he was constrained to slay his three sons, Friedrich, Reginbald and Randwer. This did not complete his crimes; but told by Sibich that his wife desired his death, he trampled her under the hoofs of his horse. This act was followed by war. His noble friend of Bern became the target of his vengeance; and though he damaged the prestige of his opponent, he afterwards regretted having been led into strife by his advisors; but was never able to realize their purpose.

ERMYN. (*Vide* "Bevis of Hampton.") A Saracen king, who befriended Bevis. When he found that Bevis wished his daughter to become a Christian, he quarrelled with him. They were afterwards reconciled. Ermyn became a Christian, and gave his crown to Bevis' son, Guy.

ERNEBOROUGH. (*Vide* "Bevis of Hampton.") Wife of Saber. She interpreted his dreams, and once went abroad to ask Sir Bevis to come back to England to help Saber.

ERNIS. (*Vide* "Guy of Warwick.") Emperor of Greece. He was besieged by the Soudan, but was relieved by Sir Guy.

ERNOUS, COUNT. A nobleman alluded to in the *Queste del Saint Graal* (*q.v.*) as the Castle Carchelois in the March of Scotland. He was slain by his three sons, who were in turn despatched by Galahad. When dying he urged Galahad to go to the assistance of the Maimed King and to undertake other adventures.

ERTHAI. (*Vide* "Gododin.") A Cymric chief slain in the battle at Cattreath. "In the van was, loud as thunder, the din of targets. . . . When the tale shall be told of the battle of Cattraeth, the people will utter sighs, long has been their grief because of the warrior's absence, there will be a dominion without a sovereign and a smoking land."

ESCORANT. A king alluded to in the romance of the *Queste del Saint Graal* (*q.v.*). On Perceval, Galahad, and Bors arriving in his kingdom he casts them into prison, thinking them to be sorcerers. They are miraculously fed by the Grail. At Escorant's death Galahad is made king of his realm.

ESCOS. A monarch alluded to in the romance of the *Grand Saint Graal* (*q.v.*) as having given his name to Scotland. The Grail company pass through his kingdom.

ESPINOGRE. A notable alluded to in Manessier's portion of the *Conte del Graal* (*q.v.*) as besieging Goon Desert (*q.v.*) in Quiquagrant. Goon Desert made a sally and slew him. Espinogre's nephew swore revenge. Donning the armour of one of Goon Desert's knights, he slew him.

ESPLANDIAN. A romance current throughout Spain during the middle ages. It tells how Amadis of Gaul (*q.v.*) and his wife Oriana of the Firm Island had in their keeping the wicked enchanter Archelous. One day the prisoner's wife entreated Amadis to set her husband free. This he did; but not without great misgivings. Soon after the news of his friend King Lisuarte's captivity reached the island, and in deep despair Amadis regretted having set Archelous free, as he attributed the misfortune to the enchanter. Hardly had the dismayed Amadis time to consider the situation when a huge mountain of fire approached the island. As it came nearer it appeared to break, and to the astonishment of all a monstrous eagle arose from the flames and floated towards them. As its huge wings touched the shore the enchantress Urganda appeared. She explained that their son Esplandian must undertake a mission of revenge, and ere questions could be put to her she had mysteriously carried the youth off. Wafted across the smooth ocean on a beautiful ship, Esplandian was thrilled with joy at his new life. At last he touched an island and going ashore he saw it to be barren. A vast tower crowned its topmost height. He found the massive structure deserted, and, on looking around, he caught sight of a sword firmly embedded in a stone. As he attempted to grasp it, the air was rent by the hideous howl of a dragon which quickly coiled its body around him. A grim struggle ensued, neither man nor beast giving way. The earth shook, and the castle rocked under the weight of their bodies. But Esplandian with one hand free was at last able to reach the magic sword the enchantress Urganda had given him. It started out at his touch, and soon with its aid he laid the dragon dead. Esplandian quitted the tower and proceeded to the shore, the light of the blade guiding his footsteps as he went. On reaching the beach a boat awaited him, he stepped on board and the frail craft brought him to a rugged country. As he wandered toward a castle which he had perceived at a distance he met with a hermit who advised him to avoid it. The old man further told him that a great

prince was a captive therein. The youth believed this monarch to be King Lisuarte, and the castle the wicked Archelous's stronghold. He proceeded on his way heedless of the kindly hermit's advice, and on arrival at the castle encountered a giant sentinel. This monster he speedily vanquished, and was about to enter the stronghold when Archelous confronted him. Enraged at the stripling's audacity, the evil enchanter ran towards him and a desperate struggle ensued. At last the young knight obtained an advantage, and with a thrust of his sword he slew the enchanter. Next came Archelous's nephew to avenge his uncle's death; but he too was slain. Arcobone, the mother of the slain enchanter, attempted to use her evil powers on the knight, but his magic sword preserved him, and at his command she led him to where the prisoner was lodged. He came upon his kinsman and released him. As they reached the shore the fleet of Matroed, eldest son of Arcobone, had anchored. Matroed advanced and engaged Esplandian in combat, both warriors being well matched. As the sun began to wane, the pagan, sorely wounded, appealed to the knight to allow him to die in peace. A holy man arrived, and as Matroed expired he implored his blessing. The stronghold of Archelous was razed to the ground, the land freed from pagan custom and the fleet of Matroed destroyed.

ESTMERE, KING. A Scottish romance. The date of this epic, which enjoyed a national reputation, appears to be obscure. We possess one fortunate clue— if a clue it be—in the general assumption that a portion at least of the romance was composed during the sovereignty of the Saracens, or Moors, over a part of Spanish territory. Taking the latest date for a basis, we can safely assume that the Moorish race lost its prestige over its Spanish possessions about the year 1491. Some critics seem to have at one time confused this romance with the *Tale of the King of Esimoreland's Marriage to the Daughter of the King of Westmoreland*, mentioned in the *Complaynt of Scotland*, 1549. But latterly such a view seems to have been weakened by the belief that the tale belongs to the ancient romance of *Kyng Horn* (*q.v.*). The legend has not come down to us in its original condition. This short epic is admired for its simplicity of style and action. The tale commences at the home of the light-hearted adventurer, King Estmere. Over a social horn of ale, he is advised to marry by his bosom friend Adler. The good-natured host replies to the effect that he would find it difficult to marry happily, since he is not easily satisfied. His friend, however, determines to pursue the matter. He remembers having heard of a King Adland and his beautiful daughter, and suggests that his host might visit the king, and succeed, if possible, in winning His Majesty's daughter. This suggestion meets with Estmere's approval, and they subsequently depart on the matrimonial mission. Arriving before Adland's palace, they are questioned on their religious tendencies. Admitting, however, that they are Christians, Estmere and his embassy are ushered into the presence of King Adland, who heartily makes them at ease. Disclosing the purpose of his visit, Estmere prevails upon his royal

host to bring forth his daughter. Adland warns the visitors that another suitor—the Spanish king, had recently journeyed to his court for the same purpose, and being refused because he was not a Christian, threatened vengeance. The daughter appears, and instantly falls in love with Estmere, who is, however, restrained by her father from taking her away. They nevertheless swear to be true to each other. King Estmere and his companion commence their return journey. They have not proceeded far, when a messenger from Adland's court overtakes them, advising Estmere to return and defend his kingly friend against an inroad of the Spanish king. He doubts the advisability of acting upon the request. But prompted by his ally, they disguised themselves as Moors, and decide to return and defend the good king and his daughter. They arrive in the guise of Moorish harpers, to find the enemy in charge of the castle, and the leader paying court to the disheartened king's daughter. Estmere, playing on his harp, succeeds in enticing the beautiful girl from the presence of the Spanish king, who in his rage scoffs at the disguised harper for his conceit and offers to try the instrument. The ruse is successful in luring the Spanish suitor to come towards Estmere, who, seeing his opportunity, slays him. The loyal followers of the dead chief immediately assail the two harpers. A desperate struggle ensues, and by means of the magic power they possess Estmere and his companion win the day. King Adland, seeing the defeat of the Saracen king and his army, does not hesitate to hand his daughter over to Estmere, who marries her. They return to England soon afterwards.

ESTMERE, KING. The principal character in the romance of that name (*q.v.*). He is possessed of a simple and pleasing manner, taking life lightly. He seriously decides, through the advice of his friend Adler, to marry. His method of accomplishing his object is very wittily expressed in the romance. After succeeding in marrying the daughter of King Adland (*q.v.*)— but not before he had slain his opponent, the Spanish king— he returned to his home, to resume his peaceful manner of living.

ESTRAGOTT. (*Vide* "Sir Ferumbras.") A huge Ethiopian in Laban's service. He killed Sabaryz at Rome.

ESTROIS DE GARILES. Alluded to in the *Queste del Saint Graal* (*q.v.*) as one of the three messengers who bore tidings from Galahad, Perceval, and Bors to the court of King Arthur.

ESTUYT OF LEGIERS. (*Vide* "Sir Otuel.") A knight of Charlemagne's, who seized a firebrand and threw it at Otuel in anger at his insulting words when he gave his message at the court of Charlemagne.

ETAIN. Second wife of Midir the Proud. Her beauty evoking the jealousy of his first wife, Fuamnach, she was by her turned into a butterfly and blown from the palace by a magic tempest. Tossed hither and thither through Ireland, after seven years she was blown through a window of the fairy palace of Angus, on the Boyne. He could not release her from the magic of Fuamnach, but during the day she fed in a beautiful bower upon honey-laden flowers, and at night in her natural form gave Angus her love. Fuamnach, however, learned of her hiding-place, and the tempest she now sent blew Etain into the drinking-cup of Etar, the wife of an Ulster chieftain. The butterfly was swallowed, and Etain was born daughter of Etar, and as such she wedded Eochy, High King of Ireland. For her remaining history, see "Midir."

ETAIN OIG. In Irish romance, daughter of Etain (*q.v.*) and wife of Cormac, King of Ulster, in the article concerning whom her story is related.

ETAR. The mortal mother of Etain (*q.v.*).

ETERSKEL. In Irish romance, King of Tara, whose cowherd protected and brought up Messbuachalla, whom the king discovered and married.

ETHAL ANUBAL. Father of Caer (*q.v.*).

ETHLINN. Daughter of Balor, King of the Fomorians (*q.v.*), in Irish romance. As her father had been informed by a druid that he would be slain by his grandson, and as Ethlinn was his only child, he imprisoned her in a lofty tower in Tory Island, in the charge of twelve matrons, who were forbidden to tell her that such beings as men existed. Balor stole a magic cow belonging to Kian (*q.v.*), who determined to be revenged upon him, and, disguising himself in woman's garb, gained access to Ethlinn. From their intercourse sprang three infants, whom Balor ordered to be drowned. But one fell from the napkin in which the trio were carried to their death, and was taken by the Druidess Birog to its father Kian, and became the great Lugh (*q.v.*).

ETHNÉ. The daughter of Elie, steward of Angus, in Irish romance. She was a beautiful handmaid of the daughter of Mananan the sea-god, who had sent his child to be brought up in the Brugh na Boyna. But while the other Danaans lived on Mananan's magic swine, she took no nourishment. It was then discovered that her moral nature had been awakened in her by the brutal desire of a chieftain of the Danaans to possess her by force, and she therefore took no faëry food. Mananan and Angus, how-ever, brought back from the East two magic cows with a never-failing supply of milk. Upon this she fed, as the animals had come from a sacred land. One day she went down with her mistress and the other maidens to bathe in the Boyne, but after arraying herself she discovered that she had lost her Veil of Invisibility, and there-fore her home and companions. Wandering up and down, she came to a church, and told her story to a monk, who brought her to St. Patrick. By him she was baptized. But as she was praying in the church one day she heard voices afar off calling her name. Attempting to reply, in her emo-tion she fell into a swoon, and regained her senses only to pine away with grief at the loss of her Danaan kindred to whom the strange voices belonged. She died upon the breast of St. Patrick, and, through the last rites ad-ministered to her by the saint, was received into heaven. The church was henceforth named Kill Ethné. The word " kill " usually means in Irish place-names the Latin *cella*, a monastic cell, shrine, or church. In this pathetic legend we can see the yearning of the early Irish Celtic Christians after the old pagan religion with its radiant and mystic environment, its beautiful women of the Dana, and their careless immortality.

Like Persephone, Ethné must con-sume no faëry food, no nurture of Hades, or she is lost. Persephone ate and became the wife of Pluto, and the young corn, like the Xilonen of the Mexicans. But Ethné does not eat in the Chris-tianized legend, which is tanta-mount to saying that she did in the pagan version.

ETLYM GLEDDYV COCH. A youth who offered his services to Peredur as a guide, alluded to in the *Mabinogi* story of *Peredur the Son of Evrawc*. Peredur arrives at the court of the Countess of Achieve-ments, and overthrows her three hundred knights, but learning that she loves Etlym, he resigns her to him. Accompanied by Etlym, Peredur comes to the Mound of Mourning, slays two out of the three hundred knights whom he finds guarding the serpent there, kills the reptile, and gives Etlym the magic stone which he finds at the spot, sending him back to his lady-love.

ETZEL. (*Vide* " Attila.")

EUDES. Uncle of Huon of Bordeaux (*q.v.*). He renounced Christianity for Mohammedanism, to the chagrin of his nephew.

EVALACH THE UNKNOWN, In Grail romance, a Saracen lord. Expresses his disbelief to Joseph in the mystery of the Immaculate Conception and the Trinity. Evalach has a vision in which appear three equal tree-trunks, which, though three, are yet truly one, and also of a room with a secret door of marble, through which a child passes without opening it. A voice tells him this is a type of the miraculous conception of Christ. He is ulti-mately converted.

EVRAWC. Father of Peredur, alluded to in the tale of *Peredur the Son of Evrawc* (*q.v.*), in the Welsh *Mabinogion*. He was slain in combat along with six of his sons, leaving Peredur and his mother without protection.

EVRIC. A Milesian farmer dwelling on the shores of Erris Bay, who befriended the swan-children of the Irish sea-god Lir (*q.v.*). Their story is supposed to have been handed down by him.

EXCALIBUR. Otherwise called Mirandoise, or in Welsh legend Caledvwlch, and in some instances Caliburn, the sword of King Arthur. The weapon is a magical one like the Gram of Odin thrust into the roof-tree of the Volsungs, or the Durandal of Roland, and the Lady of the Lake, who is its guardian, is on a par with Thetis the mother of Achilles who presents her son with armour which renders him invulnerable. The scabbard of this sword is even more wonderful than the weapon it holds. Merlin tells Arthur that it is worth ten of the blade, for so long as he carries the sheath he will not lose blood, however sore he may be wounded. Morgan le Fay, Arthur's sister, purloined the scabbard and presented it to Sir Accolon, palming off a forged scabbard on her brother. We find a like weapon in the possession of Sir Galahad. The sword was Arthur's faithful companion in many an adventure, and at the point of death he delivered it to Bedivere, with orders to cast it into a certain lake. Hesitating to lose so fine a weapon, Bedivere prevaricated thrice with the king as to having cast it into the lake, but Arthur was not to be deceived, and prayed him to do as he had been requested. At last he cast the weapon into the mere, and espied a hand and arm arise from the waters, seize it and disappear, after brandishing it three times. Spenser calls Excalibur Morddure, probably "the biter." (*Faërie Queene*, II. viii. 21.)

EYLIMI, KING. (*Vide* "Volsungs.") Father of Hjordis (*q.v.*) who wedded Sigmund (*q.v.*). He was subsequently slain by King Lyngi (*q.v.*) while defending Sigmund (*q.v.*).

F

FACHTNA. In Irish romance, the giant King of Ulster, husband of Nessa and father of Conor (*q.v.*).

FAFNIR. (*Vide* "Volsungs.") Son of Hreidmar, and brother to Otter (*q.v.*) and Regin (*q.v.*). In his lust for treasure he slew his father to obtain Otter's skin, which contained a treasure of gold rings. He eventually developed into a dragon and was slain by Sigurd.

FAIR MANE. The foster-mother of Geena mac Luga (*q.v.*) and of many of the Fianna.

FALCON. A horse possessed by Dietrich of Bern (*q.v.*).

FALIAS. One of the four cities whence the Danaans (*q.v.*) of Irish romance sprang. From this city came the Lia Fail, or Stone of Destiny, which roared beneath a rightful king, and which is now part of the British throne in Westminster Abbey.

FAMONGOMADAN. A giant leagued with Cildadan against King Lisuarte, whose daughter Oriana he demanded. Beltenebros eventually slays him and his giant son Basagante.

FAND. The Pearl of Beauty, wife of Mananan the Irish Celtic sea-god, who sought the love of Cuchulain (*q.v.*). She quarrelled with her husband, and in consequence her kingdom was besieged by three demons who threatened it with destruction. She offered her love to Cuchulain in return for his help against the invaders. Cuchulain defeated them, and dwelt for a month with Fand, after which he departed, having appointed as trysting-place on earth the strand of the Yew Tree. Emer, Cuchulain's wife, heard of the tryst, however, and arrived at the place of assignation with fifty maidens armed with knives, with the intention of slaying Cuchulain. He perceived their approach from afar, and sung to Emir of the surpassing excellences of his mistress. Fand offered to give him up, but Emer protested on her part that she should be the deserted one. Mananan the sea-god then appeared to his unfaithful spouse, and offered to take her back, and she departed with him. Mananan shook his cloak between Cuchulain and Fand, so that they might meet nevermore—a beautiful simile of the power for estrangement and division possessed by the sea. Cuchulain, on the departure of Fand, sorrowed long, refusing meat and drink, till the druids bestowed upon him a draught of forgetfulness.

FAUST or **FAUSTUS.** A sixteenth-century legend mentioned by Saxo-Grammaticus, is first alluded to by Trithemius, who, in writing to Johann Winding, describes Faust as " a fool rather than a philosopher," who fled rather than confront him. Faust boasted that were all the works of Plato and Aristotle effaced he could restore them with greater elegance. He declared that Christ's miracles were nothing to wonder at, as he could perform deeds equally as marvellous. The magician took about with him a dog which was supposed to be possessed of a devil. Melancthon describes Faust as " a disgraceful beast and sower of many devils," who studied magic at Cracow. Weiher mentions that Faust was found dead with his neck wrung, after the house in which he resided had been shaken to its foundations by a terrific din.

Faust personified the old spirit of mediæval magic as Luther personified the Protestant religion. The person around whom the magus-legend clustered was one Johann Faust, who from 1516 to 1525 resided with his friend the Abbot of Maulbronn, where the Faust-kitchen and Faust-tower still exist. He was forced to flee from Wittenberg because of his magical practices, and after many wanderings, ended his life in a village of Würtemberg. He has nothing in common with John Fust, the printer of Mainz, with whom, without any historical justification, he became latterly identified.

The oldest Faust-book appeared in Frankfort in 1587. In 1590 it was translated into English, and almost immediately afterwards appeared the *Tragicall History of Doctor Faustus*, by Christopher Marlowe, who simply dramatized the popular legend after the manner of his time, throwing into its dark shadows, however, the brilliant light of a rich poetry and deep religious fervour. Transformed by the genius of Goethe, the legend took the shape of a great world-drama, in which the deepest philosophy is combined with the most unerring worldly wisdom, and the tragic notes of human woe and passion are blent with a rich mysticism and romantic fervour. In Goethe's *Faust* the old and the modern world meet, and the whole tragedy of man is set forth with unrivalled power, pathos and skill.

FAYLINN. In Irish romance, the home of a diminutive race called "the Wee Folk," who appear to have been of the Elfin tribe. Its King was Iubdan (*q.v.*). (*Vide* "Eisirt.")

FEDELMA. A prophetess in Irish romance, who dwelt in the fairy mound of Croghan. She prophesied to Queen Maev the defeat of her foray into Ulster.

FEIREFIZ. Alluded to in the *Parzival* of Wolfram von Eschenbach as the son of Gahmuret by a heathen Eastern queen, Belakane, and thus half-brother to Percival or Parzival.

FELICE. (*Vide* "Guy of Warwick.") Daughter of Rohand. In the words of the poem she was very "fair, courteous, wise and learned." She behaved in rather a haughty and capricious way to Sir Guy, and had been married only a short time when her husband left her and went on a pilgrimage to the Holy Land. Her only child, Raynburn, was stolen. She dedicated her life after that to good works, and did not see her husband again (although he once came to the castle and received hospitality unrecognized) until he was dying, when he sent for her. She only survived him fifteen days.

FELIM. In Irish romance, son of Dall, and father of Deirdre (*q.v.*), a lord of Ulster. Whilst the king and his nobles were visiting him,

he was informed that his wife had borne him a daughter. Cathbad the druid prophesied to the assembly that the child should grow into a wondrous fair woman, and that she should wed a king, but that because of her ruin and desolation should come upon Ulster. The nobles then resolved to put her to death, but Conor the king forbade them, and said he would himself espouse her when she came of fitting age. This child was Deirdre.

FELIX (1). Prince. (*Vide* "Florice and Blanchfleur.") Ruler over Murcia, husband to the Queen of Murcia, and father of Florice. He was noted for his cruelty and unscrupulous behaviour. During his conflict with the kings of Portugal and Galicia he slew the innocent Perse, on pilgrimage with Topase to the Holy Land. He appointed Mohady, a zealous priest, as tutor to his son Florice. At Mohady's instigation Felix sent Blanchfleur to the slave market of Alexandria.

FELIX (2). Alluded to in the romance of the *Grand Saint Graal* (*q.v.*) as Governor of Syria. He took Evelach (*q.v.*) with him, and held him in high honour, until one day Evelach became angry with Felix's son, slew him and was forced to fly.

FELIXMARTE OF HYRCANIA. A slayer of giants.

FERCARTNA. Bard of Curoi, King of Munster. He leapt over a precipice with Blanid (*q.v.*) Curoi's wife, who had treacherously brought about the death of her husband through her lover Cuchulain (*q.v.*).

FERDIA. In Irish romance, son of Daman the Firbolg, and friend to Cuchulain. He joined Queen Maev in her foray against Ulster.

In the battle which ensued, Maev suggested that he should engage Cuchulain, who had vanquished all the other heroes of might. At first he would not, but she taunted him so sorely that at length he consented. The combat between them lasted four days, and on the fourth day Cuchulain, after a strenuous combat, slew him with the Gae Bolg, or belly-spear.

FERDINAND GONSALEZ, COUNT, THE ESCAPE OF. This romance, related in a Spanish historical ballad of the tenth century, is considered by many modern critics to have been of an entirely fabulous origin so informed is it with the spirit of romance and adventure. Ferdinand's wife Sancha, daughter of Garcias, King of Navarre, was a woman of great courage and resource, and through her clever strategy she was enabled to effect her husband's escape from prison on two occasions. The ballad describes the capture of the Count of Castille who was bound " hand and heel " and thrown into a dungeon by order of King Garcias. A Christian knight of Normandy, fighting against the Moors, was riding through Navarre, and hearing of the capture of Gonsalez he bribed the jailer of the prison to let him see the count. He succeeded in having an interview with him, and afterwards attended a feast given by the king on account of having made a prisoner of "the doughtiest lord in Spain." There he met Garcias' daughter, and telling her that Gonsalez had loved her for long, he urged her to liberate him. During the night when all her maids were asleep the Infanta rose, and going to the jailer she bribed him with gold and jewels to set his prisoner free. She showed Gonsalez the way to liberty, and offered to accompany him on his journey, as she feared her father's anger. Gonsalez kissed her and they both proceeded to the forest, where they met a priest, who tried to stop them, as he knew them both, and threatened to report their flight if they did not pay him a ransom. The Infanta beckoned to the priest to enter the wood, where she held him fast, while Gonsalez picked up the priest's javelin which lay on the grass and pressed it through his body to the ground, spearing him like a boar. They left him to die and continued their way on the priest's horse until they met a troop of men who turned out to be Gonsalez' own soldiers. The ballad ends with their arrival in Castille, accompanied by the horsemen with their shining pennons and bright swords. (*Vide Chronica Antigua de España ;* Lockhart, *Spanish Ballads*, 1823.)

FERGUS (1). In Irish romance, a Nemedian chief who slew the Fomorian Conann.

FERGUS (2), **SIR.** A knight of King Mark, and a friend of Sir Tristram (*q.v.*). (*Vide* " Morte d'Arthur.")

FERGUS MAC LEDA. In Irish romance a sub-King of Ulster, who delighted in exploring the depths of the lakes and rivers of Ireland. At the bottom of Loch Rury he encountered the Muirdris, or river-horse, the terror of meeting which so strongly affected him that his face was twisted awry. No monarch with a blemish might rule in Ireland, and, to save his feelings, those about him permitted no mirrors to enter his palace, so that he was unaware of his true condition. On one occasion he struck a handmaiden, who retorted that he would be better employed in striking the monster who had brought about his deformity. On hearing this Fergus called for a mirror, and, perceiving the blemish, took his sword, dived into Loch Rury, and rose again with the Muirdris's head in his hand. Throwing the bloody trophy on the bank, he indicated to the spectators that the blemish had departed, and with a lofty smile upon his face, sank into the depths and disappeared.

FERGUS MAC ROY. In Irish romance, half-brother of Fachtna (*q.v.*), King of Ulster, whom he succeeded. He took to wife his brother's spouse, Nessa, who wed him on condition that he permitted Conor, her son, to reign for one year. At the end of that period the people demanded that he should retain the throne, to which Fergus consented. He was sent by Conor to invite Naisi and Deirdre (*q.v.*) to return, and whilst guiding them home, was asked by Baruch, Lord of the Red Branch (*q.v.*), to a feast, with consequences disastrous to Naisi and Deirdre.

FERUMBRAS. This romance is a translation from the French, dating from the beginning of the fifteenth century. Its theme is that of strife between the Saracens and the Christians. Laban, King of Babylon, persecuted the Jews and drove them out of the Holy Land. Having learned that treasure of great value, intended as a present to himself, had been taken from a ship by the Romans, he vowed he would destroy Rome in revenge. He set out with a large army, accompanied by his son Ferumbras, King of Alexandria, and Floripas his daughter. They besieged Rome, which was defended bravely by Sabaryz, until by strategy an entrance was made and Sabaryz was killed. The Romans repulsed many assaults, but Ferumbras showed conspicuous ability and would probably have conquered without the help the Saracens gained by the treachery of Ispres, who commanded the principal gate. The news of the distress in Rome reached Charlemagne, who sent Sir Guy of Burgundy to its aid, but he could do nothing without assistance. Enraged at Laban, Charlemagne went to the neighbourhood of Aigremor, where Laban had encamped, and began to ravage the country. A battle followed in which the Saracens suffered severely. Ferumbras then offered to fight any of the Christians in single combat, and Olivier accepted the challenge. After a severe struggle Olivier won, and Ferumbras acknowledged himself vanquished, and embraced Christianity, being afterwards baptized by Turpin. Meanwhile, Roland and Olivier had been taken prisoners and carried to Laban, who would have slain them, but Floripas advised him to keep them as hostages for Ferumbras, and they were thrown into a dungeon. By the help of Floripas, they were drawn up out of this and concealed in her apartments. Twelve delegates from both contending parties met to arrange an exchange of prisoners. Sir Guy proposed a trial of strength, and all the Saracens were killed. The French knights carried back their heads to Laban at Aigremor, who would have killed them, had not Floripas requested she might take charge of them till the best form of punishment had been decided. She then took them to join the others in her apartments. Floripas told them she wished to marry Sir Guy, and become a Christian, to which request Sir Guy agreed, and they were betrothed. She then gave the knights armour and arranged how they could attack Laban and take the castle. Laban escaped, and attempted an assault, but was driven back. He then cut off all supply of provisions, and blockaded the castle. Floripas, however, had a magical girdle which prevented the wearer feeling hunger. This was lost, and their position became desperate. Richard of Normandy sallied out to find Charlemagne and get help, which he did eventually, and after some adventures, and nearly losing his life, which was saved by Ferumbras, Charlemagne arrived at Aigremor, and a battle took place which resulted in the total defeat of the Saracens. Laban was unhorsed, and refusing to be baptized, was executed. Floripas married Sir Guy, and half of Spain was given to them as a dowry, and the remainder to Ferumbras, and Charlemagne returned to France.

FIACHA. In Irish romance, son of Firaha. He joined the host of Maev in the foray against Ulster. When the men of Erin sent the Clan Calatin (*i.e.* the children of Calatin, the offspring of a wizard who with his twenty-seven sons formed one being) against Cuchulain, the Clan Calatin succeeded in overthrowing him, and ground his face in the gravel, but Fiacha with one stroke cut off their twenty-eight hands, after which Cuchulain hacked them into fragments. He gave to Finn a magic spear, which, when its naked blade was laid against a man's brow, filled him with a courage which rendered him invincible.

FIAL (Feeal). In Irish romance, sister of Emer (*q.v.*).

FIANNA. An Irish military order frequently alluded to in Irish romance

which flourished in the reign of Conor mac Ort in the third century A.D. It was divided mainly into the Clans Bascna and Morna (*q.v.*), which were continually fighting with each other for supremacy. Under the captaincy of Cuchulain, the Fianna had to perform several feats of strength, courage, coolness, and agility before they were received into the order ; and the candidate had to be versed in the Twelve Books of Poesy, and to be himself a bard. This order was practically exterminated in the Battle of Gowra (*q.v.*), fought as the result of the refusal of King Cairbolg (*q.v.*) to pay to the Fianna tribute for the marriage of his daughter Sgeimh Solias (Light of Beauty) (*q.v.*).

FINCHOOM. In Irish romance, Dectera's sister, foster-mother to Cuchulain (*q.v.*), mother of Conall.

FINDABAIR (of the Fair Eyebrows). In Irish romance, a daughter of Maev (*q.v.*), offered as wife to Ferdia (*q.v.*) if he would fight Cuchulain (*q.v.*).

FINEGAS. Sage and druid, from whom Finn (*q.v.*), the Irish Ossianic hero, learnt science and poetry.

FINIAS. One of the four great cities whence the Irish mythical Danaans (*q.v.*) are said to have sprung. From this city these deities brought a magic spear.

FINN MAC CUMHAL. In Irish romance, Captain of the Fianna (*q.v.*) and the centre of the Ossianic tales. His father, Cumhal, chief of the Clan Bascna (*q.v.*) had been slain at Castle-Knock, by the rival clan Morna, and his mother, and Murna of the White Neck, granddaughter of the Danaan King, Nuada of the Silver Hand (*q.v.*), succeeded in saving him from the Mornan sword. She gave him to two old women to be brought up in the wild wood. Demna was his name, but from the fairness of his skin he was known as Finn (the Fair One). His first success for his outcast clan was to slay Lia (*q.v.*), the Fiannan Treasurer, and to hand over the Treasure Bag to the Clan Bascna. Then he prepared himself for the position of his father's son by learning science and poetry from Finegas, who dwelt on the Boyne. This druid had been unable, until Finn became his pupil, to catch the Salmon of Knowledge that lived in a pool of the river. When he did succeed in catching it, he told Finn to watch while it cooled, but not to eat it. He had, however, burnt his fingers, as he turned the spit, and put one of them to his mouth, like Gwion Bach and Siegfried (*q.v.*). Seeing this, Finegas bade him eat the salmon, and Finn was filled with the wisdom of the ages. Goll mac Morna was captain of the Fianna, when Finn, a stranger, sat down among the king's warriors and the Fianna in the Great Assembly at Tara. To the king he told his name and lineage, and took service with him. Shortly after this Cormac promised him the leadership of the Fianna if he slew the fire-blowing demon that came yearly to set Tara in flames. Finn, therefore, possessed himself of the magic sword of Fiacha (*q.v.*), and as the dream-lapping music of the demon's harp began to bewitch him he placed the blade against his forehead, when the battle fury came upon him. The goblin, perceiving that Finn was uncharmed by his music, fled to Slieve Fuad, whither Finn followed. The demon was slain and his head borne back to Tara. Then the king gave orders to all the Fianna to swear allegiance to Finn as their captain, a command which was obeyed first by Goll mac Morna and then by all the rest. During the leadership of Finn the Fianna rose to a glorious eminence in the land by their mighty deeds. an eminence which later grew tyrannical, and from which they were hurled at the Battle of Gowra. But neither annalist nor poet gives a clear account of the death of Finn. Conformable to his Danaan ancestry, his passing is shadowed in a cloud ; while a popular tradition has lulled him and his great companions to a dreamless sleep in an enchanted cave whence they shall arise in the hour of their country's need, like Arthur, Barbarossa, and Charlemagne.

FINTAN. In the Ossianic cycle of Irish legend, the Salmon of Knowledge, which Finegas (*q.v.*) bade Finn (*q.v.*) eat, who was then filled with the wisdom of the ages.

FIONUALA. (*Vide* "Children of Lir.")

FIRBOLGS. In Irish romance, one of the three Nemedian (*q.v.*) surviving families, after the Fomorian victory on Tory Island, who returned, according to later tradition, to Ireland. Their name signifies " Men of the Bog," to account for which title there is a legend which states that, oppressed in Greece by their masters, they set sail for Ireland in coracles made out of the bags in which they were required to carry soil from the valleys to the hills to make the latter arable. Nennius, on the other hand, states that they came from " Spain " or the Land of the Dead. They invaded Ireland in three groups, the Firbolg, the Fir-Danaan, and the Galian. They personified dulness and stupidity, and in the first Battle of Moytura readily gave ground before the light of intelligence, represented by the Danaans (*q.v.*).

FISHER KING. (*Vide* "Amfortas.")

FLEGENTYNE. Mentioned in the *Grand Saint Graal* as wife of Nasciens (*q.v.*). She set out in search of her husband, accompanied by the old knight Corsapias and his son Helicoras. At the bidding of Christ she sets out with Mordrains, King Label's daughter, and their households for Britain, in order to be avenged upon King Crudel, who has thrown Josephes (*q.v.*) and many other Christians into prison. The captain of the ship on which they have embarked lusts after Flegentyne, and is carried off by a devil. On arriving in Britain so great is her joy that she nearly dies, swooning twelve times. She dies on the same day as her husband and Sarraquite (*q.v.*).

FLORICE, SIR. Son of Felix, King of Murcia (*q.v.*), one of the two leading characters in the romance of *Florice and Blanchfleur* (*q.v.*). Born at the same time as Blanchfleur (*q.v.*), whom he loved, their intimacy caused his tutor Mohady (*q.v.*) to prevail upon his father for his banishment. He was sent to the court of the King of Montorio, where he completed his education. But he could not rest. Being possessed of a mystic ring given him by Blanchfleur, he was forced to enter into many adventures for her sake. The first outward proof of his love toward her was the rescue of his lady, who had through the treason of Mohady and Ajoub (*q.v.*) been sentenced to death. An illness followed, and through the skill of Averroes (*q.v.*) he was preserved from death. Again his ring

clouded, which showed that his love was in danger, and through the advice of Salim (*q.v.*) he set off in pursuit of Blanchfleur, who had been shipped to Alexandria, to be sold as a slave. His journeys are very vividly depicted in the romance, and through the plotting of Dayre (*q.v.*) and the weakness of the porter to the Amiral of Babylon, he succeeded in securing his mistress. The amiral threatened to put him to death, but after much explanation befriended him, and, through the advice of the two lovers, became a Christian. They married and returned to Murcia, when Florice assumed the crown. The story is told by Boccaccio in his *Filocopo*.

FLORICE AND BLANCHFLEUR. A romance, perhaps originally of Spanish origin. Probably many tales were written around the original conception, and we find what is evidently a later Spanish version, *Flores y Blancaflor* (1512), and French versions, *Histoire Amoureuse de Flore et de Blanchefleur*, traduite de l'Espagnol (1554), *Florimint et Passerose* (c. 1565). The adventures of the lovers make the principal subject of Boccaccio's *Filocopo*, and he also employs the plot in the fifth novel of the tenth day of his *Decameron*. But he admits (l. 1, p. 6, ed. 1723) that the story existed long before. Flores and Blancaflor are mentioned as illustrious lovers by Matfres Eymengau de Bezers, a poet of Languedoc, in his *Breviari d'Amor*, dated 1288.

Perse, heir to the throne of a noble emperor, possessed of rich domains in Italy, being desirous to marry, his loyal subjects anxiously awaited his happy choice. Topase, the daughter of the Duke of Ferrara, and niece to the Duke of Milan, was the bride-elect. The two imperial houses, approving the union, hastened the marriage. The young couple met, and loved at first sight, so the nuptial bond was consecrated by the benediction of the Pope. As they were anxious for the birth of a child, a superstitious Spaniard advised the newly-wedded pair to implore Saint James to intercede on their behalf. Out of gratitude Prince Perse promised to perform a pilgrimage to the shrine of this saint, in Compostella. The following night Perse and Topase were alarmed by the vision of an angel, warning them of many calamities attending their journey. Ignoring the dream, they resumed their ill-fated visit to Galicia. Having traversed the battle-ground of the kings of Galicia and Portugal, just before the weary pilgrims entered Galicia, they rested awhile on the fringe of a forest. The Saracen Prince Felix swooped down upon the slumbering pair, slaying Perse, and taking Topase captive. Felix, surprised at her beauty, sent Topase to his queen. About the same age as Topase, Murcia readily sympathized with the young mourner in her grief, and a strong bond of friendship was soon formed. The two princesses were delivered on the same day of a boy and a girl. Murcia named her infant son Florice, and Topase gave to her daughter the name of Blanch-fleur. Weakened by sickness, sorrow, and remorse, her life was ebbing fast away. When the two children were brought before Topase, the dying mother had just power enough left to baptize her daughter with her tears, then, uttering a faint scream, she expired.

The boy and girl grew up side by side, Murcia guiding their young lives, and an attachment almost amounting to love developed. Mohady, a Saracen priest, preceptor to the young prince, seeing that his pupil had imbibed the Christian faith of his foster-sister, conspired to separate the two comrades. The Mollah succeeded in convincing Felix of the expediency of removing Florice, at which the young prince was heart-broken. The father sent his son to Montorio to complete his studies, so that his superior rank might be upheld with becoming dignity. Blanch-fleur gave her lover a ring containing a talisman, which would foretell when danger threatened. One day Mohady caught Florice in the act of breathing a prayer to the God of the Christians for the safety of his lover. The Mollah informed Felix of the necessity for taking stringent measures, and prayed Ajoub of the great mosque to concoct a plot for destroying Blanchfleur. As the unfortunate girl was accustomed to feed the poultry, Ajoub artfully contrived to poison the food, then accused Blanchfleur of poisoning the fowl placed before him. The wicked Ajoub influenced the judges and was jubilant at the sentence of death which was passed upon the innocent Blanchfleur. Meanwhile, at Montorio, the young prince displayed his prowess against two Moorish kings. But suddenly observing his talisman's brilliance clouding he hastened to Murcia, arriving just in time to see Blanchfleur being led to her death. On learning her fearful plight he challenged her guilty accuser to mortal combat. Ajoub enlisted his son's aid, who entered the lists in his stead, while Blanchfleur, veiled in black, was unable to perceive her supporter.

Florice vanquished his adversary, then, being assailed by Ajoub, he proved victorious in this second duel also. A slave confessed having been accomplice to Ajoub, thus proving Blanchfleur's innocence. Ever fearing treachery towards his lover, the young prince contracted a fever. His physician Averroes, procured through the influence of the Sultan of Algeria, relieved the worst symptoms of the malady, but insisted on Blanchfleur's presence for his patient's recovery. Felix, angry at the idea of the lovers' reunion, deported the unhappy girl to Alexandria, to be sold as a slave. His queen, indignant at such ignominy, reproached Felix, but without avail. Florice, despite his illness, set out in pursuit, the magic ring again warning him of her danger. On learning that Blanchfleur had been sold to the Amiral of Babylon, he became frantic with rage. While entertained in the city he received a ring from his host which would procure him the assistance of a trustworthy burgess named Dayre. This wealthy man then proceeded to tell Florice that his quest was in vain, because the fortress of the amiral was impregnable, being guarded by many soldiers. But the passion of Florice overshadowed all obstacles, and he determined to attack the castle of marble in which his lady love was imprisoned. Dayre, admiring the enamoured youth's brave heart, devised a clever plot. He advised Florice to gain the favour of the porter, and to pretend he was an architect examining the tower, so as to build a similar edifice in his native land. Florice straightway proceeded to the palace with his servant Salim, and so well did he succeed that he soon enlisted the aid of the porter. Blanchfleur was passionately fond of flowers, and it was the duty of the porter to supply them. Gazing at the hampers of flowers one morning, the man thought his accomplice might reach the lady's chamber in one of them. This novel scheme delighted Florice, who immediately placed himself within one. After covering Florice with leaves the porter despatched the hamper to Blanchfleur's room. The basket proving heavy for the two carriers, they set it down before the apartment of Clarice. The young prince, hearing soft footsteps coming towards him, sprang out, believing the girl to be Blanchfleur. The friendly Clarice, realizing Florice's purpose, led him to her companion's chamber. The meeting of the long-separated lovers, in which they gave vent to their pent-up feelings, showed the depth of their mutual passion. Clarice promised to help the devoted pair to escape. One morning the amiral was surprised to find Clarice in attendance instead of Blanchfleur. Being told that his servant was ill, having passed a restless night praying for the safety of her master, he felt satisfied, and rejoiced at such devotion. But next morning Blanchfleur was still missing, so the enraged amiral rushed to her chamber, and there learnt the cause of her neglect. The lovers were put on trial, and realizing that death would be the verdict, they resolved to die together. This devotion caused the amiral to revoke the stern decree, and release them. Florice revealed his high rank, and the amiral ordered the two lovers to marry, then sent the young adventurer back to his dominions. After converting the Saracen Amiral of Babylon to

Christianity, Florice departed for Murcia, on hearing of the death of his father, where he succeeded to the throne.

FLORIPAS. (*Vide* "Sir Ferumbras.") Daughter of Laban. She befriended the Christian knights, even drowning her old governess, and killing the gaoler, Britomarte, because they refused to help them. She fell in love with Sir Guy of Burgundy before she ever saw him, became a Christian and married him. She helped the Christian knights to take her father's castle and gave them her magical girdle to keep them from starving. Charlemagne gave her half of Spain as her marriage portion.

FOLLAMAN. In Irish romance, the youngest son of the Ulster King, Conor (*q.v.*). He led the ill-fated boy corps against the host of Maev (*q.v.*).

FOMORIANS. In romance, the primeval inhabitants of Ireland. Gross, cruel, misshapen monsters, they were driven out of the north seas by the people of Partholan (*q.v.*); they conquered the Nemedians (*q.v.*) on Long Island; under their leader Balor (*q.v.*) they cruelly oppressed the Danaans (*q.v.*), until in the second Battle of Moytura they were completely routed by them. The Fomorians were not a people, but they represented the fierce powers of evil, as the Danaans the enlightening strength of knowledge.

FORBAY. In Irish romance, son of Conor mac Nessa (*q.v.*). Having discovered that Maev (*q.v.*) was wont to bathe early every morning in a pool near to the landing-place of her island home, he measured the distance from the bathing-place to the mainland. Returning to Emania he practised shooting with a sling at an apple fixed on a pole at this distance from him until his aim became perfectly sure. Then with a missile from his sling he smote the queen fatally in the centre of the forehead.

FORGALL. In Irish romance, the wily Lord of Lusca, father of Emer. He fell lifeless in leaping from the rampart of a dun or building to escape Cuchulain (*q.v.*), who sought, and finally won, his daughter as his wife.

FOUR SONS OF AYMON. A romance of the Charlemagne cycle. Their names were Renaud, Richard, Alard, and Guichard. They come to court, are knighted by the king, and bid for favour till they incur his wrath. Renaud quarrels with Charles's nephew Bertolis, whom he slays. After this the brothers leap upon Bayard, a favourite horse, and gallop to their father's castle. But Aymon favours the outraged king, and consequently casts his sons adrift. During their long wanderings, they suffer extreme privation, which bring them to the feet of their mother, who attempts to shield them. But their father again banishes the brothers. They fall into the hands of Yon, King of Bordeaux, whom they assist in his war with the Saracens. Yon marries his sister to Renaud, and lets him build a strong castle named Montauban on a rock overlooking the Garonne. Charles hears of this, and is furious. He sets out to avenge his nephew's death, and besieges the castle. Siege after siege takes place, during which much blood is spilt. Yon betrays the brothers, but they retain the castle, while Renaud endeavours to make peace. Charles is obdurate. The stronghold is impregnable; but within food becomes scarce. Everything worth eating has been devoured, and now Bayard is bled to keep them alive. At last a joust between Renaud and Roland is to be the deciding point in the conflict. The combat is indecisive, a truce is called, while Roland is helped into the castle by his opponents. Charlemagne is angry at seeing them apparently on the best of terms, and determines that the siege be resumed. Renaud encounters Charles, whom he overcomes, but lets him go unhurt. Mangis, the wizard, steals the royal crown, and throwing Charles into an enchanted sleep, carries him within the castle. The amazed king wakes to find himself a prisoner, and is again approached to make peace ; but without avail. Renaud lets him go free, saying, " When it pleases God and you, we shall be friends." The brothers hold out and succeed in capturing Richard of Normandy, and, sending word to Charles, threaten their prisoner's life if peace is not forthcoming. But the king heeds not the threat until his knights rebel against his inflexibility. Peace is at last restored, the prisoner is released, and Renaud promises the king to undertake a pilgrimage to Jerusalem. In poor attire he deserts his castle and wanders to Cologne, to find a cathedral in construction. By way of pious exercise he joins the band of hodmen whom he assists. They become jealous of his marvellous strength and slay him. They cast his body into the river, but it floats miraculously, shedding an unearthly light accompanied by angelic chants. The bells of the cathedral ring of themselves, the sick are cured, and the hero is transfigured into a saint.

FRACHRA. One of the children of Lir (*q.v.*).

FRAGARACH ("The Answerer"). In Irish legend, a sword that could pierce any mail. It was one of the magical gifts brought by Lugh (*q.v.*) from the Land of the Living.

FRAINE, LAY LE (or, The Adventure of the Ash). An English translation from the French of Marie de France. Once there lived two wealthy knights, friends from infancy, who had married about the same time. One lady gave birth to twins, an event which her husband communicated to his friend. The messenger's reception was cordial enough, but he was surprised at the knight's lady's manifest disgust. So he hastened back to inform his master of the curious attitude displayed by his friend's wife. Soon afterwards this unjust lady was delivered of twin daughters. Thereupon she contrived a plot to destroy one of the infants. Soliciting her midwife's aid, she implored her to declare that only one child had been born. The horrified midwife refused to comply with such an inhuman request. So a trustworthy servant proposed to conceal the infant, and relieved the unnatural mother of her undesired burden. She bestowed great care on the upbringing of her other daughter. After the mother had placed a ring on the child's finger, the serving-maid laid her tiny charge, wrapped in a rich mantle, under the porch of an abbey at nightfall. Early the following morning the abandoned infant was discovered by the porter of the abbey, who hastened with the foundling to his wife. Hearing of the discovery, the abbess claimed the child, and educated her in the Christian faith. She named her *protégée* Fraine (meaning ash, under which tree she was discovered), and under her strict guardianship the deserted daughter blossomed into womanhood. Sir Garoun, a young knight possessed of rich lands, hearing of Fraine, went to the abbey so that he might win her. Captivated with her beauty, he resolved to enter into the religious order of the abbey to be near the maiden. Never doubting his honesty of purpose the abbess granted his request, and he soon won the heart of Fraine, who agreed to elope with her lover, taking with her the mantle and ring. Sir Garoun carried her to his castle, where they lived in perfect felicity. His knights, observing that Fraine was not his legal wife, and pointing out that he must bring forth an heir to the baronage, urged him to forsake her. Accordingly he visited a neighbouring knight, who promised Garoun his daughter's hand, the wedding to take place at his own castle. The guests arrived, and Fraine bore her sorrow patiently. The feast was attended with the utmost formality, and, strangely enough, Fraine's young rival, named Le Codre, was observed to bear a striking resemblance to her. The bride's mother, on going to inspect the bridal chamber, discovered, to her horror, the incriminating mantle, which Le Fraine had placed upon the bed. Thereupon she disclosed the relationship between them, enlightening the guests, curious as to the cause of the interrupted ceremony. Sir Garoun claimed his former love, directing the priest to dissolve his newly-formed bond with Le Codre. Thus Le Fraine was restored to her rightful position, and was wed to Sir Garoun. Her twin-sister subsequently married a neighbouring lord.

FRAINE, LE. The twin-daughter of one of the " two knights " referred to in the *Lay le Fraine* (*q.v.*) and sister to Le Codre. She at her birth was deserted by her mother. Discovered by an abbess she became an inmate of her religious house. She subsequently fled with Sir Garoun (*q.v.*), whom she afterwards married.

FRIAR BACON. A sixteenth-century English romance concerning the famous alchemist, printed entire in the *Miscellanea Antiqua Anglicana*. The traditional compilation is entirely destitute of fact. Friar Bacon, reading one day of the many conquests of England, bethought himself how he might make the island impregnable, and himself famous. After much study he resolved to make a brazen head, which should speak, and also to wall all England about with brass. Assisted by Friar Bungay, a noted magician, he formed a head of brass, shaped like a man's, so that it might speak. They conjured up a spirit to learn the gift of speech. Satan appeared, and asked them what was required. " Know," said Friar Bacon, " that we have made an artificial head of brass, which we desire should speak. As we are unable to confer speech, we therefore solicit your aid." The devil replied that only God could enlighten them. " Liar," cried Friar Bacon, " I know that thou dost dissemble, and therefore inform me directly, or we will imprison thee here on earth during our pleasure." Thus threatened, Satan consented, and told them that " by the application of a continual fume of the six hottest simples " the head would move, and in one month would speak. But if they were not within hearing when it spoke, all their labour would be lost. Being satisfied, the two magicians allowed the spirit to depart.

The learned friars prepared the simples, made the fume, and watched continually for the head to speak. Three weeks elapsed, so that they felt weary, and fain would rest. Friar Bacon called his man Miles, and entreated him to watch whilst they slept, and to call them if the brazen head spoke. Soon they were fast asleep, and Miles was alone with his charge. To keep awake, Miles got a tabor and pipe and burst into song. Suddenly the head spoke these words : " Time Is." Deeming this insignificant, Miles let the friars sleep on. " Thou brazen head, after all my master's labour dost thou requite him with two words ? " cried he. " I know Time Is, and that you shall hear." So Miles sang a song conveying the moral that there was a time for everything. " I hope we scholars know our time, when to get drunk, when to kiss our hostess, and when to pay the reckoning—that time comes seldom," pursued he. After half an hour had passed, the head again spoke these words : " Time Was." Miles still scoffed, and in scorn sang another song, telling how the head was once a kettle, now spoiled by Friar Bacon. " I know Time Was, and I know that which existed when Time was. Unless you speak wiser I will not disturb the slumbering friars." Thus Miles talked and sang until another half-hour was gone. Then the brazen head spoke again these words : " Time Is Past," and therewith fell down with a crash. A terrific din followed, accompanied by strange flashes of fire, which frightened Miles, and awoke the two friars. When the smoke vanished, they beheld the brazen

head broken and lying on the floor. Friar Bacon asked if it had spoken. " Yes," quoth Miles, " it spoke, but to no purpose. I'll teach a parrot to speak better in less time." " Out on thee, villain, thou hast undone us both ! " exclaimed Friar Bacon. " First it said, ' Time Is ! ' " " Hadst thou called us then, we had been made for ever," said Friar Bacon. " Then half an hour after it said, ' Time Was,' " continued Miles. " Why didst thou not call us then ? " asked Bungay. " Because I thought it would have told me some long tale, and then I meant to call you," answered Miles. " After another half an hour it cried, ' Time is Past,' and made such a noise that ye awakened." Friar Bacon was so enraged that he would have beaten Miles, had not Bungay restrained him. As a punishment, he struck him dumb for a whole month. Thus the great work of these learned men was overthrown by this simple fellow.

On another occasion, when the King of England was carrying on a war in France, Bacon, in response to a summons, hastened to effect the capitulation of a city for his royal master by setting fire to the state house of the beleagured town, without ever approaching the walls of the fortress. The city consequently fell.

So great was his skill in the art of magic, that he was able to bring to life the ghosts of departed warriors. On one occasion while displaying one of these scenes, he revived the persons of Pompey and Julius Cæsar, who fought a battle before several spectators. He raised the ghost of Hercules, whom he commanded to crush a venomous dragon. The battle of Troy was, on another occasion, faithfully represented. Hector with his Trojans, and Achilles with his Greeks came into deadly combat at his bidding : Hector was slain and the Trojans fled. In settling disputes he excelled. A quarrel between three brothers who fought over their deceased father's estate was ended by his skill. Having the body of the father exhumed, he ordered the three sons to shoot at it as they would at a target, and to him whose arrow went nearest the heart the estates would be given. The two elder brothers did as the friar directed, but the younger of the three hesitated, saying that his veneration for the body of his father whom he loved was too great to permit of his treating it so. The lands were awarded this faithful and reverent son. At last, after many years of magical practice, Bacon resorted to a life of seclusion ; and, after a brief retirement, died.

FRIAR RUSH. (German *Rausch*.) A house-spirit, sent from the infernal regions in the seventeenth century to keep the monks and friars in the same state of wickedness they were then in. He gained admittance as a scullion, and played the monks divers pranks. The legends of this roysterer are of German origin. " Friar Rush " probably represents the spirit of inebriety.

FRITHJOF SAGA, THE. An Icelandic semi-historical romance, probably of the eighth century, committed to writing about the end of the thirteenth century. Frithjof was the son of Thane Thorsten, the friend of King Bele of Norway. He played with the little Princess Ingebjorg, and with her was sent to the sage Hilding to learn wisdom. King Bele and

his thane, Thorsten, died, and the Princes Helgi and Halfdan then shared their father's throne. But Frithjof entered upon his rich inheritance of Framnäs, and of the three great treasures of Thorsten— his wonder-bright sword Angurvadel (*q.v.*) with its strange runes that dulled in peace and flamed in war, the arm-ring of Wayland Smith, and *Ellide* (*q.v.*) the dragonship. After the death-feast of his father he came over the sea to the grave-mound of King Bele to ask the ruling brothers for the hand of Ingebjorg their sister. But Helgi sneered, and in angry contempt the rejected suitor sundered with his sword the gold and brazen shield of the dark prince. Then he returned to his ship homewards. Frithjof, however, had a rival, and this was the old and mild King Ring, a widower. He too was refused his suit, and therefore came to give war to the princes. Helgi then shut up Ingebjorg in Baldur's temple, which no Northman would profane, and sent Hilding to persuade Frithjof to lend his aid against King Ring. Deaf to the entreaties of his old tutor to help King Bele's sons, he was moved by Ingebjorg's tears. He therefore climbed into Baldur's grove, fearing nothing for having profaned it. Then, after three days, he returned to his old playfellow to tell her that Helgi had refused his offer. All men were now against him for his sacrilegious crime, and for punishment he was bidden to wrest from Yarl Angantyr the tribute due to the sons of King Bele on pain of perpetual exile. Unable to pursuade Ingebjorg to go with him, he set out for the island ruled over by Angantyr, despite the attempt of Helgi to engulf him in the storm raised by the sea-witches Heyd and

Ham (*q.v.*). Before reaching the castle he overcame the Viking Atli (*q.v.*), but spared his life on account of his fearlessness, and became his friend. He was welcomed by Angantyr, his father's friend, who had given presents, not tribute, to King Bele, and was rewarded with a purse of gold. Remaining with the yarl until spring, he then sailed for seven days Framnäs-ward, to find it razed, burnt, and in ruins, and to learn from Hilding that King Ring had conquered and had wedded Ingebjorg. Then madness seized upon Frithjof, and he became dangerous to friend and foe alike. In the temple of Baldur, where the midsummer feast was being held, Frithjof challenged the shrinking Helgi to single combat, when noticing Ingebjorg's armlet upon the arm of the image of Baldur, he tugged it off. But the force of the wrenching overbalanced the god, and he fell into the fire. Immediately the temple took fire, which spread to the grove, which soon was ablaze. In holy terror Frithjof sought the sea, and was chased with ten warships by Helgi. Bjorn, however, had bored holes in them on the previous night, and all aboard were drowned save the dark king. Frithjof and his men then became successful vikings, but after three years he turned *Ellide*, his ship, to the Northland. Attired as a beggar, and bent with seeming age, he sat upon the bench without the hall of King Ring, who was celebrating the Yule-tide feast. But a bluff warrior seeking to make jest of the beggar, Frithjof caught him and turned him head over heels upon his feet again. Then the king bade him throw off his disguise, when he revealed himself as a young and noble warrior, richly dressed. The royal host

gave no sign of recognition, but Ingebjorg blushed and paled. Twice Frithjof had his enemy's life in his hands. But the old man had recognized him from the first, and had thus tested his faith. Finally the generous king thrust his sword into his own breast and died. But Frithjof, before wedding with Ingebjorg, sought forgiveness from Baldur, who vouchsafed him a vision of a temple. According to its design Frithjof built a temple to the god, was forgiven by him through the high priest, made Ingebjorg his bride, and took in friendship the hand of her surviving brother, Halfdan. In this saga we have another of those legends obviously superimposed upon the universal conception of the sun-myth. Following the general scheme, the hero, obscure at first, gradually rises into notoriety, wanders for a period, is attacked by madness, and finally weds in peace the beautiful maiden he has sought so long. In each of these steps we note those of the sun on his path—his obscurity at first, but promise of greatness, his climbing to power, his wandering, his dangerous and dizzy height at noon, and his final rest and peace at sunset.

FROL, LA ORGULUS, SIR. Brother to Sir Belliance. In defending his wife against some knights he was slain by Sir Lamorak (*q.v.*). (*Vide* " Morte d'Arthur.")

FROMONDIN. (*Vide* "Garin the Lorrainer.") Son of Fromont, a brave knight who was knighted in order to fight at a certain tourney. Rigaut fought him, unhorsed him, and took him prisoner. Fromondin afterwards fought with Huo of Cambrai and beat him, but granted him his life ; Bernard later stabbed H-10 to Fromondin's indignation.

FROMONT. (*Vide* "Garin the Lorrainer.") Son of Count Hardre (*q.v.*), one of Pepin's counsellors. He was at one time very friendly with the Lorrainers, but he quarrelled with Garin, on account of his intended marriage to Blanchflower (*q.v.*), and Garin never could forgive Fromont for not keeping his promise to punish the murderers of Bego (*q.v.*). Towards the end of his life Fromont met with many misfortunes, and lost many of his kinsmen and his lands in fighting with Garin.

FRUTE OF DANELAND. (*Vide* "Gudrun Lay.") One of Horant's men (*vide* "Horant") who came with him to King Hettel and formed one of the embassy sent to King Hagen (*vide* "Hagen and Hettel"). He also took part in the struggles described in "Gudrun" (*q.v.*).

FUAMNACH. Wife of Midir the Proud (*q.v.*), who took as his second bride, Etain (*q.v.*), whose great beauty and grace evoked the jealousy of Fuamnach. So by magic art she transformed her rival into a butterfly.

FURION. Nephew to Archelous (*q.v.*); was slain by Esplandian (*q.v.*) after his conquest over Archelous.

G

GAE BOLG. In Irish romance, a terrible weapon, thrown with the foot. If it entered into an enemy's body it filled every part of him with its barbs. The thrust of this sword was taught by Skatha (*q.v.*) to Cuchulain (*q.v.*).

GAHERIS (1). Nephew to King Arthur (*q.v.*). (*Vide* "Morte d'Arthur.")

GAHERIS (2), **SIR.** Son of King Lot, brother of Gawaine and Gareth, a knight of the court of Arthur, sometime friend of Sir Tristram. He was killed by Sir Lancelot in the rescue of Guinevere from the stake. (*Vide* "Morte d'Arthur.")

GAHMURET. The father of Parzival or Percival, alluded to in Wolfram von Eschenbach's *Parzival* (*q.v.*). He went to the East, took service with Baruc, and won the love of the heathen Queen Belakane, to whom he promised to return, and by whom he had a son Feirefiz (*q.v.*). Instead of returning to her he became attached to Herzeloyde, who was attracted to him by his prowess at a tournament, and whom he married on condition that he might go tourneying every month. Hearing that his old lord Baruc was in danger, he hastened to him and was slain.

GAIMAR, GEOFFREY. Translated Geoffrey of Monmouth's *Historia Regum Britanniæ* into Anglo-Norman verse shortly after it was written. This he did at the request of the lady to whose household he was attached, Constance, wife of Ralph Fitz Gilbert, a powerful baron of the North in Stephen's time. The copy of Geoffrey from which Gaimar translated was obtained through a Yorkshire baron, Walter Espec, from Robert, Earl of Gloucester, to whom the original work had been dedicated. Gaimar continued the British Chronicle by adding a metrical history of the Anglo-Saxon kings. Wace's *Brut* caused Gaimar's book to fall out of request, and only a portion of it is now known to be extant. He also translated *Havelok the Dane* (*q.v.*) from the French.

GALAAD. Son of Joseph, of the Castle of Galafort. Joseph hears a voice from heaven which calls on him to beget a son.

GALACIAN. A Saracen King alluded to in the romance of *Ogier of Denmark*. Sadone (*q.v.*) knocks out three of his teeth for opposing the freedom of Ogier.

GALAHAD, SIR. Son of Lancelot ; famous in Arthurian legend for his success in the quest of the Holy Grail. With him are associated Sir Perceval, Bors, and Lancelot. It is recorded that after the quest his soul leaves his body, and is borne heavenwards by angels, whilst his body is buried.

His first appearance seems to have been at the Round Table. He is hailed to the " Seat Perilous " on which this was written : " This is Galahad's seat." Queen Guinevere is told of the advent of the new knight, and her ladies exclaim, " He shall end the wonders of Great Britain, and through him the Maimed King shall be healed." Sir Galahad, among all the knights, is the only one who successfully draws the sword from the block of red marble on which is written that none may draw it save " the best knight in the world." Lancelot refuses to essay the venture, exclaiming that " the wonders of the Holy Grail are about to begin," although Gawain, Perceval, and others try, and signally fail. On the morrow, at King Bagdemagus's suggestion, all the questers, Galahad first, swear to maintain the quest for a

year and a day, and longer if need be. After the queen had taken leave of Lancelot, and Arthur had vainly tried to force a shield on Sir Galahad, the questers set off together and pass the first night at Vagan's Castle. After five days Sir Galahad comes to an abbey where he finds King Bagdemagus and Ywain and the rest. The abbey contains a shield which no knight save the destined one may take and go unslain or unhurt. Sir Galahad proves to be the rightful knight, and takes possession of it. King Bagdemagus would fain have taken it, but is overthrown by a White Knight, who admits Sir Galahad's rightful ownership. One of the first of Sir Galahad's allegorical adventures, as recounted in the *Quete del Saint Graal*, appears to be that he draws near a tomb in an abbey graveyard, whence issues a voice telling him not to approach and drive it out. But he does so, and smoke in man's form emerges ; on opening the tomb a dead knight's body is found lying therein. This is cast out. These things are a symbol : the hard tombstone signifies the " hardheartedness of the world " (the hardship which Jesus Christ had in this world) ; the dead body those dead in sin. The smoke was a devil who fled from Galahad because he was a virgin.

The next day Sir Galahad sets out accompanied by Melians (*q.v.*), a youth who had begged to be allowed to serve him, and whom he had knighted. They separate at a cross-road. Melians takes the left-hand road in spite of warning, comes to a tent where hangs a golden crown, seizes it, meets a strange knight who overthrows and had slain him but for Galahad coming to the rescue and overcoming first one, and then a second assailant. Melians is taken to an abbey to be tended, and learns that the two knights who almost overpowered him were his pride in taking the left-hand path, and his covetousness in carrying off the crown of gold. Galahad then enters a hermitage to pray, and hears a voice bidding him proceed to the Castle of Maidens and rid it of its many evils. He encounters on the way seven knights whom he must overcome. Such was the custom of the castle. He forces them to fight, and an old priest brings him the keys of the castle. He finds therein numberless maidens, and learns that the former lord of the castle had been, with his son, slain by the seven knights who had striven beforehand to carry off his daughter. She foretold that as they had gained the castle for a maiden's sake, they would lose it through a maiden, and be overcome by a single knight, whereupon they determined to make prisoner every maiden passing that way. Galahad delivers the captives, and puts a daughter of the former duke in possession of the castle. He learns then that the seven brothers have been slain by Gawain, Gheriot, and Ywain. Sir Galahad, after wandering about a while adventureless, encounters Sir Lancelot and Perceval, who attack him, not knowing his arms (shield). He overcomes them and hurries off, being ashamed to have fought with his friends, whom a recluse recognizes and informs him of their identity. Lancelot starts in pursuit of "The Unknown Knight."

We now find that Sir Galahad, after "numberless adventures," finds himself opposed to Gawain and Hector de Mares in a tournament; he deals the former such a blow as knocks him out of the saddle. He is brought to the ship wherein are Perceval and Bors by a damsel, who accompanies them until, fourteen days' sail from Logres, they come to a desert isle off which is another ship, on which is written (according to the *Morte d'Arthur*) that those who would enter should see they were full of faith. The damsel then tells Perceval she is his sister, daughter of King Pellehem. They enter the ship and find a rich bed with a crown at its head, and at its foot a sword six inches out of the scabbard, its tip a stone of all the colours in the world, its handle of the bones of two beasts, the serpent Papagast, the fish Orteniaus; it is covered with a cloth whereon is written that only the first of his line would grasp the sword. Perceval and Bors both essay vainly. Galahad, on being asked, sees written on the blade that he only should draw who could strike better than the others. The damsel tells the story of the sword as follows: When the ship came to the kingdom of Logres there was war between King Labor, father to the Maimed King, and King Urlain, heretofore Saracen, but newly baptized. Once Urlain, discomfited, fled to the ship, and finding therein the sword, drew it and slew King Labor (according to Birch-Hirschfeld's text, Labor slays Urlain with it). That was the first blow struck with the sword in the kingdom of Logres, and there came from it such pestilence and destruction in the land of the two kingdoms that it was afterwards called the Waste Land. When Urlain re-entered the ship he fell down dead. Galahad, further examining the sword, finds the scabbard of serpent's skin, but the hangings of poor stuff. On the scabbard is written that the wearer must surpass his fellows, and the hangings be changed only by a king's daughter and she a maid ; on turning the sword over, the other side is found black as pitch, and bearing words that he who should praise it most should blame it most in his greatest need. Further words show that King Pelles, called the Maimed King, might not be healed till Galahad came. Later in the chronicle Galahad is urged to go to the assistance of the Maimed King. Sir Perceval now seems to assume Sir Galahad's sword. Taking up the story again with Sir Galahad, we now find that he comes to an abbey wherein is King Mordrains, who knows his approach, and asks that he may die in his arms ; Galahad takes him on his breast, Mordrains dies, and all his wounds are found healed. Galahad cools the boiling fountain by putting his hand in it. Galahad delivers from the tomb where he had been burning three hundred and fifty-four years, his relative Symeu, who thus expiated his sin against Joseph of Arimathea. Galahad rides five years before he comes to the house of the Maimed King and during all the five years Perceval bears him company, and within that time they achieve the great adventures of the kingdom of Logres (i.e. cast out the evil adventures of the Island of Britain). One day they met Bors, who in the five years had not been in bed four times. The three come to Castle Corbenic. Sir Galahad alone can make the broken sword whole, and it is then given to Bors. Later in the chronicle Joseph gives the sacrament to Sir Galahad, and explains that the Grail is the dish of the Last Supper, and that Galahad shall see it more fully in the City of Sarras, whither it is going (Britain being unworthy of it), and whither he is to follow it with Perceval and Bors ; but as he must not leave the land without healing the Maimed King he is to take some of the blood off the Grail lance (q.v.) and therewith anoint his legs. Galahad asks why all may not come with him ; but Christ says they are twelve who have eaten as the Apostles were twelve, and they must separate as the Apostles separated. Galahad then heals the Maimed King, who goes into an abbey of white monks. The three companions, after sending messages to Arthur's court through Estrois de Gariles and Claudius, son of King Claudas, come to Solomon's ship, wherein they find the Holy Grail. They set sail, and on landing bury Perceval's sister, heal a cripple to help them to carry the Grail table, are cast in prison by King Escorant for a year, and are fed by the Holy Grail. At Escorant's death Galahad is made king, fashions a tree of gold and precious stones over the Grail, and prays before it every morning, as do his companions. On the anniversary of Galahad's crowning the three see before the Holy Vessel a man clad like a bishop, who begins Mass and calls Galahad to see what he had so longed to see. At the sight Galahad trembles very greatly, and he thanks God for letting him see that which tongue may not describe nor heart think, and begs that he may pass away from this earthly life to the heavenly one. The bishop then gives him the body of God, and reveals himself as Josephes, son of Joseph of Arimathea. Galahad kisses Perceval and Bors, and sends greetings to Lancelot through Bors. Galahad is borne heavenwards, and his body is buried, the vessel and the bloody lance are also borne upwards. Since then there has been no man bold enough to say that he has seen the Holy Grail. (*Vide* "Morte d'Arthur" and "Grail, Holy.")

GALICIA, KING OF. (*Vide* "Florice and Blanchfleur.*") An ally of the King of Portugal, who made war against Prince Felix, whose Saracen influence oppressed the people.

GALIHODIN, SIR. Brother to Sir Lancelot. After an inconspicuous career he was presented with the dukedom of Saintonge in France by Lancelot, who for a time assumed the rôle of ruler over that country. (*Vide* "Morte d'Arthur.")

GALIHUD, SIR. Brother to Lancelot, and knight of the Round Table. In Arthurian romance he is appointed, by his brother, overlord of the earldom of Perigot in France.

GALIHULT, SIR. Knight of the Round Table. He was noted for his prowess in tournaments. (*Vide* "Morte d'Arthur.")

GALIOIN. In Irish romance, one of the three groups of the Firbolgs (*q.v.*).

GANILO or **GUENES.** A peer of Charlemagne and stepfather of Roland. Out of his implacable hatred of his stepson he conspired with Marsile, the pagan King of Saragossa, to cut him off with the Frankish rear-guard at Roncevalles. For this he was tried by the peers, and sentenced to be torn to pieces by horses (*vide* "Song of Roland"). He reappears in Ariosto's *Orlando*

Furioso as Ganoloni, or Gano de Pontierie, the head of the race of Maganza, a tribe of traitors, who were dangerous to all with whom they were connected.

GANORT. Alluded to in the *Grand Saint Graal* (*q.v.*) as Lord of Galafort, a "Saracen" stronghold. He receives the Grail company hospitably, and shortly after their arrival he and his folk are baptized, a hundred and fifty who refuse being drowned. Over their bodies a tower is built. (*Vide* "Tower of Marvels.") The King of Northumberland, hearing of Ganort's conversion, summons him to his court, and on his refusal attacks him, but is defeated and slain.

GARACH. A battle in Irish romance, fought on the plain bearing the same name, between Queen Maev (*q.v.*) and the Ulstermen, in which the latter were victorious.

GARALAS. A knight alluded to in the *Conte del Graal* (*q.v.*) as the knight of the damsel who steals the hound mentioned in that romance. He is also the brother of the Knight of the Tomb (*q.v.*) and is overcome by Perceval.

GARCIA PEREZ DE VARGAS. This romantic poem of Spain recounts an adventure of a distinguished warrior and native of Toledo, who fought under King Ferdinand, surnamed "The Saint" during the warfare by which the Moorish power in Spain was overthrown. The incident of his valour and prowess about to be related, occurred about the beginning of the siege of Seville in the year 1248, is contained in Lockhart's *Spanish Ballads*, and is taken from the Spanish history of Juan de Mariana. King Ferdinand stood one day on the hill watching two cavaliers riding along the glen. They were Don Garcia Perez and a knight, who urged him to ride on quickly as he saw the gleam of the helm and lance of the Moorish host in the distance. Vargas returned that he was ready to meet any one, but the knight turned quickly and fled to the camp, leaving his friend alone. Seven Moors came up to him with haughty mien, and resplendent in armour, but Vargas met them calmly. The Moors, recognizing him by the Red Cross and the Tree upon his shield, did not speak. Vargas removed the casque from his head, and noticed that the scarf he had worn was gone. Thinking he had dropped it, he looked around and discovered that the Moors had picked it up and looped it on a spear. As the scarf had been given to him by his lady-love he preferred to fight for it rather than leave it with them, so he rode furiously among them and called upon them to lay down his lady's pledge. They resisted, but were ultimately overthrown, and when he returned to camp he was the proud bearer of the scarf thrown around his breast. His sword was red with blood, and seven green turbans sorely hacked, hung upon his pommel.

GARETH, SIR. Or Beaumaris, Knight of the " Round Table." He married Dame Liones (*q.v.*) of the Castle Perilous. Subsequently slain by Sir Lancelot, in the rescue of Guinever from the Stake. (*Vide* " Morte d'Arthur.")

GARIN DE MONTGLANE. A sub-cycle of the Charlemagne cycle (*q.v.*), consisting of twenty-four separate romances, eighteen of which are concerned with and included in the sub-cycle of William of Orange (*q.v.*). The first six romances of the sub-cycle recount the adventures of the House of Montglane or Narbonne. *Les Enfances Garin de Montglane* tells how Garin, son of Duke Savary of Aquitaine, fights first in Sicily, procures atonement for the wrongs of his mother, and proceeds to the court of Charlemagne. He conquers the territory of Montglane, and weds the Lady Mohiller, the details of his marriage occupying the second romance, the *Garin de Montglane* proper. By this lady he has four sons, Hernant de Beaulande, Gerard de Viana (*q.v.*), Renin de Gennes, and Milles de Poule. Each of the three first is the subject of a separate romance. *Hernant de Beaulande* tells how the hero conquers Aquitaine, marries Fregonde, and becomes the father of Aimeri de Narbonne. The *Renin de Gennes* tells of the success of its hero at Genoa, when he becomes the father of the famous Oliver and Aude. *Gerard de Viana* will be found treated under a separate heading as being important for its picture of the early quarrel of Roland and Oliver. We then pass to the third generation in *Aimeri de Narbonne*, and the events subsequent to Roncesvaux. On his return from that battle Aimeri rescues Barboune from pagan hands. He marries Hermengart, sister of the King of the Lombards, repulses the Saracens who endeavour to rescue Narbonne, and becomes the father of twelve children, one of whom is the famous William of Orange (*q.v.*).

GARIN OF ANSÉUNE. (Cycle of William of Orange.) A scion of the race of Aymery, and father of Vivian. (*Vide* " Enfances Vivian.")

GARIN THE LORRAINER. A very popular twelfth-century epic, the characters in which were genuinely historical. But it is replete with anachronisms. The story is laid in the eighth century and commences with a description of the Vandal invasion of France in the time of Charles Martel. Hervi, Duke of Metz, defeated the Saracens (or Vandals) at Soissons, and after Charles' death at Troyes, had his son, Pepin, crowned. Hervi married and had two sons—Garin the nominal hero of the poem, and Bego perhaps a greater hero. When the Vandals besieged Metz, Hervi asked Pepin's assistance, which was refused, so he offered to be vassal to Anseis of Cologne, who came to his aid and conquered the enemy. Hervi was killed, so Anseis took possession of Metz. Hervi's sons escaped to their uncle, the Bishop of Chalons. They afterwards went to the court of France, and Count Hardré brought them up with his own two sons. News came that Richard of Normandy was ravaging Beauvais, and the four young knights set out to fight for the king. They defeated Richard, subdued Flanders, and Garin added Gascony and Poitou to his territory, and gained back Metz. Then Thierry, King of Savoy, was besieged by four Moorish kings of Spain, and applied for aid to Pepin. Pepin refused, but the four knights persuaded him to let them help Thierry. Garin and Bego commanded, and a terrible battle ensued. The invaders were routed, but Thierry was mortally wounded. When dying, he offered his daughter, Blanchflower (fifteen and a half years old) to Garin in marriage, who accepted on condition of Pepin's approval. The king gave his consent, but this arrangement displeased Fromont, who quarrelled with Garin, and a

hotly contested battle took place, in which Garin was victorious. Fromont fled to his cousin Odo at St. Quentin and told his story. Droo of Flanders told him he could find as good a wife for him in the person of Hilesend, sister of Baldwin, of Flanders. Droo went to Baldwin, proposed Fromont as a husband for his sister, saying Hardré was dead and Fromont would succeed him, but concealed the fact of his having lost Soissons and his other lands. Hilesend consented to be married at once, and the day after the marriage Baldwin discovered the trick they had played on him. Although much annoyed, he made the best of it, and advised Fromont to invade Cambrai, the property of Huo, a nephew of the two Lorrainers. Isoré, Fromont's nephew, headed the invaders, and when Huo saw who was leading, he appealed to Isoré, reminding him of past services. Touched by this appeal, Isoré refused to fight, but Baldwin appeared with 30,000 men, and Huo sent a message to the king and Garin. When Huo's letter came, Garin told Pepin of Fromont's unworthy behaviour, and the king assembled his forces and marched out against him, sending a message to Bego. Bernard of Naisil had meanwhile gone to Fromont's assistance, and had attacked Aubry in Dijon. The king's message found Bego being entertained by Hardré's sons, who were unaware of their father's death. Bego set out at once, excusing himself because the king needed him, but hearing from Aubry, went first to assist him. On his way to Cambrai, he destroyed Lyons and several other towns, and, after conquering Burgundy he invaded Champagne. He then attacked Bernard at his castle of Naisil, and took him prisoner, after which he went on to besiege Verdun. He then got news that Pepin had summoned Fromont, who refused to answer for his misdeeds, and that he and Garin needed his assistance against the men of Bordeaux. He then set off for St. Quentin, pillaging every place on his way. A great battle ensued, which began with a quarrel between Bego and Isoré. Bego was wounded, and while being nursed sent Aubry to do battle for him, but on hearing he had been taken prisoner, he himself arose, and after some fighting, surrounded St. Quentin, cutting off all supplies. Bernard, still a prisoner, sent word to Fromont to make terms with Pepin. It was agreed that Fromont should plead his cause before the king. Bernard and Aubry exchanged, and the army broke up. The high court met at Paris, where many nobles arrived, the Lorrainers being in great force. Blanchflower attended. The Archbishop of Rheims advised the king rather to marry her himself than give her to Garin. After seeing how lovely she was, he consented. Next day, the king summoned Fromont, commanding him to make peace with the Lorrainers. The banns were being proclaimed between Blanchflower and Garin when a monk appeared and forbade the marriage on the score of relationship between the pair. Some altercation took place, and Fromont offered his two sisters to Garin and Bego if Blanchflower would marry his brother, but the king now said he would marry Blanchflower himself. Garin was ill pleased with this, but Bego persuaded him not to object, and the marriage took place. During the ceremony, Bernard insulted Garin, who was

holding the golden cup, and Garin gave him a heavy blow with it. A general fight took place, resulting in Fromont's men being defeated. Bernard carried a lying story about Garin to Pepin, which he believed. Garin denied it, and offered to meet Bernard in single combat, but the king refused his pledge, so Bego took up the challenge for his brother. Bego was victorious, and there was great rejoicing in Paris. Bernard escaped, and vowing vengeance on the Lorrainers, went to prepare his castle for defence. Peace was made with Fromont, but when Bernard began to ravage all the land round his castle, Fromont was asked by the king if he would side against his uncle, and he agreed. Bernard defended himself bravely and refused to surrender, till he found that his caves had been discovered by Bego and walled up. It was agreed he should keep his castle and indemnify Garin, but Bego destroyed the castle. The king reproved him for this, and gave Bernard liberty to rebuild it. Soon afterwards the queen advised the king to get wives for the Lorrainers, to prevent them marrying any of Fromont's kin, so the king went to Duke Milo of Gascony and offered suitors for the latter's daughters. The duke said they were in love with Garin and Bego, and as these were the two knights of whom the king had spoken, there was small difficulty in the way. Garin married Alice and Bego married Beatrice, and both marriages brought much happiness. Garin was married at Metz, having given up his wife's share in her father's property to Bego, and taken over all his father's lands. He had a son called Girbert, and Bego had two sons, Hernaut and

Gerin. News of these double marriages came to Thibaut, who determined to surprise Bego on his return home and carry off Beatrice. Bego, being warned of this by a pilgrim, was prepared for the ambush, and defended himself bravely. He was seriously wounded, but the Bordelais were driven off. Bego then fortified his castle of Belin, where he was besieged by overwhelming numbers. He found a messenger, Gallopin a ne'er-do-well, who went to King Pepin with the news to ask help. The queen incited the king to go to help Bego. Bernard, on attempting to make mischief, and insulting the queen, was attacked by Garin, and nearly killed by the people. Before help arrived, Bego sallied forth, with a small number of men, but would have been killed had Garin and Aubrey not come in time. The king ordered all the property of the rebels to be destroyed, which order Bego carried out. Meanwhile, Bernard showing the mark on his face left by Garin's attack, and rousing the anger of his kinsmen, they raised an army against the Lorrainers. At first the men of Bordeaux were victorious, and a tourney was proposed. Garin was too ill to accept a challenge, but Bego did, and he picked out Rigaut, son of Hervi the villein, who challenged Fromondin, son of Fromont. Bego and Aubry had lain down to rest before the combat. They were wakened by a lad who brought the news that the royalists were getting the worst of it. Bego rushed out, fighting furiously, and carried all before him. Rigaut defeated Fromondin, and won great praise for his prowess at the tourney. The Lorrainers and the Bordelais met again in combat, but peace was

made by the king, and this lasted seven years. The second song ends here.

After a time of rest in his castle, Bego began to weary to see his brother Garin, and told Beatrice he had heard of a wild boar in a wood, the head of which he would like to take to Garin. Beatrice reminded him that the wood was in the land of Count Baldwin, his enemy, and that she had a presentiment that if he went there he would never come back. Bego was quite determined to go in spite of his wife's warning, and left next day. When he reached Valenciennes he stayed with Berenger, who promised to show him where he would find the boar, and also warned him of his many enemies. The monster killed nearly all the hounds. The huntsmen lost sight of Bego, went back to Valenciennes, and Bego who pursued the boar and killed it, spent the night in the forest. Next morning he kindled a fire, which was seen by a forester who noticed Bego's rich dress and accoutrements. The forester went back to Fromont at Lens and told what he had seen to the seneschal, who sent six men with the forester to kill Bego and share the spoil. Thibaut heard of the plot and joined them. After hearing Bego's account of how he killed the boar, they attacked him and he was killed by a steel arrow shot by the forester's nephew. They left Bego alone in the forest on a bier, and on arriving at the palace all came out to see the dead boar, but Fromont saw that no ordinary huntsman could be the owner of the spoil they had brought, and sent for the body. Great was his grief and consternation when he found that Bego had been killed. He wrote to Garin, offering to have

Thibaut and all connected with the murder killed. He promised to give great treasure of gold and silver, have 10,000 Masses sung, and swore he had been ignorant of the whole thing. He sent for an abbot, a nephew of Garin, and the body was consecrated. The funeral procession then started for Metz. It was met by Rigaut, who went to Paris to tell the news to the empress, and thence back to Blaives to put it on its defence, ravaging the surrounding country. When Garin saw the bier and found Begc on it, he fainted, then threatened vengeance against Fromont. The abbot gave them Fromont's letter, and Garin first decided to see Beatrice, who was at Balin. She had heard the sad news, and saw only sorrow in the future. Bego was buried in a chapel near Berlin in a coffin of grey marble and a tomb of fine gold, with his likeness, and written above it : "This was the best that sat on charger." Garin made peace with Fromont on the understanding that he would keep his promise, but Fromont broke it afterwards, and one of his kinsmen freed the prisoners. Garin and Fromont each pleaded his cause before the king. Pepin tried to persuade them to make a truce for a certain number of years ; he had difficulty in quelling a hot fight between them at the court, and they quarrelled whenever they were not under his observation. This constant warfare, continued for a long time, the queen always taking the part of Garin and Bego even against the king. The Lorrainers in the end got the best of it, Garin despoiling the whole country, and at last the queen went on an embassy of peace to Garin. The conclusion tells of the death of Garin.

There are two versions—one which seems the more ancient is to be found in a MS. at the Arsenal Library of Paris, and which M. Dumérie assigns to the latter part of the thirteenth century. The other more popular one is by John of Flagy (q.v.), and it is guaranteed by even older MS. In both stories Garin is represented as having been attacked by overwhelming numbers, and having defended himself with superhuman courage. In one version fourteen men attacking him at once, kill him, and in the other, he is surrounded by foes while he is in a chapel. The end of the poem is to be found in Mone's *Untersuchungen zur Geschichte der Teutschen Heldensage*. There are one or two more modern poems in connection with the sub-cycle of the Lorrainers, full of love intrigues and combats with the Saracens.

The language of "Garin" and many characteristics of the poem point to a date between the eleventh and twelfth centuries. The imperial power was beginning to be acknowledged, but the story is more confined to personal combats than national valour. Some of the incidents tally with events in the reign of Louis the Fat about 1108, yet it is most probable the legend of the Lorrainers must have been made about more ancient heroes who engaged in the first struggle between the West and East. Even as far back as 814 to 843 in Nithard's history we find many names mentioned which appeared in the epic of the Lorrainers. For centuries Garin's adventures were believed to be real even to some degree by the Benedictine Calmet, in his *History of Lorraine*. The feudal system with its good and bad points is well exemplified, and the

K

quality of the love between the
sexes is higher and purer and more
domestic than it was in later years.
The religious element is not strong,
although it occurs in some touching
incidents. The dramatic power
is great, the scenes are represented to the mind's eye most
vividly, although the want of the
supernatural element is rather
remarkable, and *Garin the
Lorrainer* may be said to hold its
own in literature as a great epic.
(*Vide* Ludlow's *Popular Epics of
the Middle Ages.*)

GARLON. In Arthurian romance, a
knight who went about invisible,
slaying better knights than himself. Balin (*q.v.*) meeting with
several victims of his cruelty,
traced him to the castle of King
Pellam of Listeneise, where he
met him at table. Garlon, irritated
at Balin's close observation of
him, struck him, whereupon Balin
slew him. (*Vide* ' Pellam.")

GARNIER. In the Charlemagne
cycle of romance nephew and
ally of Garin and Bego. He suggested to William of Orange that
Nîmes could be taken by concealing his men in barrels. William
took the hint, and secured the
city by the said stratagem. (*Vide*
" Charroi de Nîmes.")

GARSIE. (*Vide* " Sir Otuel.") A
Saracen Prince, King of Lombardy, who was determined to
abolish Christianity throughout
Christendom. He sent a challenge
to Charlemagne by Sir Outel,
threatening to ravage France if
he did not renounce the Christian
faith. His army was completely
routed by Charlemagne, and he
was taken prisoner by Sir Outel,
who had become a Christian, and
fought on that side. Afterwards,
when Garsie found it expedient,

he embraced Christianity and was
baptized by Archbishop Turpin.

GAWAIN. A hero-knight frequently
alluded to in both Celtic and
Norman Arthurian romance, in
many of the incidents connected
with which he is the central figure.
It is highly probable that he was
the principal character around
which a separate sub-cycle of
adventures clustered, but the early
forms of this have in all likelihood
been merged in the greater body
of later Arthurian romance. No
long romance exists which details
his life and adventures as in the
case of Perceval or Lancelot, but
in the *Conte del Graal* of Chrétien
de Troyes and the *Parzival* of
Wolfram von Eschenbach his adventures occupy as much space
as those of the titular hero of these
poems. In the *Diu Krône* of
Heinrich von dem Turlin he
succeeds in the Grail quest where
Perceval has failed, and in the
Chevalier au Lion and *Chevalier de
la Charrette*, both by Chrétien, he
plays an important part. Gawain
is represented as the *beau-ideal* of
knightly chivalry and bravery,
whose " strength is as the strength
of ten, because his heart is pure."
In his Celtic form of Gwalchmai
ap Gwyar (Hawk of Battle), Gawain
is mentioned in the Welsh Triads
as one of the " golden-tongued
knights of the court of King
Arthur," and his powers of per-
suasion are frequently alluded to
in the Welsh Arthurian tales. In
one triad he is spoken of as one
of " the three learned ones of the
island of Britain." Whereas the
romance versions of the Arthurian
tales represent Gawain as Arthur's
nephew, Celtic tradition regards
him as a son of the king. Gwalchmai, like most of the knights of
the Round Table, was probably a

form of hero-god, demi-god, or deity in course of deterioration, and having regard to his well-known attributes it does not appear to be straining probabilities unwontedly if we derive him from some Celtic deity having affinities with that Ogmios mentioned by Lucian, who, though armed with the club and lion-skin of Hercules, was yet the "exponent of persuasive speech," drawing men after him by golden cords attached from his tongue to their ears—the prototype of the Irish Ogma (*q.v.*). Some authorities, however, describe him as the lineal successor of the sun.

GAYFEROS. In Spanish romance he appears as a kinsman of Roland, and husband of Charlemagne's daughter Melisenda, who was carried off soon after their marriage as a Moorish captive to Saragossa. He set out in search of her, but after a fruitless seven years he returned to Paris. One day, on his return, as he played dice with the emperor's admiral, Charlemagne reproved him, saying, "Were you as ready to handle arms as dice, you would go to the rescue of your wife." The insulted Gayferos, enraged at the emperor's taunt, and gathering from his speech the whereabouts of his wife, rushed off to Roland in search of horse and armour. The confused uncle was not prepared to hire his steed nor risk his worthy sword, but seeing his nephew half mad with rage he finally consented. Gayferos mounted the spirited horse and rode off in the direction of Saragossa. The journey was swiftly accomplished, and meeting no opposition at the gates of the Moorish city, he rode straight to the house in which lay his captive wife. On seeing the apparently strange knight coming toward her window, she appealed to him for help, and on his responding, and at the same time raising the vizor of his helmet, she was overjoyed to find that her deliverer was her husband. She straightway mounted the horse and the pair set off toward the city gates. A Moor, who had watched the proceedings from a distance, gave the signal of alarm, soon to be followed by the pursuit of seven columns of horsemen. Melisenda, recognizing the horse on which they rode to be Roland's, remembered that by loosening the girth, opening the breast-plate, and driving the spurs into its side, it would leap across any barrier, informed her husband of this, who hastily did as she directed, and drove the steed toward the wall, which it cleared with comparative ease. The Moors, who had hotly followed them, now gave up the chase and returned to the city. On went the rejoicing pair, who drawing near their destination were met by Montesinos their kinsman, who had journeyed forth to welcome them. Embracing each other, the party rode on to Paris, which the triumphant Don Gayferos entered with the daughter of Charlemagne, who could no more reproach him as faint-hearted. (*Vide* Lockhart's *Spanish Ballads.*)

GEENA MAC LUGA. In Irish romance, son of Luga and the warrior daughter of Finn (*q.v.*). He was nurtured by "Fair Mane," who had brought up many of the Fianna (*q.v.*) to manhood. Arrived at warrior age, he made his covenant of fealty to Finn, who gave him the captaincy of a band. But Mac Luga proved slothful, selfish, boastful, and cruel. So at last the Fians under him, complaining to

Finn, requested him to choose between themselves and Mac Luga, who was then questioned, but could not explain satisfactorily why the Fians refused him their allegiance. Then Finn taught him the Maxims of the Fianna.

GELORWYDD. The "Gem of Baptism." (*Vide* "Gododin.") The enemy mocked him, for administering extreme unction on the battle-field, with his own blood for oil.

GENERYDES, THE METRICAL ROMANCE OF. The question of authorship of the English version and the source of the story are obscure. We possess no clue as to the original ; but the present version, the MS. of which exists in the library of Trinity College, Cambridge, is dated from about 1440. The French version is more complete, but almost identical in substance. Auferius, King of India, marries Serenydes, daughter to the King of Africa. She proves unfaithful, and carries on an intrigue with her husband's steward, Sir Amelok. While hunting one day, the king strays and meets with a maiden named Sereyne, the daughter of the King of Syria. On her he begets Generydes. When old enough Generydes appears at the court of Auferius, whose wife tempts him ; but declining to give way to her he courts the disfavour of Sir Amelok. This knight makes Generydes' life so intolerable that he quits the court and proceeds to the city of Mountener, the capital of Persia. He becomes attached to the court of the Sultan Goffore, and falls in love with his daughter Clarionas. Meanwhile, Sir Amelok rebels against and seizes Auferius' capital. The King of India goes to Syria, meets once more with Sereyne,

and becomes king of that country. A son, Ismael, is born to them. The Sultan of Persia turns against Generydes and accuses him of seducing his daughter Clarionas. The King of Egypt, Belen, invades the sultan's lands and demands the hand of Clarionas. The sultan prepares to defend his city against the invader and sets Generydes free. A terrific battle ensues between the rival leaders, in which fight, an innumerable host of kings are engaged. King Belen and Generydes meet in deadly combat. After prolonging the duel over several days, the King of Egypt takes flight. Generydes recognizes his father, Auferius, and meets with his brother Ismael. Belen, King of Egypt, dies, and his son, Gwynan, succeeds him. The newly-appointed king attempts to carry off Clarionas, but Generydes frustrates the plot. A second attempt is successful. Generydes pursues Gwynan and gains access to his betrothed's chamber. They escape together, and Sir Yuell, knight to Gwynan, follows after them, but Generydes slays him. The lovers leave for Syria. Amelok, the treacherous steward, dies. Auferius falls sick and succumbs. Generydes ascends his father's throne as King of India, when he marries Clarionas.

GEOFFREY OF MONMOUTH. Archdeacon of Monmouth and later Bishop of St. Asaph, author of the famous *Historia Regum Brittaniæ*, dedicated to his patron Robert, Earl of Gloucester, which we know he had composed as early as 1139, although it is thought that he wrote a later revision of his history. In the *Historia*, Geoffrey undertook to relate the history of the Britons from the time of Brutus to the death of Cadwallader, the last of the native British kings. His material is divided into twelve books, of which five books are occupied with the Arthurian History. Geoffrey lived at a period when England was responding to the intellectual stimulus that had come to her with the Norman conquest, and when her literary life had begun to blossom afresh after a state of dormancy. This influence was due to the influx of the scholars, chroniclers, and minstrels who accompanied the Normans in their conquest of Britain. The trend of the times caused the Normans to exercise a taste for literature of a less fantastic and mysterious nature than formerly. Geoffrey was shrewd enough to perceive the direction of men's thoughts, and being possessed of high intelligence and a mind distinctly inventive, was quick to exercise a great degree of enterprise. As a Latin scholar his style clearly shows his mastery over the language. Geoffrey was a most skilful combiner of romance and history, and we see how in his book he raised a national hero, already the centre of legend and myth, to the position of a monarch, whose legends, by substituting in them Norman customs for British, became a powerful factor in the Normanizing of England. Above all, he raised the standard of literature, dignifying popular national story, and determining definitely the form of Arthurian legend. (*Vide* "Historia Regum Britanniæ.")

GEORGE A GREEN. A pound-keeper of Wakefield, who resisted Robin Hood, Will Scarlet, and Little John single-handed when they attempted to trespass on land near Wakefield. He is often alluded to as a type of resolute-mindedness, a man who would do his duty come what may.

GEORGE A GREEN, THE HISTORY OF. A prose romance, probably of Elizabethan origin, dealing with the life and adventures of George a Green, pinder or constable of Wakefield, and the supposed rival and later the friend of Robin Hood. His exploits against the rebel Earl of Kendal and Lord Bonvile, and their discomfiture are first related, after which his meeting and strife with Robin Hood and his merry men and the rivalry in beauty of their respective mistresses, Maid Marian and Beatrice, is told in spirited fashion, as is the story of the riot of shoemakers in Merry Bradstead, and the coming of King Richard Cœur de Lion to that town. The tale ends with the marriage of Beatrice and the lusty pinder.

GERARD OF COMMARCHIS. (Cycle of William of Orange.) A knight who bore a message from Vivian to his uncle William of Orange, craving succour. Guichard, younger brother of Vivian, and nephew of William of Orange (*q.v.*), when his brother was hard pressed by the Saracens at Aliscans, though only fifteen years of age, cut his way to the front to succour him. (*Vide* "Enfances Vivian.")

GERARD OF ROUSSILLION. A sub-cycle of the Charlemagne cycle, written in two texts, one Provençal of the thirteenth century, the other in Frenchified Provençal of the twelfth. Both are imperfect, the latter, which is in the Harleian collection of the British Museum, especially so. According to many authors of the twelfth and thirteenth centuries, they were very popular, as is attested by the frequent repetitions which fill their pages. The story recounts how Gerard is for sixty years at war with Charles Martel, but is constantly worsted. The poem is wearisome in the extreme, the many fights and combats being merely repetitions of each other, but the most interesting portion is that which describes Gerard's wanderings with his wife after his final defeat—perhaps a modern interpolation. It is probable that we do not possess the original conclusion of the story, as we find the countess rather tamely taking to good works, and so influencing her husband that he resolved to do likewise. *Vide* edition by Mr. Francisque Michel, 1837.

GERARD OF VIANA. One of the latest poems of the Charlemagne cycle, referred to the thirteenth century. It is written in pentameter tirades with a short line at the end of each, a fact which marks it as being still sung at the date at which it was reduced to writing. It forms part (viewed in a different relation) of the cycle of the kinship of Aymery. Its subject is the struggle of Gerard of Viana (Vienne), Aymery's father against the Emperor Charles, and it also embraces the stories of the early rivalry of Roland and Oliver, and the cementing of their friendship. Charles had sworn that he would not rise from before Viana until he had taken it. Roland whilst hawking sees a mallard under the walls of the town and lets fly his hawk, which loses itself in an orchard. Oliver, nephew of Gerard, seizes the bird, and Roland calls to him to give it back, offering him fifteen pounds weight of pure gold for its return. Oliver refuses, and Roland spurs

his steed into the moat, crosses it into the orchard, and seizing Oliver's horse by the reins asks who he is. They exchange names and lineage, and defy each other. Oliver is knighted by Gerard. At verse 323 a new branch begins, in which the early prowess of Oliver is related. For seven years Charles sits before Viana. Roland, wearying of the siege, asks him to proclaim a quintain. Oliver resolves to take part in it, and his fair sister Alda expresses a wish to see the game. Oliver strikes a blow so wonderful that Charles and the Franks are surprised. Seeing ten men approach him, Oliver fears an attack, and kills three of them. The men of Viana join in the skirmish. Roland, seeing Alda, is smitten with love for her, forgets his purpose of jousting with Oliver, and attempts to carry her off. Oliver comes to the rescue, and they break lances. Oliver stuns Roland with a blow on the head, and rescues Alda. He next unhorses a knight called Lambert, who is taken prisoner to Viana, and falls in love with Alda. But he is sent back to the Frankish lines. Oliver returns with him, and is courteously received. He suggests a peace to King Charles, but the latter's terms are so mortifying that Oliver indignantly scouts them. Roland enters the royal tent, and Oliver challenges him to combat alone on the island under Viana. He accepts the challenge on the terms that if Roland be conquered Charlemagne will depart, but if Oliver, then Gerard shall cede Viana. A "felon knight" suggests the murder of Oliver, who, on hearing this, rushes at him and breaks his neck. Being hustled in consequence by the imperial knights, Oliver seizes a stake, and lays about him to such purpose that he slays a number of them. He mounts his steed and returns to Viana. Roland has speech with Alda from the walls, and they exchange mutual expressions of regard. Roland and Oliver fight on the morrow, and, Oliver's weapons being inferior, he is worsted, but he obtains a new sword (Haultclear) from Viana, and the combat is resumed. They engage desperately, until an angel comes between them and bids them cease, telling them that they should reserve their prowess for the paynim. They pledge their love, and become fast friends. Charles, caught in an ambush, whilst hunting, by Gerard's men, grants peace, renders back Gerard's honours, and celebrates the betrothal of Roland and Alda. A Saracen incursion into Gascony is intimated, and the poem ends with a hint of the death of Roland. (*Vide Girard de Viane*, ed P. Tarbé, Reims, 1850.)

GERLINTE. Queen of Ormany, wife of King Ludwig. Mother of Hartmut and Ortrun. (*Vide* " Gudrun Lay " and " Gudrun.") She is depicted as an " evil deviless " who, determined that her son shall win Gudrun for his wife, treats her with the greatest harshness and cruelty in a vain endeavour to break her spirit. On the storming of Cassian city by Herwig's rescuing army she tries to have Gudrun slain, but later has to beg forgiveness and protection. Gudrun's attempt to save her is vain, and she is slain by the fierce Wate (*q.v.*).

GERNOT. (*Vide* " Neibelungenlied.") Son of Ute, and brother to Kriemhild, Gunther, and Giselher. He disclaimed having any hand in the death of Siegfried.

GEROLD. A clerk alluded to by Ordericus Vitalis (1075–1141) as dwelling at the court of William the Conqueror, and singing of " the holy athlete William " (of Orange).

GESTA ROMANORUM. A collection of mediæval tales designed to assist preachers to rouse languid hearers, and to infuse matter of interest into their discourses. The Franciscans and Dominicans, in carrying their doctrine to the poor, may have improved the art of illustrating homily with legend and story. The French Dominican, Vincent of Beauvais, tells in the *Mirror of History* that in his time, the thirteenth century, preachers were wont to stimulate the attention of their audiences by means of tales from Æsop and other profane authors. Among the Harleian MSS. is an ancient collection of 215 stories compiled by a preacher for the use of monastic societies. The compilation known as the *Gesta Romanorum* long retained its popularity, and was printed in 1473. Reprinted a few months later at Louvain, and again in 1480, it was translated into Dutch in 1484, and went through several editions in this country in the succeeding century. When and by whom the collection was made is unknown. Warton thought Bercheur of Poitou to be the compiler because of a passage in the *Philologia Sacra* of Salomon Glassius. The work varies by omission of tales and addition of others in different MSS., and its title " Deeds of the Romans " is a merely arbitrary one, although many of the tales deal with incidents in the lives of the various Roman emperors. Tales from the East were borrowed from the Clericus Disciplina, a Latin dialogue professedly borrowed from the Arabian fabulists, and items from an old Latin translation of the Arabian *Calilah u Damnah* were also utilized in its compilation. The *Gesta Romanorum* contains the germ of the romance of *Sir Guy of Warwick* (*q.v.*), and that of Gower's *Confessio Amantis*, and several of Chaucer's tales. Translation by C. Swan.

GIBICH. King of Worms. (*Vide* " Dietrich of Bern.")

GILBERT (1), SIR. The Bastard. In Arthurian romance a noble knight, eventually slain by Sir Meliot de Logrés (*q.v.*).

GILBERT (2). In the William of Orange cycle, son of Duke Guy of Ardane, who had been captive in the Saracen city of Orange for three years. He escapes therefrom, and his praise of the city so fires the heart of William that he resolves to go thither on a secret journey. He is guided there by Gilbert, who spoke " enough Turkish and African, Bedouin and Basque, to be interpreter."

GILLA DACAR. (The Hard Gilly.) A monarch of the Celtic other world or Land of Faëry, who figures in one of the legends connected with the Irish romance of Dermot (*q.v.*). He required warriors to fight against a rival king, and by a clever artifice decoyed several of the Fianna into his realm. Taking the shape of a deformed churl dragging after him a raw-boned mare, he induced fourteen of the Fianns to mount the animal, which speedily disappeared, carrying off the heroes. Finn and the remaining Fianna took ship in search of their companions, and, after many adventures, discerned them in Faëryland. The tale concludes with the marriage of Finn with

Tasha of the White Arms, daughter of the Faëry King, and the return to Ireland of the Fianna. Gilla Dacar is unquestionably one of those Plutonic figures of the Celtic otherworld, who, in their desire to decoy and retain mortals in their misty realm, exhibit the veritable characteristics of death-gods who have sunk from their original states as such to that of mere monarchs of faëry.

GILVAETHWY. In Welsh legend, son of Don (*q.v.*), nephew of Math (*q.v.*). He fell violently in love with Goewin (*q.v.*), his uncle's footholder. So in order to obtain her, with the aid of Gwydion (*q.v.*), his magician brother, he brought about war with Pryderi (*q.v.*) and Math, on account of the theft of the former's swine. Then when his uncle was engaged in the fight, he stole back to the palace, and forcibly made Goewin his wife. For this treachery the brothers were turned into deer for a year and a day, for the same period into wild swine, and lastly into wolves, after which they were allowed to assume their human forms and natures.

GIRALDUS CAMBRENSIS. A Welsh ecclesiastic of the twelfth century, whose writings, all of them in Latin, include sundry books of a topographical order which are of importance to students of romance. Widely known during his lifetime as Sylvester, a *soubriquet* given him by some of his enemies, his name was really Gerald de Bain ; but like the majority of mediæval authors, he Latinized it, and it is by his *nom de plume* of Giraldus Cambrensis that he is invariably known. He is supposed to have been born about 1146, and his father was one William de Bain, while on his mother's side he was lineally descended from Rhys-ap-Theodor, Prince of South Wales. As a child he showed exceptional aptitude for scholarship, and while still a mere boy he wrote Latin poems, which prove his early familiarity with Latin literature. After travelling on the Continent, he returned to England in 1172, and decided to take holy orders ; and, having been duly ordained, he was appointed to secure payments of tithes in Wales. In 1176, on the death of his uncle, the Bishop of St. David's, the Welsh clergy manifested great eagerness to make the deceased's prelate's see independent of Canterbury, and the canons nominated Giraldus for the vacant post. But the king, Henry II., strenuously opposed this measure, for political motives. Much disgusted, Giraldus left his native land for a while, and went to Paris, where he continued his theological studies. He even pushed so far afield as Bologna, but by 1180 he was on his way back, and on reaching England he went first to Canterbury, where he was entertained by the archbishop. Thereafter he proceeded to Wales, and was appointed commissary to the Bishop of St. David's, but being shocked by the misrule of the latter he soon gave up the charge, and in 1184 he became a chaplain to Henry II. The king sent him to accompany his son John on his expedition to Ireland. He was offered the bishopric of Wexford and Leighlin, and apparently at a later time the see of Ossory ; but he declined them all, and concerned himself instead with the composition of his book, *Itinerarium Hiberniæ*. This was dedicated to Henry II., and it gives an invaluable account of the existing condition of the country, while along with matter of this sort are mixed many Irish stories. Giraldus left Ireland in 1186, and two years later the king, having decided to make a Crusade, sent him and Archbishop Baldwin to preach on its behalf in Wales. He was given an enthusiastic reception, as he tells in his *Itinerarium Cambriæ* (1191), a book which has the same value as his work on Ireland. The English forces now set out for Palestine, and with them went Giraldus along with Baldwin, who intended the former to write a history of the forthcoming Crusade ; but on the death of the king Giraldus was sent back to Wales to try to quiet the unrest there, and so he had perforce to obtain absolution from the crusading vow he had taken previously. Giraldus now declared himself desirous of further theological study, but it was impossible for him to go to Paris again, the English having meanwhile declared war with the French ; and so he went instead to Lincoln, and there he lived quietly for several years, accomplishing among other things the writing of his *Gemna Ecclesiastica*. In 1189 he was created Bishop of St. David's, but he did not hold the see long, in spite of two appeals to the Pope made in person at Rome. This ended Giraldus' career in the Church, though he became reconciled with the king and the Archbishop of Canterbury. The date of his death is uncertain, but it was probably 1220, and is supposed to have occurred in London.

Literature : Besides his books on Ireland and Wales, Giraldus wrote a life of St. Hugh of Lincoln, and also one of St. David ; while other notable things from his pen are *Expugnatio Hibernica* and *De*

Rebus a se Gestis. A complete edition of his works was published in the Rolls Series (1861–77) under the editorship of J. S. Brown and J. F. Winock, and the preface contributed by the former should be consulted. (*Vide* Warton's *Anglia Sacra*, which has a chronology of Giraldus' life, and consult the biography of Sir R. C. Hoare, prefaced to his translation of *Itinerarium Cambriæ*, 1806.)

GIRARD OF LIEGE. (*Vide* "Garin the Lorrainer.") Nephew of Garin and Bego. He fought on all occasions for the Lorrainers.

GISELHER. (*Vide* "Nibelungenlied.") Brother to Gunther, Gernot, and Kriemhild. He became attached to Siegfried, after whose death, he successfully prevailed upon his sister to remain at the court of Ute, their mother.

GISLI. (*Vide* "Grettir Saga.") A braggart and fop, who was severely thrashed by Grettir.

GIUKI, KING. ("*Vide* Volsungs.") Husband to Grimhild (*q.v.*), and father of the three sons, Gunnar (*q.v.*), Hogni (*q.v.*), and Guttorm (*q.v.*), and of a daughter Gudrun (*q.v.*). He met his death through the treachery of Atli.

GLAM. (*Vide* "Grettir Saga.") An uncouth shepherd, who for a time tended Thorkall's (*q.v.*) flocks. But he too, like former shepherds upon the haunted farm, was missed one winter night, and never returned alive. His evil spirit, however, terrorized the people in winter and slaughtered both men and animals, until he was mastered by Grettir. But his dreadful grey eyes haunted the hero in the dark, and made it impossible for him to dwell alone, thus leading ultimately to his death.

GLISTENING HEATH. (*Vide* "Volsungs.") The retreat where the Dragon Fafnir (*q.v.*) dwelt.

GLORIANDA. In Carlovingian romance, the daughter of the Saracen emir Corsuble, and the betrothed of Karaheut, King of India (*q.v.*). (*Vide* "Ogier the Dane.")

GLORIETTA. A wonderful marble tower in the city of Orange (*vide* "Prise d'Orange"). William of Orange was shut up in it, besieged by thousands of Saracens, but held his own, succoured by Orable, Queen of Orange (*q.v.*), who succeeded in effecting his escape, and whom he afterwards married. The pillars were of marble, the windows carved in silver, and a golden eagle lit the whole. A wondrous spice-bearing tree perfumed the place.

GOBAN THE SMITH. In Irish romance, brother of Kian and Sawan, He corresponds to Weyland Smith in Germanic legend. He was regarded as the founder, in Ireland, of artistry and handicraft. The legends in which he figures, occur in the Irish invasion myths.

GODELBOG. (*Vide* "Gododin.") A Cymric chief. Slain at the Battle of Cattraeth, carried to the grave by his sons.

GODFREY, DUKE OF DENMARK. In Carlovingian romance, father of Ogier the Dane. He left his son as a hostage with Charlemagne. He sent back messengers from that monarch with shaven faces and tonsured crowns, wherefore the emperor resolved to hang his son Ogier (*q.v.*).

GODFREY OF BOUILLON. (*Vide* "Jerusalem Delivered.")

GODILAKE, SIR. A knight, alluded to in Arthurian romance, who frequented the tourneys of Arthur's court. (*Vide* "Morte d'Arthur.")

GODODIN, THE. An early Welsh poem, said to be written by Aneurin, giving an account of a battle fought at Gododin, and praising the Cymric chiefs who distinguished themselves. Owen, son of Urien, is the first hero whose fame is sung by the poet, although under the name of the "only son of Marro." "He was a man in mind, in years a youth, and gallant in the din of war." His armour and dress are described, and the manner of his fighting. "No quarter would he give to those whom he pursued: nor would he retreat from the combat until blood flowed; and he cut down like rushes the men who would not yield." He was evidently slain in battle. "Alas, Owain! my beloved friend; It is not meet that he should be devoured by ravens!" The Angles invaded Gododin and the Cymry were fighting to regain some of their territory. Cattraeth (probably Catterick in Yorkshire) was the scene of battle. "The heroes marched to Cattraeth, loquacious was the host . . . and after the joyful cry, silence ensued! They should have gone to churches to perform penance; the inevitable strife of death was about to pierce them." Manawyd who came from the coast of Mordei, and the son of Isgyran, and Hyveidd Hir, are among these heroes. Hyveidd Hir came from Glamorgan and swept down five battalions of Deivyr and Bryneich (Durham and Northumberland). He himself was wounded. "He had not raised the spear ere his blood streamed to the ground." Gray, in his Ode from the Welsh *The Death of Hoel*, has given a

different interpretation to the death of the son of the bard Kian who had married a daughter of a Gododin chief. The heroes marched to Cattraeth with the dawn; their peace was disturbed by those who feared them; a hundred thousand with three hundred engaged in mutual overthrow; drenched in gore, they marked the fall of the lances; the post of war was most manfully and with gallantry maintained. Before the retinue of Mynyddawg "the Courteous," Gelorwydd, the "Gem of Baptism," had extreme unction given him, his own blood being substituted for the oil. Tudvwich, a Strathclyde Briton, slaughtered the Saxons for seven days, and became their prisoner in the end. Erthal and Godebog were there, Tudvwich and Cyvwlch the Tall, Gwarthleo and Gwrueling were all slain. There were three chiefs of the Novantae (people of Wigtown, Kirkcudbright and Ayr), with five battalions of 500 men each, three levies each of three hundred knights from Eiddin (perhaps Edinburgh), three chiefs from Breitan, on the shores of the Clyde, and three from Aeron (probably Ayr). These were the confederate Cymric tribes whose chiefs crossed the Solway or marched through Strathclyde to Cumberland. Only three of these brave warriors escaped death. "But there escaped by valour from the funeral fosse, the two war-dogs of Aeron, and Cynon the dauntless, and myself, from the spilling of blood, the reward of my pure song. As translated by Gray in *The Death of Hoel*—

"To Cattraeth's vale in glittering row
  Twice two hundred warriors go;
    .   .   .   .   .
But none from Cattraeth's vale return,

> Save Aeron brave, and Conan strong
> (Bursting through the bloody throng),
> And I, the meanest of them all,
> That live to weep, and sing their fall."

Graid, the son of Hoewgi, Bud-dvan, Gwenabwy, Marchten, and the son of Gwddnen, all mighty warriors. " Not one to his native home returned." Gwlyget, an Ododin chief, was slain at Cat-traeth, and Morien was killed by a stone as he was attacking the place, but it was taken. The Cymry sent their chief counsellor, a very old man riding a piebald steed and wearing a gold chain, to meet a dwarf messenger sent by the Saxons, who proposed a com-pact, but the Cymry would not agree. " Let heaven be our pro-tection. Let his compact be death by the spear in battle." Even some of the women of the Cymry fought in this awful struggle. " Equal to three men, though a maid, was Bradwin. . . . In the engagement of wrath and carnage, Bradwin perished, she did not escape." The men of Cymry were defeated, and were forced to come to an agreement. The poem then relates the demands made on the Cymry, how the Saxon heralds stabbed a friend of Aneurin, and the revenge the Cymry took on the traitor. A battle was fought near the river Swale: "at early dawn there was a battle at the confluence of rivers " and the dwarf herald was killed. The poet then eulogizes the chiefs that were slain, the last being Morien and Gwenabwy. " Fain would I sing, ' Would that Morien had not died.' I sigh for Gwena-bwy, the son of Gwen." *The Gododin* thus ends with a lament. All, save a few of the heroes who fought so bravely, were slaughtered on the field of battle.

GOEWIN. In Welsh romance, daughter of Pebin. (*Vide* "Gil-vaethwy.")

GOLDEMAR. A fragmentary poem written by Albrecht von Kemena-ten in the thirteenth century, and connected with the Dietrich of Bern Saga-cycle (*q.v.*).

GOLEUDDYD. In British Celtic legend, wife of Kilydd ; mother of Kulhwch (*q.v.*).

GOLL MAC MORNA. In Irish ro-mance, Captain of the Fianna (*q.v.*). He was the first to swear service to the young Finn, whom he rescued later from the en-chanted cave of Conaran. For this service Keva of the White Skin, his chief's daughter, was bestowed upon him in marriage. Goll appears in the Irish Ossianic cycle.

GOLOGROS AND GAWANE, THE KNIGHTLY TALE OF. An Arthu-rian poem. It is manifestly by a Scotsman, but the author's iden-tity is uncertain, though both Huchown of the Awle Ryle and Clerk of Tranent have been sug-gested. The ascription in the latter case rests on a statement made by Dunbar, in his *Lament for the Makaris*—

> " Clerk of Tranent eik he is tane
> That made the anteris of Sir Gwane,"

but the historian Andrew of Wyn-ton speaks of Huchown as having

> " Made the gret Gest of Arthure
> And the Awntyrs of Gawane ";

and, as Wynton lived fully a century before Dunbar, his testi-mony in a matter of this sort naturally carries greater weight. Sir Frederic Madden held that the tale was largely derived from the *Perceval* of Chrestien de Troyes, but though his contention is *prima facie* tenable, it is more likely that the author, as Sir Walter Scott asserts, drew his material from legendary lore current in Scotland in his day. Moreover, it is fairly evident that *Gologros and Gawane* is no mere translation ; for it is written throughout in stanzas of thirteen lines each, intricately rhymed and full of alliteration, and it is improbable that a translator would have used so elaborate a vehicle as this. The poem carries Arthur and some of his knights through many adventures in different lands, but the most important scene is laid in France, where Sir Gologros, a knight of marvellous prowess who dwells by the Rhone, vanquishes Gawane in single combat and compels him to pay obeisance to Arthur. Leyden tells that Gologros was a very popular hero in mediæval Scotland, and the mere fact that the poem was among those published by the earliest Scottish printers, Chepman and Myllar, during the reign of James IV., goes far to show that it was widely admired at that time. The reader will find it in a volume of *Ancient Poems*, 1807, where it is given verbatim from Chepman and Myllar's edition, even the old black-letter type being reproduced, as also is the quaint trade-mark of the fathers of Scottish typography. (*Vide* articles " Huchown," and " Awntyrs of Arthur.")

GONEMANS or **GONEMANT.** Of Gelbort, Knight, in Grail romance. He takes Sir Percival into his castle, and teaches him the use of arms, and all knightly exercises. He counsels Sir Perceval to avoid over-readiness in speech and in asking questions and to cease from the habit of always " quoting his mother's counsels." He is the uncle, too, of the " damsel of surpassing beauty," Blanchefleur (*q.v.*), whom Sir Perceval afterwards defends against the encroachments of King Clamadex (*q.v.*).

GOON DESERT. A monarch alluded to in the *Conte del Graal*. He is father of the maid who bears the Grail dish. He was also brother to the Fisher King, and dwelt in Quiquagrant. He was slain by a nephew of Espinogre, whom he had killed in a most treacherous manner. His body was brought to the Fisher King's castle, whither came, too, his daughter with the sword which had slain Goon Desert. She prophesied that a knight should come who would join the fragments of the sword, and revenge the foul murder of her father. The Fisher King, taking up the fragments incautiously, was pierced through the thigh, and the wound might not heal until his brother's death was avenged.

GORIAS. In Irish romance, one of the four cities from which came the four treasures of the Danaans (*q.v.*). The invincible sword of Lugh of the Long Arm (*q.v.*) came from Gorias.

GOTELIND. (*Vide* "Nibelungenlied.") Wife of Rudiger, Margrave of Bechlarn. Mother of Dietlinde. On Kriemhild's (*q.v.*) journey to wed Etzel (*q.v.*), she is received with much affection by Gotelind and Dietlinde at Rudiger's Castle of Bechlarn. Gotelind also joins her husband in showing unstinted kindness and hospitality to Gunther and his retinue on the way to Etzel's court, giving Hagen (*q.v.*), as his choice, his famous shield which had belonged to her father, Nodung.

GOTTFRIED VON STRASSBURG. A German poet of burgher rank, who flourished about the beginning of the thirteenth century. His principal title to fame is his work *Tristan und Isolt*, the material for which he probably took from an older French version of the legend. It is undoubtedly the finest of all the Tristan romances from a literary point of view, but in depths of thought is inferior to the *Parzival* of Wolfram von Eschenbach. Gottfried, from the materials at his command, created in the most original vein a picture of human passion all-devouring and consuming, yet painted with much *naïveté*. His style is at once perspicuous and melodious, and is happily free from the wearisome digressions in which the literature of his age abounds. "He may be considered as the forerunner of that appetite for worldly and physical enjoyment, for material advancement and possession which in the fourteenth and fifteenth centuries caused Europe to degenerate into mere animalism, hypocrisy and disbelief." Gottfried left his work unfinished. Concerning his private life practically nothing is known. No poet of the thirteenth century was so widely imitated by his own and succeeding generations as Gottfried. Ulrich von Türheim and Heinrich von Frieburg both essayed continuations of *Tristan und Isolt*. The first is brief. The latter displays considerable literary skill, but is inferior to the original. (*Vide* "Tristan and Isolt.")

GOUVERNAIL, SIR. Mentioned in Arthurian romance as tutor to Sir Tristram (*q.v.*). (*Vide* "Morte d'Arthur.")

GOWRA. In Irish romance the death-field of Oscar (*q.v.*), and his opponent, Cairbry, King of Ireland.

GOWTHER, SIR. An Arthurian romance, the hero of which is the son of a fiendish knight and a gentle lady whom he had betrayed. The boy, as was predicted, proved to be of a most savage temperament, until the offending spirit was whipped out of him by means of self-inflicted penance. He then wins the love of an earl's daughter by glorious achievement in the lists, and piously builds an abbey to commemorate his conversion.

GRADASSO. (*Vide* "Orlando Innamorato," and "Orlando Furioso.") King of Sericane, attempted the enchanted castle of Atlantes, but was made prisoner. He was afterwards liberated by Bradamant. He fought with Rinaldo, but the duel was broken off. He was killed by Orlando.

GRAELENT, THE LAY OF. A tale of Brittany, a *lai* by Marie de France (*q.v.*). The *lai* is practically the same as that of Sir Launfal (*q.v.*). The Knight Graelent won great praise in the service of his lord, the King of Brittany, and his renown fired the heart of the queen. She prayed him to return her love, but loyal knight that he was, he gently refused. Her love then was turned to hatred. Impoverished and sad, he went riding one day by himself through a wood. Here he espied a milk-white hart unsurpassed in beauty, and started in her chase. Following hard upon the creature, he came to an open lawn in the centre of which stood a fountain. Herein a wonderfully beautiful maiden was bathing. After some parlance they pledged their loves, and the lady henceforth supplied him with whatever he might wish and gave him her company to his heart's content. This good fortune attended him until he forgot his promise—never to let man know of her existence. At a feast the king bade his wife stand upon the dais, and challenged all present to show him her superior in beauty. In an unlucky moment Graelent, who was of the company, boasted of his lady-love. Right wrathful were both king and queen, and the hapless knight was seized and imprisoned for a year. At the end of that period he was permitted freedom to seek this surpassing beauty, but he failed to bring her. The king then sat in hasty judgment upon him, when a page desired the court to suspend sentence, as two beautiful damsels were riding thither, perhaps to the knight's succour. These were followed by two more beautiful than they; and finally their mistress rode into the court. This was the boasted beauty, and Graelent was set free. Then his lady-love rode away, while her lover followed hard upon her track. At last they came to a river into which the maiden rode, forbidding her knight to follow. But so mighty was his love that he heeded not her words, plunged after her, and came near to drowning. Having rescued her knight, the lady once more leapt into the river and once again did Graelent follow her. This time he had surely drowned but for the beseechings of her maidens. At last both lady and knight rode off into fairyland, whence no one witnessed their return; while the noble steed the maiden had sent to Graelent sought yearly with loud neighings through the forest for his lost master.

GRAID. (*Vide* "Gododin.") Son of Hoewgi. A Cymric warrior, slain at the Battle of Cattraeth. "Motionless is the sword of Graid."

GRAIL, THE HOLY. A section of the Arthurian cycle of romance (*q.v.*), of late origin, which embodies a number of tales dealing with the search for a certain vessel of great sanctity called the Grail.

It is considered with some reason that these tales originated in early mediæval legends of the quest for talismans which conferred great boons upon the finder, as, for example, the shoes of swiftness, the cloak of invisibility, and so forth, and that these stories were interpreted in the light and spirit of mediæval Christianity and mysticism. The Grail romances were divided by the late Alfred Nutt into two classes : (1) those which are connected with the quest for certain talismans of which the Grail is only one, and which deals with the personality of the hero who achieves the quest ; (2) those which deal with the nature and history of those talismans. The first he designated "The Quest," the second "The Early History Versions." In the first class we find a mass of poetic matter known as the *Conte del Graal*, consisting of some 60,000 verses. This material was composed between 1180 and 1240. That part of it between verses 1283 and 10,601 is the work of Chrétien de Troyes, a celebrated French poet of the twelfth century, who died about 1182. He states that the source of his poetical narration was a book presented to him by a Count Philip of Flanders, who was Regent of France in 1180 –81, and who perished in the Crusades. Several continuations of Chrétien's work exist, the dates of which may be placed between 1190 and 1240. The material of these, which amounts to some 50,000 lines, deals with the origin and history of the Grail. Its nature is also described. Wolfram von Eschenbach (*q.v.*), who probably took his account from a lost French source, by one Kyot or Guyot, alludes to the Grail as a stone, and enumerates in connection with it a sword and lance. The Welsh romance of *Peredur*, speaks of the Grail as a head in a salver, and mentions a lance. In other accounts the Grail is connected with the restoration to health of certain relatives of the questing hero. Wolfram, regarding loss of health as due to sin, shows how the sin-suffering on the part of the kinsmen is dissipated by the spiritual insight of the questing hero, whose sympathies are heightened and quickened, thus enabling him to cure his relative. The scene of all these versions is laid in Britain, and the *dramatis personæ* discovered in them are wholly British, with the exception of Wolfram von Eschenbach's version, where Breton and Argevin characters are found. Coming to the accounts in the *Conte del Graal* which deal with the nature and origin of the Grail, we find that all these substantially agree that the Grail is the vessel of the Last Supper, in which Joseph of Arimathea caught the blood of Christ as He hung upon the Cross, and the Grail lance that with which the Saviour was pierced. Joseph came to Britain with Veronica, sister of Nicodemus. Becoming an-hungered, he prayed for the Grail. It appeared in answer to the summons, and all with Joseph had meat, bread, and wine in abundance. On Joseph's decease the Grail descended to his family, from whom sprang the father of Perce-

val. The accounts which deal with this aspect of the Grail legend are obviously the latest portion of the *Conte del Graal*. It is probable that the *Conte* possesses elements of both Christian and non-Christian origin, the first of which are possibly to be found in the prose romance called the *Grand St. Graal* (*c.* 1200 ?) and the *Joseph of Arimathea* and *Merlin* of Robert de Borron, written between 1170 and 1212. The Grail legend has been alluded to as a legend of the conversion of Britain. It was probably originally derived from a group of apocryphal writings including the *Evangelium Nicodemi*, a book very popular in early Britain, or perhaps in an account of the evangelization of Britain by St. Joseph, included in some documents emanating from the Abbey of Glastonbury in the twelfth century—a place traditionally connected with the Grail legend. Turning to the non-Christian element in the legend, we find the vengeance theme prominent—the redressing of wrong to a kinsman—in several of the versions. (See *Percyvelle*, *Peredur*, etc.), but also the breaking of spells and enchantments as in *Diu Krône* (*q.v.*), and, in another romance, the manner in which the Grail was regarded as a talisman to restore fertility to a desert land. This aspect of the legend may have its source in the pagan romance of Celtic Ireland and Wales, so that the Grail vessel may be connected with the Cauldron of Dagda the Irish God of Fertility or the *Lia Fail*, Stone of Destiny, now in Westminster Abbey. In fine, the Grail legend may be a Christianized version of ancient Celtic myths, affected by Christian symbolism and story. (For subject-matter of the several legends, *vide* " Peredur," " Perceval le Gallois," " Conte del Graal," " Grand St. Graal," " Sir Percyvelle," " Parzival," " Joseph of Arimathea," " Merlin," " Quete del St. Graal," " Didot Percival," and especially " Guyot.")

GRAIL SWORD. In Arthurian romance this weapon is associated with the Holy Grail. Its history commences with King David, on whose death Solomon is prompted to cherish it, but not before he has recast the pommel. After his death it falls into disuse. Solomon's wife having built a ship, she extravagantly furnishes the interior, and Solomon placed by the side of the luxurious bed the Grail sword. It is subsequently discovered by the Knights of the Quest, who prompt Galahad to assume it. Strangely enough it does not resist his interference, and is borne by him. (*Vide* " Morte d'Arthur.")

GRAM. (*Vide* " The Lay of the Volsungs.") A sword of magic thrust into a tree by Odin (*q.v.*), and pulled out by Sigmund (*q.v.*). Dag (*q.v.*) latterly became possessed of it. It bestowed upon its possessor exceptional power, and performed many miracles.

GRAND ST. GRAAL. A romance on the subject of the Holy Grail (*q.v.*), probably dating from the beginning of the thirteenth century, and thus one of the latest romances connected with the legend. A prologue states that Christ was the original author of the work. It tells how Joseph of Arimathea employed the dish used at the Last Supper to catch the blood of the Redeemer which flowed from His body before His entombment. He is cast into prison, but the dish keeps him supplied with food. He is set free by Vespasian,

and having been baptized by St. Philip, he converts many of his friends and kindred, and encloses the holy vessel in an ark. He sets out with his followers on a journey through the wilderness, and during his peregrinations is miraculously sustained by the dish. Reaching Sarras, where he converts Evelach, a native, he is placed in charge of a little band of Christians by divine command. He is pierced with a lance for venturing too near the glory of the Grail, but is healed by an angel, and the lance is preserved, as Joseph is told that the last of his kin will be struck by it also. Nasciens, brother-in-law to Evelach, undergoes many adventures with the latter, and at length discovers the sword of Solomon, with which he is wounded. Josephes, son of Joseph, leads a band to Britain, where they find Celidoine, the son of Nasciens. Joseph and his son are cast into prison by Crudel, King of North Wales, but on Evelach (who has received the Christian name of Mordrains) being instructed by Christ to deliver them, he proceeds to Britain and succeeds in freeing them. Mordrains builds a monastery, and there Perceval and Galahad meet with him, as is set forth in the tale of the Holy Grail. Brons, Joseph's brother-in-law, now enters the legend with his twelve sons, whom he brings to Josephes. As the youngest, Alain, is unmarried he is appointed guardian of the Grail at the death of Josephes. Alain, having caught a great fish with which he feeds the entire company, is called the Rich Fisher, which title becomes that of all the Grail keepers in perpetuity. Alain duly becomes the Keeper of the Grail, and places it in the castle of Corbenic,

L

for the offence of reposing in which a king is wounded through both thighs. Josue succeeds Alain as keeper, and the line of guardians is brought down to Pelles, by whose daughter Lancelot du Lac is the father of Galahad.

GRANI (1). (*Vide* "Burnt Njal.") Younger son of Gunnar (*q.v.*), by Hallgerda (*q.v.*). Having received his life from Njal's sons who slew Thrain (*q.v.*), and Hrapp (*q.v.*), he ill returned their kindness by assisting in the burning of Njal and his household.

GRANI (2). (*Vide* "Volsungs, Lay of.") A foal presented by Odin to Sigurd (*q.v.*). She performed many wonderful feats, including the conveyance of her master through the flames to Brunhild's (*q.v.*) castle.

GRANIA. In Irish romance, daughter of Cormac mac Art; betrothed to Finn (*q.v.*). She beguiled Dermot (*q.v.*) to elope with her, and after sixteen years of outlawry, followed by a short time of peace, Dermot was slain by the boar of Ben Bulben (*q.v.*). Grania latterly espoused Finn. The myth is included in the Irish Ossianic cycle.

GRASSY, SIR. (*Vide* "Bevis of Hampton.") Steward to the King of Mounbraunt. Boniface gave him a sleeping potion when he was in charge of the city, so as to enable Bevis and Josyan to escape.

GRENDEL. (Legend of Beowulf.) A giant who lived in the morass near Hirschhall, the hall of King Hrodgar (*q.v.*). He slew many warriors by night, none being able to resist him, till Beowulf, after a terrific struggle, inflicted on him his death-wound. (*Vide* "Beowulf.")

GRETTIR THE STRONG. An Icelandic saga, probably of the eleventh century. It abounds in impossibilities and incidents which are almost frankly mythical. The saga has few distinctive features, and can scarcely be regarded as in any sense a record of contemporary Icelandic life. Grettir was the second son of Asmund and Asdis and the favourite of his mother. Short and stout of stature, of uncommon strength and perverse disposition, in his father's opinion he was good for nothing. He played many tricks upon his sire, flayed the weatherwise mare Keingald, and slew Skegg in a quarrel about a lost meal-bag. For this he had a fine to pay, which matter was settled by Thorfinn, Asmund's friend, and Grettir was ordered into a three years' banishment. Provided with nothing save a sword which his mother gave him, he entered the vessel of Haflidi, which was wrecked on the island of Havamsey. Here Grettir remained for some time with its chief, Thorfinn, making friends with farmer Audun. Walking one evening with his companions he watched a fire break from a mound, and believing the mound to conceal some treasure, he went next morning to dig an entrance into the mound, which was known as the grave of Old Karr, Thorfinn's father. Working all day he came at night to the rafters of the barrow, gathered together the treasure, and was about to ascend when the dead man awoke. After a tremendous struggle with him, Grettir shore off Karr's head, and laid it at his thigh that he might not come to life again. The treasure he delivered up to Thorfinn, but sought to keep a certain short sword.

That, however, he might not have until he had done some great deed. But the weapon was soon his, for having trapped in the storeroom twelve outlaws who came at Yuletide to rob his master's home in Thorfinn's absence, he slew ten of them, the other two being later found dead of their wounds. Then he received the sword, and his name became famous in all Norway. At the beginning of spring Grettir came to Heligoland, where he stayed with Thorkel and slew a great bear that was the dread of the countryside. But he and Biorn, one of Thorkel's chief men, and a blustering, evil-tempered conceited person, were at daggers drawn. Again at spring-time Grettir started a wandering, and landed upon the island of Gartar in Drontheim Firth. He soon found his old enemy Biorn, who had started for England, but had been driven by stress of weather into this haven. They fought, and Biorn was slain. The dead man's brother Hiarandi then sought redress, but Thorfinn paid down the blood-money, reminding Yarl Svein of Grettir's good deed in slaying the outlaws. Hiarandi, however, refused the money ; but one day seeking, with the help of five others, to slay Grettir, he and four of his accomplices were despatched by their intended victim and his friend Ambiorn, sent by his kinsman Thorfinn to accompany Grettir, for whom he foresaw treachery was intended. Yarl Svein agreed to settle the matter at Tunsberg, where Gunnar, the brother of Biorn and Hiarandi, dwelt. Gunnar too sought to slay Grettir, but was sent the same road as his brothers, accompanied by two of his accomplices, the third taking flight. Madly wroth with Grettir, Yarl Svein would have hunted him from his refuge in his brother Thorstein Dromond's court. But the men of Tunsberg dissuaded him, and Grettir was banished from Norway, Thorfinn again paying the blood-money. The outlaw then made for Biarg, where his father dwelt. Hearing of the dreadful visitations of Glam, the ghost-slain shepherd of Thorhall, who owned a haunted farm in Waterdale, Grettir determined to probe the mystery of the many slaughterings there. To that end he rode over to the farm, but it was not until the third night that he found his horse dead and the stable in ruins. The next night he rolled himself in a rug with but two openings for his eyes, laid down upon a locker and awaited events. Shortly after midnight Glam appeared, and after a tremendous struggle he was mastered by Grettir, who finally shore off his head, and, as in Karr's case, laid it beside his thigh. But the evil spirit foretold to Grettir ill luck, a wandering life, and a constant dread of its terrible grey eyes. Loaded with presents, Grettir then returned to Biarg. He next set out for Norway, to seek service with King Olaf, slaying, however, ere he left, Thorbiorn the Tardy, a braggadocio, who had provoked him. But upon his way to Drontheim, the crew requiring fire, he swam ashore with a cask and procured some from a refuge-house. Here were the sons of Thorir of Garth, who, deeming him a troll, or evil spirit, set upon him with firebrands. In the scuffle they set fire to the house and its inmates. For this mishap Grettir was blamed, and was shunned by the sailors. He sought out Olaf, with whom he claimed kinship, but though the king believed in his innocence he would have no dealings with Grettir because of his ill-luck. On his way to Tunsberg he slew Snoekell, a berserk who challenged Einar in whose house Grettir was tarrying. But when he again set foot upon Framnäs he learned that Åsmund had died, Atli had been treacherously murdered by Thorbiorn Oxmain, brother of the braggadocio sailor, and he, Grettir, had been outlawed without a hearing. To avenge these things, Grettir slew Thorbiorn and his son Arnor, but being an outlaw he could not be prosecuted. Thorin of Garth then joined with Thorod Drapnastump, Thorbiorn's brother, and each set a price upon the outlaw's head. Escaping death by hanging at the hands of thirty farmers, Grettir, by the advice of Skapti, dwelt upon a lake-shore. Thither the Northlanders sent Grim and Redbeard, two ruffians, to murder the outlaw ; but these suffered defeat. Nor did the men sent by Thorir of Garth to entrap his enemy in the pass escape without many being slain and wounded by Grettir and Hallmund, his friend in need. For a short time the friends dwelt together, then Grettir began wandering again. He met the fop Gisli, and by a severe lesson cured him of his bragging. Hearing of the Yule-eve hauntings at the homestead of the priest Stein, Grettir sought out that place, guarded the home folk one Yule-eve, and flung the invading troll-wife into the stream's force. Then having regained his strength after grappling with the witch, he plunged into the force, hacked to pieces an ogre who dwelt there, and brought up the bones of Stein's two missing house-carles. These were buried in the churchyard,

and as at Thorhall's farm, so here at Sand-heaps, the haunting ceased. Some time afterwards Grettir took with him his brother Illugi, and a merry tom-fool, nicknamed Noise, to the laddered island of Drangey. Here they lived upon the mainland farmer's sheep that grazed upon the rock. Wearying of that life, Grettir went disguised to the Thing at Heronness, where he wrestled victoriously with Hialti and Thorbiorn Angle. The latter having purchased the whole island sought, by entreaties, threats, and finally sorcery, to wrest it from the outlaw. In this case by the proffered assistance of his foster-mother, the witch Thurid (q.v.), he gained the hut where Grettir lay all but helpless from a ghastly wound inflicted upon him by her agency. Then, after a protracted defence on the part of the outlaw and his brother, Noise having been beaten unconscious, Thorbiorn Angle seized the short sword and hacked off Grettir's head, thereby notching the blade. But Illugi, steadfast in his revengeful intentions, was hacked to pieces. Thorbiorn Angle took ship to Norway, and, boasting of his deed, revealed himself to Thorstein Dromond, Grettir's only surviving brother, who with his brother's sword, cleft his skull in two. Cast into prison for his murder, Thorstein by his cheery singing attracted the good services of Lady Spes (q.v.), who ransomed him and whom he afterwards courted. Her jealous husband thrice had good proof of his lady's faithlessness, but by her cunning, failing to prove his allegation before others, he summoned his wife to swear to her innocence before the bishop. Again their combined inventiveness brought the lovers off victorious, and Lady

Spes got a divorce from her husband Sigurd. Soon afterwards she wedded with Thorstein, with whom she lived happily and prosperously, until by common consent they separated to end their lives in penitence at Rome. The *Grettir Saga*, like that of *Frithjof*, is yet another legend superimposed upon the sun-myth. Grettir is the man of the sun disguised as our Icelandic hero. But, while in the *Frithjof Saga* the hero finally wins peace and happiness upon the bosom of his beloved, here, in this tale, through blood and destruction, Grettir meets a dreadful and agonizing death. In the one Saga we feel the softer, more beautiful and more peaceful influence of the sun ; in the other we are oppressed by his gigantic strength, and the feeling that even that cannot avail him when all-consuming night gapes to annihilate him.

GREY OF MACHA. In Irish romance, the horse of Cuchulain (*q.v.*).

GRIM (1). (*Vide* "Grettir Saga.") A ruffian who was sent to murder Grettir in his lonely hut, but was himself slain by his intended victim.

GRIM (2). An outlaw and lucky fisherman harboured by Hallmund (*q.v.*), who figures in the *Grettir Saga*. Grim coming upon him with a missing fish belonging to him in his hand, slew him.

GRIM (3). (*Vide* "Burnt Njal.") Second son of Njal. With his brother Helgi (*q.v.*) he went sea-roving by the Orkneys, and made friends there with the viking Kari (*q.v.*). He assisted in the slaying of Thrain (*q.v.*) and Hrapp, and that of Hanskuld, but was burnt in the Bergthorsknoll by Flosi (*q.v.*).

GRIM (4). (*Vide* "Dietrich of Bern.") A giant brother to Hilda (*q.v.*), who was equally as formidable. He was subsequently slain by Dietrich and Hildebrand.

GRIMHILD. (*Vide* "Volsungs.") Wife of King Guiki (*q.v.*) and mother of Gunnar (*q.v.*), Hogni (*q.v.*), Guttorm (*q.v.*), and Gudrun (*q.v.*). She administered to Gudrun a magic draught, under the influence of which the latter married Atli (*q.v.*).

GRINAMORE, SIR. Knight of King Arthur, brother of Liones and Linet, and friend of Sir Gareth (*q.v.*). (*Vide* "Morte d'Arthur.")

GRIOGORAS. In Arthurian romance, a knight whom Gauvain had once punished for ill-doing, and whom he finds wounded in a forest, nursed by a damsel. On the occasion Griogoras makes off with Gauvain's horse. He is alluded to in the *Conte del Graal*.

GRONW PEBYR. In Welsh legend, a stranger loved by Blodeuwedd, and finally slain by her husband Llew.

GUARINOS THE ADMIRAL. A Spanish tale of the Charlemagne cycle in ballad form. Guarinos, admiral to King Charles of France, was captured in battle by the seven Moorish Kings. They cast lots as to which of them is to win him, and the prize falls to Marlotes. Marlotes offers Guarinos wealth and his daughter as wife if he will become a Moslem. This Guarinos refuses ; he is therefore put into a dungeon and bound with iron bands. Three times only in the year does he see daylight, namely, on the three high-feast days. At the feast of John the Baptist, Marlotes raises a high target which the Moorish Knights must pierce. It is, however, so high that none of them succeed. Marlotes, in his anger at their failure, proclaims that until the spearman's prize is won, no banquet shall begin. Guarinos, in his dungeon, hears this from his jailer, and begs him to ask the king to give him his horse and armour so that he may try for the prize, willingly forfeiting his life should he fail. The king consents. Guarinos vaults into the saddle, halts before Marlotes, and pierces him with his lance. He then flies off to France.

GUDRUN (1). Third portion of Ettmuller's division of the *Gudrun Lay* (*q.v.*). (For the second portion, *vide* "Hagen and Hettel.") Gudrun was the daughter of Hettel and Hilda, King and Queen of Friesland and sister of Ortwein. She was exceptionally beautiful, and had many suitors, chief among them being King Seyfried of Moorland (afterwards spoken of as King of Carady), King Hartmut of Ormany, and King Herwig of Seeland (*q.v.*), all of whom her father rejected. Herwig marched against Hettel, and a fierce conflict took place, till Gudrun intervened. While she pleaded for peace, love stirred in her towards Herwig, and at last her parents agreed to his suit, and they were betrothed, Hilda stipulating for a year's delay. Meantime, Seyfrid ravaged Herwig's land, and Herwig, returning home, was forced to solicit aid from Hettel, who went to his assistance with his nobles. During their absence Gerlinte urged her son Hartmut and his father to attack Hegelingen and win Gudrun by force, which they did, and carried off Gudrun with many of her ladies. Queen Hilda sent the news to Herwig and Hettel, who made peace with Seyfrid and secured his aid against Hartmut. They followed Hartmut and his men to the Wulpenstrand, where a dreadful conflict took place, in which Hettel was killed. During the night, Ludwig and Hartmut with their men succeeded in embarking and escaping unseen, carrying Gudrun with them. Pursuit was useless till a younger generation grew to manhood, as the flower of Denmark was slain, so all that Queen Hilda and Herwig could do was to labour at building up another expedition. Meantime, on nearing Ormany, Ludwig bade Gudrun cease weeping and look with love on his son. "Death were preferable," declared the captive, and Ludwig in rage flung her into the sea, but Hartmut rescued her. Queen Gerlinte and her daughter Ortrun received Gudrun magnificently, but Gudrun declined to kiss Gerlinte, and the queen hated her because she persisted in her refusal to marry Hartmut. Devotedly did he love her, and throughout many years repeatedly sought to win her heart, but Gudrun steadfastly refused to forget Herwig. Whenever Hartmut in despair went away for a time, Gerlinte endeavoured to break Gudrun's spirit by all kinds of indignities and ill-treatment, forcing her and her maidens to do the lowest menial work. Ortrun, however, who loved Gudrun, did her best to help her, and pleaded her brother's cause, but kindness and cruelty alike failed to move Gudrun from her fidelity to Herwig, even Hartmut's unchanging love proving vain. For many years this continued, and Gerlinte, on Hartmut's absence on an expedition, set Gudrun to wash clothes on the sea-shore from morn till night. One of Gudrun's maidens, Hildeburg, true to her mistress through all, asked permission to share her hardships, and for six and a half years they endured this menial occupation, while Gerlinte's cruelty grew worse. She forced them to wear the thinnest of garments in icy weather. Still Gudrun's fidelity never faltered. Then, one day, a sea-maiden in the shape of a swan brought them good news of a rescuing fleet from Denmark. This fleet, completed at length, set sail for Ormany, headed by Herwig, Horant (as standard-bearer), Morung, Wate, and others, joined by Seyfried, with reinforcements. On landing in the neighbourhood of Hartmut's fortress, Herwig and Ortwein set out in a boat as messengers to Gudrun, and came upon her and Hildeburg, half-clad and washing clothes in the bitter cold. After some speech with them, mutual recognition took place, and great joy was theirs. Herwig wished to carry off the maidens at once, but Ortwein insisted on winning them by battle and " with honour," and a " hard parting " took place meantime. Gudrun having been "kissed by two kings " flung the washing into the sea and defied Gerlinte, who ordered her to be flogged. To escape this indignity, and with a view to her rescue on the morrow, Gudrun feigned to agree to wed Hartmut. Full of joy he came to her, but she asked fit robes for herself and her maidens, and bade him send messengers to summon his friends to the wedding, thus diminishing his forces. Her requests were carried out. Through the night the Hegelingen army approached the fortress, and on the morrow a fierce conflict took place, Hartmut and his knights going forth bravely to meet the enemy. Herwig and Ludwig fought, Herwig finally slaying Ludwig. Harmut and Wate engaged in combat, when suddenly Gerlinte ordered a " faithless churl " to slay Gudrun, and Hartmut, hearing her voice, ceased fighting, threatening the murderer with death, thus saving Gudrun almost at the cost of his own life. Ortrun besought Gudrun to intervene to save Hartmut's life. Herwig tried to part Wate and Hartmut, Wate striking at him in anger at the interruption, but Hartmut was saved, being made a prisoner. Wate stormed the city, fiercely slaying and plundering. Gudrun sheltered Ortrun and her maidens, and when Gerlinte also sought protection, Gudrun forgave her wrongs and tried to save her, but Wate found and slew her, only sparing Ortrun and her ladies at Gudrun's tearful prayers and expostulations. Wate also slew Heregart, a maid who had proved false to Gudrun. Lovingly was Herwig received by Gudrun, and having devastated the land, the Danes and their allies returned to Denmark, leaving Morant and Morung to keep the country, and carrying with them Hartmut and the other prisoners. (*Vide* "Gudrun Lay.")

GUDRUN (2). (*Vide* "Volsungs.") Daughter of King Giuki (*q.v.*) and Grimhild (*q.v.*), and mother of Swanhild (*q.v.*). She wedded Sigurd (*q.v.*) while the latter was under the influence of a magic potion. Her husband was slain by Guttorm (*q.v.*). Her mother again influenced her into marrying Atli (*q.v.*). She despised her second husband, whose treachery toward her brothers she repelled. She eventually succeeded by the aid of Niblung (*q.v.*) in slaying

Atli. After this she attempted to drown herself, but the sea carried her to the burg of King Jonakr (*q.v.*), who took her to wife. She lived long enough to witness the end of her kindred.

GUDRUN LAY. A German epic, embodying North German or Frisian-Danish-Norse sagas, recounting the legendary history of three generations. Ettmuller (*Gudrun Lieder*, 1841) divides the whole epic into three—*Hagene, Hagene und Hettel*, and *Gudrun*, and for convenience we have dealt more fully with the epic under these three headings. The lay tells how Hagen, son of Sigebant and Uta, King and Queen of Ireland, is carried off by a griffin, and after many vicissitudes, returns home, marries Hilda of India, and succeeds his father as king. He refuses all suitors for the hand of his daughter Hilda, but King Hettel of Denmark sends messengers who win her heart to his cause and succeed in abducting her—a willing captive—and bring her to be King Hettel's bride. Her father follows in wrath, and a great fight ensues between Hagen's men and the Danes, ending in peace being concluded. To Hilda and Hettel are born a son and daughter, Ortwein and Gudrun, the latter of whom is marvellously beautiful. She has many suitors, chief of whom are Seyfrid, King of Moorland, Hartmut, King of Ormany, and Herwig, King of Seeland; but Hettel refuses them all. Herwig attacks Hettel's fortress, wins Gudrun's love, and finally is accepted by Hettel as her future husband. Hartmut, however, carries her off to Ormany, where she is held captive for many years, during which time Hartmut, who truly loves her, endeavours in vain to induce her to forget Herwig, to whom she is faithful even when cruelly ill treated by Hartmut's mother Gerlinte, who is determined to force her to wed Hartmut. At length Herwig is able to rescue her, the poem giving a vivid and dramatic description of how this takes place. Probably the chief feature of the epic is Gudrun's fidelity, and she stands as the type of love that remains true through trial and suffering. The poem regarding her is one of the finest examples of the German epic muse. It has been preserved through the agency of the Emperor Maximilian I., who, about 1517, caused it, along with others, to be transcribed in one volume and placed in the Ambras Library in the Tyrol. It was brought to light some three hundred years later. The earliest reference to any portion of the *Gudrun* legend appears to occur in the Exeter Anglo-Saxon MS., where Heovrend the "lay-crafty man" is spoken of—apparently the Horant of *Gudrun*. An allusion to Wate's valour seems to occur in Priest Konrad's version of the *Song of Roland* (1173 to 1177). The *Gudrun Lay* cannot be taken as primarily forming a whole, nor as being the work of a single author—which accounts, doubtless, for several discrepancies in point of time, etc., which occur in the poem as it now stands. (For a short discussion of these, see *Popular Epics of the Middle Ages*, by Ludlow.) The frequent variation in proper names also indicates variety of source, or of text. The earlier portion of the poem has really little connection with the "Gudrun" portion, except as regards names. Ludlow is "inclined to think that the *Gudrun Lay* proper is the oldest portion.

He also states that a kernel of ancient legend lies in the *Hagen Lay* portion, overlaid by modern additions. The names and scenery point to the origin of the poem being Norse ; the story of the griffins indicates Oriental traditions, while Ludlow considers the fencing and the story of Gudrun's trials in captivity quite modern in character. He says, " To the thirteenth century, I believe, belongs the idea of female sufferings as subject for epic treatment ; the story of Gudrun may thus be connected with the French *Berte aux grans pièds*, and links itself on to the popular fourteenth-century tale of the *Patient Grizzel*, as treated by Boccaccio and Chaucer." A version of the legend, with variations, occurs in the *Younger Edda* of Snorre, where Hilldr the Dane, daughter of Hogni (Hagen) = Hilda, who married Hedin (Hettel). Hilldr, however, is represented as a witch, and later, ceasing to love Hedin, casts a spell upon him and her father, so that every night they rise and fight one another till dawn. This is obviously a remnant of a day-and-night myth. M. Amédée Thierry sees in this form of the legend especially a reminiscence of the history of Atilla, who = Hettel, while Hilda is Ildico, the historic bride of Attila. He also identifies her with Walther's bride Hildegrund, in the Walther-legend (*q.v.*). The carrying away of Hogni's daughter is spoken of by older Norse writers than Snorre, and also by Saxo Grammaticus. Some authorities also consider that Horant, or Hjarrandi appears in the Hamlet-myths as Orendil or Aurentil, and is " no other than Orpheus or Amphion, Pan or Wäinämöinen." For a fuller account of the MS. of *Gudrun*, and of modern German translations and theories on the poem—also some speculations as to the localities referred to in it, see *Gudrun, a Story of the North Sea* (1863), by Miss Letherbrow, Preface and Introduction.

GUIBORC. Wife of William of Orange (*q.v.*). She was originally wife to the Saracen King of Orange, Tybalt, when she was called Orable, but fell in love with William and married him. (*Vide* " Orable " and " Prise d'Orange.")

GUIELIN. A Frankish knight, nephew of William of Orange, who held the tower of Glorietta in the city of Orange along with William against the Saracens. (*Vide* " Prise d'Orange.")

GUILLARDUN. (*Vide* " Eliduc, Lay of.") Daughter of the King of Logres, who held his court near Exeter. Eliduc, having been banished from the court of Brittany, took service with the king and defeated the knight who was warring against the monarch for the hand of Guillardun. After a year the maiden had sight and speech of her father's champion, when both fell in love with each other. The obstacle to the union of the knight and the princess was his wife Guilldeluec (*q.v.*). But she discovered the secret of her lord's sadness and gloom, and craving leave to take the veil, thus permitted him to wed with Guillardun.

GUILLAUME DE LORRIS. A French troubadour of the thirteenth century. He is famous as author of the first part of the *Roman de la Rose*, concluded subsequently by Jean de Meung, but no biographical facts concerning him have come down to posterity. A French writer, M. L. Jarry, in his *Guillaume de Lorris et le Testament d'Alphonse* *de Poitiers* (1881), has attempted to identify the poet with one Guillielmus de Lorriaco, mentioned in the will of Alphonse of Poitiers ; but the writer's contentions are based on the slenderest evidence, and it is likely that Guillaume's sub-name was given him simply on account of his being a native of Lorris, a small village about equidistant from Montargis and Gien. Guillaume is credited with some four or five thousand lines of the *Roman*, and at the outset of these he describes himself as being twenty years of age when he conceived the poem, but he adds that it was not till five years later that he began to write it down. The mere fact that so young a man left his work unfinished suggests that he died prematurely, and this idea has gradually become current, a pathetic interest attaching to Guillaume accordingly. But his memory hardly requires anything of that sort to keep it fresh, for it is improbable that recognition will ever cease to be given to his verse, abounding as it does in vivid descriptions, and occasionally disclosing phraseology of exceptional beauty. The idea has been mooted sometimes that he was indebted in some measure to Ovid, and, be that as it may, his work certainly hints at obligations to his compatriot, Raoul de Houdenc. Nevertheless, Guillaume must be regarded as a man of no ordinary originality, while moreover, the *Roman de la Rose* proved the most influential of all the great Mediæval French poems, its style being imitated by endless later writers, not only in France but also elsewhere.

GUILLDELUEC. (*Vide* "Eliduc, Lay of.") Wife of Eliduc. Having discovered the beautiful maiden Guillardun whom her husband loved and whom he believed dead, Guilldeluec prayed his leave to take the veil. He therefore founded a church, installed his wife as abbess there, and wed with Guillardun.

GUINEVERE. Wife of King Arthur, and daughter of the King of Cameliard. On espousing her Arthur was warned by Merlin that she was "not wholesome for him," and this prophecy was soon fulfilled as regards her amour with Sir Lancelot du Lac. She, however, concealed her deficiencies from the king for many years, until at length his eyes were opened to her intrigues. She eventually betook herself to a nunnery, where she died after a few years' residence. She is of the breed of women who, like Helen of Troy or Deirdre, are the doom and destroyers of cities and good knights through their ill-conceived loves.

GUINGAMOUR or **GUGEMAR, LAY OF.** A romance or *lai*, attributed to Marie of France (*q.v.*). Concerning it the Bretons "had already made a lay." The Baron Oridial, Lord of Leon, had a daughter and son, Nogent and Gugemar. The lad went to take service at court, where he was knighted. He was a goodly person, but had one fault, he "took no care of love." Desirous of advancement, he set out for Flanders, and having achieved many adventures there, returned to his own country in order that he might once more behold his parents. Chancing to come upon a white doe whilst hunting, he wounded her above the hoof, but the arrow glanced and struck Gugemar in the thigh, so that he fell off his horse beside the wounded deer. The animal addressed him in human speech, and told him that never would he be healed unless by a woman who, because of her love, would suffer such pain and sorrow as no woman in the world had done before. Binding up his wound, Gugemar mounted his steed and rode to the sea-shore, where he espied a goodly vessel, which he boarded. Within it was a bed made " in the days of King Solomon," surrounded by every possible luxury. He entered the bed, and, a wind springing up, was carried out to sea. He was wafted to an ancient city, where dwelt an old king who was supremely jealous of his young and beautiful wife. Her bower was walled in with green marble, and here she dwelt with her niece, save whom no one ever entered the place. Only one man, an aged priest, possessed the key to the bower. The captive queen marked the arrival of Gugemar's ship from her garden, and her niece climbed aboard to see who was therein, returning to say that she had found a slain knight within the vessel. Beholding Gugemar, the queen immediately conceived a violent passion for him, and the knight awaking, was told the circumstances in which she lived, adding that she desired him to remain until he was cured. For a year and a half Gugemar dwelt with the lady in love, when the queen had a presentiment that she would lose him. She therefore desired him to give her a shirt upon which she put such a knot that any woman who loved him must first undo it. In turn he placed a girdle about her middle with a secret clasp and buckle which no one could undo save himself. Discovered by the king's chamberlain, Gugemar was once more committed to his ship,

which returned whence it had come, and brought him home. The lady whom he had left was placed in prison by her husband the king for the space of two years. One day she found the prison door open, and, passing out, made her way to the seashore where she found her lover's magic ship, which she entered. It carried her to a port of Brittany, where reigned as lord one Meriadus, who, departing on a warlike expedition, chanced to note the arrival of the vessel. Beholding the queen, he fell in love with her, and brought her to his castle, placing her beside his sister. Learning that she would have no man for lover who could not unclasp her girdle, Meriadus told her that in that country dwelt a knight who would wed no woman who might not undo a knot in his shirt. Meriadus made a great jousting, to which came Gugemar. He encountered his love in Meriadus' castle, and Meriadus suggested that she should attempt to untie the knot in his shirt. Gugemar sent for the garment, the knot in which she easily unravelled. Gugemar requested Meriadus to give up the queen, which he refused to do, so Gugemar left the castle in wrath, and returned with a strong force, ultimately taking the fortress and regaining his lady.

GUIROMELANT. In Arthurian romance, a knight who loves Gauvain's sister Clarissant, and with whom Gauvain arranges a combat. Gauvain is detested by Guiromelant for having slain his father. Unaware of Gauvain's identity Guiromelant asked him to bear a ring to Clarissant, who was an inmate of a magic castle. This Gauvain does. The duel between the knights is hindered, and Guiromelant weds Clarissant.

GUNNAR (1). (*Vide* "Grettir Saga.") Like his brother Hiarandi (*q.v.*), he was slain by Grettir, upon whom he sought to avenge Biorn's death.

GUNNAR (2). (*Vide* "Burnt Njal.") Dearest friend of Njal. Having married Hallgerda (*q.v.*), he suffered much ill on her account, for she was at constant feud with Njal's wife Bergthora (*q.v.*), and this brought about many slayings of the servants of both farms. Again, by stealing from the store-house of Otkell (*q.v.*) she incurred the displeasure of Gunnar, who gave her a blow on the face, an insult she never forgot. This theft led to Gunnar's death ; for Skamkell (*q.v.*), Otkell's friend, having noised it abroad that Gunnar had wept with the pain of an unintentional gash from Otkell's spear, Gunnar and his brother Kolskegg, found an opportunity to slay Otkell and Skamkell. Then the cunning Mord (*q.v.*), learning that Njal had warned his friend not to slay two in the same stock, advised Thorgeir (*q.v.*), who sought Gunnar's death, to harden the heart of Otkell's son, an honest and peace-loving youth, against his father's slayer. Gunnar slew the son and was ordered into a three years' banishment with his brother Kolskegg. But his home looked so beautiful as he was leaving it that he was unable to go, and remained at Lithend. Then Mord, Thorgeir, and Gizir the White, sought his death ; and one day before sunset, having slain his faithful hound Sam, they surrounded his house and slew him. Nor at this critical moment would Hallgerda assist him when he bade her make a bowstring of her hair. She only laughed, reminded him of the blow he had given her, and left him unaided.

GUNNLAUG SAGA. An Icelandic tale, probably of the eleventh century. Gunnlaug of the Worm-Tongue, a designation given him on account of his stinging speech, was the son of Illugi. He was sent at the age of fifteen to learn law-craft from his father's friend, Thorstein Egilson. During the three years of his studentship he and Thorstein's daughter, Helga, returned each other's love, and when upon the eve of his departure for foreign parts, Gunnlaug asked for Helga's hand. Thorstein, after much solicitation, both from father and son, agreed to hold his daughter betrothed to her lover, should he, after three years' travelling, return with a satisfactory record. Gunnlaug set sail, and, coming to Drontheim, through his sharp speech, suffered the displeasure of Yarl Eric, co-king with his brother Svein. He therefore departed from Norway, and disembarking in London, proceeded to the court of King Athelred. Having sung the praises of this monarch at court, he was made a king's man, and was gifted with a gold-embroidered scarlet cloak. He gained great renown from the slaying of one Thorom, a notorious robber of London, who had refused to return him a loan. But at the approach of spring the Icelander sailed for Iceland, and here too he sang at the Royal Court. From King Sigtrygg also he received gifts. The winter he spent with Yarl Sigurd in the Orkneys, whence he took ship for Upsala. Here he met Rafn the Skald, an Icelander, with whom he made a friendly compact. The friendship, however, was broken by Gunnlaug's disparaging criticism of Rafn's song offered to the king, and the unsuccessful singer vowed revenge. Rafn soon afterwards set sail for Iceland, and enlisted the services of his kinsman, Skapti the lawman, in a suit for the hand of Helga. At the same time Gunnlaug returned to England as promised, but was delayed there for two years by Athelred, who feared a Danish invasion. Then entering the first north-bound ship, he came to Norway. Now, Yarl Eric had heard that Gunnlaug had sung, while in the Orkneys, a song in praise of him. Gunnlaug was therefore assisted by that earl to find ship for Iceland, but here he landed several miles from Burgfrith and Helga, and was further delayed by Thord, a farmer's son, who insisted on wrestling with Gunnlaug and his companions. But the challenger, having got the better of all the companions, was thrown by Gunnlaug, who, however, sprained his ankle. The consequence of this mishap was that Helga's lover reached Burgfrith at the time of her wedding-feast with Rafn. At the following Yule-tide marriage-feast, however, Gunnlaug and Helga met, and the disappointed lover gave the unhappy bride Athelred's gold-embroidered scarlet cloak. But when summer came Gunnlaug, in the hearing of the people at the Thing, challenged Rafn to meet him on the holm of Axe river within three days. The foes met, but could not agree regarding who had prevailed. Unable to decide their quarrel, the rivals then set sail each in a ship, Rafn reaching Drontheim, Gunnlaug the court of Yarl Eric. But this monarch forebade their intended combat, until hearing that Rafn was on his way into Sweden, he sent guides with Gunnlaug to conduct him

thither. The foes again met, this time to slay each other. And Helga, lonely and sad in her father's house, plucked the golden threads from Gunnlaug's cloak. After a time she was wedded to Thorkel, to whom she bore several sons and daughters. Still her only delight was in Gunnlaug's gift, and when sickness fell upon Thorkel's homefolk she asked for the cloak, plucked out the last thread, and died in her husband's arms. (*Vide* Sir W. Cox and Jones, *Tales of Teutonic Lands.*)

GUNTER, SIR. (*Vide* " Guy of Warwick.") A gallant knight of Otho's who nearly killed Héraud in the fight with the Italians.

GUNTHER (1). (*Vide* " Nibelungenlied.") Son of King Giuki and husband of Brunhild (*q.v.*), whom Siegfried gained for him by riding through the fire-ring at Isenstein. He is afterwards king of his father's realm, and is slain by Kriemhild in vengeance for assisting in the death of Siegfried.

GUNTHER (2). (*Vide* " Nibelungenlied.") Son of Siegfried and Kriemhild, and nephew to King Gunther of Burgundy.

GUROUN, SIR. A wealthy knight. Mentioned in the *Lay le Fraine* (*q.v.*), who, to obtain the love of Le Fraine, entered an abbey, but soon after fled with his lady. He married Le Codre (*q.v.*), whom he discovered to be the sister of Le Fraine. This discovery caused him to dissolve his marriage and wed his former love, Le Fraine.

GUTTORM. (*Vide* " Volsungs.") Son of King Giuki and Grimhild (*q.v.*). He, influenced by his brother Gunnar (*q.v.*), slew Sigurd (*q.v.*), in the doing of which he met his own death.

GUY OF WARWICK, SIR. An English romance of the thirteenth century. Roland, Earl of Warwick, was renowned for his wisdom and bravery, and his laws put into practice by his worthy steward Segard were respected by all. His daughter, Felice, was famous for her beauty and her learning. Segard's son, Guy, was cupbearer to the earl and was very popular. He was handsome, strong and brave, and had been brought up in all manly graces and sports by the famous Heraud of Ardenne. The Feast of Pentecost was about to be celebrated. It began with High Mass, then there was a banquet, followed by festivities and sports. This feast lasted a fortnight. Guy was told to take charge of Felice's dinner-party, and attracted much admiration from her ladies. Even Felice noticed him and asked his name. Guy fell violently in love with Felice, although he knew that it might mean death if he dared to express his devotion. At the end of the festival he could bear it no longer and declared his love to Felice, to meet with a disdainful refusal. This caused him to fall sick. The physicians could do nothing for him, not knowing the cause of his malady which threatened to be fatal. Felice, however, in a dream saw an angel who advised her to return Guy's love; so when he again expressed his love for her and fainted, she took pity on him and promised her troth when he was knighted and had proved his valour at the tournaments. This good news had a marvellous effect on Guy. He once more attended court and was knighted by the king. Felice requiring of him to achieve a name worthy of her, Sir Guy determined to go to foreign countries in search of adventures, and under the care of Heraud and Sir Thorold and Sir Urry and a requisite retinue he left to win a name. They journeyed first to Rouen, where they found a tournament was to be held in honour of Blanchefleur, daughter of Reignier, Emperor of Germany. The prize fell to Guy, and after sending a suit of armour and a gift of money to Blanchefleur, he sent off his prizes to Roland and Felice. He then travelled through Europe, gaining distinction and renown everywhere. After a year, Heraud suggested returning to England, and they went to London and presented themselves to King Athelstane. On going home to Warwick Sir Guy hastened to Felice, hoping that now she would deem him worthy of her. Felice, however, would not promise to marry Guy until he was at such a pinnacle of glory that he was unrivalled. Sir Guy, as a true lover, followed his lady's wishes, and begged permission from Roland to go further afield in his search for glory. The earl urged him to stay, and his parents besought him not to leave them alone in their old age, but his lady's word was law, and he set out again, with the same attendants. He went to Flanders, and travelled through Spain, Germany and Lombardy, gaining prizes and fame everywhere, but he was severely wounded at Beneventum in Italy, and his enemies made a plot to take him at a disadvantage. Guy had an enemy in Otho, Duke of Pavia, who incited several Italian knights to wait in ambush in a wood where Sir Guy and his companions were to pass. A desperate combat took place, and Sir Thorold and Sir Urry were killed. Heraud was supposed to be dead, and Sir Guy was left victorious to bewail the fate of his dear friends. Indeed, he reproached Felice for having been the primary cause of this loss of life. He left the dead body as he thought of Heraud in charge of a monk for burial and found shelter in the cave of a hermit. When he was cured of his wounds he went to Saxony and travelling from there to Burgundy, intended to go on to England. He found his friend Heraud in Burgundy, disguised as a palmer, and they went together through Flanders. Then at St. Omer they heard that Segwin, Duke of Louvain, was besieged by the Emperor Reignier and was in great straits. Sir Guy with a small army went to his assistance and defeated the royalists, and the emperor then collected a huge army, and a great battle took place in which Thierry of Gurmoise distinguished himself. But the unconquerable Guy was victorious. The Emperor with a still larger army was unsuccessful and the siege was turned into a blockade. One day when the emperor was out hunting and defenceless, he encountered Sir Guy, who met him with an olive branch and said he was sure that Segwin would welcome the emperor. So the emperor went with his conqueror into the city and peace was made. Segwin married the emperor's niece. Soon after, Sir Guy heard that Ernis, Emperor of Greece, was besieged by the Soudan and that his condition was desperate. Sir Guy collected an army, was received cordially by Ernis and completely defeated the Saracens. Ernis promised to give his daughter Loret in marriage to Sir Guy. Sir Murgadour, who had fallen in love with the princess Loret by a lying story, tried to destroy Sir Guy's reputation with the emperor, and then persuaded Sir Guy that the emperor meant to kill him. Guy nearly went over to the Saracens in anger, but meeting the emperor an explanation ensued, and Sir Murgadour's treachery was revealed. Sir Guy, hearing that the Soudan meditated another attack, went out to meet him, and after a hard struggle dispersed the army. Sir Murgadour now tried another plot. He persuaded the emperor to propose a single combat between two champions, one for the Saracens, the other the Christians. Sir Guy offered to champion the Christians, and addressed the Soudan, telling him that God's curse was on all unbelievers. The Soudan, enraged, ordered Sir Guy to be killed, but Sir Guy cut off his head, and made his way back to the camp. After this he traversed Ernis' dominions with him. On their way they witnessed a fight between a dragon and a lion. Guy killed the dragon, and the lion was so grateful that it followed like a dog. Ernis, charmed with Sir Guy's bravery, was anxious for his wedding with his daughter Loret, and a day was fixed. Sir Guy had evidently forgotten for the time his love for Felice, but the sight of the wedding-ring brought it all back to him, and he became very ill, deferred the marriage, and confided to Heraud the cause of his illness. He was at a loss how to break the unwelcome news to Ernis and Loret, when an incident occurred which made it easier. Sir Murgadour killed the lion which so faithfully attended Sir Guy, and in revenge Sir Guy slew Sir Murgadour. As he was the emperor's steward this placed Ernis in an unfortunate position, as the emperor was much more powerful than he, so Sir Guy determined to leave Constantinople altogether. His next adventure was helping a knight, Sir Thierry, who was in love with Osile, daughter of the Duke of Lorraine, and by the treachery of Otho of Pavia, had been attacked and dangerously wounded, Osile having been taken to Otho. After some adventures Sir Guy united the lovers. Not long after he heard that the Duke of Lorraine and Otho were determined to take possession of the lands of Thierry's father, Aubry, in revenge, so he went to assist Thierry. He first routed the army of Lorraine and then turned upon Duke Otho's army. Otho had recourse to treachery. He sent a message to Aubry by an archbishop to say that if Thierry and Osile appeared before the emperor and apologized he would forgive them. This ruse succeeded and the party were seized unarmed by men in ambush. Sir Heraud and Thierry were carried off, but Sir Guy escaped. Sir Thierry was thrown into a dungeon at Pavia, and Osile taken by Otho. Sir Guy, wandering from place to place, arrived at the castle of Sir Amys of the Mountain, who offered him help against Otho, but Sir Guy considered such a plan as hopeless. He disguised himself and visited Otho with a valuable war-horse, only asking as reward the charge of Sir Thierry, whom he reviled. Otho appointed him jailer, and soon Sir Guy made himself known to Thierry. However, being overheard by a felon who ran to tell Duke Otho, he followed the man and killed him in the presence of the duke, excusing himself by pretending that he had attempted to carry food to Thierry. Sir Guy managed to see Osile, arranged with her to hasten her marriage with Otho, then liberated Thierry, and riding to meet the marriage procession, killed Otho and took Osile in safety to Thierry. A reconciliation was made with the Duke of Lorraine, and Thierry and Osile were married. Sir Guy then went boar-hunting, and having killed one huge boar he carried it into Flanders. Florentine, King of Flanders, sent his son to remonstrate, and Guy gave him such a severe blow with his horn that it killed the prince. He then went to the palace and was entertained by Florentine, but when the dead body of the prince was brought in, and he found it was his guest who killed him, he and his attendants nearly slew Sir Guy, who, however, escaped. Soon after this he returned to England, and had hardly received congratulations from Athelstane before he heard of a great dragon in Northumberland doing great damage. He killed it and carried the head to Athelstane. Then he went home, found his parents both dead, offered to Felice all he had gained in his travels through Christendom, and was married at once. It was only forty days after the marriage that Sir Guy began to think how much he had done for woman's love and how little in God's service, so he resolved to devote the rest of his life to penance. Felice was horrified, but could not prevent him from his purpose, so she placed a gold ring on his finger to remind him of her, and Sir Guy, dressed as a palmer, set out for the Holy Land. The first adventure he had was an encounter with a ferocious giant, Amiraunt of Ethiopia, on behalf of Earl Jonas, who, with his fifteen sons, had been warring with the Saracens. He slew the giant, and Jonas and his sons were released. Meanwhile Felice had a son, the famous Raynburn, whom she brought up very carefully under the tuition of Heraud, but he was stolen by some Saracen merchants, and they took the child with them to a heathen land under a king called Aragus. Aragus took a fancy to the child, had his education completed, and made him his chamberlain. The boy soon made himself famous by his prowess. Heraud set out to find the boy, but he was shipwrecked and thrown into a dungeon in Africa. Guy, meanwhile, had reached Constantinople, where he met a pilgrim who turned out to be Sir Thierry who had lost all his land, and was being punished by the then Duke of Pavia, who thought he had killed Otho slain by Sir Guy. Thierry began to lament Sir Guy's death. Being weak and faint with hunger, he fell asleep on Sir Guy's arm. He had a dream which Sir Guy interpreted, and he gave Thierry a sword and treasure. Sir Guy then went to the emperor and asked charity, and on being questioned told him he was blamed for punishing the innocent Thierry. He challenged the steward. The steward accepted and Sir Guy, donning armour, got his marvellous sword from Thierry. The combat was undecided by night. The steward ordered Sir Guy to be thrown into the sea during the night. This was done and Guy found himself floating in his bed. He was found by a fisherman and rescued, and the circumstances were related to the emperor. Sir Guy then killed the steward in combat, and found Thierry, who was restored by the emperor to all his possessions. Sir Guy was now anxious to return to England, and when he arrived there, he found that Athelstane was besieged in Winchester by the King of Denmark, and his only hope lay in obtaining a champion who would challenge Colbrand, a Danish giant. In a dream Athelstane was told to request the help of the first pilgrim he met at the entrance of his palace. This pilgrim was Sir Guy, and Athelstane asked his assistance. The poet tells how Sir Guy said he had come to fight for God and to make England free, and how he prayed to God for His blessing before he began the fight. The King of Denmark swore if his man fell he would never again harass England, and Athelstane that he would give up his country to the Danish king if his man were slain. It was a keen fight, and at one time Colbrand considered himself the victor and demanded the king should yield. But when he refused to lend Guy one of his strong axes to fight with, Guy seized one of his own and struck off Colbrand's right arm, and then killed him. Guy concealed his identity even after the victory, and made the king promise not to reveal it till a year had passed. Felice had been employing her time in the absence of her husband in looking after the poor. Guy visited the castle in his pilgrim's dress, and received kindness from her, and seeing her so well employed he did not make himself known to her, but went into a hermitage in the Forest of Ardennes with only a page as attendant. Warned by an angel of the near approach of death, he sent the gold ring to Felice, and begged her to come and give directions for his burial. She came to find him dying, remained with him to the end and was buried in the same grave fifteen days after.

Not only is Guy a knight-errant and slayer of noisome monsters, the doom of the wanderer presses heavily upon him, and, his bride

M

once won, he must leave her for the Holy Land. The old tale of Odysseus and Penelope is repeated, save for a sprinkling of Christian sentiment. His bride follows him shortly to the tomb. He is the sun-hero, and she the sunset which cannot linger long when the sun has gone to his rest.

GUY, SIR (1). (*Vide* " Bevis of Hampton.") Father of Sir Bevis. He married a daughter of the King of Scotland who was much younger than he, and who got her lover, Sir Murdour, to kill her husband when he was out hunting. (*Vide* also " Guy of Warwick.")

GUY, SIR (2). (*Vide* " Bevis of Hampton " and " Guy of Warwick.") Son of Bevis of Hampton. Born and baptized in a forest and brought up by a forester, he was eventually made successor to King Ermyn. He fought bravely for his father at a battle fought in London.

GUY, SIR (3). (*Vide* " Sir Ferumbras.") Duke of Burgundy. One of the twelve French peers imprisoned in Laban's palace at Aigremor. He was taken prisoner in a sally, and would have been hanged by Laban had not Roland rescued him. He married Floripas (*q.v.*).

GUYOT. Surnamed the Provençal, a French trouvère, from whose poem on the Grail legend, not now extant, the German poet Wolfram von Eschenbach (*q.v.*) took the plot of his *Parzival*. He was born in the early part of the twelfth century, and flourished between 1160 and 1180. He was a native of Anjou, and by his appellation of "Master" may be classed as a lay commoner. He appears to have completed his literary and philosophical education in that part of the south of France which in his time was known as the Province of Saint Giles, and which maintained literary and political relations with the north of Spain. He also studied for some time at Toledo in the Moorish schools, and this circumstance fully explains the Oriental colouring in his poem, which has led many scholars to believe that the Grail legend had an Eastern origin. His long residence in and acquaintance with Provence probably won him the literary nick-name of " The Provençal," but he wrote in a dialect more akin to the north than to the south of France, as can be proved from the French words borrowed from him by Wolfram which are distinctly of the *langue d'oïl*. The chief exponent of the priority of Guyot as the first writer who cast the Grail legend into literary form was Professor Bergmann of Strasburg (*The San Gréal*, Edinburgh, 1870), whose conclusions were traversed by the late Mr. Alfred Nutt. As these conclusions are, however, extremely significant, it will be well to summarize them. Professor Bergmann says that Wolfram tells us that Guyot found at Toledo an Arabian book, written by an astrologer named Flegetanis, and containing the story of the marvellous vase called Gréal, which at first hovered in the air, and afterwards, having been deposited on earth by angels, was guarded by faithful Christians. He adds, that Guyot made researches in the Latin chronicles of Brittany, Ireland, and France, and at last found the story of the Gréal related in a chronicle of Anjou. This information, furnished by the German poet, does not seem to contain much truth. It is true that Guyot, like almost all poets of his time, may, to make a show of his erudition, have spoken of Flegetanis and an Arabian book as the source from which he drew some details of his poem. But Flegetanis can by no means be an Arabian proper name, and consequently all that Wolfram relates of this pretended personage is of his own or Guyot's invention. The name of Flegetanis might be the Latin transcription of Feleke-Dânêh, a Persian compound word, which signifies astrologer or astronomer, and in this case it would be the title of an astrological work translated into Latin, and which Guyot had the opportunity of studying while at Toledo. However this may be, it is beyond doubt that the history of the fable of the Gréal existed neither in Arabian nor Spanish books nor in the Latin chronicles of France or Brittany, but owes its origin to Guyot, who invented and composed it with poetical elements, most of which, it is true, were traditional, but which he combined in a novel manner by connecting them with a philosophical idea which was his own, at the same time that it was the expression and the natural result of the tendencies and the spirit of his age. Indeed, in the time of Guyot, the two prevailing ideas of the Middle Ages, religion and feudalism, had just been realized in the clergy and knighthood. On seeing the respect and authority enjoyed by the knight and the priest, one was naturally led to think that the highest human destiny would be to unite both qualities either in the priesthood or the priest-knight. The Church herself, temporarily allured by this beautiful ideal, once attempted to realize it. She founded the order of the Templars, in which, however, she intended the ecclesiastical element to pre-

ponderate over the secular; but she soon had cause to repent the creation of an institution which daily showed more decided tendencies gradually to extinguish the sacerdotal spirit in the worldly splendour of chivalry. These tendencies were, moreover, favoured and sustained by the anti-clerical spirit of the Albigenses, who were very numerous in the south of France, where a great number of the richest establishments of the Templars existed. It was probably also under the influence of this spirit that Guyot, during his sojourn in Provence, conceived the idea of a sacerdotal chivalry and royalty, which, in his idea, were to be the guardians of the temporal and spiritual welfare of humanity, in the same manner as the Pope and the Catholic clergy represented the kingly power and the soldiery which watched over the safety of the Church. Unable to give historic reality to this idea, which appeared so beautiful to him, he desired at least to represent it through poetry. He undertook to show in his poem how the true knight, by his actions and virtues, renders himself worthy of the highest destiny which man can attain, that priestly kingship, namely, to which it was necessary to be called both by birth and the grace of God. Temporal and spiritual welfare, the guardianship of which was to be confided to a priestly knighthood, the poet represented under the symbol of a sacred vase, the limpid and transparent element, water, and by extension, the vase or basin which contained it being, according to the symbols of the East and of the Middle Ages, images of purity and truth, and consequently the symbols of wisdom and salvation.

We have elsewhere dealt with the origin of the Grail. (*Vide* "Grail, Holy.") But it may be well to remark here when dealing with the poet who first gave the legend literary form that it is with a goblet or cup containing pure water, that the future was foretold in the East and in some countries of Europe. Poetry was represented by the skalds of the North and the Breton bards under the symbolic form of a cup filled with a precious liquid ; thence the Scandinavian myth on the vase of Quasir ; thence also, among the Bretons and Welsh, the mysteries of the magic cauldron of Keridwen (*a.b.*), the goddess of poetry ; and, lastly, the celebrated goblet of Djemschid, which was nothing but the symbol of the safety, the happiness, and the abundance which the people enjoyed under the reign of this illustrious King of Persia. It is perhaps the latter myth, explained in some Arabian work, or that of the basin of Keridwen, contained in some Breton book, which determined Guyot to choose the vase as a symbol of temporal and spiritual welfare, the guardianship of which he intrusted to his priestly knighthood. In mediæval Latinity the masculine *gradalis* or neuter *gradale* means vase, goblet, or basin. The dialects of the south of France having preserved the form of Latin words almost intact, only changed the mean dental *d* into the hissing dental *s* or *z*, so that to this day, in some parts of the south, a *grasal* (masc.) or a *grazale* (fem.) signifies a basin. In the dialects of Southern France the final consonants of the syllables of Latin words have been cut off or modified ; and consequently, *grad-alis* and *grad-ale* were changed into *gra-alz* and *gra-al*. Such, indeed, was the form of these words in the Burgundian dialects, which formed the transition from the *langue d'oïl* to the *langue d'oc*. The dialects of Picardy and Normandy, which tended to sharpen the pronunciation of vowels, instead of *Graal* adopted the form of *Grëal*, which the Normans also introduced into England, and which Guyot employed. Guyot the Provençal, a native, as we have said, of the duchy of Anjou, and consequently writing in a French dialect very much akin to that of Burgundy, found in his country the expression *Graal* to designate a vase ; and what proves that he really employed it to designate a sacred vase, is the use which his immediate imitators, Chrétien de Troyes and Wolfram von Eschenbach, made of the same word. The sacred vase, or the San Grëal, the symbol of grace and salvation, was placed, according to the fiction of Guyot, in a temple guarded by Knights Templeis or Templois. This name reminds us of that of the Templars, whom the poet imitated and idealized in his poem. The temple of the Grëal was placed upon a mountain in the midst of a thick wood, which is a symbolic representation of the moral elevation and the sanctity of this place, which no one can approach except by Divine favour. And even as Mount Meru of the Hindoos and Olympus of the Greeks are placed in the mythological poetry in a mysterious distance, so has our poet placed the mountain of the Grëal at some considerable distance from his country, beyond the Pyrenees, in Spain. For that reason he gave it the Catalonian name of Mont Salvagge (wild or inaccessible mountain). The Grëal, according to Guyot, was made of a wonderful stone called Exillis, which had once been the most brilliant in the crown of the arch-angel Lucifer. This cup was brought from heaven by angels, and left to the care of Titurel, the first king of the Grëal, who trans-mitted it to Amfortas, the second king, whose sister, Herzeloide, was the mother of Parzival, the third king of the San Grëal. This genealogy of the kings of the San Grëal commences in the East, and is connected with Sennabor, an imaginary King of Armenia ; it comprises fictitious names of kings of France and princes of Spain, and ends in the house of Anjou. As this genealogy comprises nearly eleven centuries, and descends to the epoch when Guyot lived, it cannot have existed previously to this poet, and it is more than pro-bable that he invented it. If, nevertheless, Wolfram von Eschen-bach mentions that Guyot found it in a chronicle of Anjou, this indication, which doubtless was furnished to him by the romance of the Angevine poet, only proves to us that the latter wanted to exalt his native country, the duchy of Anjou, in certain details of his poem. Though the story of the San Grëal was sufficiently interest-ing by itself, and above all by the idea on which it was based, Guyot, whose chief aim was not to instruct, but to amuse the reader, wished to enrich his romance with an addi-tional poetical element in order to make it more attractive. The favourite reading of those times consisted of knightly histories and adventures ; and, precisely at that epoch, the tales of King Arthur's adventures and those of the Knights of the Round Table were spreading all over France, and fully satisfied the taste of the century for all that was adventurous, marvellous, and fantastical. Exactly as at the same epoch in Germany the poets

rejected the national epic subjects for foreign ones, so were the Breton tales preferred in France to the national traditions regarding Charlemagne and the twelve peers of France, and that the more willingly that Breton poesy actually did surpass all others by its marvellous and highly imagi-native fictions. It is, therefore, principally on that account that Guyot connected the story of the San Grëal, not with the epic cycle of Charlemagne, as he might have done, but with that of Arthur and the Knights of the Round Table. Amongst the Breton knights who broke lances with all comers, and boldly fought with dragons, giants, and against the most insurmount-able obstacles, we chiefly distin-guish three : Gawain, Geraint and Peredur. It is principally from the traditions regarding the last of the three that Guyot borrowed a great many of the incidents with which he composed the history of *Parzival*, the principal hero of his romance. It will be sufficient to point out a few striking analogies which exist between the history of *Parzival* and the Breton or Welsh tale of *Peredur*. It is true that the *Peredur* tale which is found among the *Mabinogion* or tradi-tional tales contained in the *Red Book of Hergest*, was not written till the fourteenth century ; but the foundation of it is older, and was probably known to Guyot through the traditions spread in Armorica, a province adjoining the duchy of Anjou. The proof that they were not unknown to him, is that the history of the youth of Parzival is composed of the same incidents as the history of the youth of Peredur. The details about the castle of the sick old man, and the two uncles of Peredur were reproduced more or less faithfully in the romance of Parzival. Lastly, the castle of the king of the Grëal which figures in the poems of Guyot corresponds to the marvellous castle of the Breton tale. One might even be tempted to think that Guyot had borrowed from the Breton traditions the very history of the San Grëal, since, in the tale of Peredur, a basin or a Grëal is made mention of, and even the name of Peredur might be explained as meaning "seeker of the cup," or "searcher after the Grëal." But this illusion disappears when we consider that the cup mentioned has not the slightest relation to the idea of the San Grëal, and plays in the tale but an accessory or accidental part. If, therefore, the name of Peredur really signifies seeker of the basin, it is equally a fortuitous circumstance, since it is caused neither by the sense nor the details of the tale. This name was probably very common among the Bretons, and if it had the signification which is given to it, doubtless related and alluded to the case or basin of the goddess Keridwen. Peredur was the name of the chief of the Guenedocians, who distinguished himself at the Battle of Ardderyd, and who, at a later period, transformed by tradition into a Knight of the Round Table, became the hero whose adventures and great feats are celebrated in the Welsh text referred to. It is therefore evident that the history of the San Grëal did not exist among the Bretons, or Welsh, and is entirely of Guyot's invention, who borrowed nothing from Breton traditions save, perhaps, the idea of representing the salvation of mankind by the symbol of a cup— an idea which may have been suggested to him by the myth on the vase of Keridwen. Far from borrowing the matter of his poem from foreign countries, Guyot only connected the story, which he had invented, with the Breton traditions of the cycles of Arthur, so that the fiction of the Grëal forms indeed the accessory, but nevertheless the most important part of his romance. Guyot skilfully managed to unite these two elements of different origin without, however, confounding them. Thus the Templois, who bear the dignified character of a priestly knighthood, are clearly distinct in his poem from the Knights of the Round Table, who only represent the worldly or common chivalry. More than that, Guyot did not simply imitate the Breton traditions, he embellished them and gave them more interest, endowing them with a meaning at once more poetical and more philosophical. Thus, to quote a few instances, the silence which Peredur, according to the Breton tale, keeps in presence of the marvels he sees in the palace of the sick old man, is simply caused by the vow he had made, to remain dumb until he should have obtained the hand of Angarad. In Guyot's romance, on the contrary, Parzival's silence arises from deeper causes, and forms, as it were, the knot of the whole fiction of the Grëal. The Breton tale speaks of a bleeding lance which was presented to Peredur, and was probably intended to remind him to avenge the murder of his uncle and nephews, who had been treacherously assassinated. And in reality the lance is the symbol of protection, and a bleeding body that of an appeal for revenge. The bleeding lance was therefore likely to indicate that the instrument of protection had been violated, and will consequently bleed until revenge shall have been taken. Guyot, giving a more moral and deeper meaning to the bleeding lance, connects with it one of his chief poetical fictions. By a play upon words, which was only possible in French, the old sick king who in the Breton tradition is surnamed the fisherman (*pecheur*) because he whiled away his troubles in fishing with a line, is transformed into a king sinner (*pecheur*). His sin, according to Guyot, consists in his having fought for a sensual love against a paynim prince by whose lance he was wounded as a punishment for his fault. This lance will bleed until the king shall have been cured of his wound, or until his sins shall have been expiated. The Breton tale also mentions a magic sword, which the kingly fisher gave to Peredur as a symbol of sovereignty and strength. This sword broke in the hands of the knight, which signified that he had not yet the strength required to be worthy of sovereignty. But, according to Guyot's fiction, Parzival only receives this sword when already broken, and as it is only with this sword that he can conquer the kingdom of the Grëal; the poet represents this circumstance as almost an insurmountable obstacle, which the hero nevertheless succeeds in overcoming. It is thus that Guyot managed to give to certain details, void of meaning in the Breton tradition, a moral and philosophical signification. On the whole, the romance of the Angevin poet, though destined, like all romances of chivalry, to amuse noble lords and ladies, bore a character somewhat philosophical, and on that account we must not be astonished if certain of Guyot's ideas are not in agreement with the orthodoxy of his century. This poet did not share in the hatred against the Mohammedans so energetically manifested throughout Christendom during the Crusades. The Templois do not turn their arms against the infidels; on the contrary, their intercourse with them is that of friends, companions in arms, allies and relations. This tolerance, which in the eyes of orthodoxy probably seemed criminal, appears to have been the fruit of the sojourn which Guyot had made at Toledo, in the midst of the Mohammedan Arabs. We must also remark that the Templois, though Christians, rather resemble an association formed without the pale of the Church than a Catholic community. Moreover, the apostles, saints, angels, and ceremonies of the Church, which always occupy the first rank in the religious poems of the Middle Ages, do not occupy so important a place in Guyot's poem. These heterodox and somewhat anti-clerical tendencies were perhaps contracted by the poet in the south of France, where he must frequently have come into contact with Albigenses and Templars; and it is very probable on account of this conformity of views with the sectarians of the south that he received from his contemporaries the surname or nickname of "Provençal." Lastly, we must attribute to the heterodoxy of Guyot the loss or the destruction of his romance, which was likely to have the same fate as the books of the Albigenses and the works of the Templars. Guyot's romance, however, spread rapidly, and attracted the attention of a large number of readers in France, England and Germany. What proves this is, that it was imitated in those countries shortly after its publication, and that the history of the Grëal soon formed a kind of epic tradition, which, as such, was modified and developed by several French and foreign poets. Thus Chrétien, finding in Guyot's poem the history of Percival, who, without being a Knight of the Round Table, was nevertheless in relation with it, took this episode and treated it separately, consulting, besides, as for his other romances, the original Armorican traditions. This Champenois trouvère died before he had finished his romance of *Perceval le Gallois*, which, however, is extant even now with the continuation composed by different poets. What proves that Chrétien imitated the romance of Guyot is, first, the name of Perceval which he kept for his hero, and which is nothing less than the Champenois pronunciation of the name of Parzival, which he found in Guyot's poem. This name, invented by Guyot, is doubtless derived from *farisi-fal*, a compound Persian word signifying "ignorant knight," and alludes to the ignorance of young Parzival, who, in consequence of the extreme solicitude of his mother to shelter him from every danger, had been deprived of all knightly education. Chrétien de Troyes, unacquainted with the foreign origin of this word, explains it as signifying "one who pierces or wanders through vales to seek adventures."

GWARTHLEO. (*Vide* "Gododin.") A Cymric warrior, "young, rich, ever pressing forward." He was slain at the Battle of Cattraeth.

GWAWL. In Welsh romance, the rival of Pwyll (*q.v.*) for Rhiannon's (*q.v.*) hand. For this pretension he was decoyed into a bag and baited as a badger.

GWEN. (*Vide* "Gododin.") Father of Gwenabwy. A Cymric warrior who was slain at the Battle of Cattraeth. "Over the lovely, slender, blood-stained body" of Gwen, knelt his only son, Gwenaby.

GWENABY. (*Vide* "Gododin.") Son of Gwen. A Cymric warrior slain at the Battle of Cattraeth. "He was a mighty and fierce dragon." "His land should not be ploughed, though it might become wild."

GWERN. In Welsh romance, son of Matholwch and Branwen (*q.v.*). When still a child he was made King of Ireland, but his uncle Evnissyen immediately cast him into a fire.

GWION BACH. In Welsh romance and myth, son of Gwreang. He was put by Ceridwin (*q.v.*) to stir the magic cauldron of inspiration and science, the contents of which were to be drunk by her son ; but three drops of the liquor having lighted on Gwion's fingers he sucked them and thereby became gifted with supernatural sight. Then he fled, pursued by the jealous mother. The pursued and pursuer metamorphosed themselves into a hare and a greyhound, a fish and an otter, a bird and a hawk, a grain of wheat and a black hen, which ultimately swallowed the wheat. Later Gwion became the child of Ceridwin, but being averse to slay him on account of his beauty, she put him in a bag and cast him into the sea. After some time he was drawn out by Elphin, son of Cwyddno (*q.v.*), and was called Taliesin (*q.v.*) (Radiant Brow). The cauldron, deprived of the sacred liquor, now contained only poison, which burst the vessel and killed the horses of Gwyddno Garanhir. Compare the metamorphoses of Ceridwen and

Gwion Bach with that of the Queen of Beauty and the Jinn, son of the daughter of Eblis, in the tale of *The Second Calendar* in the *Arabian Nights' Entertainments*.

GWRUELING. (*Vide* "Gododin.") A gigantic Cymric warrior. He was slain at the Battle of Cattraeth.

GWYDDNO GARANHIR. (*Vide* "Gwion Bach.")

GWYLGET. (*Vide* "Gododin.") A chief of Gododin, who joined in the banquet of Mynyddang, and fell in the Battle of Cattraeth.

GWYNN AP NUDD. A Cymric deity who appears in Welsh romance, likened to Finn (Gaelic) and to Odin (Norse). He was King of Hades, and fought every May-day until the day of doom with Gwythur ap Greidawl for Creudylad, daughter of Llud. This myth evidently represents the contest between winter and summer for the fertile earth. Later we find him figuring as the King of the Fairies.

GWYTHUR AP GREIDAWL. (*Vide* "Gwynn ap Nudd.")

H

HACON, YARL. (*Vide* "Burnt Njal.") Heathen King of Norway, and predecessor of the Christian King Olaf.

HADEBURC. (*Vide* "Nibelungen-lied.") One of the two merwomen whom Hagen found bathing by the Danube and whose garments he seized, in order to force them to prophesy concerning the future. She foretold good, but falsely, knowing the future of the Burgundians to be doomed. (*Vide* also "Sigelint.") The seizure of the garments or "swan-dress" of a valkyr, nixie, or wise woman, was generally supposed to enforce her advice or assistance.

HAERING. (*Vide* "Grettir Saga.") A nimble climber whom Thorbiorn Angle (*q.v.*) took with him to the island of Drangey in order to slay Grettir. But his wily attempt was noticed by Grettir's brother, Illugi, who chased Haering over the cliff.

HAGEN (1). The first portion of Ettmüller's division of the *Gudrun*

Lay (*q.v.*). Hagen, known as "Wild" Hagen, was the son of Sigebant and Uta, King and Queen of Ireland. At the age of seven he was carried off by a griffin, over the sea to its nest. Escaping from its young, Hagen discovered three little girls in the same plight as himself—Hilda, daughter of the King of India, Hildburg, daughter of the Lord of Portugal, the third being the daughter of the Lord of Iceland. For many years they lived as best they might, Hagen's strength growing well-nigh superhuman, till at length a passing ship rescued them. Its master, the Count of Carady, had suffered loss through King Sigebant, and, on learning who Hagen was, ordered him to be taken to Carady as a hostage. Hagen (wearing a full suit of armour which he had found some years previously on the body of a shipwrecked warrior cast up on the shore), fought and killed thirty of the count's men, and steered the ship for Ireland, where he made himself known to his parents, and great rejoicings took place in the land. Later he married the Princess Hilda, and his father abdicated in his favour. A daughter was born to him, named Hilda. She was very beautiful, but Hagen was too proud to give her to any of her many suitors. Among these was Hettel, King of Hegelingen, and the account of his wooing and Hagen's share in events forms Ettmüller's second portion of the *Gudrun Lay* (*q.v.* under heading " Hagen and Hettel").

HAGEN (2). Of Tronje. (*Vide* " Dietrich of Berne.") He was handed over to the Franks as hostage to Etzel or Attila, but effected his escape. (*Vide* also " Walther of Aquitaine.")

HAGEN (3). (*Vide* " Nibelungen-lied.") The brother of Dankwart, and uncle to Gunther. He plotted along with Brunhilde against Siegfried, whom he slew treach-erously at her instigation. Kriem-hild (*q.v.*), Siegfried's wife, after her marriage with Etzel or Attila, avenged her husband's murder by trapping and eventually slaying him. But not until after he and his followers had made dire execution at her husband's court.

HAGEN AND HETTEL. Second divi-sion of the *Gudrun Lay* (*q.v.*). For first portion, see *Hagen*. Hettel, King of Hegelingen in Ireland, hearing of the beauty of Hilda of Ireland (*q.v.*), daughter of Hagen, determined to wed her, and after discussion with his counsellors sent ambassadors to Hagen, chief of whom were Morung of Friesland (*q.v.*), Horant of Denmark (*q.v.*), Yrolt of Ortland (*q.v.*), Wate of Sturmen (*q.v.*), and Frute of Dane-land (*q.v.*). They pretended to have been exiled by Hettel, and Hagen received them hospitably.

Horant, by his marvellous sweet singing, was specially instrumental in winning Hilda's heart for Hettel, telling her that at Hettel's court were many singers finer than him-self. Having made their plans, the ambassadors told Hagen they must return home, as Hettel was now willing to be reconciled to them. Before departing they in-vited the king and his court to come down to the shore to see their treasures, and having manœuvred that Hilda should be separated from her parents during the in-spection, Hettel's messengers leapt with her (a willing captive) into their ships, and, reinforced by armed men who had been con-cealed in the vessel, they escaped from Hagen's fury, and sailed rapidly for Daneland. Hettel re-ceived his bride joyfully, but at the wedding-feast, Hagen and his men, who had followed in pursuit, came in sight, and a fierce struggle took place, in which Hettel was wounded. Wate and Hagen en-gaged in single conflict, when Hettel, his wounds bound, sug-gested peace, as both sides seemed equal in strength, and the dead lay everywhere. Hagen finally agreed and a complete reconcilia-tion was effected, Wate producing "a good root" to heal the wounded. Hettel and Hilda entertained Hagen and his men royally for twelve days, when Hagen returned thoroughly satisfied with his daughter's marriage. Hettel and Hilda lived in honour and happi-ness, there being born to them a son Ortwein, and a daughter Gudrun, the story of whose life forms Ettmüller's third division of the *Gudrun Lay*. (*Vide* " Gudrun.")

HALFDAN. In the Icelandic saga of *Frithjof* (*q.v.*), the bright and peace-loving son of King Belé, the friend of Thorsten, Frithjof's father.

HALLGERDA. (*Vide* "Burnt Njal.") Daughter of Hanskuld ; wife of Gunnar (*q.v.*). Gunnar had but newly returned from abroad, where he had acquired much fame and fortune, when, wandering among the booths at the Thing, he was accosted by a beautiful woman. The outcome of the conversation was that Gunnar sought the lady's hand from her father, and the two were married. But Hanskuld had warned the lover that his lady-love was older than he, and that she had, in revenge for a blow, encompassed the death of two husbands. Hallgerda brought much misery upon Gunnar, as she was at bitter feud with the wife of his dearest friend Njal. And having received a blow from her angry husband, on the occasion of her theft from Otkell's store, she never forgot the insult ; but in Gunnar's direst need refused, with a sneer, to lend her assistance. He was slain by his foes, and she was driven by her mother-in-law to seek a home elsewhere.

HALLMUND. (*Vide* "Grettir Saga.") The cave-dweller who guarded one end of a pass, while Grettir defended himself at the other against the men of Thorir of Garth (*q.v.*). For some time afterwards the Icelandic hero lived with Hallmund, who met his death at the hands of Grim (*q.v.* 2), whose fish he stole.

HAM. (*Vide* "Frithjof Saga.") A Norwegian storm-fiend in the form of an eagle with black wings. Helgi (*q.v.*) had sent her with the bear-like sea-witch Heyd to swallow up Frithjof (*q.v.*) as he sailed for the island of Yarl Angantyr (*q.v.*). But Frithjof drove straight for the whale upon which the fiends rode, and they were left tossing upon the waves until the sea-weed entangled them. Then the storm subsided.

HAMLET. In the days of Rorik, King of Denmark, Gervendill was Governor of Jutland, and was succeeded by his sons Horvendill and Feng. Horvendill, on his return from a Viking expedition, in which he had slain Koll, King of Norway, married Gerutha, Rorik's daughter, who bore him a son Amleth. But Feng, out of jealousy, murdered Horvendill, and persuaded Gerutha to become his wife, on the plea that he had committed the crime for no other reason than to avenge her of a husband by whom she had been hated. Amleth, afraid of sharing his father's fate, pretended to be imbecile, but the suspicion of Feng put him to various tests which are related in detail. Among other things they sought to entangle him with a young girl, his foster-sister, but his cunning saved him. When, however, Amleth slew an eavesdropper hidden, like Polonius, in his mother's room, and destroyed all traces of the deed, Feng was assured that the young man's madness was feigned. Accordingly he despatched him to England in company with two attendants, who bore a letter enjoining the king of the country to put him to death. Amleth surmised the purport of their instructions, and secretly altered the message on their wooden tablets to the effect that the king should put the attendants to death and give Amleth his daughter in marriage. After marrying the princess, Amleth returned at the end of a year to Denmark. Of the wealth he had accumulated he took with him only certain hollow sticks filled with gold. He arrived in time for a funeral feast, held to celebrate his supposed death. During the feast he plied the courtiers with wine, and executed his vengeance during their drunken sleep by fastening down over them the woollen hangings of the hall with pegs he had sharpened during his feigned madness, and then setting fire to the palace. After a long harangue to the people he was proclaimed king. Returning to England for his wife, he found that his father-in-law and Feng had been pledged to avenge the other's death. The English king, unwilling personally to carry out his pledge, sent Amleth as proxy wooer for the hand of a terrible Scottish Queen Hermuthruda, who had put all former wooers to death, but fell in love with Amleth. On his return to England, his first wife, whose love proved stronger than her resentment, told him of her father's intended revenge. In the battle which followed Amleth won the day by setting up those who had been slain the day before armed with stakes, and thus terrifying the enemy. He then returned with his two wives to Jutland, where he had to encounter the enmity of Wiglek, whom Hermuthruda married.

In his work on the semi-mythical monarchs of Denmark, Saxo-Grammaticus tells the romantic story of Hamlet or Amleth, from which Shakespeare obtained the plot of his immortal tragedy.

HAMUND. (*Vide* " The Lay of the Volsungs.") Son of Sigmund (*q.v.*) begotten on Borghild (*q.v.*), and brother to Helgi (*q.v.*).

HANSKULD (1). (*Vide* " Burnt Njal.") Son of Thrain (*q.v.*), husband of Hildegunna (*q.v.*). Hated by Mord (*q.v.*) on account of his rivalry in the priesthood, he was foully slain one morning in his field by Mord and Njal's sons. This murder brought about the burning of Njal and his household.

HANSKULD (2). Father of Hallgerda (*q.v.*).

HARDRÉ. (" Flowery-haired.") (*Vide* " Garin the Lorrainer.") One of King Pepin's older counsellors. He brought up Garin and Bego along with his two sons, Fromont and William of Montclin. He was killed by Hernais of Orleans when he did battle with Garin.

HARDRED. (Legend of Beowulf.) Son of Hygelak and Hygd, King and Queen of Gothland (*q.v.*). Beowulf acted as regent for him. (*Vide* " Beowulf.") After becoming king, he gave sanctuary to Eanmund and Eadzils, the rebellious sons of Ohtere, King of Sweden, but was slain by Eanmund, whom Hardred had advised to make peace with his father.

HARTMANN VON DER AUE. A High German poet, who is supposed to have lived about the end of the twelfth century. He was of gentle if not actually noble birth, while it is probable that his education was fairly good, for his youth was spent in a monastery, and while sojourning there he assimilated ascetic ideals which clung to him with varying degrees of tenacity throughout the rest of his life. On completing his studies with the monks he passed into the service— in what capacity is not recorded— of a nobleman whose domain was known as Aue, a place which has been identified with Obernau on the Neckar, and subsequently he went to Palestine along with a band of German crusaders. The date of his death is uncertain, but

Gottfried von Strassburg, writing in 1210, mentions him as still alive at that time ; while in a poem by Heinrich von der Turlin, *Diu Krône*, written about 1220, he is mourned for as dead.

Hartmann was a voluminous writer. He wrote two long poems dealing with the Arthurian legends, *Erec* and *Ewein*, deriving his matter in either case from the French of Chrétien de Troyes ; while it is likely that another lengthy metrical romance from Hartmann's pen, *Gregorius*, was also drawn in considerable measure from French sources. In addition to these he wrote a host of lyrics, the majority of them informed by deep religious ardour ; but the poem whereby he is chiefly remembered is *Der Arme Heinrich* ("Poor Henry"), which recounts how one smitten with leprosy was cured of his disease through the heroism of a young girl, who sacrificed her own life to save him. The poem is manifestly based on fact, while it is generally thought, indeed, that the incident occurred in the family the poet himself served. The bulk of Hartmann's work is of rather a didactic order. He strove to imbue the rough knights of his time with a moral and religious spirit, but despite his ardour in this way he hardly ever failed to attain genuine literary merit, and his poems have a degree of grace and finish not commonly found in mediæval German verse. He has always been popular, and the story of his *Arme Heinrich* has been re-told by several modern poets, notably Longfellow and Rossetti ; while seldom have his writings been out of print for any length of time. The best complete edition of them is one issued at Leipsic in 1891, while *Der Arme Heinrich* was edited with English notes by Robertson in 1895.

HARTMUT. King of Ormany. (*Vide* "Gudrun's Lay" and "Gudrun.") Son of King Ludwig and Queen Gerlinte, brother of Ortrun. Married Hildeburg. He was an unsuccessful suitor of Gudrun, attempting first to seek to win her by force, but later was persuaded to carry her off to Ormany, aided by his father and his men. He saves Gudrun from the sea (*vide* "Ludwig"), and for many years seeks with unwavering devotion to win her as his willing bride, but in vain. He fights valiantly and nobly in the struggle with Herwig's rescuing force, being almost slain by Wate (*q.v.*) and rescued by Herwig at Gudrun's request for his sister Ortrun's sake. Later, to please Gudrun and win her friendship and to conclude peace, he, at her request, weds Hildeburg.

HAVELOK THE DANE. The first complete English romance extant, translated from the French by Geoffrey Gaimar (*q.v.*), an Anglo-Norman trouvère who flourished about the middle of the twelfth century. But the French MS. from which he took it was certainly not its original form, as it undoubtedly sprang from Anglo-Danish sources. The translator states in the beginning of the tale that he had it from a Breton lay, but this Breton form appears to have been merely intermediary. The tale recounts how Athelwold, King of England, feeling death draw near, was mightily troubled concerning the future of his infant daughter. Calling his earls about him, he requested them to choose one of their number as a regent. Their choice lighted on Earl Godrch of Cornwall, who swore to protect the princess and her throne until she was of the age of twelve, when he would find her for husband the best man in England. Athelwold died, the earl received from all an oath of fidelity to the princess until her twelfth year, and established law and order throughout the land. The princess waxed very beautiful, and in time Earl Godrich thought to give her to his own son. So he took the princess, whose name was Goldeburg, from Winchester, and shut her up in the Castle of Dover, poorly fed and thinly clad. Birkabeyn, King of Denmark, being in like case to Athelwold, a dying king with three young children, a son and two daughters, made his chief adviser Godard, swear to protect Denmark and the babes until the boy reached the age of knighthood. But Godard took the children, Havelok, Swanborow and Helfedl, and shut them up where they pined for cold and hunger. He slew the little girls, and told a fisherman to cast Havelok into the sea. The fisherman took Havelok home in a bag, but he and his wife were so startled by the light which emanated from his mouth that they became his thralls. The fisherman, Grim, told Godard that Havelok was drowned and with the boy and his own children and wife embarked on his boat and was carried by a north wind to the coast of England. They landed at Lindeseye in the Humber, where he built a hut for himself and family, and gave the place his name, Grimsby. Grim made a living as a fisherman, and, when twelve years old, Havelok decided to assist him, sending the fish Grim caught to Lincoln. A great famine befell the land, and hunger stared the little family in the face. Havelok was such a

mighty eater that fish alone would not feed him, so his foster-father cut him a garment out of the sail of the boat, and sent him to Lincoln to seek his fortune. Hearing a cry of "porters, porters," he elbowed his way through a crowd and upsetting them, was employed to carry the Earl of Cornwall's meat to the castle. He was engaged as scullion by the cook there because of his strength. At the Lincoln games he overcame all at putting the stone, and his strength and meekness became proverbial throughout England. Godrich, hearing of it, resolved to wed Havelok to the Princess Goldeburg and make him his tool to degrade the princess from her queenly right to possess England, as he had sworn to Athelwold to give his daughter to " the best man in England." Goldeburg refused to be wed save to a king's son, but with threats Godrich compelled them to marry. Going to Grimsby, Havelok found that Grim was dead, but received homage from his three sons, who manfully served both him and his wife. In the night, as Goldeburg lay sorrowing over her hard lot, she espied a bright light issuing from her husband's mouth. She also saw a noble cross of red gold upon his shoulder, and heard the voice of an angel say that Havelok was a king's son and heir, and should have all England and Denmark. Havelok on his part dreamt that he was lord of the two countries. Goldeburg counselled him to return to Denmark at once, taking with him Grim's three sons, Robert, William and Hugh. Arrived in Denmark, they asked leave of Ubbe, a great earl, to trade there, and received permission to do so. Their lodging was attacked by sixty stout thieves, but Havelok, tearing up the doorpost for a weapon, made great slaughter. But, wounded in twenty places, the brothers rushed to his aid, and slew the robbers who remained. Ubbe had Havelok taken to his own castle to cure his wounds, and going into Havelok's chamber, perceived the bright light proceeding from his mouth. He then noticed Havelok's likeness to King Birkabeyn, and fell at his feet, swearing fealty. Ubbe summoned all his dependents, and telling them of Godard's treachery, did homage to Havelok. Godard was soon at bay, with the whole of Denmark arrayed against him, and he was taken and hanged. Havelok made his three foster-brothers barons, and gave Ubbe the lands of Godard. To Grim's memory he built a fair priory at Grimsby. Godrich of Cornwall, hearing of Havelok's good fortune, became alarmed, and gathered all his forces at Lincoln. A great battle was fought at Grimsby. Havelok encountering Godrich, struck off his sword-hand, and sent him in fetters to the queen. The Englishmen did homage to Goldeburg as Queen of England, and cried out that Godrich should be hanged. By judgment of his peers he was burnt at the stake. Havelok enriched all who had served him, and with Goldeburg reigned in England sixty years. They had fifteen sons and daughters, whereof all became kings and queens.

The poem is written in octosyllabic couplets with no additional syllables except an occasional double rhyme and some, though with slight, traces of alliteration. The English is good of the period. Havelok is connected with a very wide range of myth, etymologically and otherwise. He is one of the "fatal children" who are born to be kings, and to destroy those who keep them out of their rightful inheritance, and there is, therefore, only one maiden in the world, who may be his wife. The light of kingship or power shines from Havelok as it does from the heads of Servius Tullius and Æsculapius. Like the Great Lord in the Gaelic legend, or Renouart in the Charlemagne romances, he is bound to serve in the kitchen for a space, from which he soon emerges as a mighty man of his hands. Goldeburg is disgusted with the fisher's abode of her husband, as are the princesses in German or Norse legend who espouse King Thrushbeard or King Hacon Grizzlebeard. In the French version the name of Goldeburg is translated as Argentile, and Havelok has become Havelok Curan. In Warner's later poem, *Albion's England*, we have these characteristics presented to us, and Curan in order to win Argentile, becomes a scullion in the house of Ethil, who compels her to marry Curan for motives similar to those which led Godric to insist that Goldeburg should wed Havelok. Curan is the Danish hero whom the Angles designated Anlaf-cwiran, and we discover that Anlaf is identical with Havelok, whose story, as furnishing groundwork for the claim of the Danes through him to England, is connected with the story of *Guy of Warwick* (*q.v.*). The *Havelok* further presents a link with the saga of *Beowulf* (*q.v.*) as bearing a name which is only a modification of Hygelac, one of the heroes of that myth. And when we find Anlaf Latinized into Amlethus we recognize a name familiar to us all —that of Hamlet. In whom we have another dispossessed prince.

HAVGAN. Rival of Arawn (q.v.), a king of the British Celtic Hades. He was mortally wounded by Pwyll (q.v.).

HAYMON. (Vide "Four Sons of Aymon.")

HEBIS, SIR. A knight of Ireland, mentioned in Arthurian romance in the incident of Tristram's visit to King Anguish under the guise of a harper. (Vide "Morte d'Arthur.")

HECTOR DE MARES. A knight alluded to in the Queste del Graal. He meets with Gauvain, and it is foretold to both that they cannot behold the Grail for which they search, so poor are they in faith. On one occasion he fought with Perceval so fiercely that both were near death. But an angel appeared bearing the Grail and made them whole.

HEIMSKRINGLA. An abridged form of a work in Icelandic entitled Lives of the Kings of Norway, not now extant, written by Snorri Sturluson, author of the "Younger" Edda, who flourished during the first half of the thirteenth century, and founded upon Ari Thorgilsson's Book of Kings, an earlier work on Norse-Icelandic history. Snorri treated the king's lives in the spirit of the greater Icelandic sagas, and the shape in which they exist is very far from authentic, as in the Heimskringla, Snorri's work has been greatly abridged, as is known by comparison with the saga of Olaf Tryggvason where more of Snorri appears to have been retained than in Heimskringla. Snorri by no means followed Ari slavishly, and infused much imaginative colour into his version of the Lives of the Kings. Dr. Vigfusson is very severe on the Heimskringla, which he regards as a late, weak and badly made compilation from originals. But this criticism is scarcely just, as Heimskringla is a type of annals or pseudo-history of the same character with the Danish history of Saxo-Grammaticus, the Chinese History in the Five Books, the Japanese Nihongi, or the Central American Popol Vuh—that is, it consists of romantic history as does the Historia Regum Britanniæ, and is thus placed beyond criticism so far as its lack of authenticity is concerned. There is an excellent translation of Heimskringla by William Morris and Magnusson, and Carlyle utilized it in composing his Kings of Norway.

HEINE. Son of Studas. A character in the romance of Dietrich of Bern (q.v.), to whose court he was attached. Although a brave hero, he won disfavour through his greed for treasure, which subsequently led him to turn traitor. This charge caused his death.

HEINRICH VON DEM TÜRLIN. A German poet of the thirteenth century. About the year 1220 he wrote a long narrative poem entitled Die Krône (The Crown of All Adventure), and this contains incidentally a lament for the death of Hartmann von Aue, an earlier poet, by whom Heinrich's own work was considerably influenced.

HELCHE, QUEEN. (Vide "Dietrich of Bern.")

HELDENBUCH, THE. (The Book of Heroes.) Edited by Kaspar von der Roen, in the fifteenth century, but supposed by Grässe to have been first collated from earlier sources, and embellished by Wolfram von Eschenbach and Heinrich von Ofterdingen at the end of the twelfth century. Vilmar, in his

Geschichte der Deutschen National-literatur, mentions several earlier *Heldenbücher*, and greatly disparages von der Roen's collection. But it appears to have been the most complete and popular of any. The poems it contains although unequal in merit are still all of considerable interest. They are *Onit, Wolfdietrich, Etzel's Courtkeeping, Giant Sigenôt, Ecke's Journey, Dietrich and his Companions, King Laurin, The Rose Garden at Worms, The Lay of Hildebrand, The Sea Monster*, and *Duke Ernst* (all of which see under their titles or under " Dieterich of Bern ").

HELGA. (*Vide* " Burnt Njal.") Daughter of Njal ; wife of Kari (*q.v.*).

HELGA THE FAIR. (*Vide* " Gunnlaug Saga.")

HELGI (1). In the Icelandic saga of *Frithjof* (*q.v.*). The dark and vindictive son of Bele. Hating Frithjof for his superior strength as for his inferior rank, he refused to give him Ingebjorg his sister to wife. He met his end by violently entering the temple of Yumala in the land of the Finns, against whom he was warring. As he wrenched open the door the god fell headlong and crushed him in his fall.

HELGI (2). (*Vide* " Burnt Njal.") Third and youngest son of Njal ; husband of Thorhalla. With Grim (*q.v.*) his brother he went searoving near the Orkneys, fell in with Kari a Viking, who succoured them twice in their need, and whom they married to their sister Helga (*q.v.*). He assisted in the deaths of Thrain (*q.v.*) and Hrapp (*q.v.*), and in that of Hanskuld (*q.v.*). His own end he met at the hands

of Flosi, as he sought to escape a fiery death.

HELGI (3). (*Vide* " Lay of the Volsungs.") Son of Sigmund and Borghild (*q.v.*). He slew King Hunding, after which he married Sigrun, King Hogni's daughter (all of whom see). This union displeased Hodbrod (*q.v.*), whom he slew. Sigrun's father then made war upon him, but was slain. He was subsequently killed by Dag, brother of Sigrun.

HELICORAS. In Grail romance, son of Corsapias (*q.v.*) who accompanied Flegentyne (*q.v.*) in his search for her husband Nasciens. He is alluded to in the *Grand St. Graal*.

HELIUS AND HELAKE. The murderous sons of King Hermance (*q.v.*), whom they slew. (*Vide* " Morte d'Arthur.")

HELLAWES. Lady of the Castle Nigramous, a sorceress who vainly attempted to win the love of Lancelot (*q.v.*). Failing in her endeavour, she died. (*Vide* " Morte d'Arthur.")

HELYAB. Wife of Joseph of Arimathea, in Grail romance, and mother of Josephes. She bore another son to Joseph and called him Galahad (*q.v.*).

HELYAS. Alluded to in the *Queste del St. Graal* as fourth in line from Celidoine, King of Scotland in the genealogy of Lancelot and Galahad.

HENRY, ARCHBISHOP OF RHEIMS. (*Vide* " Garin the Lorrainer.") He advised Pepin to marry Blanchflower instead of giving her to Garin the Lorrainer. He incited the monks to swear they were related.

HERBRAND. Father of Hildebrand (*q.v.*). (*Vide* " Dietrich of Bern.")

N

HEREGART. (*Vide* "Gudrun Lay," third division of, under heading "Gudrun.") A young duchess, one of Gudrun's maidens, carried off with her to Ormany. She, however, deserted her mistress for one of Hartmut's retinue (*vide* "Hartmut"). On Gudrun's rescue Heregart begged for mercy, and Gudrun tried to save her, but Wate (*q.v.*) slew her for her unfaithfulness to her mistress.

HERMANCE. King of the Red City, brutally murdered by his two sons, Helius and Helake (*q.v.*). His body was placed in a barge which sailed up the Humber. Palomides and Tristran discover the body. The former, complying with the note in the dead king's hand, sails to revenge him on his wicked sons, who are subsequently slain. (*Vide* "Morte d'Arthur.")

HERMENGARD. In the Charlemagne cycle of romance, sister of King Boniface of Pavia, and wife of Aymery of Narbonne (*q.v.*). By her he had seven sons, one of whom was the famous William of Orange (*q.v.*). (*Vide* "Enfances Guillaume.")

HERMIND, SIR. Of the Delectable Isle and brother to King Hermance (*q.v.*). (*Vide* "Morte d'Arthur.")

HERMIT. Prince of the Reussen and son of Waldemar (*q.v.*). (*Vide* "Dietrich of Bern.")

HERNAIS. (*Vide* "Garin the Lorrainer.") Son of Duke Hernais of Lorraine, nephew of Garin. He killed Count Hardré at the fight after Pepin's wedding.

HERNANT DE BEAULANDE. (*Vide* "Garin de Montglane.")

HERNANT OF DOUAY. In the Charlemagne cycle of romance, a knight who fought against Raoul of Cambray (*q.v.*). Raoul cut his wrist, and blasphemed so whilst pursuing him that Hernant said to him that he prized him "no more than a mad dog." Bernier (*q.v.*), coming up, struck Raoul a deadly blow, and Hernant finished his work.

HERPIN. In the William of Orange cycle, brother of Otrant, pagan King of Nîmes. He took two oxen belonging to William of Orange when the latter came to Nîmes disguised as a merchant, and upon the paladin's complaining Herpin pulled his beard, whereupon William brained him with a blow of his fist.

HERRAT. (*Vide* "Nibelungenlied.") Wife of Dietrich of Bern; niece of Helche (wife of Etzel, King of the Huns). She was one of the ladies-in-waiting to receive Kriemhild on her arrival at Etzel's castle after her marriage to him. (*Vide* also "Dietrich of Bern.")

HERVI (THE VILLEIN). (*Vide* "Garin the Lorrainer.") He was given charge of Plessis by Bego, and he gave assistance and advice to Bego after the attack made upon him by Thibaut. He found a messenger for Bego "Manuel Galopin" to send to the king to ask his aid. He fought bravely at the siege of Bordeaux. He was the father of Rigaut, and he was wroth with his son for not entering into the truce with the Bordelais after Bego's death.

HERWIG. King of Seeland. (*Vide* "Gudrun Lay"—third division of, under heading "Gudrun.") Married Gudrun. A suitor for the hand of Gudrun, whose father Hettel at first rejected him, but Herwig marched against Hettel and after a fierce conflict they became reconciled, and Herwig and Gudrun were betrothed. Herwig returned to defend Seeland against Seyfrid (*q.v.*), and was forced to solicit aid from Hettel, during whose absence Gudrun was carried off by Hartmut (*q.v.*). Herwig's first expedition to save her ended in failure, but many years later he and his allies were able again to attack Gudrun's captors, defeating them utterly and rescuing Gudrun and her maidens. Through all her trials Gudrun remained true and faithful to Herwig, and great joy was theirs upon reunion.

HERZELOYDE. Wife of Gahmuret and mother of Parzival, alluded to in Wolfram von Eschenbach's *Parzival*. Gahmuret wed her on condition that he might go tourneying every month. On hearing of his death Herzeloyde withdrew into the forest with her son, whom she taught to hate war and chivalry.

HETTEL. King of Hegelingen (Friesland). (*Vide* "Gudrun Lay.") Married Hilda, daughter of Hagen, King of Denmark. Father of Ortwein and Gudrun. The story of his wooing and winning of Hilda of Denmark forms the second portion of Ettmüller's division of the *Gudrun Lay* (*q.v.* under heading "Hagen and Hettel"). He refused all suitors for his daughter Gudrun's hand, finally, however, accepting King Herwig of Seeland. He was killed by King Ludwig at the battle on the Wulpenstrand, in the struggle to rescue Gudrun and her ladies who had been carried off by Ludwig and his son Hartmut (*q.v.*). For fuller description of the latter part of Hettel's life see "Gudrun," as the third division of the *Gudrun Lay*.

HEVEYEDD HEN. (Alluded to in the *Mabinogion*.) According to the Welsh triads, he was the son of Bleiddan Sant of Glamorgan, and was one of the three stranger kings of Britain on whom dominion was conferred for their mighty deeds and praiseworthy qualities. In some of the pedigrees he is called the son of Caradawc Vreichvras. He was the father of Rhiannon (*q.v.*).

HEYD. (*Vide* "Frithjof Saga.") A Norwegian sea-witch or storm-fiend in the form of a white bear. With the other storm-fiend Ham (*q.v.*) she was sent by Helgi (*q.v.*) to engulf Frithjof (*q.v.*) as he sailed for the island of Yarl Angantyr (*q.v.*).

HIARANDI. (*Vide* "Grettir Saga.") Brother of Bjorn (*q.v.*). Seeking to slay Grettir, in order to avenge his brother's death, Hiarandi was himself slain.

HILDA (1). (*Vide* "Gudrun Lay.") A princess of India. Married "Wild" Hagen (*q.v.*). Mother of Hilda.

HILDA. (2). One of the three little girls found by Hagen on his escape from the griffins' nest. She is described as sweet and gentle, and as having a softening influence on Hagen's fierce nature.

HILDA (3). (*Vide* portion of the "Gudrun Lay," under heading "Hagen and Hettel.") Daughter of Hettel and Hilda, King and Queen of Hegelingen. She was very beautiful and had many suitors, all of whom her father refused. Hettel, however, sent ambassadors in disguise, who won her heart and carried her off, a willing captive, to be King Hettels' bride. Her father followed, and after fierce fighting peace was made between Hagen and Hettel, and Hilda and her husband reigned in honour and happiness, two children being born to them, Ortwein and Gudrun—for whose life see under " Gudrun " as a division of the " Gudrun Lay." Queen Hilda is also connected with the action of " Gudrun."

HILDE. (*Vide* " Dietrich of Bern.") Sister to Grim (*q.v.*) the giant. She assailed Dietrich (*q.v.*) in his struggle with her brother, but she was overcome, and met her own end.

HILDEBRAND. Brother of Ilsan the monk and tutor of Dietrich of Bern (*q.v.*) and his faithful friend. Along with his royal student he fought many bloody conflicts. He was the son of Herbrand, a vassal to the court of Dietrich. He was possessed of great might almost equal to that of his brave master Dietrich, and throughout the story he displays untiring devotion toward the hero. He subsequently married Ute (*q.v.*). (*Vide* " Dietrich of Bern.")

HILDEBURG. (*Vide* " Gudrun Lay," third division of same, under heading " Gudrun.") Married Hartmut. She was one of the three little girls found by Hagen (*q.v.*) on his escape from the griffins' nest, and one of Gudrun's maidens who was carried off with her to Ormany. She was faithful to her mistress through all trials, sharing her hardships and sufferings during the time Gerlinte (*q.v.*) forced her to wash clothes, even in the most bitter weather. She was with Gudrun when Herwig and Ortwein came as messengers from the rescuing party, and much honour was hers on the return to Hegelingen after the deliverance of Gudrun from her captors.

Gudrun at length persuaded Hartmut (*q.v.*)—a prisoner at Hegelingen—to cease to remain unwed on account of love of her, and at her suggestion he married Hildeburg. Hildeburg is always spoken of in the first part of the *Gudrun Lay* as a daughter of the King of Portugal.

HILDEGUNDA (*Vide* " Burnt Njal.") Daughter of Flosi, wife of Hanskuld (*q.v.*). Some years after her husband's death she was wedded to Kari (*q.v.*), Helga's widower.

HILDEGUNDE. (*Vide* " Dietrich of Bern," and " Walther of Aquitaine.") Daughter of the King of Burgundy. She was given to the Huns as hostage. She met Walther (*q.v.*) also a hostage. She fell in love with him and they escaped. They were pursued and a fierce fight followed. She was, however, successful in restoring peace, and with her lover she pursued her journey to Aquitaine.

HILDESWID. Daughter of King Rodgeier (*q.v.*). She was abducted from her father's court by his warrior Samson (*q.v.*), who later became king. She married her abductor, and on his winning her father's throne reigned with him as his queen. (*Vide* " Samson.")

HILDING. (*Vide* " Frithjof Saga.") The sage who taught Frithjof and Ingebjorg the wisdom of the ages and the stories of the gods.

HISTORIA BRITONUM. A work compiled towards the end of the eighth century and attributed to a supposed British pseudo-historian Nennius, on the authority of the prologue or prologues contained in some of the MSS. The earliest MS. ascribes the work to " Marius the Anachorite." It contains an account of the struggle of Arthur with the Saxon invaders of Britain, but such historical fact as it includes is so intermingled with tradition as to be of small service to the historian proper. As the basis of romance, or at least the medium through which the Arthurian legends reached later writers, such as Geoffrey of Monmouth, it is of the deepest importance and interest to students of the subject. The *Historia Britonum* makes Arthur the general or *dux bellorum* of the British hosts, perhaps the *Comes Britanniæ*, an officer elected by the Britons to command their defensive forces after the withdrawal of the Roman legions. (*Vide* "Arthur" and "Arthurian Cycle.") See Nennius, *Historia Britonum*, ed. by J. Stevenson for Eng. Hist. Soc., 1838; Arthur de la Borderie, *L'Historia Britonum atribuée a Nennius et l'Historia Brittanica avant Geoffro de Monmouth*, Paris and London, 1883; Zimmer, *Nennius Vindicatus*; San Marte, *Nennius et Gildas*.

HISTORIA REGUM BRITANNIÆ. An alleged translation from a Welsh or French Breton chronicle by Geoffrey of Monmouth (*q.v.*), which states that he procured it from a certain Walter, Archdeacon of Oxford, who got it in Brittany (and who is not to be confounded with Walter Map (*q.v.*), who at the date of the publication of the book was only eleven years of age). This statement of Geoffrey's regarding the source of the book is in some quarters regarded, but without any real foundation, as "one of the great ruses of literary history." It contains in nine books the pseudo-history of the Britons from the era of their mythical king Brutus, to the death of Cadwallader. This work,

which is often erroneously alluded to as the *Historia Britonum*, has the merit of preserving Brythonic tradition in a more complete and consistent form than elsewhere, and to it we owe the introduction of the interesting figure of Merlin the enchanter. Its popularity was immense, and it was translated into French verse by Wace, and from that source into Anglo-Saxon by Layamon. If Geoffrey was not the first to introduce these traditions to readers, he at least revived interest in them after a lapse of three centuries. His work was published about 1128, and was dedicated to the Earl of Gloucester. It was printed at Paris in 1508 and 1509, and at Heidelberg in 1578. The *Historia Regum Britanniæ* is in its material substantially the same as the *Morte D'Arthur* of Malory, which is outlined elsewhere, except that it tells of the campaigns of Arthur's father Uther against the Saxons. Uther is poisoned by the Saxons, and Arthur succeeds to the throne at the age of fifteen. So prodigal is he of his bounty to the multitude of knights who surround him, that he is compelled to harry the Saxons, Colgrin, Cheldric and Baldulph, whom with the assistance of Hoel, his nephew, King of Armorica, he subdues in many battles. His personal slaughters are immense, in one battle amounting to 420 men. He marries Guinevere, daughter of a noble Roman family, and this appears to stimulate him to further conquests. Thus he conquers Ireland, Iceland, Gothland, and Orkney, after which he enjoys twelve years of peace, during which time the fame of his court reaches the bounds of the earth. It was his desire to conquer the whole of Europe, and we find this semi-mythical

Napoleon overrunning Gaul, Norway, and Dacia, granting these kingdoms as fiefs to his trusty warriors. Another season of peace is described, during which the king acts as the glass of fashion to the whole world, holding his magnificent and enlightened court at Carleon-on-Usk. In this description we see the germ of the veritable Arthurian court of romance. Caerleon, we are told, "had a school of two hundred philosophers learned in astronomy and in the other arts," and we are led to understand that at this era Britain surpassed all other lands in wealth, magnificence and learning. Arthur is, as in other romances, the hero of a hundred exploits, each more marvellous than the last. After this not ignoble peace he makes war against the Romans, who are under the command of Lucius Hiberius, who with the aid of the Kings of the East musters an enormous force. A tremendous slaughter follows the meeting of the armies, and many of Britain's best knights are slain, but the Roman leader is killed, and his forces so shattered that Arthur meditates a march on Rome itself, and is in the act of climbing the Alps when he learns that his nephew Mordred has seized the crown of Britain and taken Guinevere unto himself. Several engagements does Arthur fight with the usurper. Having chased him into Cornwall he forces him to give battle on the banks of the river Camel, and in the desperate encounter which ensues nearly all the men of note on either side are slain. Arthur himself is sorely wounded, and is borne unto the Isle of Avalon for the healing of his wounds. This we are told, happened in the year 542 A.D.

Literature : Historia Britonum,
ed. Schulz, 1854 ; G. Ellis, *Specimens of Early English Metrical Romances ;* Dr. Sebastian Evans, translation of Geoffrey in the *Temple Classics ;* Translation of Nennius and Geoffrey in *Bohn's Series.*

HISTORY OF CHARLES THE GREAT AND ORLANDO. This chronicle was supposed during the Middle Ages to have been composed by Archbishop Turpin or Tilpin of Rheims, but in reality was written by some monk at an unknown date before the year 1122. It is of the nature of pseudo-history, and is at the root of many tales and romances of Charles and Orlando, or Roland. In 1122 Pope Calixtus II. officially declared its authenticity, probably for the good reason that it was found to be a powerful incentive to war against the infidel. So patent were the inventions contained in the work that it came to be known as the "Magnanime Mensonge," a falsehood heroic and pious. The work was quickly translated into French, and was first printed at Frankfort in 1566 in a collection of four chronographers, the *Germanicum Rerum.* Beginning with an epistle from Turpin to Lerpander, Dean of Aix-la-Chapelle, in which the supposed author intimates his objects in writing a history of his times, the work proceeds to recount the circumstances of Charles's wars with the Saracens of Spain, of the fall of Pampeluna, the destruction of the Mahometan "idols," of the churches builded by Charles, the recovery of Spain by Argolander, the emperor's war against him, and of the death and defeat of the Saracen prince. The campaign against Furra, King of Navarre, and the war with the giant Ferracute or Ferragus, are next described (*vide* " Roland and Ferragus "). The author then proceeds to relate the circumstances connected with the " War of the Masks " with Ibrahim, King of Seville, a campaign so called because of the disguise worn by the Saracens, who are defeated. The Council of Compostella is described, after which the treachery of Ganelon (*q.v.*), and the great Battle of Roncesvalles are touched upon. A poem upon Roland's rank and virtue follows. A vision seen by Turpin is then described, in which he beholds Roland carried to heaven, and Marsile (*q.v.*), a Saracen king, borne to hell. It is then recounted how the sun stood still for three days until Charlemagne punished the Saracen army. The burial of Roland is described, the council of St. Denis alluded to, and the work ends with the death of Charlemagne, who, according to the supposed Turpin, only won heaven by virtue of the many churches he had founded.

HJALPREKS. King of Denmark, father of Alf the Viking (*q.v.*). (*Vide* " Lay of the Volsungs.") He befriended Hjordis, whose son Sigurd (*q.v.*) he became fond of.

HJORDIS. Daughter of King Eylimi (*q.v.*), and second wife of Sigmund (*q.v.*). (*Vide* " Volsungs.") She, after her husband's death, dwelt with Hjalprek (*q.v.*), King of Denmark, whose son, Alf, the Viking (*q.v.*), she married, after giving birth to the dead Sigmund's son, Sigurd (*q.v.*).

HOGNI, KING. Father of Sigrun (*q.v.*) wife of Helgi (*q.v.*), and of Dag (*q.v.*). He was subsequently slain by Helgi. (*Vide* "The Lay of the Volsungs.")

HOGNI (1). (*Vide* "Volsungs.") Son of King Giuki and Grimhild (*q.v.*) and father of Niblung (*q.v.*). He with his brother Gunnar (*q.v.*) fought with Atli (*q.v.*). He was taken prisoner, and at the request of his own brother he was slain.

HOGNI (2). (*Vide* " Burnt Njal.") Elder son of Gunnar (*q.v.*). Upon his father's death he took possession of the homestead at Lithend.

HONEYSUCKLE, THE LAY OF THE. A romance of Tristan and Isonde or Iseult (*q.v.*), written by Marie de France (*q.v.*). Tristan, banished from Cornwall by King Mark, his maternal uncle, on account of his love for the queen, Isonde, dwelt a year in his own land, South Wales. Unable, however, to support life without sight of the fair Isonde, he stole back to Cornwall. Here in the deep forest he lay hid, gleaning tidings of the court and the queen from the peasants. Then he learned that at Pentecost, King Mark proposed to hold high court at Tintagel ; also that the queen would ride thither. Through the woods they must come. Tristan therefore cut a wand from a hazel-tree, peeled off the bark and carved his name upon the wood. He also wrote upon it comparing himself and the queen to the hazel-tree and the honeysuckle. As the honeysuckle might not flourish without twining itself around the hazel, so might not Isonde thrive without her knight. This he set in her path. She saw it and bidding her knights to refresh themselves, she drew aside with Brangwaine, her maiden. She then sought her lover, and each exchanged kisses till they must part. But Tristan made a lay about that meeting and called it " The Lay of the Honeysuckle."

HORANT. Lord of Daneland. (*Vide* " Gudrun Lay," second and third divisions of same, under headings " Hagen and Hettel " and " Gudrun.") Nephew of Wate of Sturmen. He came to Hegelingen to help King Hettel (*q.v.*) in his desire to win Hilda of Ireland (*q.v.*), daughter of King Hagen, and at length set out with the embassy that went to Ireland with that purpose. Specially is he famed in the poem for his most beautiful voice, and his marvellous singing created a great stir at Hagen's court, and won Hilda's heart so that she consented to go to Hettel to be his bride, on hearing that at his court are even finer singers than Horant, and that the king himself excels them all. Horant took part also in the conflicts concerning Gudrun, fighting bravely, and acting as standard-bearer to the expedition which rescued her. He is described as the "sweet singer" in the epic, and some authorities consider that he appears in the Hamlet myths as Orendil or Aurentil. (For fuller comparisons of this nature, see article on " Gudrun Lay " as a whole.)

HOWEL (1). Son of Emyr Lydaw, and Prince of Lydau, is alluded to in the tale of *Peredur Son of Evrawc* in the Welsh *Mabinogion.* He distinguished himself greatly in Arthur's wars against the Romans, and was one of the most strenuous in urging his sovereign to resist their unjust claims. When Arthur was suddenly called back to Britain by the news of Mordred's treachery, he left Howel with part of his army in Gaul to secure his possessions in that country.

HOWELL (2). King of Brittany. In the *Morte d'Arthur* father of the sisters La Belle Isonde (Iseult) and La Blanche Isond, both of whom see.

HOWEL (3). (*Vide* " Roland and Ferragus.") Earl of Nantes, slain by Ferragus in single combat.

HRAPP. (*Vide* " Burnt Njal.") A felon chased by Yarl Hacon of Norway, and succoured by Thrain (*q.v.*). Hating Grim and Helgi (*q.v.*) who had been unwilling to receive him into Thrain's ship, he was, however, slain by these and Njal's sons.

HREIDMAR. Father of Otter (*q.v.*), Regni (*q.v.*), and Fafnir (*q.v.*). He demanded blood-money from Loki (*q.v.*) for the slaughter of Otter, and received sufficient gold rings to fill Otter's skin. This was the treasure of the Niblung's, and caused his death at the hands of his son, Fafnir (*q.v.*), who coveted it. (*Vide* " Volsungs, Lay of the.")

HRODGAR. Of Jutland, King of the Skioldungs. (Legend of Beowulf.) Grandson of Skiold, and a just and good ruler. His castle, Hirschhalle, was terrorized by the monster Grendel (*q.v.*) till Beowulf slew the giant. He loaded Beowulf with rich gifts and treated him with every consideration.

HRONERAS. The height on which Beowulf was buried. (*Vide* " Beowulf.")

HRUNTUNG. The sword which Hunford gave to Beowulf (*q.v.*).

HUCHOWNE or **HUGH.** Generally described by ancient Scots writers and annalists as " of the Awle Ryale," or Royal Palace, a romance writer who flourished in Scotland in the middle of the fourteenth century. He is said by Wyntoun in his *Chronicle* to have " made " the *Great Gest of Arthure, The Pystyl of Sweet Susane* (*q.v.*), and the *Adventure of Gawane*, which latter poem is mentioned by Dunbar in his *Lament for the Makkaris* to have been written by one Clerk of Tranent. From this circumstance, and from the fact that one MS. styles the author "The Clerk," it has been inferred that Huchowne and the clerk are one and the same. Chalmers thinks that he is the "gude Schir Hew of Eglintoun" alluded to by Dunbar as the author, on account of his connection with the court of Robert the Second, but there is not sufficient proof to support this theory. Sir F. Madden claimed for him the authorship of the much admired *Syr Gawayne and the Grene Knyght* (*q.v.*), and gives it as his opinion that no one but an educated person would have been so closely acquainted with the early poetry of France as was the author of that poem. If he was indeed the "maker" of *Syr Gawayne* he was a poet of no small power, as some of his descriptions of seasonal changes will rank with the marvellous pictures of Douglas, or Henryson's clear-cut vignettes. See the various *précis* of his romances under their several entries. His style is more antique than that of the author of *Sir Tristrem* (*q.v.*), and is strongly alliterative, having mechanical affinities with Langland and the later poets of the purely English Saxon type as apart from the Norman-English writers, and he does not employ many words of French origin.

HUGH OF MANS. (*Vide* "Garin the Lorrainer.") Nephew of Garin and Bego. He went to battle with the Lorrainers.

HUNDRED KNIGHTS, KING WITH THE. Alluded to in Arthurian romance as a knight of prowess, and a frequent visitor to the court of Arthur. (*Vide* "Morte d'Arthur.")

HUNFORD. In the legend of Beowulf, a Skioldung warrior at King Hrodgar's court. On hearing Beowulf's praises sung he was jealous and spoke scornfully to the hero, but after the defeat of Grendel he made amends by giving his sword Hruntung to Beowulf as a token of friendship.

HUO OF CAMBRAI. (*Vide* "Garin the Lorrainer.") Nephew of Garin. He was one of those who went to help King Thierry of Savoy. His own fortalice was suddenly besieged by Fromont and Baldwin of Flanders in revenge for Garin taking Soissons from Fromont. He prepared his town for defence. Going out to meet the invaders he saw Isoré the grey at the head, whom he reminded of past favours, and Isoré refused to fight against him. Baldwin's forces outnumbered Huo's, so he sent to Pepin and Garin, and eventually won. He fought bravely in all the wars between the Lorrainers and Bordelais, and on more than one occasion conducted successful campaigns. He turned out with eighty knights against Fromondin and was defeated, but Fromondin granted his life. Bernard of Naisil stabbed him unnoticed, at which Fromondin was exceedingly wroth, saying that Huo was "the best man that ever drank wine."

HUON OF BORDEAUX. A romance of the Charlemagne cycle. It tells how Charlemagne was desirous of abdicating in favour of his two sons, Charlot and Lewis. To the former, of whom he was absurdly fond, and who was least worthy of the honour, he would have handed the sceptre, but his council refused to receive Charlot as king, and eventually persuaded Charlemagne to continue in the royal power. Amaury of Hauteville, however, proposed that Charlot should try his capacity for government, and that the rule of some rich province should be granted him. In making this proposal he had in view the domains of the late Duke Sevinus, who had left two young sons to the care of the Duchess Alice their mother, and as neither had paid homage to their king, he considered they should be made to yield up the province to Charlot. The council, however, persuaded Charlemagne to send for the sons. Accordingly two knights were sent to the youths, and were met with unfeigned cordiality. Their mission ended, they returned to the king, whom they informed that the young Duke Huon would eventually excel as his good father had done. The duchess made ready the two sons and sent them on their way, enjoining them to call at the Monastery of Cluny to visit the abbot, their father's brother. The good abbot received his nephews in a warm embrace, and promised to ride with them to Paris. Meanwhile a plot had been formed between Amaury and Charlot. They purposed to slay the two youths on their approach to Paris, and with this end in view they made their way into a forest through which the road passed accompanied by a troop of guards. As the two young men and their uncle drew near to the ambuscade, Girard, the younger of the two, rode on in advance. Charlot saw him approach, went forth to meet him, sought a quarrel with him and drew him from his horse. Huon had seen this and hurried to his brother's aid. He charged the cowardly Charlot with striking an unarmed rider and immediately assailed him. Although possessed of no shield and only a sword, Huon acted with great bravery, and finally slew Charlot. Amaury had watched the conflict and was not now prepared to avenge his accomplice's death, for he knew the king's weakness toward Charlot, whose death would be revenged irrespective of the pleadings of justice. Huon and the abbot attended to Girard's wounds and once more resumed their journey. They reached Paris but a few hours before Amaury and were welcomed with much magnificence by Charlemagne, to whom they related their encounter. But the king on seeing his son's corpse being carried into the court turned against his guests and would have slain them had not his councillor, the wise Duke Namo, stopped his hand and asserted that the council were the proper judges in this case. During the trial the Abbot of Cluny offered to prove with his body the lie of Amaury. The trial ended by Huon and Amaury agreeing to fight. The battle was long, the young knight proved a worthy opponent of the hardened Amaury, and at last stretched the traitor on the ground, who begged for mercy. As he helped him, however, to mount his steed, the treacherous Amaury thrust his sword into the victim's side. Huon, without thought of keeping the traitor alive to prove the treason, immediately dealt the fatal blow. Charlemagne was not satisfied, but though he forgave Huon, he commanded him to go on a perilous quest to justify his honour in his sight. The conditions were : To go to the court of the Sultan of Gaudisso, cut off the head of one of his favoured guards ; kiss three times on the lips the fair princess, and demand from the sultan four grinders from his mouth and a handful of white hair. Drastic as the conditions were, Huon lightly accepted them. The good abbot induced the young knight to first visit the Pope, who was the brother of the Duchess Alice. On his long journey after interviewing the Pope, he met with Sherasmin, who had fought with his father and who was now willing to accompany Huon on his perilous quest. Next they met with a dwarf who gave to the young prince a goblet which in the hands of a good Christian would fill with rich wine, and a horn which if blown gently would produce a feeling of harmlessness in his opponents. With these gifts they resumed their journey. One evening as they entered a Saracen town to inquire for an inn in which they might pass the night, a wealthy person stepped forward and offered his hospitality, which they accepted. His name was Floriac. He proved a good host and related how his guest's uncle, a prince of the house of Guienne, had turned Saracen. With rage did Huon demand to be taken to this guilty uncle. The following day he arrived at the court of his kinsman whom he accused of renouncing the Christian Faith. The uncle pretended not to be moved, and as they sat at dinner the magic goblet filled with rich wine and the uncle was tempted to drink against the Saracen custom. But the wine ere it touched his lips disappeared. Consternation ensued, troops poured in and the Christians were surrounded. Remembering his enchanted horn, Huon blew but gently, and instantly calm prevailed. Under this mystic in-fluence he exacted from his uncle a ring of passport to the presence of the Sultan of Gandisso. They left the court and made toward Bagdad. Huon next interrupted a struggle between a lion and a knight. Slaying the lion he found that he had saved the life of a Saracen, Prince of Hyrcania, who on being offered a draught from the goblet flung it at his rescuer and fled. That same evening they lodged under the roof of an old dame who informs them of the marriage on the morrow of the Sultan's daughter Clariminda to the prince whom he had rescued. The next day he enters the palace of Gaudisso by professing to be a Mahometan. Reflecting on his deception, the magic goblet and horn lose their charm. He attempts to remedy this by calling aloud in the name of Christ ; but his only reply is to be confronted with the spears of the guard. The ring which his uncle gave him is shown, and immediately he is conducted into the presence of the sultan, who sat at dinner. A place is allotted to him near to the princess who was attracted to him. He remembered his charge and straightway kissed her three times. The prince, who sat on the sultan's right hand, protested by attempting to wound Huon with his sword. Huon retaliated by cutting off his head. Now the sultan intervened and had the young knight cast into prison. During his confinement the princess feeds him, and he persuades her to become Christian. An attempt is made to escape ; but he has yet to obtain the sultan's teeth and part of his beard. An embassy from the Caliph of Arabia arrives at the court with the death warrant of the sultan, who was suspected of withholding the caliph's share of treasures which had fallen into his hands. To protest was useless, and according to instructions his head was severed from his body. The princess now releases her lover, the teeth are extracted, the hairs plucked, and the lovers depart for Rome. The Holy Father unites them. They arrive in France, and Huon hands over the trophies to Charlemagne, who is well pleased.

HURGANES or HURGANET. Alluded to in the *Didot-Percival* as a knight who with Gauvain and others swears to seek the Grail. He delivered a lady from a giant, but was in turn slain by one Orgoillos Delaudes, who is vanquished by Perceval and sent to Arthur's court.

HURLAME, KING. A Saracen, who assailed King Labor (*q.v.*) and

defeated him with the Grail sword. He afterwards returns to the ship for the scabbard, but is struck dead. (*Vide* "Morte d'Arthur.")

HYALLI. (*Vide* "Volsungs.") A thrall of Gunnar's.

HYGD, QUEEN. Wife of King Hygelak of Gothland (*q.v.*), alluded to in the legend of *Beowulf*. On her husband's death she advised the election of Beowulf as king, her son Hardred (*q.v.*) being but a child. This Beowulf would not accept, acting instead as regent for Hardred.

HYGELAK. (*Vide* "Beowulf.") King of Gothland, uncle of Beowulf, slain in revenging a Viking raid made by the Frisians.

HYVEIDD HIR. (*Vide* "Gododin.") Son of Bleddai Sant of Glamorgan.

I

IBRAHIM. (*Vide* "Roland and Ferragus.") King of Spain. A Pagan who cruelly persecuted the Christians and "banished the Patriarch of Jerusalem."

IGRAINE. Wife of the Duke of Tintagil in Arthurian romance, and mother of Arthur by Uther Pendragon (*q.v.*).

ILDANACH "THE ALL-CRAFTS-MAN." Surname conferred upon Lugh (*q.v.*), the Irish Celtic sun-god.

ILLUGI. (*Vide* "Grettir Saga.") Third youngest brother of Grettir.

ILLUGI, THE BLACK. (*Vide* "Gunnlaug Saga.") Father of Gunnlaug.

ILSAN. A monk, brother of Hildebrand (*q.v.*) (*vide* "Dietrich of

Bern"). He left his monastic surroundings to fight for the hero of the story, and was conspicuous in the Battle of the Rose Garden (*q.v.*).

INGEBJORG. (*Vide* "Frithjof Saga.") Beloved by, and finally wedded to, Frithjof (*q.v.*) in the Icelandic Saga which bears his name.

INOR, KING OF MOUNBRAUNT. (*Vide* "Bevis of Hampton.") Married Josyan, who was taken from him by Sir Bevis. Ascapard the giant promised to take Josyan back to him but was killed, and Inor afterwards made war on Josyan's father, but was defeated and taken prisoner. He was slain in battle by Sir Bevis.

IPOMEDON. An English romance of the fourteenth century, probably derived from a French original. It is alluded to among the romances in the Prologue of *Richard Cuer de Lyon*. In this romance we have an example of how classical nomenclature might be applied to mediæval story. Ipomedon was the son of Ermones, King of Apulia, and loved the heiress of Calabria. Ipomedon is introduced waiting in his father's hall at a great festival. The feasters speak of the Princess of Calabria, and young Ipomedon immediately forms a resolution to visit and win her. He sets forth on his travels, disguised, and instructs his followers not to address him by his own name, or to afford any information concerning him to any inquirer. They arrive at Calabria, and request to be permitted to eat with the princess. This is granted, and Ipomedon asks leave to enter the lady's service. She accepts him as her cup-bearer. As such, he dwells in her palace a long time, and forms a fast friendship with Jason, the lady's cousin. The princess thought deeply on Ipomedon, and desired to discover his name and country. She sees he comes of high lineage through his prowess in the chase, knights him, a feast of forty days' duration is held, and we conclude that the pair are affianced.

IRNAN. In Irish romance, the last of the three sorcerer-daughters of Conaran. Putting Finn under taboo to send his men in single combat against her as long as she wished, she was slain by Goll her sister's slayer.

ISABELLA. (*Vide* "Orlando Innamorato," and "Orlando Furioso.") Daughter to Galego, King of Galica, in love with Zerbino (*q.v.*). She was found by Orlando in the outlaw's cave, and delivered by him.

When her lover was slain she renounced love for religion.

ISEMBART. A being "who had long been a fish, but since the last twelvemonth had become a human monster by decree of the fairies." He is alluded to in the *Battle of Loquifer* (sub-cycle of *William of Orange*), and declares to Renouart (*q.v.*) that he is to be carried to Paynimrie and flayed alive. He is, however, overcome and slain by Renouart.

ISEULT, ISOLDE, or **ISOND** (1). Daughter of the King of Ireland, married to King Mark of Cornwall. The many adventures and his love-affairs with Sir Tristram are detailed at length in the articles "Sir Tristram" and "Morte d'Arthur."

ISEULT, ISOLDE, or **ISOND** (2). La Blanche Mains, of Brittany, rival for the love of Tristram, and, in some romances, described as sister to Iseult of Ireland. (*Vide* "Morte d'Arthur" and "Sir Tristram.")

ISORÉ THE GREY. (*Vide* "Garin the Lorrainer.") Nephew of Fromont. He besieged Cambrai, but on Huo pleading past favours, he refused to fight against him. He defended St. Quentin afterwards, and having a quarrel with Bego a great battle ensued. He hated Bego, and tried on many occasions to kill him. He was present at the fight at the wedding ceremony and in the kitchen. He was taken prisoner then, and afterwards had a great combat with Bego by whom he was slain. His heart was torn out by Bego and handed over to William of Montclin.

ISPRES. (*Vide* "Ferumbras.") A Roman who held command of the principal gate of Rome and betrayed his city to the Soudan. Ferumbras had his head cut off and carried on the point of a spear when he went into the city.

ISUMBRAS, SIR. An English romance, consisting of 130 six-lined stanzas, abridged from the MS. copy in the library of Caius College.

Once there lived a knight who from his earliest infancy was possessed of good fortune. Being remarkably strong and handsome this favoured nobleman enjoyed life as befitted one in such a unique position. Wedded to a lady equally charming, and the father of three lovely children, Sir Isumbras could well rejoice. With princely liberality he entertained continuously, but he had neglected one important matter. This fortunate knight had many virtues, on which he relied too much, ignoring one wise rule of life which he had yet to learn. In selfish pride he forgot to acknowledge the Giver of all his abundant blessings, in his arrogance attributing these to his own virtues. While hunting one day he was confronted by an angel, who reproached him with ingratitude, and warned him of the visitation of God's vengeance upon his household. Feeling the justice of the rebuke, Isumbras returned dejected to his palace. Hardly had he turned homeward when his horse dropped dead under him. Then his magnificent palace was completely wrecked, his horses and cattle were destroyed, while his wife and children escaped from the ruins insufficiently clad. His province had become a waste. Realizing the justice of the punishment, he set out on a pilgrimage to Jerusalem. Unaccustomed to such hardships, the destitute family soon wearied of their journey. Arriving at a wide but shallow river which they must cross, Isumbras proceeded to carry his children to the other side. Placing the first one under a shady tree he returned for the second child. Meanwhile the newly-conveyed child was carried off by a lion. The father on crossing with the second was horrified at such a loss. Depositing his second son in the same spot, he likewise was borne away by a leopard. The demented parents, accompanied by their third and only surviving child, wandered on. They eventually arrived at the sea-shore, where they perceived a rich vessel lying moored to the beach. Approaching it, they asked the sailors for food. But the Soudan, the owner of the galley, refused them. His attendants, observing the strangers' noble bearing, pointed out that they were evidently of exalted rank. Struck with the beauty of Isumbras' wife, the Soudan offered gold and raiment in exchange for her, but the knight indignantly refused this offer. Accustomed to being obeyed, the angry Soudan ordered Isumbras' wife to be torn from him and that the dismayed husband should take his gold, then be brutally whipped. Separated from his wife, he took his only child, and went on shore. Ascending a rocky mountain they allayed their hunger by the food they had procured, then sought repose until daybreak. The money and provisions which had been given to Isumbras were hidden in his red mantle. The sun's golden beams falling upon the bright cloth attracted an eagle, which swooped down upon the treasure and bore it off in its talons. The knight followed the flight of the bird in the hope that it might drop the useless burden, but the eagle directed its course towards the shores of Africa. Returning to his little son, Isumbras was just in time to perceive him being snatched away by a unicorn. In these sore straits he regarded this calamity as a blessing, for he had not the means to provide for the boy's maintenance. Saved from starvation as though by Providence, he humbly knelt in prayer, then continued his journey. Perceiving the forge of a smith, Isumbras entered and begged for food, but the smith refused, and told him to work for it. The knight remained with the good smith for over a year, using his spare time to make a suit of armour. He regained his lost vigour, and his health resumed its former robustness. A war between the Christians and Saracens being imminent he enlisted with the former. Despite his courage he was vanquished by the enemy, but saved through the daring of a comrade. The Christian king despatched the wounded Isumbras to a nunnery, where he received attendance. After a long sojourn there he assumed the dress of a palmer, and went on his way.

The penitent Isumbras employed the following seven years in visiting every part of the Holy Land. He led a life of continual mortification, accepting the charity of the poor, and sleeping at night in the open air. After a day spent in fruitless quest of food, an angel appeared to him with bread and wine. Feeling that his sins were forgiven he began the daily struggle with a light heart. Passing a stately castle he asked for food. Hearing that the owner was a rich queen, who daily bestowed a florin on every poor man who approached her, and frequently in necessitous cases provided lodgings, Isumbras duly applied for refuge, and his emaciated appearance gained for him instant admittance. His exemplary conduct attracted the benevolent queen, who finally resolved to retain the holy palmer in her service, who rapidly regained his wonted strength. While crossing a field one day, Isumbras discovered his long-lost treasure in a tree, and found the contents intact. Hurrying to his chambers he hid the gold. The queen, however, had observed her servant's haste in disposing of the red cloth. So after he left the apartment she caused a search to be made, and recognizing the tell-tale bundle was overjoyed to find that it belonged to her husband. Isumbras appeared, told his story, recognized his wife, fell at her feet, and the reunion was celebrated by his becoming king of the city. The Saracen subjects, unwilling to submit to the Christian yoke, declared war against their new ruler, and Isumbras entered the field. But the victory was secured by the intervention of three knights who appeared, each riding on a wild beast. The first was mounted on a lion, the second on a leopard, and the third on a unicorn. They dispersed the bewildered enemy, who fled. Isumbras approached the three knights to find that they were his lost sons. The natives then proclaimed Isumbras as their king. Soon the three adjoining kingdoms were added to his dominions, and over each he set one of his sons. The royal family then lived to enjoy in peace the reward which, through their past sufferings and humble submission they had justly reaped.

ITH. In Irish romance, son of Bregon, grandfather of Miled (*q.v.*). He looked westward one winter's eve from his father's tower in

"Spain," and saw the coast of Ireland. Setting sail thither, he landed to find that the Danaan king had been slain in battle with the Fomorians, and that his three sons were arranging the division of the land among themselves. Invited to give his judgment he did so, but as he expressed great admiration for the country, the Danaans feared his rivalry and slew him. His companions recovered the body ; and returned from " Spain " with the children of Miled to take vengeance on the murderers. Such is the legend of the coming of the Milesians into Ireland.

IUBDAN. In Ultonian romance, King of the Wee Folk. Flushed with wine, he boasted one day of the might of his strong man Glower, who could hew down a thistle at a stroke. Eisirt (q.v.), his bard, however, hinted that oversea there was a giant race, one of whom could annihilate a whole battalion of the Wee Folk. For this audacity Eisirt was cast into prison, but was liberated on promising to go to this giant land and bring back

evidence of his story. He returned with Æda (q.v.), King Fergus' (q.v.) dwarf and bard. Eisirt then put Iubdan under geise (or taboo) to go himself to the palace of Fergus and taste his porridge. At midnight the Wee King and his wife Bebo reached their destination ; and in striving to get at the porridge and be away before daybreak Iubdan fell in. There in the pot Fergus' scullions found him, and carried him and Bebo to their master. The Ulster monarch refused to let them go until the Wee Folk came in a multitude to beg the release of Iubdan. Fergus still refusing, they plagued his country. Then they promised plenty of unsown corn yearly in his plains, but all in vain. At last Fergus released Iubdan for the gift of a pair of water shoes, wearing which a man could go over or under water as freely as on dry land.

IUCHAR. In Irish romance, one of the three sons of Turenn (q.v.).

IUCHARBA. In Irish romance, one of the three sons of Turenn (q.v.).

J

JACOBUS DE VORAGINE. An Italian prelate of the Middle Ages, who wrote a number of books in Latin, notably *Legenda Aurea*, better known as *The Golden Legend*. His name was really Giacomo, but he Latinised it in accordance with the usual fashion among mediæval writers. He is supposed to have been born about 1220, while his native place is recorded to have been Varazze, a small village not far from Genoa. Becoming a Dominican friar, he soon acquired

considerable reputation as a preacher, and in course of time he was appointed Provincial of Lombardy. In 1292 the Pope, Nicholas IV., who had conceived a high opinion of him, summoned him to Rome with the intention of consecrating him Archbishop of Genoa ; but, when Jacobus arrived at the Eternal City, he found His Holiness stricken with an illness to which he succumbed a little later. The cardinals, however, determined to take the matter into their own hands, and accordingly Jacobus was consecrated soon after the following Easter. He discharged his duties well, distinguishing himself in particular by his efforts to quell the civil discords rampant at Genoa ; but his term of office was comparatively short, for he died about 1299.

According to a statement made by Sixtus of Siena, Jacobus rendered the Old and New Testaments into Italian, but no trace of these translations remains nowadays. He was also a voluminous writer of sermons, and some of these were repeatedly issued in book-form during the fifteenth century ; while he likewise compiled a lengthy historical work, *Chronicon Januense*, parts of which may be read in *Rerum Italicarum Scriptores*, edited by Muratori (1723–1738) ; and this is a book of no ordinary significance, dealing fully as it does with the myths surrounding the early history of Genoa, and with the crusading exploits of the Genoese. The *Golden Legend*, again, was one of the most popular devotional works of the Middle Ages, and was among the first writings ever printed. Numerous Latin editions thereof were published in the fifteenth century, while it was translated into French, German, and Italian, and Caxton issued an English version in 1483. Nor is the book altogether forgotten yet, and, as the reader will doubtless recall, Longfellow culled one of his poems from its pages.

JAMES I., KING OF SCOTLAND. He is included here by virtue of the ascription to him of several poems, notably *The King's Quhair*. The second son of Robert III., James was born at Dunfermline in 1394 ; and in 1402 he became heir-apparent to the Scottish throne, his elder brother being murdered in that year. Perhaps because he dreaded a like fate for his remaining son, King Robert decided not to keep James in Scotland, but to send him to France, and *en route* the young prince was captured by the English. His subsequent imprisonment at their hands seems to have been a fairly happy one, little restriction being put on his actions, and as good an education being given him as he would have received had he been freer in Scotland or France ; but a high ransom was demanded when he was ultimately released in 1423, while it was also stipulated that he should marry an English wife. Accordingly he espoused Jane Beaufort, daughter of the Duke of Somerset, and early in 1424 he returned with her to Scotland. Robert III. had been dead since 1406, and James found his native realm in a turbulent condition ; yet he strove manfully to preserve justice and to curb the nobles, and as a result of his ardour herein he was murdered at Perth in 1437.

The question whether James really composed *The King's Quhair* is debated in an article under that heading. Suffice it to say here that he was a man of keen literary tastes, as witness the statements in a book written in his own time, *The Dethe of the Kinge of Scotis*, and also the evidence of two historians who lived soon after him, Hector Boece and Walter Bower. The latter even asserts that James was a painter of great gifts, while Boece descants on the king's talents as a musician. Moreover, Alessandro Tassoni, an Italian writer of the sixteenth century, states in his *Pensiri diversi* (lib. 10, cap. 33), that James "invented a new kind of music,

o

plaintive and melancholy, different from all other, in which he has been imitated by Carlo Gesualdo, Prince of Venosa."

Literature : James's life has been repeatedly written, and probably the best of such books is J. J. Jusserand's *Romance of a King's Life,* 1896. As the reader will no doubt recall, James's tragic end is described by Swinburne in *Kate Barlass,* and by Rosetti in *The King's Tragedy.*

JANIBUS. Son of Ortgis. (*Vide* "Dietrich of Bern.") He with his father oppressed the dwarfs, but subsequently died at the hands of Dietrich and his followers.

JEAN DE MEUNG. A French author of the Middle Ages. He was born at Meung-sur-Loire, probably about 1250, and he is supposed to have died early in the fourteenth century. Little is known about his life, but it would seem that he was a cleric of some sort, while it is recorded that as a young man he entered the Sorbonne at Paris. He appears thenceforth to have lived chiefly in the French capital, and according to a Parisian tradition his home was in the Rue St. Jacques. At the outset of his career he was chiefly concerned with translation, doing an excellent French version of *Abelard and Heloïse,* and also rendering into his native tongue the *Topographia Hibernica* of Giraldus Cambrensis and St. Ailred's *De Amicitia Spirituali.* Subsequently, at the request of the French king, Philippe le Bel, he translated the *Consolatio Philosophiæ* of Boethius, a work which enjoyed extraordinary popularity in mediæval Europe ; and it was probably after completing this that he turned his attention to his *magnum opus,* namely, his continuation of the immortal poem

begun by Guillaume de Lorris, the *Roman de la Rose.* Nor did this lengthy work conclude his activities, for towards the close of his life he wrote another poem of considerable length, the *Testament de Jean de Meung,* a curious and interesting production, full of fierce satires on the Church and its dignitaries. A number of very old manuscript copies of this poem are extant, a fact which demonstrates it to have enjoyed great vogue ; and indeed Jean was widely esteemed in the France of his time, alike for his scholarship and his writings, and accordingly numerous works are ascribed to him which cannot possibly be found to be his. (*Vide* "Romance of the Rose.")

JEFFREY. (*Vide* "Garin the Lorrainer.") Count of Anjou. Nephew and companion of the two Lorrainers.

JEHAN DE SAINTRÉ. A French romance of the fifteenth century. The hero began his career in the train of a notable knight attached to the court of France, where the boy very soon attracted the notice of the king by his good looks and splendid horsemanship, and was selected as page to that royal personage. He furthermore became the favourite of a young widowed princess, the Dame des Belles-Cousines, living at the court. One day the lady commanded him to go to her room, when to the boy's amazement she lectured him on his knightly duties, and giving him twelve gold crowns bade him go to the king's tailor and obtain fresh apparel. Her attachment to the young page increased. But afraid that her intimacy might be detected, she very cunningly contrived with Jehan to treat him in public with becoming indifference.

She further entrusted him with a key with which he might enter her room secretly and also adopted a signal of placing a diamond pin between her teeth as a mark of her desire for his presence behind the secret door. This intrigue went on until by her lavishness she had succeeded in raising him to a high command in the king's service. At last he was prompted to apply for a commission of enterprise by which he might be dubbed knight, and accordingly in all his splendour he requested the honour from his royal master. The king did not hesitate, and presenting him with a bounty of two thousand crowns, increased by a contribution from the queen, he departed with a "letter of arms" to the four principal courts of Europe. The princess had sent his heralds in advance arrayed in most extravagant fashion. His passage through France excited popular admiration, until he came to Pampeluna, where the court of Aragon had its seat, his escort being continually augmented. The Spanish knights eagerly awaited his coming, and when he did arrive treated him most courteously. His prowess drew the whole court to his feet, and the queen in her admiration took from her neck a precious necklace and fastened it to the breast of her hero. He eventually tore himself from his royal admirers and returned to Paris to be greeted with applause. His lady-love especially showed him honour; but only in the quiet of her own apartments. Jehan next vanquished a dozen English knights who had landed at Calais and had carried all before them. This new victory added to the young hero's credit another laurel which shortly afterwards led to his being knighted. His father had just died, a circumstance which necessitated his becoming overlord of his estates. The princess now deemed it wise to openly display her admiration, but strangely enough her ardour had damped. Jehan left his royal master's court to win fresh laurels in the East. During his absence the princess fell ill, and under the physician's advice went to a castle she possessed in Touraine, which lay very close to her lover's inherited property. Before his return, his fickle fair one had cast her eyes on another, who was the abbot of a rich monastery. Jehan returned to his home from his glorious achievements in the East to find his rival making rapid headway. He met with the pair and found that his mistress had become cold. The abbot in his elation challenged the knight to wrestle, which, although hardly in keeping with knightly usage, he willingly accepted. The athletic abbot scored over Jehan, who was ridiculed by the princess. He meekly submitted to her scorn and in response to an invitation dined with the abbot and his lady. The Churchman forgot his position, and very wildly denounced his guest and the noble order of knighthood. The young knight calmly remonstrated, and before leaving extended his hospitality to them. He arrived at his castle and made preparations for the abbot and his lady, who duly arrived. After the repast, he brought into the banqueting chamber a huge and heavy coat of mail which he offered to his guest, challenging him to a duel. The awe-stricken abbot refused, but in vain, and donning the weighty armour he weakly attempted to face his host, who touching him lightly with his lance, drove him to the floor. The princess screamed, but unheeding her appeals, Jehan raised the visor of the abbot and slit his tongue, exclaiming : " Be thus chastised for the reviling words thy false mouth hath vomited out against the sacred order of knighthood and those who profess it." Journeying to the court of France some time after, Jehan related the story, which drew from his royal listeners marked approval. Turning to the false princess, who had listened to his narrative, he begged for her opinion : but knowing the truthfulness of his remark, she uneasily rejoined that the knight might have displayed more justice. Thus ended their amour.

JERUSALEM DELIVERED. Tasso's (1544–1595) great poem may well be included in a dictionary of romance, as it marks an epoch when European romance reached its apogee. Moreover, it cast into romantic form the story of the Crusades — a world-movement which probably did more to disseminate and foster the romantic spirit than any other. The poem is founded on the circumstances of the first Crusade, and as it opens tells how the Christian army is encamped in the plains of Tortosa.

Book I. God, in searching the hearts of the leaders, finds ambition, power and avarice the chief motives for their ardour, Godfrey alone being inspired with the pure zeal of driving the infidel from Jerusalem. An angel is sent, who appoints him general of the Christian host, and bids him call a meeting of the chiefs, to urge them to hasten their advance on Jerusalem. They meet, and in a stirring speech Godfrey recounts their various successes, which he attributes to Divine aid ; and advises them to lose no time in marching towards Jerusalem, lest the Saracen host be strengthened by help from Egypt. Peter the Hermit—originator of the Crusades—approves the speech, and with the consent of the chiefs, elects Godfrey commander of the Christian forces. He reviews the army : and the different nations, names and rank of their leaders are described. They then continue the march to the Holy City. Aladine the Saracen king, alarmed at their approach, lays waste the country, poisons the water sources and reinforces Jerusalem.

Book II. At the instigation of Ismeno the sorcerer, Aladine forcibly carries off the image of the Virgin from the Christian temple and transfers it to a Mahometan mosque. Ismeno proposes to weave a spell that will protect the city. At night the image is stolen. The king, incensed at the Christians, and unable to find the thief, declares a general massacre. Sophronia, a Christian maiden, in order to save the people, pleads guilty to the theft, and is condemned to death. Her lover, Olindo, attempts to save her by taking the blame on himself. Aladine, enraged at both, orders them to be burned. Clorinda, an Amazon, arrives to aid the Saracen King, and admires the fortitude of Sophronia when tied to the stake. She intercedes for her and her lover and obtains their pardon. Meanwhile, Godfrey with his army reach Emmaus. He receives Arogantes and Alethes, Egyptian ambassadors. Alethes in a plausible speech endeavours to dissuade Godfrey from attacking Jerusalem. His proposals are rejected, and Arogantes declares war in the name of Egypt's king.

Book III. At their first sight

of Jerusalem the Christian army is filled with deep emotion. The alarm is given, and the Saracens prepare for the enemy's attack. From the battlements, Aladine views their approach. Erminia by his side describes the names and characteristics of the various commanders. Clorinda makes the first sally, defeats a small foraging party and kills their leader Gardo. Tancred hastens to the rescue. In the *mêlée* Clorinda's helmet falls off, thus disclosing her face. Tancred is smitten with her beauty and while parleying with her a soldier, hurrying past, aims a blow at her unprotected head, inflicting a slight wound. Incensed at the deed, Tancred pursues the man. Finding pursuit useless, he turns to behold the Christians hard pressed by Argantes. Spurring to their assistance, he is joined by Dudon and Rinaldo. Dudon is killed by Argantes, but the Pagans are routed and retreat towards the city. Rinaldo, eager to avenge the death of his friend, incites his followers to scale the walls. Godfrey, with wiser counsel, commands them to wait a more favourable opportunity. He makes a noble oration over the dead warrior, and orders him to be interred with funeral honours. Finding the walls inaccessible, Godfrey sends his men into the woods to fell timber for besieging apparatus.

Book IV. Pluto summons a council of the infernal powers, and after discoursing on their former state, urges them to employ their machinations against the Christians. The fallen angels disperse to do his bidding; and in various ways are shown the evil influences of their black art. Hidraotes, King of Damascus, scheming to sow discord in the Christian host, and so weaken their power, decides to do so through a woman's wiles, and sends his niece Armida to the enemy's camp. She is brought before Godfrey, and by a feigned story of her misfortunes, endeavours to enlist his services on her behalf. To her disappointment, he refuses to do so until they relieve Jerusalem from the Saracen yoke. The decision arouses the ire of the knights, who are eager to succour beauty in distress. At their request, ten champions are selected to aid the maiden's cause. During her residence in the camp, Armida, by her beauty and cunning, captivates almost all the principal leaders.

Book V. Eustatius, with his own interests in view, praises Rinaldo's valour, and cajoles him into aspiring to the leadership of the ten knights. Gernando, coveting the command himself, and enraged at the presumption of the stripling, goads him by taunts and insolence to mortal combat. Gernando is slain, and his friend Arnaldo, exaggerating the deed to Godfrey, desires the death of the victor. Tancred upholds Rinaldo, pleads his cause, and Godfrey resolves to grant him a public trial. Tancred hastens to the tent of his friend with the news, and on Rinaldo refusing to submit to the ignominy of a trial, he persuades him to become a voluntary exile from the camp. Armida, having tried her arts in vain on Godfrey and Tancred, is now impatient for the promised aid. Godfrey is displeased at the eagerness of his knights to desert their cause and "join the maidens." The warriors are chosen by lot, and Armida departs with her escort. Many others follow in secret. Godfrey hears the disastrous news that the food supply has been seized by Arabs, and strengthens the flagging courage of his men, although far from sanguine himself.

Book VI. Argantes, impatient at the inaction, requests permission to attack the Christians. Aladine bids him curb his zeal, informing him that Solyman of Nice is collecting men from all quarters for the purpose of invading the Christian camp. Finally sanction is given to defy the enemy in single combat, and Argantes sends a challenge to the Franks. Tancred is chosen as champion, and exultingly fares forth. Espying Clorinda, who had followed Argantes' train, Tancred stops to gaze on her. Impatient at the delay, Otho spurs forwards and encounters the Saracen. He is vanquished and taken prisoner. Tancred awakes from his stupor and engages Argantes in a terrific combat which lasts till evening. They are parted by the heralds, and decide to renew the combat when their wounds are healed. Erminia, who while one time a prisoner in the Christian camp, had fallen in love with Tancred, is grieved over his wounds and resolves to visit him. She disguises herself in Clorinda's armour, and accompanied by a trusty squire leaves the city. She sends a message to Tancred, and awaits his answer. While alone, she is attacked by a scouting party of Christians, and flies. The news reaches the hero, who believing it to concern Clorinda, departs in search of her.

Book VII. Erminia, in her flight, meets an old shepherd, who befriends her. Tancred, while pursuing the supposed Clorinda, loses his way, and meeting a messenger is treacherously conducted to the castle of Armida and made prisoner. Argantes arrives on the day appointed for the fulfilment of their compact. Tancred being absent, and the flower of their chivalry already dispersed in divers ways, the remaining warriors lack the courage to take her place. Godfrey reproaches them for their cowardice, and resolves to meet Argantes. Raymond dissuades him, and after a stirring speech, despite his years, proposes to meet the Saracen. Roused by his words, the knights vie with each other in their eagerness to oppose the pagan. They cast lots and the lot falls to Raymond. He enters the lists, and the powers of good and evil influence the fight. Raymond has the advantage, when, through a breach of warfare, Beelzebub interrupts the combat, and a general battle ensues. The pagans are almost defeated, when a storm arises which turns the scale in their favour, and the Christians are routed.

Book VIII. The infernal powers, seeking to thwart the Christians, work their purpose through a Dane, who arrives with the news of a disastrous defeat of the Danes by a band of Arabs led by Solyman. Swern, their leader, is killed and the Dane is instructed to present his sword to Rinaldo, bidding him use it in his revenge on Solyman. At this point a foraging party return with undeniable proofs of Rinaldo's death. Argillan, instigated in a dream by a demon, causes civil war in the camp by throwing the suspicion of Rinaldo's supposed murder on Godfrey, and inciting the Italians to revolt. Godfrey quells the tumult by a noble speech, causes Argillan to be bound, and resolves to lose no time in attacking Jerusalem.

Book IX. Solyman, incited by

an evil spirit, with his Arabs attacks the Christian camp by night, with great slaughter. Godfrey, encouraging his men, opposes them, but the infidels are reinforced with help from Clorinda and Argantes. God forbids the infernal powers to interfere with the fight—and the battle wages with unabated fury. Argillan escapes from prison and performs valiant deeds, but is killed by Solyman. The fortunes of the day are still undecided, when the Christians receive unexpected aid from a small band of knights, and the victory is declared in their favour. The pagans are defeated, and Solyman forced to retreat, vowing future vengeance on the Christian host.

Book X. Solyman, while pursuing his way to Gaza, is accosted by Ismeno, who persuades him to return. The magician conveys him in an enchanted chariot to Jerusalem, and then conducts him through a subterranean passage to the council-hall of the Saracens, where unseen he hears their debates. Revealing himself, he is received with joy by Aladine. Meanwhile Godfrey discovers that the band of warriors who timely came to his assistance, were those who had followed Armida. One of them relates their adventures: how they were immured in dungeons, and then sent captive to Damascus. Rinaldo rescues them on the way. The news is received with joy, and Peter the Hermit, becoming inspired, prophesies the return and future glory of Rinaldo.

Book XI. On the advice of Peter the Hermit, the Christians implore the assistance of Heaven, and form a sacred procession. The pagans are first awe-stricken, and then amused at the spectacle. The call "to arms" is given. Raymond, on beholding his chief

without the customary armour, at once suspects his intention of scaling the walls, and remonstrates. Godfrey replies that on joining the sacred cause he had vowed to set aside rank and become a humble soldier. The other leaders follow his example and march on foot. The Christians reach the fortifications, and form a canopy by holding their shields aloft to ward off the enemy's missiles. Adrastus, the first to scale the walls, is wounded by an arrow. Many others follow, and are deterred by the same means. A breach is made by the battering rams. Godfrey enters, but is wounded by an arrow from Clorinda, and forced to retire. The Saracens gain courage, and almost win the day through the marvellous bravery of Solyman and Argantes. Tancred comes to the rescue, and the tide of war is turned. Godfrey is miraculously treated by an angel, and renews the attack until nightfall.

Book XII. Clorinda, eager to emulate the heroic deeds of Solyman and Argantes, resolves to burn the wooden tower of the Christians—one of their engines of warfare, which Solyman had partially destroyed the preceding day. She confides her purpose to Argantes, who, fired by her zeal, is desirous of aiding her. Arsetes, who had reared Clorinda from infancy, is warned in a dream, and endeavours to dissuade her from the enterprise; but in vain. He tells her the story of her birth, and that she was born of Christian parents. Under cover of darkness, the two adventurers sally forth and fire the tower. The Christians pursue them. Argantes reaches the city in safety; but in the confusion the gates are hastily closed, and Clorinda is left outside. Tancred, unaware of her identity, pursues her, and they engage in deadly combat. Clorinda is mortally wounded, and feeling death approaching desires to be baptized in the Christian faith. Tancred fetches water for the purpose, and as he raises her helm, recognizes the maid. His grief is intense ; and when she expires, he falls senseless by her side. He is discovered by some Christians and conveyed to the camp. Clorinda is reverently interred with funeral pomp, and Tancred recovers from his wounds. The news spreads to the Saracen host, and Argantes vows vengeance on Tancred.

Book XIII. Ismeno by his enchantments peoples the forest with demons, and commands them to guard the trees from the Christians. Godfrey sends his workmen to fell timber for besieging purposes. They are terrified and flee. Soldiers are next sent, but they also return in a panic. Alcastus boasts that no terrors can daunt him, and sets out alone for the enchanted wood. Finding his courage deserting him at the strange sights he beholds, Alcastus returns humbled and ashamed. Several of the others attempt the adventure, but in vain. Tancred next undertakes to test his courage, and passes successfully through the various ordeals which had vanquished his companions. Finally he succumbs to a new illusion which takes the form of his beloved Clorinda. The Christian army is afflicted by drought, and reduced to the last extremity. Discontent spreads among the troops, many declaring that the drought is sent by God, who is displeased with them. The Grecian commander deserts with his squadron, and many others follow. Godfrey invokes the assistance of Heaven, and help immediately comes in the shape of the much-desired rain.

Book XIV. Godfrey is shown in a dream the futility of earthly ambitions, and is inspired with fresh courage. He is counselled to recall Rinaldo, for only through him will the spell of the magic woods be broken and the waning spirit of his men strengthened. Godfrey enquires of the vision if he is to summon Rinaldo by threats or entreaties, and is told it is not seemly for a king to plead, but if others entreat he must yield. Guelpho pleads for his nephew's return, and Godfrey consents. Ubald and Charles the Dane are appointed envoys. They are instructed by Peter the Hermit to proceed to Ascalon, where they are entertained by a Christian magician, who shows them many wonders. He describes the manner in which Armida—furious at being defrauded of her prisoners by Rinaldo—ensnared him through her enchantments. He warns the knights of the dangers before them, and how they are to be avoided. He also shows them the method of delivering Rinaldo from the power of the sorceress.

Book XV. The two knights take their leave of the hermit, who presents them with the map, buckler, and golden wand, with which they are to overcome the spells of Armida. They embark in a ship steered by a beautiful maiden. She indicates the various places of interest in their voyage through the Mediterranean. On reaching the Straits of Gibraltar, Ubald questions the fair pilot about the unexplored seas beyond. She replies that since the time Hercules erected his pillars many unsuccessful attempts had been made to search the sea and countries afar. She predicts the discovery of Columbus, and the spread of the Gospel in heathen lands. They reach the Fortunate Isles, and Charles asks to be allowed to view some of the strange countries, but his request is refused. They arrive at the Island of Armida, where after giving certain instructions their guide leaves them. The knights ascend the mountain, and overcome all obstacles by aid of the golden wand. They resist the temptation of sensual allurements, and finally reach the palace of Armida.

Book XVI. Charles and Ubald wander in the maze, but consult the map and find their way out. They discover Rinaldo and his mistress in the garden. At the departure of Armida, the knights approach Rinaldo, who feels his war-like nature aroused at the sight of their armour. Beholding his own reflection in Ubald's shield, he is ashamed at the contrast, and also at Ubald's reproaches on his unmanly dalliance. He abandons his life of slothful ease and accompanies his deliverers. Armida follows them, and tries all her arts to induce Rinaldo to return, but in vain. She becomes exhausted, and faints. The warriors embark on a vessel bound for Palestine. Armida recovers from her swoon, and finds her lover gone. Grief replaces rage, and, planning revenge, she destroys her enchanted palace and takes flight to Egypt.

Book XVII. The caliph reviews his army. The auxiliary forces are described. Armida arrives when the caliph is conferring the sole command of the army on Emirenes. The troops hail him as leader. A grand banquet is given. Armida, determined to be avenged on Rinaldo, promises her hand in marriage to the warrior who kills him. A quarrel arises over the championship between Adrastus and Tisaphernes. The caliph intervenes, and bids Armida quell the disputants. Rinaldo and the two knights return to Palestine and are met by the aged hermit, who adjures Rinaldo to use his noble gifts for higher purposes. He presents him with a suit of armour, and Rinaldo is fired to emulate the famous deeds of his ancestors emblazoned on the shield. The Dane now hands him brave Sweno's sword, and bids Rinaldo avenge his death. The hermit, accompanies them to Jerusalem, predicts new glories to Rinaldo's race, and foretells the reign of Alphonso the Wise. He takes leave of the knights within sight of the camp.

Book XVIII. Rinaldo, on returning to the camp, is graciously received by Godfrey, and warmly greeted by his friends. He is granted absolution from the hermit Peter, and repairs to Mount Olivet to offer his devotions. He proceeds alone to the charmed forest ; resists the temptations, and thereby breaks the spell. The Christians commence hewing trees, and building their engines of destruction. Godfrey rescues a dove from the claws of a falcon, and intercepts a message fastened under its wing to the Saracen king, informing him of the approach of the Egyptian army. Godfrey determines to hasten the assault, and assigns to each leader his particular post. Tancred's squire Vasrino is sent as spy to the Egyptian camp. Godfrey, with a strategic movement, draws up his battering rams and towers on the enemy's strongest side. But at night he reverses the position, and in the morning the Pagans are dismayed to find their weakest defences assailed. Godfrey attacks the city, and is valiantly opposed. Great towers are reared against the walls. Ismeno uses his magic in trying to burn them ; but a wind arises and the fire is turned on the Pagans. Ismeno is killed. Rinaldo is the first to surmount the ramparts. The Archangel Michael appears to Godfrey, and shows him the spirits of former warriors assisting in the fight. A bridge is thrown across from one of the towers to the adjoining walls, and Godfrey essays the passage. Solyman opposes him, but in vain, and Godfrey plants the standard of the Cross on the walls of Jerusalem.

Book XIX. Tancred and Argantes single out each other, retire from the city and engage in a fight to the death. Argantes is slain and Tancred faints from wounds. Slaughter is rampant within the walls. The infidels take refuge in Solomon's temple. Rinaldo and his men pursue them, break down the door, and a massacre follows. Solyman and Aladine intrench themselves in David's tower, Raymond opposes them, but is knocked down helpless. Solyman urges his followers to drag Raymond within the tower. Seeing their chief's danger, the Christians attempt a rescue ; and at the appearance of Rinaldo, the Pagans reluctantly retreat to the tower. Night falls, and the strife ceases. Vasrino arrives at the Egyptian camp. He hears that some underhand plot is formed to take Godfrey's life, the nature of which he is at first unable to discover. He meets Erminia, who explains to him that a number of Pagans who had sworn to take Godfrey's life are going disguised as Christians, and will mingle among their foes. Erminia confesses to him her love for Tancred

and leaves the camp with Vasrino. They find the wounded Tancred, who recovers from his swoon, and is ministered to by Erminia. A band of soldiers appear who had been sent in search of their leader. They convey Tancred to the city, and also the body of his enemy Argantes, which he commands to be reverently interred. Vasrino seeks Godfrey, and relates the discoveries he has made in the Egyptian camp : how Rinaldo's life is sought by many a Pagan warrior, with the hope of winning Armida in reward ; and how Godfrey is to be overcome by treachery. The Christian army prepares for its encounter with the Egyptians. On the advice of Raymond an alteration is made in the dress of Godfrey's guard, with the view of thwarting the enemy's schemes.

Book XX. The Egyptian army arrives, and each side prepares for battle. Godfrey and Emirenes inspire their hosts by a spirited speech. The Christians advance. Gildippe is the first to gain distinction. She and her husband perform valorous deeds. Altamorus exacts heavy toll from the Christians. Gildippe attacks him and is wounded. Ormond, the instigator of the vile plots, leads his disguised men into Godfrey's presence. They are recognized and killed. Rinaldo defeats the Moors and Arabs with great slaughter. He passes Armida's car, and she fires her arrows at him, which glance off his armour. Armida's followers are slain, and she is unprotected from the enemy. Altamorus sees her peril, forsakes his troops, and goes to her assistance. He realizes his mistake too late, and his men are routed. Solyman views the battle from the tower, and unable to control his impatience at the inaction leaves the fortress accompanied by Aladine and his followers. Raymond is felled to the ground by Solyman, who rushes past seeking a more worthy foe. Tancred, recovering from his wounds, hears the tumult, and arrives in time to save Raymond from the Pagan horde. Raymond slays Aladine, and unfurls the banner of the Cross from the tower. Solyman, in the thick of the fight, spurs the waning courage of the Infidels. Gildippe is slain by Solyman. Edward supports her and receives his death-blow. Adrastus and Solyman are killed by Rinaldo. Tisaphernes next engages him, and after a terrific fight is also killed. When Armida sees her last champion slain, she escapes from the field. A touching scene occurs when Rinaldo surprises her in the act of attempting her own life. A mutual understanding follows with satisfaction to both. Godfrey kills Emirenes, and takes Altamorus prisoner. The sacred cause is won by the Christians, and Godfrey pays his devotions at the hallowed shrine.

JOFRID. (*Vide* " Gunnlaug Saga.") Wife of Thorstein Egilson ; mother of Helga.

JOHN OF FLAGY. The name of a scribe or poet whose name is inscribed on the best MS. of the third portion of the romance of *Garin the Lorrainer*. He appears to have been a native of Champagne. His version enjoyed great popularity, and must have been well known in Britain, as King John of France bought a copy of *Garin le Loherain* in London to beguile his captivity there. Dumeril states that eleven out of twelve MS. consulted by him reproduced it more or less faithfully.

Flagy's local knowledge gives remarkable verisimilitude to his text, and denotes that he was probably accustomed to earn his livelihood as a wandering minstrel from castle to castle. The text may be referred to the last quarter of the twelfth century.

JONAANS, JONANA, or JONAS. Alluded to in Grail romance as the fifth in line from Celidoine, and ancestor of Lancelot and Galahad. He married the daughter of King Moroneus of Wales.

JONAKR. (*Vide* " Volsungs.") Wedded to Gudrun (*q.v.*) after the death of Atli (*q.v.*).

JORMUNREK. (*Vide* " Volsungs.") King, betrothed to Swanhild (*q.v.*), who fell in love with his son Randwer (*q.v.*). This caused him to slay the lovers. He was subsequently slain by Gudrun's sons, Jonakr (*q.v.*), Saurli (*q.v.*), and Hamdir (*q.v.*).

JOSEPH OF ARIMATHEA. While he is chiefly known as the member of the Jewish Sanhedrin or Council who begged the body of Jesus for burial, he also appears in connection with the incidents of the Grail quest. He is mentioned as explaining to Evelach—a pagan—who cannot understand the Incarnation, that the Virgin was rendered pregnant by the overshadowing of the Holy Ghost through her ear, and that her virginity was no more hurt than is water when a sunbeam enters it. However, Evelach's (*q.v.*) atheistical views are not to be moved, although he afterwards has a miraculous dream and is eventually baptized. It is mentioned that Joseph cohabited with his wife, not as the lustful do, but was so filled with his love for his Saviour that he had no desire. Scenes are pictured in which Christ's passion and crucifixion are again brought before Joseph's eyes. He has a son Josephes (*q.v.*), who gives the vessel of Christ or Holy Grail into the hands of Sir Galahad. In Robert de Borron's poem, *Joseph of Arimathea*, it is related that Brons and Enygeus, who have twelve sons, are greatly troubled and consult Joseph, who prays before the Holy Vessel ; they are told that eleven will marry, and one remain single : this one is Alain. Joseph tells all about Christ's death and about the vessel to Alain, and that from him will issue an heir who is to keep the vessel ; Alain is to take charge of his brethren and sisters and go westwards. Alain, as Joseph taught him, preaches Jesus Christ. It is mentioned that God spoke to Joseph in prison concerning the Secrets of the Grail. Alain is to be called the Rich Fisher, from a great fish he caught ; he is to keep the vessel and to pass it on to the son of his son. Joseph stays three days with him, and then the good fisher goes away to " the land where he was born," and Joseph remains.

JOSEPH OF ARIMATHEA. A romance, one of a metrical trilogy, written by Robert de Borron (*q.v.*) which also includes his *Merlin*, and another poem not now extant (*c.* 1170–1212). It describes how Joseph of Arimathea collects Christ's blood in a vessel, and is cast into prison by the Jews. There he is visited by the Redeemer, who gives him the Grail vessel filled with his blood, and entrusts him with esoteric phrases of power, further instructing him to yield the vessel to three persons only, who will take it in the name of the Trinity. Joseph is released by Vespasian after many years,

and on issuing from prison converts his brother-in-law and his sister, Brons and Enygeus. Because of fleshly sin, the hand of God falls heavily upon the Christian band, and on the intercession of Joseph he is told that he must make a table to commemorate that at which Christ sat at the Last Supper. A vacant seat is to be provided at the table, which will be filled when Brons and his wife possess a son. Later, on the violent death of a wicked person who attempts to fill the seat, Joseph is told that not Brons' son but his grandson must fill the seat. Brons and Enygeus have twelve sons, all of whom marry save Alain, who is instructed to lead his brethren towards the West, at the same time being assured that his seed shall be keepers of the Grail. Joseph is further instructed that Brons must keep the Grail after his death, and must be told the words of awful power vouchsafed to him in prison. Brons having caught a fish by means of which sinners are detected, is to be called the Rich Fisher, and is to give the vessel of the Grail to his grandson. The tale practically ends with the Grail being intrusted to Brons, who sets out with it, leaving Joseph behind. The work has been carelessly copied and edited, and in places greatly abbreviated. Several prose versions exist which were brought up-to-date so far as the progress of the Grail legend had gone in their day. Inconsistencies abound, and Borron has obviously attempted to collate two versions of the legend. But the " Joseph " is the only work on the Grail, saving the Parzival of Wolfram, which exhibits any signs of having been animated by the spirit of Christian symbolism.

JOSEPH OF EXETER or **JOSEPH ISCANUS.** He dedicated to Archbishop Baldwin a Latin poem in six books upon the subject of the Trojan War, founded on Dares Phrygius (*vide* " Dictes and Dares "), and completed when Henry II. was preparing for the crusade preached by Baldwin. He wrote also on Antioches, of which there remains only a fragment, celebrating British heroes. Warton, in his *History of Poetry*, calls this writer " a miracle of his age in classical composition," praises his pure diction, sound periods, and harmonious numbers, adding that his style includes all the graces of Ovid, Statius, and Claudian.

JOSEPHES, JOSEPHE, JOSEPHUS, or **JOSAPHES.** In Grail romances, son of Joseph of Arimathea (*q.v.*). He only with his father Joseph is allowed to touch the wooden ark for the dish of the Holy Grail which the Lord commanded Joseph to make. Josephes is bidden by Christ to celebrate the Sacrament daily. He, with his father, ultimately overcome Evelach's (*q.v.*) unbelief. Evelach's land being overrun by his enemy Tholomes (*q.v.*) Josephes tells Evelach that this ill-hap is to remind him of his lowly origin. He further explains King Evelach's dreams. In the quest of the Grail, Josephes is mentioned as having been smitten in the thigh for having left his proselytizing work to trouble about the contemners of God's law, and he was told that the mark of the wound would stay with him all his life, and that the iron spear would remain in the wound so that he would limp. Josephes brings Mordrains, Sarraquite, and Nasciens to the Holy Shrine, and shows them the vessel wherein is Christ's blood. Josephes converts many people at Camelot. He comes to a hill called Hill of the Giant ; it is a Friday, and Brons is sitting next him at the Grail-table, but between the two is a space for a man to sit, and Brons, Josephes' kinsman, asks him why he does not invite some one to fill it. Josephes replies that only he who is a holier man than any present can fill that place, as it typifies Christ's seat at the Last Supper, and is empty, waiting His coming, or that of one whom He shall send. After this, Alain (*q.v.*) is the only one of Bron's twelve sons who chooses virginity and the service of the Holy Grail. Josephes, after fifteen years' wandering, comes back to Galafort, and finds his brother Galahad (not to be confounded with Sir Galahad) grown up. By Josephes' advice he is elected king. His last appearance seems to be as a bishop, when he gives the body of God to Sir Galahad and reveals himself as the son of Joseph of Arimathea.

JOSUE. In Grail romance, brother to Alain (*q.v.*), with whom he travels to the Terre Foraine, and whose daughter he marries. At the wedding so great was the power of the Grail that all present felt as if filled with the finest meats. Josue eventually becomes king and Grail Keeper.

JOSYAN. (*Vide* " Bevis of Hampton.") Daughter of Ermyn, a Saracen king. In love with Bevis for many years, and after many perilous adventures married to him. She was forced first to marry King Inor, from whom Bevis delivered her. When at Cologne, she was beset by Sir Mile in Bevis's absence, and married him only to strangle him. She was nearly burned at the stake for this. After her marriage she gave birth to twin sons in a forest, was carried off, and was rescued by Saber. She wandered about with him till she found Sir Bevis. She died at Mounbraunt, where her husband was sovereign.

K

KAI. The seneschal, or sewer of King Arthur, known in the French romances as Messire Queux or Maître Queux or Kuex, his name being thus altered to adapt it to his office of chief of the cooks. His character is usually treated as a curious mixture of courage and buffoonery, and his prowess is by no means equal to his pugnacity. He is prominent in the *Morte d'Arthur*. In his Brythonic or Welsh Celtic form of Cai ap Cynyr, he was the son of Cynyr Cainvarawc, the son of Gwron, and in the *Triads* he is alluded to as one of the three diademed chiefs of battle. In the tale of *Kilhwch and Olwen* (*vide* " Kilhwch ") in the *Mabinogion*, we meet with sure evidence of the mythological nature of Kai in the passage which states that his " breath lasted nine nights and nine days under water, and that he could exist nine nights and nine days without sleep." Moreover a wound from his sword could not be cured, he could make himself as tall as the highest tree in the forest, and so great was the heat of his nature that during rain whatever he carried remained dry. This would make it appear that Kai was originally a divine being who, through a series of mythological processes, had degenerated into a mere hero. The characteristics attributed to him would seem to point to his having originally been a rain-and-thunder deity, his watery propensities being accounted for by his pluvial affinities, and his heat by his possession of the lightning. A similar form is to be found in the Tlaloc or god of moisture of the ancient Mexicans, or in Indra a deity of the Hindus. The words " very subtle was Kai " are almost sufficient to prove his possession of the lightning.

KALAFIER. In the *Grand St. Graal*, a hater of Christians who accuses Nasciens of having killed Mordrains, and succeeds in having him and his son Celidoine cast into prison, Kalafier acting as his jailer. A miraculous hand appears from a cloud and, striking off Nasciens' fetters, transports him from the prison. Kalafier, following, is struck down by the hand. On his death-bed he orders that Celidoine be cast from the battlements, but heavenly hands bear him up, and Kalafier is smitten with fire and goes to eternal death.

KARAHEUT. In Carlovingian romance, King of India. He offered to fight Ogier the Dane on the occasion of Charlemagne's resisting a Saracen invasion of Italy, so that many lives might be spared in a general conflict, the city of Rome to be the prize of the victor. Karaheut takes Glorianda, the daughter of Corsuble, a Saracen emir, and his betrothed, to witness the combat. The combat is interrupted by the paynim, and Ogier is taken prisoner, much to the disgust of the chivalrous Indian king, who gives himself up to Charlemagne. When Ogier is freed, Karaheut is permitted to depart with Glorianda in consideration of his good faith.

KARDEI. Alluded to in the *Parzival* of Wolfram von Eschenbach as the twin brother of Loherangrin or Lohengrin.

KARI. (*Vide* "Burnt Njal.") A Viking who succoured on the seas Grim and Helgi (*q.v.*), Njal's sons. With them he made friends, and again lent his aid when Yarl Hacon was pursuing them upon a false charge. Kari married his friends' sister Helga; assisted Njal's sons in the slaying of Thrain (*q.v.*), Hrapp (*q.v.*) and Hanskuld (*q.v.*); and escaping the burning Bergthors-knoll, avenged his friends' terrible death. Finally he made friends with the leader of the burners, Flosi, whose niece, Hallgerda (*q.v.*), Hanskuld's widow, he married some time after Helga's death.

KARNIFEES. (*Vide* "Sir Otuel.") A Saracen knight, a fierce fighter. He was slain in an encounter with Sir Otuel.

KARR. (*Vide* "Grettir Saga.") The dead father of Thorfinn (*q.v.*). This evil spirit was robbed of his treasure by Grettir, and by him laid to rest.

KEELTA MAC RONAN. In Irish romance, one of the chief men of Finn. He was one of his house-stewards, a strong warrior and a golden-tongued reciter of tales and poems. Some time after he had seen St. Patrick and received the faith, he was wounded while fighting against pirates for the Fairy Folk of the Mound of Duma. For his reward they promised him youth. But this he refused, saying it would be accepting sorcery, and was healed of his wounds and all bodily evil. He represents all that is courteous, dignified, gene-rous, and valorous in paganism, in contradistinction to St. Patrick, who symbolizes all that is benign and gracious in Christianity.

KEEVAN OF THE CURLING LOCKS. The lover of Cleena (*q.v.*), who went off to hunt in the woods, leaving her to be abducted by the fairy folk.

KEINGALA. (*Vide* "Grettir Saga.") The weatherwise mare of Asmund. Her master believed in her weather prophecies, and setting his younger son, Grettir the Strong, to tend the horses, bade him be guided by this mare, who would return home before the oncoming of a storm. The lad, however, put little faith in Keingala, and as she persisted in remaining upon the cold and bitter hill-side, grazing upon the scanty grass, he determined to cure her of the habit, for he was frozen with the cold. He therefore, one morning, flayed a strip off her hide from wither to flank and then turned out the horses. The mare soon trotted stable-wards. This was repeated the next day; and as no storm was impending, Asmund himself then let out the horses when he noticed the mare's hurt.

KENVERCHYN. In Welsh romance, the owner of three hundred ravens which he left to Owain.

KET. Son of Maga (*q.v.*). In Irish romance a foremost champion of Connacht. With Conall's (*q.v.*) "brain ball," he wounded the Ulster King Conor mac Nessa (*q.v.*), which was the cause, seven years later, of Conor's death. His own end he met in single combat with Conall of the Victories.

KEVA OF THE WHITE SKIN. In Ossianic romance, daughter of Finn (*q.v.*). She became the bride of Goll mac Morna (*q.v.*).

KIAN. In Irish legend, father of Lugh (*q.v.*); brother of Sawan and Goban (*q.v.*). His magical cow with her wonderful supply of milk was stolen by Balor (*q.v.*). In revenge for this theft Kian, with the aid of Birog, a druidess, gained access to Ethlinn (*q.v.*), daughter of Balor, and became father to three sons. Two of these were drowned by their grandfather's order, the third, Lugh, escaping death by falling into a bay, whence he was rescued by Birog and wafted to his sire. Some years later, while on a mission to the fighting Danaans in Ulster, Kian fell in with the three sons of Turenn (*q.v.*), whose house was at enmity with him. Seeking to escape their notice he turned himself into a pig and joined a herd rooting in the plain. But in vain, for the brothers detected him, and he was wounded with a spear cast by the brother Brian. Conscious that death was approaching he prayed permission to regain his human shape. This was granted him, and he rejoiced in having outwitted Brian, for now the blood-fine to be paid by his slayers would be that for a man instead of for a pig. The brothers, determining that there should be no blood-stained weapon to publish the deed, stoned Kian and buried his body.

KILYDD. In Welsh legend, husband of Goleuddydd; father of Kulhwch (*q.v.*).

KIMBAY. A legendary Irish king who lived about 300 B.C. During his reign, Ulster was founded with its capital, Emain Macha (*q.v.*).

KING CONSTANT. A French romance of the thirteenth century. It relates the story of King Constant; and might also be entitled

"The Origin of the Name Constantinople." In the days when Constantinople was called Byzantium, there lived a Paynim emperor, called Muselin, who was versed in the science of astronomy. Going forth one night accompanied by a certain lord, he heard a man on the roof of his house, alternately praying that his wife— who was in childbed—would be delivered of a child, and again that she would not. The contradictory prayers went on for some time, and the emperor's curiosity was aroused. Accosting the man, he inquired the reason of the seeming inconsistency of his utterances. The man replied that he was a student of astrology, and that if the hour of birth were unpropitious, some great misfortune would overtake the child; but, on the other hand, if the hour were favourable, prosperity would be its lot. A son had now been born, he added, and to a goodly heritage. The emperor inquired the nature of the heritage. And he was told that the child would marry the emperor's daughter, and in time become king. The emperor was wroth, and privately commanded a knight to secretly abduct the child, which he did; whereupon the king stabbed the infant, vowing that it would never live to sit on his throne, and also commanded the knight to throw the child into the sea. On his way to obey the mandate, the knight's heart was touched with pity for the new-born babe, and he left him lying on a warm muck-heap before a certain abbey. The monks found the child—who was not dead—and carried him to the lord abbot. When he saw the grievous wound, he sent for physicians, and they promised to cure the child for eighty golden pieces.

In consequence of this he was called "Constant," because of his costing the abbey so great a sum. The boy grew in stature, and was of extraordinary beauty, as well as proving an apt scholar ; therefore he became a favourite of the abbot, and accompanied him when he went abroad. One day it chanced that the abbot paid a visit to the Emperor Muselin, who was greatly struck with the beauty of the lad, and desired to know about him. Whereupon the abbot related the story of the foundling. When he spoke of the dagger wound, the emperor knew that this was the child he had tried to kill. So he besought the abbot to allow the young man to enter his service. After due consultation with his monks, the abbot sanctioned the proposal, for he dared not thwart the Saracen king. When the emperor had Constant in his power, he considered how he might secretly destroy him. He therefore wrote a letter to the Castellan of Byzantium, commanding him to slay the bearer ; and sent Constant with it, who was unaware he was carrying his own death-warrant. When he arrived at the palace, it was the dinner-hour ; so he sat down to rest in the garden, till a more opportune moment, and straightway fell asleep. The young princess and her maidens were playing in the garden, and happened upon the sleeping youth. Knowing him to be the bearer of letters and anxious to learn the news, the princess softly withdrew the fatal missive. As she read the contents she was sorely grieved, for she had never beheld so comely a person as the young man before her. Taking one of her maidens into her confidence, she wrote a letter bidding the castellan give her in marriage

to the bearer of the letter ; and to proclaim high festival, and invite all the people to the wedding banquet. This done she sealed it with her father's seal, and slipped it beneath Constant's girdle. When the young man awoke and presented the letter, no one appeared more surprised when the contents were made known, than the princess. She pretended reluctance, but was overruled by the dignitaries of the realm, who dared not be party to opposing the Imperial commands. The marriage was celebrated amid great rejoicings. When the emperor returned, he found the people still feasting and merrymaking. When he heard the reason, he pondered deeply, and knew his daughter to be at the bottom of it. He came to the conclusion that it was no use striving against what was written in the stars, so he decided to make the best of it. On the death of Muselin, Constant reigned in his stead ; and his wife and all in his realm were converted from paganism to Christianity. His son was also called Constant, and it was in his reign that the city was first called Constantinople.

KING HORNE, GESTE OF. An English metrical romance, founded upon an older French romance entitled *Le Roman du Roi Horn*, of which there remain only two fragments, one of 2386, the other of 2494 lines. This French romance was written by one Maistre Thomas and is regarded by Ritson and M. de la Rue as a composition of the latter portion of the twelfth century, whereas the English adaptation dates, according to Percy, to within a century of the Conquest. But it is now admitted on all hands to be not older than the reign of Edward I. It recounts

P

how Mury, King of the Saracens, lands in the kingdom of Suddene, where he kills the king, named Allof. The queen, Godyllt, escapes ; but Mury seizes on her son, Horne, a beautiful youth of fifteen years, and puts him in a galley with two of his playmates, Achulph and Fykenylde. The vessel being driven on the coast of the kingdom of Westnesse, the young prince is found by Aylmar, king of that country, brought to court, and delivered by Athelbrus, his steward, to be educated in hawking, harping, tilting, and other courtly accomplishments. Here the Princess Rymenild falls in love with him, declares her passion, and is betrothed. Horn, in consequence of this engagement, leaves the princess for seven years, to demonstrate, according to the ritual of chivalry, that by seeking and accomplishing dangerous enterprises, he deserves her affection. He proves a most valorous and invincible knight, and at the end of seven years, having killed King Mury, recovered his father's kingdom, and achieved many signal exploits, recovers the Princess Rymenild from the hands of his treacherous knight and companion Fykenylde, carries her in triumph to his own country, and there reigns with her in great splendour and prosperity.

KING ROBERT OF SICILY. An English romance of the fourteenth century, the authorship of which is unknown. It has never been printed. It tells how King Robert of Sicily was beguiled by pride into sneering at a priest who read Mass. The father warned him of haughtiness, saying that nothing might bring him down from his high estate. An angel is sent by the Almighty to lower Robert's pride, and he, taking Robert's shape upon him, transforms the king into the likeness of his own fool. He is sent out to lie with the dogs, in which condition he envies those curs which were permitted to rest in the king's hall. At length the Emperor Valmounde sends letters to his brother King Robert, inviting him to visit along with himself their brother, the Pope of Rome. The angel in Robert's guise welcomes the messengers, and after a long and ignominious penance restores Robert to his proper shape.

Vide MS. Vernon *ut sup.* Bibl. Bodl. f. 299 ; Caius Coll. Cambs. MS. Claff. E. 147, 4 ; Brit. Mus. MS. Harleian, 525, 2, f. 35., cod. Membran.

KING ROTHER. An epic poem, the original authorship of which is ascribed by Von der Hagen to the first half of the twelfth century, but which was evidently rewritten later. The king, who dwells in the town of Bar (or Bare) by the Western sea, is advised by his courtiers to take a wife. Count Lupolt describes the beauty of Constantine's daughter, the King of Constantinople. But every man who has sought her has lost his life. Margrave Herman proposes sending Lupolt as envoy. Lupolt is willing even at the risk of his life, but begs for eleven knights to be sent with him. They cross the sea, and ride to Constantine's court, splendidly apparelled. Both king and queen receive them graciously, for their raiment proves them to be men of note. Lupolt praises the wealth and wonders of King Rother's court, and then sues for the hand of the fair princess for his master. Constantine is wroth and casts the embassy into prison. A year and a day elapses. King Rother becomes anxious about the fate of his knights, and resolves to go in search of them. Preparations are made for their departure ; they take vast treasures, and people come from far and near to join the expedition. Among them is the giant Asprian, who brings with him a troop of fellow giants. The king determines to employ strategy, and commands all who accompany him to call him Thiderich (or Dietrich), and so hide his identity. They are made welcome at Constantine's court. "Dietrich" complains to him of illtreatment from King Rother, and offers his services, and begs protection from Constantine. By the advice of his counsellors, and through fear of the giants, Constantine accepts his services, and also tells him that he holds as prisoners some of Rother's messengers. "Dietrich" distributes gifts with a lavish hand among Constantine's people, and many gather round him for the sake of the offerings. The queen is constantly reminding her lord what a powerful man this King Rother must be, and how foolish they were not to give him their daughter. A great festival is given by Constantine, and the young princess is attracted by "Dietrich's" fine appearance and costly dress. Wishing for an interview with him, and through help of a mutual artifice, he is taken to her apartments. She declares her love for King Rother, and he makes known his real identity. She replies that she cannot be sure if he is telling the truth, while "Dietrich" cunningly answers by asking to see the prisoners who will at once recognize him. After another ruse on the part of the fair lady, the prisoners are brought forth, and recognize

Rother by his playing the harp. At this time a great host from Babylon, under a heathen named Ymelot, is on its way to attack Constantinople. The twelve knights are set free, and enter Rother's corps, who joins forces with Constantine. They set out to meet the foe. Rother and his men attack the enemy during the night. The giants vanquish the heathen, and Ymelot is taken prisoner. Constantine thanks Rother for his services, and the latter suggests that a messenger should be sent to tell the ladies the good news. Constantine bids him do so himself ; so he starts for Constantinople, taking with him only his own men. Arrived there, he tells the queen that Ymelot has slain the king and his knights, and is hastening towards them. The queen and her daughter entreat Rother to take them with him. They make for the ships and hastily embark. Rother takes his daughter on board, but leaves the mother behind. In answer to her tears, he tells her that Constantine is alive and on his way home, and that Ymelot is taken prisoner. The queen is overjoyed at the news, and the ships depart amid good wishes from all. Constantine is greatly distressed at the loss of his daughter, and in the confusion Ymelot escapes. A minstrel offers to bring back the king's daughter, if he is provided with a ship and a goodly store of merchant's wares. The ship is made ready, and reaches "Bare" during the absence of King Rother. The minstrel sells his wares at the lowest prices, and proclaims that he possesses a stone of such virtue, that if a queen held it in her hand no one should die, for a mere touch of it would revive them ; even the crooked would be made straight, only she must come on board the ship. A knight, who has two deformed children, entreats the queen to make the trial. She does so, and the instant she is aboard the ship sets sail. There is grief in Bare over the loss of the lady, and when Rother arrives he gathers together an army and sails for Constantinople. Landing at a secluded part, disguised as a pilgrim, he takes with him two knights, and a good horn, which is to give warning if he is discovered ; and departs to the court of Constantine. Meeting a knight on the way, he is informed that Ymelot attacked Constantine, who, to save his kingdom, promised him Rother's wife for his son Balistruin, the compact to be sealed that night. Constantine is seated at table with Ymelot and Balistruin, by whose side, greatly grieved, sits Rother's wife. Rother and his knights mix among the crowd round the table, and the disguised king succeeds in giving his wife a ring with his name on it. They are discovered, Balistruin threatens to drown him, and Rother asks to be hanged on the hill near the wood. Rother is bound, to the bitter grief of the young queen, and all the people bewail his fate. At the gallows a rescue is made. Rother's bonds are cut, and he blows the horn which summons his own men. The heathen are routed, but Constantine's life is spared. King Rother, his queen, and all his retinue return to Bare, where a son is born, whom they call Pepin, afterwards the father of Charlemagne. The Rother story is thus connected with the Charlemagne cycle, but visibly belongs not so much to Germany proper as to Germanesque Italy, and may be said to represent a Lombard subcycle. Von der Hagen points out some analogies between *Rother* and the later poems of the Nibelungen cycle, such as *Otnit* and *Wolfdieterich,* as well as with the Norse Wilkina Saga of the thirteenth century. Ludlow believes the legend to have been originally Lombardian, not only because of the name of its hero, but because of his capital " Bar " or " Bare," which he identifies with Bari in Southern Italy. The Carlovingian connection he believes belongs to a later elaboration of the tale.

KING OF TARS. An English romance, probably of the fourteenth century, never printed. Its full title is *The Kyng of Tars, and of the Soudan of Dammias (Damascus), how the Soudan of Dammias was cristened thoru godis gras.* It recounts how the Soldan or Sultan of Damascus hears great bruit of the beauty of the daughter of the King of Tars, and dispatches ambassadors to her father craving her hand, but without success. The sultan grows very wroth at the reply of the King of Tars (Tarsus), which is pitched in opprobrious terms, and calls his parliament together. He collects a great army, and marches on the dominions of the King of Tarsus, who is a Christian monarch, whereas his would-be son-in-law is a Mussulman. The " Saracens " prevail, and the King of Tarsus flees. To prevent further bloodshed, the princess declares that she is willing to be married to the sultan, although a pagan, and notwithstanding that her father withholds his consent she finds means to escape to the sultan's court in order to cement a peace through their marriage. They are married, and the wedding is solemnized by a great tournament which they both view from a high tower. The princess is afterwards delivered of a son, who is so deformed as to be almost a monster. At length she persuades the sultan to embrace the Christian faith, and the young prince is baptized, after which he suddenly becomes a prodigy of beauty. The sultan destroys his Saracen idols with a great stone. "With sterne strokes and with grete, on Jovyn and Plotoun, on Astrot and sire Jovyn," and releases 30,000 Christians. He is attacked by the neighbouring Saracen lords, but succeeds in beating them off.

KING'S QUHAIR, THE. (*Vide* article, "James I.") A poem attributed to King James I. of Scotland. It is written in what is usually called "rhyme royal," a metre used also by Spenser, Gower, and Dunbar; and the poet tells how he wooed and won his bride, with a beauty which makes his work one of the gems of early Scottish literature. The chief evidence for ascribing the poem to the king consists in the saying of Major, a Scottish historian of the fifteenth century, who affirms that James "left behind him many writings and songs, which are to this day remembered among the Scots, and reckoned to be the best they have. He wrote an ingenious little book about the queen while he was yet in captivity and before his marriage." Clearly the author refers here to the *Quhair*, and Major's statement is in some degree corroborated by two other mediæval historians, Bower and Boece, who both assert that James was a writer. Unfortunately, however, they give no particulars about his writings; while the earliest existing manuscript of the *Quhair*, one in the Bodleian Library, is dated 1475. This is thirty-eight years after the death of the king, but that fact does not vitiate the ascription to him, for both at beginning and end of his document the scribe attributes the poem to "King James of Scotland ye first."

Major tells that the king wrote "another ingenious song of the same kind, *Yas sen*, etc." (*sic*). Now there is a poem in manuscript in the Pepysian Library which begins, "Sen that eine that workis my weilfare"; and several editors of the writings ascribed to James, assuming that the MS. is slightly mutilated and the word "Yas" gone, have contended that this poem is what Major refers to, and have therefore included it in James's works under the title of "Song on Absence." But a study of the MS. does not lead one to suppose that it has suffered much from the hand of time, or that the word in question has been erased, and accordingly the authorship of the poem remains a mystery, while equally mysterious is yet another one also referred to by Major. He speaks of the king writing "that pleasant . . . poem at Beltane"; and some writers have imagined that the poem thus cited is no other than the famous "Peblis at the Play," which begins, "At Beltane, quhen ilk bodie bownis." But here, too, the evidence in favour of the king having been the author is slight in the extreme, while the language of the poem certainly suggests a later period than James's.

Two further pieces of verse are likewise attributed to James, *Christ's Kirk on the Green* and *Good Counsel*. The ascription in the former case rests on the fact that George Bannatyne, who, in the sixteenth century, made a collection of early Scottish poems, named the king author of *Christ's Kirk*. And as regards *Good Counsel* all that can be said is that, in *The Gude and Godlie Balletis*, first published in 1567, this poem is included along with the words, "Quod King James the First."

KLINSCHOR or **KLINGSOR.** Lord of the Magic Castle wherein are kept Arthur's mother and other queens. He is nephew to Virgilius of Naples, and is overcome by Gawain. He is alluded to in the *Parzival* of Wolfram von Eschenbach.

KNIGHT OF THE LION. (Chevalier au Lion.) A French Arthurian romance, composed about 1160 by Chrétien de Troyes. Sir Ewaine had wed a fair lady, and after a week of feasting he must join his master, who had ridden forth against the heathens. The parting was one of sorrow, and with a promise on his lips that he would return by that day twelvemonth, he took his leave of his weeping wife. He joined King Arthur, and, as of old, was first in every fight. When the war ended he did not ride homeward, for the love of adventure was strong within him; but on he went, achieving fresh victories. The twelve months passed, and one day as he sat in the feasting-hall of his king, the queen reminded him of his vow to his wife. He was on the point of riding off when a damosel entered and demanded from him the ring which his wife had given him, to whom he had acted so faithlessly. Overwhelmed by his wife's anger he left the court and fled into the forest. His reason left him and, tearing off his armour, he roamed about naked and insane. In this manner he

lived for a year, and but for a kindly hermit he encountered no one. At last the fever abated and the good recluse clothed him afresh and sent him on his way. But Ewaine had changed. No more did he love conquest, and he vowed never to use his sword but for good. He left the forest and tramped many weary miles. But one night as he was about to rest he came upon a lion and a dragon which struggled fiercely. Seeing the dragon smothering the lion under his mighty bulk, the hero rushed upon the fiery monster, and with one swing of his good sword clave its body in twain. The lion arose and went toward its deliverer, licked his feet, and fawned upon him. All night long the beast kept guard over the brave knight. On the morrow, Ewaine set out on the road, accompanied by the lion, which befriended him and sought prey, on which they fed. One day they came to a castle; but the porter on seeing the lion would not drop the drawbridge, and as Ewaine would not desert his companion, he besought the lord of the castle, who made welcome both knight and beast. But sorrow reigned over the castle, the inhabitants of which were under the tyranny of a great giant who had imprisoned the four sons of their lord, and now every day came to the castle wall demanding his fair daughter. Ewaine did not hesitate to meet the giant, who, on seeing his challenger, mockingly advised him to retreat, but the good knight heeded him not, and straightway flung his spear at his opponent. The giant met his onset with his heavy iron club. Throwing him to the ground he was about to deal the fatal blow, when the lion rushed over the parapet and overthrew the giant.

Ewaine arose and cut off the oppressor's head. With tears of thankfulness the lord, his knights and their ladies rejoiced in the victory and ever after he was called " The Knight of the Lion." Soon his valour was heard of in Arthur's court, and the king at last sent forth three of his famous knights, that they might secure him to the brotherhood. Accordingly, Sir Lancelot, Sir Gawaine and Sir Kay, the boaster, rode out of the castle, each taking different paths. On they went passing town, village and dale which rang with the victor's achievements. But of his whereabouts they knew not. Sir Kay soon gave up the search, and turning his steed in the direction of the court he was confronted by the object of his search. The boaster immediately challenged Ewaine, and bringing their horses together, Ewaine sent Sir Kay grovelling in the dust. Without waiting any further he pursued his way with the faithful lion. Sadness, however, overtook him, and despite the sympathy which the beast displayed, he was on the point of slaying himself with his sword, when from a chapel on the wayside a maiden appeared. To her he told of his misfortunes, and she in turn related how the cruel Sir Salados had imprisoned her mother within his castle. Hardly had Ewaine time to offer his sympathy when the knight in question appeared, and without more ado they came together in combat. Long and fierce waxed the fight, amid a storm of thunder and lightning ; and at last Sir Salados took flight. Ewaine took up the chase until they came to Salados' castle, into which the latter took refuge. Glancing around he saw the figure of the imprisoned lady. Then Sir Salados appeared with an army of knights ; but the faithful lion bounded over the battlements, threw the wicked Salados to the ground, and scattered the knights in confusion. Ewaine now rid himself of his enemy by cutting off his head. The maiden, followed by Sir Lancelot and Sir Gawaine, rode up. " The knight of the Lion " threw off his disguise and was recognized by all. The imprisoned lady came forward and knew him to be her long-lost husband. They wept for joy, and in one kiss forgave all the sorrow of these seven years.

KNIGHT OF THE TOMB. Or, the Black Knight. A knight who dwelt in a tomb, striving against all comers for the sake of his love. He was overcome by Perceval, and driven back into his gloomy dwelling. The incident is alluded to in the *Conte del Graal* (*q.v.*).

KOLSKEGG. (*Vide* " Burnt Njal.") Brother of Gunnar (*q.v.*).

KRIEMHILD. (*Vide* " Nibelungenlied.") Wife of Siegfried and daughter of King Giuki. She married King Etzel (*q.v.*) upon the death of her first husband, upon whose slayers she meted out a terrible vengeance.

KULHWCH. In Welsh romance and myth, son of Kilydd and Goleuddydd. His stepmother, in her jealousy of him, declared that he would have no wife until he obtained Olwen, daughter of Yspaddaden Penkawr (" Hawthorn, King of Giants "). Being nephew to Arthur he sought his assistance in this quest. But Arthur, after a year devoted to the search, could find no trace of the maiden. Then Kulhwch, accompanied by Kai (*q.v.*), Bedwyr, a man of craft and cunning unequalled in swiftness and in might; Kynddelig, who was a sure guide in strange as in familiar lands; Gwrhyr, who could speak all languages, and Menw, who could throw a veil of invisibility over his party, set out to seek for Olwen. After much journeying they found themselves before a great castle, feeding in front of which was a flock of sheep, shepherded by Custennin, the ill-treated brother of Yspaddaden. The following day being Saturday, Olwen, whose footsteps gave birth to four white trefoils, came, as was her wont, to the herdsman's hut to wash her hair. Reciprocating the love of Kulhwch for her, she sent him to ask Yspaddaden for her hand in marriage. But he, aware that his end would come upon his daughter's bridal morn, sought to free himself of this suitor as of all others; and twice, as the party were leaving his hall, he cast after them a poisoned dart, which, however, some one of them caught each time and flung back at him, wounding him sorely. Then Yspaddaden named a great number of seemingly insurmountable difficulties, which Kulhwch must overcome before he could have Olwen as his wife. But the most difficult of all was the obtaining of the comb and scissors that were between the ears of Twrch Trwyth, a king transformed into a huge boar, for there were many tasks attendant on this adventure. All these wonders were performed; Kulhwch found his bride, and Goreu, the only remaining son of Custennin, beheaded Yspaddaden.

KUNHILD. Sister of Dietlieb (q.v.). (*Vide* "Dietrich of Bern.") She mysteriously disappeared, but was found later to have been taken away by Laurin (q.v.), king of the dwarfs.

KYMIDU KYMEIN-VOLL. In Welsh romance and myth, wife of Llassar Llaesgyvnewid. Matholwch (q.v.) had met this giantess and her husband with a cauldron on his back near a certain lake in Ireland. They took service with him; but at the end of a year, the country being in an uproar on account of the outrages of their children, Matholwch determined to burn the whole family. To this end he set fire to a huge iron house into which he had enticed them, and blew it to a white heat. But husband and wife forced their way through the softened iron and came across to Britain. There they were housed and well treated by Bran (q.v.), who, for his kindness, received the magic cauldron. Such was its power, that the slain, if cast into it, would regain life and limb, but not speech.

KYMON. A knight of Arthur's court. Fired with the love of chivalrous adventure, he set out one day in its quest. Reaching a magnificent castle he was generously received and entertained, and was directed to a monstrous one-eyed, one-footed black man, who set him on his way to meet his "equal in combat." Kymon found a silver bowl on a slab of marble by the side of a fountain under a great tree, as the black man had described. Following the instructions given, the knight-errant emptied the bowlful of water on the slab, when he almost succumbed to the terrific storm of hail that followed. Then syren songs burst from the throats of the birds upon the now leafless tree. At last there appeared a black knight, who worsted Kymon.

The victor, passing the shaft of his lance through the reins of the riderless horse, turned his charger's head homeward. The unfortunate knight then returned to the castle, and with a new horse set off to Caerleon. This story is to be found in the Welsh tale of the *Lady of the Fountain*, in the *Mabinogion*.

KYNDDELIG. In Cymric legend, one of Arthur's servitors. Able to guide in strange, as in familiar lands, he accompanied Kulhwch (*q.v.*) on his quest for Olwen.

L

LABAN. (*Vide* " Sir Ferumbras.") Sovereign of Babylon. He hated the Christians and persecuted them. He captured Rome and took his booty to his city of Aigremor. He fought many battles with Charlemagne, and was at last betrayed by his daughter who became a Christian. He was taken prisoner by Charlemagne, who would have saved his life if he would have been baptized, but refusing this, he was executed.

LABEL. In Grail romance, a heathen king to whose realm Celidoine, son of Nasciens, was transported by supernatural agency. (*Vide* "Kalafier.") He wins Label's favour by expounding a dream of his, but at Label's death is cast adrift in a boat with a lion. He, however, comes safe to Nascien's island. (*Vide* " Celidoine.")

LABOR, KING. Father of the Maimed King, in Arthurian romance. He was the mortal enemy of King Hurlame, who, with the Grail sword, defeats him. (*Vide* " Morte d'Arthur.")

LABRA THE MARINER-MAON. Son of Ailill (*q.v.*) and grandson of Laery (*q.v.*). When a child he was compelled by Covac (*q.v.*), his granduncle, to swallow a portion of the hearts of his father and grandfather and a mouse with her young. His speech left him, so Covac let him go. Taken to Munster to the kingdom of Feramore, he was then sent to Gaul and treated as a future king of Ireland. But the daughter of the King of Feramore, out of her passion for him, composed a beautiful poem which was set to music by Craftiny (*q.v.*), her father's harper. This Craftiny took to Gaul, and by its enchanting virtue Maon regained his speech. The exile then set out with an armed force to wrest the Irish throne from the usurper. Covac was slain. Maon received the name " Labra the Mariner," from the circumstances that he could speak (*labraidh*), and that he was the captain of the Gaulish fleet with which he invaded Ireland. Like the Greek King Midas, Labra had the ears of a horse. So, in order to keep secret this deformity, he had his hair cropped once a year by a man chosen by lot, and put to death afterwards. Once this lot fell to a poor widow's son. With tears and beseechings, however, she prevailed upon Labra to spare her son, who swore by the sun and the wind to keep the secret. But the weight of this burden was too much for him. So, with the advice of a Druid, taking a certain direction, he whispered the deadly secret to the first willow tree he came across, and returned home light-hearted as of old. One day, however, Craftiny, requiring a new harp, cut down this willow tree, and to the amazement of all in the king's hall, in response to the harper's first touch of the strings, it chimed the words : " Two horse's ears hath Labra the Mariner." The secret was out, and no one was again put to death on its account. This tale has a counterpart in Hindu romance.

LA CÔTE MALE-TAILÉ (so-called because of his ill-fitting coat). Otherwise Sir Bruinor le Noire. On entering the court of Arthur, he is treated as a scullion. A damosel, Maledisant, leads him on a quest after a wicked knight, whom he subdues. Afterwards he marries the maiden. He becomes the overlord of the Castle of Pendragon. (*Vide* " Morte d'Arthur.")

LADMER, KING OF WESTENMER. A character in the romance of *Dietwart* (*q.v.*). He entertains for a while Dietwart, who has fallen deeply in love with his daughter Minnie, to the gratification of Ladmer. He gladly consents to their marriage, and witnesses the slaying of the dragon by his Imperial son-in-law. (*Vide* " Dietwart.")

LAEG. In Irish romance, friend, messenger, and charioteer of Cuchulain (*q.v.*). He was slain by a spear aimed at Cuchulain and flung by Lewy (*q.v.*).

LAERY (1). In Irish romance, son of King Ugainy the Great. He was treacherously slain by his brother Covac (*q.v.*).

LAERY (2). The Triumphant. One of the three claimants, including

Cuchulain (*q.v.*) and Conall of the Victories (*q.v.*), of the championship of Ireland. The test, however, he was unwilling to undergo.

LAERY (3). Son of Neill, King of Ireland. In the twelfth-century *Book of the Dun Cow*, a story is related of him which states that, remaining pagan, he had a vision of Cuchulain, whom St. Patrick summoned from Hell to prove his teachings. In the end Laery accepted the Christian faith.

LAIRGNEN. In Irish romance a Connacht chief, betrothed to Deoca (*q.v.*).

LAMBAR. Alluded to in the *Queste del Saint Graal* as the father of the Maimed King or Fisher King.

LAMBERT LE TORS. A French poet, who is commonly supposed to have lived at the beginning of the twelfth century. He is remembered by virtue of his share in the *Roman d'Alexandre*, a popular epic of which a mediæval manuscript on vellum is extant in the Bibliothèque Nationale (No. 7633), and which recounts in verse of twelve syllable lines the exploits of Alexander the Great. The poet was known among his contemporaries as Lamberz li Tors, while a misprint in the sixteenth century gained him the name of Lambert le Count, and to this day he is frequently styled thus. Nothing is known about his life, but in a passage in the poem aforesaid he furnishes this sidelight on himself :

" La verté de l'estoire, si com li vois la fist,
     Un clerc de Chateaudun, Lamberz le Tors escrist,
     Que del Latin la traist et en romans la mist."

It is hard to say how much of the *Roman d'Alexandre* is really from Lambert's pen, but he is usually credited with those parts which deal with the pursuit and death of Darius, the wonders of India, the descent of Alexander to the bottom of the sea, the expedition against Porus, the voyage through the pillars of Hercules, the fight with the Amazons, and the second defeat and ultimate subjugation of Porus. Sundry other passages are probably his work also, notably those dealing with the duel between Porus and Alexander and the taking of Babylon, while he is said to have written further matter about Alexander which is now lost. His writing in general is but lightly esteemed, and he was superseded in public favour by a subsequent writer, Alexandre de Bernay, who completely re-wrote the *Roman d'Alexandre*, improving it considerably.

LAMORAK, DE GALIS, SIR. Son of King Pellinore, and Knight of the Round Table. In Arthurian romance he is mentioned as being amongst the lovers of Queen Guinevere (*q.v.*). He is also the possessor of a magic horn, which proves a source of enjoyment to King Mark (*q.v.*). He is the cause of the Queen of Orkney's death at the hands of her son Gaheris, through his familiarity with her. He subsequently dies through a wound inflicted on him by Mordred. (*Vide* " Morte d'Arthur.")

LANCE (SPEAR), THE GRAIL. Frequently referred to in Arthurian legend as the " bleeding lance." In Furnivall's text we read that Joseph opens the door of the ark and four " angels issue, two bearing burning lights, the third a cloth of red samite, the fourth a lance bleeding so hard that the drops run into a box he holds in his other hand." It is probably intended to be symbolical of the spear which the Roman soldier thrust in Jesus' side.

LANCELOT (1). A knightly character of the Arthurian cycle, who, however, does not bulk so largely in the earlier romances as his importance in Malory's *Morte d'Arthur* suggests. The original legend of his life and adventures is probably the mediæval prose work entitled *Lancelot*, a rambling romance composed of six sections. In the article dealing with Malory's *Morte d'Arthur* a summary of his history will be found. Other works in which he figures are the *Lanzelot* of Ulrich von Zatzikhoven, the *Chevalier de la Char rette* of Chrétien de Troyes, the *Diu Krône* of Heinrich von dem Turlin, *Rigomer*, and smaller poems such as *Lancelot et le cerf au pied blanc*. In the purely Celtic literature connected with the Arthurian cycle he does not appear at all. Lancelot, who is generally alluded to as Sir Lancelot du Lac, was the son of King Ban, and was brought up by the enchantress Nimue, Lady of the Lake, who succeeded in imprisoning Merlin. As a youth he came to King Arthur's court, where by his prowess he speedily achieved great renown. But it was as the lover of Guinevere, Arthur's queen, that he became widely known in the Middle Ages. In this character he first appears in the *Chevalier de la Charrette* of Chrétien, who may have invented the entire episode, although it is more probably a variant of the Tristram story (*q.v.*). The unknown author of the prose *Lancelot*, however, probably did not introduce the subject of his amours, and it had undoubtedly been altered by a later hand in order to include the love of Lancelot and the queen, as has the prose *Merlin* for the purpose of suitably linking up the first part of the cycle with the newly introduced portion. Lancelot's character in romance is that of a brave knight and generous man whose existence was overshadowed by his false love for Guinevere, which, instead of exalting his nature, emphasized his less noble qualities, whose "Honour rooted in dishonour stood."

LANCELOT (2). Alluded to in the *Grand St. Grail* as grandfather of Sir Lancelot du Lac, and seventh in descent from Celidoine.

LAUNCEOR. A knight of Ireland, and of the court of King Arthur. He was slain in battle by Balin. (*Vide* " Morte d'Arthur.")

LAUNFAL, SIR, THE LAY OF. A French romance written by Marie de France (*q v.*), who assigned a Breton origin to it. Sir Launfal was of the court of King Arthur at Carleon-on-Usk, and of high, though foreign, descent. But he was not loved by his lord, and at a feast of Pentecost, he only, of all the royal servants, received no present from the king. Riding alone one day he essayed to cross a river, but his steed trembled and stood still. He therefore laid down upon the meadow through which the river ran and sought to sleep. Tossing and turning he kept ever awake, when looking towards the river he saw two beautiful maidens approaching him, The one carried a golden basin ; the other a pure white towel. Sir Launfal immediately rose to receive them. They greeted him, and one of them bade him, in the name of her mistress, visit that lady whose pavilion was

quite near. He followed the messengers and came upon the damsel in all the glory of her beauty and splendour. Hither she had come from a far land to give Sir Launfal her love, a gift, if he were discreet, that would prove of higher worth than the riches of any king. He at once prayed that he might be her knight, and she, granting him her whole love, promised that he would have at his will anything he wished. But he must not reveal their passion. Richly clad by the lady's bounty, Sir Launfal returned to his lodging. He succoured the needy, freed the captive, and entertained the stranger lord. And at pleasure he had sight and speech of his damsel. That same year, about the feast of St. John, Launfal was disporting with other knights in an orchard that lay beneath the queen's tower. She beheld him in his manly beauty, and straightway offered him her love. But little he cared for the offer, and in all gentleness refused it. Her pride wounded, the queen reviled him, when, in an evil moment, forgetting his promise to the beautiful damsel, he acquainted the royal lady of his love. Sad and wrathful, the queen besought her husband to punish Sir Launfal. He, she said, had importuned her with his love, and, upon her denying him, had boasted of his love for a damsel more beautiful and more noble than she. The unhappy knight was, therefore, upon a certain day tried before his peers ; but at the moment of the judgment two richly dressed maidens came riding into the court and sought hospitality for their lady and themselves. The prisoner, however, knew none of them. Again, at a similar critical moment, two other damsels approached the king for the same purpose. Nor did Sir Launfal recognize these, and once more as sentence was about to be pronounced there rode into the court the flower of all the ladies in the world. Hither she had come to prove the case against the queen. Then with her lover she rode away to the island of Avalon, dim and fair. Nor were the knight and his lady heard of again.

LAURIN, or DER KLEINE ROSEN-GARTEN. A Tyrolese romance of the late thirteenth century attached to the saga-cycle of Dietrich of Bern (*q.v.*). It tells of a dwarf king who possesses a wonderful rose garden into which no one may enter without the loss of a hand and foot. Dietrich and his follower Witege enter it, and the latter rides his horse through the rose bushes. Laurin, the dwarf, appears on horseback and dismounts Witege, but is challenged by Dietrich. Hildebrand, another of Dietrich's followers, appears upon the scene, but the dwarf dons his cloak of darkness, and Dietrich is wounded by his invisible foe. Laurin is then persuaded to wrestle with Dietrich, who wrenches off the dwarf's belt, which gives him superhuman strength, and overthrows the troll. Laurin now invites all to his mountain home to behold his treasures, and provides them with a banquet, when they become intoxicated and are thrown into a dismal dungeon. They are released by Künhild, a mortal woman, whom Laurin had spirited away, who brings their weapons. The dwarfs are defeated and Laurin is taken a prisoner to Bern, where he becomes a Christian convert, and latterly is released, when Künhild is bestowed

upon him. (See *Deutsches Heldenbuch*, Pt. 1, 1866–78; McDowall, *Epics and Romances of the Middle Ages*, 1884.)

LAVAINE, SIR. Son of Sir Bernard of Astolat (*q.v.*) and brother to Elaine de Bank and Sir Tirre (*q.v.*). He is fortunate in meeting with the favour of Lancelot, who befriends him. He is afterwards very conspicuous in Arthurian romance, displaying exceptional prowess in battle. He subsequently joins Lancelot's overseas party, when he is raised to the dignity of Earl of Arminak under Lancelot's rule.

LAY OF THE LITTLE BIRD, THE. A French romance of the thirteenth century, which is a homily on covetousness. It treats of a beautiful garden, and a little bird which sang therein. The avaricious owner of the garden, hearing the bird sing, desires to possess it. He captures the bird, which begs to be released, and promises to tell him three secrets, from which he may gain much profit. The man does so, and the bird replies, first, that he is not to believe all he hears; second, not to regret what he has never lost; and lastly, never to throw between his feet what he holds in his hands. The man, greatly enraged, answers that he knew them all from infancy. The bird replies, that if the man had known the third secret, he would not have set him free. And further, that in his body was a precious jewel weighing three ounces; whoever owned it would have every wish gratified. On hearing that, the man was maddened with rage at having set the bird free. The bird adds to his chagrin by explaining that as he weighed less than half a ounce, how was it possible for a jewel weighing three ounces to be hid in his body ? Moreover, he was already regretting what he had never lost, for he never possessed the jewel. And also, believing all he heard, he had flung the bird between his feet. Advising the man to study well these three secrets, the bird took his flight, and from that day the garden began to wither, and nothing would ever grow in it.

LAYAMON. An English priest of Ernely or Arley Regis on the west bank of the Severn in Worcestershire, author of *The Brut*, the first work in English to present the legend of a Trojan conquest of Britain. From internal evidence it has been inferred that he wrote in the first decade of the thirteenth century, but nothing is known of his life or personality. It is probable that Layamon founded his poem on that of the same name by Wace (*q.v.*), but the two versions are by no means identical, as Layamon made many additions either of his own invention or drawn from other sources. The work is of a high linguistic value, presenting as it does a unique picture of the English language in the transition stage between late Saxon and the speech of Chaucer. It contains 56,800 lines, and was first published in its entirety by Sir Frederick Madden in 1847, in three volumes, containing two texts (probably separated by an interval of fifty years), translation, and glossary.

LEN. Goldsmith of Bov the Red (*q.v.*). From his name was derived the name Locha Lein, the ancient appellation of the Lakes of Killarney, by the shores of which he used to work.

LEODEGRANCE. King of Cameliard, in Arthurian romance, father of Guinevere. Arthur rescued him from King Rience of North Wales.

LEUCANS. Alluded to in the *Grand St. Grail* as Josephes, cousin, and guardian of the ark in which the Grail dish was kept.

LEVARCAM. In Ultonian romance, the nurse of Deirdre (*q.v.*).

LEWY. Son of Curoi, foe to Cuchulain (*q.v.*) on account of the rape of his mother Blanid (*q.v.*). He slew his enemy, but met his death at the hands of Conall (*q.v.*).

LIA. In Irish romance, Lord of Luchar in Connacht, treasurer of the Fianna ; later treasurer to the Morna (*q.v.*). He was slain by the lad Finn (*q.v.*), chief of the opposing clan Bascna (*q.v.*).

LIA FAIL. In Irish romance, the stone of Destiny. When the feet of rightful kings rested upon it this stone would roar for joy. It is now placed under the seat of the Coronation Throne in Westminster Abbey.

LIBELLUS MERLINI. (Little Book of Merlin.) A Latin tract on the subject of the prophecies of Merlin (*q.v.*), written by Geoffrey of Monmouth (*q.v.*), (*c.* 1135). It purported to be a translation from the Welsh into Latin, and was incorporated by Geoffrey in his *Historia Regum Britanniæ* (*q.v.*), of which it forms the Seventh Book. He had, he says in the preface, been persuaded by the urgent requests of friends to publish this translation, a statement of great likelihood, as his *Libellus* had met with immediate public recognition, contained the first information regarding the enchanter and was probably of some rarity. It is dedicated to Alexander, Bishop of Lincoln, because of the affection Geoffrey "bore to his nobility." Geoffrey prefaces his account of the prophecies with one concerning the deeds of a supernatural youth named Ambrosius, whom he had read of in Nennius, and deliberately confounded with Merlin. Vortigern, King of the Britons, asks Ambrose Merlin the meaning of a vision in which appear two dragons, red and white, in combat. Merlin replies that the Red Dragon symbolizes the British race which would be conquered by the White Dragon, emblemistic of the Saxon power. A lengthy prophetic rhapsody follows couched in cryptic terms, relating chiefly to the Saxon wars, and with this the work as given in the Seventh Book of the *Historia*, the only source through which it has come down to us—concludes. It was, however, known in Iceland before 1218, in a form independent of the *Historia* (H. G. Leach, *Modern Phililogy*, viii. pp. 607 *et seq.*). This tract must not be confounded with the *Vita Merlini*, or *Life of Merlin* (*c.* 1145 or 1148) generally, but not unquestionably, attributed to Geoffrey. (*Vide Historia Regum Britanniæ*, Book viii.)

LIBEOUS DESCONUS. (*Vide* "Lybius Desconus.")

LIETRI. (*Vide* "Garin the Lorrainer.") Abbot of St. Amand, Garin's nephew. He came with fifteen consecrated monks and thirty-six knights after Bego's death to Lens. He was so angry that he wanted to throw off his monk's dress and fight, but was satisfied by Fromont's regrets. He headed the funeral procession to Metz, and delivered Fromont's letter to Garin, then with Garin he accompanied the body to Balin. He met Fromont at St. Amant and said Garin would agree to a truce if Fromont kept his promises, but he was wroth when he heard they meditated freeing the prisoners.

LIFE OF HAROLD, KING OF ENGLAND. A romance, chiefly relating to the recovery of Harold after the battle of Hastings, and his life as a hermit, first near Dover, afterwards at Cheswardine, in Shropshire, and finally at Chester, in twenty chapters, preceded by a prologue and a table of contents followed by a brief narrative of a similar kind, which professes to have been written by a hermit of Chester. The work is imperfect at the end. The romance opens with an account of the rise of Godwin and the campaigns of Harold in Wales, the discovery of the cross at Montainte in Somerset, its removal to Waltham and the foundation of a religious house there by Harold. Harold is wounded at Hastings, and left for dead on the field of battle. Edith, his betrothed, with the help of two Franks, removes him to Winchester, where, under the skill of a Saracen woman, he is cured in two years' time. He makes a pilgrimage to Jerusalem and visits Rome; he breaks the oath extorted from him by William, and the oak tree at Rouen, under which he pledged his promise, sheds its leaves at the moment he does so. Harold returns to England after an absence of ten years; he lives as a hermit at Dover for a similar period, but, taking the name of Christin, he crosses into Chester. His death and burial take place at Waltham. William of Malmesbury, says the romance, is said to have made a mistake as to the death of Harold at Hastings, as did the canons of Waltham in identifying the body. Harold's brother, Gurtha, gave evidence before Henry II., in the presence of Canon Michael of Waltham, of his brother's existence after the great battle. The absurdity of making Harold live so late as the first year of Henry II. (when he would be 130) is too glaring. Amongst modern writers it has been suggested that the story was written to celebrate the city of Chester.

LIGHT OF BEAUTY. (*Vide* "Sgeimh Solais.")

LIJOD. Daughter of Freyja (*q.v.*) and wife of Volsung (*q.v.*). (*Vide* "Lay of the Volsungs.")

LINET, DAME. Sister of Dame Liones, wife of Sir Gareth (*q.v.*), married to Gaheris, Gareth's brother. She accompanied Sir Gareth in his ride to the release of her sister, who was a prisoner of the Red Knight. (*Vide* "Morte d'Arthur.")

LIONEL. In Arthurian romance, cousin of Lancelot, and brother of Bors, whom he quarrels with because he left him a prisoner in order to succour a distressed damsel. He is appeased by heavenly intervention.

LIONES, DAME. Of the Castle Perilous, sister of Linet. She was one time a prisoner in the Red Laundes, but was subsequently rescued by Sir Gareth, whom she married. (*Vide* "Morte d'Arthur.")

LIR. A sea-god, father of Mananan in Irish romance. He is comparable with the Greek Oceanus and the Cymric Llyr.

LOATHLY DAMSEL, THE — KUNDRIE. The Grail Messenger. One would imagine that the holder of such an office would be saint-like, but Chrestien describes her as "a damsel more hideous than could be pictured outside hell." Wolfram refers to her in his work as "Kundrie la Sorcière."

LOBEIRA, JOÃS. A mediæval Portuguese romance writer. The exact dates of his birth and death are unrecorded, and, while some authorities hold that he lived during the reign of Alphonso III., in the beginning of the thirteenth century, others contend that he belongs to a considerably later period; while one writer, Thomas Pires, the folk-lorist, has even tried to identify him with a certain Lobeira, who is known to have been living at Elvas at the beginning of the fifteenth century. Joãs Lobeira is occasionally credited with a work more frequently ascribed to another author of the same surname, Vasco de Lobeira (*q.v.*), namely, a version in Portuguese prose of the famous old French tale of *Amadis of Gaul;* but the claim on behalf of Joãs in this relation has but slender support, resting as it does on little more than the fact that, in a poem definitely proved to be his, he uses the same *ritournelle* as Oriana sings in *Amadis.*

LOBEIRA, VASCO DE. A Portuguese romancer who is credited with a version in Portuguese prose of the famous old French romance *Amadis of Gaul,* familiar in England owing to the excellent translation by W. S. Rose, 1803, and the précis of Southey. Vasco is supposed to have been born at Oporto about 1365, and is known to have died forty years later. He appears to have been a soldier besides an author, and at the outset of his career he followed the fortunes of the future King John I., who conferred the honour of knighthood on him soon after the battle of Aljubacotta in 1385. Vasco's *Amadis* enjoyed great popularity in the author's own day, and towards the close of the sixteenth century a mediæval transcript copy thereof was discovered at Lisbon, in the library of the Duke of Alveiro. This interesting document is no longer extant, unfortunately, the likelihood being that it perished in a fire which occurred at Lisbon in 1753. It is impossible to say whether Vasco's work was really based on the original French, and it is quite possible that the Portuguese gleaned the tale from some Spanish translation ; while it has been suggested, indeed, that his version of *Amadis* was in reality the work of another Lobeira, Joãs by name (*q.v.*).

LOCH. In Irish romance, son of Mofebis. Sent by Maev (*q.v.*) against Cuchulain (*q.v.*). He wounded him, but was himself slain with Cuchulain's terrible weapon, the Gae Bolg.

LOGRES, KINGDOM OF. The scene of many adventures of the knight Sir Galahad (*q.v.*).

LOKI. (*Vide* "Volsungs.") The Scandinavian god of evil. He was responsible for the death of Otter (*q.v.*).

LOMBARD, EARL. (*Vide* "Guy of Warwick.") Attacked and slew Sir Urry in a combat, but was himself killed by Sir Guy.

LOMBARDY, DUKE OF. Father of Belisante (*q.v.*), a character in the romance of *Amys and Amylion* (*q.v.*), for whose education he was responsible.

LONGIS. In Grail romance, a Roman soldier, who pierced the side of Christ whilst on the cross with the Grail lance.

LOQUIFER. In Carlovingian romance, a fairy giant, so called because he bears an enormous log as a weapon. He and Renouart (*q.v.*) agree that the issue of a campaign between the Saracens and Franks shall rest upon a single combat between them. They meet on an island near Porpaillart. Loquifer has in the hollow of his club a balm which cures all wounds at once, but Renouart succeeds in depriving him of his weapon, slays him, and takes his three swords, "the best ever forged," whilst devils carry off his soul. (*Vide* "Battle of Loquifer.")

LORET. (*Vide* "Guy of Warwick.") Princess of Greece.

LOT. King of Lothian and Orkney, alluded to frequently in Arthurian legend and romance as the husband of Arthur's sister, Margawse, and the father of Gawaine. He made war upon Arthur on several occasions, notably that of the famous battle of the eleven kings. He allied himself with Nero, brother of King Rience of North Wales, against Arthur, as he was wroth with the latter for the seduction of his wife, Margawse (*q.v.*). In the battle which ensued he was slain by Pellinore. (See Malory's *Morte d'Arthur*, Book II. Chap. 10.)

LOUIS LE DEBONAIR. Son of Charlemagne. (*Vide* "La Coronement Loeys," and the other Carlovingian romances under their several titles ; also "Charlemagne.")

LUCAS. King Arthur's butler, son of Duke Corneus. He is alluded

Q

to more frequently in the earlier history of Arthur, and along with Sir Kay and Sir Griflet had control of the king's household.

LUCHTA. In Irish romance, the carpenter of the Danaan folk.

LUCIUS. King of Rome. He warred against Arthur, and was subsequently slain by him. (*Vide* " Morte d'Arthur.")

LUDWIG. King of Ormany. (*Vide* " Gudrun Lay " and "Gudrun.") Father of Hartmut; husband of Gerlinte. He aids his son to carry off Gudrun and kills Hettel (*q.v.*) at the battle of the Wulpenstrand, escaping with Gudrun, whom he flings into the sea on her refusal to wed his son, Hartmut, who saves her. Many years later he is slain by King Herwig (*q.v.*), when he rescues Gudrun. (*Vide* " Gudrun " for fuller details.)

LUGH. In Irish romance, son of Kian (*q.v.*), father of Cuchulain (*q.v.*). He was brought up by his uncle, Goban the Smith (*q.v.*) and by Duach, King of Fairyland. Presenting himself before the palace of Tara, he announced himself as wishing to take service with Nuada of the Silver Hand (*q.v.*). After many refusals on the score of there being men already in the palace accomplished in all the arts, he at last gained admittance as Ildanach, "The All-Craftsman." He was also known as Lugh of the Long Arm. From the Land of the Living (Fairyland) he brought back the Boat of Mananan (*q.v.*), the Horse of Mananan, and Fragarach " The Answerer," a sword that was a match for any mail. Coming upon the Danaan chiefs assembled to pay tribute to the Fomorian envoys, he took the leadership

of the oppressed, when all the enemy save nine were slain. These he sent back to Balor (*q.v.*), with a message of defiance. But other magic gifts were required to ensure the victory which the druidic prophecy had foretold that Lugh would obtain over his grandfather, Balor. So instead of taking the lives of the three murderers of his father, Kian, he put them under *geis* or promise to obtain certain wonders, including the magical spear of the King of " Persia," and the pig-skin of the King of " Greece," which if laid on a patient would heal him of his wound or cure him of his sickness. Thus equipped, Lugh entered the Battle of Moytura against the Fomorians (*q.v.*), and by hurling a huge stone which pierced through the eye to the brain of Balor, fulfilled the druidic prophecy. Nuada falling in the field, Lugh succeeded him as King of the Danaans. Lugh was the Irish Sun-god ; his final conquest of the Fomorians and their leader symbolizes the victory of light and intellect over darkness. Balor was god of darkness, and brute force as embodied in the Fomorians. By his title of ".All-Craftsman," Lugh is to be compared to the Greek Apollo. He was widely worshipped by the Continental Celts. Llew Llaw Gyffes, the Cymric hero, corresponds with the Irish Lugh.

LUKAFERE. (*Vide* " Sir Ferumbras.") King of Bagdat. He paid Laban tribute, and was a very fierce fighter. He brought 10,000 Italian maids into the Saracen camp who were all slain by order of the Soudan. He wished to marry Floripas, who agreed on certain conditions which were never fulfilled. He was burned to death at Laban's palace by Duke Naymes.

LYBIUS DESCONUS. An English poem of the Arthurian cycle, which has French, German, and Italian equivalents in *Le Bel Inconnu, Wigalois*, and *Carduino*. It dates from the end of the twelfth century. Sir Lybius is a natural son of Sir Gawain, a celebrated knight of King Arthur's court, who, being brought up in a forest by his mother, is kept ignorant of his name and descent. He early exhibits marks of his courage by killing a knight in single combat, whom he encountered as he was hunting. This inspires him with a desire of seeking adventures; therefore, clothing himself in his enemy's armour, he goes to Arthur's court, to request the order of knighthood. His request granted, he obtains the promise of having the first adventure assigned him that shall offer. A damsel named Ellen, attended by a dwarf, comes to implore King Arthur's assistance, to rescue a young princess, "the Lady of Sinadone," their mistress, who is detained from her rights and confined in prison. The adventure is claimed by the young knight Sir Lybius, and the king assents. The messengers are dissatisfied, and object to his youth, but are forced to acquiesce. The first book closes with a description of the ceremony of equipping him. Sir Lybius sets out on the adventure. He is derided by the dwarf and the damsel on account of his youth. They come to the bridge of Perill, which none can pass without encountering a knight called William de la Braunch. Sir Lybius is challenged. They joust with their spears. De la Braunch is dismounted. The

battle is renewed on foot. Sir William's sword breaks, and he yields. Sir Lybius makes him swear to go and present himself to Arthur, as the first-fruits of his valour. The conquered knight sets out for Arthur's court, is met by three knights, his kinsmen, who, informed of his disgrace, vow revenge, and pursue the conqueror. The next day they overtake him. The eldest of the three attacks Sir Lybius, but is overthrown to the ground. The two other brothers assault him. Sir Lybius is wounded, yet cuts off the second brother's arm; the third yields. Sir Lybius sends them all to Arthur. In the third evening he is awakened by the dwarf, who has discovered a fire in the wood. Sir Lybius arms himself, and leaps on horseback. He finds two giants roasting a wild boar, who hold a fair lady as their captive. Sir Lybius runs one of them through with his spear, and is assaulted by the other. A fierce battle ensues. He cuts off the giant's arm, and at length his head. The rescued lady (an earl's daughter) tells him her story, and leads him to her father's castle, who entertains him with a great feast, and presents him at parting with a suit of armour and a steed. He sends the giant's head to King Arthur. Sir Lybius, maid Ellen, and the dwarf renew their journey. They see a castle crowned with human heads, and are informed it belongs to a knight called Sir Gefferen, who, in honour of his mistress, challenges all comers. He that can produce a fairer lady is to be rewarded with a milk-white falcon, but if overcome to lose his head. Sir Lybius spends the night in the adjoining town, and in the morning goes to challenge the falcon. The knights exchange their gloves. They agree to joust in the market-place. The lady and maid Ellen are placed aloft in chairs. The knights engage. Sir Gefferon is incurably hurt, and carried home on his shield. Sir Lybius sends the falcon to King Arthur and receives back a large present in florins. He stays forty days to be cured of his wounds, which he spends in feasting with the neighbouring lords. Sir Lybius proceeds for Sinadone. In a forest he meets a knight hunting, called Sir Otes de Lisle; maid Ellen, charmed with a very beautiful dog, begs Sir Lybius to bestow him upon her. Sir Otes meets them, and claims his dog. He is refused. Being unarmed, he rides to his castle, and summons his followers. They go in quest of Sir Lybius. A battle ensues. He is still victorious, and forces Sir Otes to follow the other conquered knights to King Arthur. Sir Lybius comes to a fair city and castle by a riverside, beset round with pavilions or tents. He is informed that in the castle is a beautiful lady besieged by a giant named Maugys, who keeps the bridge, and will let none pass without doing him homage. This Lybius refuses, and a battle ensues. The battle lasts a whole summer's day. The giant is slain. The citizens come out in procession to meet their deliverer. The lady invites him into her castle and falls in love with him. He forgets the Princess of Sinadone, and stays with this bewitching lady a twelvemonth. This fair sorceress intoxicates him with all kinds of sensual pleasure and detains him from the pursuit of honour. Maid Ellen by chance gets an opportunity of speaking to him, and upbraids him with

his vice and folly. He is filled with remorse, and escapes the same evening. At length he arrives at the city and castle of Sinadone, and is given to understand that he must challenge the constable of the castle to single combat before he can be received as a guest. They joust; the constable in worsted; Sir Lybius is feasted in the castle; he declares his intention of delivering their lady; and inquires the particulars of her history. "Two necromancers have built a fine palace by sorcery, and there keep her enchanted, till she will surrender her duchy to them, and yield to such base conditions as they would impose." Early on the morrow Sir Lybius sets out for the enchanted palace. He alights in the court and enters the hall. He sits down at the high table. On a sudden all the lights are quenched. It thunders and lightens. The palace shakes; the wall falls in pieces about his ears. He is dismayed and confounded, but presently hears horses neigh, and is challenged to single combat by the sorcerers. He gets to his steed. A battle ensues, with various turns of fortune. He loses his weapon, but gets a sword from one of the necromancers, and wounds the other with it. The edge of the sword being secretly poisoned, the wound proves mortal. He goes up to the surviving sorcerer, who is carried away from him by enchantment. At length he finds him, and cuts off his head. He returns to the palace to deliver the lady, but cannot find her; as he is lamenting, a window opens, through which enters a horrible serpent with wings and a woman's face. It coils round his neck and kisses him, then is suddenly converted into a very beautiful lady. She tells him she is the lady of Sinadone, and was so enchanted, till she might kiss Sir Gawain, or some one of his blood, that he has dissolved the charm, and that herself and her dominions may be his reward. The knight, whose descent is by this means discovered, joyfully accepts the offer,

makes her his bride, and then sets out with her for King Arthur's court.

LYNGI, KING. (*Vide* "Volsungs.") Son of Hunding (*q.v.*). He slew in battle Sigmund (*q.v.*) and King Eylimi (*q.v.*). He was subsequently slain by Sigurd (*q.v.*), son of Sigmund (*q.v.*).

M

MABINOGION, THE. A term employed for a collection of Welsh semi-mythological tales translated into English by Lady Charlotte Guest, and published in 1849). Of these eleven are taken from *The Red Book of Hergest*, a fourteenth-century MS. in the library of Jesus College, Oxford, whilst the *Tale of Taliesin*, included with them, is taken from a much later MS., and has no relation to the matter translated from the *Red Book*. In early Wales the aspirant to bardic honours was designated a *mabinog*, or graduate, and the traditional lore he had to master in order to assume full bardic rank was called *Mabinogi*, a well-defined corpus of mythical tales with a traditional commentary. *Mabinogion* is the plural of this term, and was employed by Lady Guest as a partly fanciful title for her collection of translations. Strictly speaking, however, only one portion of the work is entitled to the name *Mabinogi*, that portion being the connected tales of *Pwyll, Branwen, Manawyddan*, and *Math*. The rest of the work includes the tales of King Arthur and Arthurian personages known as *Rhonabwy's Dream, Peredur* and *Geraint*, the *Lady of the Fountain*, and *Kulhwch and*

Olwen, the *Taliesin* above mentioned, and the tales of *Llud and Llevelys* and *Maxen's Dream*. The veritable *Mabinogi* are semi-mythological in character, and are undoubtedly survivals of Welsh Celtic myth. In them we recognize that process or "disease of mythology" at work by which divine beings deteriorate into demigods or "hero-gods," a process which bridges the gulf betwixt mythology and romance, and which has manufactured from deities more or less well authenticated the entire knightly circle of the Table Round and the chivalry of Camelot. Few, indeed, of King Arthur's knights there are who can escape a mythological interpretation, and who may not be identified with one or other of the gods of the early Celts. (*Vide* "Arthurian Cycle," "Gawain," "Kai," "Lancelot," etc.) The fragment called *Taliesin* is probably founded upon the life of a veritable Welsh bard of the sixth century, but the verse in which it is composed belongs to different periods, whilst the prose portion merely serves to give it a certain measure of coherence. The stories of Arthur betray the Celtic spirit so far as *Kulwch and Olwen* and the *Dream of Rhonabwy* are concerned, and these were probably fixed in form about the twelfth century before Norman influences were at work on the Arthurian legend. In the *Lady of the Fountain* and *Peredur* we find that Norman influence considerably developed, but a measure of the indigenous Celtic spirit retained. *Maxen's Dream* and *Llud and Llevelys* may be described as mythi-historic, in that they preserve what would seem to be a veritable substratum of history underneath a groundwork of myth. As literature they form a link between the *Mabinogi* and the later semi-Norman form of the *Lady of the Fountain* and *Peredur*.

The *Mabinogion* appears to have been a collection of tales which provided the Welsh bards with a key to the mystic and obscure allusions so frequent in Welsh poetry. It is the remains of a literature framed by a literary caste for the purpose of preserving the mythic and heroic traditions of the race. Although the MS. dates from the fourteenth century, the tales as fixed in the shape we know them are of the period between the tenth and eleventh centuries. But this must not be taken as implying that they originate from that period, as elements in many of them hark back to the dim days of the beginnings of Aryan history. They are only examples of a class, waifs of an enormous body of mythic literature for ever lost to us, preserved by the bards of Wales under circumstances rather unfavourable to existence. If they stood alone, however, it would be exceedingly difficult, if not impossible, to arrive at their original meaning, which we are assisted in discovering by the aid

of the *Bruts* or chronicles, the *Triads*, and by the analogies of early Irish literature. The children of Don, for example, are undoubtedly to be equated with the Irish Tuatha de Danaan, and the former may, therefore, be regarded as divine beings, like their Irish congeners. Govannon, also, can be none other than the Irish smith Goibniu, the genitive of whose name is Goibnenn. Manawyddan mab Llyr is evidently the Manannan mac Lir of Ireland, the Lord of the Otherworld, if he does not figure as such in the *Mabinogi*. A well-known theory is that which holds that the Welsh Celts borrowed these tales from the Goidelic or Gaelic population which they found in Wales on their entrance into that country. Another, put forward with equal authority, is that the Irish tales were borrowed by the Welsh in the ninth century. We find that Welsh literature has no analogies with the Ulster cycle of Irish mythi-romance, which was most popular in Ireland at the period of the alleged borrowing, but with the cycle which recounts the deeds of the Tuatha de Danaan, which from the tenth century onwards had been frankly treated by the Irish as mythological matter. A far sounder theory is that which believes both Welsh and Irish myths to have been drawn from a common source before these branches of the Celtic stock had become sundered and had achieved different characteristics and a different tongue. There are indeed superficial resemblances which exhibit later borrowings, but these are easily discernible as such. The literary merit of these tales is great, remarkable for the era in which they were cast into shape. No

French, German, or English prose of the same period can compare with them in this respect, and the glamour of phantasy which they present remains unequalled in the tales of any race or time.

The various personages and divine beings alluded to in the *Mabinogion* will be found separately treated under their names, and the several tales included in it are fully dealt with under their titles. (*Vide* also the article on " Arthurian Cycle.")

MABON, SIR. (*Vide* "Sir Ferumbras.") An engineer in the service of the soudan.

MAC CECHT (1). Grandson of the Dagda, Danaan King, ruling with his two brothers, Mac Cuill and Mac Grené, over Ireland. He was slain in battle with the Milesians.

MAC CECHT (2). A warrior of Conary's (*q.v.*) party at Derga's Hostel (*q.v.*). Conary being unable to fight from great thirst, Mac Cecht went over to Ireland to seek water for him, which at last he found in Loch Gara, whereat he filled the king's golden cup. He returned to the hostel in time to slay Conary's two beheaders and to pour the water into the grateful mouth of the severed head.

MAC CUILL. In Irish romance, brother of Mac Cecht (*q.v.*).

MAC GRENÊ. In Irish romance, brother of Mac Cecht (*q.v.*).

MACHA. In Irish romance, daughter of the Red Hugh, an Ulster prince, niece of Dithorba and Kimbay (*q.v.*), the latter of whom she weds. She appears again in the following tale : A wealthy Ulster farmer, Crundchu, found in his dun a beautiful woman, who immediately took upon herself the household duties, and, Crundchu being a widower, she became his wife. One day as her husband was preparing to go to a great fair of the Ultonians, she begged him to remain at home, but upon his persisting on going, she made him promise not to mention her in the assembly. But the king's two horses winning race after race, Crundchu forgot himself, and boasted of the swiftness of his wife. He was seized, and messengers sent to bring his wife to prove his statement. As she was pregnant, she pleaded that she might not have to run, but all were bent on seeing her outrun the king's horses. She confirmed her husband's boast, gave birth to twins, and pronounced a curse of debility upon the Ultonians.

MADOR, DE LA PORTE. Cousin of Sir Patrice (*q.v.*). He accused Queen Guinever of treason against his dead cousin. He challenged the knights to defend her cause. Blindly rushing into the fray, he is defeated by Sir Lancelot (*q.v.*), who defends the queen. Later, however, he is rewarded by hearing of the actual traitor, who escapes for safety. The queen willingly pardons her accuser. (*Vide* "Morte d'Arthur.")

MAELDUN. In Irish romance, son of Ailill Edge-of-Battle (*q.v.*) He was brought up by the queen of the territory wherein stood the church to which his nun-mother belonged. Learning from his foster-mother the names of his kindred, he sought and was well received by them. One day as Maeldun with his foot planted on a blackened flagstone in the graveyard of the ruined church of Doocloone was about to try his skill at flinging the stone, he was told that his father's body lay burnt beneath. The murderers he learnt, were reavers from Leix that lay across the sea, so with the advice of a druid he set out with the destined number of seventeen men to seek this place. But his three foster-brothers importuned him to take them also, for which disobedience of the oracular command all were punished. On an island he beheld his father's slayers, but was unable to reach them, being blown out to sea. In this plight the wanderers met with many strange island adventures related in the *Book of the Dun Cow*. From the Island of the Slayers Maeldun heard a man boasting to another in an opposite island of having slain Ailill. With a rejoicing heart he was about to land, but was blown oceanward. On the Island of the Ants, they were attacked by gigantic insects. On the trees of the Island of the Great Birds sat monstrous birds, some of which the party killed and ate. An animal like a horse, with clawed feet like a hound's, lived on the Island of the Great Beast, and pelted Maeldun as he put off. Round the racecourse of the Island of the Giant Horses flew these animals, cheered on by a great multitude. They visited in turn the Island of the Stone Door, the Island of Apples, the Island of the Wondrous Beast, and the bleeding Island of the Biting Horses, huge beasts which tore each other's sides. So weary, hungry, and thirsty, they arrived at the Island of the Fiery Swine. It was covered with golden apple trees, the fruit falling down as these red swine-like animals kicked the stems. At night Maeldun and his comrades landed and gathered what they could of the

fruit, filling their boat and providing for some time against hunger and thirst. Their apples had run out when they came to the Island of the Little Cat. This was a chalk tower reaching to the clouds, with great white houses on its ramparts. Entering the largest of them, the voyagers saw a little cat leaping from one to the other of four stone pillars standing in the middle of the house. On the walls were a row of brooches of gold and silver, a row of hoop-shaped neck-torques of the same metals and a row of great swords with gold and silver hilts. But as the youngest of the foster-brothers was carrying off one of the necklaces, the cat "leaped through him like a fiery arrow," leaving nothing of him but a heap of ashes which his comrades scattered on the seashore. Black sheep on the one and white on the other side of the brazen palisade fed in the Island of the Black and the White Sheep. They were shepherded by a mighty man who would sometimes put a black with the white sheep, when it would turn white, and *vice versâ*. Maeldun flung a peeled white wand on the side of a black sheep when the rod turned black, and the strangers in terror made off from the island, without landing there. A large island was that of the Giant Cattle, with a herd of huge swine feeding in it. One of the remaining foster-brothers landed on the Island of the Black Mourners and immediately turned black, and commenced to mourn. Two of the others, seeking to bring him off, shared the same fate. So other four covered their heads with cloths, and rescued these, but not the foster-brother. Separately kings, queens, warriors, and maidens lived in the Island of the Four Fences of gold, silver, brass, and crystal. A cheese-like food, with the taste of whatever each man wished it to be, was given the sailors as they landed and a drink that wrapped them in sleep for three days. When they awoke they found themselves on the sea in their boat, with no trace of the island. When they reached the Island of the Glass Bridge, a woman, whom they had seen lift up a slab of glass and dip her pail into the water beneath, crossed the bridge and bade them welcome. She allotted them couches, one for the chief, one for each three of his men. Then she refreshed them with food and drink from her pail according to the desire of each man. Twice the men sought to woo her for Maeldun, and she promised to give them her answer the following morning. But they awoke upon an islandless sea. Hearing a great noise of crying and speaking, they rowed for a day and a night and came, without landing, to the Island of the Shouting Birds, of plumage black, brown, and speckled. They arrived at the wooded Island of the Anchorite, to find it inhabited by many birds and one solitary man clothed only in his hair. Another anchorite robed in his hair dwelt on the Island of the Miraculous Fountain. It was filled with gold and its soil was soft, white, and downy. Approaching the Island of the Smithy, they heard the noise of mighty blows upon an anvil, and the inhabitants talking about them as "little boys." So they hastily sailed away. Down through the misty waters they beheld the subaqueous island with roofed fortresses and surrounding lands. Here from a tree a monstrous beast would stretch down its long neck to seize one of the cattle which grazed around the tree, guarded though it was by an armed warrior. Dreading that the weight of their boat must drag them beneath the mist, they speedily sailed over it and came to the cliff-hedged Island of the Prophecy. The inhabitants, probably believing that Maeldun was destined to harry their country and to drive them out, screamed: "It is they! it is they!" And when the strangers left, the people cried to each other: "They are gone away! they are not!" Rising from one side of the Island of the Spouting Water, and arching it like a rainbow, was a stream into which they thrust their spears, bringing down many more salmon than they could carry away. Great and wide was the four-square Island of the Silvern Column, losing its height in heaven and its depth in the sea. As they rowed through one of the meshes of a silver net that was flung from the summit into the sea, Diuran the Rhymer hacked away a piece of the net. He vowed to offer it upon the high altar of Armagh should he ever again reach Ireland. Then they heard from the height a voice speaking in an unknown tongue. Nor could they land upon the Island of the Pedestal, for the only visible access to it was a locked door in its base. With great difficulty they escaped from the Island of the Women. There they sat down to eat with a maiden opposite each man and the queen opposite Maeldun, the marriage of the queen and her daughters with the chief and his men crowning the entertainment. Persuaded by the queen to remain and retain for ever their youth, they dwelt in that blissful state for three months. But the men wearied and longed for Ireland. So Maeldun, though he loved his bride, not wishing that the men should depart without him, escaped with them one day as his wife, as was her daily wont, was judging her folk. But she had noticed them, and cast after them a clew of twine which her husband caught. He was unable to free himself, and the boat was pulled to land. For another three months they stayed on the island. This happened again and yet again. So as his men believed that Maeldun clung to the twine purposely, one of them caught at it the fourth time, but he too was unable to loose himself. Then Diuran smote off his hand, which fell with the twine into the sea. The queen wailed and shrieked, but her captives were free. After many similar adventures they followed the bird of the Island of the Falcon, inhabited only by sheep and deer, and came to the island of the slayer of Ailill. His dwelling they entered in peace and related their adventures to his household. Maeldun returned to his kindred, and Diuran offered his piece of silver upon the altar of Armagh.

This tale is obviously of the same *genre* as those of the *Odyssey*, the voyages of St. Brandon, and the myth of Antilia, and is obviously intended to supply a tale of a " wonder-voyage," and may have been sophisticated by the *Odyssey* and similar Moorish and other Irish myths, or these latter may have developed from it.

MAEV. In Irish romance, Queen of Connacht, wife of Ailill. She was a fierce strong woman, governed by her own will, and took husband after husband, dismissing them as she chose. She figures in the Celtic myth of the night attacking the sky, found in the Irish romance of " The Cattle Raid of Quelgny," in the *Book of Leinster* and a MS. of the twelfth century. It is as follows : Taunted by Ailill (*q.v.*) that her Red Bull, Finnbenach, with white front and horns, attached itself to his herd, Maev determined to possess herself of the Ulster Brown Bull of Quelgny. She first sought, but in vain, to obtain the bull by asking a loan of it for a year in return for a very inviting offer made to Dara its owner. Then she resolved to fight for it, so she summoned her hosts. These were the mighty men of Connaught, her allies from Leinster, and the exiles from Ulster, including Conna son of Conor (*q.v.*) and Fergus mac Roy. Before the raid her spies brought word of the debility of the Ultonians (*vide* " Macha "), but from her druid diviner she foreheard of the slaughter of her hosts, and from the vision of the prophetess Fidelma of the Ulster hero Cuchulain. During the prolonged combat, in which Cuchulain fought victoriously against the heroes of Maev and others, Maev got possession of the Brown Bull, but the slaughter continued, and in the end the Ultonians routed the host of Connaught, the Brown Bull slew Finnbennach, but himself fell dead from madness, and peace was made for seven years between Maev and the men of Ulster. But she determined to be revenged upon Cuchulain for her great loss and degradation ; so she sent the six one-birth children of her wizard Calatin (*q.v.*) against the warrior to weave around him despondency and illusions. At last he was overcome. Maev was slain by Forbay (*q.v.*).

MAGA. In Irish romance, daughter of Angus Og (*q.v.*). She was the grandmother of Conor mac Nessa (*q.v.*) by her husband Ross the Red, and of the cousins Cuchulain and Conall of the Victories by her second husband, Cathbad (*q.v.*).

MAILLEFER. In Carlovingian romance, the son of Renouart (*q.v.*) and Alice, daughter of Louis le Debonair. His birth cost his mother her life, and this so grieved his father that he survived her by seven years only, and lost his reason. Maillefer was " the strongest man that was born of mother."

MAIMED KING. Mentioned in Arthurian romance as having been cured of his infirmity by the Grail spear (*q.v.*) which was entrusted to Galahad, who subsequently achieved the Holy Grail (*q.v.*). (*Vide* " Morte d'Arthur.")

MALEDISANT, DAME. Wife of Sir La Côte Male-Tailé (*q.v.*). Previous to her marriage to that adventurous knight, she accompanied him on an errand of liberation, rebuking him mercilessly the while. (*Vide* " Morte d'Arthur.")

MALORY, SIR THOMAS. The author of the great English collection of Arthurian romance, the *Morte d'Arthur*, was perhaps of Welsh origin, but nothing definite is known concerning the place and date of his birth. He completed his *Morte d'Arthur* in 1469, and it was printed by Caxton in 1485, the original being followed by two editions by Wynkyn de Worde in 1498 and 1529 respectively. Before the middle of the seventeenth century four more editions appeared, after which the popularity of the work appears to have lapsed somewhat. With the revived interest in Arthurian literature which marked the later part of the nineteenth century the *Morte d'Arthur* was edited no less than six times, notably by Wright, Strachey, and Sommer, in the latter of which the Caxton original was faithfully and studiously reproduced. Malory's original manuscript has never been discovered. The entire subject of the *Morte d'Arthur*, together with a summary of its contents, is treated in the article under that title.

See Professor Rhys's introduction to the *Everyman* edition of the *Morte d'Arthur*, and Dr. Sommer's supplement to the second volume of his edition of the same work, and Bale's *Illustrium Maioris Britanniæ Scriptorum . . . Summarium*, fol. 208 verso.

MANAAL. One of the Keepers of the Grail.

MANANAN. Son of the Irish sea-god Lir, magician and owner of strange possessions. His magical Boat " Ocean-sweeper " steered by the wishes of its occupant, his horse, Aonbarr, able to travel upon sea and land, and his sword, Fragarach, a match for any mail, were brought by Lugh (*q.v.*) from the " Land of the Living." As lord of the sea he was the Irish Charon, and his colour-changing cloak would flap on gaily as he marched with heavy tread round the camp of the hostile force invading his darling Erin. He is comparable with the Cymric Manawyddan, and bears some resemblance to the Hellenic Proteus.

MANAS. (*Vide* " Eglamour of Artoys.") The giant brother to

Sir Maroke (*q.v.*), and companion to the Boar. He was slain by Eglamour (*q.v.*).

MANAWYD. (*Vide* " Gododin.") He joined the confederation of the Cymric chiefs with Madog. He came adorned with a wreath, " his country's rod of power." He was slain in battle.

MANAWYDDAN, SON OF LLYR. A Welsh romance included by Lady Charlotte Guest in the collection known as *The Mabinogion*, and found in the fourteenth-century *Red Book of Hergest*. It is a direct continuation of the tale of *Branwen* (*q.v.*). After interring the head of Bran, Manawyddan complains to Pryderi that he is now landless. Pryderi, to comfort him, gives him his mother, Rhiannon, to wife and a part of his territory of Dyfed. Dwelling happily together, they are startled one night by a clap of thunder, and observe that the fertile country around them has been turned into a barren waste by a thunderbolt. Famine overtakes them, and they are forced to betake themselves to Loegri to support themselves by making saddles, shields, and shoes. Several times are they driven away because of the malice of the other makers of these things. Returning to their own country, they live for a month upon game, and one day their hounds follow a boar into a strange castle. Unheeding the warning of Manawyddan, Pryderi follows them. He espies a fountain to which is chained a golden goblet, which seizing, he finds that he cannot let go. Manawyddan returns to Rhiannon, who reproaches him for leaving Pryderi. She herself returns to the castle, and meets the same fate. A thunderclap is heard, and the castle and all inside it disappears. This leaves Manawyddan with Kicva, Pryderi's wife. They go once more to Loegri to be shoemakers, but once more have to leave it. Manawyddan sows some corn, which, when ripe, is carried off by night. He discovers that an army of mice are the culprits, and, seizing one, swears to hang it on Gorsedde Arberth. While he is about to do so a clerk rides up and offers to purchase the mouse. A priest, who also asks for it, meets with a like refusal, but at last Manawyddan makes a bargain for the mouse's life with a bishop. He says that he will give him the mouse if he can restore Pryderi and Rhiannon to him. This is done, the mouse turning out to be the wife of the bishop, who is himself Llwyd Kil Coed, a friend of Gwal fab Clud, and the enchantment of Dyfed, and it transpires that the seizure of Pryderi and Rhiannon were effected in revenge for the treatment of Gwawl by the father of Pryderi, as told in the tale of *Pwyll* (*q.v.*).

MANDRICARDO. (*Vide* " Orlando Innamorato " and " Orlando Furioso.") Son of Agrican, King of Tartary. This cruel prince commanded that all unable to bear arms should be put to death. While contending for a shield with Rogero he was slain.

MANES or **MANESSE, REIDIGER DE.** A Swiss scholar and anthologist. He lived at the close of the fourteenth century, and appears to have been an influential magistrate of the town of Zurich, and eventually to have become its burgomaster. Whilst acting in these capacities he won wide recognition as a scholar of literature, especially poetry, and in collaboration with his son he set himself to collecting the best poems of their own time. The result of their labours in this direction is entitled simply, *The Work of the Manesingers*, and the manuscript is still extant in Paris.

MANUEL GALOPIN. (*Vide* " Garin the Lorrainer.") Son of Count Jocelin, cousin of Garin and Bego. A worthless man, fond of wine and women. He preferred a life of pleasure to any other, but at Bego's request he went as messenger to his kinsmen and to the king and queen to ask assistance after Thibaut's attack on Bego. Bernard was so angry at the news reaching the king that he tried to kill Galopin, but the queen rescued him.

MAON. (*Vide* " Labra the Mariner.")

MAP or **MAPES, WALTER.** The most brilliant writer and literary antiquarian of his day, was born somewhere on the borders of Wales about 1143. He studied for the Church at the University of Paris, and later entered the service of Henry II. He presided at the Assizes of Gloucester as one of the Justices in Eyre, in 1173. He acted as chaplain to the king during the wars brought about by the rebellion of his sons, represented him at the court of Louis VII., attended the Council at the Lateran at Rome, in 1179, and gained promotion in the Church first as Canon of St. Paul's, then, as Precentor of Lincoln, being finally appointed Archdeacon of Oxford in 1196. He probably died about 1210. Most of his work is written in Latin. Apart from his interest in the Arthur legend, he is credited with *The Poems of Golias*, the *De Nugis Curialium*, and a prose miscellany in five books called *Distinctiones*.

These abound in mordant and satiric criticism of the Churchmen of his time, and in vivacious descriptions of its manners and customs. Some critics formerly attributed to Map the invention and compilation of the entire corpus of Arthurian romance. What Map in reality accomplished was the introduction, and perhaps the redaction, of manuscripts relatively ancient to his own time. He was a sort of twelfth-century Walter Scott, an insatiable hunter among libraries and time-worn MSS., and an ardent collector of legend and folk-lore. He probably discovered the MS. of the *Quête del St. Graal* (*q.v.*) in the Abbey of Salisbury, and from it compiled his book of that name " for the love of his lord, King Henry," who had the story translated from Latin into French. It has been advanced by the late Mr. Alfred Nutt that Henry II. attempted to " utilize the Arthur legend for his own purpose in winning over his Celtic feudatories," and that his " discovery " of the tomb of Arthur at Glastonbury in 1191 was " intended to give the *coup de grâce* to the hopes of Arthur's return and victorious championship of a Cymric revolt." Determined attempts, too, he says, were made to gain for the Church in Britain " an origin well-nigh as illustrious as that of any Church, and for the land of Britain a special sanctity as the abiding place of the holiest of Christian relics."

MAPYNE. (*Vide* " Sir Ferumbras.") A Saracen employed by the soudan to steal his daughter's magical girdle. He was discovered by Roland and decapitated.

MARCHTEN. (*Vide* " Gododin.") A Cymric warrior, slain in the Battle of Cattreath. "He would slaughter with the blade, whilst his arms were full of furze."

MARGAWSE. Sister of King Arthur by the mother's side, and wife of Lot, King of Lothian, also mother of Gawaine, Agravaine, Gaheris, and Gareth. She came on a visit of espionage to the court of Arthur, and he, unwitting that she was his sister, entered into a *liaison* with her, the fruit of which was Mordred (*q.v.*).

MARHAUS, SIR. Brother-in-law to King Anguish, of Ireland, and knight of the Round Table. He was killed in battle with Sir Tristram (*q.v.*). (*Vide* "Morte d'Arthur.")

MARIE DE FRANCE. An Anglo-Norman poetess, who wrote *circa* 1150–1175. She produced a number of *lais* or tales which she expressly states were adopted or translated from Breton sources, the events in which are placed in the Arthurian era. The *personnel* of Arthur's court is, moreover, frequently introduced. For example, Lancelot is alluded to as beloved by Guinevere under the name of Launfal ; but his love for a fairy denizen of the Isle of Avalon prevents him from responding to her passion. Gawain is also referred to, as is the love-story of Tristran in the *Lai de Chevrefoil*. These fragments are valuable because of the evidence they present of popular knowledge of the Arthurian cycle in Brittany, and critics of standing have not hesitated to accept them as the best of proof that the true cradle of the cycle is to be found in Brittany. Then the Grail legend is not alluded to. For subject-matter of *lais*, see "Guingamour," "Bisclavaret," "Sir Launfal,"

"Eliduc." See Warnke's edition of the *lais*, 1885, with storiological notes by R. Kohler ; Roquefort's edition, 2 vols., 1820, containing a version in modern French ; *Marie de France, Seven Lais*, translated by Edith Rickert, 1901 ; Jessie L. Weston (*Three Lais*), 1900.

MARIE LA VENISSIENNE. Mentioned in the *Grand St. Grail* as an old woman who brought a cloth upon which the Saviour's likeness had painted itself when she wiped His face. The mere sight of it healed Vespasian.

MARIGONDE. (*Vide* "Sir Ferumbras.") Governess to Floripas. She refused to give her mistress any aid in relieving Roland and Olivier, and was pushed by Floripas into the sea and drowned.

MARK. King of Cornwall, and husband of Isolt or Isond (*q.v.*). He was a lifelong enemy of Tristram (*q.v.*), according to the *Morte d'Arthur ;* but the romance of *Sir Tristram* (*q.v.*) makes him the model of long-suffering husbands towards his wife's lover.

MARPHISA. (See "Orlando Innamorato " and " Orlando Furioso.") A female warrior of dauntless courage. She killed nine champions of the Amazons. She unhorsed Zerbino (*q.v.*), but was afterwards unhorsed by Bradamant (*q.v.*). She revenged three damsels whom Morganor had abused. She hanged Brunello for stealing her sword.

MARPUS. One of the Keepers of the Grail, second in descent from Celidoine, and an ancestor of Lancelot.

MARQUIS WILLIAM. (*Vide* "Garin the Lorrainer.") A brother of Fromont, but a traitor. He would not give up Bego's murderers because they were kinsmen, and thereby caused great dispeace. He offered Pepin a large sum if he would not help the Lorrainers for a year, and let them fight it out. The king assented, much to the indignation of the queen. But she wrote and warned Garin, who laid an ambush for Marquis William. He might have escaped but for Garin and three friends, who attacked and killed him, treating him brutally as they said "in exchange for Bego of Berlin."

MARSILE. The pagan King of Saragossa, the last heathen stronghold in Spain, who with his allies succeeded in cutting off the rearguard of the French army at Roncesvaux, which resulted in the death of Roland and the peers. On hearing of the defeat of the Saracens by the French in the battle which succeeded Roncesvaux, he died of chagrin.

MARSIRE. (*Vide* "Sir Otuel.") A Saracen king whom Charlemagne wished to become a Christian or pay him tribute. He bribed Ganelon, who brought this message, to betray the French. He was slain by Roland in the forest of Roncesvaux.

MATH, SON OF MATHONWY. One of the tales of the *Mabinogi*, derived from ancient Welsh sources. It tells how Math, Lord of Gwynedd, in Wales, could only rest with his feet in the lap of a virgin. The girl who performs this task was Goewin, the most beautiful maiden of her time, and Gilvaethwy, son of Don, confesses his love to her under difficulties, as Math overhears every word he says. Gwydion promises his brother Gilvaethwy to raise South Wales so that Math may have to go to war and leave Goewin behind. He departs on the ostensible errand of obtaining from Pryderi some novel animals which the latter had obtained from the underworld of Annwn. These animals are swine. Disguising themselves as bards, Gwydion and his friends are received at Pryderi's court, and exchange dogs and horses made by enchantment by Gwydion for the pigs of Pryderi. These enchanted animals only keep their shapes for a short time, and Pryderi sends a punitive expedition to Gwynedd. A great battle ensues, and the men of Gwynedd are victorious. Gwydion and Pryderi fight in single combat, and the latter is slain through Gwydion's magic arts. Math discovers the treachery of Gilvaethwy and Gwydion, takes Goewin to wife, and punishes the schemers severely. They are transformed into deer for a twelvemonth, for a like space into swine, for a third term into wolves, and in each of these states they have offspring, afterwards turned into human beings by Math. Math is now compelled to seek another virgin foot-holder, and Arianrhod, daughter of Don, is put forward for the post. Math, by dint of magic, discovers that she is no virgin, and startled, she flies, giving birth to two sons, Dylan Eil Ton, who makes at once for the sea, and another, who is hidden and brought up by Gwydion, who takes him to Arianrhod's castle. His mother says that she alone will name him. Gwydion comes once more to her castle in a ship, and sends her a pair of shoes. They do not fit, and in wrath she proceeds to his vessel, where she beholds her son strike a bird. She emits the words, "With a sure hand the lion hit the bird," and Gwydion at once declares that she has named her son Llew Llaw Gyffes, " Lion of the Sure Hand." The mother now says that the boy will never be given arms except by her. Gwydion causes an enchanted hostile fleet to appear, and, in fear, Arianrhod arms Llew. Incensed at the disappearance of the fleet, Arianrhod declares that Llew shall never have a wife save of her bestowing. Math and Gwydion make a bride out of flowers, and she is called Blodeuwedd. She intrigues with Gronw Pefr, Lord of Penllyn, who instigates her to discover from Llew the only way in which he can be killed. She discovers that only a javelin worked upon for a year's time and made during masses on a Sunday, can kill him, and then he must be caught standing by a bath on a river-bank, with one foot on the back of a buck, and the other in the side of the bath. Gronw prepares the javelin, and, when it is ready, Blodeuwedd persuades her husband to show her exactly in what manner the fatal blow would have to be dealt. Gronw, from a place of concealment, casts the spear at the proper moment, and Llew flies away in the shape of a bird. Gronw then takes his place. Gwydion sets out to seek for Llew. He discovers him in the shape of an eagle, and transforms him back to his old likeness. Llew resolves upon vengeance on his wife and her lover. She flies before him with her women, who are all drowned in Llyn Morwynion, and she is turned into an owl by Gwydion. Gronw is doomed to receive a blow in the same manner as did Llew. He interposes a flat stone between his body and the javelin, which nevertheless pierces the obstruction. Gronw is killed,

and Llew finally reigns as Lord in Gwynedd. Math is the greatest of all the mythological characters to be found in the *Mabinogi*. Professor Rhys refers to him as the Celtic Zeus. We have in this tale a sun-myth, in which Llew represents the sun-hero, born in strange circumstances, obscured for a space by Gronw, the darkness, but finally victorious. (See Alfred Nutt's edition of *The Mabinogion*.)

MATHOLWCH. King of Ireland, husband of Branwen (*q.v.*), father of Gwen (*q.v.*). He figures in the Welsh tale of Kulhwch and Olwen (*q.v.*).

MATIÈRE DE FRANCE. (*Vide* " Charlemagne Cycle.") According to Jean Bodel (*q.v.*), there were three cycles of romance alone on the subjects of which a poet of his day might worthily sing—the Matière de France (the Charlemagne cycle) ; the Matèire de Bretagne (the Arthurian cycle) ; and the story of Rome la Grant (the Geste of Alexander the Great (*q.v.*)).

MELIAGANUS, SIR. Son of King Bagdemagus. (*Vide* " Morte d'Arthur.")

MELIAGRANCE, SIR. In Arthurian romance, son of King Bagdemagus (*q.v.*). He allured Queen Guinever and slew many of her knights. Lancelot subsequently released her, not without being subjected to imprisonment. He was eventually slain by Lancelot (*q.v.*). (*Vide* " Morte d'Arthur.")

MELIANS. A companion of Galahad, who had begged to be allowed to serve him and whom he had knighted. Searching for the Grail, they separate at a cross road, Melians taking the left-hand path in spite of warning. He comes to a tent where hangs a golden crown, which he seizes. But strange knights appear who would have slain him had not Galahad come to the rescue and overthrown his assailants. Melians is taken to an abbey to be healed of his wound and learns that the two knights who almost overpowered him were Pride and Covetousness.

MELIODAS. King of Liones, father of Sir Tristram, who was born of his first wife Elizabeth, sister of King Mark of Cornwall (*q.v.*). His second wife was the daughter of King Howell of Brittany (*q.v.*). (*Vide* " Morte d'Arthur.")

MELIOT, SIR, DE LOGRES. A knight in Arthurian romance, who slew Sir Gilbert the Bastard (*q.v.*). Afterwards he was subjected to the witchery of a sorceress. He was eventually released from the enchantment by Sir Lancelot (*q.v.*). (*Vide* " Morte d'Arthur.")

MELISENDRA. An old Spanish tale, the date of which is uncertain. Melisendra lies in a tower at Sansuena. She looks towards Paris, looking and waiting for Lord Gayferos, for whom she has waited seven years, and has not seen or heard of in that time. A knight appears on the road, and she makes a sign to him, asking him to take a message to Gayferos. The knight is Gayferos (*q.v.*), and she leaps from the tower and rides away with him.

MELITS (1), SIR, DE LILE. Son of the King of Denmark (*q.v.*), and knight-in-waiting upon Sir Galahad (*q.v.*). He accompanied his master on his holy mission, but returned to the court of Arthur upon losing Galahad. Later, when Lancelot takes Benwick, he is made Earl of Tursank (*q.v.*). (*Vide* " Morte d'Arthur.")

MELITS (2). (*Vide* "Dietrich of Berne.") King of the Huns, and father of Odilia (*q.v.*).

MELUSINA. The most famous of the fays of France. Having enclosed her father in a high mountain for offending her mother, she was condemned to become, every Saturday, a serpent from her waist downwards. When she married Raymond, Count of Lusignan, she made her husband vow never to visit her on a Saturday; but the jealousy of the count being excited, he hid himself on one of the forbidden days, and saw his wife's transformation. Melusina was now obliged to quit her mortal husband, and was destined to wander about as a spectre till the day of doom. It is said also that the count immured her in the dungeon of his castle.

MERLIN. A celebrated enchanter, who appears in most of the tales and romances connected with the Arthurian cycle. In his Celtic and mythical aspect he is perhaps identical with the British Celtic sky-god Nudd, and Professor Rhys suggests that he was the deity worshipped at Stonehenge. In the Celtic or Welsh form of the Arthurian legend he appears as the archdruid or wise man from whom Arthur gladly accepts counsel, but in the Norman-French, and later versions, he is regarded as a powerful necromancer or enchanter, the type of the mediæval magician. It was through his instrumentality that Uther Pendragon gained access to Igernia, wife of Gorlois, Duke of Cornwall, in the shape of her husband, and became the father of Arthur. Later he explained the uses of the sword Excalibur to Arthur, and guided him through a portion of his reign. He conceived a fatal

R

passion for the enchantress Viviana (*q.v.*), and followed her to the forest of Broceliande, in Brittany, where she charmed him into a magic sleep, from which he could never awake.

MERLIN. This romance, written by Robert de Borron, and perhaps completed by other hands, describes how Satan, chagrined at the victory of Christ over him, begets a son unlawfully upon a virgin, who is to possess the wisdom of a Socrates, but to preach anti-Christian doctrine. His name was Merlin, and it is related that at eighteen months old he saves his mother from the doom to be meted out to those guilty of unchastity. He is afterwards brought to King Vortigern, to whom he expounds the mystery of an unfinished tower. Vortigern is driven from his throne by Pendragon, with whom Merlin stands in high esteem, as also with his successor Uther Pendragon. For the latter he builds the Round Table, leaving one place to be filled in the time of Uther's successor. He aids the king in satisfying his passion upon Igerne, wife of the Duke of Cornwall, and he takes charge of Arthur, their son. When Arthur reaches adolescence, he achieves the adventure of the sword in the anvil, and is proclaimed King. " And I, Robert of Borron, writer of this book, may not speak longer of Arthur till I have told of Alain, son of Brons, and how the woes of Britain were caused ; and as the book tells so must I what man Alain was, and what life he led and of his seed and their life. And when I have spoken of these things I will tell again of Arthur." However, Robert de Borron appears to break off here and does not enlighten us as " to what man-

ner of man Alain (*q.v.*) was," nor does the MS. refer to him at all except in the most perfunctory manner.

MERSADAGE. (*Vide* " Sir Ferumbras.") King of Barbary. One of Laban's tributary kings. He helped Laban to assault the castle at Aigremor after the French knights had taken it. He was killed by Sir Guy of Burgundy.

MESSBUACHALLA. (In Irish romance.) (The cowherd's foster-child.) Only daughter of Etain Og (*q.v.*) and of Cormac (*q.v.*). About to be cast into a pit by her heirless father, the infant smiled at her appointed executioners. Thus overcome, they gave her to a cow-herd of Eterskel, King of Tara, to be brought up. Lest she might be discovered, the princess was kept in a house of wicker-work with but a roof-opening. This precaution failed, however, for one of Eterskel's subjects climbed up the side of the prison and beheld therein the fairest maiden in Ireland. Thus informed, the king ordered a wall-opening to be made and the maiden brought forth, for he believed that she was the destined mother of the son promised him by the Druid. But before she left her strange home she was visited by a god from the Land of Youth, to whom she bore Conary.

MIDIR THE PROUD. A son of the Irish god Dagda, husband of Fuamnach (*q.v.*) and of Etain (*q.v.*). He visited Etain in the shape of Ailill, her mortal husband, King Eochy's brother. But he longed to be united to her again, so he appeared one day to Eochy, and invited him to a game of chess. Having intoxicated his opponent with success, he at last suggested that the stakes should be according to the victor's pleasure. He won the game, and asked to have Etain in his arms and to obtain a kiss from her. This was granted for a year and a day hence, when Midir appeared, despite the hedge of armed men surrounding Eochy's castle, and disappeared through the roof, eloping with his former bride. For this theft the Fairy Mound of Bri-Leith, whither he had borne her, was destroyed by the incensed mortals. And on their part the people of the Land of Youth took their revenge upon Conary (*q.v.*) the great-grandson of Etain.

MILE (1). (*Vide* "Bevis of Hampton.") Son of Bevis, born and christened in a forest and brought up by a fisherman. He fought bravely for his father at the great battle in London. Married a daughter of Edgar and became King of England.

MILE (2), **SIR.** (*Vide* "Bevis of Hampton.") Married Josyan at Cologne and was strangled by her on their wedding night.

MILO. (*Vide* "Garin the Lorrainer.") Duke of Blaives, in Gascony. He had two fair daughters, and when King Pepin asked him if he would give his daughters in marriage to two counts of his court, he said they were already in love with Garin and Bego. The king, surprised, said these were the very same counts he had spoken of. So Garin married Alice, and Bego Beatrice. Milo made them co-heiresses. Garin gave up his wife's share, and took Metz and his father's lands. Beatrice and Bego afterwards lived at Blaives.

MILON, THE LAY OF. A romance written by Marie de France (*q.v.*).

Milon was a much-esteemed knight of South Wales. The fame of his prowess and courtesy came to the ears and struck the heart of the fair daughter of a lord of the same realm. The maiden therefore sent the knight the offer of her love, which he accepted, while he asked for a meeting. The lovers met often in the damsel's garden, until the maiden forgot her duty. In great distress and fear she sent to tell Milon of her predicament. He arranged that their babe when born should be sent to her sister in Northumberland. The infant should be nourished as his sister's child ; and his mother's ring was to be placed about his neck, and the story of his parents written in a letter. The babe was born and was secretly conveyed to Northumberland. Then Milon sought a land beyond the seas, and his lady-love was given in marriage to another baron. Sad was the knight when he heard of the news. But forthwith he hid a message in the feathers of his favourite swan, and commanded his servant to give it into the hands of the lady. She found the message and also read therein that the bird would return home if it were starved for three days. After a month she managed to procure secretly parchment and ink, and, denying the swan food during the allotted period, set it free. For twenty years did this swan bear secretly the messages of these lovers. Now the son grew to manhood, and left Northumberland for Brittany. Here he made friends with the rich on account of his prowess, friends with the poor out of his liberality, and friends with all by reason of his modesty. At last as the Knight Peerless, his fame reached Milon's ears. He, seeking to uphold the honour of the older knights, set sail for Brittany, and in an Easter tournament at Mont St. Michael, jousted with his unknown son. He was unhorsed, but was courteously treated by the victor. Then his eye caught the ring upon the youth's hand, and he learned that he had at last found his son. Rejoicing, they feasted together that night, and set forth next morning for Wales. The Knight Peerless offered to slay his mother's husband; and thus give the lovers into each other's arms. But that he needed not to do. For on the way to Wales, the travellers met a messenger from the lady bearing the news of her husband's death. With joy, therefore, the lovers were wed, and lived in happiness until the end.

MINNIE, PRINCESS. Daughter to King Ladmer (*q.v.*), and subsequently wife of Dietwart (*q.v.*). The romance tells us of her narrow escape from the jaws of a dragon, from which she is saved by Dietwart, who overcame the monster.

MOHADY. (*Vide* "Florice and Blanchfleur.") A noted Mollah, preceptor to Florice, son of Prince Felix. He opposed the attachment of Florice for Blanchfleur, and his religious zeal and evil disposition influenced Felix against Blanchfleur. He conspired with Ajoub to accuse the innocent maiden of a plot to poison him.

MONGAN. (*Vide* "Fothad.")

MONIAGE GUILLAUME. (William's Monkship.) A romance of the William of Orange sub-cycle of the Charlemagne saga. (*Vide* "William of Orange.") This poem is founded on the real facts of William's life, and exhibits with some humour the contrast between his knightly and monkish spirit. Its original is probably to be found in the *Novalesian Chronicle* (*q.v.*). It tells how William is warned by an angel to embrace the life monastic, but only by dint of princely presents can he obtain leave from the monks of Aniane to wear their habit. The abbot asks if he can sing and read, and the hero quaintly replies, "Yes, without looking at the book." They gown and tonsure him, and when the abbot requests him to love his brethren well he replies, "Tell them not to put me in a passion." He is regular in the performance of his monastic duties, but eats more than any two of the brethren, and, when tipsy, ill-treats them. They determine to send him to the sea-shore to purchase fish for the monastery, and in order to rid themselves of him they instigate a band of robbers to waylay him on his return in the wood of Beauclere. He is told ere he leaves the monastery that if he should be waylaid by robbers that he is not to attack them, but, on the contrary, to give everything up to them, even to his clothing. He is told, however, that he may fight if they attempt to wrest from him the very last article of his attire. He buys fish, and is waylaid by fifteen robbers. They strip William of his attire and attempt to take his breeches from him, but he immediately falls upon them, and kills seven with his bare hands. He then tears off the leg of a sumpter-horse, and proceeds to kill them all. Having slaughtered the entire band, he prays that the horse's leg may be restored, which request is miraculously granted, and, resuming his journey, he regains the monastery safe and sound, much to the consternation of the brotherhood.

He is ill received, and slays several in his wrath ; but eventually he is forgiven, and by the advice of his guardian angel quits Aniane, and, after remaining for some time with his cousin, a hermit, seeks the desert of Gellone. Other texts extend the story still further, and tell of a conflict with a giant, an imprisonment of seven years among the Saracens at Palermo, and how William returns to succour Louis, besieged in Paris by the Saracens. He returns to the wilderness, and builds a minster and a bridge over a torrent near at hand. But the devil undoes his work every day. After a month of fruitless labour, William lies in wait for the father of evil, and, seizing him, casts him into the torrent, which ever after boiled up incessantly. He then completes the bridge, and dies shortly afterwards.

MONIAGE RENOUART. (Renouart's Monkhood.) A romance of the William of Orange sub-cycle of the Charlemagne saga. It recounts the adventures of the gigantic hero as a monk. (*Vide* "William of Orange," and "Renouart.") It bears a close resemblance to the *Moniage Guillaume* (*q.v.*). Renouart enters the Abbey of Bride or Brioude, and so torments the inmates that at last they purchase four leopards, which they starve and shut up Renouart with them. He kills them, defeats the robbers of the neighbourhood, who are in league with the monks, repels an attack of Saracens, and fights his own son Maillefer (*q.v.*), who is in the Saracen ranks, but who is eventually baptized. At last he dies, and his soul is carried off by angels, his body being taken to Spain as a relic.

MORANN. In Ultonian romance, a druid who prophesied the future greatness of Setanta, later designated the Hound of Cullan, or Cuchulain (*q.v.*).

MORD. (*Vide* "Burnt Njal.") A cunning fellow, who tracked the thief from Otkell's (*q.v.*) store of goods to Hallgerda (*q.v.*). He assisted in Gunnar's (*q.v.*) murder, and had a hand in the slaying of Hanskuld. He sought to take up the case for the murdered man's friends, and pleaded in Kari's (*q.v.*) case against the burners of Njal.

MORDRAINS. Or "Slow-of-Belief." He is known in Arthurian legend as the re-baptized Evalach (*q.v.*), who could not believe in the Trinity or the Immaculate Conception. Mordrains is shown Christ's blood, along with Serraquite and Nasciens. He ultimately believes, and orders his people to be baptized or leave his land.

MORDRED. Son of Arthur by his own sister, the wife of Lot. He was slain in Cornwall in a great final battle by Arthur, whom he succeeded in seriously wounding ere he expired. The name probably signifies "Biter," and he perhaps typifies the serpent, of whom Arthur was on several occasions prophetically warned to beware. (*Vide* "Morte d'Arthur.")

MORGADOUR, SIR. (*Vide* "Guy of Warwick.") Steward to the Emperor of Germany. He was very treacherous, and was killed by Sir Guy to avenge the death of his lion, which had been slain by Morgadour.

MORGAN LE FAY. Sister of Arthur, and wife of King Urience of the Land of Gore. Arthur gave the scabbard of his sword Excalibur into her keeping, but, loving Sir Accolon, she presented it to him, making by enchantment a forged scabbard for her brother. Arthur managed to recover the real sheath, but was once again deceived by her. She also figures as a sort of Queen of the Land of Faërie, and as such has passed into French and Italian legend. At the birth of Ogier the Dane (*q.v.*) she promised that she would finally take him to dwell with her in Avillion, where she took Arthur after his last battle. She usually presents her favourites with a ring, which procures them forgetfulness, and retains them by her in much the same manner as does Venus in the legend of Tannhäuser. Her myth is a parallel of that of Eos and Tithonos, and has probably been evolved from a sun and dawn myth.

MORIATH. In Irish romance, daughter of Seoriath, the King of Feramore. (*Vide* "Labra the Mariner.")

MORIEN. (*Vide* "Gododin.") A Cymric warrior. He made an attack on the Saxon camp, and was killed by a stone thrown from the wall of the fort.

MORNA, CLAN. In Irish romance, one of the divisions of the Fianna (*q.v.*), whose Treasure Bag containing magic weapons and precious jewels of Danaan date was kept by Fia of that clan. (*Vide* "Bascna, Clan.")

MOROKE, SIR. A giant, slain by Sir Eglamour (*q.v.*). The brightness of the latter's sword was responsible for the blindness which preceded his defeat. (See "Sir Eglamour of Artoys.")

MORRIGAN. In Irish romance, the Danaan Goddess of Death and Destruction. She persecuted Cuchulain in many shapes for refusing her proffered love. At the close,

however, she became his friend, warned him before his last battle by breaking his chariot-pole, and settled on his shoulder as a crow when he was dead. She got entrance to Da Derga's Hostel. (*Vide* "Conary.")

MORTE ARTHURE. A metrical romance the authorship of which is attributed to Huchown of the Awle Ryale (*q.v.*), a Scottish poet, who lived during the middle of the fourteenth century. His authorship is, however, by no means indisputably proved. In its lines romance is treated as fact, and it tends towards chronicle-history rather than romantic narrative. The author employs as his basis the *Historia Regum Britanniæ* of Geoffrey of Monmouth, and Layamon's *Brut ;* but the whole is so coloured with the spirit of French romance that it is impossible to believe that he did not make use of Gallic sources as well. The poem is divided into three parts : (1) that which covers the period up to Arthur's defeat of Lucius, King of Rome ; (2) that which ends with the offer of the Pope to crown Arthur King of Rome ; and (3) the revolt of Mordred and Arthur's death. The first and third portions are manifestly based upon the chronicles ; but the second is unquestionably either borrowed wholesale from some Arthurian source not now extant, or else proceeded from the writer's own imagination. That the author was a man of rare imaginative ability is seen from many interpolations and original passages. The colour-scheme of his language, the rare choice of words, the writhing of the serpentine lines, are sufficient to stamp him as a fourteenth - century Swinburne. Here, indeed, is a magic of words—

the veritable wizardry of the gifted craftsman in letters who has also the wondrous gifts of eloquence and music. Of fabrics, armour, robes—all the *materiel* of romantic poetry—he writes in phrase which glitters as brightly as the gallant vesture he describes. His *rôle* is, however, that of a chronicler. For example, he does not transport Arthur to Avillion, but prosaically buries him at Glastonbury. We are led to suspect, therefore, that the bulk of his interpolations do not partake of the nature of *matière de poesie*, save through circumstances more or less fortuitous, as he had every wish to observe exactitude, and only pictured brave translunary things as he imagined they might really have existed—or, better still, mayhap he never realized that his pen was of gold. Malory paid rich tribute to his memory when he made the *Morte Arthure* the basis of the fifth book of his great work. The one slur on the work is the quite topical one of over-alliteration, which in some instances is of such an exaggerated character as to render the exact meaning exceedingly obscure.

MORTE D'ARTHUR. A collection of Arthurian tales compiled by Sir Thomas Malory (*q.v.*) in 1469. It was, however, not printed till 1485, when it was published by Caxton. There followed two editions by Wynkyn de Worde, in 1498 and 1529, and by 1650 four more editions had appeared. The *Morte d'Arthur* was undoubtedly one of the favourite romantic books of the fifteenth and sixteenth centuries, and as a specimen of mediæval English it has never been surpassed. The original manuscript has not been found. For the most part, Malory's

originals were certain French romances of the Arthurian cycle, all of which are traceable except that from which the seventh book was composed. As the *Morte d'Arthur* was the great English compendium of Arthurian lore, it has been thought proper to give an extended summary of its contents.

Book I. Uther Pendragon, King of England, sends for the Duke of Cornwall, whose wife, Igraine, he loves. He assumes the duke's shape, and visits Igraine. The duke is killed in battle against the king, when he marries Igraine. Arthur is the fruit of their marriage. The child after its birth is reared by Sir Ector and his wife. Two years after Arthur's birth King Uther dies. Merlin, through his magic power, makes the dead Uther speak, commanding that Arthur his son may succeed to the throne.

Some time afterwards, when many lords and gentlemen had assembled in London for the Christmas feast, there was placed in the great churchyard a huge stone, in the centre of which was placed a sword, with the inscription above it, " Who pulleth out this sword of the stone is rightwise king born of England." None could move the stone but Sir Arthur, who is then crowned King of England. A great war takes place, shortly after, between Arthur, King Bors, and King Ban allied against eleven northern kings. The war is ended by the intercession of Merlin. Arthur then begot on Lionel's daughter of Saman a son named Borse. A battle is fought, then the kings, Bors and Ban, take leave of Arthur to return to their own country. Merlin prophesies the death of the eleven kings all in one day. Arthur afterwards departed unto Carlion, whither came King

Lot's wife, his sister, as messenger, but really as a spy. During her stay he begot on her Mordred, unwitting that she was of the same blood as himself. The following day he chases a "questing beast." Igraine, Arthur's mother, whom he has never seen, is sent for, that they both may know each other, and a feast is held. A messenger from the Roman Empire arrives demanding tribute of Arthur, who, refusing, challenges the emperor. War ensues, and the Emperor Nero is defeated. Arthur, in passing a lake, perceives in the centre the arm and hand of a lady holding a sword, which he receives from her on rowing out. Merlin alludes to her as the Lady of the Lake. Later he issues an edict for the destruction of all children born on May-day, that Mordred may be amongst them. They are all placed on a ship, and sent to sea. The ship is driven against a castle, and all are drowned, except Mordred, who is cast upon a rock, and nourished by a good man until he is fourteen.

Book II. King Rience of North Wales wastes Arthur's lands, doing much damage. Later Rience is captured by a knight, Balin, and his brother. Balin succeeds in drawing from the sheath a sword worn by a lady of mystery, a feat none other could perform. The sword proves one of great power, and with it Balin beheads the Lady of the Lake. He also later kills his assailant, Sir Lanceor. The twelve kings, as prophesied by Merlin, are all killed in battle against Arthur in one day. Merlin prophesies a great battle at Salisbury, in which Mordred, Arthur's son, is against the king. Balin kills the invisible Knight Garlon, who is guilty of slaying two knights. After adventure in the Grail Castle, Balin is killed in combat against his brother Balan, who also dies. They are both unaware of each other's identity until just before they expire.

Book III. King Arthur is married in the Church of St. Stephen's in Camelot to Guenever, daughter of Leodigrance. Tor, the son of King Pellinore, is made knight. King Pellinore, whilst resting overnight in a wood, overhears a plot to poison King Arthur.

Book IV. Merlin becomes very fascinated with Nimue, lady of the court of King Arthur, with whom he goes overseas to visit King Ban of Benwik. He prophesies of the Knight Lancelot, son of King Ban. He (Merlin) returns with the maiden to Cornwall, where by dint of magic, she imprisons him in a stone. Five kings now make war against Arthur, destroying cities and castles, and slaying his people. After which King Arthur and two knights slay the five kings, causing their armies to flee. On the spot where they are killed, King Arthur builds the Abbey of La Beale. A fight ensues between Arthur and Sir Accolon, who has obtained the magic scabbard of the sword Excalibur. Arthur loses much blood, and is almost beaten, but for the enchantment of the Lady of the Lake, who caused the wonderful sword Excalibur to fall from the hand of Sir Accolon into that of Arthur, who wounds his opponent, and discovers his relationship, and that his sister Morgana had given the scabbard to Accolon. Later, Sir Accolon dies. Queen Morgan le Fay again steals the scabbard from Arthur while he sleeps, and, on being pursued by him, she throws it into a lake. The Lady of the Lake saves Arthur from a mantle which should have burned him. Three knights of King Arthur meet three maidens, each knight taking one, and they all make a compact to meet at the same spot twelve months afterwards, a promise which the three couples kept, after which they again separated, and came into the court of King Arthur.

Book V. King Arthur, having been at peace for some time, is again compelled to fight in defence of the empire against the aggressions of Rome. Refusing to pay taxes to the Roman Emperor, Lucius, that monarch invades Arthur's possessions in France. After a successful march, Britain is threatened. Holding a Privy Council at York to select a regent, Arthur leaves Britain to defend his foreign possessions. The regents appointed are Sir Bawdwin of Britain and Sir Constantine of Cornwall. To the latter Arthur wills the sovereignty should he never return. While crossing the sea on his way to Barflete, in Flanders, Arthur dreams of a fight between a dragon and boar, the former animal being victorious. On arriving in Flanders, Arthur kills a giant who had murdered the Duchess of Brittany. Having completed his task, Arthur then despatched messengers to the Emperor Lucius, commanding him to quit the country. The Emperor refuses, and Arthur's messengers are assailed, which causes a general conflict, resulting in victory for Arthur. Another battle takes place on the next day, and though Arthur's army is inferior in numbers, it completely annihilates the enemy. A final battle follows, in which Arthur kills the Roman Emperor Lucius, and the Sultan of Syria, the King of Egypt and of Ethiopia, are killed, with other seventeen kings. The Roman army then retreats in confusion, leaving one hundred thousand dead on the field. Arthur, with his army, then proceeds through Almaine, and so into Italy without much resistance, except at Urbino, where a battle is fought, after which Arthur enters Rome and is crowned Emperor. He and his knights return in triumph to England.

Book VI. Sir Lancelot-du-Lake, noted for his gallantry, sets out in search of adventure, and, while sleeping in the shade, is made prisoner by the enchantment of four queens, and brought to the Castle Chariot. They then offer him their love. After refusing, Lancelot escapes by the aid of a damosel, whose father is called Bagdemagus. On the arrival of Sir Lancelot, the daughter of King Bagdemagus leads him into the abbey, and sends for her father. On his coming, Lancelot explains to him how he has been betrayed, and speaks of the obligation he was under to his daughter, promising at the same time to assist the king who is at war with the King of Northgallis. Requesting the assistance of three knights, he ambushes himself in a little wood hard by the place of tournament. Seeing the King of Northgallis encounter King Bagdemagus and his knights, Lancelot rushes on the men of Northgallis, and does mighty execution, so that the party of Bagdemagus prevails. Departing from the king's castle to seek his brother, Sir Louis, who has strayed while he slept, he meets a damosel who tells him that a neighbouring knight, Sir Turquine, had imprisoned many knights of Arthur's court. She leads him to where Sir Turquine dwelt, and they encounter one another, Turquine being slain.

Lancelot frees Turquine's prisoners, and is led by the damosel to the hold of a robber knight, whom he overthrows. Coming to the castle of Tantagil, he slays two giants, who guarded it, and delivers their prisoners. Passing by a meadow where were pitched three pavilions, and dressed in the armour of Sir Kay, he jests with the knights, who lie in their tents, and overthrows them, subsequently overthrowing four knights of the Round Table. Following a hound into a castle, he finds therein a dead knight, and a lady who mourned him grievously. Returning to the forest, he meets with a damosel, who begs him to assist her brother, who is sore wounded, saying that unless he entered the Chapel Perilous, and there procured a sword and a bloody cloth, that the knight's wounds should never be healed. Lancelot, after dreadful adventures in the Chapel, procures the talismans, and cures the knight, whose name was Sir Meliot. Passing by a castle, a lady begs him to get her hawk, which had got caught in a tree. Disarming himself, he climbs into the tree, when the lady's husband attacks him. Snatching a great bough, Lancelot kills the knight with it. Pursuing his way, he observes a knight chasing his wife with intent to slay her. The knight, feigning to forgive his lady, suddenly slays her treacherously; whereupon Lancelot lays it upon him to carry the corpse of his lady with him to Rome to obtain absolution. Returning to Arthur's court, Launcelot relates his adventures.

Book VII. At the time of the feast of Pentecost, there came to the court of Arthur a young man, who requested the king's hospitality for one year, after which two other gifts would be asked of him. Arthur granted him his wish. He causes the displeasure of Sir Kay, who deems him of low blood, and who subsequently names him Beaumains. He is in reality Sir Gareth of Orkney. The year passes, during which we hear little of him, except that Sir Kay causes him to live amongst the scullions. There comes a maiden to the court, who asks for the assistance of a knight to release her sister from the tyranny of the Red Knight. Beaumains steps forward, requesting that he may be appointed to the adventure, which is one of his boons, the other being that Arthur would make him knight to Sir Lancelot. The king having granted both requests, Beaumains sets out after the maiden, who reviles him on account of his low rank. Sir Kay sets out after him, jousts with Beaumains, and is overthrown. Then Sir Lancelot, having put the young man's skill to the test, invests him with the order of knighthood. Beaumains proceeds on his errand, and is continuously abused by the maiden, who little knows of his rank. Many thrilling incidents do they experience ere the castle of the Red Knight is reached. Their first encounter after leaving Sir Lancelot is a fight with six thieves, who had imprisoned a knight. Beaumains assails them, and kills three, the others making good their escape. Proceeding on their way, Beaumains slays two knights who oppose his passage over a river. No sooner had they crossed the river, when Beaumains espies a banner, and a shield of black hanging from a tree. He is immediately assailed by the owner, a knight of the Black Laundes. The fight ends in the death of the Black Knight, and Beaumains, possessing himself of his enemy's armour and horse, rides on till he meets the brother of the slain knight, who jousts with him. Subsequently yielding, the Green Knight offers to Beaumains thirty knights, who commands them to be in readiness to serve Arthur. Then again, on proceeding, Beaumains fights the third brother— the Red Knight, who likewise yields, and likewise offers Beaumains a number of knights. The maiden continues her abuse of Beaumains, who patiently suffers her, eventually winning her respect. In passing a meadow they meet with Sir Persent, who jousts with Beaumains, yielding to his superior skill. Beaumains discloses his identity to Sir Persent and the maiden. Beaumains and the lady then depart, and when they were come to the castle in which her sister is imprisoned, a dwarf counsels them. After which Beaumains challenges the Red Knight, who warns Beaumains of the peril of his task, but he, paying little heed to the advice, assails the tyrant. The fight is of long duration. After some repose, the combat is resumed on foot, meanwhile the ladies encourage Beaumains, who speedily brings his enemy to earth. The Red Knight pleads for mercy, which is granted him on condition that the lady will be released, and that he will pay homage to Arthur.

The lady, Dame Liones, declines Sir Gareth's advances ; but no sooner had he departed than she regrets her action, whereupon she sends her brother off in search of Sir Gareth, who, being found, returns. He then makes love to the lady, which causes her sister Linet annoyance. During the night Sir Gareth is attacked by a mysterious knight, who is beheaded by him after a fierce encounter. On his recovery, some days after, Sir Gareth is attacked in like manner by the same knight, who again is beheaded. Meanwhile there arrives at the court of Arthur, Sir Gareth's mother, demanding her son. The king, not knowing of his whereabouts, sends for Dame Liones, who at the same time announces a great joust, thus hoping by these means to attract Sir Gareth. The tourney, which is attended by the king, is one of great brilliance. Sir Gareth, disguised for each encounter that he might not be recognized, changes into different armour each time. His valiant display throughout the tourney meets with such approval as to cause the king to inquire after his rank. No man knowing, Arthur is obliged to engage spies, who discover Sir Gareth's rank by the legend on his helmet. Sir Gareth, after the tourney, betakes himself to a castle for rest, where he encounters a duke, whom he slays. He furthermore slays the duke's knights who had attacked him. Departing, Sir Gareth fights with a knight, who had imprisoned thirty widows in his castle. Killing the knight, he releases the ladies, commanding them to go before King Arthur. Sir Gareth then, unknowingly, fights with his brother, and not until the intervention of Linet do they recognize each other. While they are seated, the king, his knights, and their ladies discover them, and great rejoicing ensues. Then follows a meeting between Sir Gareth and Dame Liones. After which, amidst great rejoicing, they are married.

Book VIII. We now hear of Sir Tristram de Liones, whose mother died at his birth, his father, King Meliodas, for the second time, marrying the daughter of King Howell, of Brittany. She, jealous of Tristram, tries several times to poison him, eventually being discovered by his father, who would have slain her, but for the boy's pleading. Sir Tristram is then sent to France, to be educated. After a long sojourn in that country, he returns to England, when he goes to the assistance of King Mark, of Cornwall, who is being assailed by a knight from King Anguish, of Ireland, who demands tribute. The fight is fierce and of long duration, ending in Sir Tristram wounding Sir Marhaus, who escapes, and subsequently dies. Sir Tristram is also severely wounded, and, as he is not likely to recover, by the advice of a wise woman, is sent to Ireland, where he is cured.

Disguised as a harper, and under the name of Tramtris, he appears before King Anguish, who, little knowing of his connection with Sir Marhaus' death, put him under the care of his daughter, La Beale Isond, with whom he falls in love, but he soon realizes that he has a rival—Sir Palamides. Shortly after, a tourney is announced, and Tramtris is requested to joust, which he does, completely defeating Palamides. Sir Tristram's stay is then cut short, for the queen, discovering him to be her late brother's slayer, succeeds in procuring his banishment. Sir Tristram, ere he departs from Ireland, promises Isond that he will remain faithful. Returning to Cornwall, to the court of King Mark, with whom he fights for the love of a lady, he succeeds in defeating the king. He then departs after the lady, whose husband assails him, and is eventually overcome. Sir Tristram subsequently defeats three knights, who abduct the lady, after which she

returns to her husband. King Mark, anxious to rid himself of Sir Tristram, sends him to Ireland. A storm rising, Sir Tristram is compelled to land in England, when he hears of a charge of treason against King Anguish at Arthur's court. Sir Tristram offers help to Anguish, completely defeating his adversary. Sir Tristram and Anguish then return to Ireland for the purpose of bringing back Isond, whom King Mark desires for his wife, and soon after, he, with Isond, returns to Cornwall, bringing the lady to King Mark, who subsequently marries her.

Sir Palamides, envious of King Mark, succeeds in getting Isond into his castle, when Sir Tristram attacks him, badly wounding the abductor. The queen is then restored to her husband. Hardly had this been accomplished when a watch is set on Sir Tristram, who deeply loves the queen, and, on their meeting, Sir Tristram is caught by thirty knights, who carry him as prisoner to a chapel. Releasing himself from his cords, he slays ten of the knights, and escapes. Meanwhile Isond is carried to a leper's hut. Immediately Sir Tristram hears of this, he hastens to release her, bringing her to a house in a forest, where, in his absence, she is discovered by King Mark, and is carried off. Isond having contracted leprosy, Sir Tristram departs for Brittany, in search of her sister, La Blanche, that she might have her assistance. While in Brittany, Sir Tristram meets with many adventures. Marrying Isond's sister, Sir Tristram assists King Howell in many wars, proving himself invincible. Meanwhile, a knight of Brittany goes over to King Arthur's court, relating the marriage of Sir

Tristram, which causes surprise, and Tristram is much abused by the court. The knight returns to Brittany, and Tristram and his bride set sail for Britain. Later his wife returns to her native land.

Book IX. Leaving Tristram for a space, we turn to the adventures of a young man who appeared at the court of King Arthur clad in an ill-fitting coat of cloth of gold. He is desirous of knighthood, and not wishing to divest himself of the coat until he is avenged of his father's death (to whom the coat belonged) he receives from Sir Kay the name La Côte-Male Tailé— meaning "ill-fitting coat." He soon proves his bravery in slaying a lion which had broken loose, and which, but for him, would have devoured the queen. King Arthur then knights him. He offers to assist a damsel, who has appeared at the court for help, that a quest after a dead knight might be fulfilled. The pair set out while La Côte is continuously abused by the lady, Maledisant. Meeting with ill luck in the many jousts which he has, he is eventually rewarded by success. Coming to a castle, Sir La Côte is assailed by a hundred knights. Dismounting he shows great bravery, and after slaying twelve of them he escapes by the aid of a lady. Sir Lancelot, hearing of Sir La Côte, follows him, and offers him his friendship. Shortly after, the young knight is assailed by six knights, and is taken prisoner. Sir Lancelot, once more in search of Sir La Côte, causes the Lord of the Castle to yield, releasing the prisoners. The tourney is continued, and coming to a fortress Sir La Côte decides to enter, leaving Maledisant and Sir Lancelot to watch. Having entered, the young knight after a brave defence is overcome and taken prisoner. Sir Lancelot decides to release his comrade, and having caused the Lord of the Castle to yield, frees him. Returning to King Arthur's court, Sir La Côte becomes Lord of Pendragon Castle, and marries the maiden Maledisant.

Returning to Sir Tristram, we find La Beale Isond keenly disappointed at his marriage to her sister. Writing to Sir Tristram, she beseeches him to return with his bride to his court. Meanwhile Sir Tristram is in the forest when he is met by the Lady of the Lake, who requests him to rescue King Arthur from a false lady. This he accomplishes, but refuses to disclose his identity to the king. He sails into Cornwall, and is welcomed by Isond. He discovers that Sir Kehydiers is in love with her. Thinking her a traitress, Sir Tristram puts Sir Kehydiers to flight, and then in despair he departs into the forest. He becomes insane, and lives with the shepherds, the while he kills the giant Tawless who has attacked a knight and his lady. Meanwhile at the court of King Mark it is rumoured that Sir Tristram is dead, and but for the king, Isond would have taken her life. King Mark, hearing of the madman killing the giant, has him brought to the castle. Not recognizing him as Sir Tristram, the king orders every care and nourishment to be given him, and soon Tristram recovers. Isond, desirous of beholding this strange man of whom she hears, goes with her hound to see him. Immediately the hound recognizes Sir Tristram as his old master, which causes the queen exceeding joy. Subsequently King Mark banishes Sir Tristram from Cornwall. Landing in England Sir

Tristram with Sir Dinaden discovers a plot against Sir Launcelot, and succeeds in preventing it, slaying the culprits. Time passes on, and one day Sir Tristram falls asleep by a well, and when there is met by a damsel with letters from Isond. Upon reading them he promises to reply after the tournament of the maidens which is due to take place. Entering the tourney in disguise, Sir Tristram meets with success, and after the first battle is over he wins the prize. The following day he goes over from King Arthur's side, to the King of Northgallis, that he might be revenged of Sir Palomides who is on Arthur's side. Having again achieved much success, and won renown, he hastens into the field to escape detection.

On the third day of the tourney, Sir Tristram resumes the same position, and he succeeds in unhorsing Sir Palomides. Sir Tristram continues to do much execution, until he is assailed by Sir Lancelot, who wounds him seriously, causing him to withdraw from the field. But feeling impatient, Sir Tristram returns, defeating Sir Palomides. In doing so his identity is disclosed. No sooner had Sir Tristram retired from the field, than Sir Lancelot is awarded the prize. He refuses it, and yields it to Sir Tristram. Sir Lancelot with the king and other knights go in search of Tristram, but fail to locate his whereabouts. The searchers return to Arthur's court, and seal a compact that they will not rest until Sir Tristram is found. Meanwhile Sir Palomides riding in the forest has a fall and is conveyed to the house in which are also Sir Tristram and Sir Dinaden. Later the three knights are imprisoned by their host, who is told that one of his guests killed two of his sons at the tourney. On signs of acute sickness, the three knights are released. The three depart in different directions, and Sir Tristram in lodging at a castle over night is made Queen Morgan's prisoner. The following day, on promising to defend her banner, she presents him with a symbolic shield, and he is released. Sir Tristram then hastens to a tournament, at which his shield is the centre of attraction.

Book X. Doing much execution, Tristram jousts with King Arthur, whom he severely wounds. He then departs into the forest, meeting with Palomides, whom he secures from ten knights. Sir Tristram and Palomides in departing from each other arrange to joust at a later date, which they do, without either being successful, consequently they become friends. Having continued on his journey Tristram jousts unknowing with Sir Lancelot, on which occasion their identity is disclosed. Then Lancelot brings Tristram to the court of King Arthur, where he is made welcome. Meanwhile King Mark, hearing of Tristram's popularity, decides to seek him, that by treachery he might be slain. Meeting with many adventures on his way, King Mark proves himself none other than a coward and a murderer. He, having slain several just knights, is brought before Arthur, to whom he appeals for mercy. At about this time Arthur hears of his sister's (Queen Morgan le Fay's) cruelty towards his knights at her castle. He commands several knights to assail her, which they successfully do, and succeed in abolishing the wicked custom of the place. The king announces a joust at which tourney Sir Lamorak defeats many

Knights of the Round Table, causing Arthur to congratulate him, to the displeasure of Sir Gawaine and his followers. At the request of Tristram, King Mark, by Arthur's commands, promises to love Tristram, and take him into Cornwall. Meanwhile Percival, the son of King Pellinore, appears at the court, desirous of knighthood. King Arthur having conferred the order on Percival, a maiden commands him to arise and follow her. Bringing him to the Castle Perilous, she makes him its overlord. Arthur hears of Sir Gaharis having slain his own mother, who is loved by Sir Lamorak. The king, feeling angered, banishes Sir Gaharis from the court, who pursues Sir Lamorak, intent on his slaughter. Sir Dinaden visits Sir Palomides bearing the news of Tristram's arrival in Cornwall. Meanwhile the king and his queen and Sir Lancelot receive letters from Tristram. In replying the king and Lancelot warn Tristram to beware of King Mark's treachery. King Mark also receives letters from the same source, and is much enraged at the contents, which betray his intentions towards Tristram. Replying, he rebukes Arthur with the reminder that he also can manage his household. Arthur and Lancelot annoyed at Mark's letter, the latter entrusts Sir Dinaden to compose a lay on Mark, sending Eliot the harper before him. Enraged at the harper's audacity, Mark demands an explanation. The harper in defence states that he is sent by Sir Dinaden, thereupon he is banished from the castle. Shortly afterwards King Mark and his lords are threatened, and but for Tristram, who slew the king's assailant, Sir Elias, they would have been lost. Mark,

in a fit of jealousy, murders Boudin his brother, whose wife Anglides he put to flight with her young son, Alisander, who at his coming of age is knighted, when his mother charges him to avenge his father's death. Then Sir Alisander departs for London, that he might enter Arthur's service. Proceeding on his journey he meets with many adventures, falling into the clutches of Morgan le Fay, who makes him prisoner. He however escapes by the aid of Alice la Beale Pilgrim, whom he marries, and by whom he has a son. Arriving at Arthur's court he is hailed with pleasure. Sir Galahalt, by the king's permission, announces a tournament, in which Sir Launcelot is conspicuous by his prowess. The important event, on the fourth day of the tourney, is the encounter between the King with the Hundred Knights, and those of the Round Table, ending in victory for the latter. Sir Palomides, causing much destruction amongst Arthur's court, is assailed by Sir Lamorak, who defeats him. The seventh day's tourney ends after a brilliant display in Lancelot carrying off the prize.

Returning to King Mark and Tristram the former, desirous of Tristram's end, arranges a masked tourney. This fails in its purpose, since his nephew is too skilful. Then in despair Mark, feigning sympathy with his nephew, succeeds in drugging him, and casting him into prison. The uncle is, however, made to realize his brutal conduct by the revolt of his subjects. He then forges letters purporting to have come from the Pope, requesting Mark and his army to go unto Jerusalem, and subdue the Saracens. These he sends to the imprisoned Tristram, who refuses to serve his uncle, and discovers their fraudulent manufacture. Sir Tristram is then released by Sir Percival, but soon after is again cast into prison through his love for La Beale Isond, who very soon releases her lover, and they both take ship for England, where Sir Tristram jousts in a tourney with Sir Lancelot. Succeeding in winning favour, he discloses his identity to Arthur and Lancelot, who both rejoice exceedingly.

While hunting one day Tristram hears of Mark's imprisonment by his own knights. Then follow many encounters. Meeting with Sir Dinaden he refuses to joust, but on pursuing their way Sir Palomides assails them. Tristram, knowing Sir Palomides' hate towards him, overthrows him. Palomides promises true fellowship for ever. On approaching the Castle Lonezep Tristram hears of the death of Sir Lamorak at the hands of Sir Mordred. Coming to Humber Bank, Tristram and Palomides espy a rich vessel, wherein they find the dead body of King Hermance, in whose hand is a letter. Tristram, reading it, is loath to voice its request which implores the finder to avenge the dead king on his enemies. For this achievement his castle and estate will be the reward. Seeing it impossible in face of circumstances to comply with the letter, Tristram charges Sir Palomides with the mission of revenge. Sir Palomides then proceeds on his errand, and sailing down the Humber eventually comes to a castle high up on the seashore, where he is made welcome. He is then told of the treachery of the late Hermance's sons, and how in slaying him the king commanded that a knight of the court of Arthur should avenge him and his people of his

sons' brutal deed. Palomides departs into the Red City, where he encounters his enemy. After a long and grim struggle, both sons are slain, and Palomides is acclaimed king. He, however, sets sail for Arthur's court, and meeting with Tristram, relates his adventure. The following day Tristram, Palomides, and other knights, accompanied by La Beale Isond and her suite, set out for Lonezep. Having pitched their tents Palomides successfully jousts with Sir Gilihodin, Sir Gawaine, and others.

A tourney is announced at which Arthur and his knights are well represented, and where Tristram defeats Arthur, and Palomides overthrows Lancelot, eventually winning the prize. On the second day's battle, Palomides crosses over to the opposing force, as he fears Tristram, whose ranks he had left. He, however, disguises himself afresh, and assails Tristram, who after much difficulty succeeds in unhorsing his opponent. The prize for the day goes to Tristram. Returning to their pavilions, La Beale Isond complains to Tristram of Sir Palomides' treachery towards him, but he takes little heed. The following day's battle brings to a head the quarrel between Tristram and Palomides. The tournament terminates, and all depart. Palomides, on his journey, encounters with a knight, whom he fights for the love of a lady, after which he is imprisoned for slaying another knight. Tied to a horse he is hastened to a castle. Fortunately Tristram hears of Palomides' plight, and succeeds in rescuing him. Sir Palomides' love for La Beale Isond is so great that, realizing her indifference, he decides to end his life, and departing into a forest falls asleep and sings of his love. Meanwhile Tristram happens to ride past and hearing the sleeper, wakes him. Both enraged through jealousy, they agree to fight on a certain day. In the interval, however, Tristram is hurt, which causes the postponement of the duel. Sir Palomides hearing of Tristram's accident, departs. After Tristram is healed he pursues his opponent, but fails to locate him.

Book XI. Returning to Sir Lancelot du Lake who successfully battles with a dragon, and releases a lady from enchantment, he becomes the guest of King Pellis, cousin unto Joseph of Arimathie, on whose daughter, Elaine, he begot Galahad. King Arthur returned from the continent after a successful war against Claudius, gives a feast, to which comes Elaine, of whom Queen Guenever is jealous. Rebuking Lancelot because of his love towards Elaine, the queen causes him to flee from the castle into a forest, where he goes mad. The queen in her sorrow commands a search to be made for him. In the meantime Lancelot slays Sir Goodewin, who had killed one of his squires. Afterwards Sir Percival jousts with Sir Ector, both being severely wounded. A maiden appears before them, carrying the Holy Grail through which power they are healed.

Book XII. Meanwhile Sir Lancelot wandering in the country comes one day to a pavilion and fights with a knight, its occupant, who is defeated. Realizing his victor to be Lancelot, the knight sends him to Sir Selivant who clothes him, and with him Lancelot remains. Seeing Selivant being assailed one day, Lancelot rushes forward and rescues him. Shortly afterwards Lancelot leaves the castle, and still in his insane condition engages in a chase after a boar which attacks him, but eventually getting near the boar he slays it. Almost exhausted through loss of blood, a hermit succeeds in saving Lancelot's life. Escaping from the hermitage, he comes to the city of Cadin and running into the castle court, is captured as a madman, the inmates little knowing him to be Sir Lancelot. Some time afterwards, King Pellis's nephew has the madman brought into the castle, and clothing him in his old robes, sends Lancelot into the garden. He falls asleep and is discovered by the king and his daughter Elaine. Recognizing their captive to be Lancelot, they carry him into the castle, where by the aid of the Holy Grail, he is cured of his insanity. Lancelot feeling ashamed of his recent behaviour, changes his name, desiring to be known as La Chevalier Mal Fet. He is presented with the Castle of Bliant, on the Joyous Isle, and with Elaine and their suite departs to dwell therein. Sir Percival coming to the castle jousts with Lancelot, whose name is discovered by Percival disclosing his own. Sir Lancelot then departs for Arthur's court, so that his son Galahad might receive his knighthood. His reception is of a most cordial nature. Counselled by La Beale Isond, Sir Tristram departs for the feast in honour of Lancelot's return. On his journey he meets with Sir Palomides, and remembering past differences successfully jousts with him, who being a Saracen is then christened at Carlisle. Pursuing their way the two knights arrive at Arthur's Court.

Book XIII. Sir Galahad having

S

been installed in the Siege Perilous, is visited by Arthur and his knights, who take him down to the river in the centre of which is a stone containing a sword, which no other knight is able to dislodge but himself. Having secured the sword, Sir Galahad along with the king and his knights return to the court, where in fulfilment of a prophecy, there appears in their midst the vision of the Holy Grail. The king perceiving their departure on such a perilous expedition, and realizing the loss to the court, experiences a feeling of dismay. Sir Galahad having joined in the quest, comes to an abbey wherein was King Bagdemagus, who informs him of a white shield, bearing in the centre a red cross, which on finding Bagdemagus presumes to claim despite his disqualification for such an honour. Girding around him the shield, he goes into the country, and being badly wounded, is brought back to the monastery, when the shield is, as prophesied, restored to its rightful claimant. Galahad wearing the shield, proceeds on his quest, and meeting with a knight, he is told of the origin and adventures of the white shield, how the knight Joseph of Arimathie, who took our Lord from the Cross, and departing with a large party from Jerusalem, arrived at Sarras where King Evelake was engaged in war against the Saracens. He, by the advice of Joseph, pledged his faith in the Holy Trinity, and made a shield which bestowed great power upon its owner. Joseph, accompanied by King Evelake, left for Britain. Soon after their arrival Joseph took ill, and bleeding from the nose, had the shield brought to him. In its centre he outlined a Holy Cross in his own blood,

declaring that the shield should be preserved until the last of his line was born, who would be known as Galahad. Joseph then died, and having related the story, the White Knight takes his leave of Galahad.

Resuming the journey with his squire, Sir Galahad is led by a monk to a tomb from which leapt a demoniac being, which would have attacked him but for his holy quest. The monk explains to Galahad that the creature betokens the sin of man for whose sake Christ died. Galahad then knights his squire, who is found to be Melias de Lile, the son of the King of Denmark. Proceeding, Melias is injured by a wicked knight, and taken to a priest, who heals him. Meanwhile Galahad successfully jousts with Sir Lancelot, who does not recognize his opponent until after Galahad's departure. Coming into a forest in which is an old chapel, from the broken door of which shines the light of many candles, Sir Lancelot falls asleep, dreaming that a wounded knight enters the church, where he is healed by the power of the Holy Grail, which appears as a vision. The knight recovering takes Lancelot's horse and sword, going on his way. Awaking, Lancelot realizes his loss, and the truth of the dream, and that his worldly sins are many, and that for such a Holy Mission he is all unfitted. He departs into a hermitage, and confesses his sins.

Book XIV. Meanwhile Sir Percival in search of Sir Galahad comes to the house of his aunt, who informs him of his mother's death, and relates Merlin's prophecy concerning the search for the Holy Grail. Realizing that Galahad is the chosen one, to whom is allotted the discovery of the Grail, Sir Percival decides to befriend him, and on his aunt's instruction rides on his way. Coming to a monastery where he hears mass, Percival perceives in a bed a wounded man, who is found to be King Evelake. He had landed in Britain with Joseph three hundred years ago, pursued the search of the Holy Grail, and having trespassed in the search too far, is stricken blind by the Lord, and not until Galahad had achieved the Grail would he die. Sir Percival departs, more eager in the search for Galahad than ever. He is assailed by twenty knights. Galahad strangely enough comes to his assistance, and putting the assailants to flight, hastens away before Percival could thank him. Feeling dejected over Galahad's hasty departure, Percival wanders on, and losing his horse through jousting with a knight, he is confronted by a strange woman, who supplies him with a fresh steed. The horse being bewitched leads him to a fiery and tempestuous sea, and shakes his rider off. He then plunges into the raging torrent. Percival's bewilderment is increased by the appearance of wild beasts, which approach him from all sides. Descending into the valley he witnesses an encounter between a serpent and a lion. Seeing the lion in difficulty, Percival slays the serpent. During the night, there come to him in a dream two ladies each riding on a beast, foretelling a battle which he will fight. Arising he comes to a ship wherein is a holy man, who confirms the dream. The following day another ship appears in which is a lady who informs Percival of Sir Galahad, and his adventures. He falls in love with the lady, who mysteriously disappears in a thick volume of

smoke. Feeling enraged at his faithlessness he enters the ship of the holy man, which had reappeared, and sails away.

Book XV. Meanwhile Sir Lancelot journeys from the hermitage. He sees therein a dead priest. He, as a token of good fortune, procures for himself some hair, which is cut from the dead man's head. Falling asleep by a cross he dreams that seven kings and two knights appear before him, appealing to God for recompense for their earthly achievements, when there descends out of the clouds a spirit surrounded by angels chastising them for their vain love of earthly glory. Arising, Sir Lancelot comes to a hermit, and relates his vision. The hermit describes the seven kings as Lancelot's ancestors, and one of the knights as himself who was of mighty force. The other knight is Galahad, begotten of Lancelot, who would achieve much. Lancelot submitting to his adviser's entreaties, becomes humbled, and as a holy man. The following morning Lancelot goes on his way, meeting with a company of strangely apparelled knights, who were split into two sections, and were fighting fiercely. Seeing the defeat of the weaker side, he joins them, but is eventually overthrown. With a sad and heavy heart, he departs from their company. Falling asleep under a cross there appears before him in a vision an old man, who rebukes him for his lack of faith and his evil will. Arising with an uneasy mind, he hearkens to the words of a prophet, who likens the tourney to a battle between the pure and the impure, and because Lancelot took the side of the impure knights, who were overcome, he is told that he yet lacks faith, and is still evil. Departing with renewed spiritual strength, Lancelot suffers himself to go through a burning stream, and to be beaten by a black knight in the name of the Lord.

Book XVI. We next turn to Sir Gawaine and Sir Ector, who both in search of the Holy Grail are despondent at their lack of success. They come to an old church, which they enter, and where they fall asleep. A vision appears before them signifying their unfittedness for such a sacred quest. Awaking, they are much afraid at an apparition which passes through the church, bearing a bright candle saying unto them, " Knights of evil faith, and poor belief, thou shalt not come to the adventure of the Sangrëal." Desiring an explanation to this mystery, they sorrowfully seek the aid of a hermit. On their way Sir Gawaine slays his brother, Sir Unwaine. They arrive at the hermitage, where the hermit explains the vision, and the apparition which he tells them signifies the Holy Ghost. After this good counsel they depart from the hermit. Sir Bors riding in the quest, meets with a hermit, who advises his confession, since he is on such a holy mission. This Sir Bors agrees to, and coming to a chapel he is made fit to pursue such a sacred purpose. Arrayed in a pure vestment, as a sign of his chastity, the hermit sets Bors on his way. Then follow many trials and temptations, which Bors with patience, and meekness, suffers, that he might achieve the quest. So strong is his faith, and so meek does he become during the mission, that he suffers his brother to treat him with much cruelty. During their quarrel there appears a bright flame which descends upon their shields utterly destroying

them. Thus strengthened by this mystic occurrence, which Bors attributes to God, he continues his journey. A vision appearing before him one night directs him to the coast where on entering a ship he meets Sir Percival.

Book XVII. We now return to Sir Galahad, who after rescuing Percival rides on to the Castle Carbonek, where a maiden commands him to board a ship. Doing as she bade him, Galahad meets with Sir Percival and Sir Bors. Sailing away they are driven near to a rock against which was another ship. Entering it they discover by the side of a bed a richly jewelled sword. The maiden who had accompanied them, relates the history of the mystic sword, how that it had been connected with Cain and Abel, Solomon, and David, and how it had wounded many who tried to bear it. Then Percival and Bors try to draw it from its scabbard, but they failing Galahad essays to do likewise. Realizing the nature of the weapon on which is written, " Who that draweth me shall never fail of shame of his body, nor wounded to the death, but no man shall grip the handles but one, and he shall pass all others," Galahad is induced to wear the sword. Leaving the ship, they come to a chapel. The maiden who accompanies them, and who is Percival's sister, sacrifices her life by bleeding that a sick lady might, through her blood, be healed. Placing the lady's body on board a barge it is sent to the Holy City of Sarras where the Sangrëal would be achieved. The three comrade knights then separate. Sir Lancelot at this time is commanded in a vision to go into the sea, where he should find a ship into which he must enter. Arising, and coming to the ship he finds therein Percival's sister. Taking from her dead hand, the writ which had been placed there by her mourners, he discovers how she had sacrificed her life. Remaining there for several months, Galahad arrives there causing Lancelot to rejoice.

Galahad is commanded by a voice to leave his father that the quest might be fulfilled, and departs. Lancelot, who with the ship is driven far away, comes to a rock, on which stands a castle. Commanded in a vision to leave the ship, and go to the castle, he sets forth. Meeting with a dwarf he is sorely wounded, but vanquishes his enemy. A voice reproves him for his lack of faith, and casting his armour away, he enters the Castle Carbonek. Coming to a chamber, Lancelot hears from within a beautiful singer, and thinking it to be the guardian of the Holy Grail, he tries to enter. Failing to unfasten the door, Lancelot sinks on to his knees and prays to God.

Arising, the door opens, and Lancelot stands spellbound at the scene. The room is flooded with light, from the centre of which appears a silver table, holding the Holy Vessel, which is covered with a rich cloth. Around it he perceives angels bearing candles, and from their midst, and hovering over the sacred vessel appears a priest, on each side of whom are two men, while another he holds suspended in the air. Afraid lest the suspended object should fall, Lancelot, forgetting his surroundings, rushes forward, but is cast to the ground by a hot, scorching breath which renders him insensible. He is carried outside of the chamber, where he lies until the inmates of the castle discover him. Placed upon a bed, Lancelot lies unconscious for several days. Recovering from his comatose condition, and after resting a while, he takes his leave of his friend King Pellis. Meanwhile Sir Bors had arrived at the castle in search of Lancelot who is his brother. Lancelot returns to Arthur, and relates his adventures, and how he was permitted into the presence of the Holy Grail.

Galahad, Percival, and Bors meet, and the trio enter the Castle Carbonek, where they behold the Holy Grail, and enter into holy communion. Commanded by a voice, which comes into their midst, they seat themselves at a table, and partaking of meat and drink from the holy vessel, enter into the spiritual atmosphere of the ceremony. Our Lord then appears and commands Galahad to carry the Grail forth from the castle into the Holy City of Sarras. Quitting the country with the sacred vessel, and taking the symbolic sword, Galahad accompanied by his two comrades arrives in the land of Babylon. Proceeding to Sarras, they heal a deformed man. King Estorause hearing that enchanted knights have come to his land, casts them into prison, where during their confinement they are sustained by the Holy Grail. Soon the king dies, and they are released. Galahad assuming the kingship, is shortly afterwards called away. Realizing that his time has come, Galahad bids farewell to his noble companions, and from their midst he ascends into heaven. Soon after Percival follows. Sir Bors in fulfilment of the prophecy returns to the realm of Logris to relate to Arthur and his court the adventure and mission of the Holy Grail, in the fulfilment of which Galahad and Percival had entered into the spiritual world.

After the adventure of the Holy Grail, Guenever gives a banquet to the wanderers. Meanwhile she has driven Lancelot from the court for his apathy toward her. A tragic sequel to the banquet is the death of Sir Patrise, due to poisoning. Sir Penil, hating Sir Gawaine, had hoped to dispose of his enemy by injecting poison into apples, which he knew Gawaine to be fond of. By misfortune Patrise becomes the victim of his treachery. The queen is immediately suspected, and in a fit of madness the dead man's brother, Sir Marden, charges Guenever with treason. As there is no knight present who would defend her, she appeals to Arthur, who, regretting Lancelot's absence, advises her to seek the aid of Sir Bors. Realizing the consequences should she fail to exonerate herself, she gains the favour of Bors, who reports to Lancelot the predicament of the queen. He is deprived of the adventure by Lancelot, who enters the field of combat in disguise. The challenger appears, and assailing the queen's defender is defeated. The queen is then released, and she discovers her saviour to be her old lover. Later, however, the mystery is cleared up by an enchantress who exposes Sir Penil as the murderer. Sir Marden is then appeased by the queen. Guenever riding in the country one day is captured by Sir Meliagrance. Sending a page to Lancelot, the queen is released, and being pardoned for his treason, Meliagrance offers his hospitality to the queen and her company. He on the following day accuses the queen of falsity toward her husband. Challenging his host to joust before Arthur, Lancelot is

entrapped in the castle, but is subsequently released by a lady. Arthur meanwhile is told of the scandal. Lancelot succeeds in slaying his treacherous enemy. Hardly had this scandal subsided, when through jealousy Sir Gawaine discloses to Arthur the familiarity of his queen toward Lancelot. The king gives the knight and his comrades leave to capture the lovers when together. Lancelot and the queen are trapped, but Lancelot succeeds in escaping by fighting his way through the spies. Arriving in the company of Sir Bors, he relates his misfortune, and realizing the situation of the queen, he devises a scheme of rescue. Bors, his brother, offers his help along with other knights. A spy is sent to the court that Lancelot might be prepared for action. The king dooms his wife to be burnt at the stake. Preparations are made, and the spy reports to Lancelot. He accompanied by his followers attacks the assembled throng, inflicting great slaughter. Rushing to the stake, Lancelot frees Guenever, and with her he rides away to Joyous Gard. Arthur decides to assail Lancelot's castle. Lancelot prepares for a siege. Arthur marches forward. A state of war follows, which, lasting for some time, is terminated by the intervention of the Pope through the Bishop of Rochester, who causes Lancelot to deliver Guenever up to Arthur. Forming a brilliant procession, he marches into Carlisle, and presents Guenever to Arthur before his court. Lancelot is then assailed by Gawaine. Lancelot in despair collects his loyal followers together, and departs across the sea unto Benwick, dividing his new possessions amongst his knights.

Arthur hearing of this sets sail with a great army. Landing on the shores of Benwick, and destroying everything which opposes his progress, he arrives at the city of Benwick, where Lancelot and his followers are lodged. A siege is proclaimed. Lancelot appeals to Arthur to return, but Gawaine prevailing over his uncle, prevents a reconciliation. Gawaine, boasting of his prowess, incites his enemy to joust, who defeating him on two occasions, causes Arthur and his host to depart for England. Gawaine dies during the journey back, and expresses a wish that he might receive Lancelot's forgiveness. Meanwhile, during Arthur's absence, his son, Mordred, had assumed the kingship and had attempted by false means to marry Guenever, who flees to the Tower of London. Arthur and his army are assailed by Mordred on landing at Dover. Hostilities between the rival armies commence, the first battle deciding against Mordred. Dreaming that he sees Gawaine, Arthur is advised not to meet in the combat with his son, until a month hence. Through the influence of an adder, however, the treaty is never fulfilled. The rival armies meeting together, a terrible carnage ensues, Arthur driving his enemy into Cornwall. Still pursuing Mordred, Arthur causes him to turn. Mordred inflicts the death-blow upon the king, who in turn slays his treacherous son. Arthur dies, and is interred at Glastonbury. The queen, hearing of her husband's death, becomes a nun at Almesbury. Lancelot returning from Benwick hears of Arthur's and Mordred's death. After paying homage at his late chief's tomb, he visits Guenever who persuades him to become a monk. To this

he agrees, and going to Glastonbury enters the monastery. Other noble knights follow his example. Several years having passed he is commanded by a vision to go into Almesbury, and return with Guenever's body, which is to be buried with her husband. Arising, he does as he is commanded, and returning places Guenever's body in the tomb of Arthur.

Soon after Lancelot himself dies, and by his request is buried at Joyous Gard. The remaining knights each depart to their respective lands. Sir Constantine, Sir Cador's son, is chosen King of England.

MORUNG. Of Nifland. (*Vide* " Gudrun Lay," under second portion, " Hagan and Hettel.") He it was who first told King Hettel of the beauty of Hilda, daughter of Hagan, and suggested that Hettel should seek to wed her. He was a member of the embassy which brought her to Hettel. He took part in the struggles described in " Gudrun " (*q.v.*), as the third division of the *Gudrun Lay*.

MOYS, MOYSES. Moys attempts to sit down in Galahad's seat at the Round Table, and is swallowed up by the earth. It is supposed to be reserved for a very holy man— Sir Galahad—and would seem to typify the personal absence of Christ from the table.

MURCIA, QUEEN OF. (*Vide* "Florice and Blanchfleur.") Wife to Prince Felix, ruler of Murcia, and mother of Florice. She befriended Topase, and, following the birth of Blanchfleur, she fostered the child.

MURDER OF THE MASTER OF SAINT IAGO. This mediæval Spanish romance tells how Don Fadrique (Frederick), a brother of Don Pedro, King of Castille, called "The Cruel," was one of two natural sons of the King Alphonso and a lady of the powerful family of Guzman. This woman was actually proclaimed his queen, and her sons were brought up in the Palace as princes, the real wife and mother of Pedro being treated with contempt. At the death of King Alphonso, Pedro became king, and Donna de Guzman and her sons retired to various strongholds to protect themselves from his authority. Pedro was suddenly seized by illness, and Donna de Guzman and her sons were suspected of intriguing for possession of the throne should he die. On his recovery, his mother the Queen Dowager so persuaded him, it is said, of the truth of this, that Donna de Guzman was arrested and put to death. Don Fadrique, who had obtained the rank of the Order of Saint Iago, fled to a fortress in the Coimbra, and his brother Henry to Arragon. Castille was continually in a state of rebellion through these baleful influences and also in consequence of Pedro's own cruel behaviour. Don Fadrique made friends with Pedro, and accepted an invitation to Seville to take part in a tournament. Pedro, although married to Blanche of Bourbon, deserted her for Maria de Padilla, a woman who exerted a wicked influence over him, and who is said to have instigated the cruel murder of Saint Iago in the year 1358.

There is a peculiarity in the construction of the ballad which describes this story. Fabrique at the commencement narrates his old story, and after he is executed another voice takes it up. Fadrique receives a letter from King Pedro inviting him to join in a tournament at Seville. He takes spearmen, horses and mules with him, the journey being accomplished within a week. But it has been disastrous to him, as he loses horses, mules, his fine dagger, and a faithful page is drowned in a stream. On his arrival at the gate of Seville a priest warns him from entering, and although he notices that no arrangements have been made for the tournament, and his followers are not allowed to enter the town with him, he walks up to Pedro who receives him coldly, calling him a traitor and ordering him to stand off, declaring that his time on earth was short, and that his lady required his head as a New Year's gift. He summons a yeoman to draw his sword, and the master's head is cut off and placed in a charger which is presented to Padilla as a gift from the king. Padilla having an intense hatred for Fadrique shows it in the manner she treats his head, for, after seizing it by the clotted hair, she heaps all kinds of scornful and extravagant imprecations upon it, and then flings it out of the window, urging her dog to lick the face. The mastiff tosses the head to and fro and picks it to the bone, a gaping crowd looking on. King Pedro, hearing the noise without, asks the cause of the disturbance. He is told that the master's head was torn and eaten by the mastiff, and an old woman who had nursed the two brothers upbraids him for his cruelty to his brother. He now rues the vow he had carried into effect, and disgusted with the vindictive Padilla he rushes up to her bower and carries her to a dark and deep dungeon, hurling all manner of curses upon her for being the cause of the dark and bloody deed.

MURDOUR, SIR. (*Vide* "Bevis of Hampton.") Brother of the Emperor of Allemayne and lover of Sir Guy's wife. He slew Sir Guy married his widow, and took his lands. Killed in battle by Sir Bevis.

MURIAS. In Irish romance, one of the four great cities whence came the Danaans (*q.v.*). From Murias came the cauldron of the Irish god, Dagda, a vessel that could feed a host without requiring to be refilled.

MURNA OF THE WHITE NECK. In Irish romance wife of Cumhal and mother of Finn (*q.v.*).

N

NABON, SIR. Lord of the Isle. Mentioned in Arthurian romance as a giant. He was subsequently slain by Sir Tristram (*q.v.*). His possessions then went to Sir Sagwandes. (*Vide* "Morte d'Arthur.")

NAGELRING. (*Vide* "Dietrich of Bern.") A sword presented to Dietrich by a dwarf. It proved its worthiness in his battles with giants.

NAGLING. The sword which King Hygelak gave to Beowulf (*q.v.*), on his slaying the Nixie. (*Vide* "Hygelak," and "Breka.")

NAISI. In Irish romance the son of Usna. (*Vide* "Deirdre.")

NAPLES, KING OF. A character in *The History of Roswall and Lillian* (*q.v.*), and father of Roswall. He sends his son to the King of Bealm as a punishment for releasing three lords whom he had imprisoned. Trusting his steward (*q.v.*) to accompany his disobedient son to the court of his ally, he does not live to realize the disloyal nature of his wicked servant.

NASCIENS (1). The Hermit King. He seems to have been the spiritual adviser to the "Quest of the Holy Grail." Many references are made to him in Arthurian lore. His first appearance would seem to show that he was baptized at the same time as King Evelach, and that he changed his original name, Seraphe, into that of Nasciens. Several miracles would also appear to be connected with his name, and for a fuller account concerning him we would refer to the various articles on the Grail legend. It is said that he was the first man to behold the Holy Grail, and was the ancestor of nine kings, the eighth generation of which was "as foul as a dog," owing to Nasciens' carnal sins in the days of his youth—the ninth of his line was Sir Galahad (*q.v.*) himself. In Furnivall's text we read of him advising "that no knight entering on the quest of the Holy Grail is to have with him his lady or damsel—the quest is no earthly one." In another part of the narrative Nasciens explains a dream to the heroes of the Quest. Gawain dreams he sees in a meadow one hundred and fifty bulls, all spotted, save three, one being dingy, the other two being pure white. Nasciens explains that those spotted are the ones stained by sin, the three unspotted ones are the Grail achievers, two white virgins—Galahad and Perceval—one dingy, having once sinned carnally, Bors. It is further stated in the narrative that where Nasciens is buried there Sir Galahad's shield should be kept.

NASCIENS (2). Son of Celidoine, and the daughter of King Label called after his grandfather of the same name.

NASCIENS (3). Grandson of Celidoine.

NAYMES OF BAVARIA (1). A peer of Charlemagne, celebrated for his wisdom as for his valour. In *The Song of Roland* he offers to be Charles's ambassador to Marsile, the paynim King of Saragossa, but the emperor denies his request on the ground that he is a wise man, " and shall not go so far from him." In *Ferumbras* he is alluded to as one of the twelve peers sent by Charlemagne to demand the liberation of his nephews. He was imprisoned at Aigremor, and having his beard set on fire by King Lukafere, he was so angry that he threw him on the hearth and let him burn to death.

NECHTAN, SONS OF. Warriors of Connacht, who had slain more men of Ulster than were living when Cuchulain (*q.v.*) looked down upon their dun. With his two arms the great hero wrenched away the pillar that stood before the fortress of Nechtan, and round which was a collar bidding every warrior-man to hold it *geis* (or taboo), not to depart without challenging one of the sons to single combat. Both pillar and collar he flung into the river that flowed hard by. Then one by one he slew the brothers, and fastened their heads to his chariot.

NEMED. In Irish legend son of Agnoman. He was the second man after the Partholanians (*vide* " Partholan ") to settle in Ireland. Of his people who wandered upon the sea for a year and a half only himself with four men and four

women were left to land in Ireland. He won four battles against the Fomorians (*q.v.*), but, with many of his people, died of a plague. The Fomorians then seized the rule of Ireland with a strong and cruel hand ; till the oppressed under the leadership of Fergus revolted. Finally only thirty of the Nemedians survived. These, according to ancient belief, left Ireland to die ; according to a later tradition, the Britain family of the Nemedians left its name to the Island of Great Britain, while two others returned to Ireland, at a later period, as the Firbolgs (*q.v.*), and the Danaans (*q.v.*).

NEMGLAN. In Irish romance the king of the birds of the immortal father of Conary Mor (*q.v.*). When a lad, Conary, after playing with his foster-brothers on the Plain of Liffey, had returned towards Dublin, when before him he saw a flock of beautiful birds. Upon his aiming his catapult at them they turned into armed men, but Nemglan, their chief, protected him and related his strange history and declared his *geis* or those actions of which he must beware.

NENNIUS. (*Vide* " Historia Britonum.") It is only on the authority of the two extant prologues to the *Historia Britonum* that we ascribe its authorship to one, Nennius, of whom we know little more than the name. It is, however, probable that he was a native of South Wales, who amplified and redacted about the year 826, a compilation of the seventh or eighth century, consisting of extracts from a *Life of St. Germain*, to which he added a short *History of Britain*, written in 679, which he extended, but which had been added to before his time. He is described in one of the prologues to the work as a disciple of Elhadus or Elvoduzus, Bishop of North Wales, who died in 809, and the date of the original MS., of which the authorship is assigned to him, is given as 858 A.D., but no copies are known earlier than the twelfth century. But the earliest MS. ascribes the work to one " Marcus the Anachorite, a bishop of the British nation," who wrote in 946 or 947 A.D. It is probable that Nennius was only one of the several editors of the work which bears his name.

NEROVENS, SIR DE LILE. A knight of Sir Lancelot (*q.v.*).

NESSA. In Irish romance, daughter of Echid Yellow-heel, wife of Fachtna (*q.v.*), mother of Conor (*q.v.*).

NIAM. In Irish romance wife of Connal of the Victories (*q.v.*); she tended Cuchulain (*q.v.*) during the madness brought upon him by the children of the wizard Calatin (*q.v.*), till one of these by magic set her wandering.

NIBELUNGENLIED. Nibelungennoth, or Lay of the Niblungs. A great German epic cycle belonging in its earliest actual shape to the beginning of the thirteenth century (1210). Its detached portions, however, are considered to have been composed between 1190 and 1210, whilst a Latin original, founded on ballads, or folk songs, may have been compiled between 960 and 980. The chief difficulty connected with the cycle lies in the discrepancies found between it and the legend embodied in the Edda. The motives of the various characters are essentially different, and their actions by no means similar in the older and later versions of the tale. In its present shape it consists not of a mere collection of pieces put into sequence by a compiler, but of an actual fusion of previously existing elements. There is, indeed, great difference of opinion as to whether it was to be considered as one poem or as many, but the latter conclusion is almost certainly the correct one. The spirit of the poem is one of epic wrath. Destiny looms as terribly through its most auspicious passages as in the *Œdipus* or the *Antigone* It is, indeed, the equal of the *Iliad* in tragic intensity and awfulness of *denouement*. But in unity, proportion and general adequacy it is sadly lacking. There is little doubt that the *Nibelungenlied* is a reproduction of the *Lay of the Volsungs* (*q.v.*). The few points of difference lie in the change of names. Gunnar is Gunthar, Sigurd is Sigfried, Gudrun is Kriemhild. Like Sigurd, Sigfried has bathed his body in the dragon's blood, and only one spot between his shoulders is vulnerable. He is visibly the sunhero, as is his prototype of the Volsung tale. The poem is written in quatrains, rhymed couplet and couplet, not alternately, but evidently intended for quatrains, as the verse frequently overlaps at the second line, but regularly stops at the fourth. The normal number of syllables in a line is thirteen.

At Worms in Burgundy, the noble and beautiful maiden Kriemhild lived with her mother Ute and her three brothers, Gunther, Gernot and Giselher, whose Court includes many heroes, most noteworthy being Hagen von Tronei and his brother Dankwart the Swift, Volker of Alzeye, skilled alike with sword and fiddle, Margrave Eckwart, Ortwin of Metz,

Rumolt, the "cook-master," and many others. One night Kriemhild dreams of a falcon which she nurtures, till two eagles destroy it, which dream her mother interprets as foretelling for her a noble husband, whom "may God preserve lest thou lose him too early"; thus comes the first presentiment of the terrible woe that is to follow.

Meanwhile Sigfrid of the Netherlands, the son of Sigemund and Sigelinde, a young hero famed for his valour and comeliness, has been growing to manhood, wandering through the world, doing wonderful and mighty deeds, winning the sword and treasure of the Nibelungs (*q.v.*), conquering their King Alberich and gaining possession of his "cape of darkness." Important among his exploits was the slaying of a dragon in whose blood he bathed, coming forth invulnerable save at one spot, where, unknown to him, a linden-leaf had stuck between his shoulders so that the magic fluid did not protect him in that place. (For fuller details, *vide* "Sigfrid," and "Volsunga Saga.") Hearing of Kriemhild's beauty, Sigfrid sets out with his retinue to win her. Reaching Worms, he is received with honour, but not for a year does he see Kriemhild. He enters Gunther's service, and overcomes Luitgart, King of Denmark, and Luitger, King of Saxony, who had declared war against Burgundy; proving himself the hero of the fray, and his valour is recounted to Kriemhild, whose heart glows with love and admiration. At the festivities in celebration of the victory, Sigfrid meets Kriemhild for the first time; strong is their love for one another, and when Gunther seeks Sigfrid's aid in the winning of Brunhild of Iceland

(*q.v.*), Sigfrid makes it a condition that Gunther shall consent to his union with Kriemhild. Queen Brunhild, exceedingly beautiful, and of great strength, has made it a condition that whoever would wed her must first beat her in three trials of prowess, losing his head as a penalty of failure. Sigfrid makes an expedition to the land of the Nibelungs, whose King Alberich is under an oath of fealty to him, and returns with men and treasure. Taking Gunther's place and donning the "cloak of darkness" the hero wins the trials of strength on his friend's behalf, all men, and Brunhild herself, believing Gunther to have accomplished the feat. In Scandinavian Sagas, where this legend (originally a German one) is preserved in its pagan form—Brunhild was a Valkyr, or warmaiden of the great Teutonic God Wotan, who sent her to sleep with a prick of a magic thorn, and imprisoned her within a circle of flame, through which Sigfrid, the God of Nature, Springtide and the Sun, broke, delivering the captive and taking her as his wife, soon, however, departing from her. In the "Nibelungenlied" this mythic background is either presupposed or intentionally omitted, possibly through the influence of Christianity, but we are led to understand that Brunhild had a previous claim to Sigfrid's love, and when she comes to Worms, and is betrothed to Gunther, sadness and jealousy wring her heart on seeing Sigfrid and Kriemhild also exchange the kiss. On the night of her marriage to Gunther, she wrestles with him, conquering him easily and binding him with her girdle, and next day he appeals to Sigfrid for aid. So that night Sigfrid, wearing his magic cape, contends with the bride and over-comes her, she believing him to be Gunther. Sigfrid takes from her her girdle and ring, which he gives to Kriemhild. Sigfrid takes Kriem-hild back to his own land, where they live for many years, a son being born to them, whom they name Gunther, while Brunhild also has a child named Sigfrid. Some years later, however, Brunhild still thinking of Sigfrid, persuades Gunther, that it is time Sigfrid and Kriemhild visited their Court. Gunther yields, though fearful of his deception being discovered, and sends messengers to Sigfrid, who accompanied by Kriemhild, Sigmund and his retinue, comes to Gunther's Court. Soon, how-ever, Brunhild and Kriemhild quarrel concerning the respective standing of their husbands, and each declares she will take pre-cedence of the other in procession to church. At the Minster door the climax is reached, when Kriem-hild taunts Brunhild with the fact that Sigfrid had won and deserted her, showing the girdle and ring as proof, though indeed Sigfrid had said no such thing to Kriemhild, merely stating that the ring and girdle had belonged to Brunhild. Greatly distressed, Brunhild com-plains to her husband, and great is her wrath against Sigfrid for overcoming her on behalf of Gun-ther, and for betraying her to Kriemhild. Sigfrid is very angry with Kriemhild, and, protesting his innocence, appeases Gunther. Hagen, however, finds Brunhild weeping because of the insult, and revenge is determined upon. Ort-win and Gernot join in the plot, and Gunther, weakly and hesita-tingly, agrees also, Giselher alone endeavouring to dissuade them. So a false alarm of war is raised, and an expedition arranged.

When Hagen bids farewell to Kriemhild, she recommends Sig-frid to his care. Suspecting no evil, she tells him of her husband's vulnerable spot. He induces her to mark the place, by sewing a silk cross on her husband's tunic. The conspirators next announce that peace had been made, and a hunting expedition is organised. The poem dwells at length on the hunt and Sigfrid's exploits. Rest-ing after the chase, Hagen speaks of a fountain near, and he and Sigfrid race to it, followed by Gunther. Sigfrid courteously waits until Gunther has drunk, then stoops down to the spring, when Hagen suddenly plunges his spear through Kriemhild's silken cross. Sigfrid strikes at Hagen, but falls, mortally wounded. Dying, he reproaches his mur-derers, and commends Kriemhild to Gunther, if indeed she "can still be true to any one." Hagen, resenting the insult to Brunhild, places Sigfrid's body at Kriem-hild's door. Unspeakable is her grief when she finds her beloved husband dead—Sigmund and Sig-frid's retainers rush to arms, but Kriemhild bids them bide their time till they have the murderers in their power. The Burgundians pretend that Sigfrid was slain by robbers, but as Hagen approaches the body the wounds begin to bleed, and Kriemhild knows him for her husband's slayer. Grief and revenge possess Kriemhild's soul, rendering her indifferent even to her son, so that she refuses to leave the land where her be-loved one is buried. Giselher and Sigmund and their men return to the Netherlands, Eckwart re-maining "to serve his lady till his death."

For four years Kriemhild, speak-ing never a word to Gunther nor looking on Hagen, spends her time in a chamber near the Minster, where Sigfrid lies. To propitiate her, the Nibelung treasure is sent for, but she employs it to give magnificent gifts, till Hagen, fearing that her purpose is to win hearts and power to wreak her revenge, seizes it, and with Kriemhild's brothers sinks it in the Rhine, all swearing never to divulge the secret of its whereabouts. It is important to note at this point that when the treasure of the Nibelungs comes into the land of the Burgundians they take the name of " Nibelungen " in the same way that Sigfrid was called Lord of the Nibelungs on possessing their treasure and ruling them. For which reason this latter part of the poem was at the time of its composition called "Nibelungen Not," the whole now bearing the name " Nibelungenlied." (For fuller particulars and remarks regarding the Nibelung's hoard, *vide* " Nibelung.") Many years after the murder of Sigfrid, Helche, wife of Etzel, King of the Huns (*q.v.*), having died, he wishes to marry again, and his faithful Councillor Margrave Rudiger of Bechlarn suggests Kriemhild. Etzel despatches Rudiger to win her, and the Burgundians are all in favour of the marriage, save Hagen, who fears disaster should Kriemhild gain power. She herself will not think of consenting, till Rudiger suggests that if she has the Huns to defend her none dare insult her; immediately she makes Rudiger swear to avenge her wrongs, and he does so, little dreaming of her dark schemes, and the woe his oath will bring to him and his. Etzel is a "heathen," but Rudiger assures Kriemhild that she is likely to convert him, so she goes to Hun-

gary with Rudiger, stopping at his castle Bechlarn, where live his wife Gotelind and his daughter Dietlinde. The journey to Vienna is detailed ; crossing Bavaria they rest at Passua with Krimhild's uncle, Bishop Pilgrin, and proceed by Molk to the castle of Zeizenmauer, where countless hordes under Etzel's sway join the procession. At Tulna Etzel meets them, accompanied by 24 kings and princes and a great retinue, the most noteworthy being Dietrich of Bern, King of the Goths (*q.v.*), who with his band of Wolfings is a guest at Etzel's court, Blodelin, Etzel's brother, Hawart the Bold, King of the Danes, and his retainer, Iring the True (*q.v.*), and Infrid, Landgrave of Thuringia (*q.v.*), (in history, Hermanfrid, son-in-law of Theoderic the Great), and many others. At Vienna the wedding takes place with great magnificence, but Kriemhild's heart is sad, thinking of Sigfrid. Seven years pass and she bears Etzel a son, Ortlieb. Six years later she deems the time ripe for vengeance, and causes her husband to send to invite her kindred and friends to visit his land. Etzel sends Werbel and Swemlin, his minstrels, to Gunther. He and his court decide to accept, but Hagen is "grim loath " and warns them that Kriemhild's heart is fixed on vengeance, but rather than allow them to go alone, or appear afraid, Hagen joins the expedition. Ill omens beset them, and on coming to the Danube they find its waters swollen, and Hagen, foreboding evil, searches for a ferryman. Finding two " wise women " bathing, he seizes their garments and will not return them till they prophesy concerning the future. One, Hardeburc, foretells good, but the other, Sigelint, warns him that none shall return from Hunland save the King's chaplain. The ferryman next refuses to take them across, and attacks Hagen, who kills him. Hagen tests the truth of the prophecy by flinging the chaplain into the river, and when, despite him, the man escapes, Hagen knows thenceforward that all are doomed, and breaks up the ferryboat after they land. This whole passage is intensely vivid and dramatic. In passing through Bavaria they fight with Gelfrat, and his brother Else, killing Gelfrat. Coming to Passau, where Bishop Pilgrin receives them, they reach Bechlarn, where Rudiger entertains them with unbounded hospitality and friendliness. A match is ultimately arranged between Dietlind and Giselher, and when the Burgundians leave Rudiger showers gifts upon them without stint, giving also to Gunther a suit of armour and to Gernot his favourite sword, while Hagen chooses from Gotelind a famous shield which had belonged to her dead father Nodung. Rudiger accompanies the Burgundians to Etzel's court. Dietrich and Wolfhart (*q.v.*) meet them, Dietrich warning them that Kriemhild prays daily for vengeance for Sigfrid's murder. On arrival, Hagen and Volker sit outside the palace, at sight of Hagen Kriemhild weeps, and bids Etzel's men swear to avenge her sorrow. When she descends, Hagen sits with Sigfrid's sword Balmung across his knee, and Kriemhild recognizing it demands how he has dared to come? He answers that he has come because his masters have—he is their "man." Then Kriemhild accuses him of slaying Sigfrid, and Hagen boldly admits it. Then she demands the

Nibelung treasure, which Hagen tells her is sunk in the Rhine. When going to meet her kinsmen Kriemhild kisses only Giselher, a significant fact! Next, under the guise of friendship, she requests them to deliver up their arms, but they refuse, and Kriemhild asks who has "warned" them. Dietrich replies boldly, "I am he," and Kriemhild, bitterly fearing Dietrich, goes thence. Dietrich and Hagen converse, and Etzel joins them, speaking of Hagen's father Aldrian, who with Walther of Spain was his "man," which passage is remarkable, connecting as it does the Nibelungen cycle with the Latin poem of "Walthar of Aquitain" (*q.v.*). Too lengthy to detail are the various attempts of Kriemhild to gain her end. She offers gold to any one who will slay Hagen, but the Huns fear him. Dietrich and Hildebrand both refuse to assist her, the Burgundians are her relatives and have come trusting to her good faith! Next a tournament takes place, and Volker unluckily kills a Hun, but Etzel, who looks on his guests with favour, protects them. Kriemhild bribes Blodelin, who, with 1000 men, attacks Dankwart and his retainers. Dankwart slays him, but his followers kill all Dankwart's men, the hero himself escaping with difficulty. Rushing to the hall where the rest sit feasting with the Huns, and where Ortlieb, Kriemhild's son, has been introduced to the Burgundians, in bursts Dankwart, shouting to Hagen in fury concerning what has befallen. Up rises Hagen and slays Ortlieb and his attendant and strikes off Werbel's hand, and a terrible fight takes place till at last Dietrich, at Kriemhild's entreaties, intervenes. Gunther at once permits Dietrich and his men, with Etzel, Rudiger and Kriemhild, to leave the Hall, after which the Burgundians slay all Etzel's attendants. Desperate, Etzel and Kriemhild offer heavy bribes to any one who will kill Hagen. Iring, Margrave of Denmark, bravely makes the attempt twice, but is slain, and Irnfrid and Hawart are also slain with their men. Till night-fall does the awful conflict continue, when a temporary truce is called. From the Burgundians' position inside the Hall Giselher reproaches his sister with her treachery, and Kriemhild agrees to spare her brothers, but only on condition that they deliver up Hagen. This they will not hear of, thinking death infinitely preferable to such a deed, and Kriemhild sets the Hall on fire. The Burgundians well-nigh perish, yet in the morning 600 strong, they still hold the Hall against every attack, till Kriemhild and Etzel appeal to Rudiger to aid them. He is aghast at the idea of being a traitor to his friends, having pledged his honour for their safety. Then Kriemhild demands fulfilment of an ancient oath to her. Rudiger, torn by conflicting claims of honour, has in anguish to decide to serve his sovereign, and arming his men goes reluctantly forth against the Burgundians, Giselher rejoicing to see him, supposing that he comes to aid them. But sorrowfully does Rudiger explain that he cannot help himself. They plead with him that there be not blood between them, but in sadness he feels he has no alternative, and Hagen and he exchange their shields, Hagen and Volker pledging themselves never to strike a blow at Rudiger. The conflict commences, and great is the slaughter of the Burgundians, till at last Gernot reluctantly has to engage Rudiger, and they fall by each other's hands, and all Rudiger's men are slain. Universal is the sorrow at Rudiger's death, and Dietrich sends Hildebrand (but unarmed and in peace) to inquire the reason of his being slain. Fierce Wolfhart and Dietrich's knights follow in armour, ere Dietrich can prevent it. Sadly does Hagen bewail Rudiger's death and Hildebrand asks for his body, but "of spite of Etzel" the Burgundians refuse to give it up. Wolfhart provokes a fight, and, contrary to Dietrich's orders, a conflict takes place. Dankwart perishes, Giselher and Wolfhart slay each other; Volker kills Sigstap, nephew of Dietrich, Hildebrand slays Volker, and is in turn mortally wounded by Hagen, who is heartbroken at Volker's death. At length all lie dead save Gunther and Hagen, and of the other side Hildebrand, who returns to Dietrich with the terrible news. Dietrich goes to Hagen and Gunther, and on learning how things have come about offers them safe-conduct to their own land if they will yield. They reply that it is not fitting for brave men to surrender, and after some "womanish bickering" between Hagen and Hildebrand, Dietrich, seeing Hagen's "grim mood," fights and defeats, first Hagen, then Gunther, though with difficulty, and binds them. He carries them to Kriemhild, honouring them for their bravery and bidding her spare their lives, which she says she will do. Dietrich then sadly leaves. But little mercy does Kriemhild really feel; separating Hagen and Gunther, she offers safety to Hagen if he will reveal the hiding place of the Nibelung treasure. He refuses—"whilst any of my lords live I will show the hoard to none." Quickly then does she have her brother Gunther slain, and carries his head to Hagen, but Hagen declares that all is now finished—all are dead—but never will he reveal the secret ! So to Kriemhild nothing remains but Sigfrid's sword ; seizing it she herself slays Hagen. Hildebrand, enraged at her deed, when his master Dietrich has asked for Hagen's safety, springs up to avenge "the bold one of Tronei " and slays Kriemhild. Thus in darkest gloom ends the tragic "Nibelungenlied."

NIBLUNG. (*Vide* "Volsungs.") Son of Hogni (*q.v.*). He aided Gudrun (*q.v.*), in her scheme of revenge against Atli.

NICODEMUS. Mentioned in the Grail poem of *Joseph of Arimathea*. He was sent by Pilate to see that Joseph obtained Christ's body and the Grail vessel. He assisted Joseph in taking the body from the cross and washing it, which action so angered the Jews that they attempted to imprison him, but he escapes.

NIGHTINGALE, LAY OF THE. A romance attributed to Marie de France (*q.v.*). It is already a Breton *lai*, says the story, and is known in Brittany as *Laustic*. In the town of St. Malo in that duchy dwelt two knights of great repute, one of whom had to wife a lady of passing fairness and wit. The other knight was a bachelor, and set his love upon his neighbour's wife, and presently she set her heart on him again. They were so private and careful in their love that no man guessed of it. Their houses were side by side, so that they could converse from the casements and cast letters easily to one another. The lady

would rise from her bed at night to gaze upon her lover who came to his window, and this made her lord wrathful. Inquiring the cause, he was informed by her that she loved to hear the nightingale sing. But the husband "purposed that very soon the nightingale should sing within a net," and requested his servants to set snares about the house. Soon the bird was caught in the snare, and the husband wrung its neck. But the lady wept its evil fate. She embroidered the whole story on a piece of white samite, wrapped the body of the little bird in it, and sent it to her lover. He caused a little shrine to be fashioned, and carried the body of the unhappy bird with him wherever he went.

NOIRONS. A name for Nero in the *Grand St. Graal*.

NOISE. (*Vide* "Grettir Saga.") A big, idle, empty-headed fellow who accompanied Grettir and his brother Illugi to the laddered island of Drangey.

NORTHGALES, KING OF. Recorded in Arthurian romance as a prominent figure at the court of Arthur. (*Vide* "Morte d'Arthur.")

NORTHUMBERLAND. King of, Father of Eponogris (*q.v.*). He was a frequent visitor to the court of Arthur. (*Vide* "Morte d'Arthur.")

NUADA OF THE SILVER HAND. In Irish romance King of the Danaans (*q.v.*). In a fight with the Firbolgs (*q.v.*) he lost his hand, which, however, was replaced with a silver one by an artificer. He was slain by the terrible glance of Balor (*q.v.*), the Fomorian champion. Murna of the White Neck, his granddaughter, was Finn's mother. A solar deity, he is identified with Cymric Nuad or Ludd (*q.v.*).

T

O

OCEAN SWEEPER. In Irish romance the magical boat of the sea-god, Mananan, sail-less, oarless, and steered by the wishes of its occupant. It was brought by Lugh the Sungod from the Land of the Living that lay in the unknown, misty west.

OCTAVIAN, EMPEROR. There are several different versions of this metrical romance, one of which is preserved in the library of Lincoln Cathedral, while there is only one copy of the French original known to exist—that in the Bodleian Library, dating from the fourteenth century. The story recounts how Octavian, Emperor of Rome, and his queen mourned long over the non-fulfilment of their desires for an heir to the throne. An abbey is built to the glory of God and the empress is sent thither in the hope that their prayers would be answered. The emperor receives a message announcing the birth of two sons. His joy knows no bounds, and in humble thanksgiving he attends mass in the chapel. During the service his mother, who is also present, informs him that the children over whom he is rejoicing are the sons of a knave of the castle. After imparting this story, she quits the chapel, and instructing a knave of the palace to enter the sick-chamber of the empress, she waits the arrival of her son. The emperor's joy is changed to anger: and hastening to the chamber of his queen he slays the knave, whom he believes to be the culprit. The empress, who is asleep during this deed, dreams of a dragon belching fire at her and devouring her children.

The emperor, injured at the deception, swears to put an end to the life of his unfaithful wife, and to the lives of the children, by burning them at the stake. A fire is prepared without the city and the doomed trio despatched at the appointed hour. The queen overcome by grief, appeals to heaven for succour. So pathetic is the scene that the emperor is moved by pity and finally withdraws his threat by banishing his wife and her children.

In her lonely wanderings she lies down to rest by the side of a hermit's well, and while reposing, both of her children are carried off, the first by an ape, the second by a lion. The lion, whose den is situated on a hill, had scarcely reached its lair when a griffin swoops down upon him and the child, and carries off the pair to an uninhabited island. But immediately the lion places his feet on the solitary land he retaliates on his enemy by slaying it. A fondness springs up between the lion and the child.

The distressed mother resumes her journey, and finally arriving on the coast of Greece she implores of some shepherds to give her food. This they gladly do; but anxious to procure more for themselves several of them set out in a boat for a desert island. On reaching their destination they discover a lion and a child. The lion gives chase, two of the men are devoured, the rest make good their escape and return to tell the story of their adventure. The banished queen, conscious that the child is her son, entreats the shepherds to row her across to the island. This they do with some reluctance, but the mother is rewarded by the discovery of her son, whom she brings back with her, followed by the faithful lion. The queen again sets sail, when the ship brings them to the distant shores of Jerusalem. The king of that city makes her his queen and knights her son Octavius ; while the lion, become harmless, is permitted to live.

The other child, who had been carried off by the ape, passes through the hands of several guardians. A knight slays the ape and secures the child. Some robbers encounter the knight, capture the infant and wound their opponent. They hasten to Paris and dispose of the child to Clement, emperor of that city, in return for a few pieces of gold. The foundling is christened Florent. Some time after, a giant appears before the gates of the city challenging any knight in the name of Marsabella, daughter to a Saracen king. Florent obtains his foster-father's permission to enter the fray with the boastful giant, whom he finally slays. Without waiting to receive the congratulations of the city he hastens off to claim the Saracen maiden, but her father, angered at his boldness, locks her in her room.

Florent returns to Paris, to find that the Emperor Octavian has arrived in the city. The honour of seating himself between the friendly emperors is bestowed upon him, and as the outcome to some questioning on the part of Octavian his identity becomes known, the father rejoices in his son and dubs him " Sir Florent of Rome."

Again Sir Florent attempts to gain the maiden Marsabella. War is declared between the Christians and the Saracens with Clement at the head of the former. Florent takes part, and Olyvan, chamberlain to Marsabella, directs the young knight to his mistress. She flees with her lover to Paris. The Emperor Octavian, meanwhile, is opposing a body of Saracens at Jerusalem, who have besieged the Christian inhabitants of that city. Florent joins his father's forces and finally effects an entrance into the beleaguered city. The result is the identification of the second son, Octavius and the banished queen. A reconciliation is effected, Florent marries Marsabella, and the reunited family, accompanied by the faithful lion, return to the city of Rome.

ODILIA (1). Daughter of Elsung (*q.v.*), Earl of Bern. She married Samson's (*q.v.*) second son, after a battle between her father and King Samson ; the upshot of which was the death of the two warriors. (*Vide* "King Samson.")

ODILIA (2). Wife of Dietmar (*q.v.*) and mother of Dietrich (*q.v.*). (*Vide* " Dietrich of Bern.")

OGIER THE DANE. A sub-cycle of the Charlemagne Saga. It consists of twelve branches, and belongs to the early period of the cycle. It possesses considerable epic vigour, and as a whole is one of the most notable of the incidents connected with the legendary history of the great Emperor of the West. Ogier was originally critically recognized as a Norse rover, who had been " softened " into one of Charles's peers. But it is now put forward with much probability that we must read for " Danois " " Ardenois," and that the "Dane-March" which is Ogier's country is simply the "March" of Ardenois, or the Ardennes. There certainly was an Otker at the court of Charles, but his nationality is uncertain. He became "Advocate" or protector of Liège in Belgium, and is still remembered there in legend. The people of Denmark have erected Ogier into a national hero, Holger Danske. Ludlow inclines to identify him with a certain "Algisus, son of Desiderius the Lombard, who seems to have figured as the hero of some lost epic of which the echo has come to us in the *Novalesian Chronicle*." The late Alfred Nutt believed him to be "an Arthurian hero who had strayed by accident to the court of Charlemagne," an impossible elucidation. The poem, which exists in an MS. of the twelfth century, bears the name of Raimbert de Paris. The story, however, is made up of eleven different strata, written at separate dates, the earliest placed about the middle of the work, the latest toward the end. Raimbert was responsible for nine branches, or interpolations in these branches.

Ogier, son of Duke Godfrey of Denmark has been left as a hostage with Charlemagne, but as his father has insulted the emperor through his envoys, the young man's hostageship is forfeited, and he is imprisoned in the Castle of St. Omer. While there the castellan's daughter falls in love with him, and bears him a son, Baldwinet. Charlemagne vows to have Ogier hanged, when news comes that the Saracens have taken Rome. The emperor sets forth with his army to the rescue, and Ogier is taken along with the host. He is instrumental in rescuing the French army from serious defeat. He encounters with Charlot, the son of the emperor, the Indian King Karaheut, and the Turk Sadone. But other paynims interrupt the combat, and Ogier is made prisoner. He is given into the keeping of Glorianda, daughter of Corsuble the paynim Amiral, and Karaheut, shamed that his troth with Ogier should be broken, gives himself up to Charlemagne as hostage for the young Dane's safety. The French give battle to the pagans and have all but routed them when "the host of India" arrives to succour them. Foremost among the new-comers is Brunamont of Majorca, who beats the French back. The Amiral offers to bestow Glorianda upon him because of his success, but she is faithful to Karaheut, and puts forward Ogier as his champion. Brunamont agrees. Ogier conquers the Saracen, and takes his wonderful horse Broiefort. The French then attack the Saracens, and Glorianda is taken prisoner, but she is permitted to go free with Karaheut, and the French return to their own country. The first branch of the poem which ends here is evidently in the main modern, and probably dates from the end of the twelfth century. The birth of Baldwinet and the defeat of the Saracens are evidently adopted from an older work of which a further portion is obviously lost, as Ogier's leap into fame appears as much too sudden.

The second branch of *The Song of Ogier* is considered the oldest, and forms the groundwork of the epical portion of the poem. Charlot, playing at chess with Baldwinet, Ogier's son, is checkmated by him, and in his wrath strikes the youth with the chessboard and slays him. Ogier seeks

Charlot's life, but the emperor banishes him. He attempts to kill the emperor, but slays Lother his nephew instead. He is attacked, but is rescued by Charles's twelve peers. Pursued by the emperor, Ogier wounds him, and Charles marches to attack him in his dominions. Ogier, hunted from place to place, seeks the court of Pavia in exile, where he receives great honour and estates from Didier, its monarch.

The third branch opens with a declaration of Charles to take vengeance upon Ogier and Didier his new master. Bertram is sent to warn Didier to give Ogier up to justice. He insults Ogier, who refuses to fight with him for the sake of his father, and Bertram carries back the defiance of Lombardy. Charles sets out with a great host to take Ogier. Didier summons his army. In the battle which ensues, Ogier at first drives the French back, and Charles is unhorsed. But at length the French prevail, and the Lombards fleeing, Ogier is left with five hundred knights only. He is, however, succoured by Berron and Gerin, two Lombard chiefs, with their men. But they are slain, and Ogier is forced to fly. In his flight he slays Bertram. He takes a castle single-handed, and defends it against the emperor. He fights his way out under cover of night, mounted on his steed Broiefort, and succeeds in reaching his stronghold of Castle-Fort. Charlemagne prepares to reduce it. Ogier makes a desperate sally and wounds Charles. For five years the emperor sits before the castle. Ogier sallies out by a subterranean passage, but is betrayed by a man of Pavia. Bennet, his faithful squire, is slain, and Ogier is left alone at last. He leaps his horse into the Rhone and regains his castle. He has now but ten knights, one of whom, Hardre, a traitor, takes the keys to Charles. But Ogier, who has been asleep, wakes in time, and secures the gate. He makes men-at-arms of wood, which the French take for real warriors. Seven years pass, and famine threatens Ogier. He leaves the castle to kill Charlot in bed, but slays the wrong man, and is pursued. He once more escapes and seeks his heritage in Denmark. He is surprised by Archbishop Turpin (*q.v.*), and is taken prisoner. Turpin is permitted by Charles to retain him, and does so for seven years.

In the fourth branch of the romance we are told how Brehus, King of Africa, invades France with a mighty host. Charles frees Ogier in order to have his aid against the paynim. Ogier requires to have Charlot placed in his hands, to which the emperor agrees. Broiefort, Ogier's horse, is found harnessed to a porter's cart, but is brought back to Ogier. Ogier is about to slay Charlot, who has been given up to him, when St. Michael descends and holds his sword. A general reconciliation ensues. This brings us to the end of the ninth branch, the last of those believed to have been worked up by Raimbert of Paris from earlier versions. Ogier sets out to encounter Brehus, who has a magic ointment that can heal any wound, however grievous. Brehus wearies of the combat, requests a truce, and sleeps. On the renewal of the fight, Brehus kills Broiefort, but is eventually slain by Ogier. The eleventh and twelfth branches tell of Ogier's love for the daughter of the King of England, whom he rescues from the Saracens. A great battle with the Pagans ensued, in which the French are completely victorious. Ogier marries the princess whom he has rescued, and the emperor gives him Hainault and Brabant.

A text preserved in the British Museum relates the further adventures of Ogier. It dates from the middle of the fourteenth century and tells how the hero voyages to England, later subduing the East. He subsequently undertakes a journey into the Land of Faëry, where he meets Morgan le Fay, who frees him from death. It is, indeed, chiefly in this connection with Fairyland that the later Italian poets have celebrated Ogier. He is known in English legend as the father of Sir Bevis of Hampton, and is the hero of several of the Danish ballads of the "Kæmpe-viser."

OGMA. In Irish romance, a warrior of Nuada of the Silver Hand (*q.v.*), Lugh (*q.v.*), craving admittance into Tara as a warrior, was refused on the score that in the palace there was no need of another such while Ogma dwelt there.

OISIN (Little Fawn). In Irish romance, Son of Finn (*q.v.*), father of Oscar (*q.v.*). Knowing no father, he lived till he was a lad with his mother Saba (*q.v.*), who had been changed into a hind : till one day she unwillingly followed the dark Druid, her hated lover. Alone on Ben Bulben, in Sligo, the boy was found by Finn, to whom he related his history, whence the name given him. According to the ancient Ossianic poems he lived to meet St. Patrick, and to relate to him the doings of the Fianna (*q.v.*), hence this bardic fame.

OLAF (1), **KING.** (*Vide* "Burnt Njal.") Christian King of Norway, and successor to the heathen Yarl Hacon.

OLAF (2), **KING.** (*Vide* "Grettir Saga.") Successor to Yarl Svein of Norway (*q.v.*).

OLIVER. Son of Rainier of Genoa, nephew of Gerard of Viana, and brother of Alda ; the early rival and later the inseparable companion of Roland, and one of the peers of Charlemagne. For his adventures and other matter concerning him, see "Gerard of Viana," "The Song of Roland," etc.

OLLAV FOLA. In Irish romance, a king and the most distinguished Ollav (doctor) of Ireland, whose reign is placed about the year 1000 B.C. He heads all great political and national institutions as founder. With him compare Goban the Smith. To him it was said Ireland owed her triennial Fair at Lara.

ONEYS, CHILDE. (*Vide* "Amys and Amylion.") A faithful page to Sir Amylion, whom he accompanied during his master's affliction. As a reward, he succeeded to Amylion's domains.

ONUND. (*Vide* "Gunnlanng Saga.") Father of Rafn (*q.v.*).

ORABLE. In the Charlemagne cycle of romance, Queen of Thibaut or Tybalt, the Pagan monarch of Orange. When William of Orange came secretly to the city of that name, she succoured him, and when he was captured connived at his escape. She then offered herself to him as his wife, to which he consented. She was christened under the name of Guiborc. (*Vide* "William of Orange," and "Prise d'Orange.")

ORANGE, TAKING OF. (*Vide* " Prise d'Orange.")

ORCANS. In the *Grand St. Graal*, a heathen king, to whose island Pierre, sorely wounded, drifted in a boat. His daughter, finding Pierre dying on the seashore, tended him secretly till he was healed. Her father requiring a champion, Pierre offered himself and conquered the challenger. He then converted and baptized Orcans, who took the name Lamer and married his daughter.

ORFEO, SIR. May be briefly described as a Celtic adaptation of the familiar classical story of Orpheus and Eurydice. Queen Heurodys is carried off into Fairyland in spite of all that human efforts can avail. Orfeo follows her in despair as a minstrel, but his wonderful melodies at length succeed in leading her back to the haunts of men. The tale is included in the Auchinleck MS. (*q.v.*). The subject of Orpheus and Eurydice was also utilized in Politiano's *Favola di Orfeo*, performed at the court of Mantua in 1483. It is rather an eclogue than a drama proper, but it produced a veritable revolution in Italian poetry, and its scrupulous imitation of antiquity prepared the way for the revival of the classic authors on the Italian stage.

ORGUEILLEUSE, DAME. An interesting figure in Arthurian legend as illustrating mediæval morality. Having accomplished the feat of the Ford Perilous, Gawain offers love to her, which she flouts. As Gawain feels he has done enough to win her love—and every knight served some lady be she matron or maid, he lectures her, as a grave middle-aged man might some headstrong girl, upon the duties of a well-bred woman, and upon the wrong she has done knighthood in his person. To point the moral he winds up, at mid-day in the open forest, with a proposition which the repentant scornful one can only parry by the naïve remark, " Seldom she had found it warm in the embrace of a mail-clad arm." Not only was it the lady's duty to yield after a proper delay, but at times she might even make the first advances, and be none the worse thought of. Blanchefleur (*q.v.*) comes to Perceval's bed with scarce an apology. Orgueilleuse, overcome with admiration at the Red Knight's prowess, offers him her love. True, she has doubts as to the propriety of her conduct, but when she submits them to Gawain, the favoured lover for the time being, he unhesitatingly approves her.

ORKNEY, QUEEN OF. In Arthurian romance, wife of King Lot ; sister to Arthur ; mother to Mordred, begotten of Arthur (*q.v.*), Gareth, Gawaine and Agravaine (*vide* " Morte d'Arthur "). She was subsequently slain by Gaheris, her son, because of her familiarity with Sir Lancelot.

ORLANDO. (*Vide* " Orlando Innamorato," and " Orlando Furioso.") Lord of Anglante, became mad when he discovered that Angelica had forsaken him for Medoro. He was afterwards restored to his senses by Medoro.

ORLANDO FURIOSO. A romance in Italian, in which Ariosto continues Boiardo's narrative of the amours of the Paladins at the court of Charlemagne during the fabulous wars of that monarch against the Moors. (*Vide* " Orlando Innamorato.") The various adventures of the many characters alluded to in its pages are so intricate as to render the compilation of a synopsis a task of no little complexity. The following is offered as an outline of the poem.

When Orlando arrived at the Christian camp with Angelica, Charlemagne gave her to Namus. In a general battle Agramant and Marsilius defeated the Christian Army. Angelica fled, and met Rinaldo, who fought for her with Ferrau. Escaping, she encountered Sacripant, but their conversation was interrupted by Bradamant, who challenged the pagan, unhorsed him, and departed, when Rinaldo appeared. Furious at Sacripant's seeming favour with Angelica, Rinaldo attacked the Circassian King. Angelica flying, met a hermit, who, by a magical illusion, separated the two rivals. On returning to Paris, Rinaldo was sent by Charlemagne on an embassy to England. Bradamant, seeking her lover Rogero, met Pinabello, who decoyed her into a pit. Bradamant found herself in Merlin's cave, where she beheld Melissa, who showed her in a vision all her descendants who were to be famous in history. Then she told the maiden how to deliver Rogero from the enchanted castle of Atlantes. Following Melissa's advice, Bradamant took the ring from Brunello, defeated Atlantes, then set his prisoners free. But the magician contrived Rogero's flight from Bradamant on the griffin-horse. Meanwhile Rinaldo, entertained at an abbey, heard of the misfortunes of Geneura, daughter to the King of Scotland, and undertook her defence. Dalinco related the loves of Ariodantes and Geneura, exposing the treachery of Polinesso, who had contrived to blacken Geneura's reputation, caused her to be openly accused of unchastity, and by the laws of Scotland condemned to death. Incensed at Polinesso's duplicity, Rinaldo took up her cause before the king, and entered the lists with her enemy. Being vanquished by Rinaldo, Polinesso confessed the fraud, and thus Geneura's innocence was proved. Rogero, carried by the flying-horse to Alcina's island, found a knight transformed into a myrtle. After slaying a troop of monsters who opposed his egress, Rogero was met by two ladies belonging to Alcina's palace. Conquering Eriphila, and conducted by the two damsels, he arrived at the palace, where Alcina received him with great joy. Seduced by her allurements he led a life of luxury and effeminacy, until Melissa, assuming the form of Atlantes, delivered him. He then travelled towards the country of Logistilla. Leaving Scotland, Rinaldo arrived in England, whence the Regent transported him to assist Charlemagne. Angelica, conveyed to a desolate island, then cast into a deep sleep by a hermit, was captured by mariners. Orlando, leaving Paris disguised, went out in search of Angelica, and heard how the people of Ebuda daily sacrificed a virgin to a sea-monster. He resolved to oppose these islanders, but being cast ashore by a tempest, met Olympia, who explained her expulsion from her hereditary dominions, whereupon Orlando undertook both her restoration and revenge. Rogero, journeying towards Logistilla, arrived safely at the castle, where Alcina in vain endeavoured to oppose him. He departed on the griffin-horse to Europe, visited England, and was present at the review of the forces raised to assist Charlemagne. Passing Ebuda, he beheld Angelica bound to a rock, ready to be devoured by a sea-monster. Rogero rescued Angelica, made love to her, but by aid of the magic ring she became invisible, and, deceived by Bradamant's vision, he was decoyed to the enchanted palace of Atlantes. Orlando, in pursuit of Angelica, found Olympia exposed to be devoured by the orc, a monster which he killed. Oberto, King of Ireland, married Olympia, and Orlando resumed his search for Angelica. Deluded by her likeness, he was drawn to the enchanted castle of Atlantes, where Angelica arrived, found Orlando, Sacripant, and Ferrau, all of whom she delivered by her magic ring. While Orlando and Ferrau contended, Angelica departed, followed by Sacripant; Orlando, in quest of Angelica, found a damsel detained in a cave of outlaws. He heard how Isabella, loved by Zerbino, whose trust Odorico had betrayed, was captured by these outlaws, from whom Orlando delivered her. Bradamant lamented Rogero's absence, but was comforted by Melissa, who instructed her how to deliver him from the castle of Atlantes, conducted her thither, then left her. Meanwhile Agramant prepared to muster his forces. Mandricardo, searching for Orlando, met Doralis, betrothed to Rodomont, attacked her guard, and carried her off by force. Rinaldo led the Christian army to the walls of Paris, Agramant began the assault, and Rodomont scaled the ramparts, amidst fearful slaughter of the Christians, who made a gallant defence. Astolpho, dismissed with presents from Logistilla, was conducted by Andronica and Sophrosyne on his passage home. When they reached the Persian Gulf, the knight pursued his journey by land, arrived at Egypt, and took captive Caligorant the giant. He found Gryphon and Aquilant fighting with Orilo, whom Astolpho slew, then all entered Jerusalem where Sansonetto welcomed them. Gryphon met Origilla, who, having been proved faithless, charged him with inconstancy. Rodomont continued to besiege Paris with fearful slaughter. While Agramant led his forces in by a gateway, Rinaldo came to succour the Christians, but Rodomont destroyed all with fire and sword, until opposed by Charlemagne. Gryphon, Martano, and Origillo arrived at Damascus, where a knight hospitably entertained them, and related how Lucina, loved by Norandino, was rescued from the orc by Mandricardo and Gradasso, whereupon Norandino celebrated the event by a tournament in which Gryphon overcame all opponents, but Martano by fraud obtained the prize. Rodomont, attacked by Charlemagne and his Paladins, left Paris, and repassing the Seine, heard that Doralis was carried off by Mandricardo. The emperor returned, and renewed the battle, Lurcanio being slain. Gryphon revenged his disgrace by slaying many people of Damascus. Marphisa, Astolpho, and Sansonetto, conquering all opponents at the jousts, with Aquilant and Gryphon embarked for France. Cloridano and Medoro, seeking to bury Dardinello, whom Rinaldo slew, were captured, and Cloridano killed. Angelica found Medoro wounded, healed him, became enamoured, then married him. The four knights and Marphisa, escaping shipwreck, were cast on the land of the Amazons. Marphisa, having killed nine champions, fought equally with Guido the Savage, who related how, by ancient law, every invader perished unless he conquered the Amazon's ten champions. Guido deplored his thraldom under female sway, helped the knights to escape, but when nearly overpowered Astolpho blew his magic horn, which so terrified the Amazons that all embarked. Afterwards landing, Marphisa separated from the knights, and met Gabrina, whom he defended against Pinabello, then against Zerebino, to whom he consigned Gabrina. Zerebino next fought with Hermonides, who related how Gabrina, married to Argeo, had endeavoured to seduce Philander, the brother of Hermonides, causing him to slay Argeo in mistake for Morando. Astolpho arrived at the enchanted palace of Atlantes, blew his magic horn, dissolved the enchantment, and liberated the prisoners. Rogero meeting Bradamant, departed with her, then they were asked by a damsel to deliver Richardetto from being burnt alive for unchastity, after which Rogero defeated the four knights who threatened to despoil all strangers passing that way. Bradamant after slaying Pinabello in revenge, lost herself in a wood, where Astolpho found her. Meeting her brother Alardo, she went with him to Mount Albano, then sent Hippalca to Rogero with his horse Frontino, which Rodomont afterwards took from her. Zerebino, finding Pinabello's dead body, was accused by Gabrina of the murder, doomed to death, but delivered by Orlando, who, on discovering the loves of Angelica

and Medoro, became mad with grief. Zerebino and Isabella met Almonio and Corebo, who brought Odorico to receive from Zerebino punishment for breach of faith. Mandricardo and Rodomont fought for Doralis, till, at her request, they desisted, and departed to aid Agramant. When Rogero arrived with the damsel, after slaying a hundred who opposed him, he delivered Richardetto, who accompanied him to the castle of Agrismont, where they were entertained by Aldiger. The three knights now undertook to rescue Malagigi and Vivian from the Pagans, defeated the troops of Maganza, and liberated the two prisoners. Hippalca arrived, explained how Rodomont stole Frontino from her, and when he appeared Rogero claimed his horse. Malagigi fearing for Richardetto's safety, caused a demon to enter Doralis' horse, which carried her away, followed by Mandricardo and Rodomont, pursued by Rogero and Marphisa. The four warriors, joined by Gradasso and Sacripant, attacked Charlemagne so fiercely that the Christian army fled. Rogero again claimed the shield of Hector, Rodomont and Sacripant disputed Rogero's horse Frontino, Brunello was forcibly carried off by Marphisa, and Doralis preferred Mandricardo to Rodomont, which so enraged the jealous king of Algiers, that he left the camp. At a country inn Rodomont heard how Astolpho and Jocundo, finding their consorts false, visited Flanders, France, and Albion in quest of love ; on realizing that other men's wives were also unchaste they returned home. Rodomont set out for Algiers, but seeing a deserted chapel, resolved to reside therein. Isabella arrived with the dead body of Zerbino, slain by Mandricardo. The Algerian king fell in love with her, urged her to break her vow of virginity, but she preserved her honour by telling him of a herb, which, distilled, would render him invulnerable. Medoro and Angelica, about to embark for India, were accosted by Orlando, and with great difficulty, escaped from the madman's hands. Contending for the shield of Hector, Rogero slew Mandricardo ; Bradamant, inquiring as to her lover's welfare heard tidings of the absent one by Hippalca. On arriving at Mount Albano, Rinaldo prepared with six other knights to go to assist Charlemagne, while Bradamant remained behind at Mount Albano. Meeting Guido the Savage, they were challenged by him, and Richardetto, Alardo, then Guichardo were in turn overthrown, but Rinaldo engaged him until stopped by dusk ; then all arrived at Charlemagne's camp and defeated Agramant. Thereafter Gradasso enjoined Rinaldo to finish their contest for Bayardo. Having fled to Arli, the African monarch was relieved by Marphisa, who caused Brunello to be hanged for stealing her sword. Bradamant, meeting a Gascon knight, learnt that Marphisa now usurped Rogero's affections. Leaving Mount Albano, she met Ulania, arrived at Sir Tristram's lodge, unhorsed three kings, and was hospitably received by the lord of the castle. Next morning the female warrior unhorsed the three kings a second time. While Rinaldo and Gradasso fought for Bayardo, the horse was attacked by a monstrous bird. They ceased fighting, Gradasso caught, then mounted, the affrighted steed, and embarked for his own

country. Meanwhile Astolpho, flying through the air, reached the capital of King Senapus, in Ethiopia, drove the harpies from the king's table to Hell, where he met the ghost of Lydia, punished for scorning her lover on earth. The English duke then flew to Paradise, where St. John the Evangelist instructed him how to restore Orlando to his senses, then conveyed him to the moon, where he beheld the three fatal sisters spinning the thread of life. Bradamant had now met Flordelis, and undertook to deliver Brandimart from the hands of Rodomont. This feat she accomplished in a joust with the pagan king on a bridge, then on reaching Arli, sent Flordelis with a challenge to Rogero, after which she unhorsed at three separate encounters, Perpentino, Grandonio, and Ferrau. Marphisa was next unhorsed by the intrepid damsel, and when Rogero appeared he also was attacked. The lovers then retired to a solitary grove, pursued by Marphisa, who now assaulted Bradamant. Rogero interposed, but Marphisa turned fiercely on him, until the combat was broken off by a Voice which proclaimed them brother and sister. Rogero, Bradamant, and Marphisa, meeting three damsels whose garments were clipt away, undertook their revenge. They arrived at Lemnos and heard how Morganor, on being deprived of his two sons through love of women, banished all females. The undaunted three attacked the castle, took Morganor prisoner, and Marphisa decreed that henceforth, every husband should be ruled by his wife. Astolpho, dismissed from Paradise by Orlando's wit, returned to Nubia, restored Senapus to sight, who besieged Biserta. Whereupon Agramant sent an embassy to Charlemagne, urging him to decide the war by single combat. The emperor agreed, so Rogero and Rinaldo were the champions chosen. As they contended, Agramant, by Melissas' device, broke the truce, and a general battle ensuing, the knights separated. Landing in Africa, Astolpho received Olivero, Sansonetto, Brandimart and other Christian knights, then mad Orlando entered the camp, and the English duke restored him to his senses. Agramant, sailing from Arli, was attacked by Dudon's fleet, and his ships destroyed. The African monarch escaped with Sobrino, and at the siege of Biserta, Brandimart put Agramant to flight, who, meeting Gradasso, enlisted his aid. The three pagans then challenged Orlando, Brandimart, and Olivero. Rogero, following the king to his native Africa, arrived at Marseilles, contested with Dudon, and released seven kings captured from Agramant. He embarked with them for Africa, and in a dreadful storm all perished but himself. The three Christian knights departed for Lipadusa, and left Flordelis behind in great affliction. Rogero escaped by swimming to an island, where he was entertained by a hermit, and received Christian baptism. In the combat Agramant, Gradasso and Brandimart were slain. Rinaldo, hearing from Malagigi that Angelica had left France with Medoro, resolved on pursuit. In the forest of Arden he was attacked by Jealousy, delivered by a knight, and by drinking at the fountain of Disdain, cured of his love for Angelica.

After refusing to drink of the enchanted cup offered by a Man-

tuan knight, Rinaldo embarked in a vessel, heard how the judge Anselmo had sentenced his wife Argia to death for infidelity ; but she, finding him also false, thereby became absolved. Reaching Lipadusa, Rinaldo thence proceeded with Orlando, Sobrino, and Olivero to the island of the hermit, where they met Rogero, to whom Rinaldo promised his sister Bradamant, then all departed for Marseilles, where Astolpho joined them, and together they entered Paris in triumph. Amon, having previously promised his daughter to Leon, quarrelled with his son Rinaldo, whereupon Bradamant left her father's court, and was immured in a castle. Leaving Paris to kill Leon, Rogero assisted the Bulgarians against the Greeks, whom he defeated. Whilst asleep the brave knight was seized by Unguardo, delivered over to Theodora, desirous to revenge the death of her son, killed by Rogero. After defying Leon, Bradamant returned to Amon's court, Rogero was released by Leon, then fought Bradamant in Leon's stead. Marphisa interceded for Rogero with Charlemagne, and contested Leon's claim, which Amon opposed. Searching for Rogero, Leon accosted Melissa, who conducted him to the warrior, then all returned to Charlemagne's court. The Bulgarian ambassadors offered Rogero the crown of Bulgaria, Amon and Beatrice consented to his marriage with Bradamant, and Melissa presided over the nuptials. At the festival, Rodomont appeared, challenged Rogero, who slew the fierce Saracen in the duel.

In Orlando, mad for love of Angelica, cured by disdaining those charms formerly prized, is displayed an intimate knowledge of the heart, which brooks no rival in its affections. Angelica, forsaking Orlando for Rinaldo, then espousing Medoro, represents a type of feminine fickleness, liable to form new attachments. Astolpho, transformed into a myrtle by Alcina, and recovering his former shape by Melissa, in allegory, represents the true image of the man lost through sensuality. Alcina personifies vice, by whom men are captivated; by Logistilla is meant reason, which delivers them from sin. Rogero, intoxicated with the beauty of Alcina, is seduced from virtue by the siren's alluring charms; but detecting her depravity, he ultimately escapes from her power. Bradamant, the female warrior, in love with Rogero, is a noble character, loyal to truth, zealous in every good cause, whose fidelity wins her wayward lover's heart. The most exalted sentiments of honour are expressed by Rinaldo, ever ready to succour the distressed, to avenge cruelty, or to establish justice. Isabella, in despair when her lover Zerbino is slain, with dignity upholds the sanctity of love, which she renounces for religion. Rodomont, who loved Doralis, and when discarded by her became enamoured of Isabella, whom he ultimately killed, then fell a victim to his own importunity, points the danger of defying ordained laws.

ORLANDO INNAMORATO. An Italian treatment of the Charlemagne Cycle by Count Maria Boiardo (1430–1494) (*q.v.*). The valour of Orlando, the charms displayed by Angelica, who exercises supreme power over the hearts of the knights, the marvellous adventures of the redoubtable Rodomont, excite an interest which in popularity was surpassed only by Ariosto, who continued the romance in *Orlando Furioso* (*q.v.*). Charlemagne proclaimed a solemn feast and tournament in Paris, at which many foreign princes and knights were present from various parts of the world, both pagan and Christian. On a certain day, when all the nobles and strangers were assembled, an unknown knight and lady entered the hall, attended by four giants of great stature. The lady, whose charms dazzled all the spectators, addressed herself to the emperor. She told him that her name was Angelica, that she came with her brother Uberto from a distant kingdom, attracted by the fame and the magnificence of his court; that her brother who earnestly desired to prove his valour with the warriors then present, was ready to meet any of them in the field, whether Saracen or Christian; upon condition, that whoever was unhorsed by him, should immediately become his prisoner. If he should be overthrown, he promised to depart with the giants, and leave his sister as the prize of the conqueror. The fair stranger concluded by saying that her brother would expect them at his pavilion without the city. Having received a gracious answer the lady retired with her company while every knight, captivated with her charms, felt the utmost impatience to enter the lists with the strange warrior. But above the rest, Orlando, whose eyes had been riveted on so beautiful an object, confessed the pangs of love, though he studiously endeavoured to conceal his inward emotions. Even Namus could not resist the power of such perfections, nor was Charlemagne himself wholly exempted from the general contagion. Meanwhile Malagigi, a cousin of Rinaldo, who was deeply skilled in magic, suspecting that the visit of these strangers boded no good to the Christians, had recourse to his art, and upon consulting his familiars received intelligence that the lady was daughter to Gala-phron, King of Cathay ; that the knight her brother was not called Uberto, but Argalia ; that the king their father, to effect a great design which he meditated, had procured for his son a suit of enchanted armour, a golden lance of such hidden virtue, that the least touch of it would dismount the stoutest warrior and a horse of incomparable swiftness. To these gifts he added a ring of such wonderful efficacy, that being con-veyed into the mouth, it made the person invisible, and, being worn upon the finger, had the power to frustrate all enchantments. The king, however, confided chiefly in the beauty of his daughter, not doubting that her charms would fascinate the champions of Charle-magne, and that she would bring them prisoners to the throne of Cathay. Malagigi, having heard this, conceived the design of delivering his country from the impending danger. He caused himself to be transported by his spirits to the pavilion of Argalia, whom he found asleep, with Ange-lica near him, guarded by the four giants. These he soon cast into a deep slumber by the force of his spells, and drew his sword with a determination to put an end to the life of this dangerous beauty. But as he approached her, he began to feel sensations of a very different nature, till every reso-lution, giving way to the softer

passions that inspired him from a nearer view of her charms, he could no longer resist the powerful impulse, but advanced to embrace her. Angelica, who had the ring upon her finger, which preserved her from the force of his incanta-tions, suddenly awoke, and finding herself in the arms of a man, uttered a loud cry. Argalia ran to her assistance, and seized Malagigi, while the princess made herself mistress of his magical book, and calling upon his spirits, commanded them to convey the prisoner to her father's kingdom, which was performed in an instant. In order to put an end to the dissension that had arisen in the Christian court, each champion claiming the preference to first enter the lists with Argalia, the emperor commanded that lots should be drawn. The names that appeared were Astolpho, Ferrau, Rinaldo, and next Charle-magne, who would not be excluded notwithstanding his age. After these came many more before the name of Orlando appeared. As-tolpho being armed, as the first on the list of combatants, pre-sented himself to encounter Arga-lia, was unhorsed by the golden lance, and sent prisoner into the pavilion. Next morning at day-break, Ferrau, a Spanish knight, came from the city to try his fortune, and was overthrown in the same manner. But refusing to yield to the conditions of the combat, the giants endeavoured to seize his person. These he slew, and compelled Argalia to engage him on foot. Angelica, fearing the issue of their combat, fled, when Argalia, perceiving her flight, followed her, and was as suddenly pursued by Ferrau, who, after some time, entering the forest of Arden, found Argalia asleep, who had not been able to overtake his sister. The Spaniard determined that he should not escape him, turned Argalia's horse loose, and waited, with the utmost impatience, till his enemy awoke. An obstinate battle then ensued, till victory at last declared for Ferrau. Argalia, finding himself mortally wounded, entreated that when he was dead, his body, with all his armour, might be thrown into the river, that no one might wear it after him, and reproach his memory for suffering himself to be vanquished when he was defended with impenetrable armour. Ferrau promised to grant his request, having first desired the use of his helmet for a few days, his own being demolished in the battle. After the departure of Argalia, Angelica, and Ferrau, Astolpho having recovered his liberty, mounted his horse, took the golden lance which Argalia had left behind him, and returned to the city. In his way he met Rinaldo, who was impatient to learn the issue of the combat; and having heard what had passed determined to go in search of Angelica. Orlando, who had felt no ease since the appearance of the lovely stranger, after Astolpho's return, left the court of Charlemagne, set out likewise to follow Angelica, and in his way met with various adventures. When Rinaldo first left the court of Charlemagne to follow Angelica, he entered the forest of Arden, where he came to the enchanted fountain made by Merlin the magician, to cure Sir Tristram of his passion for Isolta. But although it so happened that the knight never tasted of the water, yet the virtue of it remained ever after. Rinaldo, arriving here, drank of the fountain, and immediately found his love for Angelica changed into hatred. He then came to the other fountain, likewise the work of Merlin, called the Fountain of Love, which had the faculty of inspiring the breast with that passion. Here, tempted by the beauty of the place, he alighted from his horse, yet, as he had before quenched his thirst, he drank not of the stream, but stretching himself on the turf, soon fell into a profound sleep. Angelica, who had fled while her brother was engaged with Ferrau, was led by chance to the same place where Rinaldo lay. The princess, fatigued with her flight, and invited by the clearness of the water, drank a large draught, and conceived a violent passion for the sleeping knight, whom she stood contemplating with inexpressible pleasure, till he awakened. As soon as Rinaldo opened his eyes, and beheld Angelica, who was now become the object of his most bitter aversion, he remounted his horse, and left the place with the utmost precipitation, in spite of the most moving entreaties which the lovesick virgin urged to detain him. About this time Gradasso, King of Sericane, having long been desirous to get possession of Durindana, Orlando's sword, and of Bayardo, Rinaldo's horse, passed with a great army into France, and Orlando being absent, he defeated Charlemagne in a general battle, and made him and many of his leaders prisoners. Charlemagne promised, at the return of Orlando, to give up to him Durindana and Bayardo, but Orlando refused to resign them and challenged Gradasso to the joust, overthrowing him with the golden lance. According to the conditions of their encounter,

Charlemagne and all the prisoners were set at liberty. Gradasso then joined himself to Marsilius. After the return of Angelica to India, Agrican, King of Tartary, and father of Mandricardo, demanded her in marriage. Being refused by her, he raised a great army, and besieged her in Albracca, the capital of Cathay, inviting other nations to join him. Many gallant actions were performed at the siege. Orlando, Brandimart, Sacripant, Marphisa, Astolpho, and many others, took the part of Angelica. But Rinaldo, who at that time hated Angelica, from his having drunk of the enchanted fountain, joined himself to her enemies, in consequence of which he had several encounters with Orlando. After various successes on either side, and an infinity of adventures engaged in by the several knights during the siege, Agrican was slain by Orlando in single combat. Angelica, hearing that Rinaldo, whom she then loved, had gone to France, persuaded Orlando to accompany her thither. After her departure, the enemies of Albracca, taking advantage of the absence of Orlando, and her other brave defenders, took the city by storm, and reduced it to ashes. When Angelica, after the taking of Albracca, returned to France with Orlando, she passed again through the Forest of Arden, and, in her way, happened to drink of the fountain of hatred, which entirely obliterated her former passion. About the same time Ronaldo, meeting with the contrary fountain, drank of the waters of love. While the siege of Albracca was being carried on, Agramant, the young King of Africa, only twenty-two years of age, and the bravest knight in the dominions of Africa, except

Rodomont, King of Sarza, burning with desire to revenge the death of his father Troyano, slain by the Christians, ordered a council to be called in the city of Biserta, the capital of his empire. When thirty-two kings, his tributaries, were assembled, he proposed to them his design of invading the kingdom of Charlemagne. After many debates it was at last resolved to transport a powerful force into France, notwithstanding the prophecy of the King of Garamanta, who declared that the expedition would prove fatal to Agramant and his army. When the King of Garamanta had in vain endeavoured to dissuade Agramant from his designed invasion of France, he told the monarch that there remained but one expedient by which he might hope to meet with any success against the Christians. This was, to take with him a young hero, named Rogero, who then resided with Atlantes the magician, on Mount Carena. Agramant, having, in consequence of his advice, made many fruitless researches to find the fatal warrior, was directed, by the King of Garamanta, to procure the enchanted ring, then in possession of Angelica, daughter of Galaphron, King of Cathay, without which the retreat of Atlantes could never be discovered. Thereupon, Agramant offering great rewards to any one that would undertake this adventure, Brunello, a person of mean extraction, but well versed in the arts of fraud, engaged to perform it. Accordingly, he went to Albracca, stole the ring from the princess, and brought it to Agramant, who, in recompense for his good service, made him king of Tangitana. In this excursion, Brunello, likewise, stole Sacripant's horse, Marphisa's sword, Orlando's sword which he had won from the enchantress Falerina, and the famous horn which he had taken from Almontes. Agramant, having got possession of this precious ring, went, with all his court, to the mountain, where Atlantes was said to reside. The ring having dispelled every mist that enchantment had cast before his eyes, they soon discovered the rock on which was the wonderful dwelling. But the height forbidding all approaches to it, Agramant, by the advice of Brunello, ordered a tournament to be held on the plain at the foot of the rock. Rogero, roused by the sound of the warlike instruments, and fired with the sight of horses and armour, which he stood for some time contemplating from the summit of the rock, at last made Atlantes, though with great reluctance, descend with him to the plain. Brunello, who carefully watched the success of his project, soon espied Rogero with Atlantes, and drawing near them, entered into conversation. Brunello, being then completely armed and mounted on Frontino, observed that Rogero was struck with the beauty of his horse and armour, so he presented them to him, and the young warrior impatiently arming himself, and girding Balisarda to his side, leaped on Frontino, and entered the lists, where he overthrew every opponent, and obtained the honours of the day. All the combatants were astonished at the valour of this unknown champion, till Agramant, having at last discovered him to be Rogero, whom he had so eagerly sought for, received him with open arms, and conferred upon him the honour of knighthood. He engaged Rogero to accompany him to France, notwithstanding all the argument used by Atlantes, to dissuade the king from taking Rogero with him in that expedition. During the battle between the pagans and the Christians, Rogero so distinguished himself that Bradamant, struck with his manly deportment, was desirous to learn who he was, and received from him the account of his origin. Bradamant, in return, revealed her birth and name, and taking off her helmet, surprised the young warrior with her beauty. At this instant a band of pagans fell in with them, one of whom wounded Bradamant in the head, which was then unarmed. Rogero, who had by this time conceived a violent passion for the fair warrior, and enraged at the brutality of the action, advanced furiously to revenge it on the author. The Pagans then attacked him all at once, and Bradamant, who now began to feel the tenderest sentiments for Rogero, immediately joined him. Their united force soon vanquished their adversaries, who were either slain or put to flight. But it so happened that in the pursuit the two lovers were separated, this being their first meeting. Throughout the war the young Rogero was accompanied by Atlantes, who, since he could not divert his charge from the pursuit of glory, was prompted by his anxiety to be near him in time of danger. The enchanted castle represents the carnal appetite which holds men prisoners; by Atlantes is figured love; Brandimart and Flordelis, pagans by birth, converted to Christianity, represent patterns of conjugal affection. Sacripant, one of Angelica's most faithful lovers, affords an example of the brave and noble actions love can inspire. Angelica is a natural lively picture of the coquetry and levity of the fair sex, and never takes hold of the heart as do the more steadfast Bradamant, Flordelis, or Isabella, these models of female excellence. Astolpho, decoyed to the palace of Alcina, illustrates the danger of tampering with vice. Marphisa, who vowed to capture the three kings, Gradasso, Agrican, and Charlemagne, shows what may be accomplished by tenacity of purpose. For the continuation of the romance, see *Orlando Furioso*.

Up to 1545 the poem would seem to have been extremely popular, for between that date and the date of the *editio princeps* it had passed through no fewer than sixteen editions. But after 1545 it was never again printed until 1830, when Parrizzi published an excellent edition with notes in nine volumes.

ORTLIEB. (*Vide* "Nibelungenlied.") Son of Kriemhild and Etzel. He was born seven years after Kriemhild (*q.v.*), married Etzel (*q.v.*), King of the Huns, and he was six years old when the Burgundians came to the Court of Etzel. During a great feast Ortlieb was brought in and introduced to Gunther (*q.v.*) and his retinue, but was slain by Hagen (*q.v.*) in his wrath at the attack on Dankwart (*q.v.*), who burst into the hall telling of how he had been attacked by Blodelin (*q.v.*) by order of Kriemhild.

ORTRUN. (*Vide* "Gudrun Lay"— third division of, under heading "Gudrun.") Daughter of Ludwig and Gerlinte, King and Queen of Ormany, sister of Hartmut. Married Ortwein, brother of Gudrun. Sweet and gentle, she loved Gudrun and endeavoured to lighten the sufferings which Gerlinte inflicted upon that princess to induce her to marry Hartmut. Ortrun pled her brother's cause with Gudrun, but in vain. When Gudrun's rescuers came, she saved Ortrun and her maidens from the fury of Wate (*q.v.*), taking her with her to Hegelingen, where she prevailed upon her mother, Hilda, to receive Ortrun with kindness. Twice Ortrun induced Gudrun to intercede for Hartmut's safety,— once during the fight at Ormany, and later at Hegelingen. (*Vide* "Hartmut.")

OSANTRIX. Son of King Hermit (*q.v.*) and husband to Oda (*q.v.*). He ruled over the Wilkinmen and was a consistent enemy of Dietrich of Bern (*q.v.*). He was slain by Elgel (*q.v.*).

OSCAR. In Irish romance son of Oisin (*q.v.*), grandson of Finn (*q.v.*). The fiercest warrior of the Fianna, he was slain in single combat with, and slew the King of Ireland, Cairbry (*q.v.*), in the Battle of Gowra (*q.v.*).

OSILE. (*Vide* "Guy of Warwick.") Daughter of the Duke of Lorraine. Married Sir Thierry.

OTHO, DUKE OF PAVIA. (See "Guy of Warwick.") He was overthrown by Sir Guy at a tournament at Rouene. He placed some warriors in ambuscade for Sir Guy, but he escaped. Otho was wounded at the siege of Louvain. He acted in a very treacherous way to Thierry and Osile, and took them prisoners, but Sir Guy delivered them and killed Otho.

OTKELL. (*Vide* "Burnt Njal.") A rich and covetous farmer who, refusing to sell food to Gunnar (*q.v.*), soon afterwards found his store-house robbed and burnt. By

Mord's (q.v.) cunning Hallgerda (q.v.) was found to be the thief. She and her husband, Gunnar, were summoned to court upon the lying advice of Skamkell (q.v.), Gunnar, however, triumphing. But one day, Otkell's spear having by mishap made a gash in Gunnar's ear, Skamkell noised it abroad that Gunnar had wept. This lie brought about the death of Otkell, Skamkell, and their six companions, who were slain soon afterwards, by Gunnar and his brother Kolskegg. By Njal's wise counsels the matter of these slayings was settled to the satisfaction of all.

OTRANT. In the Charlemagne cycle, the pagan King of Nîmes. (*Vide* " Charroi de Nîmes.")

OTTER. Son of Hreidmar (q.v.), brother to Regin (q.v.) and Fafnir (q.v.). He was slain by Loki (q.v.), the Scandinavian god of evil, who covered his skin with gold rings, which his father received as blood-money. (*Vide* "The Lay of the Volsungs.")

OTUEL, SIR. An English romance of the Charlemagne cycle, probably of the thirteenth century. The theme is an account of various battles fought between the Christians and the Saracens. A Saracen King, Garsie of Lombardy, was determined to extirpate Christianity, and as Charlemagne was its greatest champion, he sent an ambassador to him in the person of Sir Otuel. He chose the occasion of a great festival when Charlemagne was surrounded by his peers and his great heroes, Roland, Olivier, and Ogier. Sir Otuel gave his master's message, which was that unless Charlemagne renounced Christianity, became a vassal to him and handed a portion of his lands to the Saracens, he would ravage all France. Sir Otuel was very haughty and insolent in manner, and made so many insulting remarks that he roused the indignation of his hearers and a knight attacked him, but he drew his famous sword Corrouge, and after having slain the man, he defied the assembly. He challenged Roland, and they agreed to meet in single combat. After a severe encounter, Roland began to have a high opinion of his antagonist, and thinking how useful he might be as an ally, he repeated an offer made by Charlemagne, that if Otuel would become a Christian, he would be given the king's daughter, the beautiful Belisent, in marriage. The king, afraid that Roland might be slain, prayed earnestly that Otuel might be converted, and immediately a miracle happened. A white culver descended on Otuel, who demanded a parley, then promising to forsake his gods, said : " To your God ich will take." He was baptized next day by Archbishop Turpin, married Belisent, and joined the Christian army. Then preparations were made for an attack upon Garsie and a day and place fixed for battle. Roland, Olivier, and Ogier went out first in search of adventure, and had an encounter with some of the fiercest Saracen knights, when Ogier was taken prisoner. Then Sir Otuel set out and met with King Clarel, whom he slew in single combat. After this the two armies met, and the Saracens were completely defeated. Ogier escaped from prison and joined Roland and Olivier in pursuit of the Saracens. King Garsie was overtaken by Otuel, and brought prisoner to Charlemagne, becoming his vassal on condition his life was spared.

Shortly after this Charlemagne fought against the Saracens under Ibrahim, King of Seville, and routed them, killing Ibrahim. After making a conquest of Spain, Charlemagne desired to return to France, but insisted first that Marsile and Baligand should either be baptized or pay him tribute. He chose Ganelon as ambassador to them, but the Saracen kings bribed him to act traitor and lead the French army into the defiles of the forest of Roncevalles. Ganelon skilfully managed so that Roland and his friends found themselves in the forest, entirely surrounded by Saracens in overwhelming numbers. They were all slain except Roland, who after finding out Marsile and killing him, was too severely wounded and too faint to do more than sound his ivory horn, hoping some friend would hear it. Sir Baldwin and Sir Terry found him, and soon after he expired. Charlemagne revenged the death of his nephew in a battle at Saragossa, when Baligand was slain, and Sir Otuel re-appeared and slew the King of Persia, while Ganelon was hanged.

OURY THE GERMAN. (*Vide* "Garin the Lorrainer.") Nephew of the two Lorrainers. He helped them in their battles against the Bordelais.

OWEN (1). In Irish romance, son of Duracht. He alone obeyed Conor's order to slay the sons of Usna (*q.v.*). Fox, one of them, carried away Deirdre (*q.v.*), the intended bride of Conor.

OWEN (2). (*Vide* "Gododin.") Son of Urien. He was a great Cymric warrior, who was slain at the Battle of Cattreath.

P

PALFREY, THE. A French romance, probably of the thirteenth century, which relates how a brave knight, named Messire William, fell in love with a fair lady of noble birth, who returned his affections. Her father objected to the union, on account of the knight's poverty. The damsel was so well guarded that they could only hold converse through a breach in the courtyard wall. The knight on these occasions always rode a beautiful grey palfrey, which became familiar with the track through the forest. This continued for some time, till he felt he must have his fate decided one way or the other. So he went to the lady's father, an aged prince, boldly asked his daughter in marriage, and was refused. He, therefore, consulted with the maiden, who advised him to request his old uncle—a very wealthy man—to intercede with her father for him; and as Messire William was his heir, to advance him money, which he would repay after his marriage. The knight complied; the uncle acceded to his wishes, and Messire William rode blithely away to a tournament. During his absence, the uncle asked the maiden in marriage for himself, and because of his wealth, her father agreed. When the knight returned, he was sorely grieved at the trick played on him. The palfrey was borrowed for the use of the wedding guests, as they had to ride some distance to church. A feast was given in honour of the wedding, the lords became heavy with wine, and slept soundly. The warder being dazed, mistook the bright moonlight night for early morn, and sounded his horn for the cavalcade to make ready The maiden was placed on the palfrey and they set forth. The guests were so drowsy with sleep that they scarcely observed where they were going. The palfrey, knowing the way, ambled along unattended, till he came to the path which led to Messire William's house and entered the well-known track without any of the party missing him. The maiden gave him the rein, and allowed him to go where he listed. After fording a river, he brought her straight to his master's castle. The warder, recognizing the horse, ran and told the knight, who, when he beheld the maiden, brought her in amid great rejoicings. The next day they were married, and when her father heard about it, he decided that it was too late to mend matters.

PALMERIN OF ENGLAND. In romance son of an Edward, one of the English kings.

PALMERINDE DE OLIVA. Succeeded to the throne of his grandfather, King of Constantinople. He won the hand of Trineus. The son of his daughter who is said to have married one of our English Edwards became known as Palmerin of England (*q.v.*).

PALOMIDES, SIR. A noble knight of Arthur's Court. He plays an important part in Arthurian romance. As a warrior he proves his prowess in all encounters, either in sport or battle. As a lover he is somewhat conspicuous as paying court to Isond (Ysolde), but in this respect he is repeatedly disappointed. He is an enemy on that account of Sir Tristram, but they possess a deep sense of each other's worth. He is a conspicuous follower after the " questing beast." (*Vide* " Morte d'Arthur.") On another occasion he undertakes the perilous task of avenging King Hermance's (*q.v.*) assassination, overcomes the assassins and restores the liberty of the Red City. He repeatedly displays a love of justice, always fulfilling his pledges in battle, or in sport. He befriends Sir Launcelot, who for a time governor of Benwick, advances him to the Duchy of Provence. (*Vide* " Morte d'Arthur.")

PARTHENAY or THE TALE OF MELU-SINE. A metrical romance translated from the French of La Condrette before 1500 A.D. The French version is superior to the English translation, the MS. of which is in the Trinity College, Cambridge. There is also a copy of the romance in prose in the British Museum, but it differs in detail from the others. The version of the MS. in Trinity College is in octosyllabic metre, and was undertaken by one named La Condrette, a Poitevin, at the request of William, Lord of Parthenay, and continued by him after this William's death in 1401 at the request of his son John of Parthenay. The romance resolves itself into five parts.

(i.) *The story of King Helmas and the Enchanted Mountain.*— Helmas was King of Albany. He married a fairy named Presine, to whom he swore that he would never see her at the time of childbirth. She gives birth to three daughters, named Melusine, Meliov, and Palestine (*vide* " Melusine.") Helmas breaks his vow, and his daughters shut him up in an enchanted mountain until death. Presine, angered at her children's behaviour, turns Melusine into a serpent every Saturday. Meliov is banished for ever to a "Sparrow-hawk Castle" in Armenia, and Palestine is directed to watch over King Helmas' treasures, which are deposited on a mountain-top in Arragon.

(ii.) *Count Raymond*, who is adopted by Amery, the youngest son of the Earl of the Forest, marries Melusine, who exacts from him a promise not to inquire whither she goes every Saturday. He, however, breaks the vow and is forgiven ; but in anger one day he calls her a serpent. She immediately departs in that form ; and afterwards the count is absolved by the Pope and becomes a hermit at Montserrat in Arragon, where he dies.

(iii.) *The Three Sons of Raymond and Melusine.*—Melusine has ten sons in all, amongst whom three of them achieve some object. Geoffrey, with the great tooth, succeeds his father as Lord of Parthenay, and slays the giants Guedon in Geurrande and Gremold in Northumberland. He also discovers the wonders of the enchanted mountain. Fromont, after committing an atrocious deed, becomes a monk ; but Geoffrey is displeased and burns him alive. Horrible, the third son, is put to death by his mother because of his wickedness. The last two, Raymond and Thierry, attain high positions. The former becomes Earl of the Forest, and the latter succeeds Geoffrey as Lord of Parthenay.

(iv.) *The Sparrow-hawk Castle.* —The lady Meliov is given the power of granting a boon to any knight who watches the deathless sparrow within the castle for three nights without sleeping. A king

of Armenia succeeds in doing so, but on asking her to become his wife she slays him.

(v.) *Palestine's Treasures.*— Palestine guards her father's treasures on the top of the mountain in Arragon, assisted by a huge serpent, a great bear and innumerable snakes. An English knight slays the bear, passes the snakes, but is devoured by the great serpent. The romance concludes with many praises of John of Parthenay, and with a lament for his father's death.

PARTHOLAN. Son of Sera. With his Queen Dalny and several companions of both sexes, he is supposed to have been the first man to land in Ireland. In Caesar we learn that the Celts boasted of descent from the God of the Dead, in the land of the mystic west. The Partholians fought victoriously with the Fomorians (*q.v.*), but were exterminated by a pestilence, perishing upon the original plain of Ireland.

PARTINAL. Lord of the Red Tower. Nephew of Espinogre and slayer of Goon Desert, whom he slew disguised as one of Goon Desert's (*q.v.*) knights. Perceval vows to avenge the murder, and coming to his castle espies a fir tree whereon hangs a shield. This Perceval casts down, whereon Partinal appears and is slain. Perceval cuts off his head and places it on the highest tower of the Grail Castle.

PARTONOPEUS DE BLOIS. A French romance dating from the thirteenth century, which has been assigned to Denis Piramus. The tale is in its essence a variation of the legend of Cupid and Psyche. Partonopeus is represented as having lived in the days of Clovis, King of France. He was seized while hunting in the Ardennes, and carried off to a mysterious castle, the inhabitants of which were invisible. Melior, empress of Constantinople, came to him at night, stipulating that he must not attempt to see her for two years and a half. After successfully fighting against the Saracens, led by Lornegur, King of Denmark, he returned to the castle, armed with an enchanted lantern which broke the spell. His consequent misfortunes had a happy termination. The tale had a continuation giving the adventures of Fursin or Anselet, the nephew of Lornegur. Partonopeus is generally assumed to be one of the Seven against Thebes.

PARZIVAL. A German Grail romance adapted from the *Conte du Graal* (*q.v.*) of Chrétien de Troyes by Wolfram von Eschenbach (*q.v.*). It tells how Gamuret, the son of Gandin, Duke of Anjou, marries, during his wanderings in the East, the Moorish queen Belacane, by whom he has a son called Feirifiz. Impelled by his desire of returning to the west, Gamuret leaves the queen and his son ; he returns to France, where, being elected Duke of Anjou, he takes for his second wife Herzeloïde ; but shortly afterwards he dies, and his second wife gives birth to a posthumous son, called Parzival. Herzeloïde, anxious to guard her son against all danger, above all against those incidental to the adventurous life of knights, retires with him to a solitude in Soltane. Parzival is destined, however, to become a model of knighthood. Notwithstanding the ignorance in which he is kept by his mother, the knightly inclination of the youth and his curiosity irresistibly manifest themselves, and having one day met with some knights of the court of Arthur, he follows them, arrives at Nantes, where Arthur was residing, and begs to be first instructed, and afterwards received, as a knight. But Parzival must instruct himself, and gain his spurs in the midst of adventures. He sets out, arrives at the court of Cundwiramour of Pelrapeire, with whom he falls in love, and who is eventually to be his wife ; he comes afterwards to the court of Amfortas, King of the Grëal, who is ill on account of a sin he committed, and whose cure will only be effected when his successor Parzival, seated with him at the banquet of the Grëal, shall ask an explanation of the wonderful things he beholds. Parzival, ignorant of this condition imposed on him by his destiny, and restrained by too much discretion, keeps silence at the banquet, and leaves the castle of Amfortas without inquiring into what he has seen. Thus frustrated, unknown to himself, and partly by his own fault, of the brilliant destiny which awaited him, he begins anew to seek adventures, until, after many a fight, he meets with his friend, Gawain, who takes him back to the court of Arthur. There Cundrie, the witch, the messenger of the San Grëal, informs him of the great wrong of his silence, not only to himself, but also to the King Amfortas, who is his uncle. Parzival, full of grief and regret, at once sets out to find again, if possible, the castle of Amfortas, and repair his fault. At the same time his friend Gawain also leaves the court of Arthur, and, after having fought in many an adventure, succeeds in freeing ladies imprisoned in the Chastel Merveil by the fierce necromancer Klingschor, the nephew of the celebrated magician, Virgil of Naples. As for Parzival, after protracted wanderings, he arrives at a hermitage at some distance from the castle and the temple of San Grëal; the hermit's name is Trevrizent, who eventually makes himself known to him as his maternal uncle. Knowing Parzival to be destined to become King of the Grëal, but not yet worthy of this dignity, he makes known to him that the Grëal is only accessible to him who is called to it by heavenly grace. He recommends him, before approaching it, to purify his soul from all sin, and seeing the good dispositions of the neophyte, he initiates him into its mysteries. The Grëal, he tells him, is made of the *lapis exillis*, gives its servants bodily and spiritual nourishment, and communicates fresh forces for a week to those who see it. Every Good Friday a dove from Heaven comes and places upon the stone a white wafer, which communicates to it mysterious virtues. A writing, which suddenly appears on the vase, always indicates who is destined to its service and guard. Parzival, thus initiated into the mysteries of the Grëal, departs to prepare himself for his high destiny. He returns to the knight of the Round Table, and strives to acquire the knightly virtues necessary to become a Templar, and King of the Grëal. At last, when he is worthy to reign, Cundrie, the witch, again appears at the court of King Arthur, and announces to him that the writing of the Grëal has pointed him out to be King of Montsalvagge. Before going to the temple of the Grëal, Parzival visits his wife Cundwiramour, who has borne him two promising sons, Loherangrin and Cardeiz. After this he directs his steps towards Montsalvagge, the Templois come out to meet him, the banquet of the San Grëal is celebrated, and the conditions imposed by destiny being fulfilled, Amfortas is cured of his disease, and transmits the royal dignity to his nephew Parzival. The new king again meets with his brother on his father's side, Feirifiz, King of India, who, wandering about in search of adventures, has chanced to come to Montsalvagge. But, being a heathen, he was ignorant of the sanctity of the place and the mystery of the San Grëal. Feirifiz, seeing at Montsalvagge Parzival's aunt, Urepanse-de-Joie, falls in love with her, and, after receiving baptism, marries her, though the decease of his first wife, Secondille, whom he had left in the East, is as yet unknown to him. The newly-married pair set out for their kingdom in India. On their way they hear of Secondille's death. Urepanse-de-Joie gives birth to a son, who receives the name of Jean-le-prêtre, Prester John. As for Parzival, he destines his son Loherangrin to succeed him one day in the kingship of the Grëal. This young man early distinguishes himself in an adventurous expedition which he undertakes into the Duchy of Brabant. Wolfram von Eschenbach ends his romance as Guyot had ended his, without telling us what becomes of the San Grëal. He only seems to hint that Prester John will succeed his cousin Loherangrin, and the kingship of the Grëal continue in the marvellous country of India.

In the romance we have just analyzed, the German poet follows exactly the same course as Guyot in the corresponding episode of his poem ; he only adds a few details of his own invention, such as, for instance, the details regarding Klingschor the necromancer, the history of Prester John, and perhaps also the history of Loherangrin.

Klingschor has become the type of the necromancer in the German poetry of the middle ages, like Merlin with the Bretons, and Virgil of Naples with the Italians and Spaniards. But the Germans modified this type in their way, after having received it from south Italy or Sicily, which was the country of Klingschor. For there is no doubt that Klingschor originally was an historical personage, like Merdhin le Gallois in Brittany, Virgil of Mantua in Italy, and Doctor Faust in Germany.

As regards the tradition of Prester John in Graal romance a fabled Pope of Eastern Christendom, it is scarcely probable that it was known to Guyot. In the twelfth century there was in China a great Mongol tribe professing Buddhism such as it had developed itself in Tibet. This religion bore in its sacerdotal hierarchy and in some religious rites and ceremonies so striking a resemblance to Catholicism, that not only the Nestorian Christians dwelling among the Mongols, but also the strangers who visited Mongolia, mistook the Buddha religion of Tibet for an Oriental Christian religion. The temporal and spiritual prince of this supposed Christian tribe took the half-Chinese, half-Mongol title of *Ouanh-kohan*, literally " prince-chief." The Nestorian Christians, who spoke the Syriac language, rendered this by the homonyms *Iouchnan-kohan*, meaning in their language, " John the Priest." Such is the origin of the tradition that there was in the

centre of Asia a Christian Church, whose popes bore the title of Prester John. This tradition spread in Europe towards the end of the twelfth century ; it was perhaps known to Guyot and Chrétien de Troyes, but neither of them connected it with the history of the San Grëal. Wolfram von Eschenbach, on the contrary, availed himself of it in his romance. He looked upon the supposed Christian Church of Asia as a continuation of the priesthood of the Grëal, which priesthood was, after the death of Loherangrin, transmitted to his cousin, Prester John. This ingenious fiction, which, on the whole, Wolfram von Eschenbach only indicated in his romance, was afterwards developed by Albrecht von Scharfenberg in his poem entitled *Titurel*.

PARZIVAL AND THE ROUND TABLE. A romance, of which a manuscript still exists in the library of the Vatican, was composed by Nicolas Wisse and Philip Colin, goldsmith of Strasburg. They dedicated it in 1336 to Ulric, Lord of Rappoltstein, in Alsace. These meistersänger chiefly followed the romance of the French poet Manessier, the continuator of Perceval le Gallois, by Chrétien de Troyes. They were also acquainted with the romances of Wolfram and of Albrecht von Scharfenberg, and placed their ambition more in being complete, and relating all kinds of amusing anecdotes, than in composing a poem faultless in conception and poetical execution.

PATRISE, SIR. A knight of Ireland, cousin of Mader de le Porte, the unfortunate victim of a poisoning tragedy at the court of Arthur. (*Vide* "Penil.") His cousin Mador gallantly attempts to avenge his death, ignorant of the real culprit. (*Vide* "Morte d'Arthur.")

PELEUR. The name in the *Queste del Saint Graal* of the Maimed King or Fisher King (*q.v.*).

PELLEAS, SIR. Of the Isles, known as "the lover." Sometime knight to Queen Guinever. He was slain by Sir Meliagrance (*q.v.*) in defending his mistress. (*Vide* "Morte d'Arthur.")

PELLES, KING. Father of Elaine, the mother of Galahad (*q.v.*). He is also alluded to in Arthurian romance as cousin to Joseph of Arimathea (*q.v.*). He plays an indirect part in the quest of the Holy Grail. He receives a wound from the Grail Sword because of his attempt to interfere with it. The sword is subsequently chosen by Galahad. His most important occupation in the holy mission is the care of the holy vessel in his castle of Corbonec. It was here that the missioners caught their first glimpse of the Grail, and from here the chosen three carried it to its resting place. Pelles was permitted within the sacred chamber, but there his holy duty ended. (*Vide* "Morte d'Arthur.")

PELLINORE, KING. In Arthurian romance, a monarch who followed after the "questing beast." (*Vide* "Morte d'Arthur.") He discovered a plot against Arthur and was subsequently slain by his son, Lamorak.

PELLOUNCES, SIR. Father to Persides, and a venerable knight of England. The defender of the "Round Table." (*Vide* "Morte d'Arthur.")

PENIL, SIR, LA SAVAGE. Cousin of Lamorak de Galis. At a banquet given by Guinever he poisoned the apples that he might be avenged upon Gawaine, whom he hated. Sir Patrise partook of the poisonous fruit and immediately dropt dead. The company little realize who is the true culprit, and accuse their hostess of treason. Subsequently, he is exposed by an enchantress and is forced to flee for safety. (*Vide* "Morte d'Arthur.")

PEPIN. (*Vide* "Garin the Lorrainer.") Son of Charles Martel (*q.v.*), King of France. He became king when he was a boy, and was ruled by his advisers, among whom Count Hardré was chief. He was constantly being asked for assistance by some of the rival families in France. He tried to make peace between the Lorrainers and the Bordelais on several occasions. He married Blanchflower, the lovely daughter of Thierry (*q.v.*), King of Savoy (*q.v.*). He had intended to allow Garin the Lorrainer to marry her, but when he saw her, he fell in love with her himself, and, by the advice of the archbishop of Rheims, married her.

PERCEVAL. An important figure in Arthurian romance. Only once (in the metrical romance of *Sir Percyvelle*) (*q.v.*) is he alluded to as the nephew of Arthur, at whose court he does not reside, except at intervals. The earliest form of the many romances which bear his name is found in the *Conte del Graal* or *Perceval* of Chrétien of Troyes, and his continuators, and the *Parzival* of Wolfram von Eschenbach, under which titles an account of his adventures and career will be found. Both these poems are undoubtedly derived from the same source, but the connection between them is slender. Perceval, brought up in the desert by his mother, and gradually

evolving into the flower of knighthood by dint of his love of high
ideals and natural spirituality, is
the hero of the two epics alluded
to above. The more sophisticated
Perceval of the Quest of the Holy
Grail is by no means so *naïf*, so
natural. The other notable romances in which Perceval figures
are the Middle English romance of
Syr Percyvelle of Galles, the prose
Pereslavaus or *Percival li Gallois*,
and a romance by Robert de
Borron, which is now only to be
found in a prose form. He is, of
course, the hero of the Grail quest
par excellence, for information on
which phase of his legend the
reader is referred to the principal
and allied articles on the Grail
(" Grail, Holy ; " *Conte del Graal ;
Parzival*, etc.). In his Brythonic
or Welsh form of Peredur ap
Evrawc, Perceval is the hero of
the story of that name, which is
summarised under its title, and
which appears in the *Mabinogion*.
In its Celtic form his legend has no
connection with the Grail story.
A chief of his name fell in the
battle of Cattraeth in the beginning
of the sixth century, according to
the bard Aneurin, and he is mentioned by Gruffydd ap Meredydd,
who flourished about the end of
the thirteenth century, in his elegy
on Tudor ap Goronwy.

PERCEVAL LI GALLOIS. A romance
of the Grail quest. It is written
in prose, and was written for a
certain John of Nesle in Flanders,
who was living in the year 1295.
Of all the tales concerning the
quest for the Holy Grail (*q.v.*) this
is the most confused. It declares
itself to be written by Joseph of
Arimathea at the bequest of an
angel, and tells how the good
knight Perceval is descended
through his mother from Joseph

of Arimathea, who kept the lance
with which Christ was pierced and
the holy vessel in which his blood
was gathered. On his father's
side Perceval was descended from
Nicodemus. The Fisher King (*vide*
" Amfortas ") was his uncle. In the
time of his youth he went to the
Fisher's castle, but does not ask
of what avail was the Holy Grail,
hence wars arise, and the king falls
into sickness. Gawain and Lancelot arrive at the Grail Castle.
Gawain goes first to that part of
it called the Castle of Enquiry,
where the sword that was used to
behead John the Baptist is preserved, but he does not speak in
the castle, where he sees the Grail
and lance. Lancelot cannot see
the Grail on account of his carnal
love for Guinevere. The Fisher
King dies suddenly, and his lands
are taken by his brother, the King
of Castle Deadly. Perceval fights
against him, conquers, and wins
the Grail Castle. He is visited by
Arthur, Gawain, and Lancelot.
Perceval latterly sails away on a
vessel with a white sail, on which
is a red lion, and never has man
learned what became of him.
This legend, ends the MS., was
found on the shores of the Moor
Adventurous, where Arthur and
Guinevere are buried.

PERCIVAL, SIR. Son of King Pellinore (*q.v.*) and knight of the
Round Table. He appears in
Arthurian romance as a man of
high chivalry and purity of life.
He is destined along with Galahad
(*q.v.*) to accomplish the Holy Grail.
This high honour is accorded to
but few, and as one of the privi-
leged he acquits his duty nobly and
well. With Bors and Galahad he
patiently and resolutely makes his
way through the intricacies of the
quest. Arriving at their mission's

end, he willingly, after seeing Galahad's ascension, submits himself to the same honour, realising that he had done the duty for the purpose of which he was born. (*Vide* " Morte d'Arthur.")

PERCYVELLE, SIR. An English metrical romance found in the Thornton MS., written shortly before the middle of the fifteenth century. It tells how Percyvelle's parents were Percyvelle and Acheflour (Arthur's sister). His father was noted for overcoming the Red Knight in a tournament, but was ultimately slain by him. His mother thereupon betakes herself to the woods with the young boy, where he receives little instruction save that of great mother Nature herself until the time of his reaching his fifteenth birthday, when his natural mother teaches him how to invoke the great Author of his surroundings. Shortly afterwards, he meets with three knights of the court of Arthur—yclept Ewayne, Gawayne, and Kay, whom—his mind filled with mysteries—he mistakes for supernatural beings. Persuaded, however, that they are but true and puissant knights of the Round Table, he resolves to go to Arthur's court himself and win his spurs. He catches a wild horse, and, returning to his mother, announces his intention. She advises him to be always courteous and respectful in his demeanour to knights when he meets them, and on his finally taking leave presents him with her ring as a token. He sets out and at length wearied by the journey, he revives his drooping spirits with meat and drink at a wayside house. Discovering a fair damoselle asleep, he exchanges his mother's ring for that of the lady's. Arriving at Arthur's court he rides straight up to the king and peremptorily demands knighthood, threatening death if refused. Arthur notices the resemblance to his father in the young man's countenance, and recalls the prophecies that he should avenge his father's untimely end. Percyvelle exhibits disquietude and reiterates his demand for knighthood. Whilst the assembled guests are regaling themselves at the banquet, the Red Knight enters the hall, and for the fifth time in as many years seizes and carries off Arthur's cup, none daring to bar his progress. Thereupon, Percyvelle, grieved at the king's discomfiture and lamentations, undertakes the quest of killing the Red Knight and recovering the cup, if the boon of knighthood be but granted him. The king acquiesces and Percyvelle immediately follows hard upon the tracks of the purloiner, who derides him, but he is wounded to death by an unerring dart. He rides up and secures the Red Knight's horse, and being unable to remove his armour recalls his mother's injunction, " out of the iron burn the tree," lights a fire to consume the corpse. Gawayne, who has followed Sir Percyvelle closely to be at hand with friendly succour, shows him how to unlace the armour, and when that is accomplished, Percyvelle casts the Red Knight's body into the now leaping flames. Bethinking himself now as great as his lord and master the king, Percyvelle disdains to return, but sends the cup back by Gawaine, and sets out again for the fields and pastures of fresh adventures. But before proceeding far on his journey he comes upon an old witch—the mother of the Red Knight as it turns out—who invokes him as her offspring. He speedily makes short work of the old beldame by running her through with his spear, and she serves as further fuel for the glowing embers of her son's death pyre. He next comes upon ten knights, who, mistaking him for the all-dreaded Red Knight, are about to fly, when hailing them and raising his vizor, he reassures them. The oldest of the knights then recounts how the Red Knight —since fifteen years agone when he had done his brother to death— bore him and his sons bitter hatred. Hearing, however, that Percyvelle had vanquished this bane of their existence, he invites him to his castle. But "adventures are to the adventurous"; scarcely were they seated at a generous repast than a messenger comes in from the Maiden-land, begging help for the Lady Lufamour against a "Sowdane" who would feign wed her. Percyvelle sets out with three of the old knight's sons, whom, however, he sends back one after the other at the end of each of the first three miles. Meantime, the king at Carebedd, lamenting for Percyvelle, also receives a message from Lufamour and gleans from it tidings of Percyvelle, and thereupon sets out with his court to follow him. On Percyvelle reaching the Sowdane's camp he is set upon by the guard, but he kills them all and then betakes himself to slumber beneath the castle wall. At dawn Lufamour's henchmen inform her of the disaster to her enemies. She perceives Percyvelle and bids her chamberlain, Hatlayne, fetch him to her chamber. Whilst seated together news is brought that the enemy has nearly succeeded in capturing the town. Percyvelle attacks them at once single-handed and spares none. He then reconnoitres four

knights—Arthur, Ewayne, Gawayne, and Kay. He pricks against them, and Gawayne receives the onslaught. They soon recognize each other and they all proceed to Lufamour's castle. The following day, the Sowdane challenges all comers ; Percyvelle, now dubbed knight by Arthur, slays him, and thereafter weds Lufamour. At the end of a year he recalls his mother's loneliness, and sets out to find her. Hearing a maiden bewailing her fate in a wood hard by, he discovers her tethered to a tree, and learns that a year before, while sleeping, a stranger had despoiled her of her ring, leaving his in exchange. Now her ring was of a stone of such virtue that neither death nor hurt could come to the wearer thereof. He unfastens her thongs, defeats the Black Knight who had bound her, reconciles them, and claims his own ring for the ring he had taken. But the Black Knight had given it to the lord of the land—a giant. Percyvelle kills the giant, and obtains the ring from the seneschal. The latter relates to him how his master, loving a fair lady, had proffered her that same ring, but she, accusing him of killing her son, hid herself in the forest and became bereft of her wits. Percyvelle assumes the skin of a goat, and after searching for her for nine days discovers her. A magic potion of the giant throws her into a three days' trance, after which, clothed and in her right mind, she returns home with her son. Percyvelle ultimately goes to the Holy Land, and there at length death overtakes the hero.

PEREDUR, THE SON OF EVRAWC. A Welsh romance included in the fourteenth century Welsh MS.,

known as *The Red Book of Hergest*.
The first portion of the tale agrees
very much with that of Chrétien
(the *Conte del Graal*) (*q.v.*) in its
sequence and the character of
its circumstances. But there is a
notable difference in the incident
which deals with what takes place
at the castle of the Fisher King.
(*Vide* " Grail," " Conte del Graal,"
and other Grail articles.) First
Peredur beholds a lance which
drips with blood, then a charger
in which a man's head is swimming
in gore. Neither of these things
answer to what he has heard of
the Holy Grail. After its description of this enterprise the Welsh
version, whilst corresponding
generally with Chrétien, has some
especial features. Peredur guards
from injury a certain castle against
the sorceries of the enchantresses
of Gloucester, one of whom hails
him as their destined conqueror.
He learns from these enchantresses
the use of arms and the knowledge
of chivalry. A considerable portion of the romance, nearly one-
third in fact, answers to nothing
in Chrétien's work or any French
version in existence. In the latter
portion, after the coming of the
ungainly damsel, the Welsh version, whilst offering in great
measure the same sequence of
circumstances as in Chrétien's and
Gautier's poems, recounts them
in a far more coherent manner.
The romance concludes with the
advent of a youth who discovers
himself as the cousin of Peredur.
He it was who had borne the head
on the charger swimming with
blood, and had taken upon himself
the guise of the ungainly damsel
who urged Peredur to continue
his quest for the Grail. His object
in bearing the bloody head in the
charger and aiding and inciting
Peredur in many adventures was

to avenge the death of his murdered cousin (whose head he bore
in the charger) upon the enchantresses of Gloucester and the laming
of the Fisher King. The Welsh
tale is thus in a large measure a
logical and straightforward version
of a hero's vengeance upon supernatural beings for the injuries
inflicted by them upon his kindred.
. . . Had we the story in a purer form
we should find that the injury, so
far as he is concerned, consists in
the enchantment of hideous and
unsexing disguise, an enchantment
from which the consummation of
the vengeance can alone free him.
The object of the talismans is
here to remind the hero of the
wrong done and to supply the
necessary weapon." *Peredur* is a
vengeance tale pure and simple.

PERIGON. (*Vide* " Sir Otuel.") King
of Persia. Killed by Sir Otuel at
the Battle of Sarragossa.

PERSANT, SIR. Brother to Sir Grina-
more, a knight of the Round
Table. He was amongst the slain
in the defence of Guinever against
Sir Meliagrance (*q.v.*). (*Vide*
" Morte d'Arthur.")

PERSE, PRINCE. (*Vide* " Florice and
Blanchfleur.") A noble heir to
rich domains in Italy. He was
married to Topase, and while
journeying to the Holy Land, was
slain by Felix (*q.v.*).

PERSIDES, SIR. Son of a worthy
knight, Sir Pellounces. He was a
friend of Tristram (*q.v.*), and displayed conspicuous prowess in
battle. (*Vide* " Morte d'Arthur.")

PETIPASE, SIR. Of Winchelsea, a
frequent visitor to the court of
Arthur. (*Vide* " Morte d'Arthur.")

PETRONE. Mentioned in the *Grand
St. Graal* as a holy man and kinsman of Joseph of Arimathea. He

christened the daughter of King Label.

PETRUS. One of the figures introduced in a casual way at the table emblematical of the Last Supper in the Legend of the Holy Grail.

PHILOSOFINE. Alluded to in Gerbert's continuation of the *Conte del Graal* as the mother of Perceval. She came to Britain with Joseph of Arimathea and bore the Grail plate as distinct from the dish itself.

PILGRIN BISHOP. Filled the see of Passanform 971 to 991, and took a great share in the conversion of the Hungarians to Christianity. He is mentioned in *Die Klage* as having had the *Nibelungenlied* story "set down in Latin letters that men might deem it true." M. Amédée Thierry has suggested that the Eddic version of the Nibelung story in which Attila is still the ferocious monarch of history may have been touched up and moralized by Bishop Pilgrin for the Hungarians, whose national hero Attila was, so as to soften all the harsher features of his character. But no Hungarian version of the *Nibelungenlied* has been preserved, and the Hungarian chronicle sensibly depart from the Nibelung account of Attila or Etzel.

PITÉ, SIR BRUESE LAUNCE. A felon knight mentioned repeatedly in Arthurian romance as a robber and seducer of women. (*Vide* "Morte d'Arthur.")

PLAINE DE FORCE, SIR; PLAINE D'AMOUR, SIR; and **PLENORIUS, SIR.** The three brothers who assail La Côte Male-tailé (*q.v.*) in his errand of succour to Dame Lyonese (*q.v.*). They are subdued and made to pay homage to King Arthur. (*Vide* "Morte d'Arthur.")

POLITIANO, ANGELO (POLITIAN). A celebrated Italian poet, who was born at Monte Pulciano on July 24th, 1454. He early exhibited extraordinary epigrammatic powers, and upon the publication of a poem on a tournament in which Julian de' Medici was the victor, in 1468, he was received by Lorenzo de' Medici into his palace, became his confident, and afterwards tutor to his children. The tournament poem commences almost in epic style, and bears every mark of the spacious thought of the age in which it was composed. But he had by no means made choice of a suitable hero, and soon abandoned the work. The technique and spirit of his verse are equal to those of Tasso or Ariosto. He represents Julian in the flower of his youth, devoted to arms, and despising love. He draws the youth surrounding him to the chase. But Love has his revenge by drawing him from the hunt by means of a beautiful white hind, which changes after a stern chase into a beautiful maiden, Simonetta. Julian becomes deeply enamoured of her, and Cupid, proud of his victory, flies to his mother in the Isle of Cyprus, and boasts of his success. The description of Venus' palace served as a model to Ariosto and Tasso for the enchanted domes of Alcina and Armida. In the second book, Simonetta, arrayed in the armour of Pallas, appears to Julian in a dream, and reminds him that only by valour can she be won. Julian awakens amidst the aspirations of glory and of love. Here Politiano relinquishes the work. Politiano revived on the modern stage the tragedies of the ancients, and created a new species of pastoral tragedy. His *Favola di Orfeo* was performed at Mantua in 1483. It was composed in two days. Later in life he abandoned poetry for philosophy. Had he elected to cultivate his real talents instead of entering a domain for which he was almost totally unfitted, he would undoubtedly have risen to a height of fame equal to that of the greatest names in Italian literature.

PORTUGAL, KING OF. (*Vide* "Florice and Blanchfleur.") An ally of the King of Galicia, who fought against Felix (*q.v*) to obtain freedom from his oppression.

PRESTER JOHN. In Grail romance a fabled pope of Eastern Christendom. As regards his tradition, it is scarcely probable that it was known to Guyot (*q.v.*). In the twelfth century there was in China a great Mongol tribe professing Buddhism such as it had developed itself in Tibet. This religion bore in its sacerdotal hierarchy and in some religious rites and ceremonies so striking a resemblance to Catholicism, that not only the Nestorian Christians dwelling among the Mongols, but also the strangers who visited Mongolia, mistook the Buddha religion of Tibet for an Oriental Christian religion. The temporal and spiritual prince of this supposed Christian folk took the half-Chinese, half-Mongol title of *Owanh-kohan*, literally prince-chief. The Nestorian Christians, who spoke the Syriac language, rendered this by the homonyms Iouchnan-kohan, meaning, in their language, John the Priest. Such is the origin of the tradition that there was in the centre of Asia a Christian Church, whose popes bore the

title of Prester John. This tradition spread in Europe towards the end of the twelfth century ; it was perhaps known to Guyot and Chrétien de Troyes, but neither of them connected it with the history of the San Graal. Wolfram von Eschenbach, on the contrary, availed himself of it in his romance. He looked upon the supposed Christian Church of Asia as a continuation of the priesthood of the Grail, which priesthood was, after the death of Loherangrin, transmitted to his cousin, Prester John. This ingenious fiction, which, on the whole, Wolfram von Eschenbach only indicated in his romance, was afterwards developed by Albrecht von Scharfenberg in his poem of *Titurel.*

PRIADAM THE BLACK. A knight who oppresses the lady of a castle whose cause is championed by Bors (*q.v.*). Bors overcomes Priadam and reinstates the lady in her possessions.

PRIMAUS. (*Vide* "Morte d'Arthur.") Formerly a Saracen leader, he was converted to Christianity by King Arthur, who defeated him, after which he became a knight of the Round Table.

PRINSAMOUR, SIR. A count of Artois and father of Crystabell (*q.v.*), a notable character in the romance of *Sir Eglamour of Artoys* (*q.v.*). He displayed much hostility toward Sir Eglamour (*q.v.*) who desired his daughter ; but to prove the latter's prowess he sent him on three adventures, which were accomplished. He banished his daughter after discovering her dishonour, and subsequently met his death by falling from a tower.

PRISE D'ORANGE. (The taking of Orange.) A romance of the

William of Orange sub-cycle of the Charlemagne saga. It was probably composed in the first quarter of the eleventh century, but modernized after 1076, and forms in its present shape the most modern branch of the sub-cycle. (*Vide* " William of Orange.") It tells how William of Orange waking in the palace of Otrant " the cursed," the Saracen king whom he has conquered, complains to Bertram, his nephew, of the quietness of the times, and of how the Saracens and Slavons " let us sleep and rest so much." A knight who has been a prisoner of the Saracens for many years arrives at Nîmes, and tells William how great a town and fortress is the Saracen city of Orange. William hearkening, covets the city, and swears a mighty oath that he will behold it. He summons Gilbert, the knight who has just regained his freedom, to accompany him thither, as he knows the language. But Gilbert tries to dissuade the fiery chief from his purpose, as does Bertram. William, however, will not be gainsaid, and they prepare to start on their journey. They disguise themselves as Saracens, and, having arrived at the gates of Orange, they declare themselves to be pilgrims come from Africa. William interviews the king, who tells him that had he " Shortnose " (William's nickname) in his power he would torture him, and cast his bones to the wind. They are conducted to the tower of Glorietta, where they admire the marble pillars and walls, the windows carved in silver, and Lady Orable, the Queen, who is dressed in scarlet cloth and is fanned by the Lady Rosianna with a silver fan. William trembles with love at sight of her, and tells

her that William Short-nose has sworn to come to the city and destroy it. But Salatré, a Saracen recently escaped from William's city of Nîmes, recognizes him and his companions Guielin and Gilbert, and makes him uncover his face by means of a blow. Aragon, the king, tells him that he will slay him and scatter his dust through the mountains, but William brains Salatré, and the three Frenchmen among them slay fourteen Saracens. The remainder they drive out, and drawing up the chains of the drawbridge, shut themselves up in the citadel of Glorietta. Orable arms the heroes, and they prepare for a stout resistance. They make great havoc among the Saracens, and Aragon offers to let them go if they will give up Glorietta. William replies that they never mean to leave. A French host sets out to succour them. Pharaoh, King of Benevent, advises that the Christians should be burnt out with Greek fire. But an old Saracen kadi, Orquenoy, reveals a subterranean passage to Aragon, by means of which he enters the citadel of Glorietta. The French make great slaughter, but are taken, and Orable begs them as her prisoners, in order that they may be devoured by snakes. The Frenchmen are imprisoned pending the arrival of other Saracen notables. Orable comes to the prisoners, saying that if William will have her for his wife she will set them free and become a Christian. William assents to this, and she takes them up to Glorietta and tells them of another secret passage leading to the Rhône. They are overheard by a Saracen who tells Aragon, who discovers William and Orable playing chess. They are at once imprisoned, and

x

are again brought before the Paynim, when William falls upon
them and does great execution.
They succeed in shutting themselves up in Glorietta a second
time, but Bertram, William's
nephew, arrives before the city,
enters it by means of the underground passage, and takes possession of it, killing Aragon. Orable
is baptized under the name of
Guibor, and marries William. For
thirty years he dwelt in Orange,
which became his own city. A
continuation of the romance is the
Enfance Vivien, which see.

PUCCI, ANTONIO. A mediæval
Italian poet. The dates of his
birth and death are not definitely
known, but it would seem that
he was born at Florence in the
middle of the fourteenth century,
and that the greater part if not
the whole of his career was spent
in his native town, where he died
eventually about 1398. He must
have been a man of comparatively
humble origin, for it is recorded
that he began his career as a bell-
ringer, and subsequently became
town-crier ; but it appears that,
at a later date, he acquired some
more important post in the service
of the municipality. An ardent
admirer of Dante, he early began
to write verse himself, and even
from the outset his work was
characterized by singular care.
In course of time he won great
favour in Florence, the public's
attention being commanded in
particular by his humorous writings, and thereafter he turned his
attention to doing a series of
martial tales which he called
Sirventes. These songs might be
either martial or political ; while
he also wrote a number of poems
based on popular legendary lore,
salient among his works of this

order being *Reine d'Oriente, Appo-
lonio di Tivo,* and *Bel Cherardino.*
Another notable work from his pen
is *Il Centiloquio,* which is a metrical
version of the chronicle of Giovanni
Villani ; while in addition he
wrote *La Guerra di Pisa,* the
subject of this last being the war
waged between the Florentines
and the Pisans from 1362 to 1365.
Pucci is generally regarded as
the supreme humorist of mediæval
Italy, while as an heroic poet he
likewise holds a tolerably high
place. His Centiloquio is contained in *Delizie Degli.*

PULCI, LUIGI. A Florentine, the
youngest of three brothers, all
poets ; he was born in 1431. He
composed and read at the table of
Lorenzo de Medici his *Morgante
Maggiore,* a chivalric romance in
verse in the form which became
peculiar to the epic poetry of
Italy, and forecasted the metre
employed by Ariosto. The poem
was published in 1485, and is
alternately vulgar or burlesque,
serious or insipid, or else religious.
The principal characters of the
romance are the same which first
appeared in the fabulous chronicle
of Turpin in the thirteenth century. His real hero is Orlando
rather than Morgante. We are
introduced to the paladin of
Charlemagne at the point when
the intrigues of Ganelon de May-
ence compel him to flee the emperor's court. (*Vide* "Song of
Roland.") Orlando encounters
three giants, two of whom he
slays, and makes the third, Morgante, prisoner. Him he converts
and baptizes, and paladin and
giant become brothers in arms.
The entire romance consists of
warlike adventures, and quite a
secondary position is given to the
theme of love. This is the less

regrettable as the constitutional coarseness of Pulci was little suited to the delineation of the tender passion. The poem terminates with the death of Orlando at Roncesvalles, and the punishment of Ganelon's treachery. Pulci is extolled by the Italian critics for the purity of his style, which for the most part consisted in fidelity to the Tuscan dialect, but there is much music in his metres, and some native splendour of diction. He died in 1487.

PWYLL, PRINCE OF DYFED. A Welsh romance included by Lady Charlotte Guest in *The Mabinogion*, and drawn from a fourteenth-century MS. known as the *Red Book of Hergest*. It recounts how Pwyll, Prince of Dyfed in Wales, was one day hunting when he encountered a pack of supernatural hounds, engaged in pulling down a deer. He drove them from the quarry, when he was confronted by their master, who rebuked him. Pwyll offered to make amends for the deed, and the stranger, who is Arawn, King of Annwn (Hades), accepts his offer, and asks him to exchange kingdoms for a space, as he is sore pressed by an adversary, Hafgan. Pwyll undertakes the rule of Annwn, and defeats Hafgan. During his stay in the Otherworld, he sleeps nightly with Arawn's wife, who, as he had taken upon him her husband's shape, did not guess of the change, but refrains from making advances to her. Having ended his labours in Annwn, Pwyll returns to earth to find that Arawn on his part has governed Dyfed well, and the monarchs once more resume their proper shapes and dwell thenceforth in fast friendship. Shortly after Pwyll, sitting on the enchanted mound of Arberth, espies Rhiannon, daughter of Hevydd Hen, to whom he gives chase. Going to her father's palace, Pwyll is asked by a certain Gwawl to grant him a boon, and upon his promising anything in his power, the youth requests Rhiannon as his bride. Rhiannon asks him to return in a year. To this he assents and duly returns. As they make merry a beggar enters the hall carrying a bag. He craves Gwawl to grant him sufficient food to fill the bag. Gwawl assents. The bag holds everything on the table, and Gwawl protesting, is told that he must enter it himself to declare that enough has been put therein. He does so, and is at once tied into it. The followers of Pwyll rush in, and on being told that the bag contains a badger, kick it violently. Gwawl offers to abandon Rhiannon if released, so is permitted to go with his men. Pwyll then weds Rhiannon. A son is born to them. He disappears, and the nurses in their terror place the bones of a cub in the bed, and declare that Rhiannon has devoured her child. In penance she is forced to stand at the castle gate, and carry strangers in on her back. A certain Teirnyon, fearing the theft of a new-foaled colt, is sitting up with it when a great arm reaches into the stable to seize it. He cuts it off. There is an outcry, and he finds an infant lying outside the stable door. Teirnyon notices his resemblance to Pwyll, who recognizes him as his son Pryderi (Trouble), and Rhiannon's misfortunes are brought to a close. Considerable mythological degradation is shown in this tale. Annwn, the Otherworld, was in the older Celtic tales a distant and shadowy realm oversea. But here it is obviously a mundane region, seemingly bordering upon Dyfed.

The portion of the story which refers to the struggle for Rhiannon between Pwyll and Gwawl may be explained by regarding Rhiannon as the moon for which the Night (Pwyll) and the Sun (Gwawl) strive, the solar hero being trapped in the bag of Night, and released again.

PYSTIL OF SWETE SUSAN, THE. A Scottish poem of the fourteenth century. It is almost certainly from the pen of Huchown of the Awle Ryle (*q.v.*), for Andrew of Wynton, in his enthusiastic eulogy of that writer contained in *The Originale Cronykl of Scotland*, names among Huchown's works

"The pystal als off Swete Susan."

It is concerned with the familiar story of Susannah and the elders recounted in the *Apocrypha* ; and it is written in stanzas of thirteen lines each, very intricately rhymed, and embodying the usual large quota of alliteration. Despite this elaborate manner, the verses mostly have the semblance of complete spontaneity, while at times they are marked by rare happiness of phraseology and beauty of cadence. Indeed the poem must be ranked as one of the best things in early Scottish literature.

Among ancient manuscript copies of *The Pystil of Swete Susan*, the most important are one in the Bodleian Library and one in the Cotton Library. The former, known from its donor's name as the Vernon manuscript, appears from the nature of the handwriting to date from about the end of the fourteenth century, while the Cotton version was probably written by a scribe of a somewhat later period. This document is shorter than the other by several stanzas, while otherwise the two disclose sundry variations.

Q

QUELGNY, THE CATTLE RAID OF. The greatest of Celtic legendary tales. (*Vide* "Meev.") Finn Mac Gorman, Bishop of Kildare, in the year 1150 included this tale in the *Book of Leinster*, of which tradition regards Fergus Mac Roy (*q.v.*) as the original writer. He was said to have written it in Ogham characters on staves of wood which a bard carried to Italy. There are many legends dealing with the recovery of this poem : one telling how it was regained from Fergus.

QUETE DEL ST. GRAAL. This romance, the author of which is unknown, recounts the adventures of Sir Lancelot's son, Galahad, who comes to Arthur's court to achieve the adventure of the Siege Perilous and the sword driven into the block. It also recounts the coming of the Holy Grail, a vessel which fills every one who sees it with such sustenance as he longs for, and of Sir Gawain's vow that he will seek it for a year and a day. The other knights of the Round Table express a desire to go with him on the quest. The adventures which happen to Galahad and the other seekers are much the same as prophesied in the *Grand St. Graal*, and tell of unholy love and the virtues of Galahad. Lancelot discovers a maimed knight in quest of the Holy Grail. It is observed, but Lancelot refuses to speak when he beholds it, for which afterwards much unhappiness is his lot. Sir Percival discovers that Mordrains, a character originally connected with the Grail, is still alive, having eaten nothing but the Lord's body for the term of 400 years, and waiting the arrival of a good knight. Lancelot goes to a castle called Corbenic, where he lies unconscious for many days as he has approached too closely to the Grail. Galahad, Percival and Bors at last come to the castle, where they are met by nine other knights. Josephes, son of Joseph of Arimathea, who first possessed the Grail, appears, and celebrates the sacrament for them all. Christ comes to Gala-had, and tells him to go to Sarras, whither the Grail is going, as Britain is unworthy of it. But first he must heal the maimed king. (*Vide* "Grail.") The trio then embark on a ship, and are thrown into prison, but are miraculously fed by the Grail. A last appearance precedes the death of Galahad, who is soon followed in death by Percival. Bors then returns to Britain, and recounts the adventures of the seekers for the Grail, which were set forth on parchment and kept in Salisbury Abbey, whence Walter Map (*q.v.*) perhaps drew the materials for the book as we possess it. (*Vide* "Grail," and "Conte del Graal.")

R

RABENSCHLACT. (*Vide* "Dietrich of Bern.")

RAFN THE SKALD. (*Vide* "Gunnlang Saga.") Son of Onund; lover of Helga.

RALPH THE COLLIER. The only Scottish romance connected with the Charlemagne cycle. At one time it was so popular as to be specially mentioned by the Scottish poet Dunbar, yet for about seventy years it was supposed to be lost, but in 1821 a copy was discovered in a volume of tracts in the Advocates' Library in Edinburgh. It dates from about the beginning of the fifteenth century, and possesses considerable poetical merit, while the characters are well outlined. Dr. Irving suggested that it might have been written by Huchowne (*q.v.*), and its resemblance to his other works substantiates this theory. It tells how Charlemagne hunting in the forest was overtaken by a storm of wind and snow, and lost his way. Much exhausted, he falls in with a collier, and asks shelter of him. The man acquiesces, and leads him home. The collier beckons the king, of whose identity he is unaware, to enter first, but on the monarch's refusing out of politeness, he takes him by the scruff of the neck and forces him in. He requests the king to be seated at table, but once more Charles gives him precedence, and the collier, telling him that he has again forgotten his manners, hits him a mighty buffet on the ear. He is, he says, a simple man, but all must do in his house as he bids them. This is an evil life, thinks Charles, and the best policy is to give in. Therefore he is silent. After an excellent supper, the collier relates his poaching experiences in the royal forests, and asks the king about himself. Charles says that he lives at court in the service of the queen, and that his name is Wymond of the Wardrobe. He invites the collier to court. The king rises at daybreak, and offers to pay for his lodging, but Ralph will not hear of it, and will only promise that he will come to court with a load of coals. On his way to court, Charles meets his paladins who have been searching for him. They all return to Paris. On the next day, Christmas morning, Ralph fills two creels with fresh charcoal and is about to set off when his wife attempts to dissuade him. Undeterred by her fears, he sets out, and is met by Sir Roland, who has been told off to look out for him. Roland asks him to follow him, but the collier, irritated at the knight's peremptory tone, says that before he does so he will know which is the better man of the twain. Roland permits him to pass, but not before the gallant man of coal has extended a challenge to him for the next day. The collier then makes his way to the palace, and asks for Wymond. As no one knows him, he pushes his way into the royal hall where the court was assembled keeping the Christmas festivals. He is dumfounded at the sight of splendour which meets his gaze. Catching sight of the king he calls out "Yonder is Wymond." The king then relates his hunting adventure to the nobles, and while this is being told the collier stands trembling in the certainty of destruction. The king ended by asking what should be done to the man who had acted thus to his liege lord. "Hang him," cried the courtiers with one accord. But Charles in his wisdom refuses to do so, and makes the collier a knight, bestowing upon him a pension of three hundred pounds a year, with a retinue of sixty squires for his company. Next

morning the newly-dubbed knight made ready to keep his tryst with Sir Roland, when he saw coming towards him, riding on a camel, the most gigantic knight he had ever seen. They encounter, their steeds are slain, and they engage on foot for an hour, when Roland appears, and rushing in between the combatants, separates them. Sir Ralph's opponent turns out to be Magog, a Saracen knight, sent by the Cham of Tartary to declare war upon France. He has fought so bravely that Roland is anxious that he should turn Christian, and succeeds in converting him. Then all three swear on their swords to be fast friends for the rest of their lives. Magog is dubbed knight under the name of Sir Gawtier, and is married to the Duchess of Anjou. Sir Ralph is appointed Marshal of France, and to mark the spot where he found the king, a hostelry is erected in the name of Saint July for sheltering those who lose their way or otherwise require its protection.

RANDVER. (*Vide* "Volsungs.") Son of King Jormunrek (*q.v.*). He fell in love with Swanhild (*q.v.*) who was betrothed to his father. For this both were slain by order of Jormunrek.

RANNVEIG. (*Vide* "Burnt Njal.") Mother of Gunnar (*q.v.*).

RAOUL OF CAMBRAY. A sub-cycle of the Charlemagne saga, dealing with the history of the lords of Vermandois. Raoul, brought up at the court of King Louis, has his birthright taken from him by Gibouin of Mans. Guerry the Red solicits Louis to give back to Raoul, who is Guerry's nephew, the lands of Cambrésis, which are his by right, but the king refuses. At length Raoul obtains consent to take the estate of the dead Count Herbert of Vermandois. His squire Bernier dislikes the task, for Count Herbert was his father's friend. Raoul cruelly burns the town and convent of Vermandois, and Bernier's mother is slain. He remonstrates with Raoul, is struck, and leaves his service. Bernier goes to his father Ybert, who marches against Raoul. In the battle which ensues Raoul is slain by Hernant and Bernier. Red Guerry swears vengeance, as does young Walter, Raoul's nephew. Guerry and Walter, after five years' time, attack Vermandois. Walter defeats Bernier. Feud follows feud. At length a peace is patched up, and Bernier becomes Guerry's man, and marries his daughter. But the king lays an ambush for the wedding guests, and gives Bernier's wife to Erchimbauld of Poitiers as his wife. The wedding day is fixed, but as the two are to be made one, Bernier bursts forth from concealment with 3000 knights and frees his wife. Time passes. Bernier and Red Guerry go on a pilgrimage. On passing the place where Raoul was slain, ancient hate surges up in Guerry's soul, and he slays Bernier by a felon stroke. Guerry, pursued by Bernier's sons, goes into exile and becomes a hermit. The poem was highly popular, but is narrow in subject, and appears to have been compiled from more than one source, and there are several obvious interpolations. Its date would seem to be the latter end of the twelfth century. It possesses great freshness and dramatic power, and may be by th same hand as *Garin the Lorrainer*.

RATHBONE. (*Vide* "Bevis of Hampton.") A thief who by using black magic stole Arundel, Bevis's horse, killed by Saber.

RAUF COILZEAR. (*Vide* "Ralph the Collier.")

RAYMOND. A French ecclesiastic and chronicler of the eleventh century, sometimes styled Raymond d'Agiles and more often Raymond d'Aguilers. He was canon of the Church of Puy, and he went to Palestine along with the first band of crusaders, acting as chaplain to the Count of Toulouse. The latter's *entourage* chanced to include a certain scholarly soldier, Ponce de Balazun, and Raymond agreed to collaborate with this person in writing an account of the expedition ; but scarcely had they commenced work ere de Balazun was killed, and, accordingly, the ecclesiastic carried out the work singlehanded. This did not prevent him, however, from taking a singularly active part in the campaign ; and he was present at the capture of Jerusalem and the battle of Ascalon ; while once, when the crusaders were besieged at Antioch in 1098, he headed a sortie, carrying the sacred lance in his hands. Subsequently, it appears, he accompanied the Count de Toulouse on a pilgrimage to the Jordan, but otherwise no information is forthcoming concerning his career. Raymond's work, written in Latin, is entitled *Historia Francorum qui ceperunt Hierusalem*, and it is the more precious because he was an eye-witness of nearly all the events he described ; while, moreover, when he differs from other historians he is invariably careful to give his reasons for so doing. His history is printed in *Gesta Dei per Francos* and in *Recueil des Historiens Occidentaux des Croisades*, while a French translation is contained in Guizot's

Memoires sur l'Histoire de France, 1824.

REALI DI FRANCIA. The substance of the French *chansons de Geste* (*q.v.*), dealing with the subject of Charlemagne and his peers, was very early naturalised in Italy, and took shape as a compilation called the *Reali di Francia*, which achieved great popularity in mediæval times, and coloured the work of Boiardo, Pulci and Ariosto. It was probably compiled by one Andrea da Barberius at the beginning of the fifteenth century. The literature which it evoked was thus almost as extensive and important as that which gave it birth, and it was more complete, inasmuch that it represented the Charlemagne legend at every stage, historic and fantastical, without a gap or omission. The Arthurian romances were highly popular in Italy, but the Carlovingian *chansons* in their native dress must have proved even more acceptable than they, judging from their comparative influence upon the literature of the peninsula. This may be observed, for example, in the frequent references of Dante to the Carlovingian heroes, whereas those concerning the Arthurians are but few.

REDBEARD. (*Vide* " Grettir Saga.") An outlaw sent by Thorir of Garth (*q.v.*) to murder Grettir in his loneliness. But Redbeard himself met the death intended for his victim.

RED BRANCH. In Ultonian legend an order of chivalry in the reign of Conor mac Nessa, with its seat in Emain Macha. These warriors were descended from Ross the Red (*q.v.*), King of Ulster, and from collateral relatives and allies. Their glory passed away with

Conor (*q.v.*) and with Cuchulain (*q.v.*).

RED GUERRY. A noble who figures in the Charlemagne cycle. He is first the implacable enemy of Bernier (*q.v.*), the squire of Raoul of Cambray, but afterwards gives him his daughter in marriage, but in the end slays him treacherously.

RED HUGH. In Irish romance an Ulster Prince, father of Macha (*q.v.*); brother of Dithorba of Kimbay (*q.v.*).

RED KNIGHT, THE (1). Figures in Arthurian legend as the knight who carries off King Arthur's cup while he sat at a banquet at Carduel, " none daring to hinder him." However, Sir Perceval (*q.v.*) follows after him, slays him and assumes his armour with the help of Sir Gawaine, who shows him how to unlace it. His body is cast into a fire kindled by Sir Perceval (or Percyvelle) and his mother—a witch—also meets with the same fate. (2). Of the Red Laundes, notable for his treachery. He imprisoned Dame Liones, who was afterwards released by Gareth (*q.v.*). (*Vide* " Morte d'Arthur.")

REGIN. Son of Hreidmar (*q.v.*), and brother to Otter (*q.v.*) and Fafnir (*q.v.*). He became tutor to Sigurd (*q.v.*), whom he accompanied on many adventures. Sigurd subsequently slew him through the advice which he received from the birds after the killing of Fafnir. (*Vide* " The Lay of the Volsungs.")

REGNIER, SIR. (*Vide* " Sir Otuel.") Chamberlain to Charlemagne. He was told by the king to take care that Sir Otuel was protected from any attack while he was acting as representative of King Garsie.

REIGNIER, Emperor of Germany. (*Vide* "Guy of Warwick.")

RENAN DE MONTAUBON. (*Vide* "Four Sons of Aymon.")

RENIER DE GENNES. (*Vide* "Garin de Montglane.")

RENOUART. In Carlovingian romance son of King Desrame, the Saracen. In his boyhood he had been taken prisoner by the Franks, and his enormous size and strength recommended him to William of Orange when he was merely a scullion in the kitchen of Louis le Debonair. He performed wonders of valour at the battle of Arleschans (*q.v.*), in which he fought against his own kin. For this he was granted the hand of the Princess Alice, daughter of King Louis. He was a great hero with the scullions and kitchen-folk of mediæval times as personifying strength, drunkenness and laziness. (*Vide* "Marriage Renouart.")

RERIR. Son of Sigi (*q.v.*) and father of Volsung (*q.v.*). He succeeded to his father's throne. (*Vide* "The Lay of the Volsungs.")

REYNALD DE AUBÉPINE. (*Vide* "Roland and Ferragus.") A brave knight slain by Ferragus in single combat.

REYNARD THE FOX. A satirical beast epic of the Middle Ages, versions of which appeared in French, German, Flemish and English. Much controversy has been waged upon the question as to whether it was originally written in French or German. The first poem on the subject is the *Reinardus Vulpes* of a Flemish priest, Nivardus of Ghent, written about 1148. Reynard or Reginhard means a hardened evil-doer. The earliest French version of the satire is lost, but traces of it are to be found in the later *Roman de Renard*. It was probably made use of by Heinrich der Glichezare, an Albatian writer, who wrote the first German version, *Reinart*, about 1180. From a French poem on the same subject written by a priest, Pierre de St. Cloud, in the beginning of the thirteenth century, came the Flemish poem of *Reinhart* by Willem. Translations and versions multiplied after this. Professor Saintsbury thinks that "the original language of the epic is French, but French of a Wadson or Picard dialect, and that it was written somewhere between the Seine and the Rhine. A number of French continuations came into being, the chief among which are *Le Couronnement Reynard, Renart Le Nouvel, Renart Le Contrefait*, and so forth.

The purpose of these later versions was a satirical one, the institution against which their shafts of scorn were levelled being the church and the nobility. The beasts represented but few bestial qualities, and are too anthropomorphic to escape detection as men thinly disguised. Renard is a "baron" of "King Noble" the lion, and his chicanery and vulpine raiding of hen-roosts appear characteristic of the habits of the thirteenth century. The ass is the Church, and other animals and birds represent various persons or institutions.

Caxton's translation was made from the low German, probably that of Gerard Leen (1479), and was printed at Westminster in 1481. It begins by relating how the animals lodged a multitude of complaints against Renard with Noble, the lion. His Majesty calls for vengeance upon the malefactor. Bruin, the bear, sent to apprehend him, comes to misfortune through Renard's cunning, as does Tybert, the cat. Grymbart, the badger, brings Renard to law before Noble, and he is adjudged to be hanged. But Renard saves himself by telling the king of a great treasure which he boasts of. Thus escaping, Renard pursues his old career of rapine. Once more the beasts lay their complaints before Noble. But for the second time Renard's crafty tongue saves him from a well-deserved doom. Iseugrim, the wolf, lodges a complaint against Renard for the ravishment of his wife. Renard accepts his challenge to do battle on a certain day. They fight, but when Renard is undermost, he so flatters Iseugrim that he releases him forthwith, whereupon Renard wounds him treacherously. In the event, Noble forgives Renard the whole of his evil deeds, and creates him second to himself in the realm.

The story of Renard was one of the most popular and widespread of the Middle Ages. By its means satire was popularized, and the way laid for reform and the gradual breaking down of privilege.

RHIANNON. (Alluded to in the *Mabinogion* story of *Pwyll, Prince of Dyfed.*) She was daughter of Meyedd Hen, and wife of Pwyll, and was nearly lost to him through the strategy of Gwawl. (*Vide* "Pwyll.") She is probably the representative of an ancient Celtic moon-goddess. After the death of Pwyll, she was bestowed by her son Pryderi upon Manawyddan, the son of Llyr, and her subsequent history is detailed in the Mabinogion tale that bears his name.

RIBESTEIN. Minister to King Ermenrich (*q.v.*). He is mentioned in the Saga of *Dietrich of Bern* (*q.v.*) as having attempted in league with Sibich (*q.v.*) to bring Ermenrich to destruction. He easily became the tool of his colleague, with whom he plunged his master's empire into war with Dietrich.

RICHARD. (*Vide* "Sir Ferumbras.") Duke of Normandy. One of the twelve peers sent by Charlemagne as a delegate about the liberation of his nephews. While prisoner in Aigremor he was deputed to sally out in search of help from Charlemagne. He found him and returned with him to the Bridge of Mantribe, which was defended by Algolupe. Richard slew the giant, and remained in Mantribe with 200 knights, while Charlemagne pushed on to Aigremor.

RIENCE. In Arthurian romance King of North Wales. He was the uncompromising foe of Arthur, and was at last taken prisoner by Balin and Balan (*q.v.*) and brought to Camelot.

RIGAUT. *Vide* "Garin the Lorrainer.") Son of Hervi the villein. He was a great rough man, but of kindly nature and high qualities. Bego chose him to fight with Fromondin at a tourney, and promised him Fromondin's horse. He defeated Fromondin and took him prisoner. He won the prize by his exploits at the tourney, and was knighted. He avenged Bego's death by ravaging the country round Haives. He refused to enter into a truce with the Bordelais and fought against Fromont, defeating him. He further raided Bourges. His grief was so great for Bego's death, that when told he was buried, he insisted on seeing the body, and when it was disinterred, he fainted.

RINALDO or **RINAUD** (1). One of the four sons of Aymon (*q.v.*). He slew Bertolais, nephew to Charlemagne (*q.v.*), and with his other brothers fled the country on his faithful steed Bayard. Charlemagne sets siege to his castle Montauban, Rinaldo making peace with Charles and goes on a pilgrimage to the Holy Land, subsequently meeting his death at the hands of some jealous workmen whom he joined in the construction of the Cathedral at Cologne.

RINALDO (2). (*Vide* "Orlando Innamorato" and "Orlando Furioso.") Son of Amon, and brother to Bradamant. He fought with Orlando for Angelica, and, inspired by her, performed prodigies of valour. He defended Geneura against Polinesso who had accused her of unchastity, slaying her enemy in the duel.

RING, KING. (*Vide* "Frithjof Saga.") The mild and gentle old king who figures in the Icelandic Saga of *Frithjof* (*q.v.*). Desiring Ingebjorg to wife, he sent messengers to ask her from her brothers Helgi and Halfdan (*q.v.*), but the former answered them with a sneer. Then the king warred upon the sons of Belé, conquered them, and married their sister. Years later, visited by Frithjof, who believed he was unknown to all in the castle save the queen, he tested the faith of his guest, and found him true. Then he thrust his sword into his own breast and renounced his wife to her lover.

ROBERT THE DEVIL. Was the son of a Duke and Duchess of Normandy, and by the time he was twenty was a prodigy of strength, which he employed, however, only for outrage and crime. At last he learnt from his mother, in explana-tion of his wicked impulses, that he was born in answer to prayers addressed to the Devil. He was directed by the Pope to a hermit, who imposed on him by way of penance that he should maintain absolute silence, feign madness, take his food from the mouth of a dog, and provoke ill-treatment from the common people without retaliating. He became court fool to the Emperor at Rome, and delivered the city from Saracen invasions in three successive years in the guise of an unknown knight, having each time been bidden to fight by a celestial messenger. The emperor's dumb daughter recovered speech to declare the identity of the court fool with the deliverer of the city, but Robert refused the hand of the princess and the imperial inheritance, and ended his days in the hermitage of his old Confessor. The French romance of *Robert le Diable* is one of the oldest versions of the legend, and apparently originated from a folk-lore source.

ROBIN HOOD. Is first mentioned by the Scottish historian Fordun, who died in 1386. According to Stow, he was an outlaw in the reign of Richard I. (twelfth century). He entertained one hundred "tall men," all good archers, with the spoil he won, but "he suffered no woman to be oppressed, violated, or otherwise molested; poor men's goods he spared, abundantly relieving them with that which by theft he got from abbeys and houses of rich carles." He was an immense favourite with the common people. Stukeley says he was Robert Fitzooth, Earl of Huntingdon. Robin Hood and Little John having had a quarrel, parted company. Little John fell into the hands of the Sheriff of Nottingham, who bound him to a tree. Meanwhile, Robin Hood met with Guy of Gisborne, who had sworn to slay the "bold forester." The two bowmen fought, but Guy was slain, and Robin Hood rode to the tree where Little John was bound. The sheriff mistook him for Guy of Gisborne, and gave him charge of the prisoner. Robin cut the cord, handed Guy's bow to Little John, and the two soon put to flight the sheriff and his men. Robin Hood was put to death treacherously by a nun, instigated to the foul deed by his kinsman, the Prior of Kirklees, Yorkshire, near Halifax. The most complete legend concerning him is preserved in the public library of Cambridge, and will be found in *Percy's Reliques of ancient English poetry.*

ROC. In Ossianic romance a steward of Angus Og (*q.v.*). His son was metamorphosed into the Boar of Ben Bulben (*q.v.*).

ROCHESTER, BISHOP OF. Mentioned in Arthurian romance. To end the hostility between Arthur (*q.v.*) and Lancelot (*q.v.*), he was instructed by the Pope to deliver to the belligerents a pair of sacred bulls, as a symbol of peace. His intercession was successful, and Lancelot readily returned Guinever (*q.v.*) to Arthur, thus bringing the war to an end. (*Vide* "Morte d'Arthur.")

RODGEIER. King of Salern, mentioned in the romance of *Samson* (*q.v.*). He ruled with wisdom and stern justice, but not for long. Samson, who was his knight, refused the hand of his daughter Hildeswid. Despite the refusal, the hero carries off Rodgeier's daughter. Rodgeier pursues Samson, at whose hands he is slain.

RODOMONT. (*Vide* "Orlando Innamorato" and "Orlando Furioso.") King of Algiers, made incredible slaughter among the Christians. He was unhorsed by Bradamant, then performed penance for this disgrace. At the festival of Rogero's marriage he challenged the bridegroom, and was slain by him.

ROGERO. (*Vide* "Orlando Innamorato" and "Orlando Furioso.") Son to Rogero of Risa, who married Galicella, daughter of Agolant. Losing both parents, he was brought up by Atlantes, a magician. For his bravery in battle, Agramant conferred upon him the honour of knighthood.

ROHAND, EARL OF WARWICK. Father of Felice, who wedded Sir Guy of Warwick (*q.v.*).

ROLAND. Peer of France. A famous champion, and nephew of Charlemagne. He is regarded as the mediæval *beau-ideal* of chivalry and personal prowess. His early rivalry and subsequent friendship with Oliver (*q.v.*) are proverbial. He commanded the rearguard of the Frankish army leaving Spain, and with Turpin, Oliver and many other peers, was cut off by the "Saracens" at Roncevalles. He was betrothed to Oliver's sister, Alda. (*Vide* "Gerard of Viana," "Song of Roland," etc.)

ROLAND AND FERRAGUS or VERNAGU. Although this English romance was written to tell the story of Roland and Ferragus, it opens with a lengthy description of Charlemagne and his enterprise in behalf of the Christians against the Saracens. The Christians had appealed to Constantius, Emperor of Constantinople, for help against the pagan Emperor, Ibrahim of

Spain. Constantius in a dream was advised to appeal to "Charles the Conqueror," who consented to visit him at Constantinople. Nothing important resulted from that visit, but some time afterwards Charles was impressed by seeing a flight of stars appearing to settle over Spain, and St. James told him in a dream that these stars were a sign that he would conquer that country, so accordingly he raised an army and besieged it. By miraculous aid, he totally defeated the Saracens, only a few towns offering any resistance. At certain great festivals, Charles displayed much magnificence, and at one of these he received a challenge from Ferragus, a general of the Soudan of Babylon, to meet him in the field at Vasers. Ferragus was an enormous man. To quote the poem, " He had twenty men's strength, and forty feet of length . . . four feet in the face . . . and fifteen in brede " (breadth). After seeing Ferragus, Charles declined the challenge, but allowed Ogier the Dane to accept it. The giant made short work with the Dane. He unhorsed him, tucked him under his arm and carried him off to the castle of Vasers. Next day, Reynald de Aubepine met the same fate, and Ferragus jeeringly called to Charles :

"Sir ! thou wonnest Spain ! Hadst thou none better tho' ? "

On the following day, Sir Constantine of Rome and Howel of Nantes, and two other knights were slain by this formidable opponent, and then Roland, against the king's wishes, determined to attack him. When Ferragus saw this great champion approaching, he exerted all his strength and succeeded in unhorsing Roland and putting him before him on his horse's neck, but in his turn Roland unhorsed Ferragus, and they both fell to the ground. They remounted, but each killing the other's horse, they had to carry on their combat on foot. This lasted till night, without any result. Next day, Roland tried a knotty oaken club, then they threw stones at each other, till the giant became very sleepy and suggested a nap. Roland agreed, but hearing alarming sounds proceeding from the giant he thought he must be in pain and sought out a stone suitable for a pillow and placed it under his head. On awaking, Ferragus was most grateful for this kind act, and they began to converse most amiably. Roland managed to extract the information that Ferragus had one vulnerable spot. Then they began to discuss their different religions, and Roland tried to teach his quondam enemy some of the Christian verities. Tiring of discussion, Ferragus said they must decide by force, so they again joined battle, which ended in victory for Roland. He pierced Ferragus with his sword in his one vulnerable part and the giant expired, calling on Mahomet.

ROMAIN. (*Vide* " Roland and Ferragus.") A knight in the service of Charlemagne. He died at Bayonne, leaving all that he had to the poor. His executor appropriated the money, and on the release of the knight from purgatory, he appeared to his former friend in a dream, threatening him with speedy punishment for his theft. While the executor was relating this vision he was carried off by demons and dashed to pieces on a rock in Navarre, where his body was found afterwards when the army passed the place.

ROMAN DE BRUT. A chronicle in verse, written by a Norman poet, Wace (*q.v.*). It occupies a sort of intermediary position between the prose chronicle and the metrical romance. It was in some measure the forerunner of many of the metrical romances on the Arthurian subject. But it must not be confounded with the pseudo-histories such as that of Geoffrey of Monmouth, for one excellent reason. What Wace set down he wrote in good faith, believing in every circumstance as a verified fact. He even took the trouble to journey to the Forest of Broceliande to verify or unmask the tales of fäery which he had heard connected with that place. And to those tales he gives a fervent denial. Therefore when he writes of Arthur, we must take him as writing of that he believes to be actual history. He is clear and minute in his details, and had a remarkable power of visualizing. In his pictures and descriptions he is as complete and full as Homer. Basing his narrative on that of Geoffrey, he yet so controlled his source as to eliminate manifest absurdities, and he moreover introduced a love-interest, obviously to gratify his patroness, Queen Eleanor, who zealously propagated in England the chivalric ideals then current in her own Southern France. Nor does he draw all his material from the *Historia* of Geoffrey. Several of the legends he adduces are certainly of Celtic (probably Breton) origin. He does not add much to our knowledge of Arthurian literature, but he smoothed over many uglinesses in the story, and gave it its French colouring. In his narrative we first encounter Merlin in the semi-mythical time of Vortigern. He appears as living in several reigns. The tale of how Uther, Arthur's father, gained access to the wife of Gorlois is dealt with. The vexing of the Britons by Octa the Saxon occupies considerable space. When we find Arthur at last there is no doubt, as in other chronicles, that he is the rightful heir. At the time of his coronation he is "a damoiseau of fifteen years." His wars with the Saxons and the people of Scotland and Ireland are recounted at length. Wace touches on "the marvellous gestes" of Arthur's reign with a critical ability wonderful for his period. "Such rhymes," he says, "are neither sheer bare lies nor gospel truths. They should not be considered an idiot's tale [good advice this, to the critics of the seventeenth and eighteenth centuries!] or given by inspiration . . . the truth stands hid in the trappings of a tale. Thus to make a delectable tune to your ear, history goes masking as fable." This is the very standpoint of Euhemerus ; and might almost have been formulated by the Müllerian school of mythologists ! The conquest of Norway by Arthur is next described, as is that of Gaul. Wace's description of Arthur's court, if more polished and Frenchified than that of Geoffrey, is still neither so magnificent nor romantic. It occupies a considerable space, after which we find the Roman campaign dealt with much as in Geoffrey and Malory. So runs the story to its end, showing great similarity to the other Arthurian pseudo-chronicles. (*Vide* "Arthurian Cycle.")

ROMAN D'ALIXANDRE, An important French romance of the twelfth century, written in mono-rhymed *laisses* of Alexandrine metre, a measure which owes its name to this poem. In style it closely resembles the *chanson de gestes*. It was probably written by two authors, Lambert li Tors, and Alexander of Bernay or Paris, and amounts to over twenty thousand lines. It contains both authentic and fabulous matter, and has counterparts in the English *King Alisaunder* (*q.v.*), and in German and Icelandic versions. It begins with Alexander's childhood. The enchanter Nectanabus is not here credited, as in some versions, with the fatherhood of the hero, but is regarded in the light of a tutor or adviser. Nicolas, King of Cæsarea (a legendary monarch), insults Alexander, and war ensues, which ends in his defeat and the gift of his kingdom to Ptolemy. Alexander threatens Athens, but is dissuaded from her destruction by Aristotle. Arriving home, he is just in time to prevent the marriage of his father with Cleopatra, whom he sends back to Egypt. The next episode is the war with Darius. After many adventures he arrives at Tarsus, which he reduces. The siege of Tyre follows, and an episode which takes up a great part of the romance is that of the "Foray of Gaza," which is almost a complete tale in itself. A visit to Jerusalem and two battles of Arbela and Issus are speedily passed over, as is the murder of Darius. Alexander passes the desert and visits the bottom of the sea in a glass chamber, after which he gives battle to Porus, Darius's ally. Here we have a lengthy description of some interest of the peoples and customs of India which furnishes us with a faithful idea of how the east appeared to the minds of mediæval folk. Porus fights again in Bactria and is beaten, after which Alexander pursues his allies Gog and Magog,

and shuts them off by his famous wall. An armistice is concluded with Porus, after which the hero travels to the Pillars of Hercules. The return to Macedon is begun, and marvels thicken. Strange beasts attack the Greek army, and the troops arrive at the valley whence none may return, Alexander only receiving permission for his men to pass through it by dooming himself. He is, however, assisted to pass it by the aid of a friend whom he sets free. Coming to the sea, sirens lure many of the host to destruction, and the three marvellous Fountains of Youth, Immortality and Resurrection are discovered. They also encounter a forest of Maidens or "Flower-women." The men who bathe in the Fountain of Youth become as men of "thirty years old." They then come to the Trees of the Sun and Moon, which oracularly foretell Alexander's death. Porus hears of this, and when the army returns to India he picks a quarrel, and the two kings engage in combat. Bucephalus is slain, but Porus also meets his death. Alexander marches on Babylon drawn in a car to which griffins are harnessed. Much slaughter takes place there, after which the incident of the Amazons is treated. Alexander returns to Tarsus and Queen Candace, and the poem concludes with the death of the world-conqueror, who is poisoned by Anipater and Divinuspater.

See edition of Michelant, Stuttgart, 1846.

ROMANCE OF THE ROSE. A French poem of the thirteenth century in two parts, the first written by Guillaume de Lorris about 1337, and the second by Jean de Meung about 1378. The romance is a product of Central France, and approximates closely in spirit to the work of the Provençals. It is essentially allegorical, and in its pages we meet such figures as Sloth, Avarice, Anger, and Pride. The great English translation was partly the work of Chaucer. The first portion, consisting of a little over four thousand lines, possesses an atmosphere of its own, and is in touch with the poetical thought of the period. The poem opens with the description of a dewy morn in May. The raconteur is strolling past a great park, when he beholds carved on its walls certain images of Hatred, Felony, Villainy, Avarice, Envy, and so forth. These are described at length, and despite their unprepossessing characters, the Lover, as he is described, fears not to enter the enclosure. He is admitted by Dame Oyseuse (Idleness), who tells him that Delight and all his train haunt the park and its environs, and that he has had the ugly images made to heighten, not to retard, enjoyment. Entering, the Lover finds himself in a veritable Eden, and beholds the companions of Delight sitting hearkening to the sweet singing of Dame Lyesse (Pleasure) surrounded by jongleurs and all manner of entertainers. Courtesy asks him to join the dance, and he acquiesces. There are present the God of Love, his bow-bearer, Sweet-Glances, who aims at the Lover but is interrupted by some one telling the tale of Narcissus. Meanwhile the Lover has espied among the flowers of the garden one which he is specially attracted to—a Rosebud. While he strains to approach it, Love aims his arrow at him, and strikes him. He yields himself prisoner, and Love locks his heart with a golden key, gives him a homily on the duties of a lover,

culled from the romances of the Table Round, and then vanishes. He cannot get at the Rose, and is in pain thereat, when there appears to him Bel-Acueil, the son of Courtesy, through whose good offices the Lover has nearly reached the object of his desires, when an ugly personage named Danger approaches, who abuses Bel-Acueil for admitting the Lover to the Rose, and turns the unfortunate swain out of the park. Reason appears to the disconsolate lover in the garb of an elderly female of dignified appearance. She upbraids him for having placed himself under the rule of Idleness, and thereby having laid himself open to the snare of love. She tells him that he has added another enemy to Danger, her own daughter Shame, not to mention Scandal. The Lover will not hearken to her, but announces that he belongs to Love, and sends her about her business. He betakes himself to his friend, who tells him that although Danger is rough and surly he may relent if spoken to softly. Danger, at first very wroth, hearkens to what he has to say, and tells him that he has no objection to his loving the Rose if he will keep out of its way. The Lover gains the powerful aid of Pity and Frankness, who plead to Danger on his behalf, so that the surly guardian permits Bel-Acueil to return to him and take him to see the Rose once again. Venus even assists him to kiss the beauteous blossom. But Shame and Scandal are aroused by these proceedings, and are assisted by Jealousy and Fear, who once more wake up Danger. Jealousy digs a trench around the Rose, and builds a tower where Bel-Acueil is imprisoned, and the unfortunate Lover, his case ten times more hopeless than ever, is left lamenting outside. At this point the work of De Lorris ends. Jean de Meung takes up the tale by introducing Reason, who holds a lengthy discussion with the Lover. Love besieges the tower where Bel-Aceuil is imprisoned, and succeeds in freeing him. Danger, however, still guards the Rose. Love invokes the aid of Venus, who sends Nature and Genius to aid him. But all to no avail, and it requires the presence of Venus herself to render it possible for the Lover to pluck the Rose at last. In this famous poem we find the amorous poetry of troubadour and trouvere enshrined in symbolism, with not a little of that satire added which was symptomatic of the period. The consummate excellence of the second part of the *Roman* has made it the object of many ardent eulogies, and the writer has been styled the Voltaire of the middle ages, while he has likewise been compared to Rabelais. The latter comparison is certainly apt, Jean being anything but prudish, and evincing in fact a strong *Macabre* instinct, a taste in which he is curiously at variance with his predecessor, de Lorris, who is essentially refined throughout if not actually idyllic. Jean is to Guillaume, in short, very much what Chaucer is to Spenser; while at the same time Jean's parts of the *Roman de la Rose* reflect a brighter intelligence than Guillaume's, an intelligence manifestly tinctured moreover by sound erudition. Over two hundred early manuscript copies of the poem are in existence, scattered over the libraries of Europe, and this diffusion must have been going on even in the author's day, for acquaintance with his work was by no means confined to his own country. The story was retold in Walloon by a mediæval Flemish poet, Henri van Aken; while it penetrated to Italy, and there it was crystallized in a sequence of sonnets by Durante, a contemporary and possibly a friend of Dante. Then, as English readers need scarcely be reminded, Chaucer is credited with a version of the tale; while, reverting to France during the reign of Henry II., the courtier poet Clément Marot rewrote the *Roman de la Rose*, and his rendering thereof won a popularity almost equal to that which the original edition had enjoyed.

ROMANCE, NATURE, ORIGIN, AND RISE OF. The true character of romance is not easily defined. The nature of epic proper is solid and serious, that of romance fantastic and mysterious. But all epic is not serious, nor is all romance fantastic, and we cannot regard such a statement as a true definition of the meaning of the term "romance," as we find the fiction of the "heroic" age shading into epic on the one hand and into pure phantasy on the other, with, in both instances, a leaning towards pseudo-history. It is true again that what we know as romance flourished during a definite era. "Romance" originally designated a story written in *roman*, that is eleventh or twelfth-century French, instead of in Latin; therefore "romance," to use the term in its strictly technical sense, is something essentially French. How far the term "romance" is to be associated with the adjective "romantic" in its modern acceptation is really beside the question, but will be dealt with in the course of this article.

But the roots of romance—the chiefest manifestation of which was the *Matièrè de Bretagne*, otherwise the Arthurian cycle (*q.v.*)—were sunk in a period still older than its own, and it owed much of its subject-matter to that Celtic world whose mythology, characters, and incidents it so successfully translated into the terms of its own time without capturing its essential spirit of forlorn and mystic beauty. It had also a direct forerunner in France—the *Chanson de Geste*, or old French pseudo-epic, best instanced by the *Matière de France*, or Charlemagne Cycle. The *Chanson de Geste* partook more of the nature of epic in its seriousness, its relation of feats of arms, and its sustained spirit of lofty heroism. We find in it much more of what is called " the romantic " by moderns, and it contained many of the germs of later romance. Indeed, the *dramatis personæ* of the romantic tales are nearly all foreshadowed in the *chansons*, the geographical science of both types is almost entirely similar, and the *chansons* are full of miracles and phantasies no less exaggerated than those to be met with in Arthurian story. Indeed, the exaggeration to be found in the *chansons* surpasses anything in the Arthurian cycle. In the *chansons* " wonder " is genuine ; in the romances it is employed in a merely theatrical manner.

But the salient difference between the types was this : the romantic school had discovered the uses of a love-interest in fiction. This it employed in a manner which has been surpassed by no body of writers. Love illuminates and emblazons the pages of the writings of the romantic school with its refined gold, making pale the sagas of the olden days when man was the mere breadwinner and woman the food-distributor

and *hausfrau*. In romantic fiction we find the relations between the sexes altered in a manner which reveals the workings of a semi-philosophic system of exceptional natural depths and power, if of little breadth of outlook. In the *Chanson de Geste*, woman, though respected as a mother and a wife in true Teutonic fashion, is still regarded as if not a saleable at least an exchangeable commodity. In romance pure she is a divinity. Thus romance is the triumph of the Gallic over the Teutonic ideal, if it is safe to apply ethnological terms to literary phases.

The origin of this change is obscure but probably it may be traced to the influence of the fostering of an " art of love " by a literary *coterie* who had imbibed the amorous teachings of Ovid, Virgil, and other classical writers. This spirit was principally communicated to society through the agency of lyric poetry, poetic contests and " courts of love " in which great ladies adjudicated upon affairs of the heart. The romance of the day reflected this spirit no less than did lyric verse. The young squire or page attendant on a knight must remain unmarried for many years for lack of means to support a wife. He therefore fixed his regard upon some lady usually in a more exalted position than himself, whom he worshipped with a reverence in which platonic affection was strangely intermingled with the most ardent feelings. In this spirit we have an almost infallible index to what constitutes romance. If a sentimental love-interest be awanting, we are justified in relegating the tale under dispute either to the realms of pseudo-epic or to that class of story which partakes of the nature of both epic and romance.

By the twelfth century the poetry and *art d'amour* of Provençe had taken vigorous hold of the French mind, and had deeply coloured French fiction. The *esprit gauloise* plus the *esprit d'amour* of the Gallic South had invaded and conquered the more Teutonic north. Love was perhaps a more natural state with these fiery southerners, and that its art should have been systematized and expressed so didactically by a people so passionate is not surprising when we think how intense was the hold it had upon them. It was indeed their " whole existence," and they felt the imperious need of a system that would dictate exactly in what manner the love-life was to be led. As the ancient Egyptian lived solely for his religion and subordinated all other interests to it, so did the Provençal subordinate everything to love, which was his religion. Thus from passion was evolved a reasoned religion of love as many religious systems have been evolved from the frenzies of fanaticism.

In such a community the older literature of love was at a premium. Ovid's *Art of Love* was its textbook, and his *Heroides* and *Metamorphoses*, as well as the works of Statius and Virgil, were also highly esteemed. The love-stories of Dido and Medea were regarded as " very precious," and these heroines as suitable mirrors in which the *grandes dames* of the period might reflect themselves.

The French romantic writers of the twelfth century form a definite school more by reason of their discovery of love as a literary asset and the circumstance that their efforts were conscious and sophisticated than from any explicit difference of subject-matter from that to be found in the *Chansons de Geste*. Their sophistication is noticeable in that it has almost entirely robbed them of the ability to see with the eyes of romance. They are in reality the least romantic body of writers conceivable. They are the Byrons of the Middle Ages—exploiting cyclads and singing of strange journeys to please a people who had newly trodden on the skirts of the Orient, with a keen eye towards profits and a keen ear towards applause. Elegant, and with a fine sense of craftsmanship, they are yet woefully deficient in knowledge of the real *matière de poesie*. They possess the narrower tricks of music and something of its spirit, but phantasy and the magic of the remote mean nothing to them. The note of the new French poetry,

" Le cor est triste dans le bois,"

would have left them unmoved. This is shown by the circumstance that they readily adopted the figures and subject-matter of Celtic myth without capturing its spirit of aloofness. Its far voices whispered nothing to souls seared and sophisticated by passion. The romance-writers as the pioneers of a new and highly involved system were too world-worn to dwell on old simplicities ; and they had not yet learned to employ that simplicity which conceals the uglinesses of art. They certainly possessed a love of strange things. But it was a love of novelty, not of remoteness, and again they were compelled to utilize the machinery of the marvellous as demanded by the popular voice. Their merit is that they faced new problems and solved them. Whereas before their time fiction had been a mere recital of tribal or family tradition they chose the world as their collecting ground for ideas, and in this they were perhaps assisted by the westward journey of world-stories. However thin and formal their efforts, they broke away from the limited enclosure of what was, when all is said and done, merely the "tribal lay." They discovered that fiction has wings. But in mounting her to seek far countries, they kept ever in sight of land, and never permitted their newly-freed Pegasus to soar into the clouds.

ROSS THE RED. King of Ulster. Husband of Maev (*q.v.*), husband of Roy, originator of the Red Branch.

ROSWALL AND LILLIAN, THE HISTORY OF. A popular Scottish romance. The date of its composition is not known nor do we possess the original MS. But it is evident by the frequency of its mention in ancient writings that it retained its popularity amongst the Scottish people much longer than many others. This is supported by the fact that less than five decades ago it was not an uncommon occurrence to hear it chanted in the streets of the Scottish capital. The first, or earliest printed edition discovered is that of 1663, followed by a reprint in 1679, since when there appears to have been quite an abundance of editions. But these vary in length causing no little confusion. While the first edition gives us 846 lines in the epic, the subsequent editions are reduced considerably in length. The tale commences with the birth of Roswall whose father is the King of Naples. The young prince is much admired for his beauty. He meets with the displeasure of his father, by releasing from imprison-

ment three foreign lords, who in return promise the young Roswall their lifelong friendship, after which they depart to their native land. The long confinement has altered their appearance considerably. The noble prince is accused of releasing his father's prisoners, and but for his mother's pleadings he would have met his death. The royal father still enraged proposes to banish his unfaithful son. This the good mother reluctantly agrees to, and after many tears the prince and his steward depart. Meanwhile arrangements have been made between the King of Naples and the King of Bealm that the latter would receive the prince into his household. The journey proves eventful. Roswall, little suspecting his steward of treachery, dismounts at a small river to drink. The steward seizes his royal master and threatens to drown him unless he resigns himself to the ruffian's dictation. Roswall must also hand over his wealth and letters. This the frightened boy agrees to, but fearing further treachery, he escapes from the disloyal steward as they approach the Castle of Bealm. Hurrying into the village the prince, finding the day far spent, resolves to seek for shelter. Approaching a small cottage which he timidly enters, he applies to a decrepit old housewife for a night's shelter. This the woman gladly accedes to, adding that her only son, who is about his own age, would welcome the stranger's companionship. Roswall is quite delighted at this humble honesty, but his royal bearing betrays him. He is forced to assume the name "Dissawar," to which the old woman demurs, as she believes him to come from royal blood. The time passes quietly away.

The old dame's son and Roswall enjoy each other's companionship, and attend the same school. The master is particularly pleased with his new pupil and shows great kindness to him. But the villainous steward begins to frequent the village, the while he assumes a royal bearing at the court of the King of Bealm. Coming one day to the school-house he observes his young master, and straightway resolves on his capture. Going to the kind old dame he mentions that her adopted son must accompany him to his master's court. She objects, but in vain, and " Dissawar " is taken away. He is brought before the court of the king of Bealm, to whom he becomes a hired servant ; nor is his identity revealed. Plodding away without a grumble, the unfortunate Roswall soon attracts the attentions of the king's daughter, who grows to love him ; but as she believes that he is not of royal blood, therefore she must love in secret. Believing, however, in her heart that this " Dissawar " is a prince in disguise, she chooses Roswall to be her chamberlain, which angers the jealous steward and gives the young prince more liberty. In all chivalrous games " Dissawar " is allowed to display his prowess. He soon meets with the king's approval, who begins to suspect the true character of his daughter's valet. The prince's parents become anxious for their son, since they have never heard from him. Meanwhile, messengers are speeding to Naples to convey to the young prince's father the knowledge of his forthcoming marriage. This felonious message had been invented by the base steward, who pretended to be the real prince, and who intended to marry Lillian the King of Bealm's daughter.

She in turn swore that no one but her " Dissawar " would she marry. The intimation of the marriage was announced at both courts, and in keeping with kingly custom a tournament was opened several days preceding the wedding day. The tourney commences in real earnest. Roswall in disguise takes a part in the battle, and meets with approval from all sides. At last the king becomes anxious. He has seen the wonderful prowess of the prince who has inflicted defeat upon all who met him. The king orders the strange knight to be captured, but the forest proves Roswall's best friend. Hastening towards it, he dismounts, resumes his disguise and proceeds to the castle. At last, the tourney draws to a close, the wedding day approaches and nothing short of a miracle will prevent its fulfilment. Lillian has resigned herself to her fate, while the steward is inwardly exultant. But the three lords, whom Roswall freed, are peers of the King of Bealm's realm, and hearing of the approaching marriage, present themselves at his court. They mix freely amongst the guests, and meet with " Dissawar," whom they readily recognise as their saviour from the prison of the King of Naples. They quickly inform Lillian, who appeals to her father to permit her to marry " Dissawar," but he pays no heed to her request. The sorrowful girl is wedded to the vile steward. The feast begins, but the king hears of the steward's impostures, while the noble lords disclose the true personality of " Dissawar." At this the king is wroth. He orders the wicked steward to be hanged, after which " Dissawar " discards his assumed name, taking his loving Lillian before the alter.

They are married. After the feasting, he takes with him his bride,
and journeys to the house of his
father, to find on his arrival that
the king has died, and his mother
in her old age is mourning her long-
lost son. The rejoicings at his
home are renewed. He and his
wife live in peace and happiness,
while their family of five grows
into maturity. (See D. Laing,
Early Scottish Metrical Romances.)

ROUND TABLE, THE. A table, said
to have been made by Merlin, at
which the knights of Arthur
habitually sat. It is mythologically
considered to represent the sun-
sphere as Arthur represents the
sun-god.

RUADAN, ST. (*Vide* "Dermot
Mackerval.")

RÜDIGER, MARGRAVE. (*Vide*
"Nibelungenlied.") Husband of
Gotlind (*q.v.*), and ambassador to
King Elgel. He went on an
embassy to Kriemhild. He refused
to turn against the Burgundians,
but was latterly slain by Hagen
in error.

RYMOUR, THOMAS. Erroneously
designated Learmonth, a poet,
romancer and seer who was probably born between 1226 and
1229, and who held the territorial
title of Ercildoune or Earlston in
Berwickshire. He is said to have
resided in a tower situated at the
western extremity of that village,
the ruins of which are still to be
seen, whilst on a stone in the front
wall of Earlston church is an
inscription in rhyme to the effect
that his "race lies in this place."
An ancient charter describes him
as "Thomas Rymor," whilst his
son is alluded to as "heir to
Thomas Rymour of Ercildoun"
in the assignation of the estate of
Ercildoun made by him to the
convent of Soltra in 1299. He
is said to have prophesied the
death of King Alexander III. of
Scotland in 1280, so that he must
have died between these two
dates. Among his countrymen he
is celebrated as a prophet or seer
as well as a poet, and many of his
saws and predictions, or at least
those ascribed to him, will be found
in the second volume of *The
Minstrelsy of the Scottish Border*.
The *Prophecies of Thomas the
Rhymer* were printed at Edinburgh
in English and Latin in 1691, and
have been re-published frequently.
He is alluded to by Fordun,
Wyntoun, Blind Harry and other
early Scottish historians, and poets,
and Robert de Brunne, an English
poet who was contemporary with
him, states that he was the author
of a metrical romance entitled
Sir Tristrem, supposed to be lost
till a copy of it was discovered in
the Auchinleck MS. (*q.v.*) in the
Advocates' Library in Edinburgh,
and published in 1804 with notes
and an introduction by Sir Walter
Scott. It is noteworthy that the
majority of the prophecies accre-
dited to "True Thomas," as he
was designated by the Scottish
peasantry, relate to the counties
of Berwick and Aberdeen, and this
lends colour to a tradition that at
one time he suffered banishment
from his patrimonial estate and
sojourned in the latter county.
The poems popularly ascribed to
him at a late date are : *The Whole
Prophecies of Scotland, England,
Ireland, France, and Denmark,
Marvellous Merlin, Beid, Berling-
ton, Waldhave, Eltrain, Bannister*,
and *Sybilla*, but it may be said
of these as of the alleged works of
many another ancient writer that
there is little ground for referring
any of them to Thomas. There is

more likelihood that the prophecies traditionally ascribed to him and current among the Scottish peasantry originally emanated from him. Regarding the question of the authenticity of his authorship of the *Tristrem* poem with which he is credited, see "Auchinleck MS."

Although Thomas is not to be regarded as a mythical hero pure and simple, yet the accretions of myth have, perhaps inevitably, crystallised around his name, or he has become the centre of a myth, probably local, and considerably older than the century which gave him birth. Like Tannhauser he is supposed to have disappeared underground at the call of "Venus," and an old ballad tells of his abduction by the Queen of Fäerie. Cox, *Mythology and Folklore*, p. 160, note, says : "No one, probably, will attribute the names Horselberg and Ercildoune to accident. In each case we have the berg, hill or down of the moon-goddess Ursel or Ursula, a name which through the forms Ursa, Arktos, and Arksha takes us back to the original word denoting splendour or brightness which gives us the Hindu Raja, and the Latin Rex, reg-is on the one side, and the Hindu Rishi with the Teutonic Bragi on the other." There would appear to be a germ of probability in the etymology, although it possesses somewhat the appearance of a Müllerian philological triumph.

S

SABA. In Ossianic romance, the wife of Finn (*q.v.*). She was the mother of Oisin (*q.v.*). She appeared to Finn as a fawn, as he was one day returning from the chase. His man-hounds, Bran and Skolawn, having gained upon her, began to play around and lick the animal : so Finn gave her protection in his Dun of Allen. Next morning he awoke to find a most beautiful woman beside his bed. She had been changed those three years, she said, by the sorceries of her hated lover, the Druid of the Fairy Folk, into a fawn. But from one of his slaves she had learned that her human shape would be restored to her, could she but reach the Dun of Allen. Finn made her his wife, and no longer found pleasure in the battle or the chase. At last, however, hearing that the Northmen's war-ships were in the Bay of Dublin, he gathered his forces and departed to attack them. On the eighth day he returned victorious, but to find Saba gone. The enchanter, in the likeness of Finn with his hounds, had lured her from the dun to give her again a fawn shape, and by his magic she was at last forced to leave her son and to follow the Druid.

SABARYZ. (*Vide* "Sir Ferumbras.") A brave Roman who defended Rome against Laban. He was killed by Estragot, King of Babylon.

SABER. (*Vide* "Bevis of Hampton.") Uncle and foster-father of Sir Bevis. He went to the Isle of Wight after Sir Guy's death, and defended it against Sir Murdour and his wife. He sent his son Terry, disguised as a pilgrim, to find Bevis. He was a great dreamer, and on several occasions was of the greatest service to Bevis, such as rescuing Josyan from Ascapard, and finding his horse Arundel.

SACRIPANT. (*Vide* "Orlando Innamorato," and "Orlando Furioso.") King of Circassia, one of the bravest and most faithful of Angelica's lovers. When this princess was besieged in Albracca by Agrican, he marched to her assistance with a numerous army, and performed many gallant actions.

SADOK, SIR. A knight at the court of King Mark (*q.v.*). Afterwards a follower of Lancelot. He was charged with the Earldom of Surlat, under Lancelot, who assumed for a while the chieftainship of that country. (*Vide* "Morte d'Arthur.")

SADONE. In Carloving an romance, a valiant pagan who seconds Karaheut (*q.v.*) in his combat with Ogier. (*Vide* "Ogier the Dane.")

SAGRAMORE LE DESIROUS, SIR. Knight of the Court of King Arthur. He was slain by Sir Meliagrance, while acting as Queen Guinever's body-guard. (*Vide* "Morte d'Arthur.")

SAIGREMORS. Knight. Mentioned in the Legend of the Holy Grail in connection with the deliverance of a damsel from ten robber knights. Some fifteen hundred verses are devoted to the doings of this doughty champion.

ST. FINNEN. An Irish abbot of the sixth century who sought hospitality from the pagan chief Tuan mac Carell (*q.v.*), and from him learnt the history of Ireland.

SALADOS. A giant knight and robber of lands. He was subdued by Sir Ewaine, Knight of the Lion (*q.v.*).

SALIM. (*Vide* "Florice and Blanchfleur.") A loyal servant to Florice. He bore messages between the two lovers. He acquainted Florice with Blanchfleur's exile to Babylon, and accompanied his master in his search for her.

SALMON OF KNOWLEDGE. (*Vide* "Fintan.")

SAM. (*Vide* "Burnt Njal.") Gunnar's (*q.v.*) faithful hound. Treacherously slain by Gunnar's murderers; before he died he gave his master warning of their approach.

SAMSON, KING (Samsing). A romance of the Amelung cycle. Once there lived a noble yarl (earl) who ruled so justly that Salern, his country, prospered. In his service was a powerful man called Samson, who displayed great might in battle. The yarl becomes king, and at a feast which followed, Samson and his loyal follower ask a boon. The king granting the warrior leave to speak is astounded at his request. Samson had asked that he might marry his master's daughter, Hildeswid. But the perplexed king could not grant such a boon to a commoner, despite his bravery. Commanding the dejected Samson to carry some sweetmeat to the room of Hildeswid, he offers the silent warrior as much consolation as he could. Samson being a fickle-tempered man obeyed the king's command without a murmur, but not without feeling that his rebellious spirit would achieve his purpose. Proceeding to Hildeswid's room, with the plate of sweetmeats, he commands her to prepare to accompany him to his home. The bewildered girl hesitates, but not for long. Realizing his ungovernable temper, she hastens to comply with his commands. They then leave the palace, and hastening through the forest arrive at Samson's dwelling. After much difficulty they are admitted into the dingy grange by an old woman, the mother of Samson. The dwelling arouses a feeling of horror in the mind of the princess, who is, however, soothed by her abductor. The old mother pleads that they have no food, and her son accuses her of miserliness. But a satisfactory meal is provided. After which Samson proceeds to deal with his pursuers, who had by this time discovered the abduction. The princess left alone becomes weary, and desiring the old woman's companionship goes in search of her. Passing from room to room she emerges upon a low-ceilinged apartment where she perceives at one end, in the dim light, the ancient dame stooping over a chest filled with gold. The princess hesitates for a moment to listen to the whispered chant of the cunning creature, but is horrified when she realizes that the wretch means to murder her for the sake of her jewels. Just then the evil crone turns round, and catching sight of the spy runs forward, grips the princess by the throat, and would have strangled her, had not Samson appeared. He in his rage draws his sword to slay his wicked mother, but, remembering he is her son, spares her. Samson vanquishes the pursuers, but is quickly assailed by the king. Proceeding through the forest the king asks of an old woman the whereabouts of Samson's dwelling. At first she refuses to divulge it, but upon being bribed she readily answers their inquiries. This old wretch is the mother of Samson. The king and his men then attack the house. Samson by his mighty strength

subdues the men and kills the king. He is sorely tempted to end his mother's life, but, despite her betrayal, refrains. The men of Salern then proceed to elect a new king. Samson hopes that he may be selected Brunstein, brother of the late Rodgeier, is chosen, who, feeling it his duty to punish the outlaw, gathers an army together and marches against Samson. But Samson is cunning, and catching the weary army asleep one night sets fire to their encampment. Brunstein perceiving through the fire and smoke the huge frame of Samson takes flight. The remnant of Brunstein's army then retreat. The fugitive king comes to the dwelling of Samson, and after conferring with Hildeswid discovers her to be his niece. She advises him, however, to flee from the wrath of her husband. But it is too late, Samson is upon him, and after a desperate struggle the unfortunate monarch is slain. Samson then proceeds to dictate to the burghers of Salern. Meanwhile he had gathered together a large host, and with the help of his uncle Dietwar he proceeds to threaten the terror-stricken district. The citizens see that there is no other alternative, and requesting the burghers to communicate with Samson, they gladly acclaim him as their king. The hero, seeing that his wishes had been complied with, sends for his wife, and together they ride into Salern, amid the greatest enthusiasm. The new ruler governs with a stern sense of justice, and administers the laws with equal regard for all his subjects. His country develops and his people prosper. Peace reigns within her borders, and commerce grows. The people learn to love their king.

But Samson thought that this prolonged peace was not a healthy sign, since military prowess was the chief glory of his age. So investing his eldest son with the regency of the kingdom, he assembles together his army and reminds his forces of their need for patriotism. In the meantime he issues a note to the proud yarl Elsung of Bern (Verona) demanding that he should pay tribute to his liege lord. Samson further demands that the earl should give his daughter Odilia to his second son. These terms the earl refuses, and makes elaborate preparations to meet the insolent Samson. In reply, the king marches his forces upon Bern. There the armies meet, and great is the slaughter. At length Samson's herculean strength prevails. After slaying the brave earl, his army gain the victory. The defeated Bernese seeing their ruler slain, wisely choose Samson as their king, thus putting an end to the hatred which embittered the struggle. The king and his host commence their return journey. The victory satisfies Samson, who made captive the dead king's daughter. She at first refuses to accept his son, but the king's wrath frightened her, and, yielding in mortal fear, Odilia consents to wed the prince. Samson then assures her of peace and protection. These arrangements made, the king and his victorious host proceed. But on the way, Samson fell ill. The wounds that the earl had inflicted upon him began to pain him, forcing him to rest at a wayside village. He grew worse, the wounds would not heal, and after a short and painful struggle, Samson yielded to death, naming his youngest son ruler of the Rhineland, with Fritilayung as his residence.

SANCHAN TORPEST. Chief bard of Ireland in the reign of the High King Guary. He figures in Sir S. Ferguson's *Lays of the Western Gael*, a poem combining the legends that bear upon the " Tain " or " Cattle Raid of Quelgny " (*q.v.*). Taunted at the feast by the king that he could not recite the " Tain," Sanchan Torpest determined to recover the poem, and to that end sought Ireland and Alba (Scotland) for traces of it. But he could only find fragments of the lay, and therefore sent his two sons to Italy to learn what had befallen the staff-book. At Loch Ein, however, the elder brother discovered Fergus mac Roy's grave, and at the expense of his life and love recovered for his father the long-lost lay.

SANAZZARO GIACOMO, author of the celebrated *Arcadia*, was born at Naples in 1458. He belonged to a distinguished family, but did not inherit any fortune, owing all that he possessed to the favour of the Neapolitan royal family. He distinguished himself in classical studies in early life, but the love of a lady, Carmosina Bonifacia, determined him to praise her in his native tongue. Her he praised in his *Arcadia*, and in many sonnets, and when she died, he returned to his Latin verses. King Frederic gave him the delightful Villa Mergolina, a fairy-like residence, where the poet attempted to realize his dreams of happiness in an Arcadia of his own. The wars of the French and Spaniards overwhelmed him in common ruin with his benefactors. He sold all his possessions to relieve the necessities of King Frederic when that dethroned monarch was sent as a hostage to France, whither Sanazzaro followed him, and shared his exile from 1501 to 1505. Returning to Italy on the death of Frederic, he passed the rest of his life in a village on the slopes of Vesuvius. His *Arcadia*, on which his reputation principally depends, was commenced in early youth, and published in 1504, when he was forty-six. A species of romantic pastoral in prose serves to connect twelve romantic and pastoral scenes, and twelve eclogues of shepherds in arcadia. In the seventh Sanazzaro himself appears in *Arcadia*, recounts the exploits of his family, and how love had driven him into exile. The ancient *Arcadia* is to Sannazaro nothing more than the poetical world of his own age. He awakes in the twelfth eclogue as from a dream. The execution is elegant in the extreme, and if some of the sentiments expressed are somewhat trite and affected, they do not lack warmth and nature. The stanzas in which each eclogue ends are in the lyric form of canzoni, and some of them are instinct with beautiful music. Sanazzaro died in 1530.

SARRAQUITE, QUEEN. Queen of Sarras (*q.v.*). In the *Grand St. Graal* it is recounted how she was secretly a Christian, as Christ had appeared to her. She had been baptized although she feared to avow her faith to her husband. Josephes (*q.v.*) brings her with her husband, now baptized under the name of Mordrains, to the Grail shrine and shows them the Grail. Later she sends messengers in search of Nasciens and her husband whom she regains. She dies on the same day as Nasciens and Flegentyne.

SARRAS. A town in the Holy Land from which the *Saracens* are said to derive their nomenclature. It is mentioned in the Legend of the Graal (or Grail) in connection with Joseph.

SATYN, KING OF. Father of Adaranta (*q.v.*), in whose land lived the boar which was slain by Eglamour (*q.v.*). (*Vide* "Eglamour of Artoys.")

SAURLI. (*Vide* "Volsungs.") Son of Gudrun (*q.v.*). He and his brother avenged Swanhild's (*q.v.*) death by slaying King Jormunrek (*q.v.*).

SAWAN. In Irish romance, brother of Kian and Goban (*q.v.*).

SAXO GRAMMATICUS. A Danish historian and poet. belonged to a family of warriors. his father and grandfather having served under Valdemar I., King of Denmark. Brought up for the priesthood, Saxo entered the service of Archbishop Absalon about 1180, and remained in that capacity until that prelate's death in 1201. It was at the archbishop's instigation that he began, about 1185, to write the history of the Danish Christian kings from the time of Sweyn Astridson (d. 1076), but later Absalon prevailed on him to write also a history of the earlier heathen times, and to combine both into a great work, *Gesta Danorum*, or *Historia Danica*. The archbishop died before the work was finished. and therefore the preface, written about 1208, dedicates the work to his successor Archbishop Andreas, and to King Waldemar. Saxo, from his apprenticeship as the archbishop's secretary, had acquired a brilliant but somewhat euphuistic style, and wrote fine Latin verses, but otherwise he does not seem to have had any very great learning or extensive reading. His sources are partly Danish traditions and songs, partly the statements of

Archbishop Absalon, partly the accounts of Icelanders, and lastly, lists of Danish kings and short chronicles, which furnished him with some reliable chronological facts.

The first nine books of the *Gesta Danorum* comprise traditions of kings and heroes of the semi-mythical period up to about 950 A.D. Here we have traditions about Fredfrode, Amleth (Hamlet) and Ferye, about Hrolfr Kraki, Hadding, the giant Starkather, Harald Hildefaun and Ragnarr Lodbrok. In this earlier history Saxo has also embodied myths of national gods who in tradition had become Danish Kings, for instance, Baldar and Hother, and of foreign heroes likewise incorporated in Danish history, as the Gothic Jormunrek (A.S. Eormenrie) the Anglian Vermund (A. S. Garmund) and Uffe (A.S. Offa), the German Hedin, and Hild and others. Frequently the narrative is interrupted by translations of poems, which Saxo had used as authentic sources, although they are often only a few generations older than himself. In the later books (X.–XVI.) of his work he follows to a greater extent historical accounts, and the more he approaches his own time the fuller and the more trustworthy his relation becomes. Especially brilliant is his treatment of the history of King Valdemar and of Absalon. But his patriotism often makes him partial to his countrymen and his want of critical sense often blinds him to historical truth.

Saxo's work was widely read during the middle ages, and several extracts of it were made for smaller chronicles. It was published for the first time, from a MS. afterwards lost, at Paris in 1514, by the Danish humanist Christiern Pedersen. This edition was reprinted at Basle, 1534, and at Frankfort, 1576. There is an English translation by O. Elton and F. W. Powell (London, 1894).

SCHIR WILLIAM WALLACE. A long poem recounting the military and other exploits of Wallace the Scottish hero, written during the fifteenth century by Blind Harry, but based chiefly on traditions handed down orally since Wallace's own period, the end of the thirteenth century. (*Vide* "Blind Harry.")

SEAT PERILLOUS. The seat left empty at the Round Table for Sir Galahad, son of Lancelot (*q.v.*). It probably received its soubriquet of "perillous" on account of the untimely end which met would-be occupiers of the seat, such as that which befell Moyses (*q.v.*) when the earth opened up and swallowed him on his aspiring to seat himself thereon.

SEGARD OF WALLINGFORD. (*Vide* "Guy of Warwick.") Steward and counsellor of the Earl of Warwick, and father of Sir Guy.

SEGWIN. (*Vide* "Guy of Warwick.") Duke of Louvain.

SEMION. In Irish romance son of Stariat. He settled in Ireland, and from him descended all the Firbolgs and other two tribes.

SERA. (The West.) In Irish legend father of Partholan (*q.v.*).

SERAPHE. The quondam name of Nasciens (*q.v.*) before he was converted.

SETANTA. In Irish myth, the earliest name of Cuchullin (*q.v.*). The maiden Dectera (*q.v.*) had disappeared with her fifty companions from the Court of Conor (*q.v.*). After three years the king and his nobles were lured by a flock of birds to the Fairy Mound of Angus on the Boyne, where one of them met Lugh (*q.v.*) and the long-lost maidens. Next morning in the shelter-hut the Ulster warriors found a new-born infant boy. With Conall (*q.v.*) his senior, he was nursed by Dectera's sister, Finchboom, Conall's mother. In the Court of Conor he learnt the warrior's art. It was when a boy that the name Cuchullin was given him. Being late to arrive at the feast of Cullan (*q.v.*) he was attacked by, but slew that Smith's enormous watch-hound. He then took the place of the hound until its whelps might be trained to guard the palace, hence his name "The Hound of Cullan." (*Vide* "Cuchullin.")

SEVEN WISE MASTERS, THE. A cycle of stories of Oriental origin. They tell how a Roman Emperor causes his son to be educated away from the court in the seven liberal arts by "seven wise masters." On his return to court his stepmother the empress accuses him to her husband, and seeks to bring about his death by seven stories which she relates to the emperor; but her narrative is each time confuted by tales of the craft of women related by the sages. Finally the prince's lips are unsealed, the truth exposed, and the wicked empress is executed. This cycle of stories, which appears in many European languages, is of Eastern origin. An analogous collection occurs in Sanskrit, but the Indian original is unknown. Travelling from the east by way of Arabic, Persian, Syriac, and Greek, it was known as the *Book of Sindibad*, and was translated from Greek into Latin in the twelfth century by Jean de Haute-

seille, a monk of the Abbey of Hauteseille, with the title of *Dolopathus*. Three metrical romances exist in English, probably based on the French. The most important of these is *The Seven Sages*, by John Rolland of Dalkeith, edited for the Bannatyne Club. (Edinburgh, 1837.)

SEYFRID OF MOORLAND. King of Carady. (*Vide* "Gudrun Lay" and "Gudrun.") One of the suitors for Gudrun's hand. While Herwig (*q.v.*) is attacking Hegelingen, Seyfrid ravages Seeland, till Herwig, aided by Hettel (*q.v.*), drives him back. On Gudrun's abduction by Hartmut and Ludwig (*q.v.*), peace is made between Seyfrid and Herwig, and Seyfrid aids in the unsuccessful attempt to rescue her. He brings men and pinnaces to the later expedition which rescues Gudrun from Ormany, and finally weds a sister of Herwig.

SGEIMH SOLAIS. (Light of Beauty.) Daughter of Cairbry (*q.v.*), in Irish romance, she was asked in marriage by a son of the King of the Decies. On the arrangement of the alliance the Fianna (*q.v.*), claimed a tribute of twenty ingots of gold, and by the exorbitancy of their claim precipitated hostilities, which resulted in the Battle of Gowra (*q.v.*) (Garristown, co. Dublin), in which the Fianna were almost exterminated, and Cairbry and Oscar (*q.v.*) slew each other.

SIBICH. (*Vide* "Dietrich of Bern.") A marshal of the realm of Ermenrich (*q.v.*). His avarice knew no bounds, and he plotted to secure his master's downfall. Through his wicked influence the empire was plunged into war. He was assisted in his vile work by another minister of the realm named Ribestein (*q.v.*), whom he bribed. His chief aim was to embroil his master in war against Dietrich. In this he was successful ; but not to the satisfaction of his own ends. His master was defeated, and he almost suffered death ; but for his former services he was saved.

SIDHE, PEOPLE OF THE. (Fairy Mounds.) In Irish romance, the Danaans (*q.v.*) in the later fairy state.

SIDRAC. A French romance current in England in the early part of the fourteenth century and fully described as *Le Livere Sydrac le Philosophe le quel Lom appele le livere de la funtane de totes science.* It appears to have been very popular from the frequency with which its MS. are met with. It is in reality a system of natural philosophy, and treats of the virtues of plants. It undoubtedly originates from an Arabian source, probably an offshoot of the literature of the Moors in Spain. Sidrac, the philosopher of this system, was astronomer to an Eastern king. He lived 870 years after Noah, of whose book of astronomy he was possessed. He converts Bocchus an idolatrous king of India, to the Christian faith, and by him is invited to build a mighty tower against the invasions of a rival monarch. After the death of Bocchus this book of Sidrac fell into the hands of a Chaldean renowned for piety. It then successively becomes the property of King Madian, Namaan the Assyrian, and Grypho, Archbishop of Samaria The latter had a priest named Demetrius, who brought it into Spain, and here it was translated from Greek into Latin. This translation was said

to be made at Toledo by Roger de Palermo, a minorite friar in the thirteenth century. A King of Spain then commanded it to be translated from Latin into Arabic, and sent it as a most valuable present to Emir Elmomenim, Lord of Tunis. It was next given to Frederick II., Emperor of Germany, famous in the Crusades. This work, which is of considerable length, was translated into English verse by Hugh Campeden, under the title *The Historie of King Bocchus and Sydrack* in 1510. It is in the " minstrel metre," and possesses neither elegance of diction nor harmony of versification.

SIEGE OF MILAN, THE. Written in twelve stanzas in English. It is perfect in the middle and at the end, 1602 lines remaining. No French original is known of this poem. The Saracens under Sultan Arabas, after plundering Rome and other cities, take Milan. The Lord of Milan, Sir Alantine, hastens to Charlemagne, who sends Roland with an army to Milan. The French are defeated ; Richard of Normancy is killed, and Roland and three other paladins are taken prisoners. The captives are brought before Arabas, who taunts them by ordering a crucifix to be burned. Miraculous flames burst forth from it which blind the Saracens. Guy of Burgundy slaughters Arabas, and the prisoners ride back to France upon celestial horses.

Charlemagne himself prepares to march on Milan. Meanwhile the Saracens have crowned " Sir Garcy " (the Garsile of the French *Otinel* (*q.v.*)) as their Sultan.

The Saracens meet the army of Charlemagne, and are driven back on Milan ; the French prepare a siege of the city, and at this juncture the poem breaks off.

Edited for the Early English Text Society by Sydney J. Werrtage. It forms the bulk of the volume called *The English Charlemagne Romances*, Part II. (1880).

SIEGFRIED. ("Nibelungenlied.") Son of King Siegmund of Xanten. He divided the treasure of the Nibelungs between Nibelung and Schillung, slew both brothers, and overcame the dwarf Alberich (*q.v.*), he slew a dragon and bathed in the blood, whereby his skin being turned to horn, no weapon could harm him. He married Kriemhild of Burgundy, and won Brunhild of Isenstein (*q.v.*) for Gunther, his brother-in-law. But Brunhild loved him, and out of jealousy for Kriemhild urged her husband to slay him, a murder which was effected by stealth. He is the great hero of the earlier portions of the *Nibelungenlied*.

SIGEBANT. (*Vide* "Gudrun Lay.") King of Ireland, father of Hagen (*q.v.*).

SIGEHER. A son of the Emperor Dietwart (*q.v.*). He is mentioned in the legend as being the only son of a family of forty-four, who survived the death of his parents, who are said to have lived for five hundred years. (*Vide* "Dietwart.")

SIGELINT. (See "Nibelungenlied.") One of the two merwomen whose raiment Hagen seized when he found them bathing by the Danube, and wished to compel them to foretell the future. She contradicted the false prophecy of her companion (*vide* "Hadebruc"), and foretold that none of the Burgundians should ever return to their land, save only the King's chaplain, which prophecy was fulfilled.

SIGENÔT. A High German poem, probably of Tyrolese origin, dating from the latter part of the thirteenth century, and part of the Saga cycle relating to Dietrich of Bern (*q.v.*). It recounts how Dietrich riding through the forest encountered the sleeping giant Sigenôt, whom he awakened roughly. Sigenôt felled him with his club and cast him into a deep snake-infested pit. Hildebrand, a follower of Dietrich's, next encountered the giant, who seized him also, and would have thrown him beside his master, had his prisoner not espied Dietrich's sword at the mouth of the pit. He seized it, and slew the giant, subsequently rescuing Dietrich with the aid of a dwarf Eggerich. See *Deutsche Heldenbuch*, Berlin, 1866–1878; E. Henrici, *Das Deutsche Heldenbuch*, vol. vii. of Kirschner's *Deutsche National Litterratur*; J. M. Ludlow. *Popular Epics of the Middle Ages*, London and Cambridge, 1865.

SIGENÔT. (*Vide* "Dietrich of Bern.") A giant related to Grim (*q.v.*). He unsuccessfully attempted to avenge Grim's death, but met his own end at the hands of Dietrich and Hildebrand (*q.v.*).

SIGGEIR. King of the Goths (*vide* "Volsungs"), who married Signy (*q.v.*) daughter of Volsung (*q.v.*). He attempted to destroy Sigmund (*q.v.*), and Sinfjötli (*q.v.*), but his own treachery brought him to his death. His wife Signy (*q.v.*) perished also at the same time.

SIGI. Son of Odin, and father of Rerir (*q.v.*), a character in "The Lay of the Volsungs" (*q.v.*) who, forced to flee from his father's wrath, settled in Hunland. He was slain by his own followers.

SIGMUND. (*Vide* "Volsungs"), son of Volsung (*q.v.*), father of Sinfjötli (*q.v.*) by his sister Signy (*q.v.*). He wedded Borghid (*q.v.*) who bore him two sons, Helgi (*q.v.*) and Hammund (*q.v.*). He afterwards destroyed her for poisoning Sinfjötli. He then married Hjordis (*q.v.*) daughter of King Eylimi (*q.v.*), who gave birth to Sigurd (*q.v.*) after his death. He was latterly assailed by King Lyngi (*q.v.*), a rival in love, who slew him and King Eylimi.

SIGNY. (*Vide* "Volsungs.") The daughter of Volsung (*q.v.*). She married King Siggeir (*q.v.*), to whom she bore two children, who, by her wish, were slain by Sigmund (*q.v.*) her brother. Disguised as a witch she dwelt for several days with her brother, and afterwards bore to him Sinfjötli (*q.v.*). She subsequently perished with King Siggeir her husband, when her brother set fire to his dwelling.

SIGURD. Son of Sigmund (*q.v.*) and Hjordis (*q.v.*). (*Vide* "Volsungs.") He was born at the court of Hjalprek (*q.v.*) after his father's death. He became very powerful. His tutor Regin (*q.v.*) accompanied him on many of his exploits. He received the foal Grani from Odin. He revenged his father's death by slaying King Lyng (*q.v.*) and the sons of Hunding, after which he overcame the dragon Fafnir (*q.v.*), whose heart he ate this endowing him with the power of understanding the language of birds. These advised him to slay Regin, which he did. He then raised Brunhild (*q.v.*) from the trance into which Odin had placed her. He tried to win her love, but having drunk a potion which made him forget her, he wedded Gudrun (*q.v.*), daughter of King Giuki

(*q.v.*) and his queen Grimhild (*q.v.*). Later in the shape of Gunnar (*q.v.*) he rode through the flames on to Brunhild's castle, and thus won her for Gunnar. He afterwards repented of his deception, but Brunhild had by then learned the truth. He was slain by Gunnar's brother Guttorm at the request of Brunhild, and in turn slew the murderer.

SIGURD. (*Vide* "Grettir Saga.") Husband of Lady Spes (*q.v.*).

SIGWARIDES, SIR, LORD OF THE ISLE. A noble knight in Arthurian romance, and husband of an unfaithful wife. He is slain by Sir Lancelot in the rescue of Queen Guinever from the stake. (*Vide* "Morte d'Arthur.")

SINEND. In Irish legend daughter of Lodan, and thus granddaughter of Lir (*q.v.*). She went to a certain well named Connla's well, under the sea (that is in the Land of Faërie), by which the hazel trees of the science of poetry blossomed. Omitting certain rites in drawing nigh it, she was overwhelmed by the waters, and washed up on the shores of the river Shannon, where she died, giving to the river its name.

SINFJÖTLI. (*Vide* "Volsungs.") Son of Signy (*q.v.*) begotten of Sigmund (*q.v.*) her brother. He met his death through Borghild's (*q.v.*) treachery.

SIR GAWAYNE AND THE GRENE KNYGHT. One of a number of English metrical romances on the subject of Gawayne. The romance relates that as King Arthur and his knights sat down to dine one New Year Day a strangely apparelled horseman entered the hall. In height and fierceness of regard no knight could equal him. He bore in one hand a bunch of holly, and in the other a well-sharpened axe. Everything that he wore, and even the trappings of his horse, were of green. The king had not seen such a strange sight before, and in haste to welcome the fierce visitor he asked him to join in the feast. But the knight refused, for he had come to test the bravery of the king's champions. Brandishing the axe in the air, he challenged any one of the assembled knights to deal him a blow on the neck with the weapon, on condition that on the same day one year hence the acceptor would submit to a similar blow at his own hands. The amazed on-lookers could not allow this challenge to go unheeded, and to the relief of all, Gawayne arose and accepted it. The Green Knight dismounted, laid bare his neck, and commanded Gawayne to strike. Down came the sharp blow, cutting through skin and bone, and sending the severed head rolling along the floor. The headless knight took the axe, picked up the head and mounted his steed. As he rode towards the door the head turned round and warned Gawayne on his peril not to fail to be at the Green Chapel next New Year Day. The court talked long about this adventure. But as the year rolled on Gawayne only was mindful of the event. Soon the year drew to a close, and after a farewell carousal the sad but brave-hearted knight set off for the Green Chapel. He wandered over hill and through dale, but the meeting-place appeared not in sight. One evening as his weary horse led him through a forest he espied through a clearing of the branches a many-towered castle. On he spurred his steed until he came within sight of the drawbridge, which in response to his signals was let down. Here he was lodged, and as his host assured him that the chapel was near at hand, he did not hesitate to prolong his stay, for it yet wanted six days ere the New Year. Every morning his good host went to the hunt, and during his absence his wife tempted her guest. But Gawayne remained virtuous. The last morning of his stay duly arrived, and as he would not respond to his temptress she presented him with a green buckle. This he concealed from the gaze of his host by fastening it under his armour, and resumed his fatal journey accompanied by a servant to lead the way. At last the servant halted, and, pointing in the direction of the chapel, bade the knight go on alone. With an ill-boding he came to a cave almost concealed by evergreens, and deeming this to be the Green Chapel he dismounted and peered within. Nothing but green met his gaze, and at last raising a shout, he was answered by the Green Knight calling him to come forward. On he went without faltering, but believing none the less that his last moment had come. The greeting from the Green Knight, whose head rested as soundly as ever on his body, was cordial, and anxious to end the suspense, he commanded the fated knight to doff his helmet and lay bare his neck. This done, the Green Knight swung the axe, but Gawayne flinched. The Green Knight uttered a word of warning, and once more swinging his weapon, brought it down upon Sir Gawayne's neck. To Gawayne's surprise his head was still secure, for the axe had but bruised the skin. Then he turned to the

z

Green Knight and beheld him to be his good host, who told him that his name was Sir Bernlake, and in his house lived Morgan-le-Fay, who had led his wife to tempt his guest. But now that he had proved a man of valour and noble virtue he could not suffer so young a head to roll in the dust. The two knights parted, and Gawayne rode back to the court of Arthur.

The substance of this tale is almost identical with that in which the Irish hero Cuchulain takes up the challenge by the demon called "The Terrible" (q.v.), cuts off the monster's head, and next day submits to a like test himself, escaping unharmed. It is noticeable that "The Terrible" is a water spirit, and the garb and dwelling of the Green Knight would seem to point to the circumstance that he had a similar origin. That the Arthurian story is founded upon the Irish one is obvious, and this would appear to afford an illustration of some value concerning the presumed Irish source of many Arthurian tales.

SKAMKELL. (*Vide* "Burnt Njal.") The fawning friend of Otkell (q.v.) ; with whom he was slain by Gunnar (q.v.) and Kolskegg (q.v.).

SKARP-HEDINN. (*Vide* "Burnt Njal.") Eldest son of Njal. He avenged Gunnar's death ; assisted in the slaying of Thrain (q.v.) and Hrapp (q.v.), and in that of Hanskuld (q.v.). For this murder he was burnt with his parents and his brother Grim (q.v.) in Njal's home.

SKATHA. In Irish romance a mighty woman—warrior of the Land of Shadows (Skye ?). To her went many Irish warriors to learn feats of war, the last two being the crossing of the Bridge of Leaps which led to her dun or dwelling, and the use of the Gae Bolg (q.v.). Cuchullin (q.v.) accomplished the first, and was taught the second.

SKEGGI. (*Vide* "Grettir Saga.") One of the company that went with Thorkel to the king. Both he and Grettir lost their meal-bags on the way. But Skeggi finding one, Grettir demanded it of him, the quarrel ending in Skeggi's death and in a three years' banishment for the victor.

SKENA. In Irish romance wife of Amergin (q.v.), son of Miled (q.v.). As the Milesians were sailing for Ireland she died on the way, and was buried at Inverskena, the ancient name of the Kenmare River.

SKAPTI. (*Vide* "Grettir Saga.") The lawman and friend of Grettir.

SOLOMON'S SHIP. The ship on which in Arthurian legend Sir Galahad's (q.v.) sword was found. The legend tells how the heroes came upon the sword at the foot of a rich bed with its blade six inches out of the scabbard. Galahad examining the sword finds the scabbard made of serpent's skin. He also sees written on the blade that none should draw it who could not strike better than the others. Sir Perceval's sister supplies hangings made of her own hair and names the sword "The Sword of Strange Hangings," and the scabbard "Memory of Blood," and Galahad girds on the weapon.

SONG OF ROLAND, THE. A poem of the eleventh century, and the first recorded of the Carlovingian cycle. The earliest text extant which purports to be written by Turold or Théroulde (*q.v.*), is preserved at Oxford, in the Bodleian Library. The *Song* is not the work of a finished poet, but its lofty tone of courage, patriotism and devotion to duty as well as its affecting and impressive native nobility place it among the great epic poems of the world. The resolve of the valiant few to face the hosts of Saracens who confront them, and the strong but simple language in which they exhort each other must appeal powerfully to every brave man, whilst the sorrow of the paladins for those who have fallen and the affecting circumstances of the deaths of Roland, Oliver, and Turpin are scarcely to be read with dry eyes. The childlike honesty and transparency of the whole work is marvellously refreshing, and the military spirit with which it is infused stirs the heart like a trumpet-call. *The Song of Roland* is to be regarded as Norman in its origin, and was probably written by a certain Théroulde, tutor of William the Conqueror. It was certainly chanted by the Norman warrior Taillefer, as he rushed on the Saxons at the battle of Hastings, and the improbable theory of M. Génin is that the Oxford MS., after passing through Taillefer's hands, was deposited in an MS. chest by a second Théroulde, Abbot of Peterborough, who died in 1098. But the Oxford MS. is manifestly not the original, nor is it the first work of its kind, as can be proved by internal evidence. The *Song* tells the story of Roncevaux, which combat it is now considered was a Basque ambush to cut off the retreating French rearguard in the Pyrenees, and not a Saracen strategem, as the poem has it. The Basque song of *Alta-bicar* enshrines the memory of the fight among the Pyrenean peasantry. The battle took place in 778 A.D. according to the *Annales* of Eginhard, Charlemagne's chronicler.

The *Song* begins by stating that at the period of its commencement the emperor had been " full seven years in Spain," and had conquered that land as far as the sea. He only requires to reduce Saragossa, which is held by King Marsile, who worships Mahomet. Marsile calls his lords to council as to how he may best rid himself of Charles. Blancadrin advises him to send a friendly embassy to the emperor, offering to go and do fealty to him at Michaelmas and receive baptism, and further to give hostages. The Franks will then depart, and Marsile need not keep his promises. The hostages will be hanged, but it is better so than that the Moors should lose Spain the bright. The advice is taken, and envoys are sent with the mendacious message. They arrive at where Charles is, surrounded by his peers, whom he calls into council. Roland dislikes the terms, and suspects treason. Ganilo, Roland's stepfather, and a traitor, presses the assembly to accept them. Roland then suggests that Ganilo himself should proceed to Marsile's headquarters and come to an arrangement with him. This enrages Count Ganilo, and he resolves to destroy Roland, whom he hates, and Oliver with him. He takes his leave on his errand, hate of Roland in his heart. He comes to where Marsile is, and tells him that Charlemagne will give him one-half Spain in fee if he becomes a Christian, the other half he will give to Roland, his nephew. At the instance of Blancadrin Marsile bribes Ganilo to assist him in the destruction of Roland. Ganilo, who desires nothing better, tells him that Roland will be in command of the rearguard of the French, only 20,000 men in all, and that when they retreat into their own country, imagining that Marsile has surrendered, the Moorish king should raise 100,000 men and cut off the French and slay Roland. So would Charles lose " the right hand of his body." Ganilo then returns to the emperor Charles, and tells him that Marsile has agreed to become his man, and will follow him to France in a month's time. The French then depart for " sweet France." The pagans follow in their wake, four hundred thousand strong. Oliver in the rearguard says to his friend Roland that he hears a noise of trumpets afar off. He mounts a high pine-tree, and espies the paynim host. He cannot count even the troops of them. They draw near. The Franks form in battle array. Archbishop Turpin addresses them, absolves them, and for penance commands them " to strike." The battle begins by a single combat between Roland and Asbron, whom the Frankish knight slays with a mighty stroke. The combat waxes furious. The French knights do tremendous execution. The Archbishop kills Siglorel the enchanter, who, led by Jupiter (mistaken by the author for a Moorish deity), has already been in Hell. The pagans die by hundreds and by thousands. In France there is a mighty tempest, prophetic of the great loss which that land will suffer through the slaying of her best warriors. Now comes King Marsile with full thirty troops to the rescue of those who flee. So valiant are the French, however, that victory seems long to remain with them.

But after four successful encounters, the French knights are all slain save sixty. Roland says to Oliver that he will blow his horn for the purpose of attracting the French vanguard with the emperor, but Oliver dissuades him, saying that it would be shame to crave succour. Turpin, the archbishop, says that it is useless, for by the time Charles arrives they will all be cut to pieces. But, nevertheless, the king may avenge them. So Roland blows his ivory horn, and Charles hears it thirty leagues away. He recognizes it, but Ganilo laughs him to scorn. The emperor in wrath sees through Ganilo's treachery, has him seized, and returns to assist the rearguard. The French under Roland knowing that they will receive no quarter, and asking none, renew the fight like lions. The Saracen Marganice strikes Oliver from behind, but is slain by him. Oliver loses much blood, and when Roland comes nigh he mistakes him for a Saracen, and deals him a terrible blow, as does Vivien to William of Orange in the *Covenant Vivien*. Oliver feels that death is nigh, descends from horseback, and lies down on the ground. He expires. Roland laments over him " full sweetly." All the French are now slain save the doughty archbishop and Walter of Luz. Roland returns to the fray. He does great execution. He weakens. His temples are burst by his blowing of the horn, which once more he sounds. The French host approaching replies with a fanfare of sixty thousand trumpets, the sound of which reaches the hard-pressed warriors. Roland and Turpin stand together. The archbishop goes off and searches the field for the bodies of the peers, finds them, and places them in a row. Roland faints, and

Turpin trys to find water for him. But so weak is the archbishop that he falls dead of his many wounds. Roland feels that death is near. He ascends a tree under which are four blocks of marble. A Saracen thinking him at his last gasp seizes him and his sword, but is slain. He cannot see any more. He strikes ten blows on a rock with his sword Durandel—the last blows of a proud, dying man. He lies down and turns his head to the pagan folk, that all should say that he died a conqueror. Roland is dead. The emperor reaches Roncevaux. He is amazed at the slaughter. He calls for the peers, but finds all slain. The French pursue the fleeing Saracens. The amiral (Emir-al-mumenim) of Alexandria, Baligant, comes to the succour of Marsile, and rides at once to meet the emperor. Charles, meanwhile, finds the body of Roland. The French bury their dead, but the hearts of Roland, Oliver, and Turpin are taken out and placed in urns, and their bodies, wound in stag-leather, are placed upon carts. The Saracen army approaches. The combat becomes general, and the French do wonders. Charles slays Baligant, the pagans flee, and the French pursue. Brami-domie, Marsile's wife, sees the rout from the towers of Saragossa, and cries out that all is lost. On hearing her, Marsile turns his face to the wall and dies of chagrin, giving his soul to the devils. The emperor breaks down the gates of the city and enters it. The inhabitants are baptized by force, and the queen is led a prisoner to France, where she is converted. Leaving a garrison at Saragossa, Charles departs. He buries Ro-land, Oliver and Turpin in St. Roman's Church at Blaye. He

tries Ganilo. During the trial Alda, a fair damsel enters the hall and asks for Roland. She is the sister of Oliver, and Roland's betrothed. (*Vide* "Gerard de Viana.") On hearing of his death she suddenly expires. The barons agree that Ganilo should be freed. But Thierry opposes this. Pin-abel, Ganilo's kinsman, takes ex-ception to this, and the twain fight. Thierry slays Pinabel. Ganilo is sentenced to be torn to pieces by horses. At night the emperor is lying in his vaulted chamber when he has a visit from St. Gabriel, who bids him summon all his hosts that he may go into the land of Syria to the succour of King Vivian, who is besieged by pagans. The emperor fain would not go. "God," he cries, "so painful is my life." And with this hint at his bitter sorrow for his nephew and his repugnance to further slaughter the *Song* ends.

SONG OF THE SAXONS, THE. A ro-mance of the Carlovingian cycle, and fifth in number of the *Romans des Douze Pairs de France*. It was composed by Jean Bodel, a poet of Artois, who flourished to-wards the middle of the thirteenth century, though, indeed, in a Turin MS. the authorship seems to be claimed by one Guerris. It lies upon the borderland between traditional history and pure romance. The subject is his-torical — Charlemagne's invasion of Saxony on his return from Roncevaux. The work is scarcely to be considered as original, despite the contempt which the author throws upon the "villein joglers" who "could neither tell the verse of it nor the song." And is almost certainly founded on the ruder songs of the joglers, as the subject is treated in several poems which are as old if not even more ancient than the "Song" itself. However, the opening of the poem shows clearly that it belongs not to an age of mere songful activity, but to a period of literary composition. There are but three subjects worthy of song, says the bard—of France (that is of Charlemagne) of Britain (of Arthur) and of Rome the Great (of the Gesta Romanorum). Charlemagne receives news of a Saxon invasion. The heathen have taken Cologne, have killed Duke Milo, and have carried off Helissend, promised bride of Nerard of Montdidier. The barons of Herupe (the north-west provinces of modern France) refuse to march against the foe until Charles first introduces into Herupe "our customs and our laws." They are at last appeased, and Charles invades Saxony, reaching the banks of "Rune the deep," beyond which lies the Saxon king Guiteclin's palace of Tremoigne, supposed to be Dortmund in Westphalia. After a siege of two years and more the barons grumble, and ask Charles to call out the men of Herupe to their assistance. This is done, and the men of Herupe respond loyally. They ask where they are to lodge their troops, and the emperor points to the other side of the "Rune," to the Saxon lines. The Herupians take him at his word, and seize the position after a tremendous struggle. A bridge is built, and the army passes over it; the Saxons are discomfited, and Charlemagne kills Guiteclin in single combat. At this point "the slender vein of historic truth which runs through the poem may be considered as quite exhausted." Sebile, the wife of Guiteclin, has taken the captive Helissend as her

favourite, and with her and other ladies, establishes herself on the banks of the river to act as decoys to the Franks and to turn them "to folly." She falls in love with Baldwin, a nephew of Charlemagne's to whom she sends a love-message. On the death of her husband, Guiteclin, she is given in marriage to Baldwin by the emperor, and the twain are crowned King and Queen of Saxony. Helissend is united to Berard, a Frankish champion. The two sons of Guiteclin with one hundred thousand Russians and Bulgarians and the giant Ferabrus of Russia, march on Tremoigne to avenge Guiteclin's death. Baldwin has but fifteen thousand troops to oppose them, but refuses to send for succour to Charlemagne, who has returned to his dominions. At length he is prevailed upon to do so, and attacks the invaders with five thousand men, putting their vanguard to flight. Baldwin refuses to re-enter the city, although attacked by the main force of the paynim. He kills Ferabrus, and unhorses one of Guiteclin's sons. But numbers tell, and the Franks are forced to retreat into Tremoigne. The messenger despatched to Charlemagne comes up with him at Cologne, and the emperor starts in haste for Saxony with ten thousand men. Arrived at the beleaguered city, Charlemagne attempts to effect a junction with his nephew, who boldly throws himself into the pagan ranks and slays large numbers. Uncle and nephew join forces, and the battle is renewed with fury. Baldwin, mortally wounded, cleaves a Saxon to the shoulders and dies. Charlemagne bitterly inveighs against fate at his nephew's death, and quits the field. He is met by

Sebile, who inquires concerning her husband. Charlemagne shows her his corpse and she faints away. Her lament is most beautiful and impassioned. Charles that night rode the rounds himself, armed cap-à-pie. Finally the men of Herupe come up in force and rout the Saxons. An abbey is founded on the field, and is entered by Sebile. Dyalos, a baptized Saxon king, receives custody of the kingdom, and the emperor returns with the bodies of Baldwin and Berard. The poem as it stands is not to be considered as original, as the compiler refers to MS. authority at the convent of St. Faro at Meaux on two occasions, and the subject is certainly referred to in poems which are older or at least of equal antiquity with the *Song of the Saxons*, for example *The Four Sons of Aymon*, in which Charlemagne is made to refer to the summoning of the men of Herupe and the conquest of Guiteclin.

SOTÉ. In the Icelandic Saga of *Frithjof* (*q.v.*), the Viking who stole Wayland's armlet from Thorsten.

SOUDAN. (*Vide* "Guy of Warwick.") Saracen emperor. He besieged Greece, but was defeated by Ernis, who obtained the assistance of Sir Guy. Sir Guy afterwards cut off his head, and carried it to Ernis.

SPES, LADY. (*Vide* "Grettir Saga.") She ransomed Thorstein Dromond (*q.v.*), Grettir's brother, from prison and death, and finally wedded him.

STARN. In Irish romance son of Sera (*q.v.*), brother of Partholan (*q.v.*), original father of Tuan MacCarell (*q.v.*).

STEIN (1). (*Vide* "Grettir Saga.") The priest of Sandheaps whose homestead was rid of the spirits which haunted it by Grettir.

STEIN (2). The lawman who succeded Skapti, who figures in the same tale.

STORY OF BEYOND THE SEA. A French romance of the twelfth century. A certain Count of Ponthieu had a very fair daughter and by his second wife a son. In the same county there dwelt at the same time a dame of Dommare who had a noble and much beloved son, named Thibault. This youth was heir to the Count of St. Pol, but without inheritance during his uncle's lifetime. But his valiant bearing won him a post in the household of the Count of Ponthieu; and his lord prospering through this servant's prowess rewarded him with the hand of his daughter. For five years the pair lived happily; but at the end of that period they set out for the shrine of St. James, the Apostle of Spain, to pray him to send them a child. The road lay through a dangerous forest, and the lady and her lord entering that forest alone were sorely insulted by robbers. The lady was shamed, and in her madness and anger sought to slay the knight. But he returned home with her, having honoured St. James, and treated her as gently and honourably as before. All these sore mishaps during his pilgrimage the Count of Ponthieu heard from his son-in-law; and in his wrath thrust his lovely daughter into a tub, secured the top of it and cast it into the sea. A Flanders merchantman came in the tub's path. These traders with the Saracen hoisted the tub on board; and seeing the lady gain fresh life and beauty with their care and nurture, gifted the Soudan of Ammaire with this lovely prize. In return he greatly forwarded their business. The lady abjured her faith and was wedded to the paynim lord. For two and a half years these two lived in happiness, rejoicing in their little son and daughter. Meantime the lady's father, husband, and brother sorrowed greatly for her fate ; and securing each the cross upon their mantles made devout pilgrimage to all the sacred places in the Holy Land. Then having served for a year in the Temple, they took ship at Acre for the return journey. Fate, however, sent a storm, which cast them into the hands of the Soudan. In grievous plight they were all three, since they had so firmly bound themselves together during the storm, that they were taken together and thrown into the same dungeon. The Soudan, as was the paynim wont, in celebrating his birthday granted his people any captive they wished as a target for their arrows. One after another these three unhappy Frenchmen were demanded as the people's prize ; but the Sultana, knowing her captives, sought them as gifts from her lord. The people were satisfied with another of the French captives. Now, having cautiously disclosed her identity to her prisoners, she schemed for their and her deliverance. Her Christian husband she sent to the wars with the Soudan, where he acquitted himself so gloriously that he gained his favour. Then falling ill with child she requested permission to breathe her native air, as her condition demanded it. Therefore, having received leave to sail to France and to take her three captives and her little son with her, she landed at Brindisi. A message was sent back to the Soudan that she would not return. All five then sought absolution of the Pontiff at Rome ; and the bishop christened the child William, and remarried Thibault and Ponthieu's daughter. In time William married the daughter of Raoul des Preause and became Lord of Preause ; Count Ponthieu's son died ; Thibault and his lady had two sons who became heirs to the realms of Ponthieu and St. Pol ; the daughter of the Soudan was wedded to a brave Turk, Malakin of Baudas. This lady gave birth to the mother of the Sultan Saladin, a courteous, wise, honourable and conquering lord.

SUALTAM. Father of Cuchullin in Irish romance. After the carnage of Murthemne (*vide* " Cuchullin "), he took the Grey of Macha, his son's matchless steed, and attempted to rouse the province of Ulster. But as he rode through the land, crying that its inhabitants were in the direst peril through immediate invasion, the people only stared at him stupidly as even did King Cathbad and his court. In wrath Sualtam turned his horse's head to leave the royal precincts, when the animal stumbled, and Sualtam's neck coming into sharp contact with his shield, his head was shorn off and fell to the ground. But even then it continued to exhort Cathbad and his peers to take immediate action if Ulster was to be saved, until the " curse of Ulster," the stupidity and glamour which had been put upon the people by Macha (*q.v.*) was lifted, and Conor rose and sware a mighty oath to "restore every woman to her hearth and every cow to its byre."

SUPPINABILES, SIR. A knight of Brittany. He paid a visit to England during Tristram's sojourn in Brittany, and returned to relate the scandal about Tristram at Arthur's court. (*Vide* " Morte d Arthur.")

SVEIN. (*Vide* " Gunnlaug Saga.") Co-ruler of Norway with his brother Yarl Eric.

SWANHILD (1). (*Vide* "Volsungs.") Daughter of Gudrun (*q.v.*). She was betrothed to King Jormunrek (*q.v.*). On her voyage to his court she fell in love with Randver (*q.v.*), but on their arrival, she and her lover were put to death by the king.

SWANHILD (2). (*Vide* "Dietrich of Bern.") Second wife of King Ermenrich (*q.v.*). She met death at the hands of her husband, who, at the suggestion of his marshal Sibich (*q.v.*), trampled her under his horse.

SYR DEGORE. An English romance probably of the thirteenth century. It recounts how a king's daughter of England who is extremely beautiful, is asked in marriage by the monarchs of various kingdoms. Her father publishes it abroad that only he who can unhorse him at a tournament will be adjudged worthy of the lady. The suitors all prove unsuccessful in this. During a journey to his wife's tomb the king, whose daughter accompanies him, loses her. She has strayed into the forest, and has there encountered a knight, who prevails over her chastity, and at parting gives her a sword without a point and a pair of gloves which will fit no hands but her own. (Compare the myths of Hercules and Cuchullin.) At length she finds the road to her father's castle, where she is delivered of a boy. She places him in a cradle, with money and the gloves given her by the stranger knight along with a letter, and consigns him to one of her maidens who leaves him in a wood near a hermitage. The hermit discovers the infant in the morning, reads the letter, educates him until the age of twenty years, and then sends him into the world, giving him the gloves, which he tells him will fit no lady but his mother. The youth, who is called Degore, sets out in search of adventure, and saves an earl from a terrible dragon, which he slays. The earl invites him to his palace, dubs him knight, supplies him with a horse and armour, and offers him half his territory. Sir Degore refuses this offer unless the gloves which he has received from the hermit will fit any lady of the court. But they will fit none of them. He proceeds on his way, and meets with a large train of knights who, he is informed, are going to tourney with the king of England who would give his daughter to that knight who could conquer him in single combat. Sir Degore accompanies them, overthrows the king, and obtains the princess. He marries her, but immediately after the ceremony he bethinks him of the gloves, and tries them on her hands. She draws them on with the greatest ease, declares to Degore that he is her son, and gives him an account of his birth. Giving Degore his father's pointless sword, she puts it into his mind to find his sire. He sets forward on this search, and on the way comes to a castle, where he is entertained by fifteen beautiful damsels. The lady of the castle tries every artifice to tempt him to remain, but to no avail. Degore rejects all her temptations, and proceeds on his journey. In a forest he meets a knight richly accoutred, who asks him why he has presumed to enter his forest without permission. They fight, and the strange knight observing the curious sword carried by his adversary, calls a halt. He fits the sword to a point which he had always kept, and which had formerly broken off in an encounter with a giant. By this circumstance he discovers Degore to be his son. They both return to England, and Sir Degore's father is married to the princess, his mother. This romance bears a close resemblance to various world-tales more or less well known. The pledges or tokens given by the stranger knight to

his lady-love are reminiscent of those bestowed on their mistresses by Hercules, Abraham, and the father of Cuchullin. The marriage of the son to his mother is parallel to some degree in the myth of Œdipus, and the combat between son and sire is of widespread character, being found in the tales of Sohrab and Rustem, and the *Hildebrandeslied*. (*Vide* "Dietrich of Bern") The romance was printed by one William Copeland in 1560.

T

TAIN BO CUAILGNE (thawn bo quelgny). The Cattle Raid of Quelgny. (*Vide* "Maev.")

TALTIU or **TELTA.** Daughter of the King of the Land of the Dead, and wife of Eoch Mac Erc, a Firbolg (*q.v.*) king In Irish legend she is spoken of as having a palace at Telltown, called after her, where in the middle ages a great fair was annually held.

TANNHÄUSER. A German legend of the middle ages once popular in ballad form, and sung in the district of Entlibuch as late as the year 1830. The story may be traced in its literary form as far back as the fourteenth century. But it is obvious from its details that it possesses a far greater antiquity. It recounts the adventures of a minnesinger or minstrel, who, in the course of his wanderings, comes to the Hörselberg or hill of Venus, into which he is invited to enter, and where he remains for a space wallowing in the joys of Hell, and forgetful of his better nature. In time, however, he becomes aware of the

wickedness in which he is dwelling, and quits the court of Venus. With the object of obtaining absolution for his sins he travels to Rome, and seeks mercy from Pope Urban IV. But the Pope tells him that the papal staff he holds might blossom as soon as mercy be extended to such a sinner as he. Tannhäuser in despair returns to Venus. But three days afterwards the Pope's staff blossoms and he sends messengers to every country in the hope of saving the minstrel. But to no avail, for he cannot be found. As has been indicated, the story possesses a mythological basis. It is connected with the Hörselberg near Eisenach, in which the Lady Holda, a German earth-goddess, later confounded with Venus, was supposed to dwell. As in the similar legend of Thomas the Rhymer (*q.v.*), we have in the Hörselberg, or the Ercildoun of the Scots seer, the berg, hill, or doun of the moon-goddess Ursula. The goddess of night is always regarded as a being of singular beauty and seductive power. It is evident that we have, then, to deal with an ancient pagan myth on which has been superimposed a later legend, coloured by modern or mediæval and Christian thought, and the original hero of which has been displaced by a hero of later popularity. Tannhäuser was a veritable minnesinger of the middle of the thirteenth century, who resided at the court of the Austrian duke Frederick II., the Quarrelsome. On the death of that prince he attached himself to Duke Otto II. of Bavaria, and having lived prodigally, was forced to lead a wandering existence. He was highly in favour among the minnesingers of his time, and his restless and intemperate life seems to have marked him out as a probable hero for such an adventure as has been attributed to him. He was the author of many ballads of considerable excellence, which are published in the second part of the *Minnesinger* (collection by Von der Hagen, Leipsic, 1838), and in the sixth volume of Haupt's *Zeitschrift fur deutsches Alterthum*, Leipsic, 1848.

Literature : The version of the legend which may be regarded as the most authentic is that given in Uhland's *Alte hoch und nieder- deutsche Volkslieder* (Stuttgart, 1845). See also Kornmann, *Mons Veneris*, Frankfort, 1614 ; Grasse, *Die Sage, vom Ritter Tannhäuser* (Dresden and Leipsic, 1846). See also the allusions in Grimm and the *Heldenbuch*.

TASSO, TORQUATO. Descendant of the illustrious house of the Torre- giani, was born at Sorento, on March 11th, 1544. His father Bernardo Tasso, was a faithful adherent of Ferrante of San- feverina, prince of Salerno. He was also a man of literary ability, for he wrote in prose and verse ; a gift his son inherited in a more marked degree. Torquato's mother was Portia di Rossi, who was also of good parentage. Young Tasso showed early signs of genius, and was committed to the care of Manritio Catanio, who assiduously cultivated his pupil's studious tastes. After the death of Sanfeverina, Bernardo returned to Italy, and entered the service of Guglielmo Gonzaga, duke of Mantua. Shortly after, his wife died, and Bernardo sent his son to the University of Padua. While still a student at Padua, he wrote the poem of *Rinaldo*, which was published in his eighteenth year. This initial success decided him in his poetical career : a decision which offended his father, who had hoped that his son might turn his studies to a more profit- able market. While at Padua, Tasso formed the design of his celebrated poem "Jerusalem De- livered" (*q.v.*). He finished it a few years later while residing at the palace of his patron, the Duke of Ferrara ; but in the interval he had published a pastoral poem called "Arminta." Tasso was in his thirtieth year when he completed *Jerusalem Delivered*, but it was to his lasting regret prematurely printed by his patron, and before he had time to make the final corrections. The poem met with great success, and was translated into several languages. The drop of bitterness in his cup of elation was the death of his father at Mantua. After this, good fortune seemed to desert him. His *Jerusalem Delivered* was severely censured, and the aca- demy of Crusca published a scathing criticism on the poem. Becoming entangled in an affair of honour, he was arrested by the

Duke of Ferrara. After a year's imprisonment, he effected his escape, and fled to Turin. He was discovered by the Duke of Savoy, who showed him great kindness. Being suspicious of his friendship, he set out for Rome, where he stayed with his old friend, Manritio Catanio. Desirous of beholding his native country, he journeyed to Sorrento, where he stayed some time with a widowed sister. In the hope of obtaining his writings, which were in the duke's possessions, he again returned to Ferrara. But his attempts to do so were futile, and he was imprisoned for seven years, and nearly lost his reason. The only apparent motive for the duke's harsh treatment was that Tasso had aspired to the hand of the princess Leonora, the duke's sister. On his release, he stayed for some time at Naples, and also at Bifaccio, where his melancholy took the form as was then thought of possession by a familiar spirit. He afterwards returned to Naples, where he composed and published his poem *Jerusalem Conquered*. Tasso was now fêted and welcomed by the high dignitaries of the Church of Rome, and the pope granted him the honour of being crowned with laurel in the Capitol. He had a foreboding that the ceremony would not take place, a presage which came true; for in the midst of the preparations he was seized with a fatal illness. He died at Rome in his fifty-second year, and was buried in the church of St. Oimphrius, 1595.

TAWLESS. The Giant killed by Tristram (*q.v.*) during the latter's period of insanity. (*Vide* "Morte d'Arthur.")

TERRIBLE, THE. (*Vide* "Briccriu.")

TERRY, SIR. (*Vide* "Sir Otuel.") A knight of Charlemagne. He along with Sir Baldwin heard Roland's horn and finding him dying in the forest of Roncesvalles, attended to him.

THEODORIC THE OSTROGOTH. (*Vide* "Dietrich of Bern.")

THIBAUT. (*Vide* "Garin the Lorrainer.") Knight of Plaissis. He had hoped to marry Beatrice, and when he heard of the marriage to Bego he determined to lay an ambush for them on their way home from Blaives. A pilgrim having warned Bego, he prepared as far as possible, but he was outnumbered and was severely wounded. Unless help had come to Bego he would indeed have been slain. Thibaut was present at Lens when a forester brought him news of Bego whom he had seen in the forest, and he joined the men who went out to kill him. Fromont put Thibaut in prison for this, but William of Montclin pleaded for him as he was a kinsman. William of Blanchfort afterwards freed the prisoners. Thibaut was killed by Hernaud in battle.

THIDREKS SAGA. A prose version of the "Dietrich of Bern Saga-cycle" (*q.v.*), written in Icelandic in the middle of the thirteenth century from poems and tales then current in Germany, and later re-edited and extended by another hand. Commencing with Dietrich's ancestry, we are given the history of his youth and his friendship with Hildebrand, and how he forced the dwarf Alberich to give him his sword Nagelring, and like deeds of emprise. The story then digresses to include the *Wilkina Saga*, a group of tales concerning the Sclavonic monarch Wilkina. This is followed by the *Wayland*

Smith legend (*q.v.*), Wayland or Wailand being the grandson of Wilkina. The birth of Witege, Wayland's son, is described, and we return to the story of Dietrich. Witege comes to Bern to challenge Dietrich. He receives the magic sword Mimung from Hildebrand, and is on the point of worsting Dietrich when Hildebrand intervenes, and Witege remains at the court of Bern as Dietrich's friend. Dietrich, smarting under his defeat, rides forth alone on adventure bound, and after vanquishing two giants slays an elephant and a dragon. We next find Dietrich, like Arthur, the central figure of a court to which heroes eager for fame arrive in large numbers. Dietrich joins Attila in a war against Santrix, King of Wilkinaland, and later undertakes other similar expeditions. Still another digression deals with the youthful adventures of Siegfried (*q.v.*), the hero of the *Nibelungenlied*. Hearing that Siegfried is at the court of Isung, King of Bertangaland, Dietrich challenges him to a series of combats between his own and Isung's heroes. For two days Dietrich and Siegfried fight, but on the third Dietrich employs the magic sword Mimung, and overcomes him, whereupon Siegfried becomes his henchman. At this point a number of minor interludes are introduced, such as the stories of *Herbort and Hilda, Walter of Aquitaine* (*q.v.*), and *Hildegund,* and so forth. When the saga is once more resumed it is told how Ermenrich, the uncle of Dietrich, having dishonoured the wife of one Sibecke, that person contrived the deaths of Ermenrich's three sons and two nephews by means of false accusations. He instigates Ermenrich to request Dietrich to pay him tribute as a test of his

loyalty as a nephew. Dietrich refuses, and Ermenrich marches an army against him. Dietrich flies to the court of Attila, and engages in many expeditions on behalf of the Hunnish monarch. After an exile of a score of years, Attila provides him with an army which defeats that of Ermenrich, at the cost of the death of his younger brother and Attila's two sons. Once more the *dramatis personæ* of the *Nibelungenlied* (*q.v.*) are brought upon the scene. This digression commences with the quarrel between Brunhild and Kriemhild and the incidents surrounding the death of Siegfried are recounted. Dietrich holds aloof from the schemes of Kriemhild, but when his companion Rüdiger is slain, he sides against the Burgundians and takes Hagen, their last survivor.

Returning to Berne mourning the loss of all his men save Hildebrand, they hear of the death of Ermenrich. Dietrich regains his throne at last, and the remainder of the saga deals with extravagant adventures, ending with the deaths of its principal characters.

THIERRY, SIR. (*Vide* "Guy of Warwick.") A knight who served under the Duke of Lorraine. He was in love with Osile, daughter of the duke and was carrying her off when he was attacked by men sent by Duke Otho and nearly killed. He was rescued by Sir Guy, who befriended him and carried him through the many adventures he and Osile experienced before they were eventually married, and reconciled to the duke. He afterwards lost his possessions, and being met by Sir Guy fell asleep beside him. A white weasel came out of his mouth, went to a rock near, then came back and ran down his throat again. Sir Guy went to the same spot as the weasel and found a sword and treasure which he gave to Thierry, and afterwards fought for him and got him reinstated.

THIERRY, KING OF SAVOY. Mentioned in *Garin the Lorrainer*. Four Moorish kings besieged Savoy, and he appealed to Pepin for help which was at first refused. But four young knights persuaded Pepin to let them go. He agreed, and gave the command to the two Lorrainers. The Saracens were defeated, but King Thierry was fatally wounded. When dying, he grieved that his daughter was not married, and as he considered that Garin had saved his country, he asked him to espouse her, which Garin agreed to do, with Pepin's consent.

THOLOMES, KING. In Grail romance, he wars successfully against Evelach (*q.v.*), whom he takes prisoner, and defeats his army. The White Knight appears on the scene and performs prodigies of valour, overcomes Tholomes, rescues Evelach, whose armies become victorious

THOMAS. A mediæval English author, sometimes known as Thomas of Brittany. He is remembered by his metrical versions of *King Horn* and *Tristan and Iseult*, but nothing is recorded concerning his life, while even the period at which he lived has never been determined, some authorities placing him in the second half of the thirteenth century, but others holding that he belongs to the reign of Richard I., who was crowned in 1189. He wrote in French, and the style and tenor of his output proclaim him to have been influenced by the French

romance *Adénes le Roi;* but his own nationality is matter for conjecture, and the likelihood is that, like several other English authors of the middle ages, he emanated from a family which had come to England in the train of some Norman baron. It has frequently been suggested that he was the original author of *King Horn*, but it is probable that long ere the advent of Thomas the tale was familiar throughout England, and that his work consisted simply in gleaning it orally and writing it down, at the same time augmenting it. A certain popularity would seem to have been gained by his version, for numerous mediæval manuscript copies are extant, one being in the Cambridge University Library and one in the Harleian collection in the British Museum ; while another is among the vast batch of manuscripts bequeathed to the Bodleian Library by Francis Donce (1757–1834), and the story was printed from the latter by Joseph Ritson in *Early English Romances*, 1802. The manuscripts which Donce left behind him at death also included a copy of Thomas's *Tristan and Iseult*, but, by some curious mischance, this did not find its way into the Bodleian although the library was its legitimate legatee. The present domicile of this document is unknown, but at one time it passed through the hands of the French historian, Francisque Michel, who had it duly printed and published along with a preface from his own pen, 1835. A good deal shorter than most other versions of the story, Thomas's *Tristan* nevertheless enjoyed considerable vogue in the author's time, and it is supposed to have been laid under contribution by a number of immediately subsequent writers on the theme, salient among these being the German romancer, Gottfried von Strassburg (fl. 1310). He avows a debt to one Thomas of Brittany, and hence the frequent bestowal of that name on the English Thomas, but it is possible that they were two wholly different men.

THOMAS A READING, THE PLEASANT HISTORIE OF. This prose tale, dating probably from Elizabethan times, recounts the doings of the fraternity of tailors and clothiers in the reign of Henry I. It possesses but little central plot, and consists of a series of episodes connected with the several members of the confraternity and their wives. So far from the portion which recounts the doings of Thomas, the tailor of Reading, being "pleasant," it deals with the rather melodramatic circumstances surrounding his murder by the host and hostess of an inn where he lodges, who precipitate him from his bed in an upper chamber through a trap-door into a brewing-tub full of boiling water which stands in the kitchen beneath. The tale well exemplifies the Elizabethan rage for murder-stories, and, save for a goodly spice of mother-wit, is commonplace and rather rambling in tone, much resembling the chap-book type of story.

THOMASSIN VON ZITCLARIA. An ecclesiastic and poet who lived about the end of the twelfth century. Though bearing a German name, and writing in German, he was a native of Aquilée in Frioul. The work by which he is remembered is *Der Welsche Gast*, a poem of almost fifteen thousand verses; and, apart from its literary worth, it is valuable as being typical of the High-German speech of the author's time, and more particularly for the vast amount of information it contains concerning feudal manners and customs. Among the people who figure therein is Walther von der Vogelweide, a minnesinger whose name is universally familiar on account of Longfellow's poem about him.

Literature : See the edition of *Der Welsche Gast* annotated by Ruckert (1852), and also *Zeitschrift fur Deutsche Philologie*, vol. ii. p. 431.

THORBIORN ANGLE. (*Vide* "Grettir Saga.") A bonder who bought up all the island of Drangey, and sought by promises, threats, and craft, to wrest it from Grettir. At last, by the assistance of his witch foster-mother Thurid, he came upon the great Icelandic outlaw, and with Old Karr's sword smote off Grettir's head. But this murder was avenged upon him by Thorstein Dromond (*q.v.*), Grettir's brother.

THORBIORN THE TARDY. (*Vide* "Grettir Saga.") Icelandic sailor. A braggart who, by jeering at Asmund, Grettir's father, provoked the son to slay him.

THORBIORN OXMAIN. (*Vide* "Grettir Saga.") Brother of Thorbiorn the Tardy (*q.v.*). He avenged the death of his brother by Grettir upon that hero's brother, Atli. He knocked one harvest eve upon Atli's door, all being from home save the son and his mother Asdis; then hiding upon one side, he pierced the unsuspecting Atli with his spear. But during the outlawry of Grettir, Thorbiorn and his son Arnor were slain by him.

THORD. (*Vide* "Gunnlaug Saga.") A son of a Hraunhaven farmer, who challenged Gunnlaug and his companions to a wrestling match. The victorious Gunnlaug sprained his ankle, however, and was thus delayed in keeping his tryst with Helgi (*q.v.*).

THORFINN. (*Vide* "Grettir Saga.") Lord of the Island of Haramsey. He harboured Grettir who slew by a trick twelve berserks that had come in his host's absence to rob his homestead and carry off his womenfolk. This kindness Thorfinn never forgot, and paid for Grettir several blood-fines.

THORGEIR. (*Vide* "Burnt Njal.") A kinsman of a man slain by Gunnar (*q.v.*). Desiring to avenge this man's death Thorgeir sought the advice of Mord (*q.v.*). Now this cunning fellow knew that Njal had warned his friend not to slay twice in the same stock. He therefore advised Thorgeir to work upon the son of the dead Otkell (*q.v.*), slain by Gunnar, to avenge his father's death. Gunnar's end was near, for he slew the youth.

THORGERD. (*Vide* "Gunnlaug Saga.") Sister to Thorstein Egilson. Privy to her sister-in-law Jofrid's deception, she, gave her brother's child Helga to a woman on her homestead to be brought up ; and presented the maiden to her father when six years old. Thorstein then took the child to his heart and his home.

THORHALL. (*Vide* "Grettir Saga.") The owner of the haunted farm in Waterdale, Iceland.

THORHALLA. (*Vide* "Burnt Njal.") Wife of Helgi (*q.v.*), Njal's youngest son.

THORIR (1). (*Vide* "Grettir Saga.") Chief of the berserks who intended to steal the womenfolk of Thorfinn in his absence.

THORIR (2) OF GARTH. (Also in "Grettir Saga.") Father of the men who were accidentally burned in their refuge-house by Grettir.

THORIR (3) OF THE PASS. (Also in "Grettir Saga.") Father of Gunnar and Thorgeir, who were slain by Atli in self-defence.

THORKEL. (*Vide* "Grettir Saga.") Son of the dead Old Karr (*q.v.*), and one time host of Grettir.

THORN, THE LAY OF. A *lai* of Brittany, written by Marie de France (*q.v.*). A certain king in Brittany had a son. This child dearly loved his step-mother's daughter, and she returned his love, which time changed into a stronger and deeper affection. The pair were found clasped in each other's arms when the queen shut up her daughter, whom she reprimanded with the greatest severity. Unable to endure his friend's grief and imprisonment, the prince sought knighthood of his father and leave to depart to a foreign land. This the king granted, but prayed him to stay yet a year about the court that he might assist at tournaments. During this time neither prince nor princess had sight of each other. Eight days before the Feast of St. John, the prince was dubbed knight. The king spent the day at the chase, and after the evening feast listened to the minstrel's songs. In the company was a maiden who told of an adventure that awaited the bold at the Ford of the Thorn upon St. John's Eve. The young knight desired to achieve this adventure, and this news reached the ears of his friend. Stealing to the orchard she sat upon the roots of a tree and prayed God to help him. Then she fell into a sleep several times, and at last was borne by strange means to the Ford of the Thorn. Here she beheld her knight, who at first did not recognize her. At the ford he won a red-eared white steed from a red-armoured lord, and jousted with two other knights, to his own glory. With the maiden he returned to his father, related his adventures, and the loving pair were wed.

THOROLD, SIR. (*Vide* " Guy of Warwick.") A brave knight who accompanied Sir Guy on his travels. He was killed in the fight with the Italians.

THOROM. (*Vide* " Gunnlaug Saga.") A powerful robber of London, who borrowed money from Gunnlaug, having no intention of returning it. Gunnlaug then did battle with Thorom, and with King Athelred's gift, a sword that was proof against witchcraft, slew him.

THORSTEIN DROMOND. (*Vide* " Grettir Saga.") The second brother of Grettir. He scarcely figures in the saga until we meet him seeking out Thorbiorn Angle. Having slain him and thus avenged Grettir's foul death, Thorstein was cast into prison to await capital punishment. But his cheery singing attracted Lady Spes (*q.v.*), who ransomed him, and having cleverly brought about a divorce from her husband, finally wed with her lover. Both by common consent ended their days in a penitential cell in Rome.

THORSTEIN EGILSON. (*Vide* " Gunnlaug Saga.") Father of Helga, husband of Jodfrid. One night he had a dream, to the effect that upon his house-roof there sat a lovely white swan. From the north there flew an eagle, black of eye, which cooed lovingly to her. Then from the south came another eagle, and he too sought her love; whereupon, the rivals fought fiercely together until both fell dead, leaving the swan sad and lonely. Thorstein's friend, the skipper of a merchant ship, interpreted the dream thus. The swan was his friend's daughter, to be born to him, and the eagles two youths who would contend for her love. Ill-pleased at such a reading of his dream, Thorstein commanded his wife to nurture their unborn infant if it were a manchild, but to cast it forth if it were a woman-child. But the mother could not renounce the little maiden, and sent her to Thorstein's sister Thorgerd. The infant was given to a woman on the sister's homestead to be nourished; and at the age of six was presented by Thorgerd to her father, who at once loved the beautiful child. Thorstein thanked his wife and sister for their deception, and carried the child home with him.

THORSTEN. (*Vide* " Frithjof Saga.") Father of Frithjof (*q.v.*); thane and friend of King Belé.

THRAIN. (*Vide* " Burnt Njal.") Son-in-law of Hallgerda (*q.v.*). He brought upon Grim and Helgi, Njal's sons, much trouble on account of Hrapp (*q.v.*), a felon whom he succoured against their wishes. The brothers made peace with the king, and thus added to Hrapp's hatred of them that of Thrain. Both Thrain and Hrapp, however, were slain by Njal's sons.

THREE KINGS OF COLOGNE. The three Magi, called Gaspar, Melchior, and Balthazar. They are alluded to by other names, but those given are the most generally accepted. They are supposed to be those " Kings of the East " who

2 A

appeared at the birth of our
Saviour, and skulls said to be
theirs are preserved in Cologne
Cathedral.

THREE KINGS' SONS, THE. A prose
romance translated from the
French in forty-five chapters.
The three kings' sons are Philip of
France, Humphrey of England,
and David of Scotland. Philip
leaves his father—King Charles—
secretly and serves against the
Grand Turk under Ferant the
seneschal of the King of Sicily.
Philip calls himself "La Des-
pŭrŭeŭ," but the Princess Iolante
of Sicily gives him the title of
"Le Surnome." The King of
Sicily appeals for help, and com-
panies of French, English, and
Scottish troops are sent to his aid
under David of Scotland. David,
however, is shipwrecked and falls
into the hands of the Turks, but
he escapes and serves under
Ferant, calling himself "Athis."
Humphrey is also led to join the
same service, and takes the name
of "Ector." The King of Sicily
is elected Emperor of Germany.
The Turks are defeated: the
Grand Turk turns Christian and
marries the sister of Humphrey,
King of England; but after his
death his people retract from their
allegiance. He leaves no children.

A tournament is held for the
hand of Iolante, and Philip now
becomes the King of France and
marries the princess.

The French MS. was transcribed
at Hesdin in 1463 by David Aubert,
librarian to Philip the Good, Duke
of Burgundy.

THURID. (*Vide* "Grettir Saga.")
A witch and foster-mother of
Thorbiorn Angle (*q.v.*). Casting
spells upon a tree-trunk, she sent
it floating to Drangey Island, that
Grettir might take it for firewood.

Several times he shunned the evil-
looking log, but at last it was
brought to the hut by his unwitting
comrade Noise. As Grettir sought
to hew it his sword glanced flat-
wise and struck him a ghastly
wound in the thigh which proved
dangerous, and rendered him helpless against his enemies.

TIERNA. Abbot of Clonmacnois, in
Ireland, an Irish historian who
flourished in the eleventh century,
and who critically separated the
elements of romance and fact in
Irish history.

TIRRE. Son of Sir Bernard of Astolat
(*q.v.*). (*Vide* "Morte d'Arthur.")

TITUREL. A German Grail, romance of the end of the thirteenth
century, composed for the most
part by Albrecht von Scharfenberg
(*q.v.*). This romance, one of the
most popular of the middle ages,
and a masterpiece of poetry and
piety, contains several pieces from
two or three different poets. The
most remarkable of these pieces
are the fragments composed by
Wolfram von Eschenbach for his
poem *Titurel*, left unfinished. As
regards the details of the history
of the Grail, Albrecht generally
followed the fable invented by
Guyot, and reproduced by Wolfram; but other details of his
romance show that he was also
acquainted with the version of
Walter Mapes. Thus, in Albrecht's
Titurel, the San Graal has not, as
in Guyot, a purely symbolic significance, but is identified with the
vessel of the Holy Supper. The
sacerdotal and not the chivalric
spirit preponderates in it. Orthodoxy, asceticism, and intolerance
towards the infidels are in striking
contrast with the philosophic and
conciliatory spirit prevailing in
the romance of the Angevin poet.

Albrecht, above all, delights in developing the history of Prester John, and adorning it with all the prestige of his poetry. This history, for which Wolfram had but few data, and which, for this reason, he had only indicated in his *Parzival*, could now be considerably amplified by means of the new information furnished to the poet by the reports of the Pope's legate and the French ambassadors who had returned from the East. Jean du Plan de Carpin, of the order of the Minorites, had been sent by Pope Innocent IV. to Mongol Tartary, where he had stayed from 1245 to 1247. A new embassy, headed by the Franciscan friar William de Rubruquis had been sent to Mongolia by Saint Louis in 1253. Lastly, the reports of the celebrated travellers Nicolo Polo and Marco Polo perhaps also furnished Albrecht with some new and interesting details. He exerts his utmost talent to trace in the history of Prester John the brilliant picture of a true sacerdotal government, and we may say that, if Guyot depicted in his romance his ideal of chivalry, Albrecht von Scharfenberg endeavoured to express his ideal, or perhaps the ideal which his age had conceived, of priesthood and ecclesiastical hierarchy. Moreover, this important subject, which transported the reader into the land of wonders, to the centre of Asia, at the same time presented to the poet a favourable opportunity to exhibit his knowledge of geography, history, and natural sciences—a kind of knowledge which he indeed possessed extensively, and of which, like most poets of the middle ages, he did not fail to be somewhat vain. The romance of Albrecht von Scharfenberg embraces a more extensive area than

that of Wolfram von Eschenbach, without, however, being superior to the latter in conception or poetical execution. The following are the principal features that compose the romance of Titurel. Parille, the son of Sennabor of Cappadocia, having embraced the Christian faith with his brothers and sisters, assists the Emperor Vespasian at the siege and capture of Jerusalem. As a reward for his services, the emperor gives him his daughter Argusilla in marriage ; and moreover, gives him the kingdom of France in fief. Parille has a son, Titurisone, who marries Eligabel of Arragon. The son of Titurisone and Eligabel is called Titurel, a name composed and contracted from those of his father and mother. An angel from heaven announces that God has chosen Titurel to be the defender of the faith and the guardian of the San Graal. The youth receives an education at once pious and knightly, and after having fought with his father against the infidels in Spain, is conducted by angels to Montsalvagge. There he builds the magnificent chapel in which the San Graal, on descending from heaven, has placed itself of its own accord. Titurel marries the Princess Richoude of Spain ; he watches over the San Graal, and propagates the Christian faith among the infidels. When old, his son Frimutel is designated as the King of the Grail by an inscription which appears on the sacred vase. Frimutel marries Clarissa of Grenada, and has five children by her. These are Amfortas, who succeeds his father in the kingship of the Grail ; Trevrizent, the wise hermit ; Tchoysiane, who becomes the mother of Sigune, and who dies on giving birth to this child ; Herzeloïde, the mother of Parzival ; and lastly, Urepanse de Joie, who marries Feirifiz, and becomes the mother of John the Priest. The beautiful Sigune is brought up at the court of her aunt Herzeloïde, and betrothed to Tchionatulander. This young knight distinguishes himself in the East by his bravery, and stands in friendly relationship with the Knights of the Round Table. He delivers, conjointly with King Arthur, the kingdom of Canvoleis, invaded by the Duke Orilus, but is killed by this enemy in single combat. Sigune is inconsolable for the death of her betrothed ; she has his body embalmed, places it among the branches of a lime tree, and sits by it a prey to the most poignant grief. There her cousin Parzival finds her, and she informs him of the fault he committed by his too great discretion at the banquet of the San Graal. Full of regret, Parzival desires to repair his fault ; after many efforts and many an adventure, he at last obtains the kingship of the Grail at Montsalvagge. In the mean time, the West, more and more given up to sin, is no longer worthy of possessing the sacred vase. Parzival thinks of transporting it to the East. He takes the San Graal, embarks at Marseilles with the Templois, and arrives at the court of his brother Feirifiz, in India. The latter draws an enchanting picture of the riches and sanctity of Prester John, who is the spiritual and temporal chief of a neighbouring country in India. Parzival consents to entrust this personage with the Grail ; but the sacred cup manifests the desire that Parzival should remain king, and only change his name into that of Prester John. Consequently, Parzival and the Templois settle in India ; they implore the San Graal that the palace and chapel of Montsalvagge be also transported to India. Their prayer is granted ; on the following day both palace and chapel, miraculously transported through the air during the night, are placed more beautiful and brilliant in India, and the chapel again holds the sacred cup of the Grail. After the death of Parzival, the son of Feirifiz and Urepanse de Joie becomes Priest John. After the disappearance of the Grail in the West, King Arthur and the Knights of the Round Table go in search of it : they travel over the world, but in vain ; they cannot find it ; it is for ever hidden in the far East.

TOM A LINCOLN, THE RED ROSE KNIGHT. An Elizabethan prose romance detailing the adventures of Tom a Lincoln, a natural son of King Arthur. The king loved fair Angelica, the daughter of one of his earls, and the fruit of their love was Tom, who was transported at birth by the midwife to the hut of a poor shepherd who brought him up. The lad became such a mighty outlaw that the king sent for him, and, hearing that he was his own son, advanced him in his service, and gave him the command of an army against the King of Portugal, who had murdered the British envoys at his court. Tom acquitted himself so well that he inflicted a severe defeat upon the Portuguese arms, and returned to London, where he received a notable welcome, and traversed the streets of the capital in triumph. Tom, on adventure bound, penetrated to fairy land, where he was royally entertained by the maiden queen of that realm, who bore him a son, as did her ladies to other of his knights. They departed, promising to return. The Red Rose Knight then journeyed to the court of Prester John (*q.v.*), and there slew a dragon which guarded a golden tree. He was accompanied in these adventures by Sir Lancelot du Lake, one of his father's knights, to whom he confided that he loved the fair Anglitora, Prester John's daughter. Prester John would in no wise hearken to his suit, so Tom persuaded Anglitora to fly with him. They took ship from the realms of Prester John. Cælia, the Fairy Queen, beholding the ship of the Red Rose Knight pass her island, and persuaded that he would not return, cast herself into the sea, and her drowned corpse was found floating on the waves by her former lover. On Cælia's body was found a letter addressed to Tom a Lincoln, bidding him farewell. Her body was taken to England for sepulture. Coming to Pendragon Castle, Arthur's seat in Wales, Tom was gladly welcomed by his father. The second part of the history relates how King Arthur on his death-bed told Tom the secret of his birth, and introduced him to Angelica, his mother. Anglitora, his wife, ashamed of her marriage, returned secretly to her father's court with her son, the Black Knight. Arthur's Queen, Guinevere, in her hatred of Tom, issued a decree that no one should associate with him in all the realm. Making a vow that he would not cut his hair, lie in bed, eat other food than bread, and have no other drink than water until he regained his lady's love, Tom set out to discover her whereabouts. Meanwhile Angelica, Tom's mother, is put to death by order of Guinevere, who herself died shortly after. The Lady Anglitora, wandering in search of her father's dominions, came to a certain castle, and became the mistress of its owner for seven years. The Black Knight gave himself to hunting, and so wild did he grow that he became a veritable Orson. Tom a Lincoln, encountering a black slave of Anglitora's, learned from him that she was living in shame with the Knight of the Castle. Tom, proceeding to the castle, was met by his wife, who dissembled her knowledge of him, and sent him to a lowly chamber, where he was lodged. That night Anglitora and her paramour slew the Red Rose Knight, and buried his body in a dunghill. The spirit of Tom appeared to his son, the Black Knight, as he lay in the wilderness, and apprised him of his mother's crime, whereupon the Black Knight returned to the castle and slew his mother.

The son of Cælia, Queen of Faerie and the Red Rose Knight, who was known as the Faeyrie Knight, journeying in quest of adventure, encountered the Black Knight lying asleep upon his father's grave. Learning their relationship, they took quest together, and came to a pagan city where they were imprisoned, but whence they escaped by making a rope of their hair and climbing therewith over the walls. The Faeyrie Knight sustained severe injury by a fall, but, recovering, the brothers pursued their way, and eventually came to England, where they were gallantly entertained. They raised a fair abbey at Lincoln, their father's birthplace, where, after pious lives they were eventually laid in death.

The romance is briskly told, and abounds in picturesque passages. But the Elizabethan spirit o tragedy and prolixity is present throughout, and somewhat mars the story.

TOPASE. (*Vide* " Florice and Blanchfleur.") Daughter to the Duke of Ferrarra, niece to the Duke of Milan, and wife of Prince Perse. She was the mother of Blanchfleur, and accompanied her husband to the shrine of Saint James. Felix sent her to the court of his queen, where she gave birth to Blanchfleur, dying shortly afterwards.

TOR, SIR. Son of King Pellinore and the wife of Aries the cowherd, a knight of the court of King Arthur. He was slain by Sir Lancelot. (*Vide* " Morte d'Arthur.")

TORRENT OF PORTUGAL. An English metrical romance of the fifteenth century published in 1842 by Halliwell from an MS. in the Cheetham Library at Manchester, very incorrectly written, and, from the number of blunders and omissions, conjectured to have been taken down from dictation. A few short fragments also exist in a printed edition in the Bodleian Library. No other copy of the romance is recorded. The tale is probably a later edition of an older English romance, itself translated from the French, as many allusions are made throughout the poem to " the boke of Rome " (that is, " romance "). The tale recounts how Torrent, the son of a noble of Portugal, was, by the death of his father, left early the master of his own devices. Dwelling at the court of the King of Portugal, Torrent becomes enamoured of his daughter, and did many doughty feats of arms for her fair fame. The king, not relishing his suit, sends him on various dangerous quests, ostensibly for the love of his daughter Desonelle, in which Torrent succeeds in slaying two dragons and several giants. On returning from one of these expeditions Desonelle, fain to show her appreciation of the deeds he has done in her name, grants him her love. The king despatches him upon another adventure, and whilst he is gone, the Princess Desonelle bears him twin sons. Enraged at her loss of chastity, her father casts her into the sea along with her babes. But she succeeds in making the shore of a far country, where her children are reft from her. One is seized by a griffin, and is afterwards discovered by Saint Antony, a hermit, who carries it to his father, the King of Greece. The other child is found by the King of Jerusalem, playing with a leopard Desonelle is met by the King of Nazareth, who recognizes her, and carries her back to his wife with many marks of respect. Sir Torrent has meanwhile proceeded to Norway to meet a giant who torments that country. He slays the monster and returns to Portugal, where he hears what has happened to Desonelle. Collecting his friends and vassals, he falls upon the king, and commits him to the seas, where he is drowned. He then sets out for the East to war for the Cross. After successfully laying siege to several pagan cities he comes to one defended by Hoberlious, his son, found by the King of Jerusalem, who takes him prisoner. At his plaint, however, Hobertious sets him free. The King of Greece hears of his warlike fame, and proclaims a tourney to which Torrent and Hobertious betake themselves. Here they do mighty deeds, and meet Torrent's other son, Antony Fitz-Griffin, and Desonelle. All are reunited, and sail back to

Portugal, where Torrent and Desonelle are married, and he reigns
over the country. His sons are
proclaimed the heirs of the kings
of Greece and Jerusalem, and
after a well-spent reign Torrent
dies and

"Leyth in Rome in a feire abbey."

TOWER OF MARVELS. A tower
built over the remains of 150
" Saracens " of Galafort by order
of Ganort, Lord of Galafort and
the Grail company. These unbelievers were drowned because
they would not be baptized along
with others of Ganort's folk. It
was prophesied that a king named
Arthur should reign, that from
one blow of a sword adventures
should arise lasting twelve years,
until the last descendant of Nasciens should end them, and that
till that time no knight of Arthur's
house should enter the tower
without having to fight as good a
man as himself. Thus should it
be till he who was to end the
adventures appeared. So they
built the tower, and it remained
until Lancelot destroyed it as
(says the *Grand Saint Graal*) the
Tale of Arthur's Death relates.

TREBUCET or TRIBUET. The smith
who mends Sir Perceval's broken
sword. He adjures him to guard
it carefully, as no prince or conqueror " had a better one." He
appears to dwell near a lake into
which he dips the sword, whence
it emerges whole.

TRENDORN. In Irish romance, the
servant of Conor (*q.v.*). He told
his master of the beauty of Deirdre,
but in spying upon her he was
blinded in one eye by Naisi.

TRIAMOUR, SIR. An English romance, a copy of which is preserved in the British Museum.

Two other copies exist in the
Bodleian Library, Oxford, and an
MS. in the public library of Cambridge. Arados, King of Arragon,
who reigned over an obedient
people, shared his reign with the
affectionate and beautiful Margaret. But their perfect happiness was not complete. They
longed for an heir to the throne.
Arados suggests a visit to the
Holy Land, but his wife refuses
to join in such a perilous undertaking. The good king is determined to go, and unconscious
that his prayers for an heir have
been heard, he sets out on the
long journey. It unfortunately
happens that Arados had left
Marrock, his steward, to super-
intend the destinies of his kingdom. This man, anxious to seduce the unprotected queen, makes
love to her. She soon realizes that
her husband's regent, instead of
cherishing the confidence of his
sovereign, is possessed of a criminal
passion towards her. The wicked
Marrock is quickly made to reflect
upon his honourable charge. Then
seeing the queen will not stoop to
his purpose, he decides to change
his plan. Approaching her with
an air of humiliation, he appeals
for her forgiveness in the hope
that his treason will be concealed
from her husband. The queen
readily forgives him, but he, departing from her presence, vows
vengeance upon her. Meanwhile
the king accomplishes his vow,
by the slaughter of numberless
Saracens, and returns to his
people. He is overjoyed at again
being with his wife, who is daily
expecting the birth of a child.
The sly Marrock boldly asserts
that the child to whose birth he
looks forward had been begotten
in adultery. The king reproaches
his steward with negligence, but

Marrock strengthens the untruth by rejoining that he slew the knight in whose arms he had found Margaret. The king, incensed at this story, does not believe the queen, who pleads for the sake of her child. Arados, in his mad haste, banishes his wife from the court. This hasty decision pleases the wicked Marrock, who prepares a plan for capturing the rejected queen. A certain Sir Roger is commanded to act as a body-guard to the unfortunate queen, taking with him a dog. Amidst great sorrow the doleful procession leaves the palace of Arados. Marrock had previously set out, hoping to be rewarded for his successful villainy. The retinue slowly wends its way along a country road. The steward, posting himself in a forest, awaits its passage. The procession arriving at the spot is suddenly attacked. Sir Roger, altogether defenceless, makes a brave attempt to overcome the villainous steward, but is slain. Having completed his dastardly work, the steward goes in search of Margaret, who had meanwhile hid herself. Unable to locate her, the disappointed murderer retraces his steps towards Arragon. The queen then leaves her hiding-place to find that the faithful dog had scraped out a grave for his dead master. She reverently buries the noble Roger, while the dog refuses to quit the remains. Unable to entice the beast from the spot, the queen resumes her journey to Hungary. Approaching the entrance to a wood, she alights from her horse, and gives birth to a son. This new joy erases from her memory the sense of her husband's injustice, and her present unprotected position. The mother washes the child, after which she falls asleep. In this state she is discovered by a Hungarian knight, Sir Bernard de Mauservyne. Amazed at the sleeper's beauty, and presuming her to be of noble parentage, he wakens the queen, offering her his hospitality. To this generous knight she looks for help ; and gladly accompanies him to his castle. To the queen he appoints a retinue suitable to her rank, while her son is christened Triamour. Great attention is paid to the child, who receives an education befitting his rank. The dog, which Margaret had been forced to abandon at the grave of Sir Roger, guards with increasing devotion the remains of his master. Seeking his daily subsistence, as his chance of prey diminishes the length of his chase gradually increases, and at the close of the seventh year, at the festival of Christmas, he suddenly appears in the hall of the King of Arragon. Such an apparition excites the curiosity of Arados, who faintly recollects having seen the dog. The animal becomes accustomed to return every day, and after receiving his pittance returns to his post. The king, now fully recollecting the dog, orders his steward to follow after him, but no sooner does Marrock appear in answer to his master's summons than the dog springs upon him, the murderer of his master. Soon the unlucky steward is torn to pieces. This proves to the king that Marrock is the murderer. The dog after completing the revenge hastens off to his post, followed by the king's attendants. The remains of Sir Roger are removed to a more suitable resting-place, within the precincts of Arragon ; and the body of Marrock is paraded throughout the city and then hung upon a gibbet. The dog meanwhile expires at the tomb of his master. King Arados is brought to regard these recent events as proof of his wife's innocence. Soon he despatches messengers throughout the land in search of her, but without avail. In the meantime the young Triamour completes his education; and now accomplished in the arts of chivalry, he expresses a wish to display his prowess. Nor has he long to wait ere his wishes are gratified. The King of Hungary dies at an advanced age, and is succeeded by his only daughter Helen, who has just entered her fifteenth year. To one so young the responsibility of wielding the sceptre over vast dominions causes her advisers to suggest to their queen the advisability of marriage. But the young queen is beset by youthful nobles who are desirous of wedding her. So, wisely announcing a tournament, she decides by this method to select the victor. To this tourney is attracted a brilliant array of knights, every country sending forth a detachment. Amongst them arrive the young Triamour and King Arados. The day opens in brilliant array. The young queen, set high upon a tower, watches the progress of the conflict with keen attention. Triamour soon attracts the gaze of the queen, who vainly tries to discover his lineage. The tourney proceeds for three days, at the end of which young Triamour is proclaimed the victor. Sir James, son of the German Emperor, having been defeated by the young victor, determines to slay him. Approaching Triamour as he leaves the field Sir James wounds him. But he is defended by Arados, who kills his despicable assailant.

Triamour returns thanks to Arados, and hastens off to the care of his mother. Helen, disappointed at the disappearance of the victor, endeavours to locate his residence, but without success. The competitors repair to the palace to hear the decision of the fair Helen, who declares herself bound by the conditions of the tournament, which she herself had fixed. And as the victor is not forthcoming she must be permitted to withhold her decision for one year and a day, after which, on the non-appearance of the victor, another tourney would be necessary to decide her choice. This mandate produces satisfaction. The beautiful Helen mourns the disappearance of her lover. But war clouds gather and Sir James's death must be avenged. The bereaved father decides to assail Arados, whom he knows to be an accessory to the deed, although not the actual slayer of his son. This action was sufficient to draw Triamour to the aid of Sir Arados, whose relationship to himself had not yet been divulged. Success attends the German forces until they arrive at the gates of Arragon, where a large force had meanwhile congregated. Triamour sets forth to assist King Arados, who had saved his life. The king greets the young adventurer, and invests him with the order of knighthood. Meanwhile the German army has reduced the defenders of the city to a state of despair. Sir Triamour soon alters the fortune of the war by defeating the Germans, and causing them to disperse in confusion. The land of King Arados is then freed of the enemy, and amid popular jubilation, the victorious knight sets out for Hungary. Approaching the city he slays two giants who had tried to impede his journey. He enters the city to learn that another tourney for the hand of the fair Helen is in progress. This spurs him to action. He enters the field, and rapidly assails another giant who proves to be the brother of those whom he had previously encountered. The queen witnesses his entry and soon learns that he is the original victor, and the knight whom she loves. Triamour again proves his claim to the honour of her hand, and after a long struggle he successfully overcomes the giant, winning the day. His victory is received by all as a confirmation of his rightful claim to their queen. The wedding shortly afterwards takes place, to the satisfaction of his mother, Margaret, and the people of Hungary. Arados appears at the coronation of the beloved pair, when he is rewarded for all his past sufferings by the recovery of his faithful Margaret, and the pleasure of embracing his son, to whom he owes the preservation of his life and kingdom.

TRIGAMOUR. (*Vide* "Triamour.")

TRISTREM. A romance attributed to Thomas Rymour (*q.v.*), and discovered in a vellum MS., by Ritson, in the Advocates' Library at Edinburgh. (See "Auchinleck MS.") After stating that he heard the tale from Thomas's own lips, the author tells of a feud between two Cymric chieftains, Duke Morgan and Rouland Rise, Lord of Ermonie. A truce being agreed upon, they resolve to visit the court of King Mark of Cornwall, where Rouland gains the love of Blanche Flour, the king's sister. From this union springs Tristrem. Duke Morgan breaks the truce, and Rouland is slain. Blanche Flour, inconsolable

at his loss, expires, and leaves the infant Tristrem in the charge of Rohard, a faithful vassal, to whom she entrusts a ring well known to his Uncle Mark. Morgan seizes Ermonie, and Rohand pays him homage. To secure Tristrem's safety he brings him up as his own son. A Norwegian vessel puts in at the port near which they dwell, and Tristrem wins such treasure by beating its captain at chess that to avoid payment of the debt the Norsemen sail off with him. A dreadful tempest arises, and the captain attributing it to his shabby treatment of the young prisoner sets him ashore on the coast of Cornwall, with all the treasure he has won, along with his tutor, who was also seized. His skill in venerie or hunting and his playing of the harp endear him to King Mark, to whose court he comes. At length Rohand traces him to the court of Cornwall, and informs Mark of the youth's real history, which is confirmed by the production of the ring of Blanche Flour. Mark knights him, and provides him with men wherewith to regain his patrimonial estates. This he succeeds in doing, and returns to Cornwall. He finds Mark threatened by the King of Ireland for non-payment of tribute. Tristrem slays the Irish ambassador, a giant named Moraunt, but is wounded in the thigh. He is declared his uncle's heir to the Cornish crown, but his wound, which was inflicted by a poisoned weapon, becomes so offensive that no one may remain with him save his servant Gouvernayl. Tristrem leaves Cornwall and arrives at Dublin, where he takes the name of Tremtris. His fame as a harper soon reaches the ears of the queen, who pays him a visit and cures his wound by means of a medicated bath. He undertakes to instruct her daughter Ysonde in poetry and music, and after a year spent thus he returns to Cornwall. His praises of Ysonde so stir Mark's heart that he desires to have her to wife, and he sends Tristrem to Ireland to ask her hand. Arrived at Dublin they find the people in terror of a monstrous dragon which Tristrem slays. He is, however, poisoned by the dragon's breath, and the king's steward pretends to have slain the monster, producing its head. But Tristrem recovers his senses, and is carried to the palace, where it is discovered that he is the veritable dragon-slayer. His sword is broken, and Ysonde sees that a piece of it corresponds to the piece found in the skull of her Uncle Moraunt, whom Tristrem slew. She and the queen not recognizing him, attempt his life, but are restrained by the king. Explanations follow, and Tristrem departs with Ysonde and her maiden Brengwain for Cornwall. On their departure the queen entrusts Brengwain with a love potion to be given to Ysonde and the King of Cornwall, but in error she gives it to Tristrem, Ysonde also partaking. They are seized by a violent mutual passion; Mark and Ysonde are wedded on the arrival of the latter in Cornwall. An Irish lover of Ysonde's comes to Mark's court, and brings a harp of cunning upon which he refuses to play unless Mark grants him a boon. This the king rashly does. The harper demands Ysonde in fulfilment of his promise, and carries her off to his ship. But Tristrem takes up his ivory rote, and plays so skilfully that Ysonde begs to be put ashore, feigning sickness. Tristrem places her upon his horse and disappears in the forest, where they sojourn seven nights. He then restores Ysonde to his uncle, whose suspicions are not excited until a revelation is made by a companion of Tristrem's, Meriadock, who acts as the Iago of the story. Ysonde, to prove her innocence, offers to undergo the ordeal by fire. The trial is appointed to take place at Westminster, and when about to cross the Thames, she spies her lover disguised as a peasant, and asks him to carry her from the shore to the vessel in which she must cross. When the oath preparatory to the ordeal is administered she swears that no man other than her husband had used greater familiarity with her than the peasant who had carried her from the shore to the vessel. Mark is satisfied, and foregoes the application of the ordeal. Tristrem retires into Wales, and enters the service of King Triamour, whose daughter Blanche Flour is sought in marriage by Urgan, the brother of Duke Morgan. Being rejected, Urgan seizes Triamour's possessions, but they are regained by Tristrem, who slays the usurper. His uncle recalls him to Cornwall and makes him High Steward; but the old fatal love-spell brings him once more into guilt with the queen, and both are banished by Mark. They dwell in a cave in the forest, and live on the spoils of Tristrem's spear. Once more they are pardoned by Mark, and Tristrem goes to Spain, Ermonie, and Brittany, where he makes a song upon Ysonde. The daughter of the king of that realm is also called Ysonde, and imagining that the song has been made about her, is offered to Tristrem by her father. Tristrem accepts her, but the marriage remains unconsummated. After many adventures in Brittany he is accused of cruelty to his wife, by her brother, Ganhardin, who desires to know why the union has not been consummated. Tristrem tells him that he loves a fairer lady, and Ganhardin, desirous of seeing her, sets forth with him to accomplish that object. They meet Ysonde and Brengwain, with the latter of whom Ganhardin falls in love. They are watched by spies, and the queen and her maiden return to court and Ganhardin to Brittany. But Tristrem remains in Cornwall. A tournament is proclaimed, and Tristrem with Ganhardin, who returns, vanquishes all comers. The champions return to Brittany, where Tristrem receives an arrow in his old wound. (Here the matter of the Auchinleck MS. ends, but the conclusion is supplied by Sir Walter Scott, who collated it with a similar French MS. as follows): The wound can only be cured by Ysonde of Cornwall, and Tristrem requests Ganhardin to take his ring to her, and to hoist a black sail on his ship on his return should he not succeed in bringing her back with him. Ysonde returns with Ganhardin, and a white sail is displayed. But Ysonde of Brittany tells Tristrem that a black sail has been hoisted, whereupon, concluding that Ysonde of Cornwall has forsaken him, he sinks back in despair and dies. The queen on landing is informed of his death, and rushing to where his body lies, casts herself down beside it and expires. Upon the marvellously human and epic nature of this stirring and pathetic tale of hopeless passion there is no necessity to enlarge. It has been selected for condensation as being the most complete, even in its truncated condition, of all the Tristrem romances, and especially as it is of British origin, and easily accessible to British readers. But some other considerations are perhaps worthy of attention. In all probability the tale was modelled upon that of Lancelot and Guinevere. It is clear that the lovers in both tales are merely counterparts. Tristrem is one of the "fatal children" who, born in sorrow, like Macduff and Sigurd, is scarcely seen by his mother, who names him "the Unhappy." But the darkness of his infancy is dispelled by the glorious nature of his manhood. Tristrem is the mighty hunter and harper, a parallel with Orpheus, Amphion, Hermes, and Sigurd. He is wounded with the poisoned weapon of Moraunt (for the violet-tinted rays of the morning sun are called Ios, or Ion, from the word oe, homonym for a spear and for poison), and we see in his relations with King Mark and Ysonde a reproduction of those witnessed in the *Volsunga Saga*, where Sigurd, Brynhild, and Gunnar stand in like relation to one another. But, like Sigurd, he must woo his bride for another, yet is he, like him, doomed to wed another woman whom he does not love, who in the event becomes his deadly foe. Like Herakles, he is able to slay single-handed scores of assailants, it skills not how many. His is the irresistible power of the sun, for he is unquestionably one of the many "Sons of the Sun," "Men of the Sun," or "Sun-heroes," with whom the student is constantly brought into contact in the study of myth, folklore and romance.

TUAN MAC CARELL. An Irish legendary personage, the story of whose metamorphoses is to be found in the "Book of the Dun Cow," a manuscript written about the year 1100 A.D. Tuan mac Carell, an Irish chief of the sixth century, having returned St. Finnen's visit, invited him and his disciples to his fortress. Here he related to them the history of Ireland; of the Partholanians (*q.v.*), he alone remained alive after the great pestilence, wandering in lonely Ireland. Now disgusting in appearance and miserable, he awoke one morning to find himself changed into a young stag. He was king of the stags during the Nemedian occupation of Ireland. Again, weary with extreme old age, he was given the form of a wild boar, and became king of his kind. Then Semion (*q.v.*), son of Stariat, settled in Ireland. From him descended the Firbolgs (*q.v.*), and two other tribes. As an eagle he beheld the incoming of the divine Danaans (*q.v.*), and their conquerors, the sons of Miled (*q.v.*). Then in the form of a salmon he was caught and carried to the wife of Carell (*q.v.*). Born of her he became man, son of Carell.

TUDVWICH HIR. (*Vide* "Gododin.") Son of Kilydd (elsewhere called son of Prince Kelyddon, and therefore a Strathclyde Briton from Caledon). He had lost his land, and with a strong retinue boasted he would disperse the invaders. He made havoc with the Saxons for seven days, and then was taken prisoner. "His valour should have kept him a free man; his memory is cherished by his fair companions."

TURENN, QUEST OF THE SONS OF. A tale of Lugh (*q.v.*), the Irish sun-god. (*Vide* also "Kian.")

TUROLD or **THÉROULDE.** (*Vide* "Song of Roland.")

TURPIN or **TILPIN.** The warrior Archbishop of Rhiems, and one of Charlemagne's peers. A stout fighter, he died at Roncesvaux with Roland and Oliver. (*Vide* "Song of Roland.") There is attributed to him a fabulous *Chronicle*, which he certainly never compiled. He baptized Ferumbras. He was one of those who unsuccessfully remonstrated with Charlemagne at his decision about the liberation of his nephews. Charlemagne sent for him to baptize Laban the Soudan, but Laban assaulted the archbishop and was so violent that he was executed instead. He died of his wounds at Roncesvaux. He also baptized Sir Otuel when he turned proselyte, and Garsie when he embraced Christianity. He was saying mass for the souls of the dead when he declared he heard the songs of the angels who carried Roland's soul up to heaven. He heard of Roland's death from some black fiends, who were carrying King Marsire's soul to the lower regions.

TURQUINE, SIR. In Arthurian romance, a powerful warrior, and an oppressor of good knights. He eventually met his death at the hands of Sir Lancelot (*q.v.*). (*Vide* "Morte d'Arthur.")

TWO LOVERS, THE LAY OF. A Breton romance written by Marie de France (*q.v.*). The King of Normandy, who built the town of Pistres, had only one daughter, whom, his wife being dead, he cherished dearly. Many a suitor sought the maiden's hand. The king, therefore, fearing lest his child might be carried off, had it proclaimed that only he who without rest or stay could carry the princess to the pinnacle of the mountain that reared itself near the city should wed his daughter. Many essayed the task, but unsuccessfully. There was a certain squire, however, who, having set his heart upon the maiden, had his love returned. Now she desiring to have him for her husband, though she refused to flee with him, sent him with letters to her aunt in Saleone, who was very cunning in the knowledge of medicine. Armed with a strength-giving potion, the young lover returned to Pistres to ask for the hand of the princess. Amused at the stripling's self-confidence, the king summoned a large company to behold the ascent of the youth with his beloved. Nor did she forget aught that might help him, dressing but thinly and fasting. With joy in his breast and courage in his heart, he climbed swiftly till near the summit he flagged. Fearing to take the potion in the public eye, he had given the philtre to the maiden. But though she urged him to drink it, he would not. At last, almost upon the pinnacle his heart burst, and he lay dead. The unhappy maiden loudly bewailed her lover. Upon the barren mount she flung away the philtre, and there grew up many a saving herb. As the lovers did not return, the king went to seek them, and coming upon them dead in each other's arms, swooned away. When he recovered after three days he buried them upon the mountain, and gave it the name of the "Mountain of the Two Lovers."

TYREN. In Irish romance, sister to Murna, mother of Finn. She was changed into a hound by the witchcraft of a fairy woman who loved her husband Ullan. The two hounds of Finn were her children, who were born as dogs after her metamorphosis.

U

UGAINY THE GREAT. Ruler of Ireland in romance, father of Laery and Conal (*q.v.*).

ULFIUS. A knight of King Arthur, one of the earliest mentioned as having any connection with him. He accompanied Arthur's father, Uther Pendragon, when he entered the castle of Tintagil in the shape of the Duke of Tintagil in order to have access to the duke's wife, Igraine, mother of Arthur. He afterwards assisted Arthur mightily in the famous battle of the eleven kings alluded to in the first book of Malory's *Morte d'Arthur*. He is usually accompanied by his companion Sir Brastias, and what is said of the one is usually said also of the other.

URBAN OF THE BLACK THORN. Alluded to in the *Didot-Perceval* as the guardian of a certain ford which his lady had set him to watch. He challenges the passage of Perceval, who overthrew him. His lady comes to his aid with her maidens in the shape of birds. Perceval slays one which becomes a woman, and is carried off by the others to Avallon.

URIEN, KING. Husband of Morgan le Fay and father of Sir Gawain. (*Vide* " Morte d'Arthur.")

URIENS or URIENCE. King of the Land of Gore in Arthurian romance, and husband of Arthur's sister, Morgan le Fay. He leagued himself with the eleven kings (*q.v.*), against Arthur. Morgan attempted to slay him, but was prevented by her son Uwaine.

URRE, SIR. Knight of Hungary. He was severely wounded in a fray with a noble knight whom he slew, causing the fallen champion's mother to take vengeance by exercising her powers of sorcery over him, which prevented his wounds from healing. According to Arthurian romance, he goes to England, where, after vain attempts by Arthur and his knights, it is discovered that no one can heal him excepting Lancelot (*q.v.*), who later entrusted him with the Earldom of Estratse in the land of Benwick, over which Lancelot ruled for a while. (*Vide* " Morte d'Arthur.")

URRY, SIR. (*Vide* " Guy of Warwick.") Sent by Roland to travel with Sir Guy. He was killed in the affray with the Italians.

USNA. In Irish romance, father of Naisi (*q.v.*).

UTA. (*Vide* " Gudrun Lay.") Wife of King Sigebant of Ireland (*q.v.*), and mother of Hagen (*q.v.*).

UTE (1). (Uote.) Wife of Hildebrand (*q.v.*). (*Vide* " Dietrich of Bern.")

UTE (2). (*Vide* " Nibelungenlied.") Mother of Kriemhild. She interprets Kriemhild's dream of a falcon (which she nurtures for a time till two eagles swoop upon it and destroy it), as representing a noble husband " whom may God preserve lest thou lose him too early."

UTHER PENDRAGON. King of Britain, and father of Arthur by Igraine, wife of the Duke of Tintagil, afterwards his own wife. He procured access to her in the shape of her husband by means of Merlin's magic arts. Within two years he fell sick of a great malady, and willed that their child, then unknown, should be King of Britain.

UWAINE, SIR. Son of King Uriens, and Knight of the " Round Table." He met his death in combat with his brother Gawaine (*q.v.*). (*Vide* " Morte d'Arthur.")

V

VALENTINE AND ORSON. Sons of Bellisant, sister of King Pepin and wife of Alexander, Emperor of Constantinople. The twin brothers were born in a wood, near Orleans, and while their mother went in search of Orson, who had been carried off by a bear, Pepin happened to find Valentine and took him under his charge. Valentine married Clerimond, niece of the Green Knight. Orson was suckled by the bear, and when he grew to manhood he became the terror of France, and was called the *Wild Man of the Forest*. He was reclaimed by Valentine, overthrew the Green Knight, and married Fizon, the daughter of Duke Savary of Aquitaine. The romance, which is of very considerable antiquity, will be found in the *Bibliothèque de Romans*.

VIATDUR. Daughter of Constantine (*q.v.*), Emperor of Rome. She is mentioned in the romance of *Eglamour of Artoys* (*q.v.*), as having healed Eglamour of his poisoned wounds caused through his encounter with a dragon (*q.v.*).

VIRGILIUS. In the *Gesta Romanorum*. Virgil is represented as a mighty but benevolent enchanter. This is the character which tradition always gives him, and it is this traditional character that furnishes Dante with his conception of making Virgil his guide through the infernal regions. The Virgil of romance was wise, and as craft was considered a part of wisdom, especially where the overreaching of the spirits of evil was concerned, so he is represented by mediæval writers as outwitting the Demon. On one occasion, it is said, he saw an imp in a hole close by a mountain, and the imp promised to teach the poet the black art if he released him. Virgil did so, and after learning all the imp could teach him, expressed amazement that one of such imposing stature could be squeezed into so small a rift. The evil spirit said, " Oh, that is not wonderful," and crept into the hole to show Virgil how it was done—whereupon Virgil closed up the hole and kept him imprisoned there.

VIRGINAL, DIETRICH'S ERSTE AUSFAHRT, and **DIETRICH UND SEINE GESELLEN.** Similar versions of a Tyrolese tale, dating about the end of the thirteenth century and connected with the saga-cycle of *Dietrich of Bern* (*q.v.*). The poem, a prolonged and dreary account of feast and folly, tells of Dietrich's captivity among the giants, and the rescue of a maiden from their fortresses, the whole obviously compiled for the purpose of recital at court. It consists of no less than 14,000 lines, and is rambling and contradictory in character. Dietrich is informed in his court at Berne that Virginal, Queen of Jeraspunt, is oppressed by the Saracen Orkise, and sets forth to free her with Hildebrand, his companion. They lose each other, and Hildebrand comes upon a maiden of Virginal's, who has been left in the forest as tribute to the Saracens. The infidel appears, but is slain by Hildebrand. Meanwhile Dietrich has met and fought with Orkise's followers, from whom he is rescued by Hildebrand. Virginal invites the heroes to her court, but *en route* they encounter a fierce dragon which they slay, freeing a warrior named Rentnim from its clutches. They halt at Rentnim's father's castle, where they make merry for a space. Setting out once more for Jeraspunt, Dietrich, riding on ahead, is felled and imprisoned by a giant in the service of Duke Nitger, whose sister saves him from the other giants in the Duke's pay. Hildebrand arrives before Nitger's castle with a large army, the giants are slain and Dietrich is delivered. Nitger is pardoned for his sister's sake, and all proceed to Virginal's palace, where they engage in a lengthy round of festivities, Dietrich finally taking Virginal back to Bern as his wife.

VIVIANE or **VIVIANA.** Merlin, having become enamoured of Viviane, daughter of Dyonas (probably Dylan, the Brythonic sea-god), was so incautious as to impart to her the secrets of his magical arts, being driven to do so by fate, although fully aware of his folly. Weary of his importunity, she resolved to rid herself of him for ever, and obtained from him the secret whereby she might imprison him "without chains and without a tower," and by means of enchantment alone. One day whilst in the Forest of Broceliande she imprisoned Merlin with his own spell, and he was never afterwards beheld by mortal man. (*Vide* "Merlin.") Viviane is famous under the name of the Lady of the Lake as the guardian of the young Lancelot (*q.v.*). (*Vide* also "Broceliande" and "Morte d'Arthur.") She is in some romances alluded to as Nimue.

VOLSUNG. Son of Rerir (*q.v.*), husband of Lijod (*q.v.*), who bore him twins, a son and a daughter : Sigmund (*q.v.*), and Signy (*q.v.*). He met his death at the hands of King Siggeir (*q.v.*). (*Vide* "The Lay of the Volsungs.")

VOLSUNGS, LAY OF THE. So-called, or Volsunga Saga, an early Teutonic epic, probably a development of certain Edda tales as the *Nibelungenlied* is a development of it. It is likely that the epic arose from elements current as story about the eighth century. These elements are to be found in the *Elder Edda*, compiled by Seemund between 1056 and 1121. The personages of the *Volsunga Saga* are alluded to in the *Song of Hundla* in the first volume of the *Edda*, where Sigurd is mentioned as the slayer of Fafnir, and in a later stanza we find the names of Gunnar and Haugn. The group of poems referring especially to the legend occurs, however, among the heroic pieces of the second volume. Thus the Sigurd cycle proper opens with the tales called "Sigurd, Fafnir's bane." This is probably of late date, perhaps

the tenth century. The tale of Fafnir proper (*Fafnisbana II.*) partly in prose, precedes the *Tale of Brynhild, Budli's Daughter*. Then follows the *Third Tale of Sigurd*, the *First Tale of Gudrun, Second Tale of Gudrun, Third Tale of Gudrun, The Tale of Atla*, and other minor lays from which the Volsung story group was subsequently formed.

Sigi was the son of Odin. Having slain a thrall he was forced to flee his father's domain, but carved out one for himself in Hunland. In old age he was slain by those of his household, and was succeeded by his son Rerir, who overcame the rebels. In later life Rerir was troubled because he had no son. But Freyja gave an apple to Rerir's wife, so that she conceived, and after six years' labour, bore Volsung. He wedded Lijod, the handmaiden of Freyja, and she bore him twins—a son and daughter, Sigmund and Signy. Siggeir, King of Gothland, came oversea to request Signy for his wife when she had arrived at a marriageable age. In the great hall of the Volsungs stood the oak Branstock, which overshadowed the entire apartment, and in this place Volsung held a mighty feast for Siggeir, to whom he gave Signy. But she held him in loathing. On the day of the wedding-feast there entered a stranger (Odin) who thrust a great sword into the trunk of the oak Branstock, saying, "Whoso plucketh out this sword shall have the same in gift from me, and will find that better brand he never bare." All essayed to pull out the brand, but only Sigmund succeeded. King Siggeir desired to buy the sword, but Sigmund refused to sell it. He then departed with Signy,

2 B

after extracting a promise from Volsung that he and his sons should pay a visit to Gothland in three months' time. On their arrival there, they were warned by Signy that Siggeir meant them harm. The men of Gothland attacked them, slaying all save the ten sons of Volsung, whom they took captive. He placed them in a wood, and caused a great beam to be laid over them so that they could not stir. Every night a she-wolf came to the wood and killed one of the brothers. Sigmund was the last, and he succeeded in beating her off and freeing himself. He dwelt in the woods, and received food from Signy, who sent both her sons to him. He killed them because of their cowardice. Changing shapes with a wise woman, she dwelt for three days with Sigmund, and afterwards bore to him Sinfjötli. Him also she sent to her brother, who trained him to a fierce and hardy life. They dressed themselves in wolf-skins, and attacked men in the forest for their wealth. Agreeing to slay King Siggeir, they secreted themselves between the casks of ale in his hall. Discovered by the king's children they slew them, and cast their bodies into the hall at Siggeir's feet. They were captured after a stern resistance and buried in a large mound, with a great stone between them. But as the earth was cast upon them, Signy threw an armful of straw into it, in which a sword was concealed. They sawed through the stone with the blade, and cut through the earth, thus escaping. Then they heaped wood around Siggeir's palace and set it afire. Signy came to the window, and told Sigmund that he was the father of Sinfjötli. They rush back among the flames for the joy of seeing King Siggeir burn. Sigmund and Sinfjötli, then journeyed to Hunland, and put down a man there who reigned in Volsung's room. And Sigmund reigned over Hunland, and took to wife Borghild, who bore him two sons, Helgi and Hamund. Sinfjötli strove with Borghild's brother for the sake of a woman, and slew him. Wherefore Borghild poisoned him, and was put away by Sigmund, who married Hjordis, daughter of King Eylimi. King Lyngi, a rival for her hand, warred upon him, and both were slain. Ere he died he conjured Hjordis to save the shards of his good sword Gram for the son she was yet to bear. Alf the Viking landing at that juncture, Hjordis requested him to ship her with her treasure to King Hjalprek's palace in Denmark, and this he did. The lay then tells how Helgi, the son of Sigmund by Borghild, when he came to manhood went against King Hunding and slew him and took his lands. He fell in love with Sigrun, King Hogni's daughter, but she was betrothed to Hodbrod, son of King Granmar, whom she despised. Helgi made an expedition against Granmar, slew Hodbrod, and wedded Sigrun. But Hogni, Sigrun's father, came against him because he had taken his daughter, and was slain. Helgi, however, spared Dag, his son; but Dag borrowed Odin's spear, and slew Helgi. Sigrun buried Helgi, but lay with him in his burial mound, so that she sickened and died. We now return to Hjordis, who dwelt in Hjalprek's palace in Denmark. There she bore dead Sigmund's son, and called him Sigurd. Regin was his tutor, and from him he learned magic. His mother married with

Alf, King Hjalprek's son. He received the foal Grani from Odin. Regin told him of the dragon Fafnir which dwelt on Glistening Heath, and guarded a great treasure. Fafnir and Otter were brothers of Regin. Loki, the god of evil, slew Otter and was forced to fill his skin with gold rings by Hreidmar, his father. Loki caused the dwarf Andvari to pay this fine with his treasure, but Andvari retained one ring. But that also he was forced to give up, and this ring proved baneful, for Fafnir murdered his father for the treasure, and grovelled until he became a dragon. Regin forged a great sword to arm Sigurd against Fafnir, but it broke. Then went Sigurd to his mother, Hjordis, and asked for the shards of his father's sword Gram, which Regin welded again. To avenge his father, Sigurd set sail for Hunland, and slew Lyngi and the sons of Hunding, winning back his father's realm. Returning to Denmark, he set out with Regin in quest of Fafnir. He dug pits, and hid himself in one of them. Smiting upwards, he slew the dragon. Regin requested him to cut out Fafnir's heart and roast it. But as it spluttered in the fire it burnt Sigurd's finger, then he placed it to his mouth. Immediately he was able to comprehend the speech of birds, which warned him to slay Regin who meditated his death. So he smote off his head. Sigurd then ate of Fafnir's heart and put by the rest. He then secured the treasure, which he placed on his horse's back. Passing the mountain Hindfell, he saw a great light go up from it. Climbing the height he beheld a great castle, about which all was desolation. Within he came upon a fair maiden clad in armour, lying fast asleep. She was called Brynhild. He awakened her, and told her his name. She told him that when Helm Gunnar strove with Agnar that she desired to assist the latter against the will of Odin. So Odin had pierced her with the sleepthorn, and doomed her when she woke to love but to possess not, to wed, but not to have her will. Yet she had vowed to wed only a man who knew not fear. They plighted their troth, and Sigurd rode away, journeying until he came to the dwelling of a chief named Heimar who had wedded Bekkhild, a sister of Brynhild. Brynhild came to Heimar's castle to see her sister, and during her stay embroidered upon a cloth the deeds of Sigurd. At this task he espied her, but was advised by Alswid, Heimar's son, to cease to think of her, as she was a "warmaid." But he went to Brynhild and sat beside her. She told him that they might never abide together. Sigurd was sorrowful, but gave her Andvari's ring in pledge, the luckless ring of Fafnir's hoard. South of the Rhine dwelt King Giuki and his queen Grimhild. They had three sons, Gunnar, Hogni, and Guttorm, and a daughter Gudrun. Gudrun dreamed an evil dream, concerning which she consulted Brynhild. She told her that she dreamed that she had captured a hart with golden hair, and that a fierce woman took him from her, and that in this woman she recognized Brynhild herself, who shot the deer, and placed a wolf-cub on her lap instead. Brynhild read her dream as follows: that she would take Sigurd to wife, but should not have him long, and that a great strife should come between Gudrun and herself. Sigurd left King Heimar's hall, and travelled to that of King Giuki. Grimhild, his queen, desired Sigurd for her daughter Gudrun, and gave him a potion which caused him to forget Brynhild. Sigurd was wed to Gudrun. Grimhild then put it into Gunnar's heart to win Brynhild. But Gunnar might not win through the flames that surrounded her castle. Sigurd then took upon himself the likeness of Gunnar, and rode through the flames. Brynhild, because of her oath, was forced to wed Sigurd in the shape of Gunnar. They exchanged rings, and Sigurd departed. Then King Giuki made a feast for Gunnar to which came Brynhild, who was married to Gunnar. Then Sigurd's memory returned when all too late, and a great gloom fell upon him. Brynhild and Gudrun quarrelled some time afterwards, and Gudrun told her that Sigurd had rode through the fire for her in Gunnar's shape. Brynhild fell sick on hearing this, and attempted Gunnar's life. She fell into a heavy sleep, and, Gudrun pitying her, sent Sigurd to waken her. He confessed to her that Gudrun had grown dear to him, but that rather than Brynhild should die, he would put Gudrun away and wed with her. Brynhild requested Gunnar to slay Sigurd in Gudrun's arms. Gunnar fed his younger brother, Guttorm, on wolf's meat and set him to slay Sigurd in bed. In this he succeeded, but was also slain himself. So sharp was Gudrun's sorrow that she might not weep until she saw Sigurd's corpse. Brynhild in her dreadful grief thrust herself through with her sword and died. And Gunnar built a mighty pile of wood, and laid thereon the bodies of Sigurd and Brynhild which were consumed by the bale-fire. Gudrun, with

bitterness in her heart against her brethren, went into the moors to mourn alone. Later she betook herself to the palace of King Alf of Denmark, where she remained for seven years. Grimhild, her mother, journeying hither with her sons, gave her a magic draught which caused her to forget her woes. Shortly afterwards she was wed to King Atli, Brynhild's brother. Atli, desiring the treasure of Fafnir as a dowry with Gudrun, sent messengers to the Giukings to come to his realm, in order that he might slay them. But Gudrun sent a runic message to Gunnar warning him of her husband's purpose. A messenger altered this in such a manner that it appeared as a request that Gudrun's brothers should come. On their arrival at the court of Atli they found the town full of armed men, and received curt greeting from the king, who called upon them to give up Sigurd's gold. A terrific combat arose. The Giukings did tremendous execution, until only Gunnar and Hogni were left alive. In the end they were borne down by force of numbers and bound. Atli proposed to slay Hjalli, a thrall of Gunnar's, but he begged so piteously for his life that Hogni asked to be slain in his stead. Gunnar and Hogni were led away to prison, and placed in dungeons apart. Atli offered to spare Gunnar if he would tell him where Sigurd's gold might be found. This Gunnar promised to do if Atli brought him the heart of his brother Hogni. Atli did so, and Gunnar said, " Now I alone know where the treasure is ; and the secret is safe." Gunnar was cast into a pit of vipers. But Gudrun lowered a harp down to him, and upon this he played so skilfully with his feet that he charmed all the snakes asleep, save one, which stung him to death. At Gudrun's request Atli made a great funeral feast for her brethren. Whilst at the feast Atli requested Gudrun to bring their children to him. She retorted that he had just eaten of their flesh and drunk of their blood, for she had slain them in revenge for the death of her brethren, and given him them to eat. Sick at heart, Atli took himself to bed. But Niblung, the son of Hogni, and Gudrun took council, and stabbed him in his sleep, then set the palace afire. So perished Atli and all his folk with him. Gudrun, weary of life, attempted to drown herself in the sea, which carried her to the burg of King Jonakr, who took her to wife. She sent for Swanhild, her daughter by Sigurd, who was asked by King Jormunrek in marriage. Jonakr consented, but in the voyage to Jormunrek's court she fell in love with Randver his son, and on their arrival at Jormunrek's dominions both were slain by the king's order. But Gudrun's sons by Jonakr, Saurli and Hamdir, avenged her death by the slaughter of Jormunrek and his folk, in which combat, however, they were themselves slain. Gudrun, hearing of this, fell into despair, musing how all her kindred had been cut off root and branch, and with a call to Sigurd upon her lips she died. Her sorrow-bound heart thawed at last in the funeral pyre.

The *Volsunga Saga* recounts in a complicated form the world-tale of the battle between light and darkness. Like Arthur and Theseus, Sigmund alone can draw the sword Gram from the oak Branstock, a weapon from the same armoury as the sun-swords and arrows of Phœbus, Achilles, Arthur and Roland. The death of the deadly viper which lurks in the meal-bag kneaded by Sinfjötli is the slaying of the darkness of night or winter. The capture of the heaven-gods Loki (flame), Odin and Hahnir by the father of the otter and their golden ransom which fills the otterskin until not a white hair is visible, typifies the freeing of the earth from the fetters of ice, and the spreading of the golden sunshine of summer over it. Andvari's ring, which multiplies itself, symbolizes the reproductive faculty of nature. Brynhild, the Valkyrie, is the peerless maiden who has slept in a charmed slumber caused by the thorn of winter thrust into her hand by Odin like the Rakshas' claw which leaves Surya Bai, the sun-maiden, senseless in Hindu myth. Helgi (who according to the Sagaman was to be born again), Sigmund and Sigurd are all men of the sun, who, although in the story they do not return as some sun-heroes do, prove by their statements that in some earlier version they were alluded to as arising again. Gudrun, the sun-bride, becomes the wife of two other kings, the gloaming and the darkness. As Medea slew the children of Iason after she had sent the death-robe to Glauke, she gives Atli his children's flesh to eat. She then marries Jonakr, lord of the winter-land, and she passes away in an autumn twilight. The entire series of incidents belongs to the great tragedy of the year, and the drama of the four seasons—the eternal tale-basis of primitive man.

Literature : Cox, *Mythology of the Aryan Nations*, Bk. 1, Ch. xii. ; Dasent, *Popular Tales from the Norse* (introduction) ; Müller, *Chips from a German Workshop ;*

Vigfussen and Powell, *Corpus Poeticum Boreale ;* W. Morris and E. Magnusson, *The Volsunga Saga* (Camelot Library) ; W. Morris, *Sigurd the Volsung ;* Cox and Jones, *Tales from Teutonic Lands* ; Ludlow, *Popular Epics of the Middle Ages.*

VOYAGE À JERUSALEM (Charlemagne's voyage). A poem of the Charlemagne cycle (*c.* 1115), "which serves well to illustrate the fading away into a mere fable of the personality of the great emperor." It is probably one of the best known among British literati, as a MS. of it exists in the British Museum (King's Library, 16, E. VIII.). The subject of the poem is the imaginary voyage of Charles to Jerusalem and Constantinople. Charles, told by his wife that there is one monarch more kingly than he, Hugo the Strong, Emperor of Greece, is deeply wounded. The Frankish king resolves to see his rival. He, therefore, proclaims as an excuse, a pilgrimage to Jerusalem. Eighty thousand men accompany him, and reach the Holy City safely. They afterwards proceed to Constantinople, where they are greeted by Hugo, the magnificence of whose surroundings strikes the Franks with awe. After a sumptuous feast Hugo takes Charles and his peers into his sleeping apartment. The French begin to brag, a common custom with the Teutonic warriors of the early Middle Ages, and each of them vaunts that he can accomplish some feat more or less possible. A spy of Hugo's overhears them, and acquaints his master with what they have said. As all the vaunts emitted by the Franks have been more or less offensive to Hugo, he swears that unless they make them true he will have them all executed. He reproaches them with their abuse of his hospitality, and intimates his decision to them. Charles, in his despair, has his relics brought. An angel appears to him, commands him never more to brag, but tells him to be of good heart, for this time all the vauntings of the Franks shall come true. The brags are fulfilled to the letter, and Hugo is so struck with the circumstance that he becomes Charles's man, and agrees to hold his kingdom of him, as "God must love him." Great festivities are celebrated, the Franks return to France, and Charles forgives his queen "for the love of the sepulchre." The Abbé de la Rue judges from the language of this romance that it is "much earlier" than any other of the same class, and the latest date he will allow for it is the first decade of the twelfth century. This is agreed to by Michel. Ludlow thinks that according to the language and metre the poem is to be referred to the middle of the twelfth century, and perhaps even to its latter half. He also finds in it an echo of the "tumbling of the Greek emperor from the throne by Baldwin and his Flemings" during the Fourth Crusade. Its fantastic character, too, seems to him to denote a period subsequent to the popularity of the Arthurian cycle. Viewed as an Anglo-Norman poem, it may, perhaps, be questioned whether the spirit of Charlemagne's voyage is not one of satire upon France. "The rivalry of the Third Crusade between Richard and Philip—a rivalry which was national as well as personal—is perhaps here visible."

(See *Voyage à Jerusalem*, ed.

E. Koschwitz, 1883 ; Ludlow, *Popular Epics of the Middle Ages*, London and Cambridge, 1865. The romance has also been edited from the MS. in the British Museum by Michel and Pickering, 1836.

W

WACE, RICHARD (or, according to some authorities Robert), The most famous of the early writers of British pseudo-history in romance verse, was a native of Jersey, where he was born of a good family, probably in the last decade of the eleventh century. His father was one of the Norman barons who accompanied the Conqueror to England and fought at Hastings. Educated for the Church at Caen, he completed his studies in various other parts of France, and after visiting England he returned to Caen, where he occupied the remainder of his life in writing his romance poems. Late in life he was made a canon of Bayeaux on the recommendation of Henry II. The first of his " chronicles " is the *Brut d'Angleterre*, a translation into romance octosyllabic verse of the *Historia Regum Britanniæ* of Geoffrey of Monmouth, although it contains many things which are not to be found in that work. (*Vide* " Brut d'Angleterre.") This poem Wace presented to Eleanor of Aquitaine, the queen of Henry II. His other great work is the *Roman de Rou*, or the *Romance of Rollo*, a chronicle of the Dukes of Normandy, and he also wrote poems on the subjects of the Virgin and the *Life of Saint Nicholas*. There is reason for believing that he lived to an advanced age.

Literature : Pluquet, *Notice sur la Vie et les Ecrits de Robert Wace*, 1824. (See also under " Brut d'Angleterre.")

WACHILDE. A mermaid (*vide* " Dietrich of Bern "), who assisted Wittich to escape from Dietrich by taking him to her submarine castle.

WALCHTHEOV. Wife of King Hrodgar (*q.v.*) of Jutland. She gave Beowulf (*q.v.*) a gold cup and a ring and necklace in gratitude for his slaying Grendel.

WALDEMAR. King of the Reussen and son of Hermit (*q.v.*). He owed allegiance to Dietrich of Bern (*q.v.*), towards whom he was friendly. Latterly he was persuaded to turn against the hero of Bern, with whom he fought to his own misfortune.

WALTHAR OF AQUITAIN.—WALTHARIUS OR WALTHAR OF AQUITAIN. A Latin poem ascribed by Fauriel to the eighth or ninth century, and by Grimm and Schmeller to the tenth. It is probably the work of a monk, and is connected with the latter *Nibelungenlied*, which contains repeated allusions to it. Attila, King of the Huns, invades the Kingdom of the Franks ruled by Gibich. The latter is advised to pay tribute, and give hostages. His son Gunthar being too young, he sends instead a noble youth named Hagan, along with great treasure. The Huns next attack the Burgundians, and are also successful, King Herric giving his only daughter, the beautiful Hildegund, as hostage. The Aquitainians also coming under the power of the war-like Attila, King Alphue pays tribute and gives his only son Walthar—already affianced to Hildegund—as hostage. On returning to his capital, Attila shows great kindness to his hostages, and brings them up as his own children. The young men are instructed in all the war-like arts, till they surpass the Huns in prowess. On hearing news of Gibich's death and of Gunthar's succession, Hagan escapes. The queen fearing Walthar might follow his example suggests to Attila that Walthar should marry a Hunnish maiden. He pleads his unworthiness of the honour, and its interference with his military duties. The king is satisfied with his excuse, which seems confirmed in a victory gained by the army under Walthar. He persuades Hildegund to flee with him, saying he would have escaped before, but for his reluctance to leave her behind. As she has charge of the treasure he bids her fill two large chests with Hunnish money, take out a complete suit of armour and have them in readiness for their flight. On the day of their departure, Walthar gives a grand feast to the king and all his household. The wine is circulated freely, till the whole court is in a state of drunken helplessness. Walthar saddles his war-horse "Lion," and with the maiden and the treasure makes his escape. When the Huns awake from their stupor, the absence of the pair is discovered, and King Attila offers a large reward to any one who will pursue and capture Walthar. But none venture : Walthar's strength and valour are too well known. Still pursuing their flight, living on birds and fish, Walthar and Hildegund reach the Rhine, near Worms.

In return for ferrying them across, Walthar gives the ferryman fish, and he sells them to King Gunthar's cook. The king delighted at their flavour, inquires where they came from. The ferryman is summoned, and he relates his ferrying across of the armed warrior, the fair maiden, and the horse laden with the two chests. Hagan, who is at the table, declares it must be his old comrade Walthar, and Gunthar, thinking this a good chance to get back his father's treasure, sets out in search of him, accompanied by Hagan and twelve of his bravest chiefs. Meanwhile, Walthar in his flight comes upon a cave, wherein he decides to spend the night. Removing his heavy armour, and bidding Hildegund keep watch, and rouse him if she sees any one approaching, he takes his much-needed rest. But Gunthar is on his track, and Hagan warns him that Walthar roused is not an easy enemy to deal with. Hildegund sees them coming, and wakens Walthar, who puts on his armour. She thinks they are Huns, and implores Walthar to kill her, rather than let her fall into their hands. He expresses his belief that God will save them from their enemies. Recognizing Hagan's helmet, he discovers they are Franks. On Hagan's advice, they hold parley with him. Walthar's life will be granted on condition he gives up the treasure, the maiden, and also his horse. Walthar refuses, but promises to send the king a hundred armlets of red metal, if he will let him go. Hagan advises the king to accept the offer, because of a dream he had the previous night. The king taunts him with cowardice, and Hagan waxing wroth declares he will share neither the fight nor the spoil, and retires to a neighbouring hill to watch the fray. Walthar's encampment was situated in such a manner that only one man could attack him at a time, and he vanquishes each of his enemies in single combat, among them Hagan's nephew, and only the king and Hagan remain. Gunthar pleads with Hagan to avenge his friends, which the latter at last promises to do, but determines to use strategem. They decide to tempt Walthar into the open, by pretending to go away. The ruse is successful. They meet and engage in deadly combat. Gunthar loses a leg, Hagan an eye, and Walthar his right hand. Weakness makes the heroes lay down their arms. Hildegund binds their wounds, and brings them wine. A better understanding is arrived at between them. The Franks return to Worms, Walthar to Aquitain, where his marriage is celebrated with Hildegund. After his father's death, he rules the people wisely for many years.

WANDERING JEW, THE. A mediæval German legend, which from its wide diffusion and popular character partakes largely of the character of romance. The earliest mention extant of the Wandering Jew is to be found in the book of the chronicles of the Abbey of St. Albans, which was copied and continued by Matthew Paris. He records that in the year 1228, " a certain Archbishop of Armenia Major came on a pilgrimage to England to see the relics of the saints, and visit the sacred places in the kingdom, as he had done in others ; he also produced letters of recommendation from His Holiness the Pope, to the religious men and prelates of the churches, in which they were enjoined to receive and entertain him with due reverence and honour. On his arrival, he went to St. Albans, where he was received with all respect by the abbot and monks ; at this place, being fatigued with his journey, he remained some days to rest himself and his followers, and a conversation was commenced between him and the inhabitants of the convent, by means of their interpreters, during which he made many inquiries concerning the religion and religious observances of their country, and related many strange things concerning Eastern countries. In the course of conversation he was asked whether he had ever seen or heard anything of Joseph, a man of whom there was much talk in the world, who, when our Lord suffered, was present and spoke to Him, and who is still alive, in evidence of the Christian faith ; in reply to which, a knight in his retinue, who was his interpreter, replied, speaking in French, ' My lord well knows that man, and a little before he took his way to the Western countries, the said Joseph ate at the table of my lord the Archbishop in Armenia, and he had often seen and held converse with him.' He was then asked about what had passed between Christ and the same Joseph, to which he replied, ' At the time of the suffering of Jesus Christ, He was seized by the Jews, and led into the hall of judgment before Pilate, the governor, that He might be judged by him on the accusation of the Jews ; and Pilate, finding no cause for adjudging Him to death, said to them, " Take Him and judge Him according to your law ; " the shouts of the Jews, however, increasing, he, at their request, released unto them Barabbas, and delivered Jesus to them to be crucified. When, therefore, the Jews were dragging Jesus forth, and had reached the door, Cartăphĭlus, a porter of the hall, in Pilate's service, as Jesus was going out of the door, impiously struck Him on the back with his hand, and said in mockery, " Go quicker, Jesus, go quicker ; why do you loiter ? " and Jesus, looking back on him with a severe countenance, said to him, " I am going, and you will wait till I return." ' And according, as our Lord said, this Cartăphĭlus is still awaiting His return. At the time of our Lord's suffering he was thirty years old, and when he attains the age of a hundred years, he always returns to the same age as he was when our Lord suffered. After Christ's death, when the Catholic faith gained ground, this Cartăphĭlus was baptized by Ananias (who also baptized the Apostle Paul), and was called Joseph. He often dwells in both divisions of Armenia, and other Eastern countries, passing his time amidst the bishops and other prelates of the Church ; he is a man of holy conversation and religious ; a man of few words, and circumspect in his behaviour ; for he does not speak at all unless when questioned by the bishops and religious men ; and then he tells of the events of old times, and of the events which occurred at the suffering and resurrection of our Lord, and of the witnesses of the resurrection, namely, those who rose with Christ, and went into the holy city, and appeared unto men. He also tells of the creed of the Apostles, and of their separation and preaching. And all this he relates without smiling or levity of conversation, as one who is well practised in sorrow and the fear of God, always looking forward with fear to the coming of

Jesus Christ, lest at the Last Judgment he should find Him in anger whom, when on His way to death, he had provoked to just vengeance. Numbers came to him from different parts of the world, enjoying his society and conversation ; and to them, if they are men of authority, he explains all doubts on the matters on which he is questioned. He refuses all gifts that are offered to him, being content with slight food and clothing. He places his hope of salvation on the fact that he sinned through ignorance, for the Lord when suffering prayed for His enemies in these words, ' Father, forgive them, for they know not what they do.' "

Much about the same date Philip Mouskes, afterwards Bishop of Tournay, wrote his rhymed chronicle (1242), which contains a similar account of the Jew, derived from the same Armenian prelate. He says that this man having visited the shrine of " St. Tumas de Kantorbire," and then having paid his devotions at " Monseignour St. Jake," he went on to Cologne to see the heads of the three Kings. The version told in the Netherlands much resembled that related at S. Albans.

Curiously enough, we next hear of him in the East, where he is confounded with the prophet Elijah. Early in the century he appeared to an Arab Fadhilah, under peculiar circumstances. After the Arabs had captured the city of Elvān, Fadhilah, at the head of three hundred horsemen, pitched his tents, late in the evening, between two mountains. Fadhilah having begun his evening prayer with a loud voice, heard the words " Allah akbar " (God is great) repeated distinctly, and each word of his prayer was followed in a similar manner. Fadhilah, not believing this to be the result of an echo, was much astonished, and cried out, " O thou ! whether thou art of the angel ranks, or whether thou art of some other order of spirits, it is well, the power of God be with thee ; but if thou art a man, then let mine eyes light upon thee, that I may rejoice in thy presence and society." Scarcely had he spoken these words, before an aged man with bald head stood before him, holding a staff in his hand, and much resembling a dervish in appearance. After having courteously saluted him, Fadhilah asked the old man who he was. Thereupon the stranger answered, " Bassi Hadhret Issa, I am here by command of the Lord Jesus, who has left me in this world, that I may live therein until He comes a second time to earth. I wait for this Lord who is the Fountain of Happiness, and in obedience to His command I dwell behind yon mountain." When Fadhilah heard these words, he asked when the Lord Jesus would appear, and the old man replied that His appearing would be at the end of the world, at the Last Judgment. But this only increased Fadhilah's curiosity, so that he inquired the signs of the approach of the end of all things, whereupon Zerib Bar Elīa gave him an account of the general, social, and moral dissolution, which would be the climax of this world's history. In 1547 he was seen in Europe, if we are to believe the following narration : " Paul von Eitzen, doctor of the Holy Scriptures, and Bishop of Schleswig, related as true for some years past, that when he was young, having studied at Wittemberg, he returned home to his parents in Hamburg in the winter of the

year 1547, and that on the following Sunday, in church, he observed a tall man with his hair hanging over his shoulders, standing barefoot during the sermon, over against the pulpit, listening with deepest attention to the discourse, and, whenever the name of Jesus was mentioned, bowing himself profoundly, and humbly, with sighs and beating of the breast. He had no other clothing in the bitter cold of the winter, except a pair of hose which were in tatters about his feet, and a coat with a girdle which reached to his feet ; and his general appearance was that of a man of fifty years. And many people, some of high degree and title, have seen this same man in England, France, Italy, Hungary, Persia, Spain, Poland, Moscow, Lapland, Sweden, Denmark, Scotland, and other places. Every one wondered over the man. Now after the sermon, the said Doctor inquired diligently where the stranger was to be found, and when he had sought him out, he inquired of him privately whence he came, and how long that winter he had been in the place. Thereupon he replied modestly, that he was a Jew by birth, a native of Jerusalem, by name Ahăsŭerus, by trade a shoemaker ; he had been present at the crucifixion of Christ, and has lived ever since, travelling through various lands and cities, the which he substantiated by accounts he gave ; he related also the circumstances of Christ's transference from Pilate to Herod, and the final crucifixion, together with other details not recorded in the Evangelists and historians ; he gave accounts of the changes of government in many countries, especially of the East, through several centuries, and moreover he detailed the labours and deaths of the holy Apostles of Christ most circumstantially. Now when Doctor Paul von Eitzen heard this with profound astonishment, on account of its incredible novelty, he inquired further, in order that he might obtain more accurate information. Then the man answered that he had lived in Jerusalem at the time of the crucifixion of Christ, whom he had regarded as a deceiver of the people and a heretic; he had seen Him with his own eyes, and had done his best, along with others, to bring this deceiver, as he regarded Him, to justice, and to have Him put out of the way. When the sentence had been pronounced by Pilate, Christ was about to be dragged past his house; then he ran home, and called together his household to have a look at Christ, and see what sort of a person He was. This having been done, he had his little child on his arm, and was standing in his doorway to have a sight of the Lord Jesus Christ. As then, Christ was led by, bowed under the weight of the heavy cross, He tried to rest a little, and stood still a moment; but the shoemaker, in zeal and rage, and for the sake of obtaining credit among the other Jews, drove the Lord Christ forward, and told Him to hasten on His way. Jesus obeying, looked at him, and said, 'I shall stand and rest, but thou shalt go till the last day.' At these words the man set down the child; and unable to remain where he was, he followed Christ, and saw how cruelly He was crucified, how He suffered, how He died. As soon as this had taken place, it came upon him suddenly that he could no more return to Jerusalem, nor see again his wife and child, but must go

forth into foreign lands, one after another, like a mournful pilgrim. Now, when, years after, he returned to Jerusalem, he found it ruined and utterly razed, so that not one stone was left standing on another; and he could not recognize former localities. He believes that it is God's purpose in thus driving him about in miserable life, and preserving him undying, to present him before the Jews at the end, as a living token, so that the godless and unbelieving may remember the death of Christ, and be turned to repentance. For his part he would well rejoice were God in heaven to release him from this vale of tears. After this conversation, Doctor Paul von Eitzen, along with the rector of the school of Hamburg, who was well read in history, and a traveller, questioned him about events which had taken place in the East since the death of Christ, and he was able to give them much information on many ancient matters; so that it was impossible not to be convinced of the truth of his story, and to see, that what seems impossible with men is, after all, possible with God. Since the Jew has had his life extended, he has become silent and reserved, and only answers direct questions. When invited to become any one's guest, he eats little, and drinks in great moderation; then hurries on, never remaining long in one place. When at Hamburg, Dantzig, and elsewhere money has been offered him, he never took more than two skillings ($4\frac{1}{4}d$.), and at once distributed it to the poor, as a token that he needed no money, for God would provide for him, as he rued the sins he had committed in ignorance. During the period of his stay in Hamburg and Dantzig he was never seen to laugh. In whatever land he travelled he spoke its language, and when he spoke Saxon, it was like a native Saxon. Many people came from different places to Hamburg and Dantzig in order to see and hear this man, and were convinced that the providence of God was exercised in this individual in a very remarkable manner. He gladly listened to God's word, or heard it spoken of always with great gravity and compunction, and he ever reverenced with sighs the pronunciation of the name of God, or of Jesus Christ, and could not endure to hear curses, but whenever he heard any one swear by God's death or pains, he waxed indignant, and exclaimed, with vehemence and with sighs, 'Wretched man and miserable creature, thus to misuse the name of thy Lord and God, and His bitter sufferings and passion. Hadst thou seen, as I have, how heavy and bitter were the pangs and wounds of thy Lord, endured for thee and me, thou wouldst rather undergo great pain thyself than thus take His sacred name in vain!' Such is the account given to me by Doctor Paul von Eitzen, with many circumstantial proofs, and corroborated by certain of my own old acquaintances who saw this same individual with their own eyes in Hamburg. In the year 1575, the Secretary Christopher Krause, and Master Jacob von Holstein, legates to the Court of Spain, and afterwards sent into the Netherlands to pay the soldiers serving his Majesty in that country, related on their return home to Schleswig, and confirmed with solemn oaths, that they had come across the same mysterious individual at Madrid, in Spain, in appearance, manner of life, habits, clothing, just the same as he had appeared in Hamburg. They said that they had spoken with him, and that many people of all classes had conversed with him, and found him to speak good Spanish. In the year 1599, in December, a reliable person wrote from Brunswick to Strasburg that the same-mentioned strange person had been seen alive at Vienna in Austria, and that he had started for Poland and Dantzig; and that he purposed going on to Moscow. This Ahãsŭerus was at Lubeck in 1601, also about the same date in Revel in Livonia, and in Cracow in Poland. In Moscow he was seen of many and spoken to by many. What thoughtful God-fearing persons are to think of the said person, is at their option. God's works are wondrous and past finding out, and are manifested day by day, only to be revealed in full at the last great day of account." Thus ends the narrative of Doctor von Eitzen.

In 1604, the Jew seems to have appeared in Paris. Rudolph Botereus says under this date: "I fear lest I be accused of giving ear to old wives' fables, if I insert in these pages what is reported all over Europe of the Jews, coeval with the Saviour Christ; however, nothing is more common, and our popular histories have not scrupled to assert it. Following the lead of those who wrote our annals I may say that he who appeared not in one century only, in Spain, Italy, and Germany, was also in this year seen and recognized as the same individual who had appeared in Hamburg in the year 1566. The common people, bold in spreading reports, relate many things of him; and this I allude to, lest any thing should be left unsaid." J. C. Bulenger puts the date of the Hamburg visit earlier. " It was reported at this time that a Jew of the time of Christ was wandering without food and drink, having for a thousand and odd years been a vagabond and outcast, condemned by God to rove, because he, of that generation of vipers was the first to cry out for the crucifixion of Christ and the release of Barabbas ; and also because soon after, when Christ, panting under the burden of the rood, sought to rest before his workshop (he was a cobbler), the fellow ordered him off with acerbity. Thereupon Christ replied : ' Because thou grudgest Me such a moment of rest, I shall enter into My rest, but thou shalt wander restless.' At once frantic and agitated he fled through the whole earth, and on the same account to this day he journeys through the world. It was this person who was seen in Hamburg in 1564. Credat Judæus Apella ! I did not see him or hear anything authentic concerning him at that time when I was in Paris ! "

We must regard the legend of the Wandering Jew as the epic of the Semite people in the middle ages. It is obvious from the versions just quoted that the story has no foundation in fact. It is a mediæval legend, pure and simple, and bears the stamp of the middle ages strongly upon it. The burgher of Germany, Poland, or Austria or the citizen of Paris or Padua noticing the Jewish Pedlar in his locality, would see in the stranger who avoided all unnecessary converse that outcast whose impious act had condemned him to wander for ever until the day upon which the dreadful curse was lifted and his wanderings would end. But the legend of the Wandering Jew has its mythical side as well as a purely legendary one, and this side is perhaps the more interesting of the two.

In some parts of Germany we find the Wandering Jew identified with the Wild Huntsman, whilst in several French districts that mythical character is regarded as the wind of night, which, rioting through the night-bound country seems to the peasant crouching in his hut, to bring in his train a howling pack of hounds with which he chases a spectral deer. The blast is his horn, which, rushing through the valleys, creates a hollow, booming sound, not unlike a great bugle. In this legend we have in all probability the clue to the mythological side of the story of the Wandering Jew. In this connection he is almost certainly the wind which, constantly wandering round the world seldom halts for long in one place. Or, perhaps the idea of the Wandering Jew has become confounded or fused with that of the idea of the wind. Of course to commence with the two ideas would be quite distinct, and it would only be when the myth had attained a respectable antiquity that it would become confounded with the idea of the wind. The likeness between the two conceptions would be too great to escape the popular mind, always ready to confound similar stories or legendary ideas. From a literary point of view, the legend of the Wandering Jew has been treated with considerable skill by Eugene Sué and Croly.

WASTE CITY, KING OF THE. He is mentioned in the Grail legends as " hating all Christian folk." He seems to have employed a " hideous hag " to do his evil deeds, whom Percival overcomes.

WASTE LAND. Mentioned in Arthurian legend as bringing destruction and pestilence. Bliocadrans' child, Percival, is brought up in this forest by his mother, who warns him against "men covered with iron — they are devils."

WATE OF STURMEN. (*Vide* "Gudrun Lay," 2nd and 3rd divisions of, under headings "Hagen and Hettel," and "Gudrun.") Uncle of Horant, Lord of Daneland. He brought up King Hettel (*q.v.*), and later formed one of the embassy sent by him to win Hilda of Ireland (*q.v.*). He is described as a grim warrior, more used to fighting than to court life; he won the friendship of King Hagen (*q.v.*), chiefly through his skilful swordsmanship. He took part in all the conflicts connected with the winning of Hilda for Hettel, and on the reconciliation produced a healing root to cure the wounded. (*Vide* "Hagen and Hettel" for details.) He brought up Hettel's son Ortwein, and fought fiercely in all the battles to secure the freedom of Gudrun, proving a terror to the enemy. At the rescue of Gudrun he slaughtered relentlessly, slaying even women—Gerlinte (*q.v.*) and Heregart (*q.v.*). He was a mighty warrior, but fierce and bloodthirsty, never willing to show mercy, and loth that anyone else should do so. Ludlow considers that a description of Wate's valour occurs in Priest Conrad's version of the *Song of Roland* (1173 to 1177).

WAYLAND'S ARMLET. (*Vide* "Frithjof Saga.") A strange gift of Wayland Smith to an ancestor of Thorsten, the father of the Icelandic hero Frithjof (*q.v.*). But the Viking Soté stole the armlet from Thorsten, and was pursued to Britain by the thane and his royal friend King Belé. Here in a cavern they beheld the spirit of the dead Soté sitting upon the mast of his ship, swathed in fire, and scouring in vain his bloody sword blade. On his arm was the ring which Thorsten at a terrible and untold cost wrested from him. This armlet became one of the three possessions of Frithjof.

WERE-WOLF, THE LAY OF THE. A Breton romance written by Marie de France (*q.v.*). The Were-Wolf, named Bisclavaret in Brittany and Garwa in Normandy, is a human being transformed by art-magic into a fearsome, man-devouring beast that lurks in the woods. This lay tells of a baron who lay near to the heart of his lord, and was loved and esteemed of all. Greatly did he love his wife and greatly she loved him. But she would fain know what kept him from her side three days in each week. Importuned, he at last related to her his secret. He became, during those days a were-wolf, having concealed his clothes in a hidden spot, because if he did not find them again he would remain a beast for ever. Of this secret, too, she got possession, and fearing to live longer with her husband, gave to a lover the affection he had so long asked of her. She further instructed him how he might spoil the were-wolf of his vesture. The two were wed, and for more than a year no one heard about the king's favourite noble. But one day as the monarch was hunting in the woods, he made up upon the were-wolf, who, with human gestures, prayed protection. Marvelling at the creature's supplication, the king forbade his companions to molest it, and returned to his court, followed by the strange animal. Day by day he grew fonder of his quarry, nor was there any one who did not make much of the beast. Once, however, at a great feast given by the king to his nobles and vassals, the animal flew at the knight of the lady who had betrayed her former lord. And again when that lady visited the king in a certain lodge, whither he had taken the wolf with him, Bisclavaret tore off her nose. A cunning counsellor surmised some reason for this fierceness on the animal's part. He therefore advised the king to put both the knight and his wife in surety, and demand of them what they knew concerning the wolf. They were forced to tell the truth, and by the same wise lord's counsel Bisclavaret's clothing was laid before him. But the animal, ashamed to become man again in the public view, took, as it were, no heed of the raiment. The king shut it up in a private apartment for a time, and upon entering that apartment found his lost knight sleeping upon the royal bed like a child. Great was the joy of all at the recovery of the noble. But his false wife and her lover were banished from the realm.

WICHSTAN. A warrior of Gothland mentioned in the legend of *Beowulf* (*q.v.*). He avenged King Hardred's murder by slaying Eanmund. (*Vide* "Hardred" and "Eanmund.") Beowulf was his dearest friend and in that hero's struggle with the dragon, Wichstan was the only warrior brave enough to go to the king's aid, which he did so effectually that Beowulf was able to slay the dragon. Beowulf bade Wichstan carry the dragon's treasure out of the cave, and after doing this, Wichstan in

sorrow watched his master breathe his last.

WIELAND or WAYLAND. The smith, a famous character in German mythological romance, and father of Weltich (*q.v.*), whom he trained in the art of warfare and sent to the court of Dietrich of Bern (*q.v.*). Before he despatched his son he presented him with the good sword Miming, and told him of a mermaid, who married his great-grandfather King Wilkinus. To her he must apply when in difficulty. He is further referred to in the Sigfried (*q.v.*), story as being in company with a smith named Mimer, when Sigfried joins the smithy. We find his workmanship much praised in the Beowolf (*q.v.*) tales, and his armour, which the hero wears, proves impregnable against the onslaught of Grendal (*q.v.*) the giantess and the dragon. He is the supernatural and semi-divine smith of the Teutonic peoples as Vulcan is that of the Romans and Hephaistos of the Greeks, and his smithy is traditionally referred to as being underground.

WILKINA SAGA. (*Vide* "Thidrekssaga.")

WILLIAM OF MALMESBURY. An English chronicler of the twelfth century whose voluminous writings, all of them in Latin, are of the utmost value as historical documents, and are likewise of considerable moment to the student of early romantic literature. Little is known of William's life, but it is probable that he was born about 1090, and sundry passages in his books suggest that Somerset was his native shire. He spent his childhood in Malmesbury Abbey, and it is recorded that, while still a mere boy, he showed such erudition that he was employed by the abbot to aid in forming and arranging the monastery's library. Espousing the monastic life, and incited to scholarship by his father, William soon became famous for his knowledge of logic, medicine, ethics, and many other branches of learning. In course of time, accordingly, he was appointed librarian at Malmesbury, and thenceforth he gave his activities chiefly to historical research. By 1125 he had finished his two most important works, *Gesta Regum Anglorum* and *Gesta Pontificum Anglorum,* while at a subsequent date he compiled a history of the Abbey of Glastonbury, which was not far from his own. He seems, indeed, to have been connected with the former in some way, for he refers to it as the monastery "wherein I am a professed soldier of Heaven," and the probability is that he stayed at Glastonbury for a while with a view to studying its records the more thoroughly. Be that as it may, he was twice offered the Abbacy of Malmesbury, but he declined on both occasions, continuing to pursue his historical studies ; while he also found a certain amount of time for travel, making a pilgrimage once to Rome, and likewise visiting many parts of England. The year of his death is not definitely known, but it is commonly supposed to have been 1143. William's *Gesta Regum Anglorum* begins with the shadowy dawn of English history, and ends at the year 1127 ; while the chronicler wrote a sequel thereto entitled *Historia Novella,* and this extends to the year 1142. The historian was personally acquainted with most of the leading men of his own day, namely the reigns of Henry I. and Stephen ; but, while this gives

his writing on that period an especial significance, the opening parts of his *Gesta Regum* are perhaps equally important. The two great abbeys with which William was connected were treasure-houses of historical material, documentary and legendary ; and thus the author was enabled to draw freely on the oldest ballad literature of England, while it is even probable, as John Richard Green points out, that he utilized many things now lost. Hence the interest which his works hold for the scholar of romance, while his *Gestis Pontificum Anglorum* is literally the foundation on which all ensuing writers on English ecclesiastical history have built.

Literature : Gesta Regum and *Historia Novella* were first printed in 1596, and the former has been repeatedly published during recent times, the best such edition being one edited by Professor Stubbs in the Rolls Series (1887–89). The editor's preface to this is important, while the student should also consult the *Life and Writings* of William of Malmesbury by W. de Gray Birch (transaction of the Royal Society of Literature, Vol. X., new series). The significance of William's histories has been amply recognized, and they have been utilized by all the best English historians, notably Green in his *History of the English People.*

WILLIAM OF ORANGE. A sub-cycle of the Charlemagne epic, which later expanded into an "enormous and incoherent" cycle of the kinship of *Garin of Montglane* (*q.v.*), and *Aymery of Narbonne,* and which was connected through the former with the sub-cycle of the Lorrainers (*q.v.*). The various poems of which it is composed are chiefly referred to the eleventh

2 c

century, and include *Enfances Guillaume*, *Departement des Enfans Aimeri*, *La Mort Aymeri de Narbonne*, *Siege de Narbonne*, *Le Charroi de Nimes*, *Prise d'Orange*, *Enfances Vivien*, *Le Covenant Vivien*, *Aliscans*, *Le Moniage Guillaume I.*, *Le Moniage Guillaume II.*, *Le Moniage Renouart*, *Le Bataille de Loquifer*. It is obvious that the central figure in these romances is a composite one, whose historic personality is far from clear. Indeed, the cycle is replete with anachronisms and brings together districts separated by the width of France in most incongruous proximity. William is alluded to as an historical personage by chroniclers of the reigns of Louis le Debonair and Charlemagne, but the individual mentioned by them, later became confounded with other Williams, among them William *Fierabras*, William "Shortnose," William of Toulouse, William I. of Provence, and a William of Bezalu. The veritable William with whom these others were afterwards confounded, was put in the place of Count Orso of Toulouse when the latter was surprised and defeated by Adelori the Gascon. He quelled that chief, and as Duke of Aquitaine became standard-bearer of the empire. In 793 he inflicted a heavy check upon the " Saracens," and assisted in the taking of Barcelona by Louis in 801. He founded the Abbey of Gellone, which he entered, and where he died May 28, 812. His life was written by St. Cerdo, disciple of St. Benedict of Anniane, in 823 or 824. His exploits became the theme of song about the end of the eleventh century. The cycle of the children of *Garin of Montglane* and *Amyery of Narbonne* which has grown around

William of Orange comprises no less than 120,000 lines, the latest portions being in Alexandrines with a short line at the close. There is a large variety of texts. For the matter of the sub-cycle, see the titles of the several romances which compose it.

Literature : Becker, *Die altfranzösische Wilhelmsage*, Halle, 1896 ; Jonckbloet, *Guillaume d'Orange*, 1854 ; Gautier, *Epopées Françaises*, Vol. IV. For works on the various romances of the sub-cycle, see under their titles.

WILLIAM OF PALERMO. This French metrical romance was written at the desire of a Countess Yolande, daughter of Baldwin IV., count of Flanders. The English poem in alliterative verse was written about 1350 by a poet called William, at the desire of Humphrey Bohun, Earl of Hereford (d. 1361). Guillaume, a foundling supposed to be of low degree, is brought up at the court of the Emperor of Rome, and loves his daughter Melior who is destined for a Greek prince. The lovers flee into the woods disguised in bear-skins. Alfonso, who is Guillaume's cousin and a Spanish prince, has been changed into a wolf by his stepmother's enchantments. He provides food and protection for the fugitives, and Guillaume eventually triumphs over Alfonso's father, and wins back from him his kingdom. The benevolent were-wolf is disenchanted, and marries Guillaume's sister.

WILLIAM (" the proud one of Montclin "). (*Vide* "Garin the Lorrainer.") Son of Count Hardré, and one of the four young knights who fought against Richard of Normandy, and the "four kings " who besieged Thierry, King of

Savoy. He joined with Bernard of Naisil after his fight with Garin, and he also fought with Bego, whom he was most anxious to kill, but he made peace afterwards with Garin. One of his sons became Garin's godchild, and got from him a market at Metz. He fought against Garin at the attack made upon him in which he was slain.

WITTICH, SON OF WILLAND. A notable character in the story of Dietrich of Bern (*q.v.*), towards whom he was a faithful ally. His deeds of heroism won him high renown. He took part in the successful Battle of the Rose Garden (*q.v.*), but in the march to Etzel he was taken prisoner. His release was followed by his marriage to Bolfiana. He subsequently offended his royal master, who pursued him to the sea, into which he plunged, and was received by the mermaid Wachilde (*q.v.*).

WOLFHART. (*Vide* "Dietrich of Bern.") A follower of Dietrich of Bern (*q.v.*). He figured conspicuously in the battle of the Great Rose Garden (*q.v.*). He also took part in the unfortunate war against Ermenrich (*q.v.*).

WOLFRAM VON ESCHENBACH. Author of the Arthurian romance of *Parzival* (*q.v.*), was born at the small town of Eschenbach near Ansbach, and died about 1220. He was descended from a poor but noble family, and speedily found his place among that circle of poets who at the end of the twelfth century clustered around the brilliant court of Hermann, Landgrave of Thuringia. Although Wolfram wrote many of his poems at the Wartburg near Eisenach, he did not reside there permanently, as he found it necessary on occasion to follow the fortunes of Count Wertheim, his feudal lord. He is in no way to be confounded with the class of strolling minstrels who thronged the Thuringian court, whose methods literary and social he strongly condemns in his *Parzival*. That his muse was by no means venal is proved by the circumstances that not one of his poems is dedicated to a prince, although his *Parzival* is very appropriately dedicated to a noble lady whom he loved, and whose name he has not disclosed. His great epic of *Parzival* was composed about the year 1204, and his *Willehalm* (a translation of the French "William of Orange" sub-cycle of the Charlemagne cycle), probably in 1215–1216. No further facts concerning him have come down to us. His work proves him to have been the possessor of a nature spiritual, exalted and deeply imbued with the true spirit of poetry, and though his *Parzival* does not possess the literary polish of the similar poem of Chrétien de Troyes, it is more poetic in conception and richer in human interest and pathos. (*Vide* "Parzival.")

Y

YELLOW BOOK OF LECAN. An Irish manuscript of the ninth century containing the tale of Cuchulain and Connla (*q.v.*).

YLIAS. (*Vide* "Dietrich of Bern.")

Son of King Hermit (*q.v.*), and Yarl of the Greeks.

YONEC, THE LAY OF. A French *lai* written by Marie de France (*q.v.*). The Lord of Chepstow, an old man, had wedded a young, beautiful and gay wife. In his jealousy he had shut her up in a tower and set his widowed sister to guard her. For seven years the unhappy lady dwelt in this plight until one day she gave vent to her sorrow when the old woman was out of hearing. A hawk flew in at the window and became transformed into a handsome knight. Her terror over, she grew to love the stranger. She felt a new joy in her life and regained her lost beauty. This the jealous husband noticed, and by a snare learned the cause. In wrath, he set four sharp swords against the window ; and, as he foresaw, the unwitting bird met his death-wound upon them. Distracted, the lady could not be comforted, and when the hawk flew away she leapt from the window, twenty feet to the ground. Following his flight by the blood-drops she at last found him in his palace in a silver city. The dying knight prayed her to be gone before his folk slew her as the cause of their lord's death. He put his ring upon her finger, telling her that as long as she wore it her husband would not think of her ; and giving her his sword bade her render it to none till their son should be esteemed a brave and worthy knight. Then would she and her lord go to a feast, and would lodge in an abbey where should be seen a fair tomb. Here would the son learn his history, and here he would be girt with the sword. With difficulty the lady reached her tower, unheeded of her lord ; and in due time gave birth to a son, whom she named Yonec. He grew up unmatched for beauty, generosity and skill with the spear. Time drew on and he was dubbed knight. That same year he went with his mother and her husband to observe the festival of Aaron. On the way to Carleon the company were lodged in an abbey where they beheld a very beautiful and elaborate tomb. The son learned that herein lay his father, and taking the sword from his mother he smote off her husband's head. The lady died upon the tomb, was buried beside her lover ; and Yonec was proclaimed king of that realm.

YOUTH. In Irish romance the maiden who put the love spot upon Dermot's (*q.v.*) brow.

YROLT OF ORTLAND. (*Vide* "Gudrun Lay," and "Hagen and Hettel.") One of the embassy from King Hettel to win Hilda, daughter of Hagen. He takes part in the action described in "Gudrun."

YWAIN. Son of King Uriens, in Grail legend, the adulterer ; also referred to as Owain, Ewayne, Yones. Sir Galahad finds King Bagdemagus and Ywain and "li aoutres" at an abbey in the course of his quest.

Z

ZERBINO. Son of the King of Scotland, a character in Ariosto's *Orlando Furioso.* He it was who gathered together the arms and weapons which Orlando in his madness had left scattered on the field. He formed them into a trophy to be preserved for the hero when he should be restored to reason, but omitted to include among them the sword of Orlando, which was called Durandal. This had been secured by the evil Moor, Manricardo, whom he met and challenged. The weapons of Manricardo were charmed, so that the armour of Zerbino was shattered at each blow, and, mortally wounded, he expired in the arms of Isabel, his betrothed.

BIBLIOGRAPHY OF STANDARD WORKS ON MEDIÆVAL ROMANCE.

ENGLISH AND SCOTS ROMANCE.

Catalogue of Romances in the British Museum, Ward, 1883.
Specimens of Early English Metrical Romances, George Ellis, 1805.
Reliques of Ancient English Poetry, Thomas Percy, 1774.
Publications of the Roxburghe Club.
Publications of the Bannatyne Club.
Publications of the Maitland Club.
Publications of the Abbotsford Club.
Publications of the Early English Text Society.
Early Scottish Metrical Tales, David Laing, 1826.
The Ancient Popular Poetry of Scotland, David Laing, 1822.
Early English Prose Romances, William J. Thoms.
Early Prose Romances, ed. Prof. Henry Morley.
    (The two preceding works are published in one volume in the "Early
       Novelists" Library, ed. E. A. Baker.)
English Writers, Henry Morley, 1866.
Specimens of Early English, Skeat, 1887.
Ritson, Ancient English Metrical Romances, 1802.
Chronicle of Scottish Poetry, Sibbald, 1802.
Metrical Romances, Weber, 1810.
Select Pieces of Early Popular Poetry, Utterson, 1817.
Ancient Metrical Tales, Hartshorne, 1829.
Havelok the Dane, Sir Frederick Madden, 1828 (Roxburghe Club).
William the Werewolf, Sir Frederick Madden, 1832 (Roxburghe Club).
The Buik of Alexander the Great, 1834 (Bannatyne Club).
The Seven Sagas in Scotch Metre, John Rolland of Dalkieth, 1837 (Bannatyne
    Club).
Sir Bevis of Hamtoun, 1838 (Maitland Club).
Clariodus, 1830 (Maitland Club).
Rowland and Vernagu, 1836 (Abbotsford Club).
History of English Poetry, Warton, 1778.
Cambridge History of English Literature, vol. i.
Flourishing of Romance and Rise of Allegory, Prof. Saintsbury, 1897
    (deals with romance generally).
Epic and Romance, Prof. Ker, 1896 (also general in treatment).
Guide to the Middle English Metrical Romances, Billings, 1901.

ARTHURIAN ROMANCES.

Historia Britonum, Nennius (Eng. Hist. Society).
Historia Regum Britanniæ, Geoffrey of Monmouth (S. Evans, 1903).

Li Romans de Brut, Wace (ed. by Leroux de Lincy, 1835–38).
Brut, Layamon (ed. Sir Frederick Madden), 1847.
The Round Table Before Wace, Prof. A. Brown (Harvard Studies and
Notes, vol. viii.).
The Round Table, Dr. Lewis Mott (Publ. Mod. Lang. Assoc. of America).
Merlin (ed. Dr. Oskar Sommer), 1894.
Merlin, Suite de (from the Huth MS., ed. by G. Paris and J. Ulrich), 1890–91.
Le Morte Arthur, ed. Furnivall, 1854 ; (Roxburghe Club), 1819 ; J. D.
Bruce, 1903 ; Hemmingway, Boston, 1912.
Morte Arthure, Halliwell, 1847 ; Banks, 1900.
Le Morte d'Arthur, Sir Thomas Malory (ed. Dr. Oskar Sommer), 1889–90–91.
Survey of Arthurian Romance, Jessie L. Weston, 1905.
Syr Gawayne (ed. Sir Fredk. Madden).
Syr Gawayne and the Grene Knyght (ed. R. Morriss, E.E.T.S.).
Sir Gawain, a study on the Legend, by Jessie L. Weston, 1897 (Grimm
Library).
Diu Krône, Heinrich von dem Türlin, ed. Scholl, 1852.
Le Conte del Graal, Chretien de Troyes (ed. Potvin—very scarce), 1866–71.
Parzival, Wolfram von Eschenbach, ed. Lachmann ; ed. Bartsch, 1875–77.
The High History of the Holy Grail (Perceval li Gallois), trans. by Sebastian
Evans, 1898.
Romans de la Table Round, Paulin Paris.
Queste del Saint Graal (ed. Furnivall), 1864.
Tristan, Gottfried von Strassburg (ed. Bechstein) 1889.
Le Roman en Prose de Tristan, E. Löseth, 1892.
Der Heutige Stand der Tristan Forschung, Dr. Röttiger, 1897.
Lais, Marie de France (ed. Warncke), 1885.
Iwein, Hartmann von Aue (ed. Bech), 1888.
Le Saint-Graal, Hucher, 1875–78.
Die Sage vom Graal, Birch-Hirschfeld, 1877.
Studies on the Legend of the Holy Grail, Nutt, 1888.
Die französischen Gralromane, Heinzel.
Sage v. heil. Gral, 1898, Wechssler.
Glastonbury et Avalon, Ferd. Lot, in *Romania*, vol. xxvii.
The Parzival of Wolfram von Eschenbach, J. L. Weston.
Les derniers travaux Allemands sur la légende du Saint Graal, A. Nutt (see
Folk-Lore, 1892).
Arthurian Legend, Rhys.

CELTIC ROMANCE.

Cours de Littérature celtique, d'Arbois de Jubainville.
Celtic Britain, Rhys.
A Literary History of Ireland, Hyde, 1899.
Silva Gadelica, O'Grady.
Old Celtic Romances, Joyce, 1894.
Literature of the Kymry, Stephens, 1876.
The Mabinogion, Lady Charlotte Guest (ed. Nutt), 1902.
Hibbert Lectures, Rhys, 1888.
Four Ancient Books of Wales (ed. Skene), 1868.
Myvyrian Archæology, 1801.

The Black Book of Carmarthen (ed. Evans).
Mythology of the British Islands, Squire, 1905.
Transactions of the Ossianic Society, Dublin, 1854-61.
The Voyage of Bran, A. Nutt, 1895-97.
The Cuchullin Saga in Irish Literature, 1898.
Gods and Fighting Men, Lady Gregory, 1904.

French Romance.

(*Note.*—Numerous French romances have been translated into English, and are included in the list of English and Arthurian romances given above.)

Roman de Renart (ed. Méon et Chabaille), 1826-35 ; ed. Martin. 1882-87.
Roman de la Rose (ed. Michel), 1864.
Aucassin et Nicolette (trans. A. Lang), 1887 ; (trans. A. Bourdillon), 1887.
Classiques français du moyen âge (6 vols. publ. 1911, rest in progress).
Des Ouvrages inedits de la littérature française du moyen âge, Crapelet, 1834.
Le Roman de Meliador, Froissart (ed. A. Longuas), 1895.
Melanges de littérature française du moyen âge, Gaston, Paris (ed. Mario Roques), 1910-11.
Romania (a publication devoted to the study of French romantic literature, founded in 1872).
Histoire de la Littérature Française, Lauson, 1895.
Histoire de la Langue et de la Littérature Française (ed. Petit de Juleville).
Specimens of Old French, Paget Toynbee, 1892.
Le Roman de Troie, Benoit de Sainte-More (ed. Joly), 1870.
Alexandre le Grand dans la Littérature Française au Moyen Age, Paul Meyer, 1886.
Roman d'Alixandre (ed. Michelant), 1846.
Nouvelles Françaises du Quatorzième siècle, Moland and d'Héricault, Bibliothèque Elzévirienne, 1856.
Troilus (ed. Moland and d'Héricault, as above).
Fabliaux et Contes, Meon, 1808.
Chatelaine de Vergi, S. Reynaud, *Romania,* vol. xxi., 1892.

Charlemagne Romances.
(Chansons de Geste.)

Les Epopées Françaises, Leon Gautier, 1878-82.
L'Histoire poetique de Charlemagne, Gaston Paris, 1865.
Bibliographie des Chansons de Geste, Gautier, 1877.
Popular Epics of the Middle Ages, Ludlow, 1865.
Couronnement Looys (ed. E. Langlois), 1888.
Lyf of Charles the Grete (Early Eng. Text Society).
Turpin's Chronicle (ed. F. Castels), 1880.
Fierabras (in Recueil des Ancien Poètes de la France, vol. iv.), 1860 ; English trans. in Early Eng. Text Society.
Chanson de Roland (ed. Leon Gautier).
The Song of Roland, by A. Way and F. Spencer, 1895.
Chanson des Saisnes, J. Bodel (ed. F. Michel), 1835.

Girard de Viènne (ed. P. Tarbé), 1850.
Ogier le Danois (Chevalerie Ogier), ed. J. Barrois, 1842.
Die alt-französische Wilhelmsage, Prof. Becker, 1896.
Guillaume d'Orange, Jonckbloet, 1854.

GERMAN.

(Several German romances are noted under the heading " Arthurian."
Such works as refer to both German and Norse literature are marked
with an asterisk.)

Heldensage, Rassmann, 1863.
*Nordische, Heldenromane, von der Hagen, 1873.
*Die Prosaische Edda, Wilken, 1878.
*Volsunga Saga, Magnusson and Morris, 1870 (in English).
Nibelungenlied (ed. Bartsch), 1895 ; Shumway, 1909.
*Gudrun, Martin, 1902.
*Corpus Poeticum Boreale, Vigfusson and Powell, 1883.
Denkmäler deutscher Poesie und Prosa, Müllenhoff and Scherer, 1892.
Althoch deutsches Lesebuch, 1901.
German Classics, Max Müller, 1886.
Deutsches Heldenbuch (in five parts), 1866–78.
Altdeutsche und Altnordische Heldensagen, 1872.
Das deutsche Heldenbuch, Henrici (in vol. vii. of Kürschner's *Deutsche
National-Litteratur*).
Theodoric the Goth, T. Hodgkin.
Epics and Romances of the Middle Ages, M. W. Macdowall, London, 1884.
Deutsche Heldensagen, O. L. Jiriczek, 1898.
*Northern Hero-Legends, M. Bentinck-Smith, 1902.
*Tales from Teutonic Lands, Cox and Jones.
Curious Myths of the Middle Ages, Baring-Gould.

NORSE AND ICELANDIC.

(Most of these are included under " German," as dealing with both
literatures.)

Sturlunga Saga (Vigfusson), 1879.
The Story of Burnt Njal, Dasent, 1861.
Historia Danica, Saxo-Grammaticus (ed. F. York Powell), 1894.

SPANISH.

Romancero Castellano (ed. G. B. Depping), 1844.
Silva de varios romances, Sarragossa, 1550.
La Flor de varios y nuevos romances, A. de Villatta, Valencia, 1593.
Poesias escogidas de nuestros cancioneros y romanceros antiguos, Madrid,
1796.
Tesoros de los romanceros, Paris, 1838.
Sarmiento, Memorias para la historia de la poesia
Poesias selectas Castellanos, Madrid, 1817.
Romancero de romances, Duran, Madrid, 1832.

Spanish Ballads, Lockhart, 1823.
Poesias Castellanos Anteriores al siglo XV., 1842.
The Cid (trans. by Southey), in several cheap editions.

ITALIAN.

Literature of the South of Europe, Sismondi (Eng. trans. by T. Roscoe), 1823.
Studj sulla Letteratura Italiana dei Primi secoli, d'Ancona, 1891.
Il Fonte dell' Ariosto, Pio Rajna.
Orlando Furioso, Ariosto (Eng. trans. by Hoole).
Carduino, A. Pucci (ed. Rajna), 1873.
Storie Nerbonese, M. I. G. Isola, 1887.
Reali di Francia, Andrea da Barberino (ed. P. Rajna and G. Vandelli), 1872–1901.
Jerusalem Delivered, Tasso (Eng. trans. by Hoole).
Historia Trojana, Guido de Colonna, 1477 (Oxford ed. by Rood, 1480).
Memoirs of Politiano, W. P. Greswell.
Della Poésie di Antonio Pucci, Fra Ildefonso di San Luigi, 1772.
Orlando Innamorato, Boiardo (Panizzi), 1830.

PRINTED BY WILLIAM CLOWES AND SONS, LIMITED, LONDON AND BECCLES.

WESTFIELD COLLEGE
LIBRARY
UNIVERSITY OF LONDON